Exam Ref 70-740 Installation, Storage and Compute with Windows Server 2016

Craig Zacker

Exam Ref 70-740 Installation, Storage, and Compute with Windows Server 2016

Published with the authorization of Microsoft Corporation by:
Pearson Education, Inc.

Copyright © 2017 by Craig Zacker

All rights reserved. Printed in the United States of America. This publication is protected by copyright, and permission must be obtained from the publisher prior to any prohibited reproduction, storage in a retrieval system, or transmission in any form or by any means, electronic, mechanical, photocopying, recording, or likewise. For information regarding permissions, request forms, and the appropriate contacts within the Pearson Education Global Rights & Permissions Department, please visit www.pearsoned.com/permissions/. No patent liability is assumed with respect to the use of the information contained herein. Although every precaution has been taken in the preparation of this book, the publisher and author assume no responsibility for errors or omissions. Nor is any liability assumed for damages resulting from the use of the information contained herein.

ISBN-13: 978-0-7356-9882-6
ISBN-10: 0-7356-9882-1

Library of Congress Control Number: 2016962646

6 18

Trademarks

Microsoft and the trademarks listed at https://www.microsoft.com on the "Trademarks" webpage are trademarks of the Microsoft group of companies. All other marks are property of their respective owners.

Warning and Disclaimer

Every effort has been made to make this book as complete and as accurate as possible, but no warranty or fitness is implied. The information provided is on an "as is" basis. The authors, the publisher, and Microsoft Corporation shall have neither liability nor responsibility to any person or entity with respect to any loss or damages arising from the information contained in this book or programs accompanying it.

Special Sales

For information about buying this title in bulk quantities, or for special sales opportunities (which may include electronic versions; custom cover designs; and content particular to your business, training goals, marketing focus, or branding interests), please contact our corporate sales department at corpsales@pearsoned.com or (800) 382-3419.

For government sales inquiries, please contact governmentsales@pearsoned.com.

For questions about sales outside the U.S., please contact intlcs@pearson.com.

Editor-in-Chief	Greg Wiegand
Acquisitions Editor	Trina MacDonald
Development Editor	Rick Kughen
Managing Editor	Sandra Schroeder
Senior Project Editor	Tracey Croom
Editorial Production	Backstop Media
Copy Editor	Christina Rudloff
Indexer	Julie Grady
Proofreader	Christina Rudloff
Technical Editor	Ajay Kakkar
Cover Designer	Twist Creative, Seattle

Contents at a glance

	Introduction	xv
	Preparing for the exam	xix
CHAPTER 1	Install Windows Servers in host and compute environments	1
CHAPTER 2	Implement storage solutions	81
CHAPTER 3	Implement Hyper-V	165
CHAPTER 4	Implement Windows containers	259
CHAPTER 5	Implement high availability	297
CHAPTER 6	Maintain and monitor server environments	387
	Index	445

Contents

Introduction   **xv**

Organization of this book xvi

Microsoft certifications xvi

Free ebooks from Microsoft Press xvi

Microsoft Virtual Academy xvi

Quick access to online references xvii

Errata, updates, & book support xvii

We want to hear from you xvii

Stay in touch xvii

Preparing for the exam   *xix*

Chapter 1   Install Windows Servers in host and compute environments   **1**

Skill 1.1: Install, upgrade, and migrate servers and workloads 1

    Determine Windows Server 2016 installation requirements   2

    Determine appropriate Windows Server 2016 editions per workloads   4

    Install Windows Server 2016   6

    Install Windows Server 2016 features and roles   11

    Install and configure Windows Server Core   17

    Manage Windows Server Core installations using Windows PowerShell, command line, and remote management capabilities   21

What do you think of this book? We want to hear from you!

Microsoft is interested in hearing your feedback so we can continually improve our books and learning resources for you. To participate in a brief online survey, please visit:

https://aka.ms/tellpress

Implement Windows PowerShell Desired State Configuration
(DSC) to install and maintain integrity of installed environments 26

Perform upgrades and migrations of servers and core workloads
from Windows Server 2008 and Windows Server 2012 to
Windows Server 2016 27

Determine the appropriate activation model for server installation 35

Skill 1.2: Install and configure Nano Server 42

Determine appropriate usage scenarios and requirements
for Nano Server 43

Install Nano Server 44

Implement Roles and Features on Nano Server 48

Manage and configure Nano Server 50

Managing Nano Server remotely using PowerShell 55

Skill 1.3: Create, manage, and maintain images for deployment 58

Plan for Windows Server virtualization 58

Plan for Linux and FreeBSD deployments 61

Assess virtualization workloads using the Microsoft
Assessment and Planning (MAP) Toolkit 61

Determine considerations for deploying workloads into
virtualized environments 69

Update images with patches, hotfixes, and drivers 70

Install Roles and Features in offline images 75

Manage and maintain Windows Server Core, Nano Server
images, and VHDs using Windows PowerShell 76

Chapter summary 79

Thought experiment. 80

Thought experiment answer. 80

Chapter 2 Implement storage solutions 81

Skill 2.1: Configure disks and volumes. 81

Configure sector sizes appropriate for various workloads 82

Configure GUID partition table (GPT) disks 84

Create VHD and VHDX files using Server Manager or
Windows PowerShell 88

Mount Virtual Hard Disks (VHDs) 91

	Determine when to use NTFS and ReFS File Systems	93
	Configure NFS and SMB shares using Server Manager	95
	Configure SMB share and session settings using Windows PowerShell	106
	Configure SMB server and SMB client configuration settings using Windows PowerShell	108
	Configure file and folder permissions	112

Skill 2.2: Implement server storage 123

    Configure storage pools   123

    Implement simple, mirror, and parity storage layout options for disks or enclosures   125

    Configure tiered storage   131

    Configure iSCSI target and initiator   133

    Configure iSNS   140

    Configure Datacenter Bridging (DCB)   142

    Configure Multipath I/O (MPIO)   145

    Determine usage scenarios for Storage Replica   148

    Implement Storage Replica for server-to-server, cluster-to-cluster, and stretch cluster scenarios   151

Skill 2.3: Implement data deduplication 155

    Implement and configure deduplication   155

    Determine appropriate usage scenarios for deduplication   158

    Monitor deduplication   160

    Implement a backup and restore solution with deduplication   162

Chapter summary 162

Thought experiment..164

Thought experiment answer.....................................164

Chapter 3 Implement Hyper-V   165

Skill 3.1: Install and configure Hyper-V............................165

    Determine hardware and compatibility requirements for installing Hyper-V   166

    Install Hyper-V   170

    Install management tools   172

Upgrade from existing versions of Hyper-V	173
Delegate virtual machine management	174
Perform remote management of Hyper-V hosts	174
Configure virtual machines using Windows PowerShell Direct	180
Implement nested virtualization	181

Skill 3.2: Configure virtual machine (VM) settings 182

Creating a virtual machine	182
Add or remove memory in running a VM	185
Configure dynamic memory	186
Configure Non-Uniform Memory Access (NUMA) support	189
Configure smart paging	192
Configure resource metering	193
Manage Integration Services	195
Create and configure Generation 1 and 2 VMs and determine appropriate usage scenarios	197
Implement enhanced session mode	199
Create Linux and FreeBSD VMs	201
Install and configure Linux Integration Services (LIS)	204
Install and configure FreeBSD Integration Services (BIS)	205
Implement Secure Boot for Windows and Linux environments	205
Move and convert VMs from previous versions of Hyper-V to Windows Server 2016 Hyper-V	208
Export and import VMs	209
Implement Discrete Device Assignment (DDA)	212

Skill 3.3: Configure Hyper-V storage 213

Create VHDs and VHDX files using Hyper-V Manager	214
Create shared VHDX files	220
Configure differencing disks	222
Modify virtual hard disks	223
Configure pass-through disks	225
Resize a virtual hard disk	226
Manage checkpoints	228
Implement production checkpoints	230

Implement a virtual fibre channel adapter	231
Configure Storage Quality of Service (QoS)	233

Skill 3.4: Configure Hyper-V networking 235

Add and remove virtual network interface cards (vNICs)	236
Configure Hyper-V virtual switches	238
Optimize network performance	243
Configure MAC addresses	244
Configure network isolation	246
Configure synthetic and legacy virtual network adapters	247
Configure NIC teaming in VMs	249
Configure virtual machine queue (VMQ)	251
Enable Remote Direct Memory Access (RDMA) on network adapters bound to a Hyper-V virtual switch using Switch Embedded Teaming (SET)	253
Configure bandwidth management	254

Chapter summary 256

Thought experiment..258

Thought experiment answer......................................258

Chapter 4   Implement Windows containers   259

Skill 4.1: Deploy Windows containers 259

Determine installation requirements and appropriate scenarios for Windows containers	260
Install and configure Windows Server Container Host in physical or virtualized environments	261
Install and configure Windows Server container host to Windows Server Core or Nano Server in a physical or virtualized environment	264
Install Docker on Windows Server and Nano Server	266
Configure Docker Daemon start-up options	269
Configure Windows PowerShell for use with containers	270
Install a base operating system	271
Tag an image	272
Uninstall an operating system image	273

    Create Windows Server containers 274
    Create Hyper-V containers 275

  Skill 4.2: Manage Windows containers 277
    Manage Windows or Linux containers using the Docker daemon 277
    Manage Windows or Linux containers using Windows PowerShell 279
    Manage container networking 281
    Manage container data volumes 286
    Manage resource control 287
    Create new container images using Dockerfile 289
    Manage container images using DockerHub Repository for public and private scenarios 291
    Manage container images using Microsoft Azure 293

  Chapter summary 293

  Thought experiment. 295

  Thought experiment answer. 295

Chapter 5 Implement high availability 297

  Skill 5.1: Implement high availability and disaster recovery options in Hyper-V 297
    Implement Hyper-V Replica 298
    Implement live migration 303
    Implement shared nothing live migration 307
    Configure CredSSP or Kerberos authentication protocol for Live Migration 308
    Implement storage migration 309

  Skill 5.2: Implement failover clustering 311
    Implement workgroup, single, and multi domain clusters 314
    Configure quorum 317
    Configure cluster networking 321
    Restore single node or cluster configuration 324
    Configure cluster storage 326
    Implement cluster-aware updating 328
    Implement cluster operating system rolling upgrade 332

Configure and optimize clustered shared volumes (CSVs)	333
Configure clusters without network names	337
Implement Scale-Out File Server (SoFS)	337
Determine different scenarios for the use of SoFS vs. clustered file server	341
Determine usage scenarios for implementing guest clustering	341
Implement a clustered Storage Spaces solution using shared SAS storage enclosures	342
Implement Storage Replica	345
Implement cloud witness	345
Implement VM resiliency	348
Implement shared VHDX as a storage solution for guest clusters	349

Skill 5.3: Implement Storage Spaces Direct 352

Determine scenario requirements for implementing Storage Spaces Direct	352
Enable Storage Spaces direct using Windows PowerShell	354
Implement a disaggregated Storage Spaces Direct scenario in a cluster	355
Implement a hyper-converged Storage Spaces Direct scenario in a cluster	357

Skill 5.4: Manage failover clustering 359

Configure role-specific settings, including continuously available shares	359
Configure VM monitoring	361
Configure failover and preference settings	364
Implement stretch and site-aware failover clusters	365
Enable and configure node fairness	367

Skill 5.5: Manage VM movement in clustered nodes 369

Perform a live migration	369
Perform a quick migration	370
Perform a storage migration	371
Import, export, and copy VMs	372
Configure VM network health protection	373
Configure drain on shutdown	374

Skill 5.6: Implement Network Load Balancing (NLB) 375

    Configure NLB prerequisites   375

    Install NLB nodes   377

    Configure affinity   381

    Configure port rules   382

    Configure cluster operation mode   384

    Upgrade an NLB cluster   384

Chapter summary 385

Thought experiment 386

Thought experiment answer......................................386

Chapter 6 Maintain and monitor server environments 387

Skill 6.1: Maintain server installations 387

    Implement Windows Server Update Services (WSUS) solutions   388

    Configure WSUS groups   398

    Manage patch management in mixed environments   401

    Implement an antimalware solution with Windows Defender   405

    Integrate Windows Defender with WSUS and Windows Update   409

    Perform backup and restore operations using Windows Server Backup   411

    Determine backup strategies for different Windows Server roles and workloads, including Hyper-V Host, Hyper-V Guests, Active Directory, File Servers, and Web Servers using Windows Server 2016 native tools and solutions   421

Skill 6.2: Monitor server installations 425

    Monitor workloads using Performance Monitor   425

    Configure data collector sets   431

    Determine appropriate CPU, memory, disk, and networking counters for storage and compute workloads   433

    Configure alerts   438

    Monitor workloads using Resource Monitor   440

Chapter summary 442
Thought experiment 443
Thought experiment answer 443

Index   *445*

What do you think of this book? We want to hear from you!
Microsoft is interested in hearing your feedback so we can continually improve our books and learning resources for you. To participate in a brief online survey, please visit:

https://aka.ms/tellpress

Introduction

Many Windows Server books take the approach of teaching you every detail about the product. Such books end up being huge and tough to read. Not to mention that remembering everything you read is incredibly challenging. That's why those books aren't the best choice for preparing for a certification exam such as the Microsoft Exam 70-740, "Installation, Storage, and Compute with Windows Server 2016." For this book, we focus on your review of the Windows Server skills that you need to maximize your chances of passing the exam. Our goal is to cover all of the skills measured on the exam, while bringing a real-world focus to the information. This book shouldn't be your only resource for exam preparation, but it can be your primary resource. We recommend combining the information in this book with some hands-on work in a lab environment (or as part of your job in a real-world environment).

The 70-740 exam is geared toward IT professionals who have a minimum of 3 years of experience working with Windows Server. That doesn't mean you can't take and pass the exam with less experience, but it probably means that it will be harder. Of course, everyone is different. It is possible to get the knowledge and skills required to pass the 70-740 exam in fewer than 3 years. But whether you are a senior-level Windows Server administrator or just a couple of years into your Windows Server journey, we think you'll find the information in this book valuable as your primary exam prep resource.

This book covers every major topic area found on the exam, but it does not cover every exam question. Only the Microsoft exam team has access to the exam questions, and Microsoft regularly adds new questions to the exam, making it impossible to cover specific questions. You should consider this book a supplement to your relevant real-world experience and other study materials. If you encounter a topic in this book that you do not feel completely comfortable with, use the "Need more review?" links you'll find in the text to find more information and take the time to research and study the topic. Great information is available on MSDN, TechNet, and in blogs and forums.

Organization of this book

This book is organized by the "Skills measured" list published for the exam. The "Skills measured" list is available for each exam on the Microsoft Learning website: *https://aka.ms/examlist*. Each chapter in this book corresponds to a major topic area in the list, and the technical tasks in each topic area determine a chapter's organization. If an exam covers six major topic areas, for example, the book will contain six chapters.

Microsoft certifications

Microsoft certifications distinguish you by proving your command of a broad set of skills and experience with current Microsoft products and technologies. The exams and corresponding certifications are developed to validate your mastery of critical competencies as you design and develop, or implement and support, solutions with Microsoft products and technologies both on-premises and in the cloud. Certification brings a variety of benefits to the individual and to employers and organizations.

> **MORE INFO**   **ALL MICROSOFT CERTIFICATIONS**
>
> For information about Microsoft certifications, including a full list of available certifications, go to *https://www.microsoft.com/learning*.

Free ebooks from Microsoft Press

From technical overviews to in-depth information on special topics, the free ebooks from Microsoft Press cover a wide range of topics. These ebooks are available in PDF, EPUB, and Mobi for Kindle formats, ready for you to download at:

https://aka.ms/mspressfree

Check back often to see what is new!

Microsoft Virtual Academy

Build your knowledge of Microsoft technologies with free expert-led online training from Microsoft Virtual Academy (MVA). MVA offers a comprehensive library of videos, live events, and more to help you learn the latest technologies and prepare for certification exams. You'll find what you need here:

https://www.microsoftvirtualacademy.com

Quick access to online references

Throughout this book are addresses to webpages that the author has recommended you visit for more information. Some of these addresses (also known as URLs) can be painstaking to type into a web browser, so we've compiled all of them into a single list that readers of the print edition can refer to while they read.

Download the list at *https://aka.ms/examref740/downloads*.

The URLs are organized by chapter and heading. Every time you come across a URL in the book, find the hyperlink in the list to go directly to the webpage.

Errata, updates, & book support

We've made every effort to ensure the accuracy of this book and its companion content. You can access updates to this book—in the form of a list of submitted errata and their related corrections—at:

https://aka.ms/examref740/errata

If you discover an error that is not already listed, please submit it to us at the same page.

If you need additional support, email Microsoft Press Book Support at *mspinput@microsoft.com*.

Please note that product support for Microsoft software and hardware is not offered through the previous addresses. For help with Microsoft software or hardware, go to *http://support.microsoft.com*.

We want to hear from you

At Microsoft Press, your satisfaction is our top priority, and your feedback our most valuable asset. Please tell us what you think of this book at:

https://aka.ms/tellpress

We know you're busy, so we've kept it short with just a few questions. Your answers go directly to the editors at Microsoft Press. (No personal information will be requested.) Thanks in advance for your input!

Stay in touch

Let's keep the conversation going! We're on Twitter: *http://twitter.com/MicrosoftPress*.

Important: How to use this book to study for the exam

Certification exams validate your on-the-job experience and product knowledge. To gauge your readiness to take an exam, use this Exam Ref to help you check your understanding of the skills tested by the exam. Determine the topics you know well and the areas in which you need more experience. To help you refresh your skills in specific areas, we have also provided "Need more review?" pointers, which direct you to more in-depth information outside the book.

The Exam Ref is not a substitute for hands-on experience. This book is not designed to teach you new skills.

We recommend that you round out your exam preparation by using a combination of available study materials and courses. Learn more about available classroom training at *https://www.microsoft.com/learning*. Microsoft Official Practice Tests are available for many exams at *https://aka.ms/practicetests*. You can also find free online courses and live events from Microsoft Virtual Academy at *https://www.microsoftvirtualacademy.com*.

This book is organized by the "Skills measured" list published for the exam. The "Skills measured" list for each exam is available on the Microsoft Learning website: *https://aka.ms/examlist*.

Note that this Exam Ref is based on this publicly available information and the author's experience. To safeguard the integrity of the exam, authors do not have access to the exam questions.

CHAPTER 1

Install Windows Servers in host and compute environments

Windows Server 2016 provides administrators with a variety of ways to deploy servers. You can install the operating system on a physical computer, as always, but you can also create a virtual deployment, using Hyper-V virtual machines and also the new Nano Server installation option.

Skills in this chapter:

- Install, upgrade, and migrate servers and workloads
- Install and configure Nano Server
- Create, manage, and maintain images for deployment

> **IMPORTANT**
> *Have you read page xix?*
> It contains valuable information regarding the skills you need to pass the exam.

Skill 1.1: Install, upgrade, and migrate servers and workloads

There is more to installing Windows Server 2016 than running a setup wizard. Deploying servers, however you choose to do it, requires careful planning before you touch any hardware. This planning includes selecting the proper operating system edition and the best installation option for your organization's needs. If you have existing servers running prior Windows Server versions, you must decide how to upgrade or migrate them to Windows Server 2016.

> **This section covers how to:**
> - Determine Windows Server 2016 installation requirements
> - Determine appropriate Windows Server 2016 editions per workloads
> - Install Windows Server 2016
> - Install Windows Server 2016 features and roles
> - Install and configure Windows Server Core
> - Manage Windows Server Core installations using Windows PowerShell, command line, and remote management capabilities
> - Implement Windows PowerShell Desired State Configuration (DSC) to install and maintain integrity of installed environments
> - Perform upgrades and migrations of servers and core workloads from Windows Server 2008 and Windows Server 2012 to Windows Server 2016
> - Determine the appropriate activation model for server installation, such as Automatic Virtual Machine Activation (AVMA), Key Management Service (KMS), and Active Directory-based Activation

Determine Windows Server 2016 installation requirements

Planning a Windows Server 2016 installation requires several important decisions that affect not only the initial deployment of the server, but also its ongoing maintenance. While the Windows installation process is relatively simple, there are options to be considered both before you purchase the server hardware and the operating system, and after the initial installation is complete.

Some of the questions you must consider when planning a server deployment are as follows:

- **Which Windows Server 2016 edition should you install?** Microsoft provides Windows Server 2016 in several editions, which vary in the features they include, the resources they support, and the cost of the license. The details of the editions are described later in this chapter.

- **Which installation option should you use?** Most of the Windows Server 2016 editions include two installation options: Desktop Experience and Server Core. Desktop Experience includes all of the Windows features and a full graphical user interface (GUI). Server Core has a minimal user interface and a significantly reduced resource footprint, so it can utilize less memory and disk space than a Desktop Experience installation. There is also a third installation option, Nano Server, which requires an even smaller resource footprint, but this option does not appear in the initial installation wizard; you deploy Nano Server later, using Windows PowerShell.

- **Which roles and features does the server need?** The type and number of roles and features you plan to install can greatly affect the hardware resources the server will need, as well as the edition you purchase. For example, complex roles such as

Active Directory Certificate Services and Failover Clustering typically require additional resources and are not available in all editions. Third-party applications also affect resource utilization.

- **What virtualization strategy should you use?** The increased emphasis on virtualization in enterprise networking has profoundly altered the server deployment process. The ease with which administrators can migrate virtual machines from one host server to another has led then to consider not only what roles the physical server runs, but what roles could be needed on any virtual servers it is hosting. It is also important to consider what resources could be required if a server has to host additional virtual machines during a disaster situation.

By answering these questions, you can begin to determine what resources a server will need. Microsoft publishes minimum hardware requirements for a Windows Server 2016 installation, but it is difficult to predict just what resources a server will need to run efficiently, once you have installed all of the roles, features, and applications it requires to function.

Minimum hardware requirements

If your computer does not meet the following minimum hardware specifications, Windows Server 2016 will not install correctly (or possibly not install at all):

- Processor: 1.4-GHz 64-bit
- RAM: 512 MB ECC for Server Core, 2 GB ECC for Server with Desktop Experience
- Disk space: 32 GB minimum on a SATA or comparable drive
- Network adapter: Ethernet, with gigabit throughput
- Monitor: Super VGA (1024 x 768) or higher resolution
- Keyboard and mouse (or other compatible pointing device)
- Internet access

32 GB of available disk space should be considered the absolute minimum. A minimal Server Core installation with only the Web Server (IIS) role added should install successfully in 32 GB, but using the Desktop Experience installation option and installing additional roles will require more storage.

Windows Server 2016 does not support the use of the ATA, PATA, IDE, or EIDE interfaces for boot, page, or data drives. The system partition also needs additional space if you install the system over a network or if the computer has more than 16 GB of RAM. The additional disk space is required for paging, hibernation, and dump files.

> *NOTE* **INSTALLING A MINIMUM HARDWARE CONFIGURATION**
>
> A Windows Server 2016 installation on a virtual machine with the minimum single processor core and 512 MB of RAM fails. However, you can allocate more memory for the installation and then reduce it 512 MB afterwards, and the operating system runs.

Maximum hardware and virtualization limits

Virtualization has complicated the issue of the maximum hardware configurations supported by Windows Server 2016. It's no longer a simple matter of how many processors, how much memory, and largest possible disk size. While processor maximums were at one time measured in the number of sockets, now they refer to numbers of cores and logical processors. There are now also different maximums for physical and virtual machines in some resources.

The maximum hardware configurations for Windows Server 2016 are as follows:

- **Processors**   A server host supports up to 512 logical processors (LPs) if Hyper-V is installed.
- **Memory**   Up to 24 terabytes per host server and up to 12 terabytes per virtual machine.
- **VHDX size**   Up to 64 terabytes.
- **Virtual machines**   Up to 1,024 per host server.
- **Virtual machine processors**   Up to 240 per virtual machine.

> **NOTE UNDERSTANDING LPS**
>
> Intel processors have a feature called hyperthreading, which enables a single core to process two threads simultaneously when Hyper-V is running. Thus, an Intel processor is considered to have two LPs per core when Hyper-V is running and one LP per core when it is not. In an AMD processor with multiple cores, each core is equivalent to one LP.

Determine appropriate Windows Server 2016 editions per workloads

Windows Server 2016 is available in multiple editions, with varying prices and features. To select an edition for your server deployment, you should consider the following questions:

- What roles and features will you need to run on the server?
- How will you obtain licenses for the servers?
- Will you be running Windows Server 2016 on virtual or physical machines?

The current trend in server deployment is to use relatively small servers that perform a single task, rather than large servers that perform many tasks. In cloud deployments, whether public, private, or hybrid, it is common to see virtual machines performing one role, such as a web server or a DNS server. It is for this reason that Microsoft introduced the Server Core installation option in Windows Server 2008 and Nano Server in Windows Server 2016, so that virtual machines could function with a smaller resource footprint.

Before you choose an installation option, however, you must select the appropriate Windows Server 2016 edition for the server workload you intend to implement. The Windows Server 2016 editions are as follows:

- **Windows Server 2016 Datacenter**   The Datacenter edition is intended for large and powerful servers in a highly virtualized environment. The license allows for an unlim-

ited number of operating system environments (OSEs) or Hyper-V containers. The Datacenter edition also includes additional features not available in the other editions, such as Storage Spaces Direct, Storage Replica, shielded virtual machines, and a new networking stack with additional virtualization options.

- **Windows Server 2016 Standard**   The Standard edition license allows for two OSEs and includes the same core set of features as the Datacenter edition. However, it lacks the new storage and networking features listed in the Datacenter description.

- **Windows Server 2016 Essentials**   The Essentials edition includes nearly all the features in the Standard and Datacenter editions; it does not include the Server Core installation option. The Essentials edition is also limited to one OSE (physical or virtual) and a maximum of 25 users and 50 devices. Unlike the Standard and Datacenter editions, Essential includes a configuration wizard that installs and configures Active Directory Domain Services and other essential components needed for a single-server network.

- **Windows Server 2016 MultiPoint Premium Server**   Available only through academic licensing, the Multipoint edition enables multiple users to access a single server installation.

- **Windows Storage Server 2016 Server**   Available only through original equipment manufacturer (OEM) channels, the Storage Server edition is bundled as part of a dedicated storage hardware solution.

- **Windows Hyper-V Server 2016**   Available at no cost, the Hyper-V Server edition is a hypervisor-only download, without a graphical interface, that hosts virtual machines as its only function.

> **NOTE   UNDERSTANDING OSES**
>
> Microsoft now uses the term operating system environment (OSE) to refer to the Windows instances running on a computer. An OSE can be physical or virtual. For example, a server running one virtual machine in Hyper-V would be using two OSEs because the physical server installation counts for one.

In Windows Server 2012, the Datacenter and Standard editions were functionally identical. The only difference was in the number of Hyper-V virtual machines the license authorized you to create. In Windows Server 2016, the Datacenter edition includes several new features that could affect your decision to choose that edition over Standard. The features in the Datacenter edition that are not included in the Standard edition are as follows:

- **Storage Spaces Direct**   Enables administrators to use relatively inexpensive drive arrays to create high-availability storage solutions. Instead of using an expensive array or controller with built-in storage management intelligence, the intelligence is incorporated into the operating system, enabling the use of inexpensive JBOD (just a bunch of disks) arrays.

- **Storage Replica**   Provides storage-agnostic, synchronous or asynchronous volume replication between local or remote servers, using the Server Message Blocks Version 3 protocol.
- **Shielded virtual machines**   Provides VMs with protection from compromised administrators that have access to the Hyper-V host computer by encrypting the VM state and its virtual disks.
- **Network controller**   Provides a central automation point for network infrastructure configuration, monitoring, and troubleshooting.

For most organizations, the selection of an edition will be based on cost. The Essentials edition is inexpensive and easy to deploy, but it is limited in its features. For a small organization, it can be ideal, however.

For medium to large-sized organizations, the typical choice is between the Standard and Datacenter editions. If the new Datacenter features are not important to you, the decision will likely be based on your virtualization strategy. If the plan is for a server to run a relatively small number of virtual machines, it could be more economical to purchase multiple Standard edition licenses than one Datacenter license. At the current prices, you can purchase up to seven Standard licenses (with two OSEs each) for less than the cost of a single Datacenter license.

Another issue to consider is your organization's potential for growth. If you intend to run 10 virtual machines now, it could be better to spend a few hundred dollars more for a Datacenter license, which provides unlimited OSEs for future expansion, rather than five Standard licenses.

EXAM TIP

The 70-740 exam can include licensing questions in which you must determine which Windows edition and how many licenses are needed to support a specific number of virtual machines on a Hyper-V server, while minimizing the licensing cost.

Install Windows Server 2016

The process of installing Windows Server 2016 can be relatively simple, when you are performing a clean installation on a single, new computer. It can also be extremely complex, when you are automating a mass deployment or migrating existing servers to the new operating system.

Performing a clean installation

A clean installation—also called a bare-metal installation—is when you are installing an operating system on a computer that does not already have one. To do this, you must have the operating system files on a bootable installation medium. Windows Server 2016 is still available on a bootable DVD, but most administrators download the installation package as a disk image file with an ISO extension.

- To install an ISO on a physical computer, you have to burn it to a removable disk, such as a flash drive or a DVD. You can do this on any other computer running Windows Server 2016 or Windows 10 by selecting the ISO in File Manager, and then selecting the Disk Image Tools\Manage menu, and clicking the Burn button.

- To install Windows Server 2016 on a virtual machine in Hyper-V, you can use the ISO file directly. When you create a VM, you can specify the ISO as you configure the virtual DVD drive. When you start the VM, the ISO appears and functions as a bootable disk on the system.

Once you have a bootable disk, you can perform a clean installation of Windows Server 2016 on a physical machine using the following procedure.

1. Turn on the computer and insert the Windows Server 2016 installation flash drive or disk.
2. Press any key to boot from the installation medium (if necessary). A progress indicator screen appears as Windows loads files.

> **NOTE MODIFYING BIOS SETTINGS**
>
> The device that a PC uses to boot is specified in its system (or BIOS) settings. In some cases, you could have to modify these settings to enable the computer to boot from the installation medium you are using. If you are not familiar with the operation of a particular computer, watch the screen carefully as the system starts and look for an instruction specifying what key to press to access the system settings.

3. The computer loads the graphical user interface and the Windows Setup page appears, as shown in Figure 1-1.

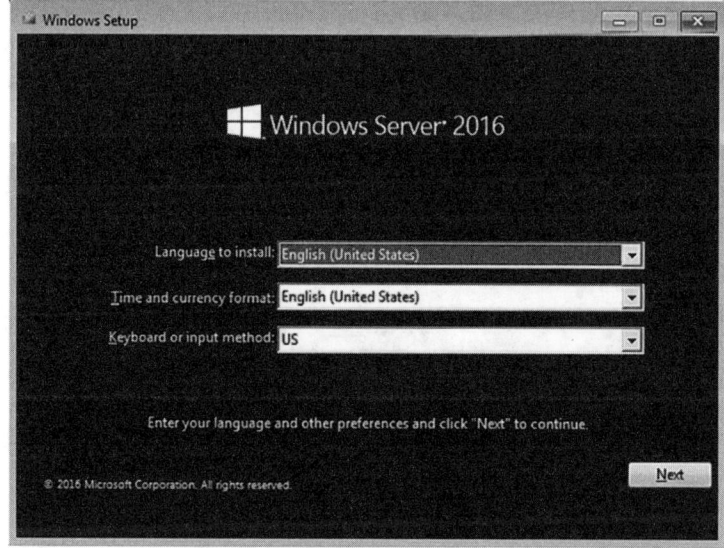

FIGURE 1-1 The Windows Setup page

4. Using the drop-down lists provided, select the appropriate Language To Install, Time And Currency Format, and Keyboard Or Input Method, and then click Next. Another Windows Setup page appears.

5. Click Install Now. The Windows Setup Wizard appears, displaying the Select The Operating System You Want To Install page.
6. Select the operating system edition and installation option you want to install and click Next. The Applicable Notices And License Terms page appears.
7. Select the I Accept The License Terms check box and click Next. The Which Type Of Installation Do You Want page appears, as shown in Figure 1-2.

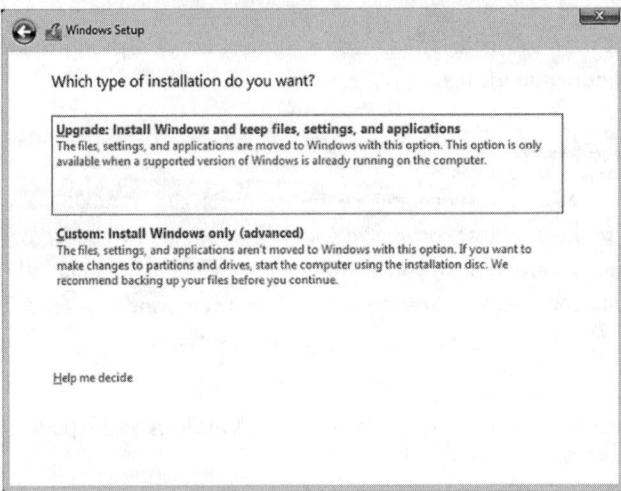

FIGURE 1-2 The Which Type Of Installation Do You Want page

8. Because you are performing a clean installation and not an upgrade, click the Custom: Install Windows Only (Advanced) option. The Where Do You Want To Install Windows page appears, as shown in Figure 1-3.

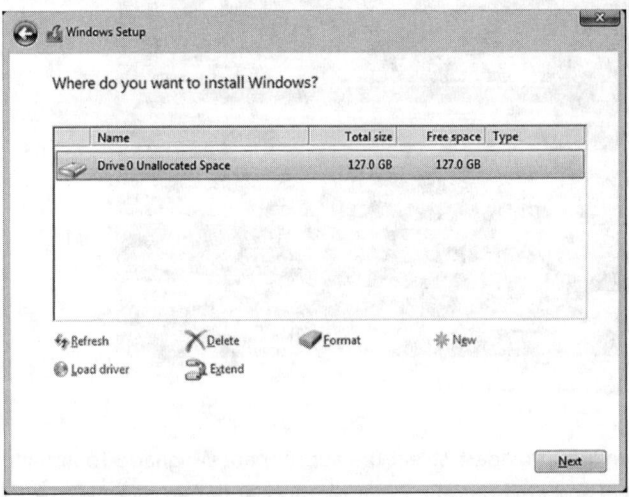

FIGURE 1-3 The Where Do You Want To Install Windows page

9. From the list provided, select the partition on which you want to install Windows Server 2016, or select an area of unallocated disk space where the Setup program can create a new partition. Then click Next. The Installing Windows page appears.

10. After several minutes, during which the Setup program installs Windows Server 2016, the computer restarts and the Customize Settings page appears, as shown in Figure 1-4.

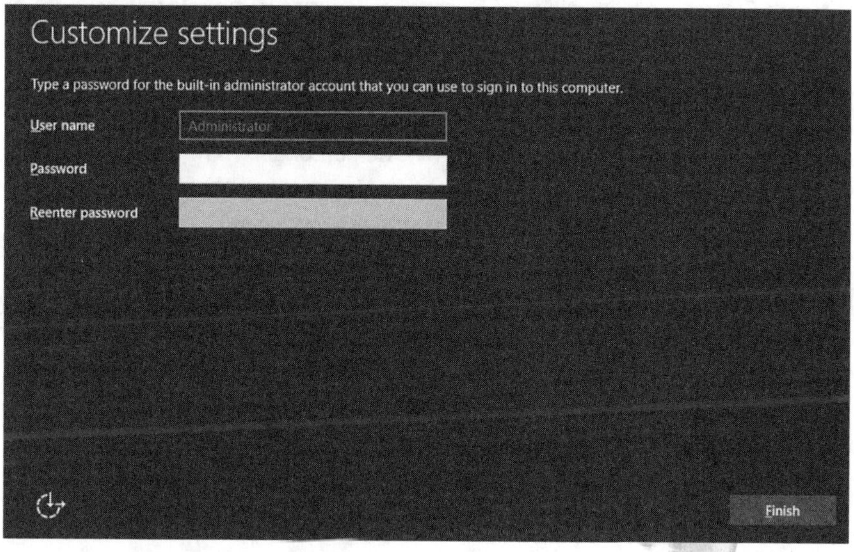

FIGURE 1-4 The Customize Settings page

11. In the Password and Reenter Password text boxes, type the password to be associated with the system's local Administrator account and press Enter. The system finalizes the installation and the Windows lock screen appears.

Working with partitions

In some cases, as you install Windows Server 2016, you could find it necessary to work with your disks and partitions. For this reason, the Setup program includes controls on the Where Do You Want To Install Windows page that enable you to create, manage, and delete the partitions on your disks.

The buttons on the page have the following functions:

- **Refresh** Displays partitions that are available as the result of a newly loaded driver.
- **Load driver** Enables you to add disk drivers from an external medium, such as a CD-ROM, DVD, or USB drive.
- **Delete** Removes an existing partition from a disk, permanently erasing all its data. You might want to delete partitions to consolidate unallocated disk space, enabling you to create a new, larger partition.

- **Extend** Enables you to make an existing partition larger, as long as unallocated space is available immediately following the selected partition on the disk.
- **Format** Enables you to format an existing partition on a disk, thereby erasing all its data. You do not need to format any new partitions you create for the install, but you might want to format an existing partition to eliminate unwanted files before installing Windows Server 2016 on it.
- **New** Creates a new partition of a user-specified size in the selected area of unallocated space.

Sometimes, during an installation, you might see no partitions listed at all on the Where Do You Want To Install Windows page. This page lists the partitions on all the computer's disk drives that the Setup program can detect with its default drivers. If no partitions appear, it is because the computer's disk controller requires a device driver that is not included in the Windows default driver set. Some high-end controllers, such as those for disk arrays, require their own drivers, which you can install during the Setup process.

Check the disk controller manufacturer's website for a driver supporting Windows Server 2016, or another recent version of Windows Server, and use the following procedure to install it.

1. On the Where Do You Want To Install Windows page, click the Load Driver button. A Load Driver message box appears, as shown in Figure 1-5.

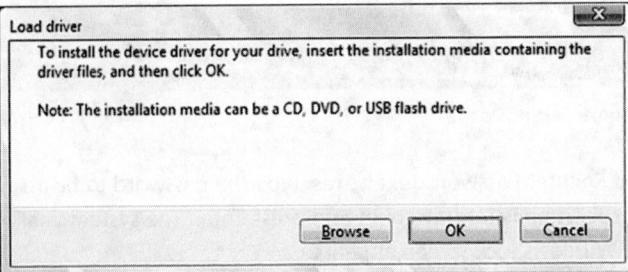

FIGURE 1-5 The Load Driver message box

2. Insert the storage medium containing the driver into the computer. You can supply drivers on a CD, DVD, USB flash drive, or floppy disk.
3. Click OK if the driver is in the root directory of the storage medium, or Browse if you need to locate the driver in the directory structure of the disk. A list of the drivers found on the disk appears on the Select The Driver To Install page.
4. Select one of the drivers in the list, and click Next.
5. When the driver loads, the partitions and unallocated space on the associated disks appear in the list on the Where Do You Want To Install Windows page.
6. Select the partition or area of unallocated space where you want to install Windows Server 2016, and then continue with the rest of the installation procedure, as covered earlier in this chapter.

Performing a mass deployment

When you have a large number of servers to install, you can conceivably mount a disk and perform a manual installation on each one, but that can become impractical. For a mass operating system deployment, you can use a server-based technology, such as Windows Deployment Services (WDS), to deploy image files automatically.

WDS is a role included with Windows Server 2016, which you can use to provide disk images to clients on the network. For this to work, however, the client must have some way to contact the WDS server and initiate the process. WDS enables you to create boot images, which you can burn to removable disks, but this still requires you to travel to each computer and run through the installation process.

A better way of deploying the WDS boot image is to use the *Preboot Execution Environment (PXE)* feature included with most network interface adapters. PXE is built into the adapter's firmware and enables a computer with no operating system to discover a Dynamic Host Configuration Protocol (DHCP) server on the network and request a configuration from it. The DHCP server supplies the client with the IP address of a WDS server, which the client then uses to connect to the server and download a boot image. The client system can then boot from that image and run a WDS client program that initiates the operating system installation.

Installing and configuring an automated software deployment service, such as WDS or System Center Configuration Manager, can be a complex task in itself. It is up to the administrators to decide whether the number of servers they have to deploy is worth the time and expense.

Install Windows Server 2016 features and roles

Windows Server 2016 includes predefined combinations of services, called *roles*, which are designed to configure the server to perform specific tasks. The operating system also includes other, smaller components called *features*. Windows Server 2016 can run as many roles as it has the hardware resources to support, but the current trend is toward more specialized servers that run only one or two roles.

To add roles and features in Windows Server 2016, you can use a graphical wizard in the Server Manager console, or you can install them from the Windows PowerShell command line, as described in the following sections.

Using Server Manager to install roles

To install roles and services on a computer running Windows Server 2016 with Server Manager, use the following procedure:

1. In Server Manager, open the Manage menu and select Add Roles And Features. The Add Roles And Features Wizard launches.
2. Bypass the Before You Begin page to proceed to the Select Installation Type page, as shown in Figure 1-6.

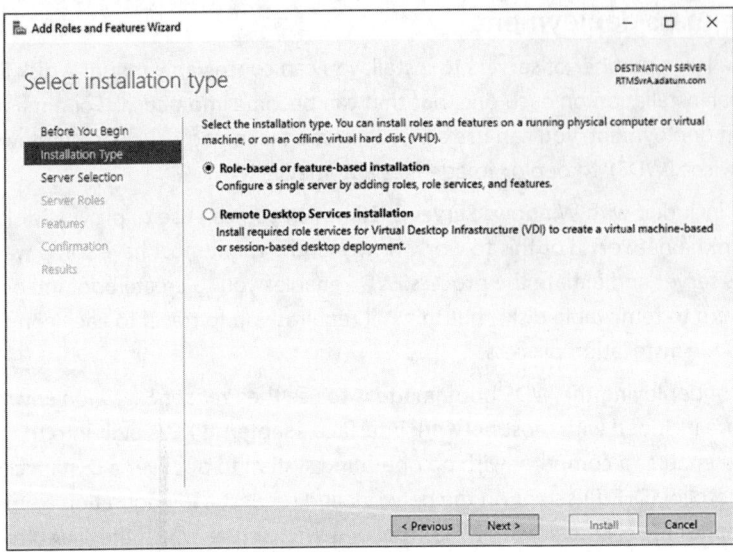

FIGURE 1-6 The Select Installation Type page in the Add Roles And Features Wizard

3. Click Next to accept the default Role-Based or Feature-Based Installation option selected. The Select Destination Server page appears, as shown in Figure 1-7.

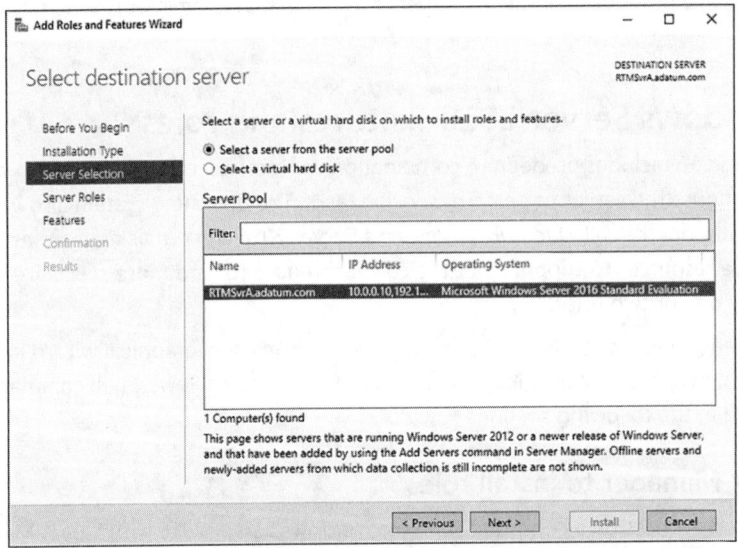

FIGURE 1-7 The Select Destination Server page in the Add Roles And Features Wizard

4. Click Next to accept the default server settings. The Select Server Roles page opens, as shown in Figure 1-8.

NOTE **CONFIGURING MULTIPLE SERVERS**

When you first run Server Manager, only the local server appears on the Select Destination Server page. However, you can add other servers to Server Manager, enabling you to manage them remotely. When you do this, you can use the Add Roles And Features Wizard to install components to any server you have added, though you cannot use it to install components to multiple servers at once. You can, however, do this by using the Install-WindowsFeature cmdlet in Windows PowerShell.

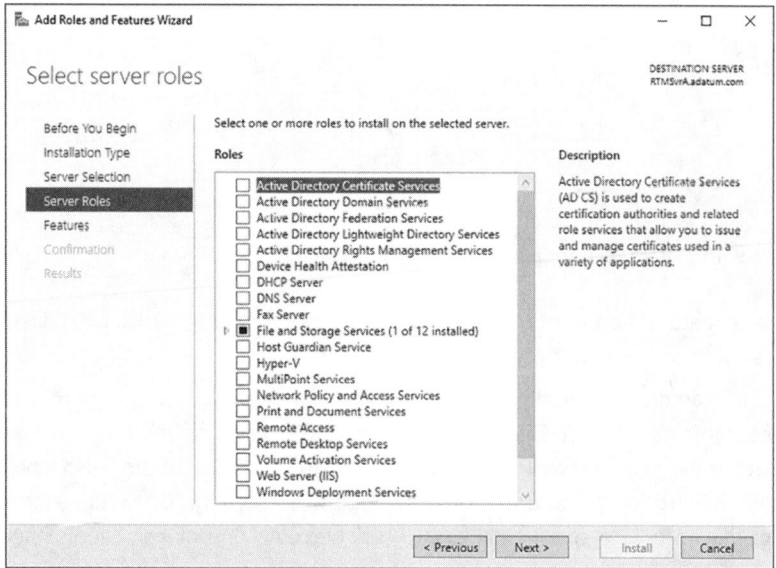

FIGURE 1-8 The Select Server Roles page in the Add Roles And Features Wizard

5. Select the role or roles you want to install on the selected server. If the roles you select have other roles or features as dependencies, an Add Features That Are Required dialog box appears.

6. Click Add Features to accept the dependencies, and then click Next to open the Select Features page, as shown in Figure 1-9.

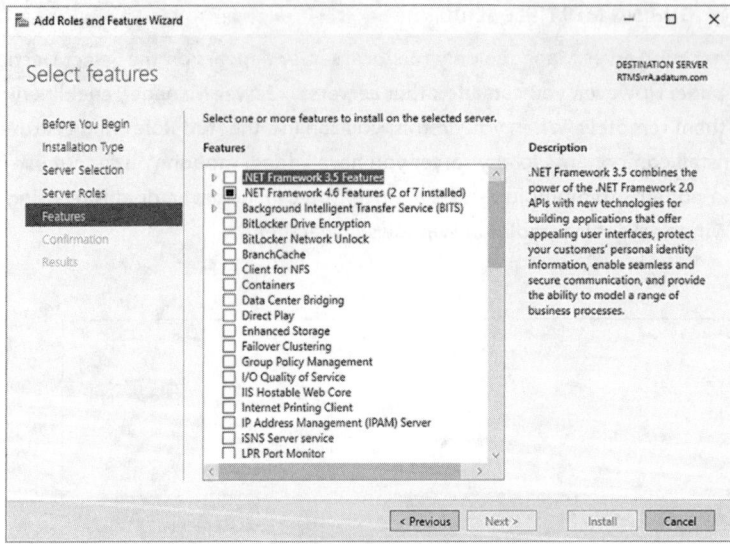

FIGURE 1-9 The Select Features page in the Add Roles And Features Wizard

7. Select any features you want to install on the selected server and click Next. Dependencies could also appear for your feature selections.

8. The wizard can display additional pages specific to the roles or features you have selected. Most roles have a Select Role Services page, on which you can select which elements of the role you want to install, as shown in Figure 1-10. Some also have pages that contain introductory information or configuration settings. Complete each of the role-specific or feature-specific pages and click Next. A Confirm Installation Selections page appears.

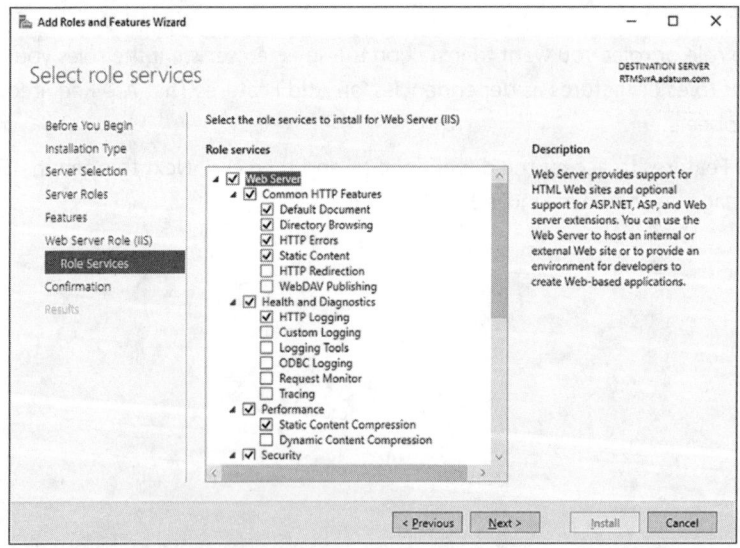

FIGURE 1-10 A Select Role Services page in the Add Roles And Features Wizard

9. On the Confirm Installation Selections page, you can perform the following optional tasks:
    - **Restart The Destination Server Automatically If Required** Selecting this check box causes the server to restart automatically when the installation is completed, if the selected roles and features require it.
    - **Export Configuration Settings** Creates an XML script containing the procedures performed by the wizard. You can use the script to install the same configuration on another server by using Windows PowerShell.
    - **Specify An Alternate Source Path** Specifies the location of an image file containing the software needed to install the selected roles and features. In a default Windows Server 2016 installation, this is not necessary, but if you have previously deleted the source files from the system using Features on Demand, you will need an image file to install roles and features.
10. Click Install to open the Installation Progress page. Depending on the roles and features you have selected, the wizard might display hyperlinks to the tools or wizards needed to perform required post installation tasks. When the installation is complete, click Close to complete the wizard.

Using Windows PowerShell to install roles

For administrators who prefer working from the command line, or for those working on systems using the Server Core installation option, it is also possible to install roles and features using the Install-WindowsFeature cmdlet in Windows PowerShell. The basic syntax of the cmdlet is as follows:

```
install-windowsfeature -name featurename [-includeallsubfeature]
[-includemanagementtools]
```

To install a role or feature, you must use a PowerShell session with administrative privileges. Then, you must determine the correct name to use for the role or feature you want to install. To do this, you can list all of the available roles and features available in Windows by running the Get-WindowsFeature cmdlet, the first part of which is shown in Figure 1-11.

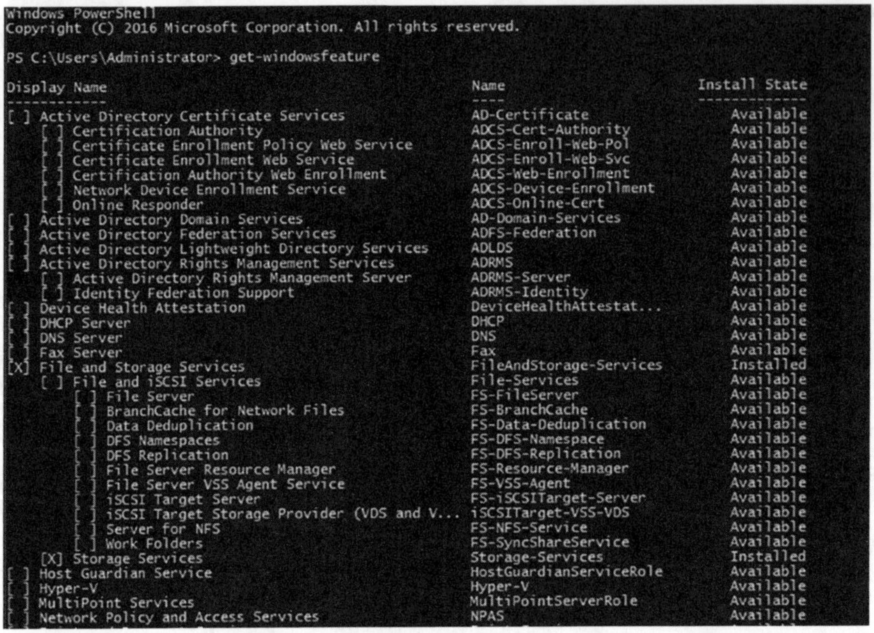

FIGURE 1-11 Output from the Get-WindowsFeature cmdlet

> ***NOTE*** **POWERSHELL TERMINOLOGY**
>
> Windows PowerShell, in its command language, does not distinguish between roles and features, as Server Manager does. All of the components are referred to as features and are installed using the Install-WindowsFeature cmdlet. There are no cmdlets that use the term role.

The resulting list displays all of the roles first, and then all of the features. The Name column specifies the exact string you should use in the Name parameter of your Install-WindowsFeature command line.

The check boxes specify which components are currently installed on the system. The list is indented to show which components are subordinate role services or subfeatures, so that you can install specific elements of a role, just as you can in Server Manager. You can also add the IncludeAllSubFeature parameter to install all of the subordinate components for a role.

Unlike Server Manager, which automatically includes the management tools associated with a role when you install it, the Install-WindowsFeature cmdlet does not. If you want to install the Microsoft Management Console snap-in or other tools used to manage a role or feature, you must add the IncludeManagementTools parameter on the command line.

Install and configure Windows Server Core

For many network administrators, running a graphical user interface (GUI) on a server that will spend its life in a data center or server closet seems like a waste of resources. In many cases, administrators rarely have to touch servers after their initial installation and configuration, except to check logs, which can be done remotely. Server Core is an installation option in Windows Server 2016 that eliminates most of the GUI, leaving a default screen with only a command line interface, as shown in Figure 1-12.

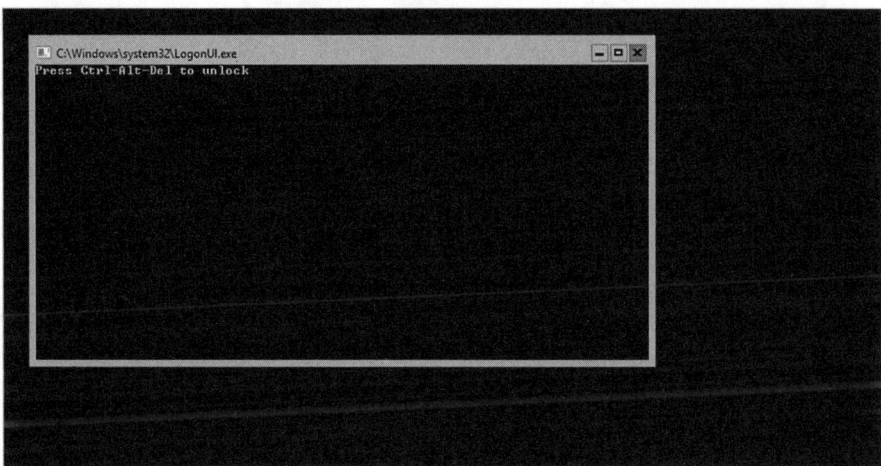

FIGURE 1-12 The default Server Core screen in Windows Server 2016

Installing Server Core

When you install Windows Server 2016, the Select The Operating System You Want To Install page of the Windows Setup Wizard appears, with the Server Core option selected by default, as shown in Figure 1-13. Unlike Windows Server 2012 R2, the term Server Core does not appear on the page; the full GUI option is identified by the term Desktop Experience. (In Windows Server 2012 R2, the options are called Server With A GUI and Server Core Installation.) With the exception of this page, the operating system installation is the same as for the Desktop Experience option, described earlier in this chapter.

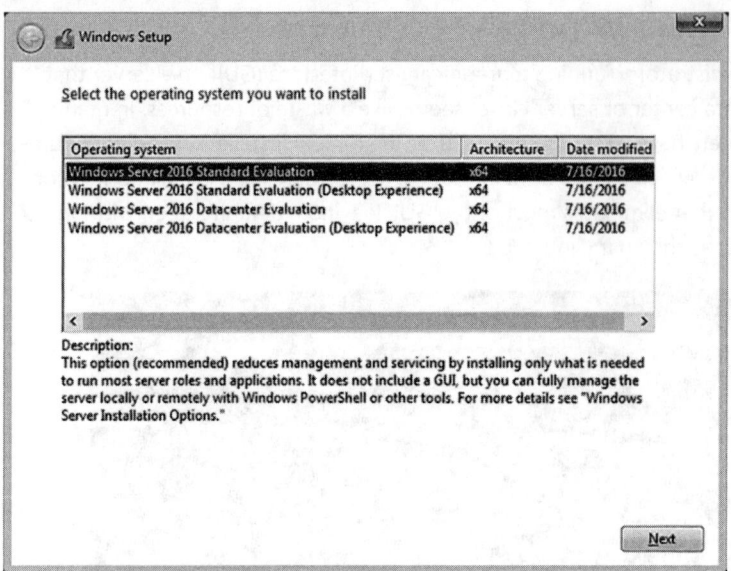

FIGURE 1-13 The Select The Operating System You Want To Install page of the Windows Setup Wizard

EXAM TIP

In Windows Server 2016, you can no longer add or remove the GUI elements after the operating system installation. In addition, there is no Minimal Server Interface option, as in Windows Server 2012 R2. This means that, at installation time, you must choose between a full graphical interface, similar to that of Windows 10, and a command line only. In Windows Server 2012 R2, it was possible to install and configure the server using the full GUI option, and then remove GUI features once the server was up and running. This is no longer possible. Administrators familiar with this practice should be aware of the change when taking Exam 70-740.

When you select the Windows Server Core installation option, you get a stripped-down version of the operating system. There is no Taskbar, no Explorer shell, no Server Manager, no Microsoft Management Console, and virtually no other graphical applications.

However, the advantages of running servers using the Server Core option are several, including the following:

- **Hardware resource conservation** Server Core eliminates some of the most memory- and processor-intensive elements of the Windows Server 2016 operating system, thus devoting more of the system resources to running applications and essential services.

- **Reduced disk space** Server Core requires less disk space for the installed operating system elements, as well as less storage space devoted to memory swapping, which maximizes the utilization of the server's storage resources.

- **Fewer updates** The graphical elements of Windows Server 2016 are among the most frequently updated features, so running Server Core reduces the number of updates that administrators must apply. Fewer updates also means fewer server restarts and less downtime.
- **Reduced attack surface** The less software there is running on the computer, the fewer entrances there are available for attackers to exploit. Server Core reduces the potential openings presented by the operating system, increasing its overall security.

Configuring Server Core

To work interactively with a computer installed using the Server Core option, you can use the CMD command line interface, or you can use Windows PowerShell. It is also possible to connect to the server remotely, using graphical tools such as Server Manager and MMC snap-ins.

Immediately after the installation, however, you might be forced to perform some basic post-installation tasks interactively, such as configuring the network adapter, renaming the computer, and joining the server to a domain. To complete these tasks on a computer running Server Core using Windows PowerShell, you must first type **powershell** in the CMD window to invoke a PowerShell session.

If your network does not have a DHCP server to automatically configure the computer's network adapter, you can do it manually with the New-NetIpAddress cmdlet. First, you must discover the interface index of the adapter by using the Get-NetAdapter cmdlet, which produces the output shown in Figure 1-14.

```
PS C:\Users\Administrator> get-netadapter

Name          InterfaceDescription                 ifIndex Status   MacAddress          LinkSpeed
----          --------------------                 ------- ------   ----------          ---------
Ethernet 2    Microsoft Hyper-V Network Adapter #2       6 Up       00-15-5D-02-01-32    10 Gbps
Ethernet      Microsoft Hyper-V Network Adapter          4 Up       00-15-5D-02-01-30    10 Gbps


PS C:\Users\Administrator>
```

FIGURE 1-14 Output of the Get-NetAdapter cmdlet

With this information, you can select the interface of the adapter you want to configure and use a command like the following to configure it:

```
new-netipaddress -interfaceindex 6 -ipaddress 192.168.0.200 -prefixlength 24
-defaultgateway 192.168.0.1
```

The functions of the command line parameters are as follows:

- **interfaceindex** Identifies the adapter in the computer to be configured, using index numbers displayed by the Get-NetAdapter cmdlet.
- **ipaddress** Specifies the IP address to be assigned to the adapter.
- **prefixlength** Specifies the subnet mask value to be associated with the IP address. The numeral specifies the number of network bits in the IP address. For example, a prefixlength value of 24 is the equivalent of a subnet mask value of 255.255.255.0.

- **defaultgateway** Specifies the IP address of a local router that the computer should use to access other networks.

The resulting output is shown in Figure 1-15.

```
PS C:\Users\Administrator> new-netipaddress -interfaceindex 4 -ipaddress 10.0.0.200 -prefixlength 24 -defaultgateway 10.0.0.1

IPAddress         : 10.0.0.200
InterfaceIndex    : 4
InterfaceAlias    : Ethernet
AddressFamily     : IPv4
Type              : Unicast
PrefixLength      : 24
PrefixOrigin      : Manual
SuffixOrigin      : Manual
AddressState      : Tentative
ValidLifetime     : Infinite ([TimeSpan]::MaxValue)
PreferredLifetime : Infinite ([TimeSpan]::MaxValue)
SkipAsSource      : False
PolicyStore       : ActiveStore

IPAddress         : 10.0.0.200
InterfaceIndex    : 4
InterfaceAlias    : Ethernet
AddressFamily     : IPv4
Type              : Unicast
PrefixLength      : 24
PrefixOrigin      : Manual
SuffixOrigin      : Manual
AddressState      : Invalid
ValidLifetime     : Infinite ([TimeSpan]::MaxValue)
PreferredLifetime : Infinite ([TimeSpan]::MaxValue)
SkipAsSource      : False
PolicyStore       : PersistentStore
```

FIGURE 1-15 Output of the New-NetIpAddress cmdlet

To configure the DNS server addresses for the adapter, you use the Set-DnsClient-ServerAddress cmdlet, as in the following example:

```
Set-dnsclientserveraddress -interfaceindex 6 -serveraddresses
("192.168.0.1","192.168.0.2")
```

To rename the computer and join it to a domain, you can use the Add-Computer cmdlet, as in the following example:

```
add-computer -domainname adatum.com -newname ServerB -credential adatum\administrator
```

The functions of the command line parameters are as follows:

- **domainname** Specifies the name of the domain that you want the computer to join
- **newname** Specifies a computer name that you want to assign to the computer
- **credential** Specifies the domain and account names for a domain user with domain join privileges

Manage Windows Server Core installations using Windows PowerShell, command line, and remote management capabilities

Although most of the standard graphical utilities are not available on a computer installed using the Server Core option, there are still many ways to manage the server, both locally and remotely. In the previous section, you learned how to configure the network adapter and join a domain using Windows PowerShell cmdlets. There are thousands of other PowerShell cmdlets available on a Server Core computer, which can perform virtually any tasks that the graphical tools can, except display results in a fancy, colorful window. PowerShell also provides a powerful scripting capability that you can use to automate complex tasks.

To display a long list of the PowerShell cmdlets available, run the Get-Command cmdlet. To learn how to use any one of the cmdlets, run the Get-help cmdlet with the name of the cmdlet about which you want to learn.

In addition to Windows PowerShell, Server Core also includes the standard CMD command shell, which you can use to run any of the command line programs included with Windows Server 2016.

For example, as an alternative to the Add-Computer PowerShell cmdlet, you can use the Netdom.exe tool from the command prompt to rename a computer and join it to a domain. To rename a computer, you use the following command:

```
netdom renamecomputer %computername% /newname: newcomputername
```

To restart the computer after changing its name, you use the Shutdown.exe tool, as follows:

```
shutdown /r
```

To join a computer to a domain using Netdom.exe, use the following command:

```
netdom join %computername% /domain: domainname /userd: username /passwordd:*
```

In this command, the asterisk (*) in the /password parameter causes the program to prompt you for the password to the user account you specified.

Using remote PowerShell

For Server Core computers that are locked in server closets or data centers, or that are at remote locations, you can access their PowerShell prompts remotely. In Windows Server 2016, the Windows Remote Management (WinRM) service is enabled by default, so you can create a remote PowerShell session using the New-PsSession cmdlet, as in the following example:

```
new-pssession -computername rtmsvrd
```

In this example, Rtmsvrd is the remote Server Core computer you want to manage. Running this command creates a connection to remote computer and assigns it an ID number as shown in Figure 1-16.

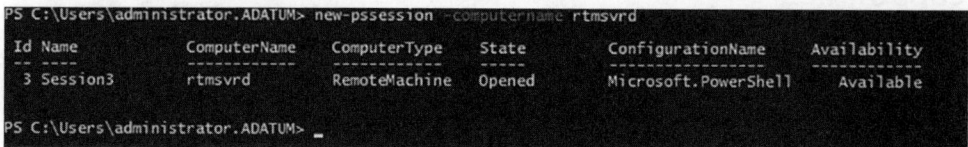

FIGURE 1-16 Output of the New-PsSession cmdlet

Once you have created the session, you can connect to it using the Enter-PsSession cmdlet, specifying the ID number of the session you just created, as shown in Figure 1-17. Notice that the command prompt changes to indicate the name of the computer you are working on.

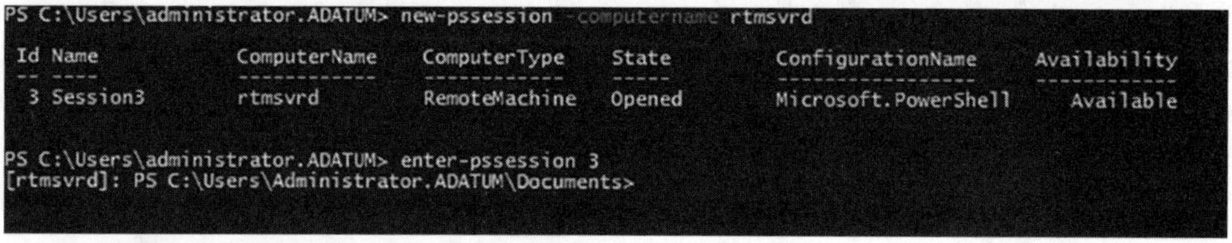

FIGURE 1-17 Output of the Enter-PsSession cmdlet

While you are connected to the session, the commands you type are running on the remote computer, configuring the remote computer's settings, and utilizing the remote computer's resources.

To leave the session and return to the local PowerShell prompt, you run the Exit-PsSession cmdlet, or just type exit. When you do this, the session remains in force, however, and you can return to it by running the Enter-PsSession cmdlet again. To terminate the session, run the Disconnect-PsSession cmdlet.

Using Server Manager remotely

For administrators who are not comfortable working at the CMD or PowerShell command line, it is possible to use graphical management tools on another system to manage a computer running Server Core. The Server Manager console included with the Windows Server 2016 Desktop Experience installation option enables you to add multiple servers to its interface, add and remove roles and features on any server, and monitor the installed roles.

To add servers in Server Manager, use the following procedure.

1. Open Server Manager and, in the left pane, click All Servers. The Servers pane appears, as shown in Figure 1-18.

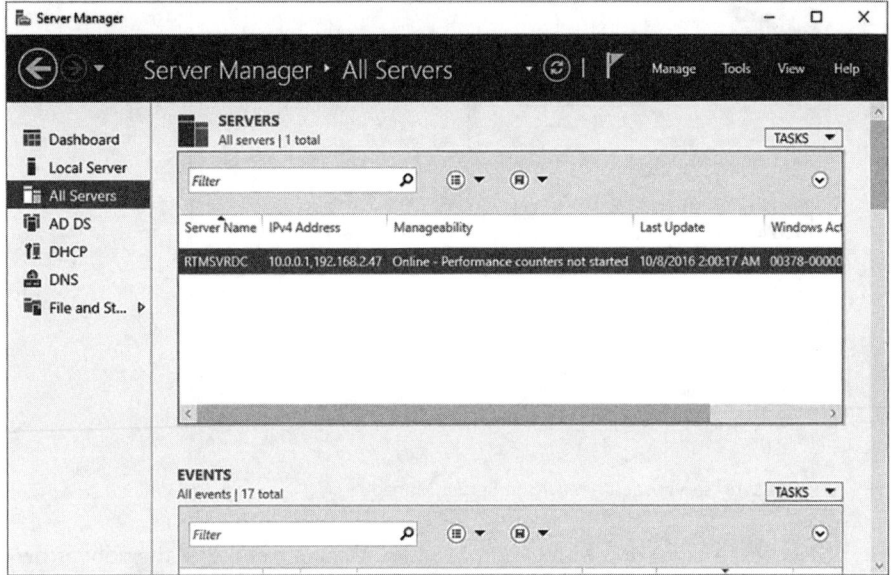

FIGURE 1-18 The Servers pane in Server Manager

2. From the Manage menu, select Add Servers. The Add Servers dialog box appears.
3. Select one of the following tabs to search for servers:
   - **Active Directory**   Enables you to search for servers running specific Windows versions in specific Active Directory locations
   - **DNS**   Enables you to search the Domain Name System (DNS) for servers
   - **Import**   Enables you to supply a text file specifying server names

4. Select search parameters or supply a text file to display a list of available servers, as shown in Figure 1-19.

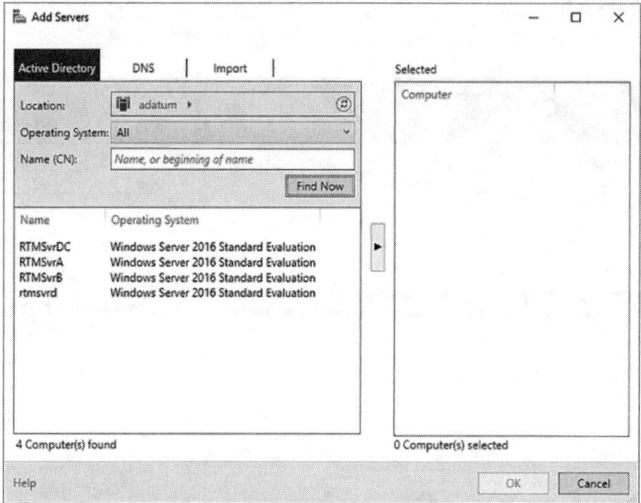

FIGURE 1-19 Server search results in Server Manager

5. Select each server you wish to add to Server Manager, and click the right arrow button to add each to the Selected list.
6. Click OK. The servers in the Selected list appear in the Servers pane, as shown in Figure 1-20.

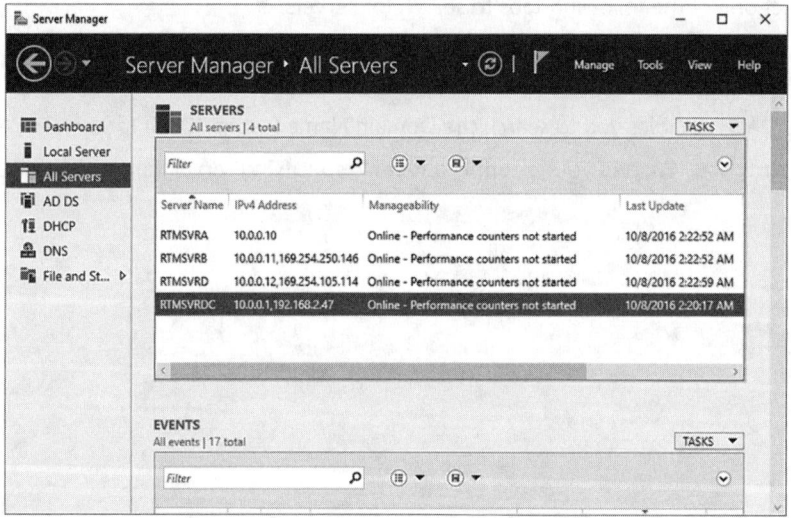

FIGURE 1-20 The Servers pane in Server Manager, with servers

Using MMC snap-ins remotely

Many of the Microsoft Management Console snap-ins used to administer Windows services have the ability to connect to another computer and manage it remotely. For example, you can use the Event Viewer console on a Desktop Experience Windows installation to connect a computer running Server Core and view its logs.

To connect an MMC snap-in to another system, click Connect To Another Computer in the Actions pane, to display the Select Computer dialog box, shown in Figure 1-21. Select the Another Computer option and enter or browse to the name of the computer you want to manage.

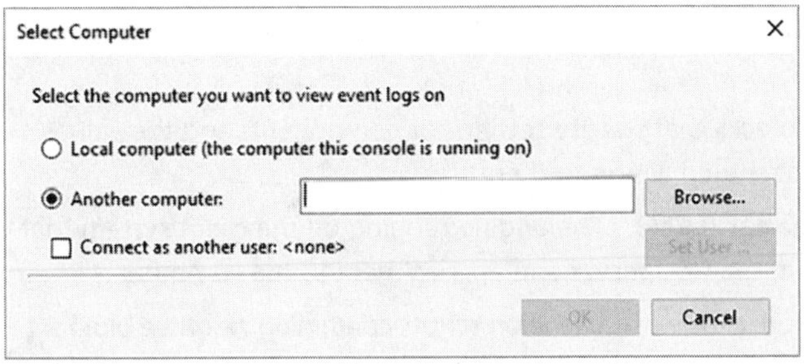

FIGURE 1-21 The Select Computer dialog box

With Windows Server 2016 in its default configuration, an attempt to manage it with an MMC snap-in on another computer generates an error. This is because MMC uses the Distributed Component Object Model (DCOM) for remote management, and the communication settings for DCOM are not enabled by default. To connect to a remote system with MMC, you must enable the following rules in Windows Firewall on the system to be managed:

- COM+ Network Access (DCOM-In)
- Remote Event Log Management (NP-In)
- Remote Event Log Management (RPC)
- Remote Event Log Management (RPC-EPMAP)

To enable these firewall rules on a computer running Server Core, you use the Set-NetFirewallRule cmdlet in Windows PowerShell, as follows:

```
set-netfirewallrule -name complusnetworkaccess-dcom-in -enabled true
set-netfirewallrule -name remoteeventlogsvc-in-tcp -enabled true
set-netfirewallrule -name remoteeventlogsvc-np-in-tcp -enabled true
set-netfirewallrule -name remoteeventlogsvc-rpcss-in-tcp -enabled true
```

Once these rules are enabled, you are able to connect MMC snap-ins to the remote server.

Implement Windows PowerShell Desired State Configuration (DSC) to install and maintain integrity of installed environments

Desired State Configuration (DSC) is a Windows PowerShell feature that uses script files to apply, monitor, and maintain a specific system configuration. The script files are stored on a central DSC server. Clients either pull the scripts from the server, or the server pushes them to the clients.

DSC consists of three components, as follows:

- **Configurations**   PowerShell scripts that contain node blocks specifying the names of the computers to be configured and resource blocks specifying the property settings to be applied
- **Resources**   The building blocks that specify settings or components and the values that the configuration script should assign to them
- **Local Configuration Manager (LCM)**   The engine running on the client system that receives configurations from the DSC server and applies them to the computer

To implement DSC, administrators create configuration scripts containing resource blocks, compile them into modules, and deploy them on a central file server or web server. The LCM running on the clients then receives the configuration modules from the server, using a push or pull architecture, and applies them to the system. The LCM also maintains the system configuration by monitoring the system, ensuring that the required resource settings are maintained, and reapplying them if necessary. DSC configurations are *idempotent*, meaning that the scripts can be applied to a system repeatedly without generating errors or other undesirable results.

Creating DSC configuration scripts

A simple DSC configuration script to configure the client's DNS server address can appear as shown in Listing 1-1. This is only the basic model for a configuration. Actual configuration scripts are often far more complicated and contain complete system configurations.

LISTING 1-1 Sample DSC configuration script

```
Configuration DnsClient
{
    Import-DscResource -ModuleName "xNetworking"
    Node ("ServerA","ServerB")
    {
        xDnsServerAddress DnsServer
        {
            Address        = 10.0.0.1
            AddressFamily  = "Ipv4"
            InterfaceAlias = "Ethernet"
        }
    }
}
```

The commands in this particular script perform the following functions:

- **Configuration**   Specifies the name of the configuration, in this case DnsClient
- **Import-DscResource**   Loads a module called xNetworking
- **Node**   Specifies the names of the computers to be configured, in this case ServerA and ServerB
- **xDnsServerAddress**   Specifies the resource in the module to be configured, in this case DnsServer
- **Address**   Specifies the DNS server address that is the property for the resource, in this case 10.0.0.1
- **AddressFamily**   Identifies the IP version of the DNS address, in this case Ipv4
- **InterfaceAlias**   Identifies the network adapter in the node systems to be configured

When you run the configuration script, PowerShell creates a Management Object Format (MOF) file for each computer specified in the Node block. The MOF files are the actual scripts that are distributed to the DSC clients.

When DSC applies this configuration to a client system, the LCM checks to see if the IPv4 DNS Server Address for the specified network adapter is configured correctly. If it is, nothing happens. If it is not, then the LCM configures it.

Deploying DSC configurations

To deploy a DSC configuration module to clients, you must decide between using a pull or a push architecture. In a pull architecture, the MOF files are stored on a Pull Server, which is an SMB server or an IIS web server with an OData interface, set up with its own DSC configuration.

Once you have published the MOF files on the Pull Server, you configure the LCM on the client computers with a configuration script that specifies the URL of the Pull Server and creates a scheduled task. When both the DSC server and the client are properly configured, the scheduled task on the client causes the LCM to periodically check the Pull Server for configurations and examine the local system for compliance. When necessary, the LCM downloads configuration files from the Pull Server and applies them to the client computer.

In a push architecture, you run the Start-DscConfiguration cmdlet on the server, specifying the location where the MOF files are stored in the Path parameter. By default, the cmdlet pushes the specified configuration to all of the clients that have MOF files in the specified path.

Perform upgrades and migrations of servers and core workloads from Windows Server 2008 and Windows Server 2012 to Windows Server 2016

If you have downlevel servers on which you want to run Windows Server 2016, you have two choices: upgrade or migrate. An upgrade is a type of Windows Server 2016 installation that you perform on your existing server. At the end of the process, you have a computer running Windows Server 2016 with all of your roles, applications, configuration settings, and data files intact. A migration is when you perform a clean Windows Server 2016 installation on a new computer and transfer all of your roles, applications, configuration settings, and data files from the old computer to the new one. Microsoft recommends that you perform migrations, rather than upgrades, wherever possible.

Upgrading servers

An in-place upgrade is the most complicated form of Windows Server 2016 installation. It is also the lengthiest and the most likely to experience problems during its execution. During an in-place upgrade, the Setup program creates a new Windows folder and installs the Windows Server 2016 operating system files into it.

This is only half of the process, however. The program must then migrate the applications, files, and settings from the old operating system. This calls for a variety of procedures, such as importing the user profiles, copying all pertinent settings from the old registry to the new one, locating applications and data files, and updating device drivers with new versions.

Thus, the upgrade is really not an upgrade at all, but rather an internal migration between two operating systems installed in the same computer. The potential for problems during an upgrade comes from the fact that the original operating system is relegated to a directory called Windows.old during the process, making it difficult to return the computer to its original configuration. In a migration between two computers, the original system remains unchanged and is still usable, should a problem occur.

While in-place upgrades often proceed smoothly, the complexity of the upgrade process and the large number of variables involved means that many things can potentially go wrong. To minimize the risks involved, administrators must take the upgrade process seriously, prepare the system beforehand, and have the ability to troubleshoot any problems that might arise.

Upgrade paths

In most cases, you can upgrade a computer running Windows Server 2012 or Windows Server 2012 R2 to an equivalent Windows Server 2016 edition. However, there are some limitations to the upgrade process, as follows:

- **Versions**   Upgrades from Windows Server 2012 and Windows Server 2012 R2 to Windows Server 2016 are supported. There is no direct upgrade path from any versions prior to Windows Server 2012. However, it is possible to perform a two-step upgrade, from 2008 to 2012, and from 2012 to 2016, for example.
- **Editions**   Upgrades between equivalent operating system editions are supported, as are upgrades from Windows Server 2012 Standard or Windows Server 2012 R2 Standard to Windows Server 2016 Datacenter. Upgrades from the Datacenter editions to the Standard edition are not supported.

- **Installation options** Upgrades between computers running the Server Core and the full GUI installation options are not supported, in either direction. Upgrades between Nano Servers and other Windows Server installation options are also not supported.
- **Platforms** Upgrades from 32-bit to 64-bit versions of Windows Server have never been supported. As Windows Server 2008 was the last server version to be available in 32-bit, there is no upgrade path to Windows Server 2016 anyway.
- **Languages** Upgrades from one language Windows version to another are not supported, regardless of the version.
- **Workstations** Upgrades from the Windows workstation operating systems to Windows Server 2016 are not supported, regardless of the version.

In any of these unsupported cases, the Windows Setup program does not permit an upgrade to proceed, but it offers to perform a clean installation.

Preparing to upgrade

Before you begin an in-place upgrade to Windows Server 2016, you should perform a number of preliminary procedures to anticipate possible difficulties and protect your server data.

Consider the following before you perform any upgrade to Windows Server 2016:

- **Check hardware compatibility** Make sure that the server meets the minimum hardware requirements for a Windows Server 2016 installation. Generally speaking, if Windows Server 2012 or Windows Server 2012 R2 is running satisfactorily, your hardware should be sufficient to run Windows Server 2016. If you are planning hardware upgrades, such as installing additional memory, you should complete them and test them thoroughly before performing the upgrade, or wait until after the upgrade is complete and thoroughly tested.
- **Remove NIC Teaming** Windows Server 2016 does not preserve NIC teams during the upgrade process. If your existing server uses NIC teaming, you should remove all of the teams before performing the upgrade and recreate them afterwards.
- **Check disk space** Make sure that sufficient free disk space is available on the partition where the old operating system is installed. During the upgrade procedure, the partition needs sufficient disk space to hold both operating systems simultaneously. After the upgrade is completed successfully, you can remove the old files, freeing up some additional space.
- **Confirm that software is signed** All kernel-mode software on the server, including device drivers, must be digitally signed, or the upgrade won't proceed. If you cannot locate a software update for any signed application or driver, you must uninstall the application or driver before you proceed with the installation.
- **Check application compatibility** The Setup program displays a What Needs Your Attention page that can point out possible application compatibility problems. You can sometimes solve these problems by updating or upgrading the applications. Create an inventory of the software products installed on the server and check the manufac-

turers' websites for updates, availability of upgrades, and announcements regarding support for Windows Server 2016. In an enterprise environment, you should test all applications for Windows Server 2016 compatibility, no matter what the manufacturer says, before you perform any operating system upgrades.

- **Install Windows updates** Make sure that the old operating system is fully updated with the latest patches before you proceed with the upgrade.
- **Ensure computer functionality** Make sure that Windows Server 2012 or Windows Server 2012 R2 is running properly on the computer before you begin the upgrade process. Check the Event Viewer console for warnings and errors. You must start an in-place upgrade from within the existing operating system, so you cannot count on Windows Server 2016 to correct any problems that prevent the computer from starting or running the Setup program.
- **Perform a full backup** Before you perform any upgrade procedure, you should back up the entire system, preferably using a product with a disaster recovery feature, so that you can return the server to its original state, if necessary. At the very least, you should back up your essential data files. Removable hard drives make this a simple process, even if the computer does not have a suitable backup device.
- **Purchase Windows Server 2016** Be sure to purchase the appropriate Windows Server 2016 license for the upgrade, and that you have the installation medium and the product key handy (if needed).

Performing an upgrade installation

Once the system is prepared and you have all of the necessary components, the actual in-place upgrade procedure is similar to that of a clean installation, except that it takes longer.

Instead of booting the system using a flash drive or installation disk, you start the old operating system in the normal manner and run the Windows Server 2016 Setup.exe program. The Windows Setup Wizard appears, and the installation process begins.

The first difference is that a Choose What To Keep page appears, as shown in Figure 1-22. This page prompts you to choose between two options, Keep Personal Files And Apps, which is an upgrade, and Nothing, which is a clean installation.

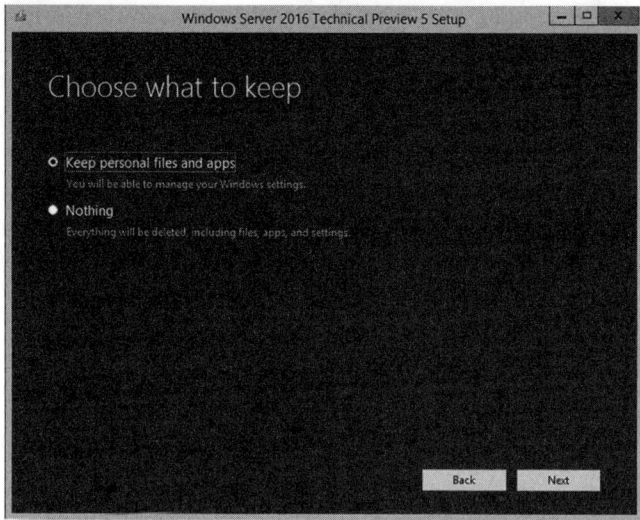

FIGURE 1-22 The Choose What To Keep page

Then, the What Needs Your Attention page appears, as shown in Figure 1-23, informing you of any known driver or application incompatibilities.

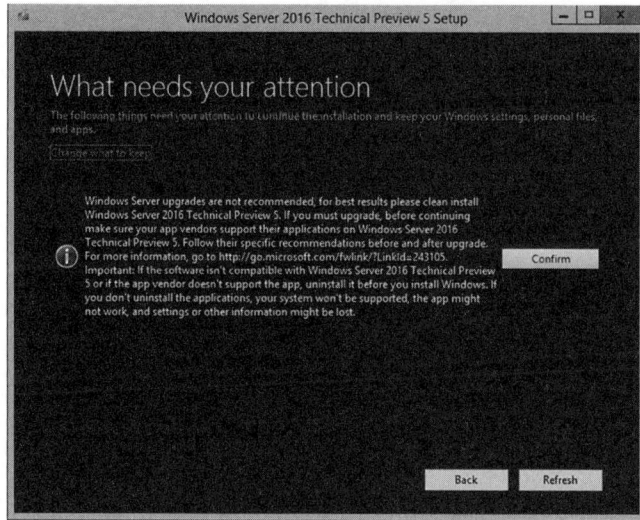

FIGURE 1-23 The What Needs Your Attention page

If the compatibility information provided by the Setup program indicates any potential problems, you might have to close the Setup program to update, upgrade, or uninstall an incompatible application.

After you click Install, the Setup program upgrades Windows Server 2012 or Windows Server 2012 R2 to Windows Server 2016 and restarts the computer several times. Depending on what is installed on the server, it can be quite a while before the system finalizes the installation and the Windows sign-on screen appears.

Migrating roles

Migration is the preferred method of replacing an existing server with one running Windows Server 2016. Unlike an in-place upgrade, a migration copies vital information from an existing server to a clean Windows Server 2016 installation. The existing server is left intact, and the new server has no leftover artifacts of the previous operating system.

During a migration, virtually all the restrictions listed earlier concerning upgrades do not apply. Using the Windows Server Migration Tools and migration guides supplied with Windows Server 2016, you can migrate data between servers under any of the following conditions:

- **Between versions**   You can migrate data from any Windows Server version since Windows Server 2008 to Windows Server 2016. This includes migrations from one server running Windows Server 2016 to another.
- **Between platforms**   You can migrate data from an x86- or x64-based server to an x64-based server running Windows Server 2016.
- **Between editions**   You can migrate data between servers running different Windows Server editions.
- **Between physical and virtual machines**   You can migrate data from a physical machine to a virtual one, or the reverse.
- **Between installation options**   You can migrate data from a computer running the Windows Server 2012 or Windows Server 2012 R2 Server Core installation option to a full GUI system running Windows Server 2016. You can also migrate data from a full GUI system to Windows Server 2016 Server Core.

> *NOTE* **MIGRATION LIMITATIONS**
>
> Windows Server 2016 does not support migrations between different language versions of the operating system. You also cannot migrate data from Server Core installations of Windows Server 2008, because Server Core in that version does not include support for Microsoft .NET Framework.

Migrating Windows servers is substantially different from any migrations you might have performed on Windows workstations. Rather than running a single migration procedure that copies all applications and user data from the source to the destination computer at once, in a server migration, you migrate roles or role services individually.

Windows Server 2016 includes a collection of migration guides that provide detailed, individualized instructions for the migration of each role supported by Windows Server 2016.

Some roles require the use of the Windows Server Migration Tools, while others have their own migration capabilities built in. Typically, this takes the form of a tool that saves all of the role settings and data to a file that you can copy to the new server and import.

Installing Windows Server Migration Tools

Windows Server Migration Tools is a Windows Server 2016 feature that consists of five Windows PowerShell cmdlets and help files that enable administrators to migrate certain roles between servers.

The five cmdlets included in Windows Server Migration Tools are as follows:

- **Export-SmigServerSetting**   Exports certain Windows features and operating system settings to a migration store.
- **Get-SmigServerFeature**   Displays a list of Windows features that can be migrated from the local server or from a migration store.
- **Import-SmigServerSetting**   Imports certain Windows features and operating system settings from a migration store and applies them to the local server.
- **Receive-SmigServerData**   Enables a destination server to receive migrated files, folders, permissions, and share properties from a source server. The Send-SmigServerData cmdlet must be running on the source server at the same time.
- **Send-SmigServerData**   Migrates files, folders, permissions, and share properties from a source server to a destination server. The Receive-SmigServerData cmdlet must be running on the destination server at the same time.

Before you can use the migration tools cmdlets, you must install the Windows Server Migration Tools feature on the destination server that is running Windows Server 2016, and then copy the appropriate version of the tools to the source server.

Windows Server Migration Tools is a standard feature that you install on Windows Server 2016 using the Add Roles And Features Wizard in Server Manager or by using the Install-WindowsFeature cmdlet in Windows PowerShell, as follows:

```
install-windowsfeature migration
```

After you install the Windows Server Migration Tools feature on the destination server, you must create a distribution folder containing the tools for the source server. This distribution folder contains the appropriate files for the operating system running on the source server.

To create the distribution folder on a server running Windows Server 2016 with the Windows Server Migration Tools feature already installed, use the following procedure.

1. Open a Command Prompt window with administrative privileges.
2. Switch to the directory containing the Windows Server Migration Tools files with the following command:

    ```
    cd\windows\system32\ServerMigrationTools
    ```

3. Run the SmigDeploy.exe program with the appropriate command line switches for the platform and operating system version of the source server, using the following syntax:

```
SmigDeploy.exe /package /architecture [x86|amd64]
/os [WS16|WS12R2|WS12|WS08|WS08R2|WS03] /path foldername
```

The SmigDeploy.exe program creates a new folder in the directory you specify for the foldername variable, assigning it a name and location based on the command-line switches you specify. For example, if you enter the following command and press Enter, the program creates a folder called c:\temp\SMT_ws12R2_amd64 containing the Server Migration Tools.

```
SmigDeploy.exe /package /architecture amd64 /os WS12R2 /path c:\temp
```

After you create the distribution folder, copy it to the source server by any standard means, and then register Windows Server Migration Tools on the source server by running the SmigDeploy.exe program from a command prompt with administrative privileges.

When you execute SmigDeploy.exe, the program registers the Windows Server Migration Tools on the source server and opens a Windows PowerShell window in which you can use those tools.

Using migration guides

After you install the Windows Server Migration Tools on both the source and the destination servers, you can proceed to migrate data between the two. Using the migration tools, you can migrate certain roles, features, shares, operating system settings, and other data from the source server to the destination server running Windows Server 2016.

Migrating all the Windows Server roles does not involve any one procedure, whether the roles have their own migration tools or not. Instead, Microsoft provides detailed migration guides for individual roles, and sometimes for individual role services within a role.

A typical migration guide contains elements such as the following:

- **Compatibility notes** Lists or tables containing specific circumstances under which the guide procedures apply, and circumstances under which they do not apply. These include notes regarding migrations between different operating system versions, platforms, and installation options.
- **Guide contents** A list of the sections appearing in the migration guide.
- **Migration overview** A high-level list of the procedures required to complete the migration, linked to the instructions for the procedures themselves.
- **Migration requirements** A list of the software, permissions, and other elements needed to complete the migration, as well as the estimated amount of time required.
- **Pre-migration tasks** Detailed instructions for procedures you must complete before beginning the actual migration, including installation of required software and backup of existing data.
- **Migration procedures** Detailed instructions for the individual procedures you must perform to complete the migration.

- **Post-migration procedures** Instructions for removing or disabling a role from the source server or restoring the systems to their previous states.

Determine the appropriate activation model for server installation

When you purchase a retail copy of Windows Server 2016, it comes with a 25-character product key. You type the key in during the operating system installation, and Windows later activates it by connecting to a Microsoft server and validating it. For network administrators responsible for dozens or hundreds of servers, however, typing a different key on each computer and keeping track of them afterwards is highly impractical. To address this problem, Microsoft provides several volume activation models that can simplify this aspect of a mass deployment, such as the following:

- Multiple Activation Keys (MAK)
- Key Management Service (KMS)
- Active Directory-Based Activation

The following sections examine each of these volume activation methods.

> **NOTE LICENSING AND ACTIVATION**
>
> It is important to understand that the Microsoft software validation process consists of two separate parts: purchasing the software licenses and activating the product keys associated with the licenses. The Volume Activation mechanisms described here are only the means to activate the product keys you have already obtained through a Volume Licensing program. The mechanisms have nothing to do with the actual purchase of the licenses.

Multiple Activation Keys (MAKs)

A *multiple activation key (MAK)* is essentially a product key that you can use to activate multiple Windows systems. Designed for relatively small networks, such as those that do not meet the KMS activation threshold, MAK activation eliminates the need for administrators to obtain and manage an individual product key for each computer.

When you enter into a MAK Volume Licensing agreement with Microsoft, you can obtain a product key that supports the specific number of licenses you have purchased. If you purchase additional licenses at a later time, you can add them to your existing MAK.

Because you use the same MAK for multiple computers, you can incorporate the product key into an operating system image or specify it in a deployment script. The same key is then copied to all of the computers.

There are two ways to utilize a MAK when activating Windows computers, as follows:

- **MAK Independent** In this mode, each computer using the MAK must perform an individual activation with Microsoft, using either an Internet connection or by telephone. Administrators can incorporate the MAK into a Windows deployment script, so that all of the newly installed computers receive the key and activate it as soon as they are connected to the Internet. This option is also suitable for computers that are not connected to the corporate network, because it requires no internal server connection.

- **MAK Proxy** In this mode, Windows computers receive a MAK from a system running the Volume Activation Management Tool (VAMT). The VAMT collects installation IDs from the target computers, sends them to Microsoft using a single connection, and receives confirmation IDs in return, which it deploys to the targets. Proxy authentication is intended for systems that do not have direct access to the Internet, either for security reasons or because they are part of a laboratory or classroom environment.

Key Management Service (KMS)

The *Key Management Service (KMS)* is a client/server application that enables client computers to activate their licensed operating system products by communicating with a KMS host computer on the local network. Clients do not require access to the Internet to complete the activation process; however, the computer functioning as the KMS host does.

KMS is Microsoft's recommended activation method for large networks. Unlike Multiple Activation Key (MAK) activations, in which a server functions as a proxy by performing individual activation transactions for its clients, the KMS host functions as an actual activating authority for the computers on the network. Once the KMS host's own product key is validated, the host activates the client products itself, and renews those product activations on a regular basis.

For network administrators, this means that they can perform mass operating system deployments without having to specify an individual product key for each computer and without having to complete a separate Internet transaction for each activation. Once the installation of the licensed operating system is complete, the client computers locate a KMS host on the network and activate their products automatically. No further interaction is required at either the client or the KMS host end.

KMS limitations

Before deciding to choose KMS for your network's volume activations, you should be aware of limitations that might prevent you from using it. The version of KMS included in Windows Server 2016 and Windows 10 can activate Windows Vista and later versions, Windows Server 2008 and later versions, and Office 2010 and later versions. However, if you use Windows 10 as the KMS host, you can only activate the workstation versions of Windows, not the server versions.

KMS also requires a minimum of 25 workstation systems or five server systems as clients. This is called the *activation threshold*. As computers send their activation requests to the KMS host, the host maintains a request count, and does not perform any activations until that count reaches the minimum requirement. When the host has not reached the minimum, clients repeat their requests every two hours to determine the host's current activation count. In addition, if the activation count of an operational KMS host ever drops below the minimum, the KMS host stops performing activations until it recovers.

KMS hosts maintain a cache of activation requests that totals twice the number of the activation threshold. Therefore, a host maintains a record of its 50 most recent workstation requests, to help prevent it from dropping below the minimum required. For this reason, Microsoft recommends that networks using KMS have at least 50 computers. Networks consisting of less than 50 computers should use other mechanisms for volume activation.

Unlike individual and MAK activations, which are one-time occurrences, KMS activations expire in 180 days. This is known as the *activation validity interval*. The clients attempt to renew their activations every seven days. If they fail to reactivate, their product activations expire.

Installing a KMS host

A single KMS host can manage the activations for a network of virtually any size, but many organizations maintain two, for fault tolerance purposes. To install a KMS host on a computer running Windows Server 2016, you must add the Volume Activation Services role and then configure the Volume Activation Tools.

To install a KMS host on Windows Server 2016, you must first obtain a KMS host key from the Microsoft Volume Licensing Service Center. Then complete the following procedure.

1. Using an account with administrative privileges, launch Server Manager and use the Add Roles And Features Wizard to install the Volume Activation Services role, including its corequisite features.

2. When the installation of the role is completed, click the Volume Activation Tools link. The Volume Activation Tools Wizard appears, displaying the Select Volume Activation Method page, as shown in Figure 1-24.

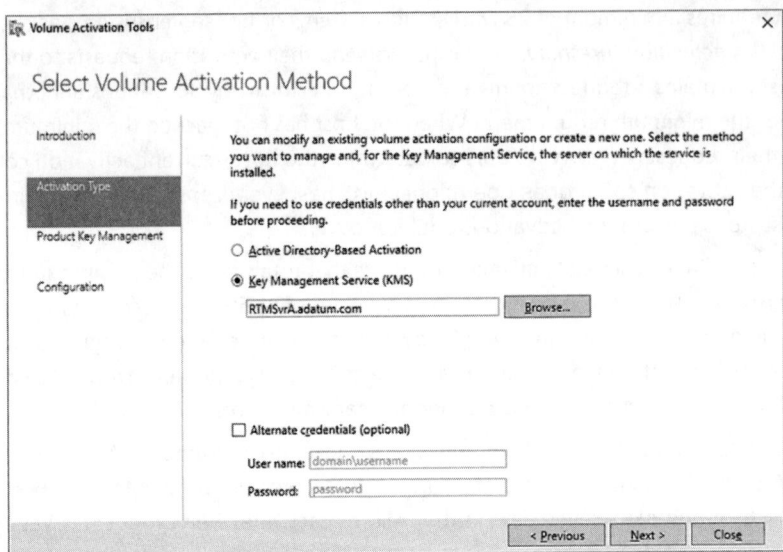

FIGURE 1-24 The Volume Activation Method page in the Volume Activation Tools Wizard

3. Click Next to accept the local system as the KMS server. The Manage KMS Host page appears, as shown in Figure 1-25.

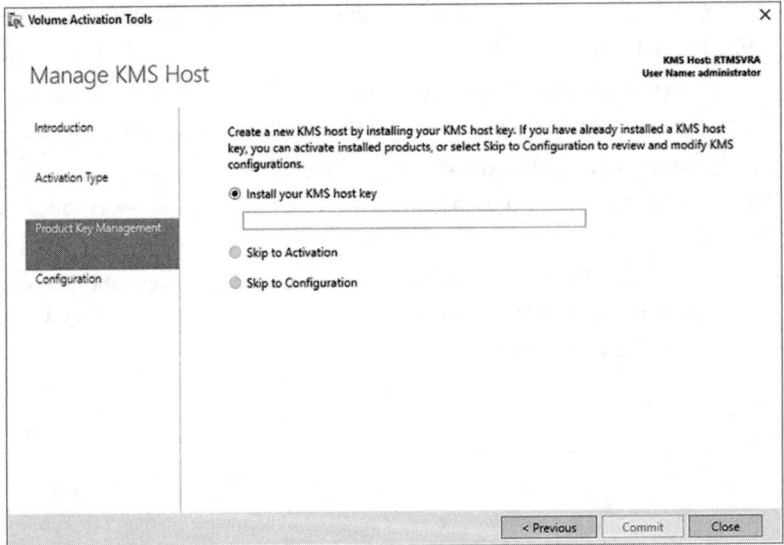

FIGURE 1-25 The Manage KMS Host page in the Volume Activation Tools Wizard

4. Type your KMS host key in the text box and click Commit. The Product Key Installation Succeeded page appears.

5. Click Activate Products. The Activate Product page appears.

6. Leave the Activate Online option selected and click Commit. The wizard activates the key and the Activation Succeeded page appears.
7. Click Close.

> **NOTE KMS COMMUNICATIONS**
> A computer functioning as a KMS host must allow traffic through TCP port 1688. Be sure to configure any firewalls to allow this traffic.

Once the KMS host is installed and configured, and its host key activated, it is ready to activate clients on the network. Which products the KMS host is capable of activating—and which operating systems can function as the KMS host—depends on the host key itself. When you enter into a volume licensing agreement with Microsoft, you specify which operating systems you intend to run, as well as how many computers you intend to deploy, and Microsoft provides you with a KMS host key for the appropriate volume product group.

For clients to connect to a KMS host, they must be able to find it, and they do this by using the Domain Name System (DNS). Once the KMS host is activated, it creates an SRV resource record that identifies the computer as such. The KMS clients on the network can then find the host by performing standard DNS queries.

Configuring KMS clients

Volume licensed editions of Windows, such as the Enterprise editions, use KMS to activate the operating system by default. After a mass deployment of these operating systems, authentication occurs automatically as long as the clients can locate and connect to an operational KMS host.

If you have computers running Windows editions that are not KMS clients by default, such as computers with retail, MAK, or KMS host licenses, you can configure them to be KMS clients by giving them *generic volume licensing keys (GVLKs)* published by Microsoft.

Active Directory-based activation

In Windows Server 2012 and Windows 8, Microsoft introduced a third volume activation method, called Active Directory-based activation. *Active Directory-based activation* is essentially similar to KMS, except that it uses Active Directory Domain Services (AD DS) for communication and data storage instead of a KMS host. Once you have configured your AD DS forest to provide Active Directory-based activation, computers with GVLKs are activated automatically when they join the domain.

Active Directory can only activate licenses for Windows Server 2016, Windows Server 2012 R2, Windows Server 2012, Windows 10, Windows 8.1, Windows 8, and any newer Windows versions. For earlier Windows versions, such as Windows Server 2008 R2 and Windows 7, you must use a standard KMS host or MAK licenses.

To support Active Directory-based activation, you must have at least one domain controller running Windows Server 2016, Windows Server 2012 R2, or Windows Server 2012, and your forest schema must be at the Windows Server 2012 level, at minimum. This means that if your network has AD DS domain controllers running Windows Server 2008 R2 or earlier, you must either raise the forest functional level to at least Windows Server 2012 or update the schema to at least the Windows Server 2012 level using the Adprep.exe tool.

The procedure for configuring Active Directory-based activation is nearly the same as that for installing a KMS host, as detailed earlier. You must add the Volume Licensing Services role on a computer running Windows Server 2016, Windows Server 2012 R2, or Windows Server 2012, and then run the Volume Activation Tools Wizard. The primary difference is that on the Select Volume Activation Method page, you select the Active Directory–Based Activation option, as shown in Figure 1-26.

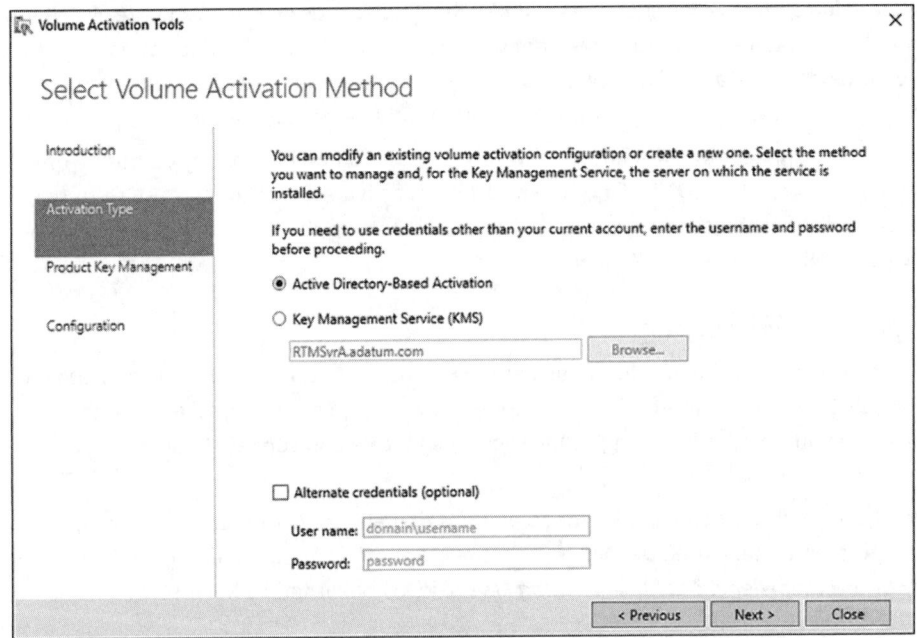

FIGURE 1-26 The Volume Activation Method page in the Volume Activation Tools Wizard

On the Manage Activation Objects page, shown in Figure 1-27, you supply your KMS host key and specify a name for the new activation object that is created in AD DS. Once the host key is activated, the wizard creates an activation object in your AD DS domain. When the Activation Succeeded page appears, click Close, and AD DS is ready to activate clients.

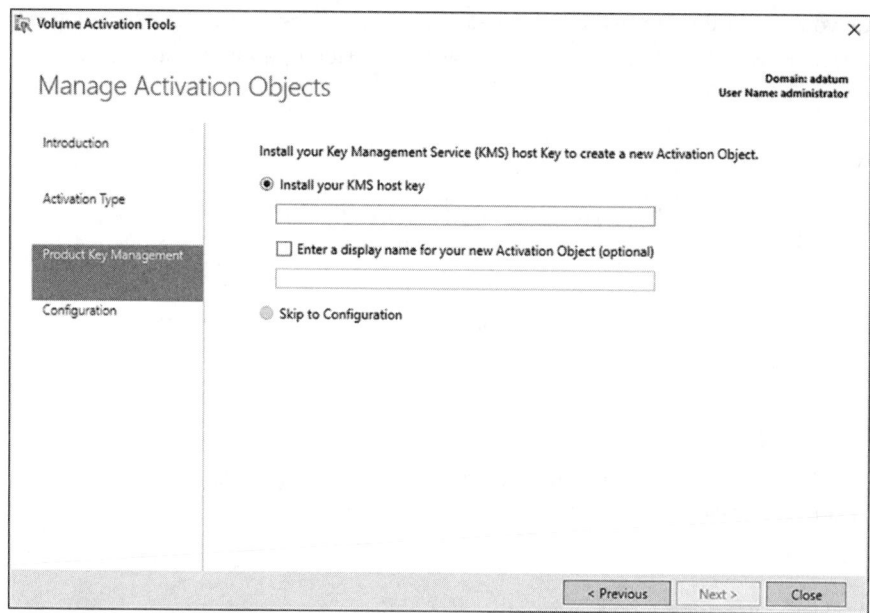

FIGURE 1-27 The Manage Activation Objects page in the Volume Activation Tools Wizard

Using Automatic Virtual Machine Activation (AVMA)

Automatic Virtual Machine Activation (AVMA) is a mechanism that simplifies the process of activating the virtual machines (VMs) you create on a properly activated Hyper-V server. Instead of having to enter and manage a product key for each individual VM, AVMA creates a binding between the host server and the activation mechanism on each VM. The VMs are activated automatically and remain activated, even when they are migrated to other Hyper-V servers.

Because the host server is functioning as the activation agent for its VMs, AVMA can activate client VMs when there is no Internet connection, or when the server is at a remote location. Administrators can monitor the activation status of the VMs from the host server, even when they have no access to the VMs themselves.

To use AVMA, you must be running the Datacenter edition of Windows Server 2016 or Windows Server 2012 R2 on your Hyper-V host server. The virtual machines on that server can be running the Datacenter, Standard, or Essential edition of Windows Server 2016 (on a Windows Server 2016 host only) or Windows Server 2012 R2.

After you install the Hyper-V role on the host server, you can create virtual machine running one of the supported operating systems in the usual manner. Then, you must install an AVMA key from a command prompt with administrative privileges, using the following syntax:

```
slmgr /ipk AVMAkey
```

The value you use for the AVMAkey variable depends on the operating system running on the virtual machine. Microsoft publishes keys for each supported operating system and edition, as shown in Table 1-1.

TABLE 1-1 AVMA keys

Edition	Windows Server 2016	Windows Server 2012 R2
Datacenter	TMJ3Y-NTRTM-FJYXT-T22BY-CWG3J	Y4TGP-NPTV9-HTC2H-7MGQ3-DV4TW
Standard	C3RCX-M6NRP-6CXC9-TW2F2-4RHYD	DBGBW-NPF86-BJVTX-K3WKJ-MTB6V
Essentials	B4YNW-62DX9-W8V6M-82649-MHBKQ	K2XGM-NMBT3-2R6Q8-WF2FK-P36R2

Quick check

Which of the following are the correct activation thresholds for the Key Management System (KMS)?

1. 5 workstations
2. 5 servers
3. 25 workstations
4. 25 servers

Quick check answer

KMS requires a minimum of 25 workstation systems or (#3) 5 server systems as clients. This is called the activation threshold.

Skill 1.2: Install and configure Nano Server

Server Core, first included in the Windows Server 2008 release, was a scaled-down installation option that required less memory and less storage. It also had reduced maintenance requirements and a smaller attack surface. Server Core has no Windows Explorer shell, so you must administer it using the command and PowerShell prompts, and by remote management.

In Windows Server 2016, Microsoft released *Nano Server*, another installation option that is scaled down even further. Nano Server is headless; it has no local user interface, no 32-bit application support, and only the most basic configuration controls. There is no support for Remote Desktop; to administer the system, you use Windows Remote Management (WinRM) remote PowerShell connections, and Windows Management Interface (WMI) tools.

> **This section covers how to:**
> - Determine appropriate usage scenarios and requirements for Nano Server
> - Install Nano Server
> - Implement Roles and Features on Nano Server
> - Manage and configure Nano Server
> - Manage Nano Server remotely using Windows PowerShell

Determine appropriate usage scenarios and requirements for Nano Server

Nano Server is designed to provide cloud-based infrastructure services with a minimal resource, management, and attack footprint. The two basic scenarios for Nano Server deployments are as follows:

- Server cloud infrastructure services, such as Hyper-V, Failover Clustering, Scale-Out File Servers, DNS, and Internet Information Services (IIS)
- Born-in-the-cloud applications running on virtual machines, in containers, or on physical servers, using development platforms that do not require a graphical interface

Nano Server has an extremely small footprint that enables the server to boot in a few seconds, dramatically faster than Windows Server or Server Core; requires fewer updates; and provides a much smaller attack surface. By default, Nano Server runs less than half as many services and processes as a full Windows Server installation, and far fewer than Server Core, as well as maintaining fewer open ports.

Microsoft has a commitment to cloud-based services—whether public, private, or hybrid—and this has led to the need for highly efficient servers dedicated to specific tasks. One of the largest obstacles in this pursuit was the relatively large size of the Windows Server resource footprint, even in Server Core. Nano Server is designed to provide a more efficient virtual machine-based infrastructure with reduced hardware resource storage requirements, minimal downtime, and simplified maintenance.

When running as a Hyper-V virtual machine, Nano Server is remarkably efficient. By purely empirical standards, a Nano Server VM uses less than half the assigned memory of a lightly loaded member server running the full Windows Server Desktop Experience, and less than a Server Core system as well. For demonstration purposes, Microsoft was able to run over 3,400 VMs, with 128 MB of RAM each, on a single server with eight 20-core processors and 1 terabyte of memory.

The headless nature of the Nano Server design does not mean that administrators are limited to PowerShell and Command Prompt management tools, although these are certainly available. You can connect to a Nano Server remotely using the standard Windows graphical tools, if desired, including Hyper-V Manager and other Microsoft Management Console (MMC) snap-ins, Server Manager, and even the System Center consoles.

The main shortcoming of the Nano Server design, at least at this point in its development, is its relatively limited utility. The server supports only a small subset of the roles and features in the full Windows Server product. However, the roles that are supported in Nano Server are particularly well-suited to cloud deployments. You can run IIS web servers, file servers, and Hyper-V servers, and, with the clustering and container support provided, these services are both resilient and highly scalable.

Install Nano Server

There is no wizard for installing Nano Server, as there is for Windows Server and Server Core. You install the operating system by creating a Virtual Hard Disk (VHD) on another computer from the PowerShell command line. Then you use the VHD to create a Hyper-V virtual machine or a boot drive for a physical server.

Windows Server 2016 includes a Nano Server directory on its installation disk or in its image file, which contains the Nano Server image, a PowerShell module, and a subdirectory containing the package files for the roles and features the operating system supports. Importing the PowerShell module provides the cmdlets you use to create and edit Nano Server images. The package files contain specially created versions of the roles and features that you can install directly to the VHD file. Despite their similarity to the versions used by Windows Server and Server Core, the Nano Server roles are not interchangeable. You cannot install roles from the full Windows Server product on a Nano Server system.

Creating a Nano Server image

To create a new Nano Server image, you open a PowerShell session with administrative privileges on a computer with the Windows Server 2016 installation media loaded or mounted. Then, you switch to the NanoServer folder on the installation disk and import the Windows PowerShell module required to provide the cmdlets for Nano Server, using the following command:

```
import-module .\nanoserverimagegenerator -verbose
```

Importing the module provides you with access to the New-NanoServerImage cmdlet, which you use to create a Nano Server VHD file.

To run the New-NanoServerImage cmdlet, use the following basic syntax:

```
new-nanoserverimage -deploymenttype guest|host -edition standard|datacenter -mediapath root -targetpath path\filename -computername name
```

The required parameters for the New-NanoServerImage cmdlet are as follows:

- **DeploymentType** Specifies whether the image file should be used on a Hyper-V virtual machine (Guest) or a physical server (Host).
- **Edition** Specifies whether to install the Standard or Datacenter edition of Nano Server.
- **MediaPath** Specifies the path to the root of the Windows Server 2016 installation disk or mounted image.

- **BasePath** Specifies a path on the local system where the cmdlet creates a copy of the installation files from the location specified in the MediaPath parameter. Once the copy is created, you can use the BasePath parameter only for future New-NanoServerImage commands and omit the MediaPath parameter. This parameter is optional.
- **TargetPath** Species the full path and filename of the new image to be created. The filename extension (.vhd or .vhdx) specifies whether the new image should be Generation 1 or Generation 2.
- **ComputerName** Specifies the computer name that should be assigned to the new image.

An example of the command to create a standard, Generation 2 Nano Server image with the computer name Nano1, for use on a virtual machine, would be as follows:

```
new-nanoserverimage -deploymenttype guest -edition standard -mediapath d:\ -targetpath c:\temp\nanoserver1.vhdx -computername nano1
```

As the command runs, it prompts you for a password that will be applied to the Administrator account in the Nano Server image. The output generated by the cmdlet appears as shown in Figure 1-28.

```
Windows(R) Image to Virtual Hard Disk Converter for Windows(R) 10
Copyright (C) Microsoft Corporation.    All rights reserved.
Version 10.0.14300.1000.amd64fre.rs1_release_svc.160324-1723

INFO    : Looking for the requested Windows image in the WIM file
INFO    : Image 1 selected (ServerStandardNano)...
INFO    : Creating sparse disk...
INFO    : Attaching VHDX...
INFO    : Initializing disk...
INFO    : Creating EFI system partition...
INFO    : Formatting system volume...
INFO    : Setting system partition as ESP...
INFO    : Creating MSR partition...
INFO    : Creating windows partition...
INFO    : Formatting windows volume...
INFO    : Windows path (F:) has been assigned.
INFO    : System volume location: E:
INFO    : Applying image to VHDX. This could take a while...
INFO    : Image was applied successfully.
INFO    : Making image bootable...
INFO    : Drive is bootable.  Cleaning up...
INFO    : Closing VHDX...
INFO    : Closing Windows image...
INFO    : Done.
Done. The log is at: C:\Users\ADMINI~1.CON\AppData\Local\Temp\NanoServerImageGenerator.log
```

Figure 1-28 PowerShell output from New-NanoServerImage cmdlet

Joining a domain

To create a new Nano Server image that is a member of a domain, you are essentially performing an offline domain join. To do this, you must have access to the domain the Nano Server will join, so that you can harvest a domain provisioning file, called a *blob*, and apply it to the newly created VHD file.

The New-NanoServerImage cmdlet supports a DomainName parameter, which you can use when you are creating the image on a computer that is a member of the domain, and you are logged on using an account that has the privileges needed to create domain computer accounts. You specify the DomainName parameter on the New-NanoServerImage command line with the name of the domain the new image will join, as in the following example:

```
new-nanoserverimage -deploymenttype guest -edition standard -mediapath d:\ -targetpath
c:\temp\nanoserver2.vhdx -computername nano2 -domainname contoso
```

Once the command processing completes and the new image is created, a new Computer object appears in Active Directory, as shown in Figure 1-29.

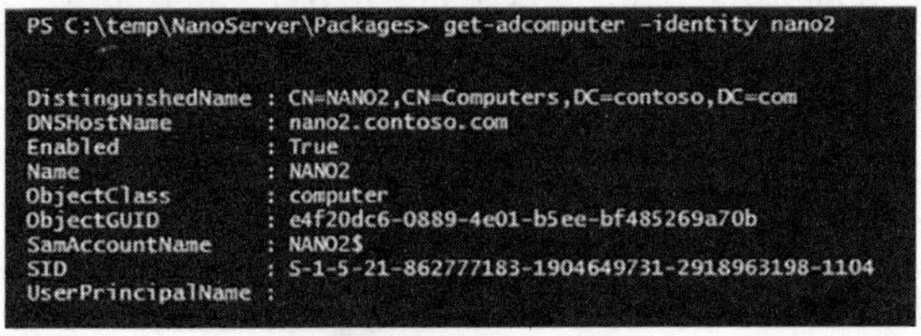

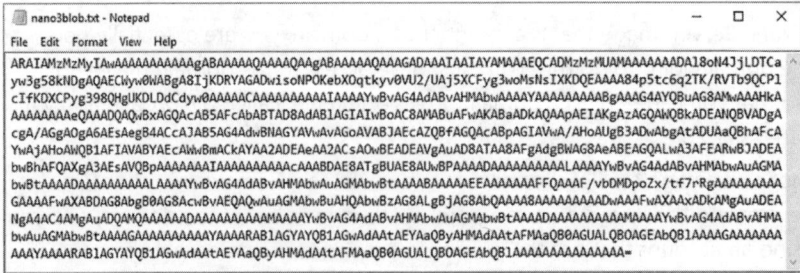

FIGURE 1-29 New Nano Server computer account in Active Directory

> **NOTE** **REUSING A DOMAIN COMPUTER NAME**
>
> If a computer account with the name specified in the ComputerName parameter already exists in Active Directory, you can configure a Nano Server image to reuse that account by adding the ReuseDomainNode parameter to the New-NanoServerImage command line.

It is possible to join a new Nano Server image to a domain when creating it on a computer that is not a domain member, but the process is more complicated. In this case, you have to harvest the blob file on a domain member computer, and then copy it to the computer where you intend to run New-NanoServerImage.

You create a blob file with the Djoin.exe tool included with Windows Server 2016, using the following syntax:

```
djoin /provision /domain domainname /machine computername /savefile filename.txt
```

An example, of a Djoin provisioning command would be as follows:

```
djoin /provision /domain contoso /machine nano3 /savefile nano3blob.txt
```

Provisioning the computer in this way creates the computer account in the domain and creates a text file using the name you specified in the Djoin command. Although the blob is a text file, the information it contains is encoded, as shown in Figure 1-30.

FIGURE 1-30 Contents of a blob file created by Djoin.exe

After you copy the blob file to the computer where you will create the new Nano Server image, you run the New-NanoServerImage cmdlet with the DomainBlobPath parameter, specifying the location of the blob file, as in the following example:

```
new-nanoserverimage -deploymenttype guest -edition standard -mediapath d:\ -targetpath
c:\temp\nanoserver2.vhdx -computername nano2 -domainblobpath c:\temp\nano3blob.txt
```

Creating a NanoServer VM

Once you have created a Nano Server VHD or VHDX image file using the New-NanoServerImage cmdlet, you can proceed to deploy it. In the case of a virtual machine (for which you specified Guest in the DeploymentType parameter), you create a new VM in Hyper-V, using the Nano Server VHD or VHDX image file as its virtual disk file, instead of creating a new one.

If you create the VM using the New Virtual Machine Wizard in Hyper-V Manager, you select the Use An Existing Virtual Hard Disk option on the Connect Virtual Hard Disk page, and select the Nano Server image file you created, as shown in Figure 1-31.

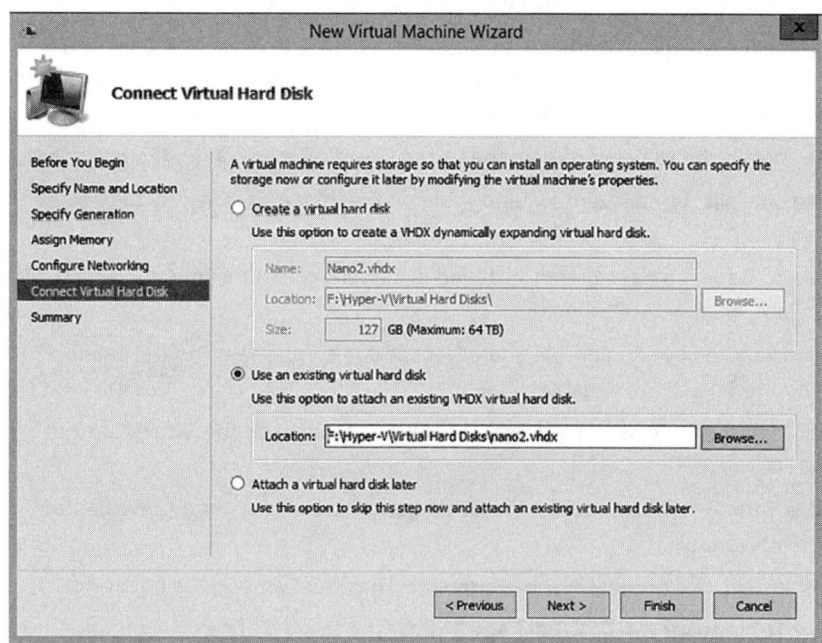

FIGURE 1-31 Using a Nano Server VHDX image file to create a virtual machine

If you use the New-VM PowerShell cmdlet to create the virtual machine, you use the VHDPath parameter to specify the name and location of the Nano Server image file, as in the following example:

```
new-vm -name "nano2" -generation 2 -memorystartupbytes 1GB -vhdpath "f:\hyper-v\virtual
hard disks\nano2.vhdx"
```

> **NOTE** **CREATING THE CORRECT GENERATION VM**
>
> As mentioned earlier, the file extension you supply in the TargetPath parameter specifies whether the New-NanoServerImage cmdlet creates a Generation 1 or Generation 2 image. When creating the new virtual machine in Hyper-V, be sure to specify a Generation 1 VM for a VHD file or a Generation 2 VM for a VHDX file.

Implement Roles and Features on Nano Server

All of the optional software components that you can add to a Nano Server VHD file are supplied as packages. The NanoServer directory on the Windows Server 2016 installation media has a subdirectory called Packages, which contains all of the individual cabinet (CAB) files containing the drivers, roles, features, and other components that you can add to a VHD.

After the New-NanoServerImage cmdlet creates a VHD file, it adds any packages you have specified in the command. For example, the Guest drivers specified by the DeploymentType parameter are provided as a package, which the cmdlet installs to the VHD file.

To install additional packages provided with Nano Server, such as those containing roles and features, you can add optional parameters to the New-NanoServerImage command line. The optional parameters for the New-NanoServerImage cmdlet are as follows:

- **Compute** Installs the Hyper-V role on the image specified by the TargetPath variable.
- **Clustering** Installs the Failover Clustering role on the image specified by the TargetPath variable.
- **OEMDrivers** Adds the basic drivers included in Server Core to the image specified by the TargetPath variable.
- **Storage** Installs the File Server role and other storage components on the image specified by the TargetPath variable.
- **Defender** Installs Windows Defender on the image specified by the TargetPath variable.
- **Containers** Installs host support for Windows Containers on the image specified by the TargetPath variable.
- **Packages** Installs one or more Nano Center packages from among the following:
    - **Microsoft-NanoServer-DSC-Package** Installs the Desired State Configuration (DSC) package on the image specified by the TargetPath variable.
    - **Microsoft-NanoServer-DNS-Package** Installs the DNS Server role on the image specified by the TargetPath variable.
    - **Microsoft-NanoServer-IIS-Package** Installs the IIS role on the image specified by the TargetPath variable.

- **Microsoft-NanoServer-SCVMM-Package** Installs the System Center Virtual Machine Manager agent on the image specified by the TargetPath variable.
- **Microsoft-NanoServer-SCVMM-Compute-Package** Installs the Hyper-V role on the image specified by the TargetPath variable, so that is it manageable with System Center Virtual Machine Manager. Do not use with the Compute parameter.
- **Microsoft-NanoServer-NPDS-Package** Installs the Network Performance Diagnostics Service on the image specified by the TargetPath variable.
- **Microsoft-NanoServer-DCB-Package** Installs Data Center Bridging on the image specified by the TargetPath variable.
- **Microsoft-NanoServer-SecureStartup-Package** Installs Secure Startup on the image specified by the TargetPath variable.
- **Microsoft-NanoServer-ShieldedVM-Package** Installs the Shielded Virtual Machine package on the image specified by the TargetPath variable (Datacenter edition only).

To add a role or feature to an existing Nano Server VHD file, you can use the Edit-NanoServerImage cmdlet, which is similar the New-NanoServerImage cmdlet used to create the VHD file. The syntax is as follows:

```
edit-nanoserverimage -basepath path -targetpath path\filename -packages name
```

The parameters for the Edit-NanoServerImage cmdlet are as follows:

- **BasePath** Specifies the path on the local system where you have previously created a copy of the Nano Server installation files using the New-NanoServerImage cmdlet with the BasePath parameter.
- **TargetPath** Species the full path and filename of an existing Nano Server image to be modified.
- **Packages** Specifies one or more Nano Center packages to be installed to the image file specified in the TargetPath parameter. The possible values for the parameter are the same as those listed earlier for the New-NanoServerImage cmdlet, or you can specify CAB files you have downloaded or created yourself.

For example, the command to add the Web Server (IIS) role to an image file would appear like the following:

```
edit-nanoserverimage -basepath c:\nanoserver\base -targetpath c:\nanoserver\nano1.vhdx
-packages microsoft-nanoserver-iis-package
```

> ✓ **Quick check**
>
> You are planning to deploy a Nano Server to function as a Hyper-V server for your network. Which of the following parameters should you include on the New-NanoServerImage command line?
>
> 1. /containers
> 2. /packages
> 3. /compute
> 4. /clustering
>
> **Quick check answer**
>
> When you run New-NanoServerImage with the /compute parameter (#3), the cmdlet applies the Hyper-V role to the new image file.

Manage and configure Nano Server

Once you have deployed the VHD image in a virtual machine and started the Nano Server system, a simple, character-based authentication screen appears, as shown in Figure 1-32.

FIGURE 1-32 The Nano Server authentication screen

After you log on, the Nano Server Recovery Console screen appears, as shown in Figure 1-33. This screen provides only the minimal controls you might need to configure the system's remote administration client capabilities.

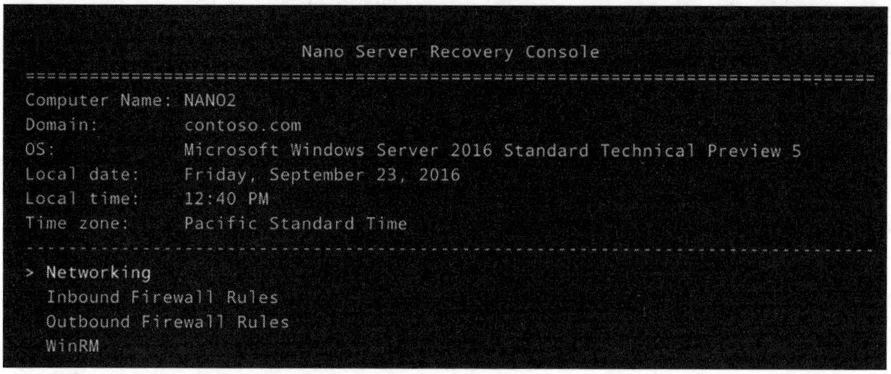

```
                    Nano Server Recovery Console
==============================================================================
Computer Name: NANO2
Domain:        contoso.com
OS:            Microsoft Windows Server 2016 Standard Technical Preview 5
Local date:    Friday, September 23, 2016
Local time:    12:40 PM
Time zone:     Pacific Standard Time
------------------------------------------------------------------------------
> Networking
  Inbound Firewall Rules
  Outbound Firewall Rules
  WinRM
```

FIGURE 1-33 The Nano Server Recovery Console screen

You can configure the network interfaces, set Windows Firewall rules, and configure Windows remote Management (WinRM). Once the system is ready to listen for calls from remote management tools, there is nothing more to do from the Nano Server console. All subsequent administration occurs remotely.

Configuring a Nano Server IP address

As with the other Windows Server installation options, Nano Server has its Dynamic Host Configuration Protocol (DHCP) client enabled by default. If you have a DHCP server on your network, Nano Server will obtain an IP address from it and configure the system's network adapter automatically. If no DHCP server is available, you can configure the network adapter manually, using parameters in the New-NanoServerImage command line, or using one of the few functions available in the Nano Server Recovery Console.

You can configure a network adapter in a Nano Server as you create the VHD image file, by specifying the IP configuration settings on the New-NanoServerImage command line. You can also modify the settings in an existing VHD file using the Edit-NanoServerImage cmdlet. The parameters to use with both cmdlets are as follows:

- **InterfaceNameOrIndex** Identifies the network adapter in the Nano Server to which the settings in the following parameters should be applied. In a machine with a single network interface adapter, the value Ethernet should be sufficient.
- **Ipv4Address** Specifies the IPv4 address to be assigned to the network adapter identified by the InterfaceNameOrIndex parameter.
- **Ipv4SubnetMask** Specifies the Subnet Mask value associated with the IP address specified in the Ipv4Address parameter.
- **Ipv4Gateway** Specifies the IP address of a router on the local network where the IP address specified in the Ipv4Address parameter is located, that provides access to other networks.
- **Ipv4Dns** Specifies the IP address of the DNS server that the system should use to locate resources.

An example of the New-NanoServerImage command line including these parameters would be as follows:

```
new-nanoserverimage -deploymenttype guest -edition standard -mediapath d:\ -targetpath
c:\temp\nanoserver4.vhdx -computername nano4 -domain contoso.com -interfacenameorindex
ethernet -ipv4address 192.168.10.41 -ipv4subnetmask 255.255.255.0 -ipv4gateway
192.168.10.1 -ipv4dns 192.168.10.2
```

To manually configure the network adapter to use a static IP address from the Nano Server Recovery Console, after the image has been created and deployed, use the following procedure:

1. Select the Networking item and press Enter.

> *NOTE* **USING THE NANO SERVER RECOVERY CONSOLE INTERFACE**
>
> The Nano Server Recovery Console has no support for the mouse, and even its keyboard support is limited. Number pads are not supported, nor are CapsLk and NumLk keys. To navigate the interface, you use the cursor keys or the Tab key to highlight an option and press Enter to select it. The legend at the bottom of the screen specifies additional key combinations.

2. On the Network Settings screen, select a network adapter, and press Enter.
3. On the Network Adapter Settings screen, shown in Figure 1-34, press F11 to configure the IPv4 settings for the adapter.

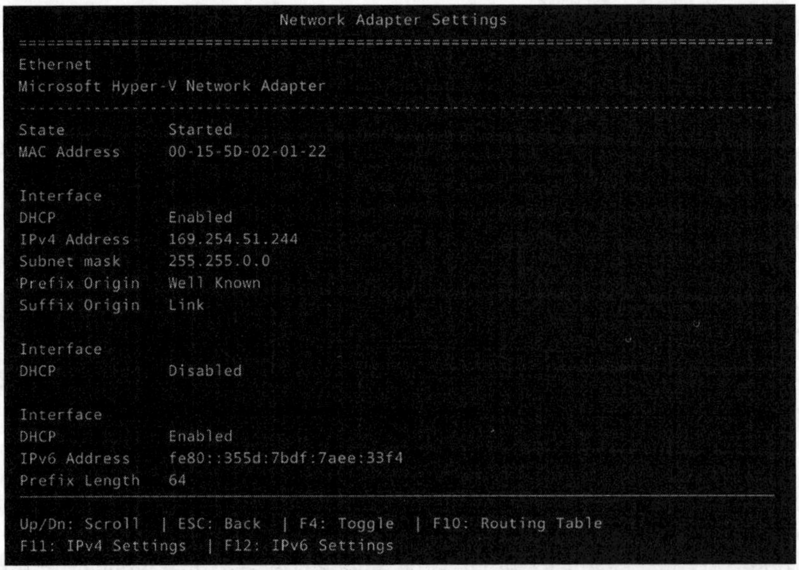

FIGURE 1-34 The Network Adapter Settings screen in the Nano Server Recovery Console

4. On the IP Configuration screen, press F4 to toggle the DHCP client to Disabled, as shown in Figure 1-35.

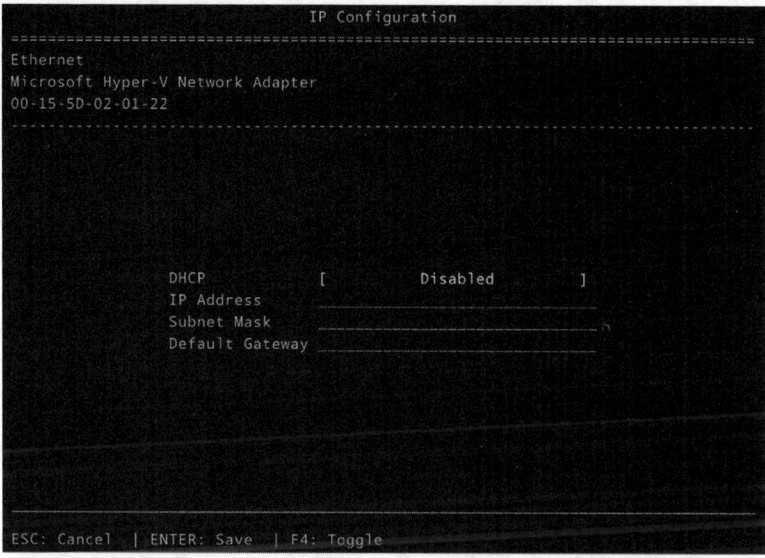

FIGURE 1-35 The IP Configuration screen in the Nano Server Recovery Console

5. Press the Tab key to advance to the IP Address field, and type an IP address for the adapter.
6. Press the Tab key to advance to the Subnet Mask field, and type the mask associated with the IP address.
7. Press the Tab key to advance to the Default Gateway field, and type the address of a router on the network.
8. Press Enter to save your settings.
9. Press Enter again to confirm the Save.
10. Press Esc to return to the Network Adapter Settings screen.
11. Press F12 to configure IPv6 Settings or F10 to modify the routing table, if necessary.
12. Press Esc twice to return to the Nano Server Recovery Console.

> **NOTE CONFIGURING A DNS SERVER ADDRESS**
> Unusually, there is no way to specify a DNS server address in the Nano Server Recovery Console interface. To configure the DNS server address for an initial Nano Server configuration, you must use the Ipv4Dns parameter on the New-NanoServerImage or Edit-NanoServerImage command line or use DHCP to supply the address.

Configuring firewall rules

Depending on what remote tools you intend to use to manage Nano Server, you might have to work with Windows Firewall rules to provide appropriate access to the computer. The local interface on Nano Server enables you to enable or disable existing firewall rules, both inbound and outbound, to open and close ports as needed.

On the Nano Server Recovery Console screen, when you select Inbound Firewall Rules or Outbound Firewall Rules, you see a scrollable screen containing all of the default rules on the system, as shown in Figure 1-36.

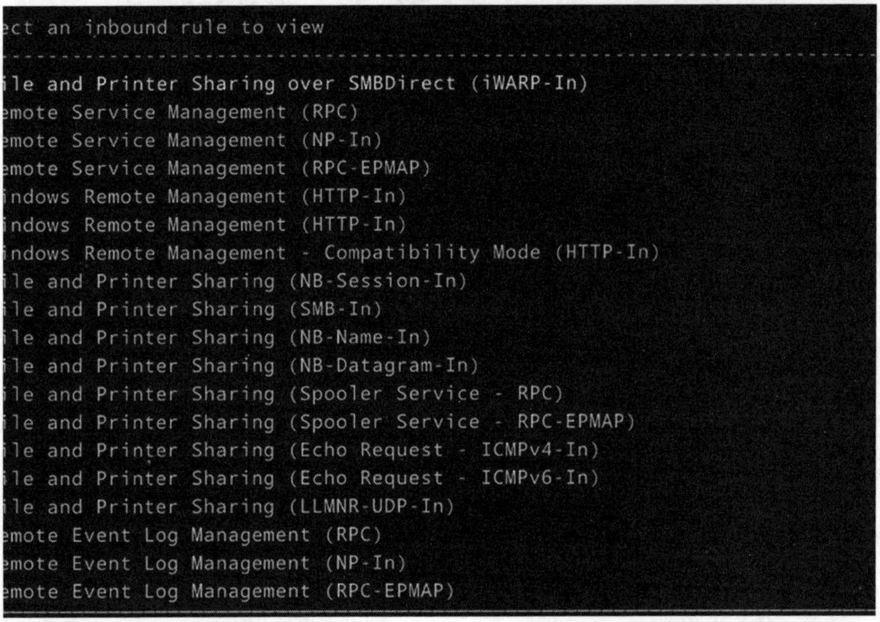

```
ect an inbound rule to view
----------------------------------------------------------
ile and Printer Sharing over SMBDirect (iWARP-In)
emote Service Management (RPC)
emote Service Management (NP-In)
emote Service Management (RPC-EPMAP)
indows Remote Management (HTTP-In)
indows Remote Management (HTTP-In)
indows Remote Management - Compatibility Mode (HTTP-In)
ile and Printer Sharing (NB-Session-In)
ile and Printer Sharing (SMB-In)
ile and Printer Sharing (NB-Name-In)
ile and Printer Sharing (NB-Datagram-In)
ile and Printer Sharing (Spooler Service - RPC)
ile and Printer Sharing (Spooler Service - RPC-EPMAP)
ile and Printer Sharing (Echo Request - ICMPv4-In)
ile and Printer Sharing (Echo Request - ICMPv6-In)
ile and Printer Sharing (LLMNR-UDP-In)
emote Event Log Management (RPC)
emote Event Log Management (NP-In)
emote Event Log Management (RPC-EPMAP)
```

FIGURE 1-36 The Firewall Rules screen in the Nano Server Recovery Console

Selecting a rule displays a Firewall Rule Details screen that contains information about the rule, including the port affected by the rule and whether it is currently enabled, as shown in Figure 1-37. You can then press the F4 key to enable or disable the rule.

4. On the IP Configuration screen, press F4 to toggle the DHCP client to Disabled, as shown in Figure 1-35.

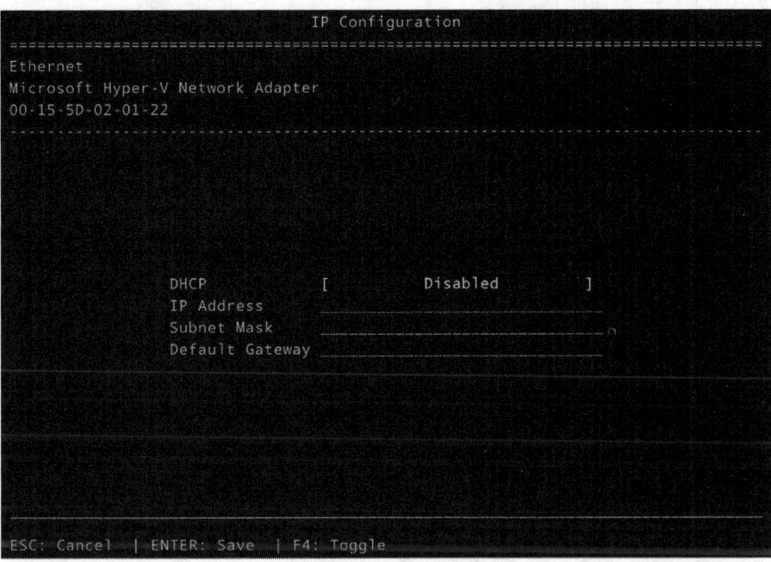

FIGURE 1-35 The IP Configuration screen in the Nano Server Recovery Console

5. Press the Tab key to advance to the IP Address field, and type an IP address for the adapter.
6. Press the Tab key to advance to the Subnet Mask field, and type the mask associated with the IP address.
7. Press the Tab key to advance to the Default Gateway field, and type the address of a router on the network.
8. Press Enter to save your settings.
9. Press Enter again to confirm the Save.
10. Press Esc to return to the Network Adapter Settings screen.
11. Press F12 to configure IPv6 Settings or F10 to modify the routing table, if necessary.
12. Press Esc twice to return to the Nano Server Recovery Console.

> *NOTE* **CONFIGURING A DNS SERVER ADDRESS**
>
> Unusually, there is no way to specify a DNS server address in the Nano Server Recovery Console interface. To configure the DNS server address for an initial Nano Server configuration, you must use the Ipv4Dns parameter on the New-NanoServerImage or Edit-NanoServerImage command line or use DHCP to supply the address.

Configuring firewall rules

Depending on what remote tools you intend to use to manage Nano Server, you might have to work with Windows Firewall rules to provide appropriate access to the computer. The local interface on Nano Server enables you to enable or disable existing firewall rules, both inbound and outbound, to open and close ports as needed.

On the Nano Server Recovery Console screen, when you select Inbound Firewall Rules or Outbound Firewall Rules, you see a scrollable screen containing all of the default rules on the system, as shown in Figure 1-36.

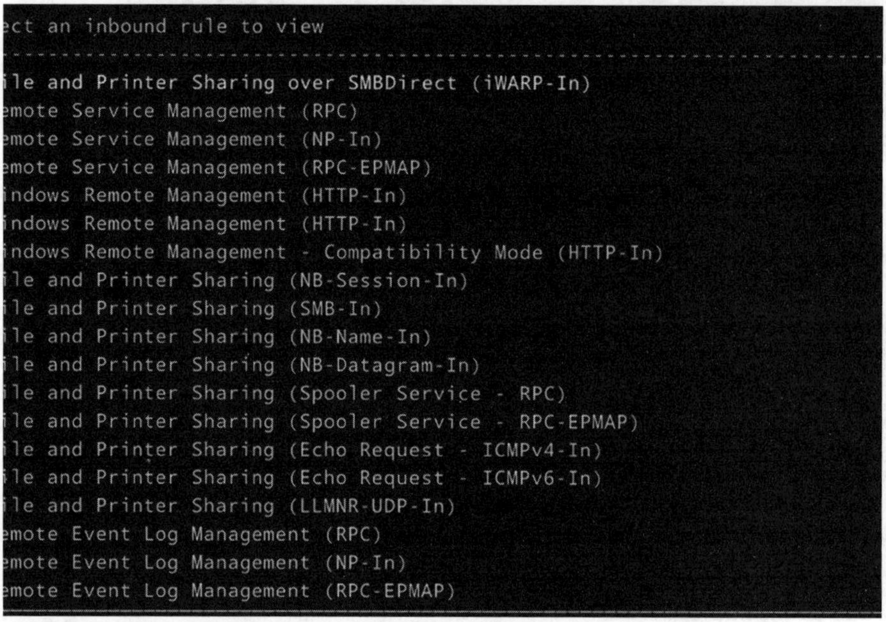

```
ct an inbound rule to view
--------------------------------------------------
le and Printer Sharing over SMBDirect (iWARP-In)
mote Service Management (RPC)
mote Service Management (NP-In)
mote Service Management (RPC-EPMAP)
ndows Remote Management (HTTP-In)
ndows Remote Management (HTTP-In)
ndows Remote Management - Compatibility Mode (HTTP-In)
le and Printer Sharing (NB-Session-In)
le and Printer Sharing (SMB-In)
le and Printer Sharing (NB-Name-In)
le and Printer Sharing (NB-Datagram-In)
le and Printer Sharing (Spooler Service - RPC)
le and Printer Sharing (Spooler Service - RPC-EPMAP)
le and Printer Sharing (Echo Request - ICMPv4-In)
le and Printer Sharing (Echo Request - ICMPv6-In)
le and Printer Sharing (LLMNR-UDP-In)
mote Event Log Management (RPC)
mote Event Log Management (NP-In)
mote Event Log Management (RPC-EPMAP)
```

FIGURE 1-36 The Firewall Rules screen in the Nano Server Recovery Console

Selecting a rule displays a Firewall Rule Details screen that contains information about the rule, including the port affected by the rule and whether it is currently enabled, as shown in Figure 1-37. You can then press the F4 key to enable or disable the rule.

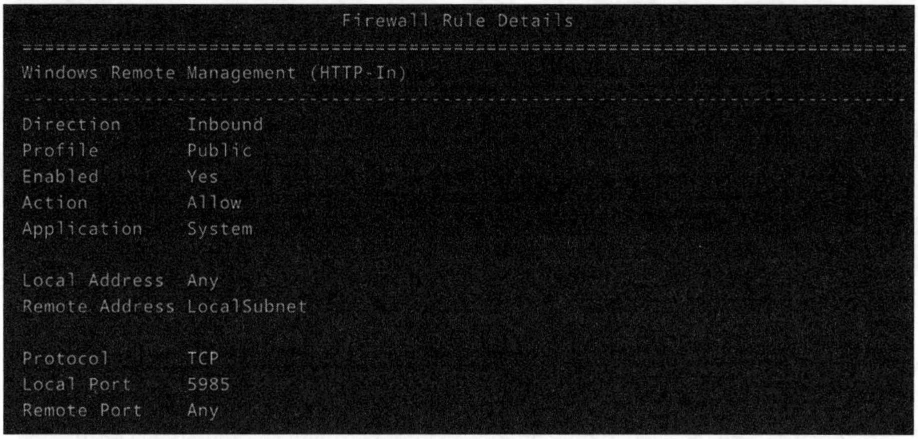

```
                    Firewall Rule Details
================================================================
Windows Remote Management (HTTP-In)
----------------------------------------------------------------
Direction         Inbound
Profile           Public
Enabled           Yes
Action            Allow
Application       System

Local Address     Any
Remote Address    LocalSubnet

Protocol          TCP
Local Port        5985
Remote Port       Any
```

FIGURE 1-37 The Firewall Rule Details screen in the Nano Server Recovery Console

This interface does not provide full administrative access to Windows Firewall. It is intended only to provide you with sufficient control to gain remote access to the Nano Server. You can activate or deactivate an existing rule, but you cannot modify rules themselves or create new ones. Once you have remote access to the Nano Server, you can use standard tools, such as the Windows Firewall with Advanced Security console or the Windows PowerShell cmdlets, to exercise complete control over the firewall.

Configuring Windows Remote Management

The WinRM entry on the Nano Server Recovery Console screen provides only a single function, the ability to reset the WinRM service and firewall to their default settings, in the event that the Nano Server configuration is preventing you from establishing a connection with a remote management tool.

Managing Nano Server remotely using PowerShell

In most cases, a newly-installed Nano Server with a proper network adapter configuration should be ready to listen for incoming connection requests from remote management tools. For example, to connect to a Nano Server using Windows PowerShell, you create a PowerShell session with the New-PSSession cmdlet, using following basic syntax:

```
new-pssession -computername name -credential domain\username
```

The values you use for the ComputerName and Credential parameters in this command depend on whether the Nano Server is already a member of a domain. For a domain-joined Nano Server, you should be able to connect by specifying the fully-qualified domain name of the Nano Server and a domain account name, as in the following example:

```
new-pssession -computername nano4.contoso.com -credential contoso\administrator
```

The cmdlet will prompt for a password for the Administrator account and create a new session, as shown in Figure 1-38. The output from the cmdlet specifies the ID for the session, which you will use to connect to it.

```
PS C:\temp\NanoServer> new-pssession -ComputerName "nano4.contoso.com" -Credential contoso\administrator

Id Name            ComputerName    ComputerType    State     ConfigurationName       Availability
-- ----            ------------    ------------    -----     -----------------       ------------
16 Session16       nano4.contos... RemoteMachine   Opened    Microsoft.PowerShell    Available


PS C:\temp\NanoServer>
```

FIGURE 1-38 Creating a PowerShell session to a Nano Server

When the Nano Server is not joined to a domain, the process of creating a new session can be more complicated. First, you must consider whether or not the computer name of the Nano Server can be resolved. If the network adapter has been configured by DHCP, you can probably use the computer's name in the ComputerName parameter, as in the following example:

```
new-pssession -computername nano4 -credential -\administrator
```

Omitting the domain name from the Credential parameter will cause the cmdlet to prompt you for the local account password.

If you have manually configured the network adapter, you might have to use the IP address of the Nano Server instead of its computer name, as in the following example:

```
new-pssession -computername 192.168.10.41 -credential -\administrator
```

Second, you will most likely have to add the Nano Server to the computer's Trusted Hosts list in the Windows Remote Management implementation. Otherwise, the cmdlet will try to use Kerberos to authenticate the session, which will fail in the case of a non-domain-joined host.

To add a computer to the Trusted Hosts list using PowerShell, you specify its name or IP address in the Set-Item cmdlet, as in the following example:

```
set-item wsman:\localhost\client\trustedhosts "192.168.10.41"
```

You can also use the Winrm.exe tool from the command prompt, as follows:

```
winrm set winrm/config/client @{TrustedHosts="192.168.10.41"}
```

Once you have successfully created a PowerShell session, you can connect to it using the Enter-PSSession cmdlet, specifying the ID displayed in the New-PSSession output, as in the following example:

```
enter-pssession -id 16
```

When you successfully connect to the session, the command prompt changes to include the remote computer name, as shown in Figure 1-39.

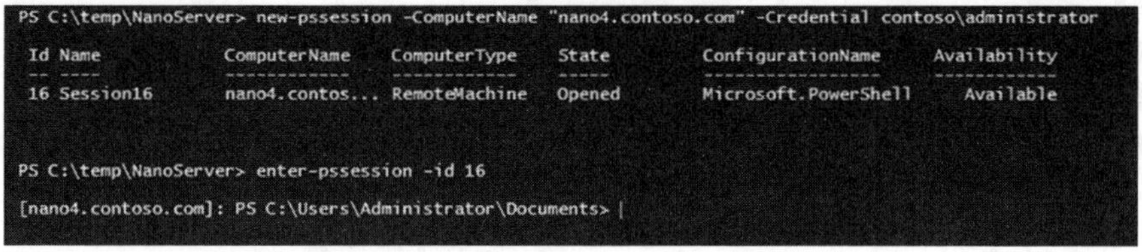

```
PS C:\temp\NanoServer> new-pssession -ComputerName "nano4.contoso.com" -Credential contoso\administrator

Id Name            ComputerName     ComputerType    State    ConfigurationName      Availability
-- ----            ------------     ------------    -----    -----------------      ------------
16 Session16       nano4.contos...  RemoteMachine   Opened   Microsoft.PowerShell   Available


PS C:\temp\NanoServer> enter-pssession -id 16
[nano4.contoso.com]: PS C:\Users\Administrator\Documents>
```

FIGURE 1-39 Connecting to a PowerShell session on a Nano Server

Once you have connected to the session, you are working with the PowerShell resources of the Nano Server. The Windows PowerShell 5.1 version included in Windows Server 2016 now exists in two editions: Desktop and Core. The full version of Windows Server 2016 and Server Core both include the Desktop edition. Nano Server includes the PowerShell Core edition, as displayed in the $PSVersionTable variable, shown in Figure 1-40.

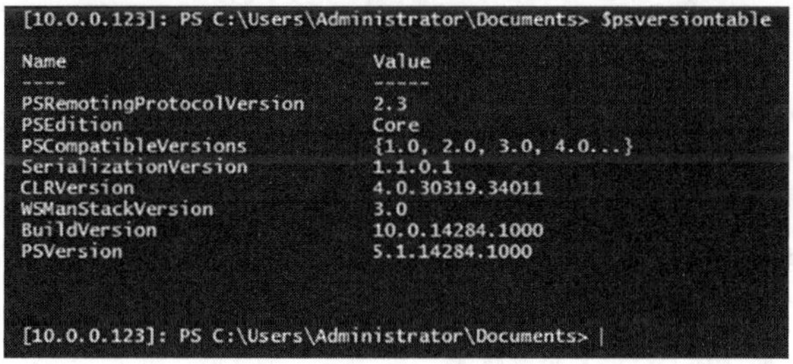

```
[10.0.0.123]: PS C:\Users\Administrator\Documents> $psversiontable

Name                           Value
----                           -----
PSRemotingProtocolVersion      2.3
PSEdition                      Core
PSCompatibleVersions           {1.0, 2.0, 3.0, 4.0...}
SerializationVersion           1.1.0.1
CLRVersion                     4.0.30319.34011
WSManStackVersion              3.0
BuildVersion                   10.0.14284.1000
PSVersion                      5.1.14284.1000


[10.0.0.123]: PS C:\Users\Administrator\Documents>
```

FIGURE 1-40 Contents of the $PSVersionTable variable

PowerShell Core is a subset of PowerShell Desktop, omitting many of its features. Administrators and developers with existing PowerShell code should test it on a PowerShell Core implementation.

> **NEED MORE REVIEW?** **POWERSHELL CORE FEATURE OMISSIONS**
>
> For a list of the features not included in PowerShell Core, see *https://technet.microsoft.com/en-us/windows-server-docs/get-started/powershell-on-nano-server*.

To disconnect from a connected session, you can use the Exit-PSSession cmdlet, or just type Exit. The command prompt returns to its original form, and you are back working with the host computer.

Skill 1.3: Create, manage, and maintain images for deployment

Creating virtualized server environments is a task that requires the consideration not only of the hardware you will use, but also the needs of your organization. One of the advantages of virtual machines is that you can work with their virtual hard disks offline, to apply updates and features.

> **This section covers how to:**
> - Plan for Windows Server virtualization
> - Plan for Linux and FreeBSD deployments
> - Assess virtualization workloads using the Microsoft Assessment and Planning (MAP) Toolkit
> - Determine considerations for deploying workloads into virtualized environments
> - Update images with patches, hotfixes, and drivers
> - Install roles and features in offline images
> - Manage and maintain Windows Server Core, Nano Server images, and VHDs using Windows PowerShell

Plan for Windows Server virtualization

Virtualization has become an important tool in network administration. With the cost of high-performance host servers relatively low, it is possible to deploy many virtual servers on a single computer. The advantages of this are numerous, including the following:

- **Hardware compatibility** Because the hardware in a virtual machine is virtual, driver compatibility issues are all but eliminated. Instead of equipping separate computers with the hardware they need, and dealing with the inevitable driver installation and maintenance issues that arise, virtual machines deploy in minutes and requires no driver maintenance.
- **Smaller datacenters** A data center with 10 host server computers in it can be smaller than one with 50 or more physical servers. It is also easier and less expensive to power and cool, resulting in environmental benefits and cost savings.
- **Upgradability** As workloads evolve, virtualization makes it a simple matter to add as much memory or storage to a virtual machine as it needs.
- **Provisioning** Deployment of new virtual servers can be accomplished in hours, rather than the days needed to approve, obtain, and install hardware for a new physical server.

- **Efficiency** Virtual machines enable you to utilize the resources of the host server more efficiently. Physical servers dedicated to a single application rarely run at high capacity; much of the time, it is 20 percent or less. By running several VMs on a single host, you can adjust the resources devoted to each one and utilize more of those resources much of the time.
- **Uptime** Technologies such as live migration and failover clustering are far easier to implement in a virtual server environment than they are with physical computers. This means that administrators can more easily keep virtual servers running, even when unplanned outages occur.
- **Maintenance** When running fewer physical computers, there are fewer updates to install and it is easier to maintain a flat environment with one physical server model rather than many. All of these things contribute to reduced maintenance costs.
- **Disaster recovery** Because virtual machines can easily be migrated from one server to another, recovery from a catastrophic hardware failure that brings down a host server can be as simply as activating a replica of the VM on another server.
- **Testing** Virtual machines make it a simple matter to set up an isolated lab environment for the testing and evaluation of server configurations, software products, and updates.
- **Isolated applications** Deploying a large number of applications on physical servers requires either a separate computer for each application or a lot of compatibility testing. With virtualization, you can easily deploy a separate VM for each application and modify the virtual hardware resources devoted to each one as needed.
- **Cloud migration** Virtual servers abstract away the computer's underlying hardware, so that the eventual migration of servers to a private or public cloud is a relatively simple matter.
- **Return on Investment (ROI)** All of these factors contribute to an ROI that should offset the cost of the virtualization project. During the design phase of the project, ROI should be an important consideration.

If you are considering using a visualized environment for your enterprise, the planning phase should include several important questions, covered next.

Which servers should you virtualize?

Defining the scope of your virtualization project, by deciding which of your servers should be virtualized and when, is a critical part of the planning process. When you are building a new network from scratch, you can easily deploy all of your servers virtually, implementing only applications and technologies that are compatible with the virtual environment. Things don't often work out that easily, though. For many administrators, virtualization is a matter of adapting existing physical servers to a virtual world.

You can start the virtualization process easily by deploying any new servers required as virtual machines. Instead of purchasing a physical server for a single application, you can consider a better equipped model for use as a Hyper-V host server. You then have the hardware platform needed to deploy multiple VMs for your future needs.

The next step is to consider the question of whether you should consider converting your existing physical servers to VMs. This process, sometimes called *P2V migration*, requires that you consider the requirements of your organization, as well as the technical aspects of the process.

Which servers should you migrate first?

Prioritizing the virtualization project is an important part of the plan, both because it is often a learning process for the administrators performing the migrations and because you must consider the organization's business requirements. You might consider classifying your existing servers according to the following priorities:

- **Low risk**   The first migrations to virtual servers should be those with functions that are not crucial to everyday business, such as development and test platforms. These initial migrations can enable administrators to develop a protocol for the process of converting a physical machine to a virtual one.
- **Non-critical**   The next priority should be servers running applications that are not critical to business operations. For example, web servers that are part of a server farm can be interrupted because there are other servers there to take up the slack.
- **Higher use**   Systems that are frequently used but not critical to business should be the next priority, such as virtual private networking (VPN) servers.
- **Business critical**   The last servers to be migrated should be those running business critical workloads. By this time, the administrators performing the migrations should have sufficient experience to handle any issues that might occur. For servers that work with frequently changing data, such as email and database servers, the migration will typically have to be performed offline.

How will you migrate physical servers to virtual servers?

The final consideration is that of the actual migration from a physical server to a virtual one. This migration process consists of converting the contents of the physical hard disks in the existing server to the virtual hard disks (VHDs) that Hyper-V uses. There are many software tools available to perform this type of conversion, which you should evaluate and test before committing any important data to them.

This part of the virtualization process should consist of the development of a carefully documented protocol for the actual conversion process, which will be followed for all of the subsequent migrations.

Plan for Linux and FreeBSD deployments

The Hyper-V service in Windows Server 2016 supports the creation of guest virtual machines running various Linux and FreeBSD operating systems. In this case, the word "supported" means more than that Hyper-V will allow you to install a Linux or FreeBSD operating system on a virtual machine. Microsoft is willing to provide technical support for users with issues involving the running of these OSes on Hyper-V.

Choosing a distribution

Windows Server 2016 supports FreeBSD and a large number of Linux distributions, all in several versions. Performance levels and feature availability varies depending on the OS and the version you choose, so selecting an appropriate distribution for your needs and the correct version is critical.

To obtain the best performance from VMs running Linux or FreeBSD, you should use the drivers for Hyper-V-specific devices that were developed by Microsoft. Hyper-V can emulate the native Linux and FreeBSD devices, but these do not provide the same level of performance, nor do they support many of the Hyper-V virtual machine management capabilities.

The drivers for the Hyper-V-specific devices are called Linux Integration Services (LIS) and FreeBSD Integration Services (BIS). The more recent versions of the Linux and FreeBSD distributions have LIS and BIS integrated into their respective kernels, which simplifies the installation process. For older versions, downloadable LIS and BIS packages are available from the Microsoft Download Center at *http://www.microsoft.com/download*.

> *NOTE* **SUPPORTED LINUX AND FREEBSD DISTRIBUTIONS**
>
> For complete listings of the Linux and FreeBSD distributions supported as Hyper-V guests and the LIS or BIS features supported, see *https://technet.microsoft.com/en-us/windows-server-docs/compute/hyper-v/supported-linux-and-freebsd-virtual-machines-for-hyper-v-on-windows*.

Feature support varies among Linux distributions, depending on the version of the guest operating system and that of the host operating system. For example, Hyper-V in Windows Server 2016 adds support for Secure Boot in Linux guests, which was not available in previous versions.

Assess virtualization workloads using the Microsoft Assessment and Planning (MAP) Toolkit

Deploying Windows devices and enterprise applications on a large network can often mean evaluating a large number of existing computers, to determine whether they have the appropriate hardware for the operating system.

Performing and maintaining a hardware inventory can be a daunting task, especially when you have computers and other networked devices with many different hardware configurations, located at distant sites. Microsoft provides a free tool that you can use for this purpose, called the *Microsoft Assessment and Planning (MAP) Toolkit*.

MAP Toolkit is an inventory, assessment, and reporting tool that enables you to discover and evaluate the hardware and software on servers and workstations, in the context of various assessment and deployment scenarios.

The primary functions provided by MAP are as follows:

- Migration planning
- Consolidation/virtualization
- Private/public cloud planning
- Software usage tracking

Unlike some other products of its type, MAP is capable of performing an inventory on computers with no agent software required on the client side. This means that you can install MAP on one system, and it connects to any or all of the other computers on your network using standard technologies, such as Active Directory Domain Services (AD DS), Windows Management Instrumentation (WMI), Remote Registry Service, Secure Shell (SSH), and the Computer Browser service. Once connected, MAP discovers information about the computers' hardware, software, and performance, as well as the network infrastructure, and adds it to a database.

The MAP discovery process can detect all of the Windows versions going back to Windows Server 2003 and Windows XP, and all versions of Microsoft Office. The toolkit also detects some products that are not from Microsoft, such as VMWare virtualization servers and selected Linux distributions. In addition to operating systems, MAP can detect a wide range of Microsoft server applications, including SQL Server, Exchange, SharePoint, and Visual Studio.

Once MAP has gathered information about the systems running on the network, it can evaluate the inventory and generate reports that perform a variety of tasks. One of the primary functions of the MAP Toolkit is to analyze the hardware of the computers on the network and determine their readiness for an upgrade to the latest version of the operating system. The assessment evaluates the hardware in the computers and compares it to the system requirements for the new operating system. MAP also ascertains whether appropriate drivers are available for all of the devices installed in the computers.

In addition to evaluating a computer's readiness for an operating system upgrade, MAP Toolkit can also perform tasks that can help you to plan a virtualization project, including the following:

- Identify virtual machines running on both Hyper-V and VMware and gather detailed information about their hosts and guests.
- Perform a detailed assessment of server utilization and prepare recommendations for server consolidation and virtual machine placement using Hyper-V.
- Discover and identify Linux operating systems and their underlying hardware and plan for their virtualization using Hyper-V.

Installing the MAP Toolkit

The MAP Toolkit has several installation and licensing prerequisites that you must meet before you can successfully install the software. MAP is essentially a database application based on Microsoft SQL Server 2012 Express, a scaled-down, free version of SQL Server 2012. MAP can run on any of the following operating systems:

- Windows 10 (Professional and Enterprise editions only)
- Windows 8.1 (Pro and Enterprise editions only)
- Windows 8 (Professional and Enterprise editions only)
- Windows 7 with Service Pack 1 (Professional, Enterprise, and Ultimate editions only)
- Windows Server 2016
- Windows Server 2012 R2
- Windows Server 2012
- Windows Server 2008 R2 with Service Pack 1

The minimum hardware configuration for a computer running MAP is as follows:

- Dual-core 1.5GHz processor
- 2.0 GB of RAM
- 1 GB of available disk space
- Network adapter card
- Graphics adapter that supports 1024x768 or higher resolution

Before installing MAP on a Windows computer, you should install all of the available updates for the operating system, plus .NET Framework 4.5, which you can obtain from the Microsoft Download Center.

The MAP Toolkit installation program checks for these prerequisites before it allows the setup program to proceed. Reporting is the primary function of the MAP Toolkit once it has gathered data about the devices on the network. The reports that MAP generates take the form of Excel spreadsheets, so you must have Microsoft Excel or the free Excel Viewer application to open them.

Running MapSetup.exe

The MAP Toolkit is available as a free download from the Microsoft Download Center at *http://www.microsoft.com/download*. When you run the MapSetup.exe program, the Microsoft Assessment and Planning Toolkit Setup Wizard appears.

After you accept the license terms and select the folder where you want to install the toolkit, the wizard installs the MAP program itself and enables you to create a new MAP database or use an existing one, as shown in Figure 1-41.

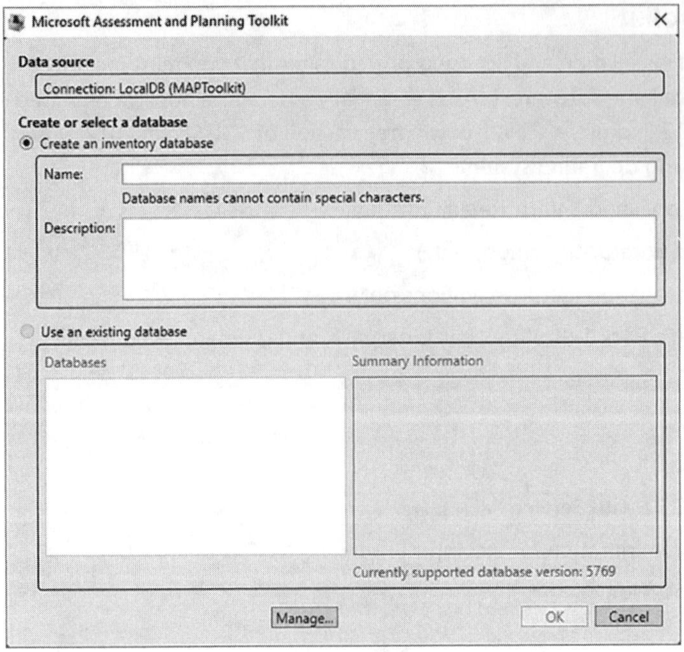

FIGURE 1-41 Creating a MAP database

> **NOTE MAP TOOLKIT DATABASES**
>
> By default, the MAP Toolkit Setup Wizard installs the SQL Server 2012 Express database manager and creates an instance called LocalDB, where MAP stores the information it gathers about the network. In most cases, this default configuration is sufficient for a network of up to 20,000 nodes. However, for larger networks, it is also possible to use a copy of SQL Server 2012 Standard that you have already installed in the computer. To use SQL Server 2012 Standard with MAP, you must install SQL Server first and create a non-default instance called "MAPS." You cannot point MAP to an existing SQL Server instance that is not called "MAPS," nor can you point MAP to a SQL Server installation running on another computer.

Collecting inventory information

MAP uses a console-based interface to configure its information gathering and report processing tasks. When you start MAP, the Microsoft Assessment and Planning Toolkit console appears, as shown in Figure 1-42.

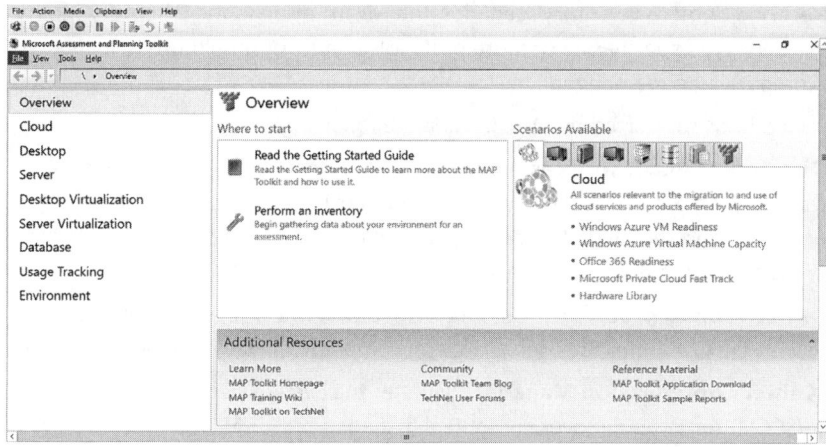

FIGURE 1-42 The Microsoft Assessment and Planning Toolkit console

Once you have configured MAP with a database, you can select one of several methods for collecting inventory information from the computers on the network. Clicking Perform An Inventory on the console's Overview page launches the Inventory And Assessment Wizard. This wizard is the starting point for all inventory scenarios. The Inventory Scenarios page, shown in Figure 1-43, lists the basic types of information discoverable by MAP and specifies the collector technologies that the program uses to probe the network. A *collector technology* specifies the means and the protocol by which MAP communicates with the other computers on the network.

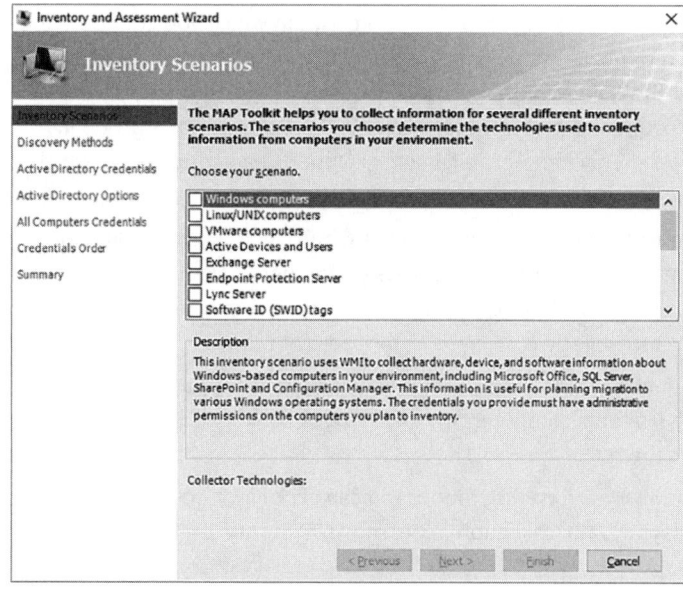

FIGURE 1-43 The Inventory Scenarios page

After you select one or more inventory scenarios, the wizard displays the Discovery Methods page. On this page, you specify one or more protocols that MAP should use to locate and connect to the computers on the network.

The discovery methods supported by MAP include the following:

- **Active Directory Domain Services**   Queries a domain controller using the Lightweight Directory Access Protocol (LDAP) for computers located in specific domains, containers, or organizational units. Use this method if all of the computers you want to inventory are located in Active Directory domains.
- **Windows networking protocols**   Uses the Win32 LAN Manager interface to communicate with the Computer Browser service on computers in workgroups or domains.
- **System Center Configuration Manager**   Queries the System Center Configuration Manager (SCCM) server to discover computers managed by SCCM. You must supply credentials for an account with access to the Configuration Manager WMI provider on the server.
- **Scan an IP address range**   Queries up to 100,000 devices using IP addresses within a specified range. This enables the wizard to connect to computers without credentials and regardless of their operating systems.
- **Manually enter computer names**   Enables you to inventory a small number of computers by entering their computer names, NetBIOS names, or fully-qualified domain names (FQDNs).
- **Import computer names from a file**   Enables you to specify the name of a text file containing up to 120,000 computer names, NetBIOS names, FQDNs, or IPv4 addresses.

Making selections on this page causes the wizard to add pages in which you configure the discovery method or supply credentials. For example, when you select the Active Directory Domain Services discovery method, an Active Directory Credentials page appears, on which you must supply a domain account and password for a user in the Domain Users group in each domain you intend to query. Then, an Active Directory Options page appears, in which you can select specific domains, containers, and organizational units.

Depending on which inventory scenario you select in the wizard, you must supply appropriate credentials that MAP needs to access the computers on the network and their software. In some cases, you must also configure the target computers to accept the communication protocol used by the collector technology.

On the All Computers Credentials page of the wizard, you can create multiple account entries, providing access to the various computers on the network, and specifying the order in which the MAP Toolkit uses them.

Once you have completed the wizard configuration, you can click Finish to start the inventory process. The wizard displays a Data Collection page, shown in Figure 1-44, which tracks the progress of the inventory.

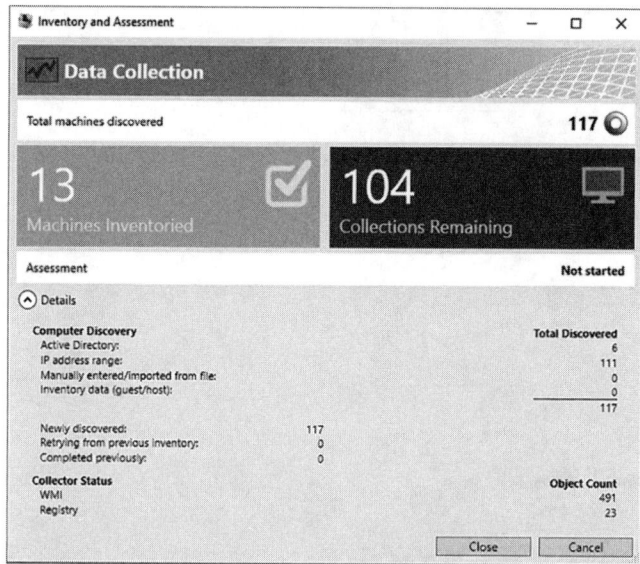

FIGURE 1-44 The Data Collection page

Once you have performed a hardware inventory, you can view the Server Virtualization page (shown in Figure 1-45), which guides you through the rest of the data collection procedure.

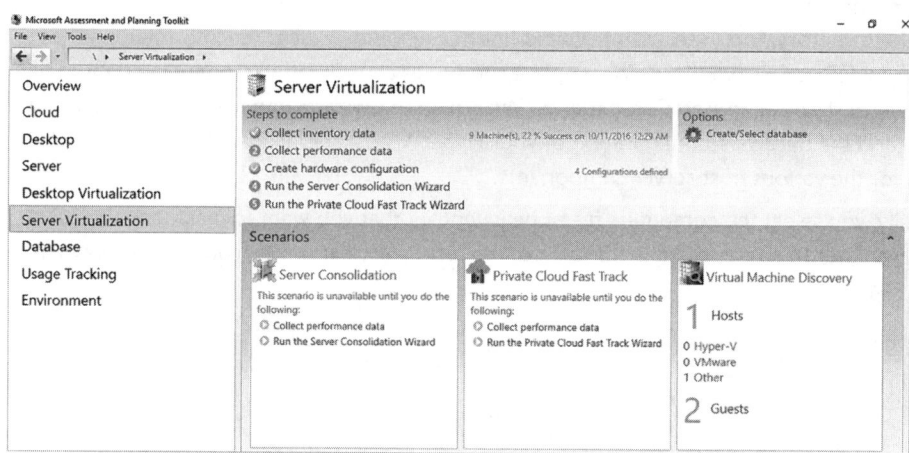

FIGURE 1-45 The Inventory Scenarios page

Clicking Collect Performance Data launches the Performance Metrics Wizard. This wizard collects performance data from the computers on the network over a period of time, which you specify on the Collection Configuration page.

You select the computers from which you want to collect data and supply credentials, as you did earlier. Once the wizard begins, it samples performance counter data from each computer every five minutes, as shown in Figure 1-46, until the specified time expires.

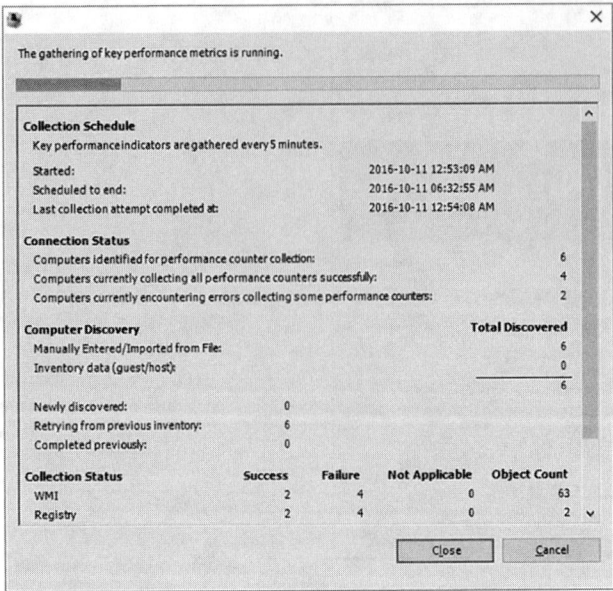

FIGURE 1-46 The Performance Metrics Wizard

Evaluating results

Once the Inventory And Assessment Wizard finishes running, it saves the information it has discovered to the SQL database. To complete the server consolidation scenario, you must run the Server Virtualization And Consolidation Wizard. In this wizard, you specify the operating system and the hardware configuration of your Hyper-V host server, as well as a utilization ceiling for the various host server components.

Finally, you select the computers from the inventory that you want to include in the assessment. After the assessment is completed, the results appear on the console, as shown in Figure 1-47.

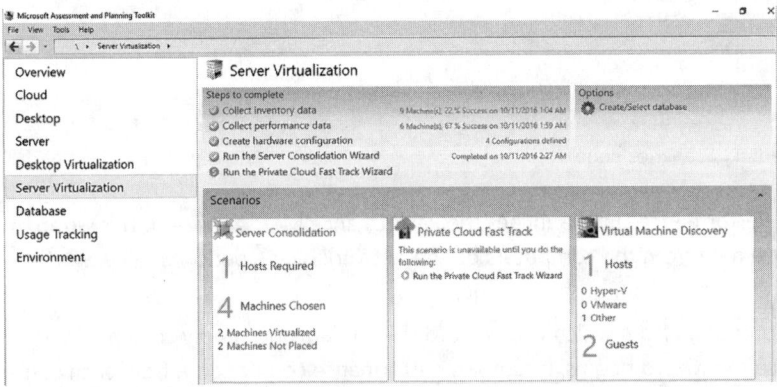

FIGURE 1-47 The completed Server Virtualization page

The MAP Toolkit also creates reports as Excel workbooks, which in this scenario provides details about the recommended server consolidation strategy, as shown in Figure 1-48.

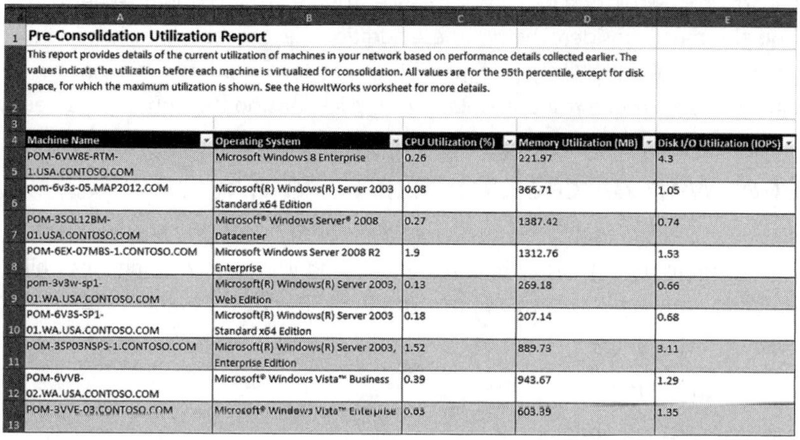

Pre-Consolidation Utilization Report

This report provides details of the current utilization of machines in your network based on performance details collected earlier. The values indicate the utilization before each machine is virtualized for consolidation. All values are for the 95th percentile, except for disk space, for which the maximum utilization is shown. See the HowItWorks worksheet for more details.

Machine Name	Operating System	CPU Utilization (%)	Memory Utilization (MB)	Disk I/O Utilization (IOPS)
POM-6VW8E-RTM-1.USA.CONTOSO.COM	Microsoft Windows 8 Enterprise	0.26	221.97	4.3
pom-6v3s-05.MAP2012.COM	Microsoft(R) Windows(R) Server 2003 Standard x64 Edition	0.08	366.71	1.05
POM-3SQL12BM-01.USA.CONTOSO.COM	Microsoft® Windows Server® 2008 Datacenter	0.27	1387.42	0.74
POM-6EX-07MBS-1.CONTOSO.COM	Microsoft Windows Server 2008 R2 Enterprise	1.9	1312.76	1.53
pom-3v3w-sp1-01.WA.USA.CONTOSO.COM	Microsoft(R) Windows(R) Server 2003, Web Edition	0.13	269.18	0.66
POM-6V3S-SP1-01.WA.USA.CONTOSO.COM	Microsoft(R) Windows(R) Server 2003 Standard x64 Edition	0.18	207.14	0.68
POM-3SP03NSPS-1.CONTOSO.COM	Microsoft(R) Windows(R) Server 2003, Enterprise Edition	1.52	889.73	3.11
POM-6VVB-02.WA.USA.CONTOSO.COM	Microsoft® Windows Vista™ Business	0.39	943.67	1.29
POM-3VVE-03.CONTOSO.COM	Microsoft® Windows Vista™ Enterprise	0.63	603.39	1.35

FIGURE 1-48 The Server Consolidation report

Determine considerations for deploying workloads into virtualized environments

Many of the workloads used on today's networks can easily be converted from physical to virtual servers, but not all of them can be, and even more important, not all of them should be. To determine which existing servers are the best candidates for virtualization, consider first the following resource utilization factors:

- **Memory** Applications that have large memory requirements might not be good candidates for virtualization, because they might consume an inordinate amount of the host server's memory resources. For example, an application that uses 32 GB of memory would not be cost effective on a VM running on a host server with 48 GB total.
- **Processor** Much like the memory requirement, an application that consistently uses a large amount of the physical server's CPU capacity might not be efficient on a virtual machine because it could leave too few of the host server's processor capacity for other VMs.
- **Network** Network throughput is a critical factor in a virtualization project because you must consider the combined requirements of all the virtual machines running on the server. You must consider the combined network throughput requirements of all the virtual machines running on the host server to make sure that they do not overwhelm the capacity of the physical network adapters. This is often the reason why administrators cannot deploy dozens of VMs on a single host server.
- **Storage** Physical servers with a high storage throughput might not work well in a virtualized environment because they could slow down the input/output (I/O) performance of the other VMs.

Enhancing the hardware configuration of the host server can mitigate all of these factors. For example, you could purchase a physical computer with 512 GB of memory instead of 48 GB, or several multicore processors, or a high performance storage array, or multiple network connections, but you also must consider whether these additional expenses are worth it. The higher the hardware costs go, the less likely that the ROI will pay for the project. It might be more economical just to leave certain resource-intensive applications on their physical servers.

Update images with patches, hotfixes, and drivers

Windows includes a command line tool called *Deployment Image Servicing and Management (DISM.exe)* that enables you to modify virtual hard disk (VHD) and Windows Imaging files while they are offline. With that same tool, you can also perform the following maintenance tasks:

- Add and remove device drivers
- Add and remove language packs
- Add and remove packaged updates
- Add and remove files and folders
- Enable or disable operating system features
- Execute answer files
- Add or remove app packages

Administrators can use this capability in several ways. If you capture images from reference computers so that you can use them to deploy new computers, those images will eventually become outdated. At first, you can apply operating system and application updates to your deployed workstations as they are released. However, eventually, deploying new workstations become increasingly difficult because of all the updates and changes you must apply to each one. When this happens, it is time to consider updating your image files, and this is when an alternative to recapturing new images is welcome.

The 10.0 version of DISM.exe included in Windows Server 2016 can service images of the following operating systems:

- Windows 10
- Windows 8.1
- Windows 8
- Windows 7
- Windows Server 2016
- Windows Server 2012 R2
- Windows Server 2012
- Windows Server 2008 R2
- Windows Server 2008 SP2
- Windows Preinstallation Environment (Windows PE) 5.0

- Windows PE 4.0
- Windows 3.0

While DISM was originally designed to service WIM images, like the ones on the Windows installation disks, many (but not all) of its functions also work with virtual hard disk (VHD and VHDX) images. For example, you can use DISM.exe to mount VHD or VHDX images and add or remove drivers and packages, as well as enable and disable Windows features. In addition to working with image files in their offline state, you can also use DISM to perform certain functions on the computer's currently running operating system.

Mounting an image

The standard procedure for modifying image files offline is to mount an image to a folder, make changes to the expanded files, and then commit the changes back to the image file. To modify an image file using DISM.exe, you must first mount it to a folder. This process creates copies of all the files in the image in their expanded form. You can then work with the copies, making any changes you need.

To mount an image, open a command prompt with administrative privileges and use the following syntax:

```
dism /mount-image /imagefile:filename /index:# /name:imagename /mountdir:pathname
```

The functions of the parameters are as follows:

- **/mount-image**   Specifies that the command should mount an image to a folder
- **/imagefile:filename**   Specifies the name and location of the image file you want to mount
- **/index:#**   Specifies the number of the image within the WIM file that you want to mount
- **/name:imagename**   Specifies the name of the image within the WIM file that you want to mount
- **/mountdir:pathname**   Specifies a location on the local disk where you want to mount the image

A typical mount command would appear as follows:

```
Dism /mount-image /imagefile:c:\images\install.wim /index:4 /mountdir:c:\mount
```

This command takes the fourth image in the Install.wim file, found in the C:\Images folder, and mounts it in the C:\Mount folder. The result of the command is as shown in Figure 1-49.

```
C:\Windows\system32>dism /mount-image /imagefile:c:\images\install.wim /index:4 /mountdir:c:\mount

Deployment Image Servicing and Management tool
Version: 10.0.14393.0

Mounting image
[==========================100.0%==========================]
The operation completed successfully.

C:\Windows\system32>
```

FIGURE 1-49 Mounting an image using DISM.exe

> **NOTE MOUNTING READ/WRITE IMAGES**
>
> If you mount an image directly from a read-only source, such as a Windows installation DVD, the DISM.exe program mounts the image in read-only mode. You can't make any changes to the image, even though it is mounted to a folder on a read/write hard disk. To modify the image from a Windows disk, you must first copy the Install.wim file from the DVD to a hard disk.

WIM files can contain multiple images, but you can only mount one of the images in the file at a time. This is the reason for the /index and /name options on the command line. To determine the index number or name value for a specific image in a file containing more than one, you can use the following command:

```
dism /get-imageinfo /imagefile:x:\filename
```

Once the image is mounted, you can proceed to work with it, as shown in the following sections.

Adding drivers to an image file

For a workstation with a storage host adapter or other hardware device that Windows Server 2016 does not support natively, an administrator might find it easier to add a device driver for the adapter to an existing image file rather than capture a new one. This would be especially true if there are several workstation configurations with different drivers involved.

To add a driver to an image file that you have already mounted, use a DISM command with the following syntax:

```
dism /image:foldername /add-driver /driver:drivername [/recurse]
```

- **/image:foldername** Specifies the location of the mounted image that you want to modify.
- **/add-driver** Indicates that you want to add a driver to the image specified by the /image parameter.
- **/driver:drivername** Specifies the location of the driver to be added to the image, either as a path to the driver file (with an .inf extension) or to the folder where the driver is located.
- **/recurse** When you specify a folder without a file name in the /driver option, causes the program to search for drivers in the subdirectories of the folder specified in the /driver parameter.

> **NOTE** **THE /IMAGE PARAMETER**
>
> Once you have mounted an image using DISM.exe, nearly all of the commands you use to work with the image begin with the /image parameter, with which you specify the mount location, so that DISM knows what image it should access. For some commands, you can substitute the /online option for the /image option, to service the currently running operating system. The commands that you can perform with the /online option depend on the Windows version that is currently running.

An example of the command is shown in Figure 1-50.

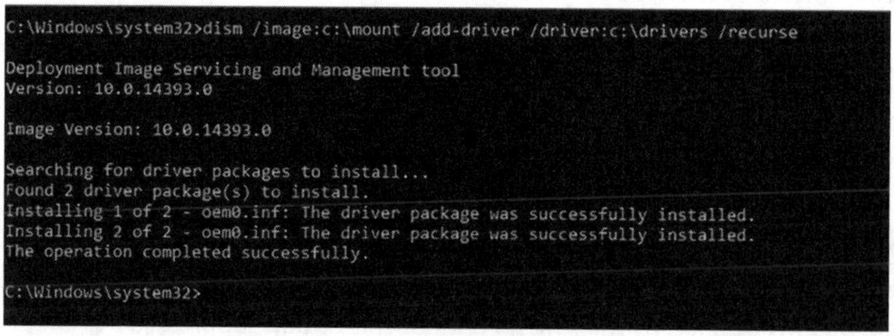

```
C:\Windows\system32>dism /image:c:\mount /add-driver /driver:c:\drivers /recurse

Deployment Image Servicing and Management tool
Version: 10.0.14393.0

Image Version: 10.0.14393.0

Searching for driver packages to install...
Found 2 driver package(s) to install.
Installing 1 of 2 - oem0.inf: The driver package was successfully installed.
Installing 2 of 2 - oem0.inf: The driver package was successfully installed.
The operation completed successfully.

C:\Windows\system32>
```

FIGURE 1-50 Adding a driver with DISM.exe

> **NOTE** **INSTALLING DRIVERS**
>
> DISM.exe can only manage drivers that include a Windows Information file (with an .Inf extension). If you have drivers packaged as executable (.exe) files or Microsoft Windows Installer (.msi) packages, you cannot add them to an image using the /add-driver parameter. You can however, use Windows System Image Manager (SIM) to create an answer file that installs these drivers and then apply the answer file to the image using DISM with the /Apply-Unattend parameter.

During the driver addition process, DISM renames the driver files with consecutively numbered file names, such as oem1.inf and oem2.inf. From that point on, you must use the new file names when referring to the drivers on the command line. To display information about the drivers in an image, use the following command:

```
dism /image:c:\mount /get-drivers
```

You can also use the /Get-DriverInfo option to display detailed information about a specific driver, as in the following example:

```
dism /image:c:\mount /get-driverinfo /driver:c:\drivers\driver.inf
```

Once you know this information, you can remove a driver from an image by substituting the /Remove-Driver option instead of /Add-Driver. An example would appear as follows:

```
dism /image:c:\mount /remove-driver /driver:oem1.inf
```

Adding updates to an image file

In roughly the same way that you can add drivers to a mounted image, you can also add operating system updates, such as hotfixes and language packs, which have been packaged as cabinet (CAB) or Windows Update Stand-Alone Installer (MSU) files.

To add an update to a mounted image, you use a command like the following:

```
dism /image:c:\mount /add-package /packagepath:c:\updates\package.msu [/ignorecheck]
```

- **/image:c:\mount**   Specifies the location of the image that you want to modify.
- **/add-package**   Indicates that you want to add a package to the image specified by the /image parameter.
- **/packagepath:c:\updates\package.msu**   Specifies the location of the package to be added to the image. This option can point to a single CAB or MSU file, a folder that contains a single expanded CAB or a single MSU file, or a folder containing multiple CAB or MSU files. If the option points to a folder containing a CAB or MSU file, the program recursively checks any subdirectories for additional packages.
- **/ignorecheck**   By default, DISM checks each package file to determine if it applies to the operating system specified by the /image option. This option suppresses this check and applies the package regardless of the operating system version.

DISM.exe can only add packages that take the form of cabinet (.cab) or Windows Update Stand-alone Installer (.msu) files.

> **NOTE FINDING CABS AND MSUS**
> Although it might seem as though most of the updates that you can download from the Microsoft Download center do not qualify for addition to mounted images, because they are executable (.exe) or sector-based image (.iso) files, these packages often do contain appropriate .cab or .msu files inside the archive. You can expand an executable archive or mount an .iso file to access the files inside.

You can specify multiple /packagepath options in a single DISM command, to install multiple packages. The program installs the packages in the order in which they appear on the command line.

To remove a package from an image file, you can use the /remove-package option, with the /packagepath option specifying the package you want to remove. You can also use the /get-packages option, to display information about all of the packages in an image, or the /get-packageinfo option, to display information about a specific package.

Committing and unmounting images

When you have made all of your modifications to the mounted image, you must commit the changes you made to the mounted copy back to the original Windows Imaging file and unmount the image, using a command like the following:

```
dism /unmount-image /mountdir:c:\mount /commit
```

The result of the command is shown in Figure 1-51. The /commit parameter causes DISM to save the changes you made. To abandon the changes and unmount the image without saving, use the /discard parameter instead of /commit.

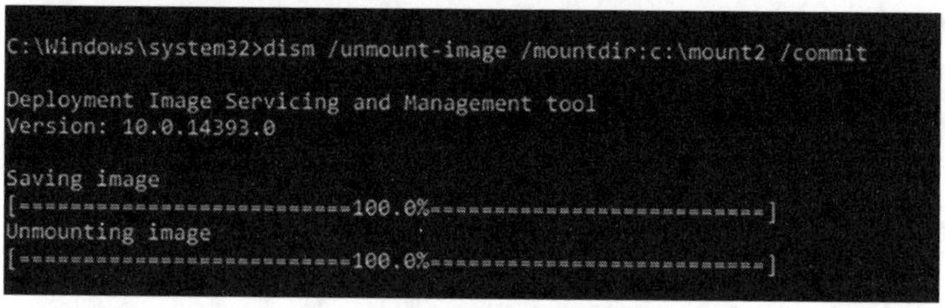

FIGURE 1-51 Unmounting an image with DISM.exe

Install Roles and Features in offline images

DISM also enables you to enable and disable Windows features in a mounted image. To do this, you must first determine the exact name of the feature using DISM with the /get-features option, as in the following example:

```
dism /image:c:\mount /get-features
```

The result of this command is a long list of Windows features, the beginning of which is shown in Figure 1-52.

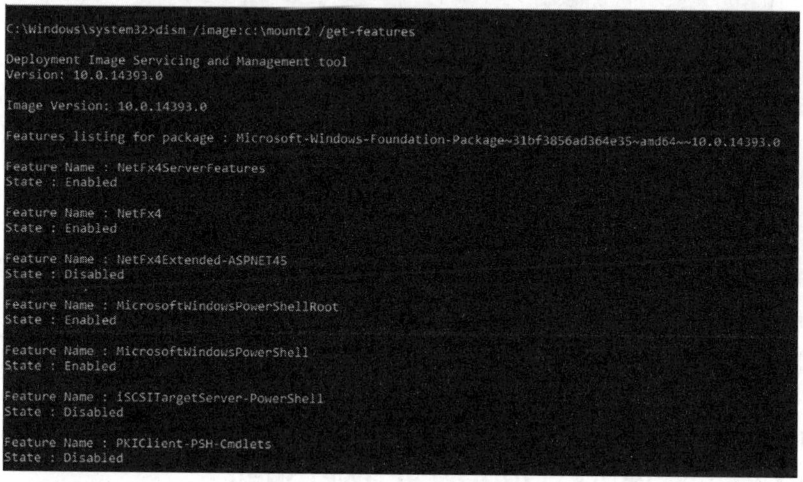

FIGURE 1-52 Displaying Windows features with DISM.exe

Once you have found the feature you want to add, you must create a DISM command using the /enable-feature option and the exact feature name, as shown in the /get-features list, which you insert into the /featurename option.

The syntax for the DISM /enable-feature command is as follows:

```
dism /image:folder /enable-feature /featurename:feature [/packagename:package] [/source:path] [/all]
```

- **/image:folder**   Specifies the location of the image that you want to modify.
- **/enable-feature**   Indicates that you want to enable a Windows feature in the image specified by the /image parameter.
- **/featurename:feature**   Specifies the name of the feature you want to enable, using the name specified by the /get-features option.
- **[/packagename:package]**   Specifies the name of the feature's parent package. This option is not needed when enabling a Windows Foundation feature.
- **[/source:path]**   Specifies the path to the files needed to re-enable a feature that has previously been removed. This can be the /Windows folder in a mounted image or a Windows side-by-side (SxS) folder.
- **[/all]**   Causes the program to enable all of the parent features for the specified feature.

An example of an /enable-feature command is shown in Figure 1-53.

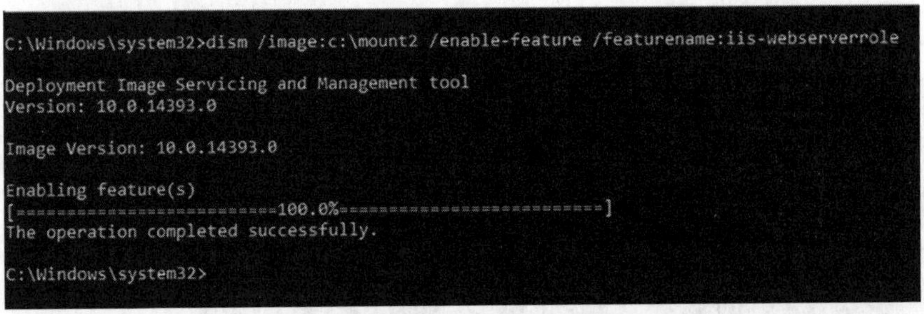

```
C:\Windows\system32>dism /image:c:\mount2 /enable-feature /featurename:iis-webserverrole

Deployment Image Servicing and Management tool
Version: 10.0.14393.0

Image Version: 10.0.14393.0

Enabling feature(s)
[==========================100.0%==========================]
The operation completed successfully.

C:\Windows\system32>
```

FIGURE 1-53 Enabling a feature using DISM.exe

You can include multiple /featurename options in a single DISM command, as long as the features you specify all have the same common parent. For example, you can enable several IIS features at once, but you cannot enable an IIS and a Hyper-V feature in the same command.

The /disable-feature command functions in the same way as /enable-feature and uses the same basic syntax.

Manage and maintain Windows Server Core, Nano Server images, and VHDs using Windows PowerShell

As noted earlier in this chapter, the Windows Server 2016 Server Core installation option relies heavily on Windows PowerShell for system management and maintenance. On a Server Core system, Windows PowerShell and the CMD command prompt are your only choices for interactive management on the local console.

The Nano Server installation option relies on PowerShell for the creation of the image files that you use to deploy Nano Servers. You can also use the Edit-NanoServerImage cmdlet to modify those image files by configuring their network adapter settings and adding role and feature packages.

Windows includes a DISM module for Windows PowerShell that enables you to perform most of the same modifications on VHD image files as the DISM.exe command line executable.

Many of the Windows PowerShell cmdlets in the DISM module correspond directly to their command line equivalents and use exactly the same options and syntax. Some are slightly different, however. Table 1-2 lists the DISM.exe command line options and their equivalent Windows PowerShell cmdlets.

TABLE 1-2 Windows PowerShell equivalents for basic DISM.exe command line options

Dism.exe command	DISM cmdlet
Dism.exe /Append-Image	Add-WindowsImage
Dism.exe /Apply-Image	Expand-WindowsImage
Dism.exe /Capture-Image	New-WindowsImage
Dism.exe /Commit-Image	Save-WindowsImage
Dism.exe /Export-Image	Export-WindowsImage
Dism.exe /Get-ImageInfo	Get-WindowsImage
Dism.exe /Get-MountedImageInfo	Get-WindowsImage -Mounted
Dism.exe /List-Image	Get-WindowsImageContent
Dism.exe /Mount-Image	Mount-WindowsImage
Dism.exe /Remove-Image	Remove-WindowsImage
Dism.exe /Remount-Image	Mount-WindowsImage -Remount
Dism.exe /Unmount-Image	Dismount-WindowsImage
Dism.exe /Image:foldername /Add-Driver	Add-WindowsDriver
Dism.exe /Image:foldername /Add-Package	Add-WindowsPackage
Dism.exe /Image:foldername /Add-ProvisionedAppxPackage	Add-AppxProvisionedPackage
Dism.exe /Image:foldername /Apply-Unattend	Apply-WindowsUnattend
Dism.exe /Image:foldername /Disable-Feature	Disable-WindowsOptionalFeature
Dism.exe /Image:foldername /Enable-Feature	Enable-WindowsOptionalFeature
Dism.exe /Image:foldername /Export-Driver	Export-WindowsDriver

Dism.exe /Image:foldername /Get-Driverinfo	Get-WindowsDriver -Driver
Dism.exe /Image:foldername /Get-Drivers	Get-WindowsDriver
Dism.exe /Image:foldername /Get-Featureinfo	Get-WindowsOptionalFeature -FeatureName
Dism.exe /Image:foldername /Get-Features	Get-WindowsOptionalFeature
Dism.exe /Image:foldername /Get-Packageinfo	Get-WindowsPackage -PackagePath | -PackageName
Dism.exe /Image:foldername /Get-Packages	Get-WindowsPackage
Dism.exe /Image:foldername /Get-ProvisionedAppxPackages	Get-AppxProvisionedPackage
Dism.exe /Image:foldername /Remove-Driver	Remove-WindowsDriver
Dism.exe /Image:foldername /Remove-Package	Remove-WindowsPackage
Dism.exe /Image:foldername /Remove-ProvisionedAppxPackage	Remove-AppxProvisionedPackage
Dism.exe /Image:foldername /Set-ProvisionedAppxDataFile	Set-AppXProvisionedDataFile

 Quick check

Which of the following are the correct activation thresholds for the Key Management System (KMS)?

1. 5 workstations
2. 5 servers
3. 25 workstations
4. 25 servers

Quick check answer

KMS requires a minimum of 25 workstation systems (#3) or 5 server systems as clients. This is called the activation threshold.

Chapter summary

- Windows Server 2016 is available in multiple editions that vary in features, capabilities, market, and price.
- Installing Windows Server 2016 on a single computer is usually simple, but mass deployments can be extremely complex.
- Windows Server 2016 includes a collection of roles and features, which you can install using Server Manager or Windows PowerShell.
- Server Core is an installation option that provides a reduced resource footprint, which you manage remotely or from the command line.
- An upgrade is when you install Windows Server 2016 on a computer running an earlier version of Windows. A migration is when you transfer the roles, settings, and data from an existing server to a new one.
- After installation, the Windows Server 2016 operating system must be activated, and there are several ways to do that, including the Key Management Service (KMS) and Active Directory-Based Activation.
- Nano Server is a Windows Server 2016 installation option that provides a stripped-down, headless server.
- To install Nano Server, you create a VHD image file using PowerShell and deploy it as Hyper-V virtual machine.
- Nano Server includes a limited selection of roles and features, which are not interchangeable with those used by the other Windows Server installation options.
- To manage Nano Server, you use remote installation tools from another computer.
- Virtualizing Windows servers requires a careful planning process that takes business factors into account, as well as technical factors.
- Windows Server 2016 Hyper-V provides support for FreeBSD and many Linux operating system distributions. The integration services that provide support for many of Hyper-V's features are integrated into the kernels of the latest FreeBSD and Linux versions.
- The MAP Toolkit includes a series of wizards that collect information about the configuration and performance of the computers on your network. Using that information, the toolkit can create a server consolidation report that specifies which of your servers should be migrated to virtual machines.
- When developing a virtualization plan, you should consider not only when [articular workloads should be migrated to virtual machines, but if they should be migrated.
- To update image files by adding patches, hotfixes, and features, you can use the DISM. exe command line tool.

Thought experiment

In this thought experiment, demonstrate your skills and knowledge of the topics covered in this chapter. You can find answer to this thought experiment in the next section.

Alice is responsible for deploying four new computers, which run Windows Server 2016. The computers function as Hyper-V servers and run as a cluster. To ensure that all of the computers are installed and configured identically, Alice has copied the Install.wim file from a Windows Server 2016 installation image to her working computer. Her intention is to mount the image using DISM.exe, add all of the drivers the computers need, and enable the Hyper-V role.

Alice mounts the image she needs to a local directory called c:\winsvr using the DISM /mount-image command. Then she adds the required drivers using the /add-drivers command. Both of these procedures complete flawlessly. Next, she attempts to enable the Hyper-V role using the following command:

```
dism /image:c:\winsvr /enable-feature /featurename:Hyper-V
```

This time, the command fails. What must Alice do to successfully enable the Hyper-V role using DISM? After she determines how to install Hyper-V successfully, what must Alice do before she can deploy the image to the computers?

Thought experiment answer

This section contains the solution to the thought experiment.

Alice must use the DISM /get-features command to list the available features in the image. When she does so, she discovers that the correct name for the role is Microsoft-Hyper-V. She must use this name in the /featurename option. After she installs Hyper-V, Alice must commit her changes to the image file an unmount it, using the following command:

```
dism /unmount-image /mountdir:c:\winsvr /commit
```

CHAPTER 2

Implement storage solutions

Enhancing the storage infrastructure in Windows Server has been a clear priority for the operating system developers for some years. Windows Server 2016 maintains many of the venerable storage mechanisms and management tools from previous versions, deprecates others, but also builds on these foundations with new capabilities that enable administrators to build larger and more reliable storage systems.

Skills in this chapter:
- Configure disks and volumes
- Implement server storage
- Implement data deduplication

Skill 2.1: Configure disks and volumes

Many of the fundamental storage technologies in Windows Server 2016 are unchanged from the previous version. However, it is still common for certification exams to test your knowledge of these technologies because they involve some of the most common tasks performed by server administrators.

> **This section covers how to:**
> - Configure sector sizes appropriate for various workloads
> - Configure GUID partition table (GPT) disks
> - Create VHD and VHDX files using Server Manager or Windows PowerShell
> - Mount virtual hard disks
> - Determine when to use NTFS and ReFS file systems
> - Configure NFS and SMB shares using Server Manager
> - Configure SMB share and session settings using Windows PowerShell
> - Configure SMB server and SMB client configuration settings using Windows PowerShell
> - Configure file and folder permissions

Configure sector sizes appropriate for various workloads

In its correct usage, a disk sector is a subdivision of a track. Each platter of a hard disk drive is split into circular tracks, and each track is split into sectors, as shown in Figure 2-1. Hard disks traditionally use 512-byte sectors, although new Advanced Format disks use 4,096-byte sectors. The sector size is created during the manufacture of the drive; it cannot be changed.

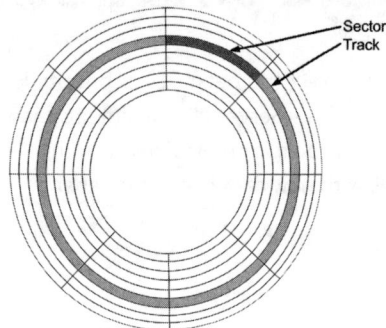

FIGURE 2-1 On a hard disk platter, a sector is a segment of a track

You can, however, change the *allocation unit* size of a disk volume, which is often incorrectly called a sector. Allocation unit is the Windows term, but it is also commonly called a block or a cluster. An allocation unit is the smallest amount of disk space that the computer can allocate when storing a file. For example, storing a 10-kilobyte file on a disk with an allocation unit size of 4 kilobytes requires three allocation units, or 12 kilobytes. Allocation units cannot be split among files, so this means that 2 kilobytes of storage space is wasted in what is called *slack space*.

You select the allocation unit size of a volume when you format it, as shown in Figure 2-2. Selecting an allocation unit size for a workload is a tradeoff between slack space and drive efficiency. You typically select an allocation unit size based on the average size of the files that you intend to store on the volume. If you select a larger allocation unit size, any small files that you store on the volume incurs a larger amount of space wasted.

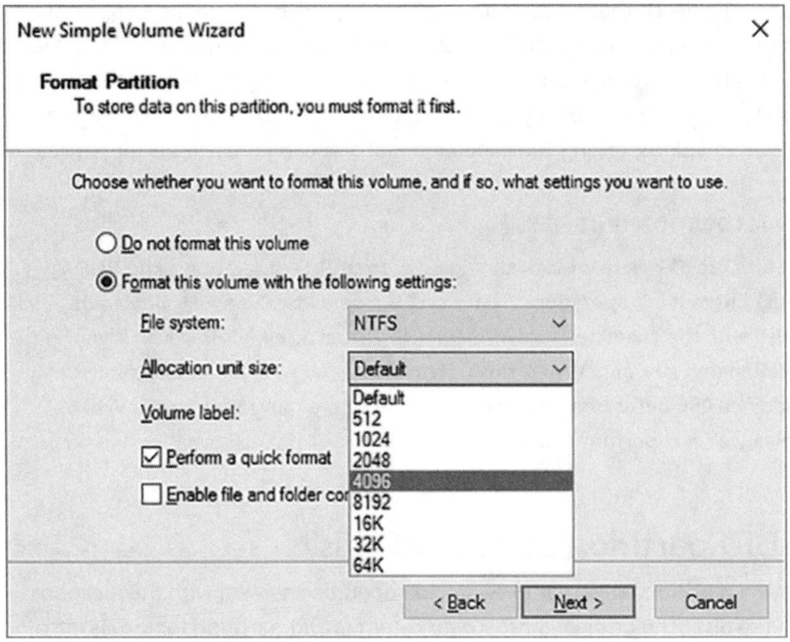

FIGURE 2-2 The Format Partition page of the New Simple Volume Wizard

For example, storing the 10 KB file mentioned earlier on a volume with a 4 KB allocation unit size wastes 2 KB. If the volume has a 64 KB allocation unit size, only one allocation unit is needed, but 54 KB of storage space would be wasted. Multiply that by thousands of files and you end up wasting a substantial part of the volume.

On the other hand, if you are storing a 1-megabyte file on a volume with a 4 KB allocation unit size, 250 allocation units are required. If the volume uses a 64 KB allocation unit size, the file only requires 16 allocation units. To access the file, the drive must seek and read each allocation unit individually. Seeking and reading 250 allocation units is inherently less efficient than seeking and reading 16 allocation units, so the drive performs better.

Also, the issue is complicated by the degree of fragmentation on the volume. The more a volume is written and rewritten, the more likely it is that the allocation units for a file are not adjacent to each other, and the drive has to pick up its heads and place them at a new location to read each allocation unit.

Hard disks have grown so large that the difference between allocation unit sizes does not matter all that much. For a typical volume, the average amount of slack space per file is half of the allocation unit size. For example, on a volume with a 4 KB allocation unit size, the slack space averages 2 KB per file. On a volume with a 64 KB allocation unit size, the slack space averages 32 KB per file. If you store 10,000 files on each volume, the wasted space is 20 MB on the 4 KB volume, and 312 MB on the 64 KB volume. On a disk that is 2 TB or larger, the loss of 300 MB is not such a big deal, especially when you achieve better efficiency in the bargain.

This does not mean, however, that by formatting all of your drives to use the maximum 64 KB allocation unit size, you realize a dramatic improvement in drive performance. The default allocation unit size for an NTFS volume under 16 TB is 4,096 bytes, or 4 KB, and this is usually appropriate for a system drive. However, if you have volumes on which you store mostly large files, such as databases or videos, raising the allocation unit size can enhance performance.

> *NOTE* **HYPER-V ALLOCATION UNIT SIZES**
>
> In Hyper-V, VHD files use 512-byte internal disk input/output (I/O) operations, and VHDX files use 4,096 byte internal I/O operations. Therefore, the default 4,096 NTFS allocation unit size aligns well with the characteristics of the VHDX virtual disk file. However, if you use a 64 KB allocation unit size on a VHDX, the system must read each 64 KB allocation unit, cache it, modify 4,096 bytes of it, and then write the whole thing back to the VHDX file, which negatively affects performance.

Configure GUID partition table (GPT) disks

Hard disk drives have a partition table that provides the operating system with the locations of the partitions on the disk. The original *master boot record (MBR)* partition table was introduced in 1983. It is still supported by Windows, and it is still used on many computers. The MBR partition table has shortcomings, however, which is why the *GUID partition table (GPT)* was created in the late 1990s.

When you add a new hard disk to a computer running Windows Server 2016, your first step after installing the hardware is to initialize the disk. When you launch the Disk Management snap-in, the tool detects the new disk and presents the Initialize Disk dialog box, as shown in Figure 2-3.

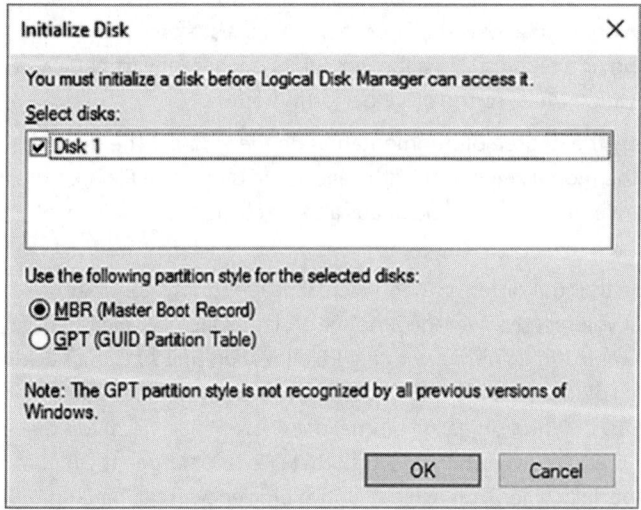

FIGURE 2-3 The Initialize Disk dialog box in the Disk Management snap-in

This dialog box provides the following options:

- **Master Boot Record (MBR)** The MBR partition style has been around since PC DOS 2.0, before Windows, and provides the most compatibility. It is still a common partition style for x86-based and x64-based computers.
- **GUID Partition Table (GPT)** GPT has existed since the late 1990s, but no x86 versions of Windows prior to Windows Server 2008 and Windows Vista support it. Today, most operating systems support GPT, including Windows Server 2016.

MBR shortcomings

Selecting the MBR option creates a boot sector at the beginning of the disk that points to the locations of the partitions and provides a boot loader for the operating system. Because this vital information is stored in only one place on the disk, if that boot sector is corrupted or overwritten, the disk is not recognized by the operating system. This partition style was the industry standard for many years and is still supported by nearly all operating systems.

The MBR disk partitioning style supports volumes up to 2 TB in size, and up to four primary partitions. The size limitation is due to the 32-bit maximum size of the partition entries in the MBR boot sector. At the time the MBR style was designed, the idea of a 2 TB hard drive was pure fantasy, but today they are commonplace, making this limitation a major shortcoming.

The four-partition limit is also a disadvantage for some. Beginning with PC DOS 3.3 in 1987, if you wanted more than four partitions on an MBR drive, you had to create three primary partitions and make the fourth an extended partition. You could then create multiple logical drives on the extended partition, as shown in Vol4, Vol5, and Vol6 in Figure 2-4. This is a workaround that exists in the MBR partition style to this day.

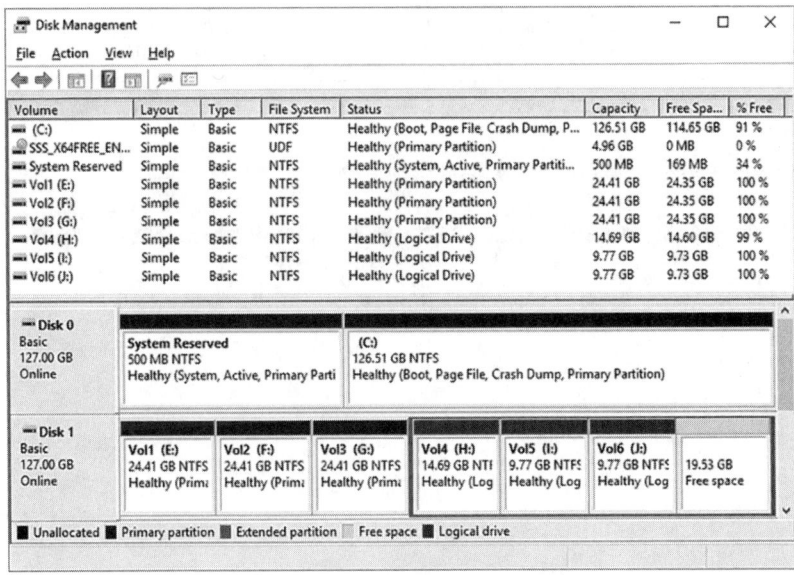

FIGURE 2-4 An MBR disk in the Disk Management snap-in

GPT advantages

The GUID partition table style is so named because each of the partitions on the disk has a globally-unique identifier (GUID). GPT is part of the *Unified Extensible Firmware Interface (UEFI)* developed by Intel in the late 1990s to replace the venerable Basic Input/Output System (BIOS) firmware standard.

GPT varies from MBR in that the partitioning information is stored in multiple places spread throughout the disk, along with cyclical redundancy check (CRC) information that makes it possible to detect corruption in the partition table and recover the data from another location. This makes the GPT partitioning style more robust than MBR.

Most importantly, GPT disks are not limited to 2 TB, as are MBR disks. The GPT disk partitioning style supports volumes up to 18 exabytes (1 exabyte = 1 billion gigabytes, or 2^{60} bytes).

GPT is also not subject to the four-partition limit of MBR. The GPT specification permits an unlimited number of partitions, but the Windows GPT implementation limits the number of partitions to 128 per disk. Therefore, it is possible to create a GPT disk with six partitions, as shown in Figure 2-5.

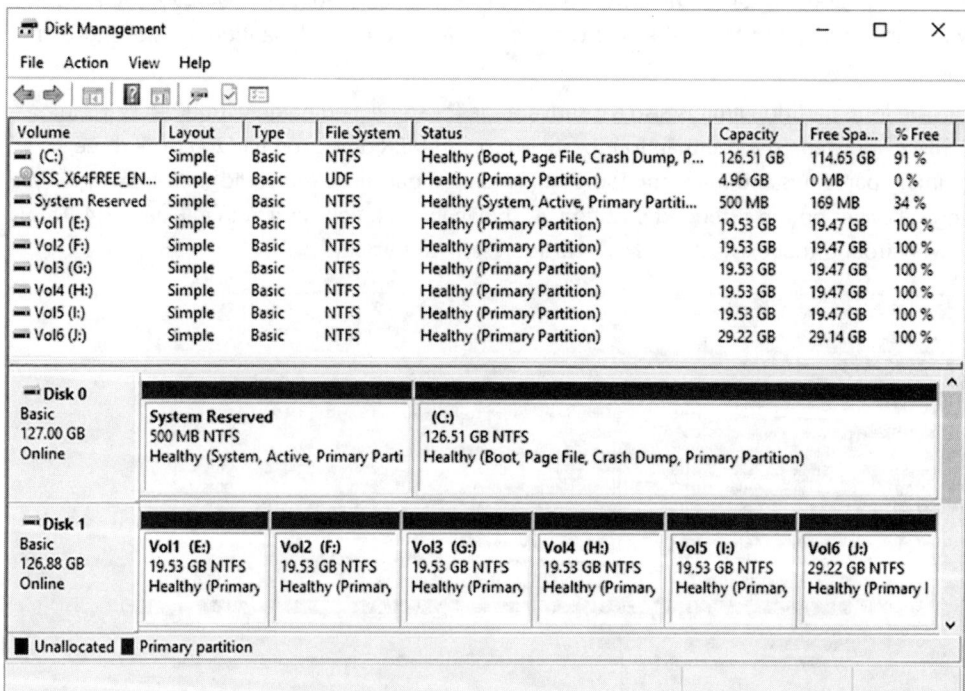

FIGURE 2-5 A GPT disk in the Disk Management snap-in

Selecting a partition style

Unless the computer's architecture provides support for an Extensible Firmware Interface (EFI)-based boot partition, it is not possible to boot from a GPT disk. If this is the case, the system drive must be an MBR disk, and you can use GPT only on separate non-bootable disks used for data storage.

Before Windows Server 2008 and Windows Vista, all x86-based Windows computers could use only the MBR partition style. Computers based on the x64 platform could use either the MBR or GPT partition style, if the GPT disk was not the boot disk.

Now that hard disk drives larger than 2 TB are readily available, the selection of a partition style is more critical than ever. When you initialize a physical disk using the traditional Disk Management snap-in, MBR is the default partition style, as it always has been. You can also use the snap-in to convert a disk between MBR and GPT partition styles, although you can do so only on disks that do not have partitions or volumes created on them.

When you use Server Manager to initialize a disk in Windows Server 2016, it uses the GPT partition style, whether the disk is physical or virtual. Server Manager has no controls supporting MBR, although it does display the partition style in the Disks tile.

Table 2-1 compares some of the characteristics of the MBR and GPT partition styles.

TABLE 2-1 MBR and GPT Partition Style Comparison

Master Boot Record (MBR)	GUID partition table (GPT)
Supports up to four primary partitions or three primary partitions and one extended partition, with unlimited logical drives on the extended partition	Supports up to 128 primary partitions
Supports volumes up to 2 terabytes	Supports volumes up to 18 exabytes
Hidden (unpartitioned) sectors store data critical to platform operation	Partitions store data critical to platform operation
Replication and cyclical redundancy checks (CRCs) are not features of the MBR partition table	Replication and CRC protection of the partition table provide increased reliability

Booting from GPT disks

The main compatibility issue with the partition styles is the ability to boot from a GPT disk. Windows can only boot from a GPT disk if the computer has UEFI firmware and if it is running a 64-bit version of Windows. Servers must be running at least Windows Server 2008, and workstations must be running at least Windows Vista.

Nearly all of the servers on the market today have UEFI firmware, and Windows Server 2016 is available only in a 64-bit version. If you are running older hardware, you must confirm that the computer is UEFI-compatible before you can boot from a GPT disk.

If you cannot boot from a GPT disk, you can still use MBR for your partition style on the boot disk and GPT for the other hard disks in the computer. GPT is essential if your other disks are larger than 2 TB in size.

In Windows Server 2016 Hyper-V, Generation 1 virtual machines emulate the BIOS boot firmware and must boot from a virtual MBR disk. You can create additional virtual GPT disks, just as in a physical computer. When you create a Generation 2 VM, however, the firmware is UEFI and the boot disk uses the GPT partition style. You can create additional virtual disks using either the GPT or MBR partition style, although there is no compelling reason to use MBR.

Create VHD and VHDX files using Server Manager or Windows PowerShell

Hyper-V relies on the Virtual Hard Disk (VHD) format to store virtual disk data in files that can easily be transferred from one computer to another. You can create new VHD files on a computer running Hyper-V by using the New Virtual Hard Disk Wizard, but it is also possible to create and use VHDs on computers that are not running the Hyper-V role.

Windows Server 2016 supports two types of virtual hard disk images, differentiated by their file name extensions, as follows:

- **VHD**   VHD images are limited to maximum size of 2 TB and are compatible with servers running Windows Server 2008 or later, or workstations running Windows 7 or later.

- **VHDX**   VHDX image files can be as large as 64 TB, and they also support 4 KB logical sector sizes, to provide compatibility with new 4 KB native drives. VHDX files are not backward compatible and can be read only by servers running Windows Server 2012, or later or workstations running Windows 8 or later.

Creating VHD or VHDX files using Disk Management

The Disk Management snap-in in Windows Server 2016 enables you to create VHD and VHDX files, and mount them on the computer. As soon as a VHD or VHDX file is mounted, you can treat it just like a physical disk and use it to store data. Dismounting a VHD or VHDX packages the stored data in the file, so you can copy or move it as needed.

To create a VHD in Disk Management, use the following procedure.

1. Log on to Windows Server 2016, using an account with Administrator privileges. The Server Manager window appears.
2. Click Tools, and Computer Management.
3. In the Computer Management console, click Disk Management. The Disk Management snap-in appears.

> *NOTE* **LAUNCHING DISK MANAGEMENT**
>
> You can also launch the Disk Management snap-in by right-clicking the Start button, and selecting Disk Management from the context menu that appears, or by executing the Diskmgmt.msc file.

4. From the Action menu, select Create VHD. The Create And Attach Virtual Hard Disk dialog box appears, as shown in Figure 2-6.

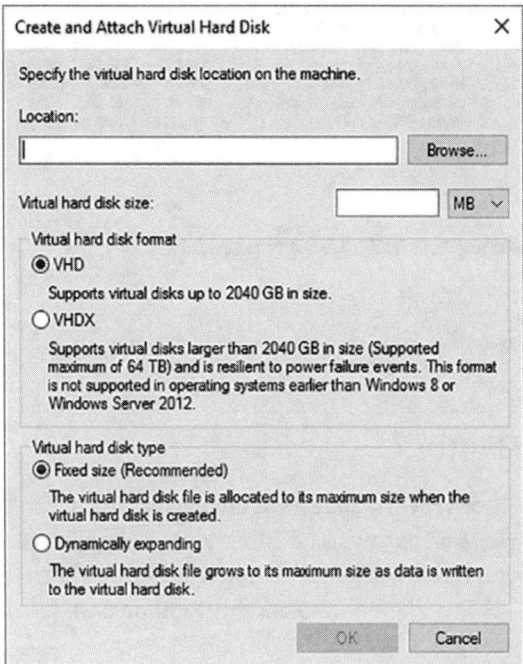

FIGURE 2-6 The Create And Attach Virtual Hard Disk dialog box

5. In the Location text box, specify the path and name for the file you want to create.
6. In the Virtual Hard Disk Size text box, specify the maximum size of the disk you want to create.
7. In the Virtual Hard Disk Format box, select the VHD or VHDX option.
8. Select one of the following Virtual Hard Disk Type options:
   - **Fixed Size**   Allocates all disk space for the entire size of the VHD or VHDX file at once
   - **Dynamically Expanding**   Allocates disk space to the VHD or VHDX file as you add data to the virtual hard disk
9. Click OK. The system creates the VHD or VHDX file and attaches it, so that it appears as a new disk in the snap-in, as shown in Figure 2-7.

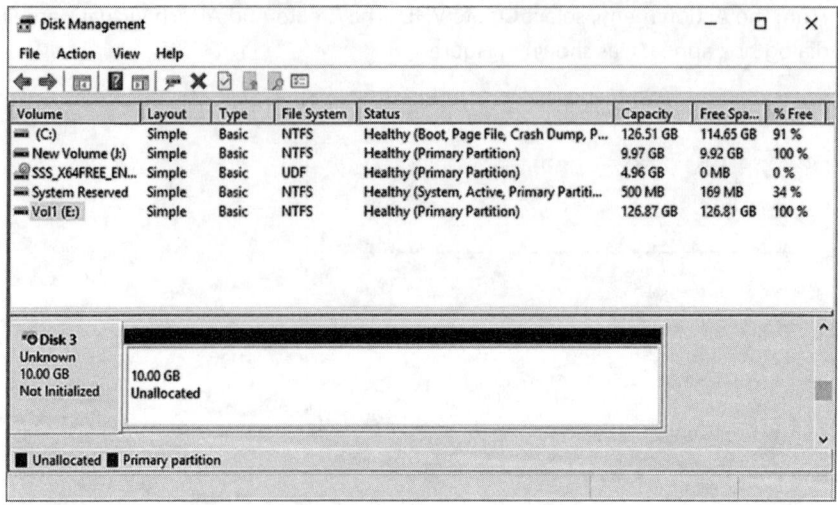

FIGURE 2-7 A newly created and attached VHD

After you create and attach the VHD or VHDX, it appears as an uninitialized disk in the Disk Management snap-in and in Server Manager. By using either tool, you can initialize the disk and create volumes on it, just as you would a physical disk. After storing data on the volumes, you can detach the VHD or VHDX and move it to another location or mount it on a Hyper-V virtual machine.

Creating VHD or VHDX files using Windows PowerShell

To create a VHD or VHDX in Windows PowerShell, you use the New-VHD cmdlet, which is included in the Hyper-V module. This module is installed as part of the Hyper-V Management Tools feature. If you do not have Hyper-V installed on your system, you can add just the PowerShell tools with the following command:

```
install-windowsfeature -name hyper-v-powershell
```

This module includes cmdlets that enable you to list, create, mount, merge, and resize VHDs. To create a new VHD, you can use the New-VHD cmdlet as in the following example:

```
new-vhd -path c:\data\disk1.vhdx -sizebytes 10gb
```

This simple command creates a 10 gigabyte VHDX disk called Disk1 in the c:\data folder. To configure other VHD features, you can use any of the following parameters:

- **Path** Specifies the location where the VHD is to be created and its filename. The filename extension you use specifies whether to create a VHD or a VHDX file.
- **SizeBytes** Specifies the size if the VHD to be created, or in the case of a dynamic disk, the maximum size. You can specify sizes using the following abbreviations: MB, GB, TB.

- **Fixed** Allocates all of the storage space specified in the SizeBytes parameter immediately on creating the VHD.
- **Dynamic** Creates a small-sized VHD and enables it to expand as needed to the maximum size specified in the SizeBytes parameter.
- **Differencing** Creates a differencing disk for the parent specified in the ParentPath parameter.
- **ParentPath** Specifies the location and filename of the parent disk for which a differencing disk is to be created.
- **SourceDisk** Specifies the location and filename of a physical disk to be copied to the new VHD upon creation.

To create a VHD and prepare it for use with one command, you can combine New-VHD with other cmdlets using the pipe character, as in the following example:

```
new-vhd -path c:\data\disk1.vhdx -sizebytes 256gb -dynamic | mount-vhd -passthru |
initialize-disk -passthru | new-partition -driveletter x -usemaximumsize | format-volume
-filesystem ntfs -filesystemlabel data1 -confirm:$false -force
```

This command creates a new 256 gigabyte dynamic VHDX file in the c:\data folder, mounts the disk, initializes the disk, creates a partition using drive letter X, and finally formats the partition using the NTFS file system. On completion of this command, the new VHD is ready to receive data.

Mount Virtual Hard Disks (VHDs)

One of the advantages of VHD and VHDX files is that you can easily move them to any system. In addition, you can mount a VHD or VHDX file on a physical or virtual machine and access it through the file system, using a standard drive letter. Mounting an image file provides you with full read/write capabilities, enabling you to access single files or entire folders as needed.

To mount a VHD or VHDX file, you can use the Disk Management snap-in, or Windows PowerShell cmdlets.

Mounting a VHD or VHDX with Disk Management

You can mount or dismount an existing VHD or VHDX file using the Disk Management snap-in, which uses the terms Attach and Detach instead. To mount a file, use the following procedure.

1. Log on to Windows Server 2016, using an account with Administrator privileges. The Server Manager window appears.
2. Click Tools, and Computer Management.
3. In the Computer Management console, click Disk Management. The Disk Management snap-in appears.

4. From the Action menu, click Attach VHD. The Attach Virtual Hard Disk dialog box appears, as shown in Figure 2-8.

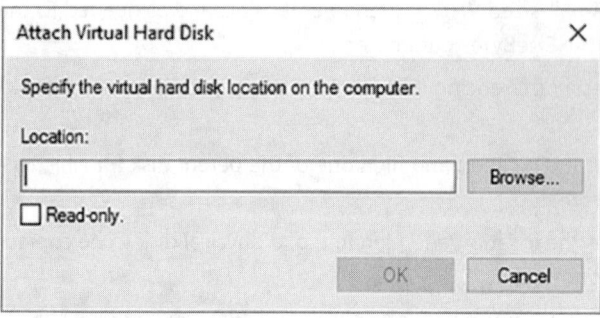

FIGURE 2-8 The Attach Virtual Hard Disk dialog box

5. In the Location text box, type or browse to the location and filename of the VHD or VHDX file to be mounted and click OK. The mounted disk appears in the Disk Management console.

If the virtual disk has already been initialized, partitioned, and formatted, its volumes appear using their assigned drive letters, and are ready for use. If the disk is still in its raw state, you must initialize it, create a volume, and format it using the file system of your choice before you can use it to store data.

When you are finished using the disk, you can select it and choose Detach VHD from the Action menu. Any changes you have made to the disk or its contents are saved back to the original VHD or VHDX file.

Mounting a VHD or VHDX with Windows PowerShell

There are two PowerShell cmdlets you can use to mount an existing VHD or VHDX files. Their syntaxes are similar, but not identical. The Mount-DiskImage cmdlet is part of the Storage module, and is found on all computers running Windows Server 2016. The Mount-VHD cmdlet is part of the Hyper-V module, and is only available on systems that have the Hyper-V management tools installed.

To mount a VHD or VHDX file with the Mount-DiskImage cmdlet, use the following syntax:

```
mount-diskimage -imagepath filename
```

To dismount a mounted image, you can use the Dismount-DiskImage cmdlet with the same imagepath parameter.

To mount a VHD or VHDX file with the Mount-VHD cmdlet, use the following syntax:

```
mount-vhd -path filename
```

To dismount a mounted image, you can use the Dismount-VHD cmdlet with the same path parameter.

Examples of the command lines for the two cmdlets are as follows:

```
mount-diskimage -imagepath c:\temp\diskimage.vhdx
```

```
mount-vhd -path c:\temp\diskimage.vhdx
```

Determine when to use NTFS and ReFS File Systems

To organize and store data or programs on a hard drive, you must install a file system, the underlying disk drive structure that enables you to store information on your computer. You install file systems by formatting a volume on the hard disk, as shown in Figure 2-9. In Windows Server 2016, five file system options are available, but only NTFS and ReFS are suitable for use on a modern server.

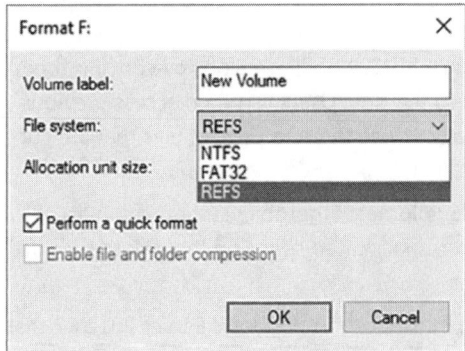

FIGURE 2-9 Formatting a volume using ReFS

NTFS has been the default file system for the Windows Server operating systems since the Windows NT 3.1 release in 1993. The primary advantage of NTFS over the FAT file systems it replaces is the ability to authorize user access to files and folders using permissions stored in discretionary access control lists (DACLs).

NTFS also supports long file names and larger files and volumes than FAT. The maximum size for an NTFS volume using the default 4KB allocation unit size is 16 TB; with the maximum 64 KB allocation units, the maximum volume size is 256 TB.

> **NOTE FAT FILE SYSTEMS**
>
> Because the FAT (File Allocation Table) file systems lack the security that NTFS provides, any user who gains access to your computer can read any file without restriction. FAT file systems also have disk size limitations. FAT32 cannot handle a partition greater than 32 GB, or a file greater than 4 GB. FAT cannot handle a hard disk greater than 4 GB, or a file greater than 2 GB. Because of these limitations, the only viable reason for using FAT16 or FAT32 is the need to dual boot the computer with a non-Windows operating system or a previous version of Windows that does not support NTFS, which is not a likely configuration for a server.

In addition to these capabilities, NTFS also includes the following additional features:

- **File compression** NTFS supports transparent, on-the-fly compression, but only for volumes using the 4 KB allocation unit size. The rate of compression is based on the type of file, with those containing repetitive bit patterns compressing more than those that don't. Volume size, number of files, and write frequency can all affect the efficiency of the compression system, which can be significantly processor-intensive.

- **Encrypting File System (EFS)** NTFS can provide on-the-fly encryption of selected files and folders using the public key belonging to a specific user. The file system then decrypts the files on demand with the user's public key. EFS and NTFS compression are mutually exclusive; files can be compressed or encrypted, but not both.

- **Quotas** Administrators can impose a quota governing the amount of storage space allowed to a specific user and specify the thresholds at which the user should receive a warning and be denied access.

- **Volume Shadow Copy** NTFS can maintain a history of file versions by copying them to an alternate location as they are written to the disk. Users can then access previous versions as needed, and backup applications can use them to protect files that are currently in use.

- **Resizing** Users can shrink or expand NTFS volumes (other than system volumes), if there is sufficient free space in the volume or unallocated space on the disk to support the requested action.

ReFS (Resilient File System) is a new file system introduced in Windows Server 2012 R2 that offers practically unlimited file and volume sizes and an increased resiliency that eliminates the need for error-checking tools, such as Chkdsk.exe. The maximum ReFS volume size is 2^{80} bytes, or 1 yobibyte. The maximum file size is 16 exabytes (or one million terabytes), which is far larger than any storage technology available today can provide. But then again, who expected to be talking about terabyte drives a few years ago?

ReFS uses checksums to protect the metadata on a volume and, optionally, the data itself. Periodic checks occur in the background, while the volume is in use. When corruption is detected, the system repairs it immediately, without the need to take the drive offline.

The error detection and repair capabilities of ReFS make it particularly useful in Storage Spaces pools. In a storage pool that uses a mirror or parity space, a corrupted file detected on a ReFS volume can be repaired automatically using the duplicate mirror or parity data. On Hyper-V virtual disks, ReFS implements checkpointing and backups as file system metadata operations, increasing their speed and efficiency.

ReFS uses the same system of permissions as NTFS, and is completely compatible with existing ACLs. However, ReFS does not include support for NTFS features such as file compression, Encrypted File System (EFS), and disk quotas. ReFS disks also cannot be read by any operating systems older than Windows Server 2012 and Windows 8.1.

Improvements in ReFS in Windows Server 2016, and particularly its improvements in Hyper-V use, have led Microsoft to state that it is now the preferred data volume for the operating system. System drives and volumes requiring compression, encryption, and other NTFS-only features should continue to use that file system, but all others can benefit from the resiliency that ReFS provides.

Configure NFS and SMB shares using Server Manager

Sharing server folders enables network users to access them. After you initialize, partition, and format your disks on a file server, you must create shares for users to be able to access those disks over the network.

Before you begin to create shares, you should devise a sharing strategy that consists of answers to questions like the following:

- Which disk folders are you sharing?
- What names are you assigning to the shares?
- What share permissions are you granting to your users?
- What Offline Files settings are you using for the shares?

If you are the designated Creator Owner of a folder, you can share it in Windows Server 2016 by right-clicking the folder in any File Explorer window, selecting Share With, and then Specific People from the context menu, and following the instructions in the File Sharing dialog box, as shown in Figure 2-10.

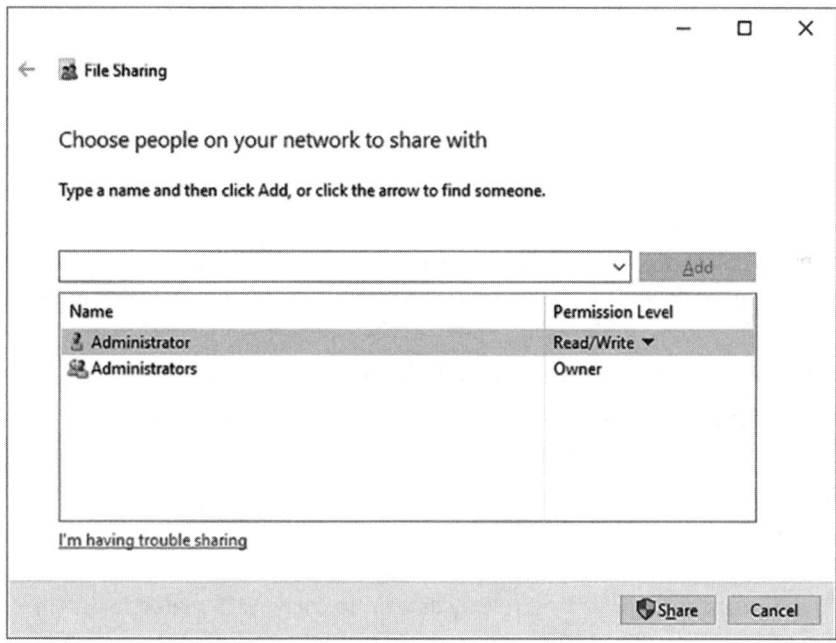

FIGURE 2-10 The File Sharing dialog box

This method of creating shares provides a simplified interface that contains only limited control over elements such as share permissions. You can specify only that the share users receive Read or Read/Write permissions to the share.

If you are not the Creator Owner of the folder, you can access the Sharing tab of the folder's Properties sheet instead. Clicking the Share button on this tab launches the same File Sharing dialog box, but clicking the Advanced Sharing button and selecting the Share This Folder check box displays the dialog box shown in Figure 2-11. Clicking the Permissions button in the Advanced Sharing dialog box provides you with greater control over share permissions through the standard Windows security interface.

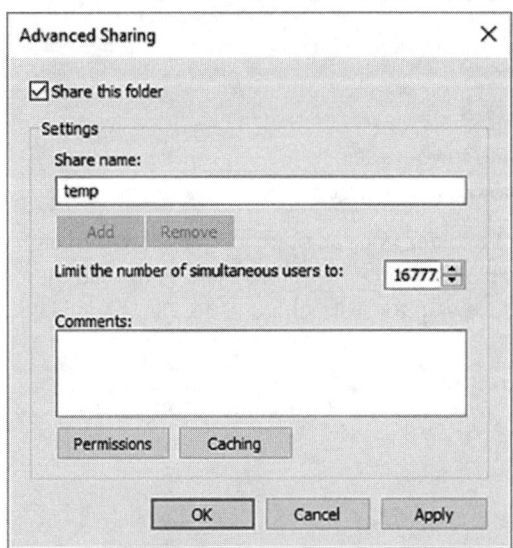

FIGURE 2-11 The Advanced Sharing dialog box

However, to take control of the shares on all of your disks and all of your servers so that you can exercise full control over their properties, use the File And Storage Services page in Server Manager.

Windows Server 2016 supports two types of folder shares:

- **Server Message Blocks (SMB)** An application layer protocol that has long been the standard for file and printer sharing on Windows networks.
- **Network File System (NFS)** A standardized file system protocol typically used by UNIX and Linux distributions.

When you install Windows Server 2016, the setup program installs the Storage Services role service in the File and Storage Services role by default. To create SMB shared folders in Server Manager, however, you must first install the File Server role service. When you create your first folder share using File Explorer, the system automatically installs the File Server role service.

To create NFS shares, you must install the Server for NFS role service. To install either of these role services, you can use the Add Roles And Features Wizard in Server Manager, or the Install-WindowsFeature cmdlet in Windows PowerShell, as in the following commands:

```
install-windowsfeature -name fs-fileserver
```

```
install-windowsfeature -name fs-nfs-service
```

Creating an SMB share

To create an SMB share using Server Manager, use the following procedure.

1. Log on to Windows Server 2016, using an account with Administrator privileges. The Server Manager window appears.
2. Click the File and Storage Services icon and, in the submenu that appears, click Shares. The Shares page appears, as shown in Figure 2-12.

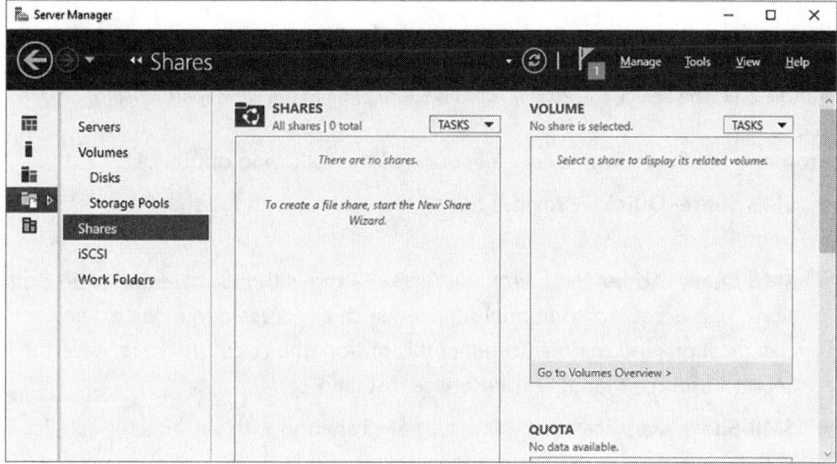

FIGURE 2-12 The Shares page in Server Manager

3. From the Tasks menu in the Shares tile, select New Share. The New Share Wizard appears, displaying the Select The Profile For This Share page, as shown in Figure 2-13.

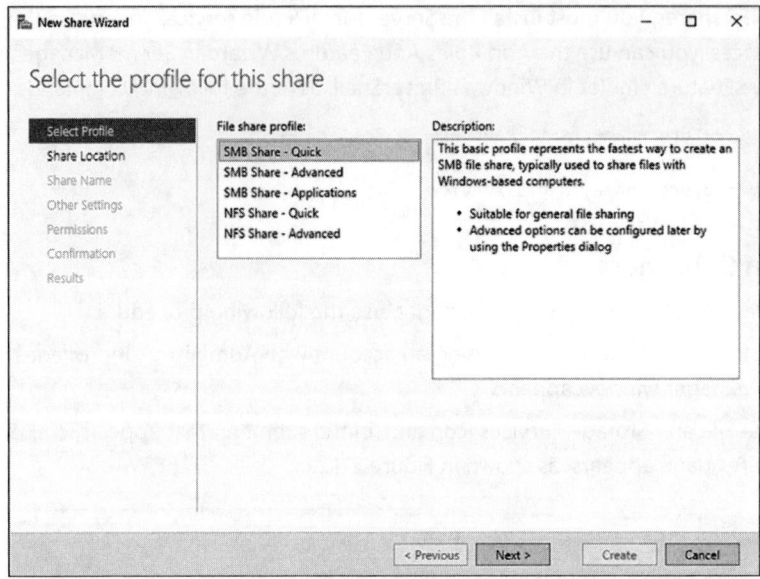

FIGURE 2-13 The Select The Profile For This Share page in the New Share Wizard

4. From the File Share Profile list, select one of the following options:

   - **SMB Share–Quick**   Provides basic SMB sharing with full share and NTFS permissions.
   - **SMB Share–Advanced**   Provides SMB sharing with full share and NTFS permissions, plus access to additional services, such as access-denied assistance, folder classification, and quotas. To select this option, the computer must have the File Server Resource Manager role service installed.
   - **SMB Share–Applications**   Provides SMB sharing with settings suitable for Hyper-V, databases, and other applications.

5. Click Next. The Select The Server And Path For This Share page appears, as shown in Figure 2-14.

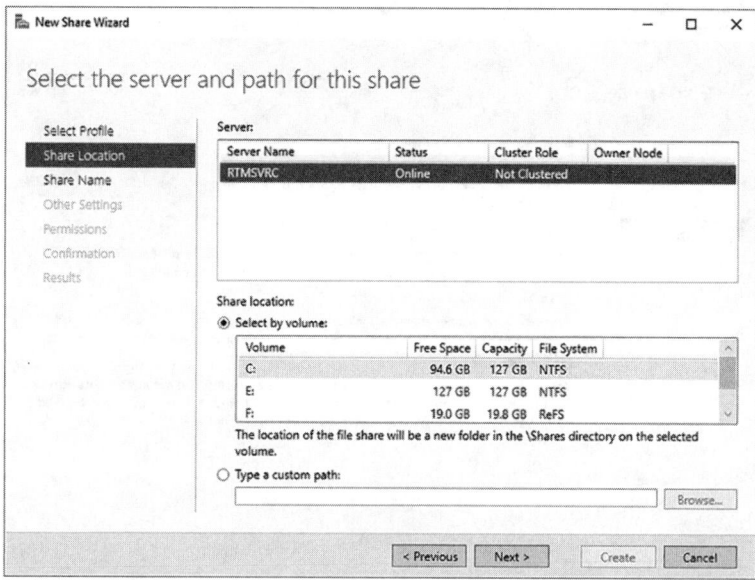

FIGURE 2-14 The Select The Server And Path For This Share page of the New Share Wizard

6. Select the server on which you want to create the share, and then either select a volume on the server or specify a path to the folder you want to share. Then click Next. The Specify Share Name page appears.

7. In the Share Name text box, specify the name you want to assign to the share and click Next. The Configure Share Settings Page appears.

8. Select any, or all of the following options:

    - **Enable Access-Based Enumeration**   Applies filters to shared folders based on the individual user's permissions to the files and subfolders in the share. Users who cannot access a shared resource cannot see that resource on the network. This feature prevents users from searching through files and folders they cannot access.

    - **Allow Caching Of Share**   Enables client systems to maintain local copies of files they access from server shares. When a client selects the Always Available Offline option for a server-based file, folder, or share, the client system copies the selected data to the local drive and updates it regularly, so that the client user can always access it, even if the server is offline.

    - **Enable BranchCache On The File Share**   Enables client computers at remote locations running BranchCache to cache files accessed from this share, so that other computers at the remote location can access them.

    - **Encrypt Data Access**   Causes the server to encrypt the files in the share before transmitting them to the remote client.

9. Click Next. The Specify Permissions To Control Access page appears, as shown in Figure 2-15.

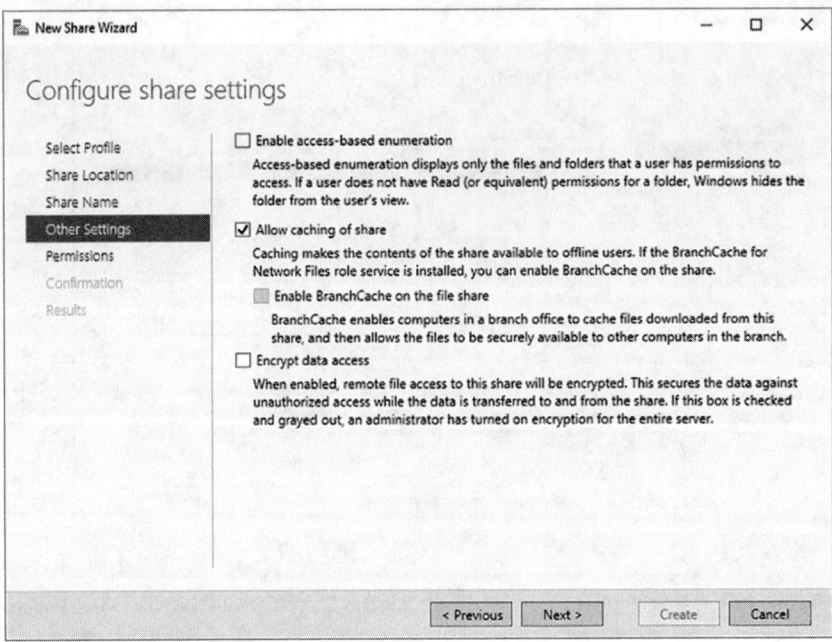

FIGURE 2-15 The Specify Permissions To Control Access page of the New Share Wizard

10. Modify the default share and NTFS permissions as needed, and click Next. The Confirm Selections page appears.
11. Click Create. The View Results page appears as the wizard creates the share.
12. Click Close. The new share appears in the Shares tile of the Shares page in Server Manager.

You can use the tile to manage a share by right-clicking it and opening its Properties sheet, or by clicking Stop Sharing. The Properties sheet for a share in Server Manager (see Figure 2-16) provides access to the same controls found on the Specify Permissions *To Control Access and Configure Share Settings pages in the New Share Wizard.*

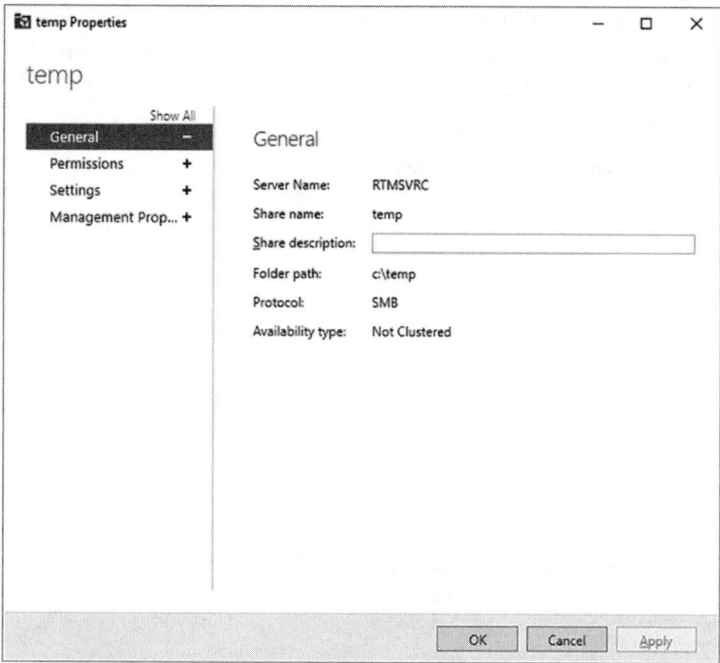

FIGURE 2-16 A share's Properties sheet in Server Manager

Creating an NFS share

To create an NFS share using Server Manager, use the following procedure.

1. Log on to Windows Server 2016, using an account with Administrator privileges. The Server Manager window appears.
2. Click the File And Storage Services icon and, in the submenu that appears, Click Shares. The Shares page appears.
3. From the Tasks menu in the Shares tile, select New Share. The New Share Wizard appears, displaying the Select The Profile For This Share page.
4. From the File Share Profile list, select one of the following options:
   - **NFS Share–Quick**   Provides basic NFS sharing with authentication and permissions.
   - **NFS Share–Advanced**   Provides NFS sharing with full share and NTFS permissions, plus access to additional services, such as access-denied assistance, folder classification, and quotas. To select this option, the computer must have the File Server Resource Manager role service installed.
5. Click Next. The Select The Server And Path For This Share page appears.

6. Select the server on which you want to create the share, and then either select a volume on the server or specify a path to the folder you want to share. Then click Next. The Specify Share Name page appears.
7. In the Share Name text box, specify the name you want to assign to the share and click Next. The Specify Authentication Methods page appears, as shown in Figure 2-17.

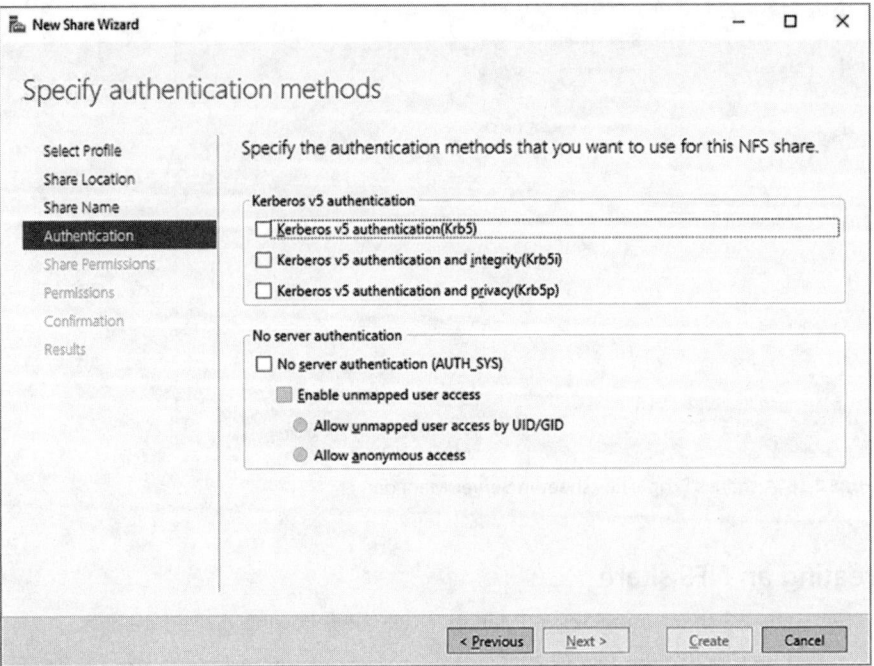

FIGURE 2-17 The Specify Authentication Methods page of the New Share Wizard

8. Select the check boxes for the authentication methods you want to use for share access, if any.
9. Click Next. The Specify The Share Permissions page appears.
10. Click Add. The Add Permissions dialog box appears, as shown in Figure 2-18.

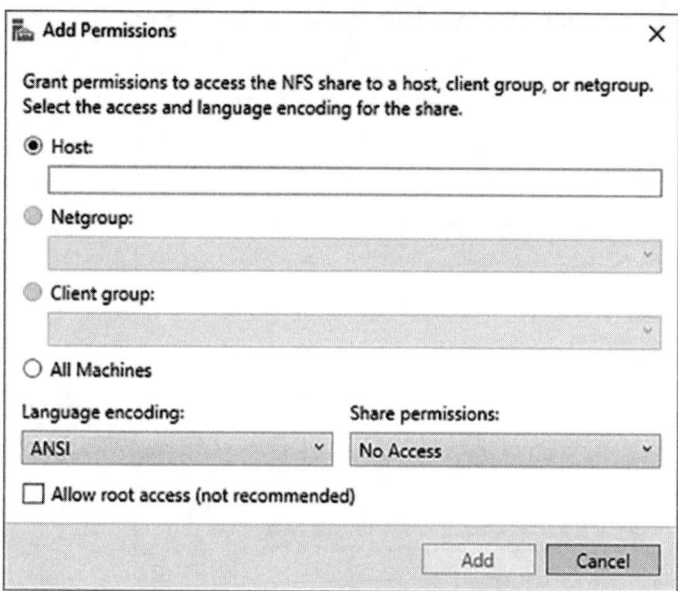

FIGURE 2-18 The Add Permissions dialog box

11. Specify the name of a host to be granted permission to the share or select the All Machines option. In the Share Permissions drop-down list, specify whether the selected host(s) should receive Read/Write, No Access, or Read Only access.
12. Click Add. The host is added to the wizard page. Repeat steps 10 to 12 to add more hosts, if necessary.
13. Click Next. The Specify Permissions To Control Access page appears.
14. Modify the default NTFS permissions as needed and click Next. The Confirm Selections page appears.
15. Click Create. The View Results page appears as the wizard creates the share.
16. Click Close. The new share appears in the Shares tile of the Shares page in Server Manager.

Creating advanced shares

When you select the SMB Share-Advanced or NFS Share-Advanced profile, two additional pages appear in the New Share Wizard. The first is a Specify Folder Management Properties page, as shown in Figure 2-19, on which you can select Folder Usage property values for the share. These values identify the type of data stored in the shared folder. You can use them to configure classification rules in the File Server Resource Manager (FSRM) that perform actions on files based on their classification properties. You can also specify the email addresses of the folder's owner or administrator, which are notified when a user is denied access to the share.

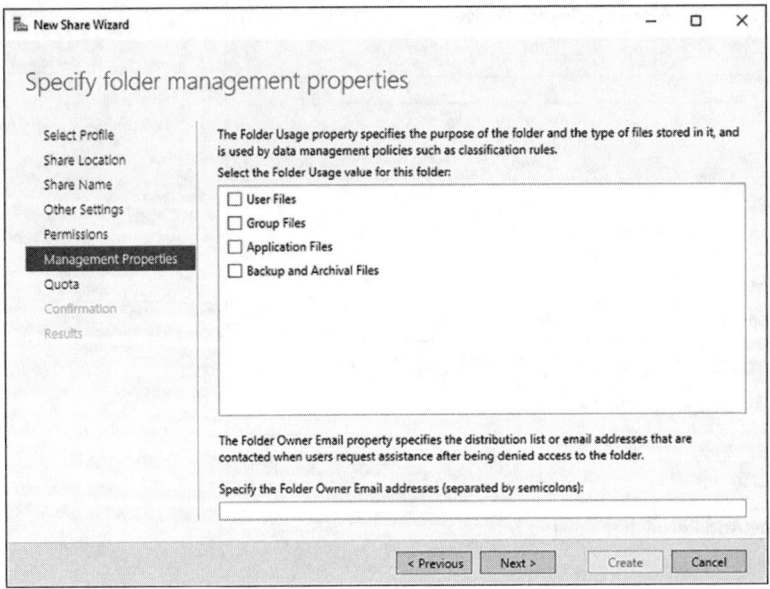

FIGURE 2-19 The Specify Folder Management Properties page of the New Share Wizard

The second added page is the Apply A Quota To A Folder Or Volume page, on which you can select a quota to be applied to the share from the list of predefined quota templates. For more granular control of quotas, you must use FSRM.

Configuring share permissions

On Windows systems, shared folders have their own permission system, which is completely independent from the NTFS and other permission systems. For network users to access a share on a file server, an administrator must grant them the appropriate share permissions. By default, the Everyone special identity receives the Allow Read share permission to any new shares you create using File Explorer. In shares you create using Server Manager, the Everyone special identity receives the Allow Full Control share permission.

It is important to understand that network users can possess the share permissions required to access a folder, but still be denied access to it because they lack the necessary NTFS permissions. The opposite is also true; users with the correct NTFS permissions cannot access a share over the network if they lack the required share permissions. You should also understand that share permissions only control access to a share over the network, while NTFS permissions control access both over the network and on the local machine.

When you create an SMB share using Server Manager, you can use the Specify Permissions To Control Access page to configure both NTFS and share permissions for the shared folder. Clicking Customize Permissions opens the Advanced Security Settings dialog box for the shared folder. The Permissions tab that is selected by default displays the NTFS permissions. To configure the share permissions for the folder, select the Share tab, as shown in Figure 2-20.

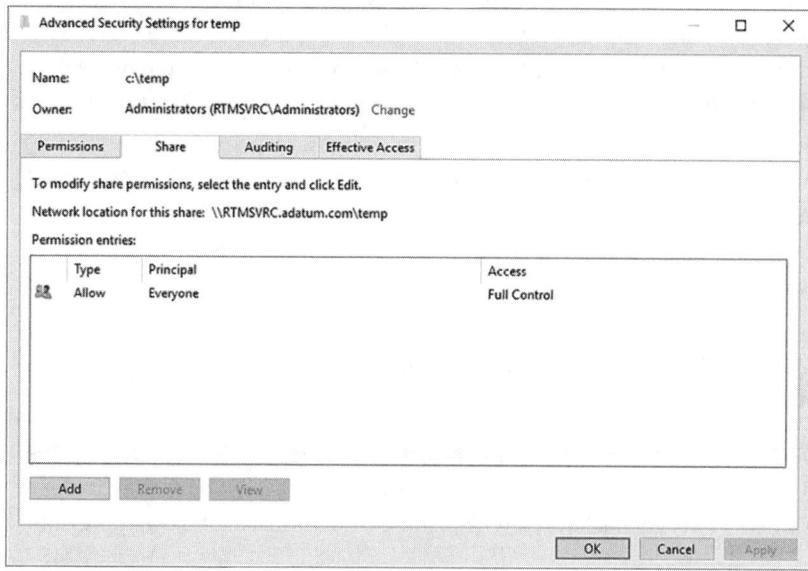

FIGURE 2-20 The Share tab on the Advanced Security Settings dialog box

Clicking the Add button opens a Permission Entry dialog box for the folder, on which you select a principal—a user or group to receive the permissions—and the permissions you want the principal to receive.

The Windows share permission system is relatively simple and has only three permissions. The permissions and the abilities they grant to users are listed in Table 2-2.

TABLE 2-2 Share permissions and their functions

Share permission	Allows or denies security principals the ability to:
Full Control	■ Change file permissions ■ Take ownership of files ■ Perform all tasks allowed by the Change permission
Change	■ Create folders ■ Add files to folders ■ Change data in files ■ Append data to files ■ Change file attributes ■ Delete folders and files ■ Perform all actions permitted by the Read permission
Read	■ Display folder names, filenames, file data and attributes ■ Execute program files ■ Access other folders within the shared folder

When assigning share permissions, you must also be aware that they do not combine like NTFS permissions. If you grant a user named Alice the Allow Read and Allow Change permissions to the shared C:\Documents\Alice folder and later deny her all three permissions to the shared C:\Documents folder, the Deny permissions prevent her from accessing any files through the C:\Documents share, including those in the C:\Documents\Alice folder. However, she can still access her files through the C:\Documents\Alice share because of the Allow permissions. In other words, the C:\Documents\Alice share does not inherit the Deny permissions from the C:\Documents share.

When you create an NFS share using the New Share Wizard in Server Manager, the Specify Permissions To Control Access page provides access only to the NTFS permissions. This is because you have already configured the share permissions for the NFS share on the Specify The Share Permissions page on the wizard.

Configure SMB share and session settings using Windows PowerShell

For those who prefer to work from the command line, Windows Server 2016 includes a Windows PowerShell module called SmbShare, which you can use to create and manage folder shares. To create a new share, you use the New-SmbShare cmdlet with the following basic syntax:

```
new-smbshare -name sharename -path pathname [-fullaccess groupname] [-readaccess groupname] [-changeaccess groupname] [-noaccess groupname]
```

For example, to create a new share called Data from the C:\Docs folder with the Allow Full Control permission granted to the Everyone special identity, use the following command:

```
new-smbshare -name data -path c:\docs -fullaccess everyone
```

In addition to the access parameters listed here, there are other parameters you can include on the command line, to implement features available in the New Share Wizard, including the following:

- **ConcurrentUserLimit #** Specifies the maximum number of users that can connect to the share simultaneously. A value of 0 allows unlimited users.
- **CachingMode value** Specifies the type of offline file caching permitted to share clients, using the following values:
    - **None** Disables offline file caching at the client
    - **Manual** Enables users to select files for offline caching
    - **Programs** Automatically caches programs and documents offline
    - **Documents** Automatically caches documents offline
    - **BranchCache** Enables BranchCache caching on the remote client
- **EncryptData True|False** Causes the server to encrypt the files in the share before transmitting them to the remote client

- **FolderEnumerationMode AccessBased|Unrestricted** Implements or disables access-based enumeration. The default setting is Unrestricted.
- **Temporary** Causes the share to persist only to the next computer restart

Managing sessions

Once you have created a share, by any means, you can monitor and manage its use using PowerShell cmdlets. For example, running the Get-SmbSession cmdlet displays all the current client sessions that are connected to the server's shares, as shown in Figure 2-21.

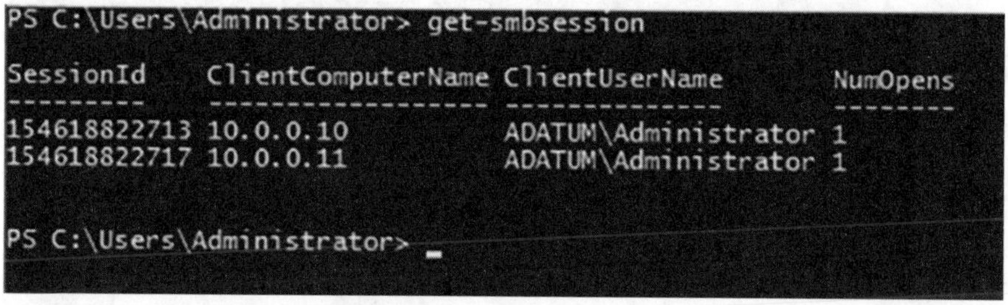

```
PS C:\Users\Administrator> get-smbsession

SessionId      ClientComputerName  ClientUserName        NumOpens
---------      ------------------  --------------        --------
154618822713   10.0.0.10           ADATUM\Administrator  1
154618822717   10.0.0.11           ADATUM\Administrator  1


PS C:\Users\Administrator>
```

FIGURE 2-21 Output of the Get-SmbSession cmdlet

With the information in this listing, you can terminate a specific session using the Close-SmbSession cmdlet, as in the following example, which uses the Session ID to specify the session to close.

```
close-smbsession -sessionid 154618822713
```

By default, the cmdlet displays a warning, prompting you to confirm that you want to terminate the session, as shown in Figure 2-22. Adding the Force parameter to the command line eliminates the prompt. There is no warning displayed on the client computer, and closing the session can cause any work in progress by the client to be lost.

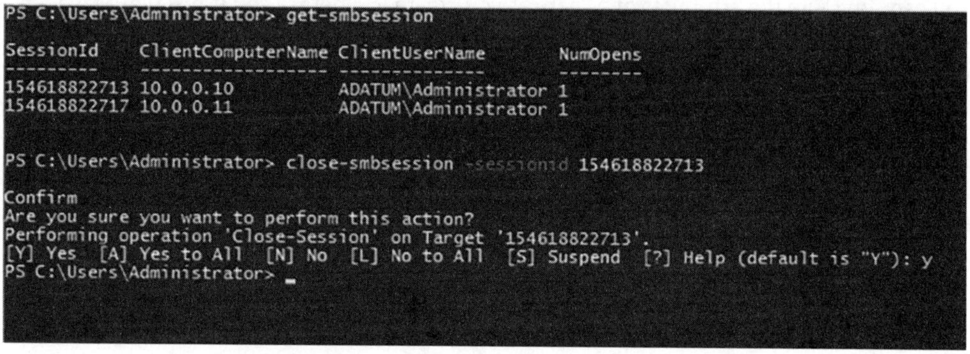

```
PS C:\Users\Administrator> get-smbsession

SessionId      ClientComputerName  ClientUserName        NumOpens
---------      ------------------  --------------        --------
154618822713   10.0.0.10           ADATUM\Administrator  1
154618822717   10.0.0.11           ADATUM\Administrator  1


PS C:\Users\Administrator> close-smbsession -sessionid 154618822713

Confirm
Are you sure you want to perform this action?
Performing operation 'Close-Session' on Target '154618822713'.
[Y] Yes  [A] Yes to All  [N] No  [L] No to All  [S] Suspend  [?] Help (default is "Y"): y
PS C:\Users\Administrator>
```

FIGURE 2-22 Output of the Close-SmbSession cmdlet

You can also close sessions based on the other information in the Get-SmbSession output, as shown in the following examples.

```
close-smbsession -clientcomputername 10.0.0.11
```

```
close-smbsession -clientusername adatum\Administrator
```

In addition to listing sessions, you can also use the Get-SmbOpenFile cmdlet to display the files that clients are currently accessing, as shown in Figure 2-23.

```
PS C:\Users\Administrator> get-smbopenfile

FileId         SessionId       Path                  ShareRelativePath  ClientComputerName  ClientUserName
------         ---------       ----                  -----------------  ------------------  --------------
154618822929   154618822721    c:\temp\                                 10.0.0.10           ADATUM\Administrator
154618822953   154618822717    c:\temp\                                 10.0.0.11           ADATUM\Administrator
154618822961   154618822717    c:\temp\disk2.vhdx    disk2.vhdx         10.0.0.11           ADATUM\Administrator

PS C:\Users\Administrator>
```

FIGURE 2-23 Output of the Get-SmbOpenFile cmdlet

To forcefully close an open file, you can use the Close-SmbOpenFile cmdlet, as in the following example:

```
close-smbopenfile -fileid 154618822961
```

Removing a share

To terminate a share completely, along with all its sessions, you can use the Remove-Smb-Share cmdlet, specifying the name of the share on the command line, as in the following example:

```
remove-smbshare -name data
```

Configure SMB server and SMB client configuration settings using Windows PowerShell

You can configure the attributes of a share as you create it, whether you use Server Manager or PowerShell to do so, but you can also modify a share's configuration settings at any time after its creation using other cmdlets in the SmbShare PowerShell module.

Setting share permissions

You can modify the share permissions for a specific share, using the following cmdlets:

- **Get-SmbShareAccess** Displays the access control list for a named share, as shown in Figure 2-24.

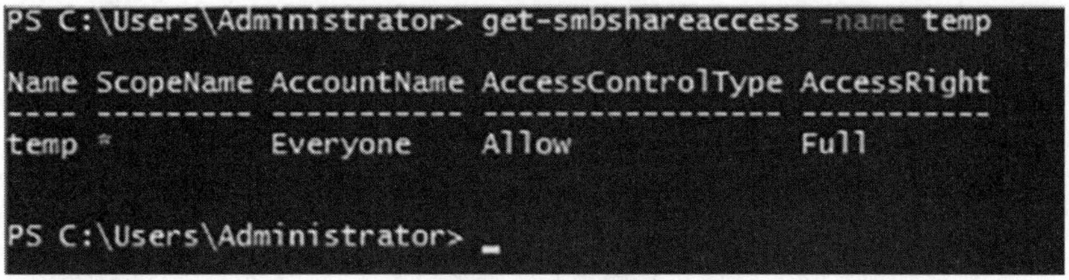

```
PS C:\Users\Administrator> get-smbshareaccess -name temp

Name ScopeName AccountName AccessControlType AccessRight
---- --------- ----------- ----------------- -----------
temp *         Everyone    Allow             Full


PS C:\Users\Administrator>
```

FIGURE 2-24 Output of the Get-SmbShareAccess cmdlet

- **Grant-SmbShareAccess** Adds an Allow access control entry to the ACL for a named share, as in the following example:

  ```
  grant-smbshareaccess -name data -accountname adatum\administrator -accessright
  full
  ```

- **Revoke-SmbShareAccess** Removes all the Allow permissions for a specified security principal from a named share, as in the following example:

  ```
  revoke-smbshareaccess -name data -accountname adatum\administrator
  ```

- **Block-SmbShareAccess** Adds an Deny access control entry to the ACL for a named share, as in the following example:

  ```
  block-smbshareaccess -name data -accountname adatum\administrator -accessright
  full
  ```

- **Unblock-SmbShareAccess** Removes all of the Deny permissions for a specified security principal from a named share, as in the following example:

  ```
  unblock-smbshareaccess -name data -accountname adatum\administrator
  ```

Configuring SMB server configuration settings

The SmbShare PowerShell module in Windows Server 2012 introduced the Set-SmbServerConfiguration cmdlet, which enables administrators to configure many underlying settings for the SMB server implementation. To display all the current server configuration settings, run the Get-SmbServerConfiguration cmdlet, as shown in Figure 2-25.

```
PS C:\Users\Administrator> get-smbserverconfiguration

AnnounceComment                :
AnnounceServer                 : False
AsynchronousCredits            : 512
AuditSmb1Access                : False
AutoDisconnectTimeout          : 15
AutoShareServer                : True
AutoShareWorkstation           : True
CachedOpenLimit                : 10
DurableHandleV2TimeoutInSeconds : 180
EnableAuthenticateUserSharing  : False
EnableDownlevelTimewarp        : False
EnableForcedLogoff             : True
EnableLeasing                  : True
EnableMultiChannel             : True
EnableOplocks                  : True
EnableSecuritySignature        : False
EnableSMB1Protocol             : True
EnableSMB2Protocol             : True
EnableStrictNameChecking       : True
EncryptData                    : False
IrpStackSize                   : 15
KeepAliveTime                  : 2
MaxChannelPerSession           : 32
MaxMpxCount                    : 50
MaxSessionPerConnection        : 16384
MaxThreadsPerQueue             : 20
MaxWorkItems                   : 1
NullSessionPipes               :
NullSessionShares              :
OplockBreakWait                : 35
PendingClientTimeoutInSeconds  : 120
RejectUnencryptedAccess        : True
RequireSecuritySignature       : False
ServerHidden                   : True
Smb2CreditsMax                 : 8192
Smb2CreditsMin                 : 512
SmbServerNameHardeningLevel    : 0
TreatHostAsStableStorage       : False
ValidateAliasNotCircular       : True
ValidateShareScope             : True
ValidateShareScopeNotAliased   : True
ValidateTargetName             : True

PS C:\Users\Administrator>
```

FIGURE 2-25 Output of the Get-SmbServerConfiguration cmdlet

For example, you can specify what versions of the SMB protocol the server should use by running commands like the following:

```
set-SmbServerConfiguration -enablesmb1protocol $false
```

```
set-SmbServerConfiguration -enablesmb2protocol $false
```

Windows Server 2016 uses SMB version 3, but the previous versions are available to support down level clients. Note that there is no separate parameter for enabling SMB version 3 by itself, because version 3 cannot run without version 2.

SMB versions 2 and 3 provide many features that can enhance the performance of the protocol, including data encryption and multichannel link aggregation. Disabling SMB version 1 with the first command ensures that your clients are using the latest SMB versions and are taking advantage of the new features. SMB version 1 is not needed unless you have clients running Windows XP or earlier.

The latter example disables SMB versions 2 and 3, leaving the server to use only the original SMB version 1. This disables a number of advanced SMB features, which can be temporarily useful for troubleshooting purposes.

When your server is running SMB version 3, you can enable encryption of SMB sessions for the entire server or for a specific share on the server, using the following commands:

```
set-smbserverconfiguration -encryptdata $true
```

```
set-smbserverconfiguration -name data -encryptdata $true
```

When encryption is enabled, the default behavior of the server is to reject a connection from any client that does not support SMB version 3 encryption. You can override this behavior using the following command:

```
set-SmbServerConfiguration -rejectunencryptedaccess $false
```

There are dozens of other parameters you can use with the Set-SmbServerConfiguration cmdlet. To display them and their functions, run the following command:

```
get-help set-smbserverconfiguration -detailed
```

Configuring SMB client configuration settings

Just as you can configure SMB server configuration settings using Windows PowerShell, you can configure SMB client configuration settings as well. Running the Get-SmbClientConfiguration cmdlet displays a list of the available settings, as shown in Figure 2-26.

```
PS C:\Users\Administrator> get-smbclientconfiguration

ConnectionCountPerRssNetworkInterface : 4
DirectoryCacheEntriesMax              : 16
DirectoryCacheEntrySizeMax            : 65536
DirectoryCacheLifetime                : 10
DormantFileLimit                      : 1023
EnableBandwidthThrottling             : True
EnableByteRangeLockingOnReadOnlyFiles : True
EnableInsecureGuestLogons             : True
EnableLargeMtu                        : True
EnableLoadBalanceScaleOut             : True
EnableMultiChannel                    : True
EnableSecuritySignature               : True
ExtendedSessionTimeout                : 1000
FileInfoCacheEntriesMax               : 64
FileInfoCacheLifetime                 : 10
FileNotFoundCacheEntriesMax           : 128
FileNotFoundCacheLifetime             : 5
KeepConn                              : 600
MaxCmds                               : 50
MaximumConnectionCountPerServer       : 32
OplocksDisabled                       : False
RequireSecuritySignature              : False
SessionTimeout                        : 60
UseOpportunisticLocking               : True
WindowSizeThreshold                   : 1

PS C:\Users\Administrator>
```

FIGURE 2-26 Output of the Get-SmbClientConfiguration cmdlet

As with the SMB server configuration parameters, most of these settings do not require modification for normal use. However, if you are exploring the enhancements in the newer SMB versions, you might want to disable certain features temporarily, for testing purposes.

For example, the new multichannel capability in SMB can enable your computers to realize greater communication throughput and fault tolerance, but the feature has hardware requirements for both the client and server computer, such as multiple network adapters or adapters configured to use NIC Teaming.

SMB multichannel is enabled by default; if your computers are equipped to use it, they are. However, if you are unsure whether the feature is operating on your systems, you can test it by disabling multichannel using the following command:

```
set-smbclientconfiguration -enablemultichannel $false
```

If your SMB connections slow down because of this command, this means that multichannel was working; and you can enable it again by changing $false to $true. If there is no change in SMB performance with multichannel disabled, there is a problem elsewhere that you must troubleshoot.

Configure file and folder permissions

Windows Server 2016 uses permissions to control access to all NTFS files and folders, shares, registry keys, and AD DS objects. Each of these permission systems is wholly independent from the others, but the interfaces you use to manage them are similar.

To store the permissions, each element has an *access control list (ACL)*. An ACL is a collection of individual permission assignments called *access control entries (ACEs)*. Each ACE consists of a *security principal* (the name of the user, group, or computer granted the permissions) and the specific permissions assigned to that security principal. When you manage permissions in any of the Windows Server 2016 permission systems, you are creating and modifying the ACEs in an ACL.

It is critically important to understand that, in all Windows operating systems, permissions are stored as part of the protected element, not the security principal that is granted access. For example, when you grant a user the NTFS permissions needed to access a file, the ACE you create is stored in the file's ACL; it is not part of the user account. You can move the file to a different NTFS drive, and its permissions go with it.

To manage permissions in Windows Server 2016, you use a tab in the protected element's Properties sheet, like the one shown in Figure 2-27, with the security principals listed at the top and the permissions associated with them at the bottom. Share permissions are typically found on a Share Permissions tab, and NTFS permissions are located on a Security tab. All Windows permission systems use the same basic interface, although the permissions themselves vary. Server Manager also provides access to NTFS and share permissions, using a slightly different interface.

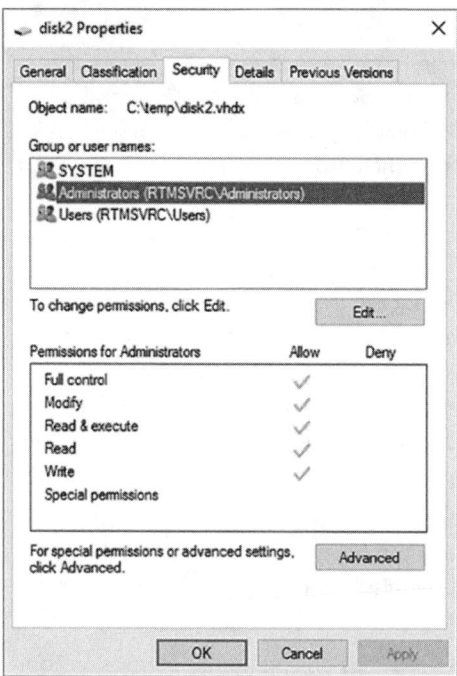

FIGURE 2-27 The Security tab of a file's Properties sheet

> **NOTE COMBINING NTFS AND SHARE PERMISSIONS**
>
> Share permissions provide limited protection, but this might be sufficient on some small networks. Share permissions might also be the only alternative on a computer with FAT32 drives, because the FAT file system does not have its own permissions. However, on networks already possessing a well-planned system of NTFS permissions, share permissions are not necessary. In a case like this, you can safely grant the Full Control share permission to Everyone, and allow the NTFS permissions to provide security. Adding share permissions to the mix would only complicate the administration process, without providing any additional protection.

In the NTFS permission system, which ReFS also supports, the security principals involved are users and groups, which Windows refers to using *security identifiers (SIDs)*. When a user attempts to access an NTFS file or folder, the system reads the user's security access token, which contains the SIDs for the user's account and all groups to which the user belongs. The system then compares these SIDs to those stored in the file or folder's ACEs, to determine what access the user should have. This process is called *authorization*.

> ***NOTE* ASSIGNING PERMISSIONS**
>
> While the security principals to which you can assign NTFS file and folder permissions can be users or groups, Microsoft recommends as a best practice that you not assign permissions to individual users, but to groups instead. This enables you to maintain your permission strategy by simply adding users to and removing them from groups.

Basic and advanced permissions

The permission systems in Windows Server 2016 are not like the keys to a lock, which provide either full access or no access at all. Windows permissions are designed to be granular, enabling you to grant specific degrees of access to security principals. For example, you can use NTFS permissions to control not only who has access to a spreadsheet, but also the degree of access. You might grant Ralph permission to read and modify the spreadsheet, but Alice can only read it, and Ed cannot see it at all.

To provide this granularity, each Windows permission system has an assortment of permissions that you can assign to a security principal in any combination. Depending on the permission system, there might be dozens of different permissions available for a single system element.

To make the system more manageable, Windows provides preconfigured permission combinations that are suitable for most common access control scenarios. When you open the Properties sheet for a system element and look at its Security tab, the NTFS permissions you see are called *basic permissions*. Basic permissions are combinations of *advanced permissions*, which provide the most granular control over the element.

> **EXAM TIP**
>
> Prior to Windows Server 2012, basic permissions were known as standard permissions, and advanced permissions were known as special permissions. Candidates for certification exams should be aware of these alternative terms.

The NTFS permission system has 14 advanced permissions that you can assign to a folder or file. However, it also has six basic permissions that are various combinations of the 14 advanced permissions. You can choose to work with either the basic or advanced permissions, and even assign both permission types in a single ACE, to create a customized combination. However, most users only work with basic permissions. Many administrators rarely, if ever, work directly with advanced permissions.

If you do find it necessary to work with advanced permissions directly, Windows makes it possible. When you click the Advanced button on the Security tab of any file or folder's Properties sheet, you can access the ACEs for the selected system element directly, using the Advanced Security Settings dialog box, as shown in Figure 2-28. Server Manager provides access to the same dialog box through a share's Properties sheet.

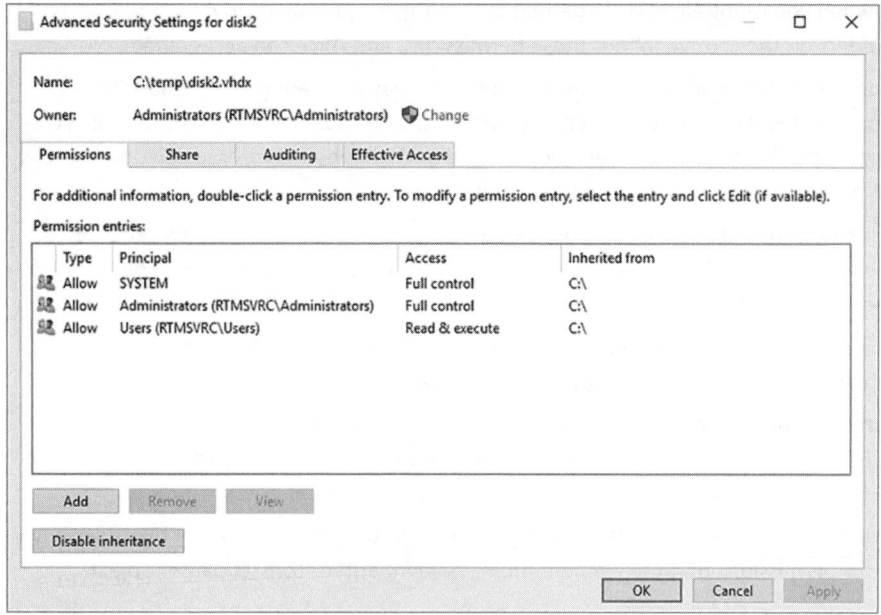

FIGURE 2-28 The Advanced Security Settings dialog box

Allowing and denying permissions

When you assign permissions to a system element, you are, in effect, creating a new ACE in the element's ACL. There are two types of ACE: Allow and Deny. This makes it possible to approach permission management tasks from two directions:

- **Additive**   Start with no permissions and then grant Allow permissions to individual security principals to provide them with the access they need.
- **Subtractive**   Start by granting all possible Allow permissions to individual security principals, providing them with full control over the system element, and then grant them Deny permissions for the access you do not want them to have.

Most administrators prefer the additive approach because Windows, by default, attempts to limit access to important system elements by withholding permissions. In a properly designed permission hierarchy, the use of Deny permissions is often not needed at all. Many administrators frown on their use, because combining Allow and Deny permissions in the same hierarchy can often make determining the effective permissions for a specific system element difficult.

Inheriting permissions

The most important principle in permission management is that permissions tend to run downward through a hierarchy. This is called *permission inheritance*. Permission inheritance means that parent elements pass their permissions down to their subordinate elements. For example, when you grant Alice Allow permissions to the root of the D drive, all the folders and subfolders on the D drive inherit those permissions, and Alice can access them.

The principle of inheritance simplifies the permission assignment process enormously. Without it, you would have to grant security principals individual Allow permissions for every file, folder, share, object, and key they need to access. With inheritance, you can grant access to an entire file system by creating one set of Allow permissions.

In most cases, whether consciously or not, system administrators take inheritance into account when they design their file systems. The location of a system element in a hierarchy is often based on how the administrators plan to assign permissions.

In some situations, you might want to prevent subordinate elements from inheriting permissions from their parents. You can do this in two ways:

- **Turn off inheritance**   When you assign advanced permissions, you can configure an ACE not to pass permissions down to its subordinate elements. While not recommended by Microsoft best practices, this effectively blocks the inheritance process.
- **Deny permissions**   Assigning a Deny permission to a system element overrides any Allow permissions that the element might have inherited from its parent objects.

Understanding effective access

A security principal can receive permissions in many ways, and it is important for administrators to understand how these permissions interact. The combination of Allow permissions and Deny permissions that a security principal receives for a given system element, whether explicitly assigned, inherited, or received through a group membership, is called the *effective access* for that element. Because a security principal can receive permissions from so many sources, conflict for those permissions happens often, so there are rules that define how the permissions combine to form the effective access. These rules are as follows:

- **Allow permissions are cumulative**   When a security principal receives Allow permissions from more than one source, the permissions are combined to form the effective access permissions. For example, if Alice receives the Allow Read and Allow List Folder Contents permissions for a folder by inheriting them from its parent folder, and receives the Allow Write and Allow Modify permissions to the same folder from a group membership, Alice's effective access for the folder is the combination of all four permissions.
- **Deny permissions override Allow permissions**   When a security principal receives Allow permissions, whether explicitly, by inheritance, or from a group, you can override those permissions by granting the principal Deny permissions of the same type. For example, if Alice receives the Allow Read and Allow List Folder Contents permissions for a particular folder by inheritance, and receives the Allow Write and Allow Modify permissions to the same folder from a group membership, explicitly granting the Deny permissions to that folder prevents her from accessing it in any way.

- **Explicit permissions take precedence over inherited permissions** When a security principal receives permissions by inheriting them from a parent or from group memberships, you can override them by explicitly assigning contradicting permissions to the security principal itself. For example, if Alice inherits the Deny Full Access permission for a folder, explicitly assigning her user account the Allow Full Access permission to that folder overrides the denial.

Of course, rather than examine and evaluate all possible permission sources, you can just open the Advanced Security Settings dialog box, and click the Effective Access tab. On this tab, you can select a user, group, or device and view its effective access, with or without the influence provided by specific groups, as shown in Figure 2-29.

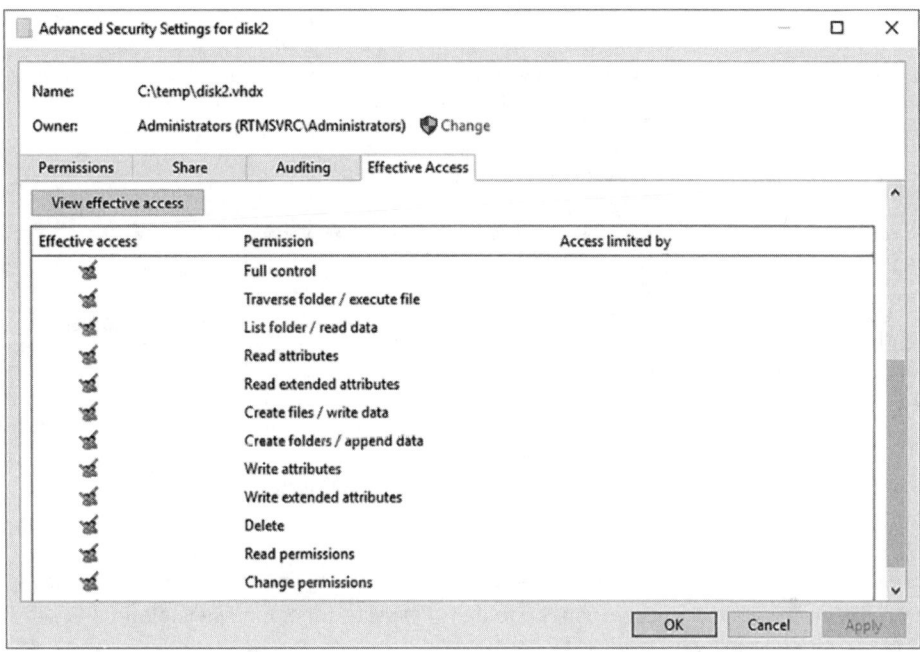

FIGURE 2-29 The Effective Access tab of the Advanced Security Settings dialog box

Assigning basic NTFS permissions

Most file server administrators work with basic NTFS permissions almost exclusively because most common access-control tasks do not require them to work directly with advanced permissions. Table 2-3 lists the basic permissions that you can assign to NTFS files or folders, and the capabilities that they grant to their possessors.

TABLE 2-3 NTFS basic permissions

Standard permission	When applied to a folder, enables a security principal to:	When applied to a file, enables a security principal to:
Full Control	▪ Modify the folder permissions ▪ Take ownership of the folder ▪ Delete subfolders and files contained in the folder ▪ Perform all actions associated with all the other NTFS folder permissions	▪ Modify the file permissions ▪ Take ownership of the file ▪ Perform all actions associated with all the other NTFS file permissions
Modify	▪ Delete the folder ▪ Perform all actions associated with the Write and the Read & Execute permissions	▪ Modify the file ▪ Delete the file ▪ Perform all actions associated with the Write and the Read & Execute permissions
Read and Execute	▪ Navigate through restricted folders to reach other files and folders ▪ Perform all actions associated with the Read and List Folder Contents permissions	▪ Perform all actions associated with the Read permission ▪ Run applications
List Folder Contents	▪ View the names of the files and subfolders contained in the folder	▪ Not applicable
Read	▪ See the files and subfolders contained in the folder ▪ View the folder's ownership, permissions, and attributes	▪ Read the file contents ▪ View the file's ownership, permissions, and attributes
Write	▪ Create new files and subfolders inside the folder ▪ Modify the folder attributes ▪ View the folder's ownership and permissions	▪ Overwrite the file ▪ Modify the file attributes ▪ View the file's ownership and permissions

To assign basic NTFS permissions to a shared folder, the options are essentially the same as with share permissions. You can open the folder's Properties sheet in File Explorer and select the Security tab, or you can open a share's Properties sheet in Server Manager, as in the following procedure.

1. Log on to Windows Server 2016, using an account with domain administrative privileges. The Server Manager window appears.

2. Click the File and Storage Services icon and, in the submenu that appears, click Shares. The Shares page appears.

> **NOTE ASSIGNING PERMISSIONS TO ANY FILE**
>
> NTFS permissions are not limited to shared folders. Every file and folder on an NTFS volume has an ACL. While this procedure describes the process of assigning permissions to a shared folder, you can open the Properties sheet for any file or folder in a File Explorer window, click the Security tab, and work with its NTFS permissions in the same way.

3. In the Shares tile, right-click a share and, from the context menu, select Properties. The Properties sheet for the share appears.
4. Click Permissions. The Permissions page appears.
5. Click Customize Permissions. The Advanced Security Settings dialog box for the shared folder appears, displaying the Permissions tab, as shown in Figure 2-30. This dialog box is as close as the Windows graphical interface can come to displaying the contents of an ACL. Each line in the Permission Entries list is essentially an ACE and includes the following information:
    - **Type** Specifies whether the entry allows or denies the permission.
    - **Principal** Specifies the name of the user, group, or device receiving the permission.
    - **Access** Specifies the name of the permission assigned to the security principal. If the entry is used to assign multiple advanced permissions, the word Special appears in this field.
    - **Inherited From** Specifies whether the permission is inherited and, if so, from where it is inherited.
    - **Applies To** Specifies whether the permission is to be inherited by subordinate objects and, if so, by which ones.

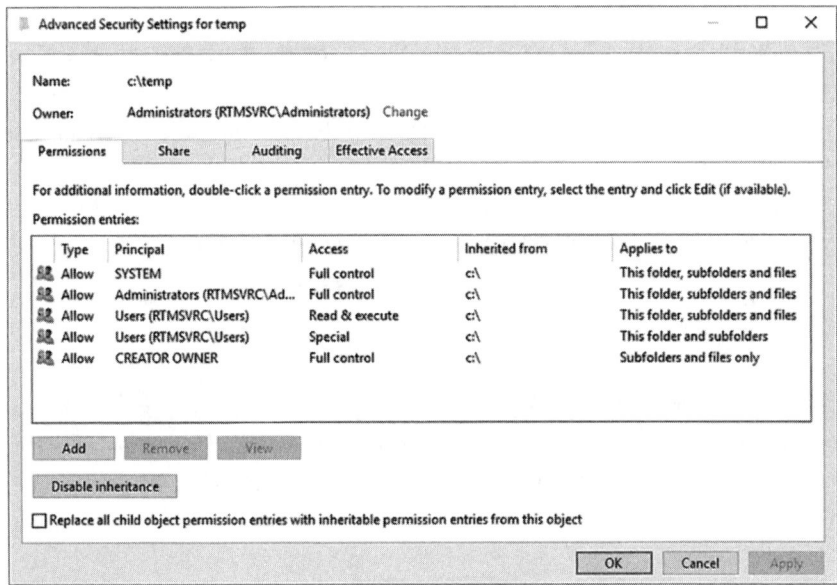

FIGURE 2-30 The Advanced Security Settings dialog box for a shared folder

6. Click Add. A Permission Entry dialog box for the share appears.
7. Click the Select A Principal link to display the Select User, Computer, Service Account, or Group dialog box.

8. Type the name of or search for the security principal to which you want to assign share permissions and click OK. The Permission Entry dialog box displays the security principal you specified as shown in Figure 2-31.

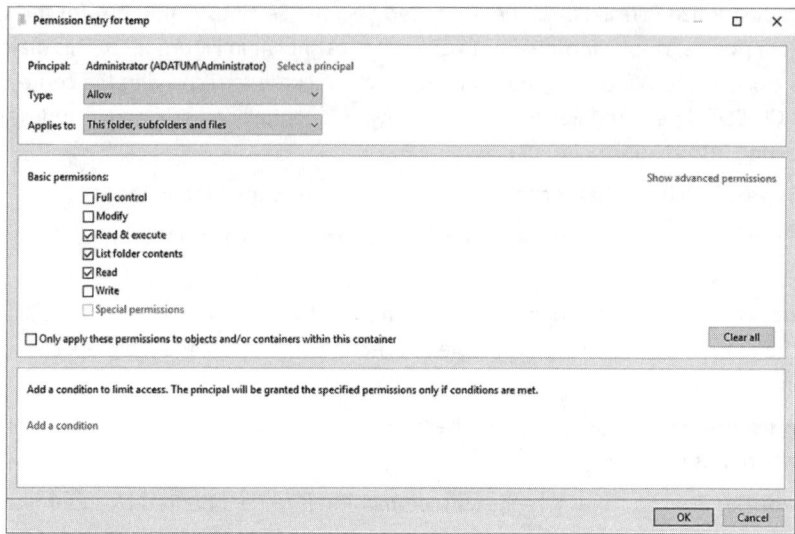

FIGURE 2-31 The Permission Entry dialog box

9. From the Type drop-down list, select the type of permissions you want to assign (Allow or Deny).
10. From the Applies To drop-down list, specify which subfolders and files should inherit the permissions you are assigning.
11. Select the check boxes for the basic permissions you want to assign and click OK. The Advanced Security Settings dialog box displays the new access control entry you just created.
12. Click OK to close the Advanced Security Settings dialog box.
13. Click OK to close the Properties sheet.

> **NOTE LARGE PERMISSION ASSIGNMENTS**
>
> Assigning permissions to a single folder takes only a moment, but for a folder with many files and subfolders subordinate to it, the process can take a long time, because the system must modify the ACL of each folder and file.

Assigning advanced NTFS permissions

In Windows Server 2016, the interface for managing advanced permissions is integrated into the same interface you use to manage basic permissions. In the Permission Entry dialog box, clicking the Show Advanced Permissions link changes the list of basic permissions to a list of advanced permissions. You can then assign advanced permissions in any combination, just as you would basic permissions.

Table 2-4 lists the NTFS advanced permissions that you can assign to files and folders, and the capabilities they grant to their possessors.

TABLE 2-4 NTFS advanced permissions

Advances permission	Functions
Full Control	■ The Full Control permission allows or denies security principals all of the other advanced permissions.
Traverse Folder/ Execute File	■ The Traverse Folder permission allows or denies security principals the ability to move through folders that they do not have permission to access, so they can reach files or folders that they do have permission to access. This permission applies only to folders. ■ The Execute File permission allows or denies security principals the ability to run program files. This permission applies only to files.
List Folder/ Read Data	■ The List Folder permission allows or denies security principals the ability to view the file and subfolder names within a folder. This permission applies only to folders. ■ The Read Data permission allows or denies security principals the ability to view the contents of a file. This permission applies only to files.
Read Attributes	■ Allows or denies security principals the ability to view the NTFS attributes of a file or folder.
Read Extended Attributes	■ Allows or denies security principals the ability to view the extended attributes of a file or folder.
Create Files/ Write Data	■ The Create Files permission allows or denies security principals the ability to create files within the folder. This permission applies only to folders. ■ The Write Data permission allows or denies security principals the ability to modify the file and overwrite existing content. This permission applies only to files.
Create Folders/ Append Data	■ The Create Folders permission allows or denies security principals the ability to create subfolders within a folder. This permission applies only to folders. ■ The Append Data permission allows or denies security principals the ability to add data to the end of the file but not to modify, delete, or overwrite existing data in the file. This permission applies only to files.
Write Attributes	■ Allows or denies security principals the ability to modify the NTFS attributes of a file or folder.
Write Extended Attributes	■ Allows or denies security principals the ability to modify the extended attributes of a file or folder.
Delete Subfolders and Files	■ Allows or denies security principals the ability to delete subfolders and files, even if the Delete permission has not been granted on the subfolder or file.
Delete	■ Allows or denies security principals the ability to delete the file or folder.
Read Permissions	■ Allows or denies security principals the ability to read the permissions for the file or folder.
Change Permissions	■ Allows or denies security principals the ability to modify the permissions for the file or folder.
Take Ownership	■ Allows or denies security principals the ability to take ownership of the file or folder.
Synchronize	■ Allows or denies different threads of multithreaded, multiprocessor programs to wait on the handle for the file or folder and synchronize with another thread that might signal it.

Understanding resource ownership

As you study the NTFS permission system, you might realize that it seems possible to lock out a file or folder—that is, assign a combination of permissions that permits access to no one at all, leaving the file or folder inaccessible. In fact, this is true.

A user with administrative privileges can revoke his or her own permissions, as well as everyone else's, preventing them from accessing a resource. However, the NTFS permissions system includes a "back door" that prevents these orphaned files and folders from remaining permanently inaccessible.

Every file and folder on an NTFS drive has an owner, and the owner always can modify the permissions for the file or folder, even if the owner has no permissions him or herself. By default, the owner of a file or folder is the user account that created it. However, any account possessing the Take Ownership advanced permission (or the Full Control basic permission) can take ownership of the file or folder.

The Administrator user can take ownership of any file or folder, even those from which the previous owner has revoked all Administrator permissions. After the Administrator user takes ownership of a file or folder, he or she cannot assign ownership back to the previous owner. This prevents the Administrator account from accessing other users' files undetected.

The other purpose for file and folder ownership is to calculate disk quotas. When you set quotas specifying the maximum amount of disk space particular users can consume, Windows calculates a user's current disk consumption by adding the sizes of all the files and folders that the user owns.

To change the ownership of a file or folder, you must open the Effective Access tab of the Advanced Security Settings dialog box and select the Change link by the Owner setting.

 Quick check

Petrina, a new hire in the IT department, approaches you, her supervisor, with her eyes wide and her face pale. A few minutes earlier, the company's Chief Financial Officer called the help desk and asked Petrina to give his new assistant the permissions needed to access his personal budget spreadsheet. As she was attempting to assign the permissions, she accidentally deleted the BUDGET_USERS group from the spreadsheet's access control list. Petrina is terrified because that group was the only entry in the file's ACL. Now, no one can access the spreadsheet file, not even the CFO or the Administrator account. Is there any way to regain access to the file, and if so, how?

Quick check answer

If no one has permission to access an NTFS file, it is still possible to rescue it. The owner of a file always retains the ability to assign permissions to that file. Petrina simply must identify the file's owner, and ask that person to assign her the Allow Full Control permission. Then, she can take the steps needed to rebuild the permissions for the file.

Skill 2.2: Implement server storage

Windows Server 2016 includes a variety of advanced storage technologies that administrators can use to equip servers with massive amounts of storage space, both inside and outside of the computer. These technologies also provide various fault tolerance mechanisms, which can maintain data availability when equipment failures and other disasters occur.

> **This section covers how to:**
> - Configure storage pools
> - Implement simple, mirror, and parity storage layout options for disks or enclosures
> - Expand storage pools
> - Configure Tiered Storage
> - Configure iSCSI target and initiator
> - Configure iSNS
> - Configure Datacenter Bridging (DCB)
> - Configure Multi-Path IO (MPIO)
> - Determine usage scenarios for Storage Replica
> - Implement Storage Replica for server-to-server, cluster-to-cluster, and stretch cluster scenarios

Configure storage pools

Windows Server 2016 includes a disk virtualization technology called Storage Spaces, which enables a server to combine the storage space from individual physical disks and allocate that space to create virtual disks of any size supported by the hardware. This type of virtualization is a feature often found in storage area network (SAN) and network attached storage (NAS) technologies, which require a substantial investment in specialized hardware and administrative skill. Storage Spaces provides similar capabilities, using standard direct-attached disk drives or simple external just-a-bunch-of-disks (JBOD) arrays.

Storage Spaces uses unallocated disk space on server drives to create storage pools. A *storage pool* can span multiple drives invisibly, providing an accumulated storage resource that you can expand or reduce as needed by adding disks to or removing them from the pool. By using the space in the pool, you can create *virtual disks* of any size.

After creating a virtual disk, you can create volumes on it, just as you would on a physical disk. Server Manager provides the tools needed to create and manage storage pools and virtual disks, as well as the capability to create volumes and file system shares, with some limitations.

To create a storage pool in Server Manager, use the following procedure.

1. Log on to Windows Server 2016, using an account with administrative privileges. The Server Manager console appears.
2. Click File and Storage Services, and on the submenu that appears, click Storage Pools. The Storage Pools page appears, as shown in Figure 2-32.

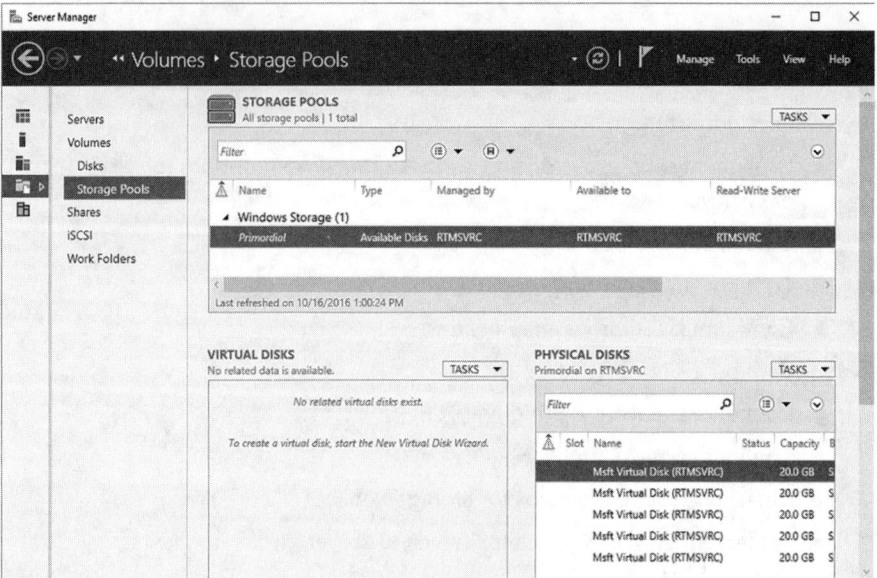

FIGURE 2-32 The Storage Pools page in Server Manager

3. In the Storage Pools tile, click Tasks, New Storage Pool. The New Storage Pool Wizard appears, displaying the Before You Begin page.
4. Click Next. The Specify A Storage Pool Name And Subsystem page appears.
5. In the Name text box, type a name for the pool and click Next. The Select Physical Disks For The Storage Pool page appears, as shown in Figure 2-33.

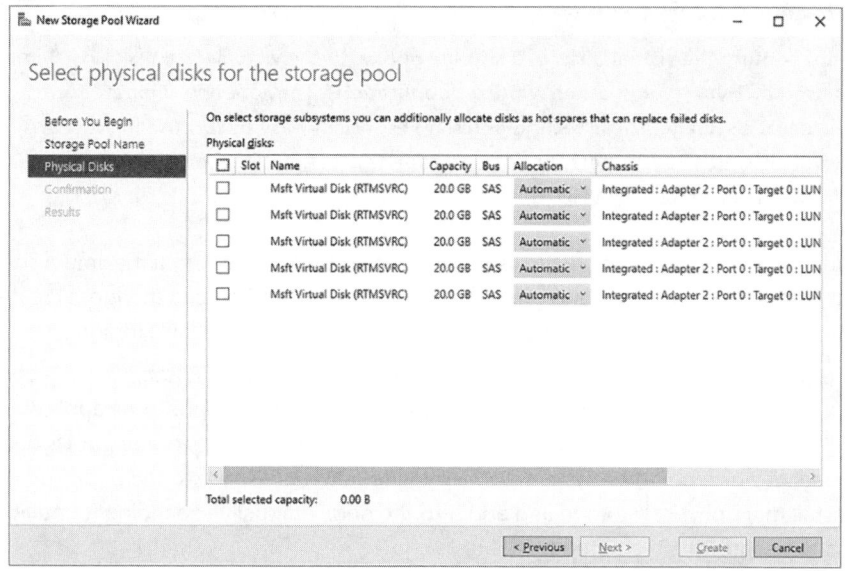

FIGURE 2-33 The Select Physical Disks For The Storage Pool page in Server Manager

> **NOTE   ADDING PHYSICAL DISKS**
>
> For a physical disk to be eligible for addition to a storage pool, it must be online and initialized, but there must be no volumes on it. In the Disk Management, the entire disk should appear as Unallocated Space.

1. Select the check boxes for the physical disks you want to add to the pool and click Next. The Confirm Selections page appears.
2. Click Create. The wizard creates the storage pool.
3. Click Close. The new pool appears in the Storage Pools tile.

By creating a storage pool, you have combined the storage space of the physical disks you selected. You can now create any number of virtual disks out of the pooled storage that need not correspond to the storage sizes of the individual physical disks.

Implement simple, mirror, and parity storage layout options for disks or enclosures

Once you have created a storage pool, you can create virtual disks using that pooled storage. A virtual disk behaves much like a physical disk, except that the actual bits might be stored on any number of physical drives in the system. Virtual disks can also provide fault tolerance by using the physical disks in the storage pool to hold mirrored or parity data.

> **NOTE** **VIRTUAL DISKS AND VHDS**
>
> Do not confuse the virtual disks in a storage pool with the virtual hard disk (VHD) image files used by Hyper-V and other Windows applications. They are two separate forms of virtualized storage. These technologies are especially easy to confuse in Windows PowerShell, which has cmdlets for both. Storage Spaces cmdlets use the noun VirtualDisk, while Hyper-V cmdlets use VHD.

Virtual disks can also be *thinly provisioned*, meaning that you specify a maximum size for the disk, but it starts out small and grows as you add data to it. You can therefore create a virtual disk with a maximum size that is larger than that of your available storage space.

For example, if you plan to allocate a maximum of 10 TB for your database files, you can create a thin 10 TB virtual disk, even if you only have a 2 TB storage pool. The application using the disk will function normally, gradually adding data until the storage pool is nearly consumed, at which point the system notifies you to add more space to the pool. You can then install more physical storage and add it to the pool, gradually expanding it until it can support the entire 10 TB required by the disk.

Creating a virtual disk

To create a simple virtual disk, use the following procedure.

1. In Server Manager, on the Storage Pools page, in the Storage Pools tile, select a pool you have created earlier.
2. In the Virtual Disks tile, click Tasks, New Virtual Disk. A Select The Storage Pool dialog box appears.
3. Select the pool you want to use and click OK. The New Virtual Disk Wizard appears, displaying the Before You Begin page.
4. Click Next. The Select The Storage Pool page appears.
5. Click Next. The Specify The Virtual Disk Name page appears.
6. In the Name text box, type a name for the virtual disk and click Next. The Specify Enclosure Resiliency page appears.
7. Click Next. Select The Storage Layout page appears, as shown in Figure 2-34.

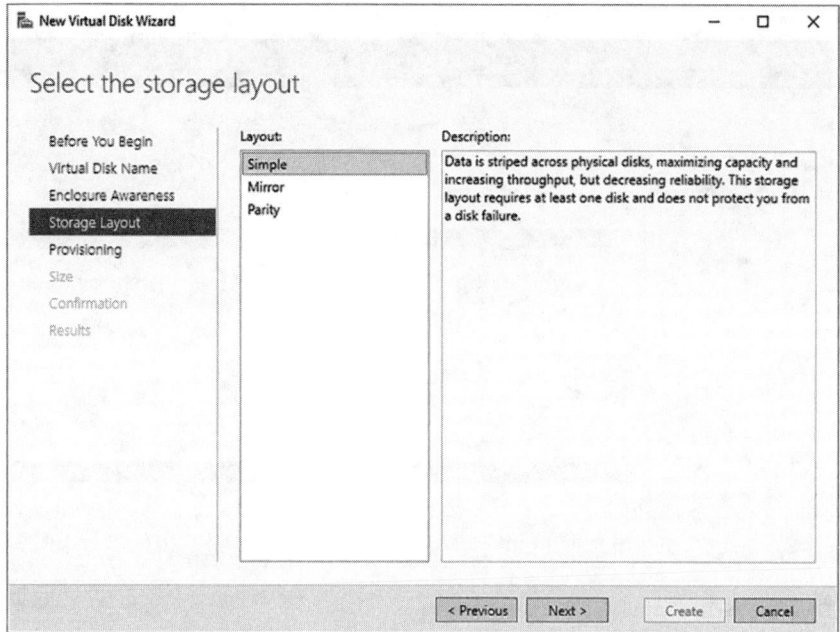

FIGURE 2-34 The Select The Storage Layout page

8. In the Layout list, select Simple and click Next. The Specify The Provisioning Type page appears.

9. Select one of the following options and click Next. The Specify The Size Of The Virtual Disk page appears.

   - **Thin**   You specify a maximum size for the virtual disk, but the system creates a small disk and allocates additional space to it as needed. This option is best suited to situations in which you do not yet have enough physical space to create the virtual disk you will need, but you plan to add more later.

   - **Fixed**   You specify a size for the virtual disk and the system allocates all of the physical disk space needed to create it immediately.

10. Specify a size for the virtual disk or select the Maximum Size option to use all of the space in the storage pool. Then click Next. The Confirm Selections page appears.

11. Click Create. The wizard creates the virtual disk and the View Results page appears. Clear the Create A Volume When This Wizard Closes check box.

12. Click Close. The virtual disk appears in the Virtual Disks tile on the Storage Pools page, as shown in Figure 2-35.

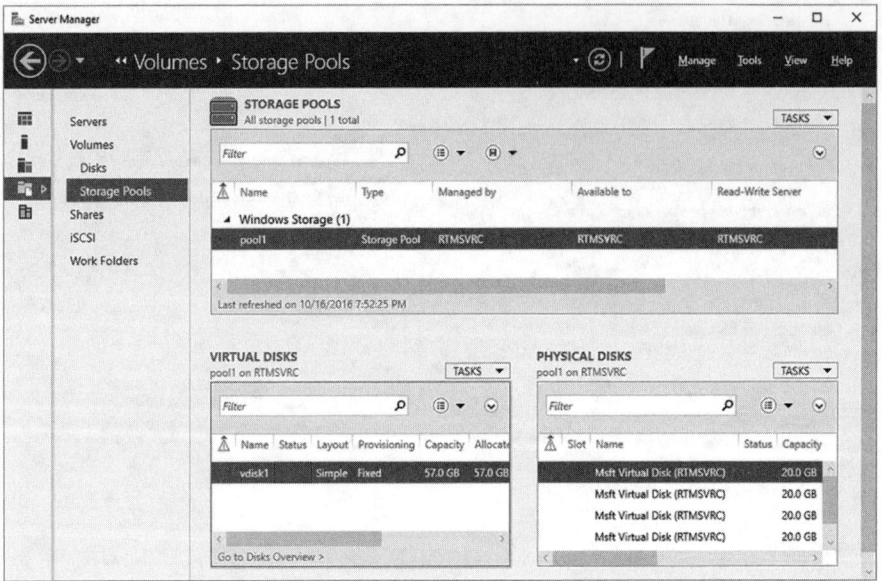

FIGURE 2-35 The populated Storage Pools page

Once you have created a virtual disk, you can right-click it in the Virtual Disks tile and select New Volume to launch the New Volume Wizard. At this point, the process of creating a volume is identical to that of creating it directly on a physical disk.

Fault tolerance in storage spaces

Depending on the nature of your organization and your data, fault tolerance for your file servers might be a convenience or an absolute requirement. For some businesses, a server hard drive failure might mean a few hours of lost productivity. For an order-entry department, it could mean lost income. For a hospital records department, it could mean lost lives. Depending on where in this range your organization falls, you might consider using a fault-tolerance mechanism to make sure that your users always have access to their applications and data.

The essence of fault tolerance is immediate redundancy. If one copy of a file becomes unavailable due to a disk error or failure, another copy is online, ready to take its place almost immediately. When you create a virtual disk in a storage pool, the Select The Storage Layout page of the wizard offers three options, as follows:

- **Simple** The computer stripes the data across all of the disks in the pool, maximizing performance and economy, but providing no fault tolerance.
- **Mirror** The computer writes the same data to two or three different physical disks, so that if a disk failure occurs, there is always a copy available for immediate access. Mirroring data incurs little or no performance penalty, but it is an expensive form of

fault tolerance, because you are paying for two or three times the price for the storage space you need.

- **Parity** The computer stripes the data across three or more physical disks in the pool along with parity information, which the system can use to recreate the data if a physical disk fails. Performance is slightly reduced, because the server is writing additional parity data, but this option is less expensive than mirroring.

When you select the Mirror option, a Configure The Resiliency Settings page is added to the wizard, as shown in Figure 2-36. The Two-Way Mirror option requires two physical disks and provides protection against a single disk failure. The Three-Way Mirror option requires five physical disks and provides protection against the failure of two disk.

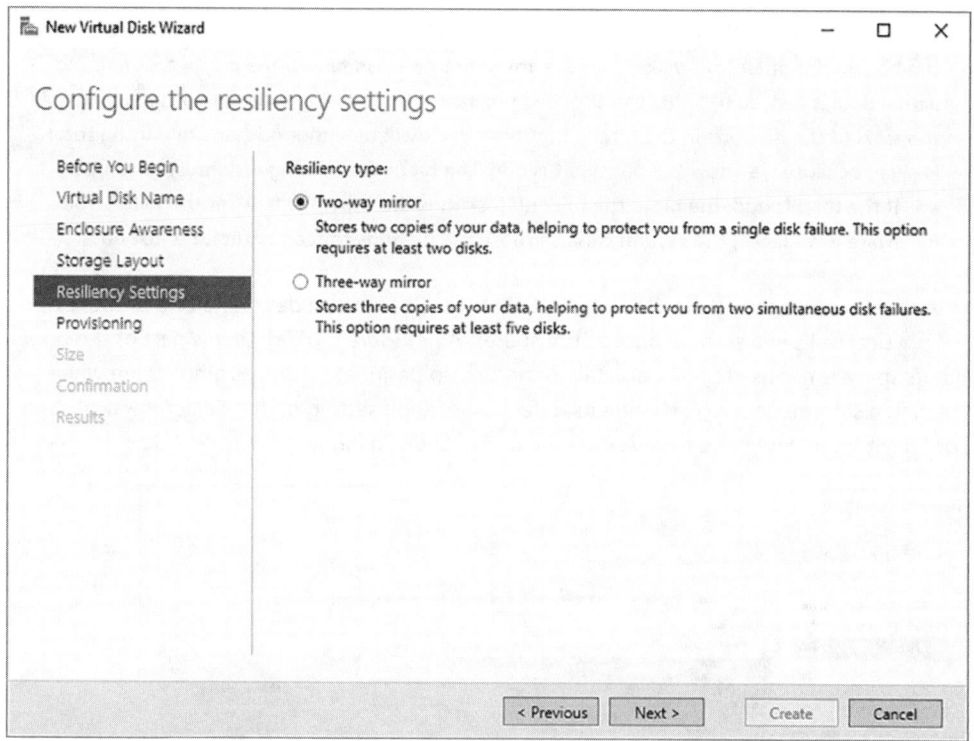

FIGURE 2-36 The Configure The Resiliency Settings page, in which you select between two-way and three-way mirroring

Choosing the Parity option on the Select The Storage Layout page requires no additional configuration. However, if your storage pool does not contain enough physical disks to support the layout, the wizard displays an error and forces you to select another option.

> **NOTE** **UNDERSTANDING PARITY**
>
> *Parity* is a mathematical algorithm that some disk storage technologies use to provide data redundancy in their disk write operations. To calculate the parity information for a drive array, the system takes the values for the same data bit on each drive in the array and adds them together, to determine whether the total is odd or even. The system then uses the resulting total to calculate a value for a parity bit corresponding to those data bits. The system then repeats the process for every bit location on the drives. If one drive is lost due to a hardware failure, the system can restore each lost data bit by calculating its value using the remaining data bits and the parity bit.
>
> For example, in an array with five disks, suppose the first four disks have the values 1, 1, 0, and 1 for their first bit. The total of the four bits is 3, an odd number, so the system sets the first bit of the fifth disk, the parity disk, to 0, indicating an odd result for the total of the bits on the other four disks. Suppose then that one disk fails. If the parity disk fails, no actual data is lost, so data I/O can proceed normally. If one of the four data disks is lost, the total of the first bits in the remaining three disks will be either odd or even. If the total is even, because we know the parity bit is odd, the bit in the missing disk must have been a 1. If the total is odd, the bit in the missing disk must have been a 0. After the failed disk hardware is replaced, the system can use these calculations to reconstruct the lost data.

Another way to provide fault tolerance in Storage Spaces is to designate one or more of the physical disks in a storage pool as hot spares. A *hot spare* is a disk that is part of the pool, but its space is not used until a disk failure occurs. To designate a disk as a hot spare while creating a storage pool, you change its default Allocation setting on the Select Physical Disks For The Storage Pool page from Automatic to Hot Spare, as shown in Figure 2-37.

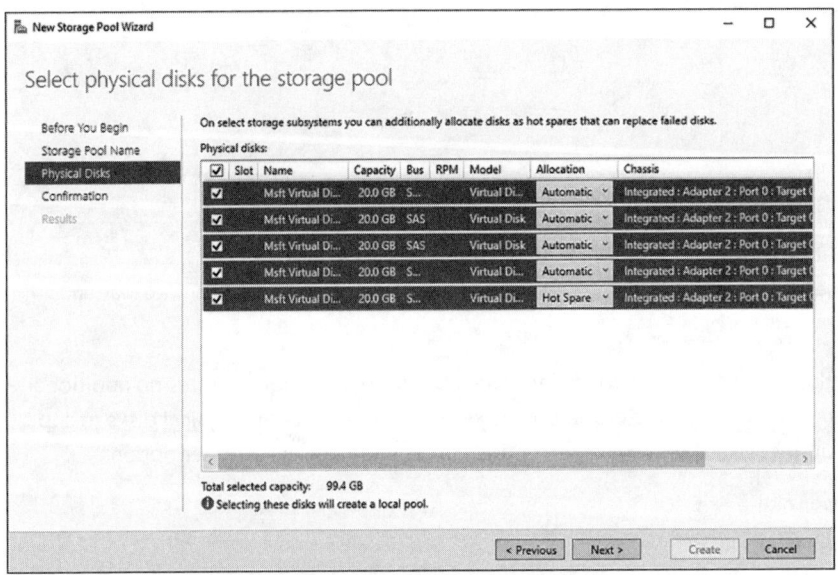

FIGURE 2-37 The Select Physical Disks For The Storage Pool page, with a hot spare

When a physical hard drive reports a write error to the operating system (usually after silently recovering from several failures), it marks the disk as failed and activates a hot spare, if one exists. In the case of a read error, the system will try to recover from the failure, if possible, by writing the missing data back to the disk using a mirror or parity copy. If this fails, the write error procedure begins.

Expand storage pools

One of the advantages of Storage Spaces is that you can expand a storage pool at any time by adding physical disks. The disks can be new ones that you've installed in the server or its storage array, or you can repurpose existing disks by deleting any volumes on them. When you add a physical disk to an existing storage pool, the new space is simply added to it. If you have created a pool that is larger than the physical disk space available in the computer, the space on the added disk does to make up the difference.

To expand an existing storage pool, use the following procedure.

1. In Server Manager, on the Storage Pools page, select an existing pool in the Storage Pools tile.
2. Right-click the existing pool and, from the context menu, select Add Physical Disk. The Add Physical Disk dialog box appears, as shown in Figure 2-38.

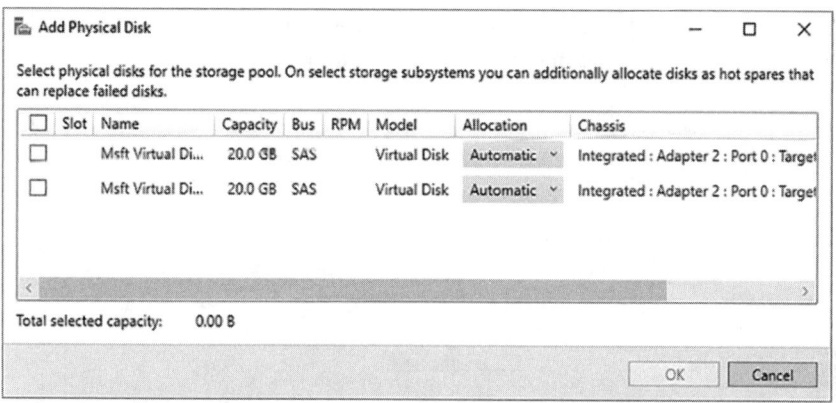

FIGURE 2-38 The Add Physical Disk dialog box

3. Select the disk(s) that you want to add to the pool and click OK. The storage space from the new disks is added to the storage pool.

Configure tiered storage

Tiered storage, in Windows Server 2016, is a Storage Spaces feature that enables administrators to use their higher-performance storage devices for their most commonly used files. To use tiered storage in Windows Server 2016, you create a storage pool that contains both solid state drives (SSDs) and standard hard disk drives (HDDs). SSDs are faster than HDDs, but they are also more expensive. You then create a virtual disk that includes space from both drive types. Once users begin storing data on the virtual disk, the system transparently copies the most frequently-used files from the HDDs to the SSDs, thus providing improved access times for those files.

When you create a virtual disk in Server Manager, using the New Virtual Disk Wizard, the Specify The Virtual Disk Name page includes a Create Storage Tiers On This Virtual Disk check box. The check box is only enabled when the storage pool contains both SSD and HDD physical disks. You also must have enough physical disks of each type to support the layout you intend to use when you create the virtual disk. For example, to create a tiered virtual disk with a two-way mirror layout, you must have a minimum of two SSDs and two HDDs available.

> **NOTE RECOGNIZING MEDIA TYPES**
>
> Windows recognizes the types of storage devices installed in, or connected to, the computer and assigns them media types—SSD and HDD—so that Storage Spaces can determine which devices to use for each tier. In situations where the system fails to identify the drives correctly (such as when you create VHDs on the physical disks for use in Hyper-V virtual machines), you can manually set the media type using the Set-PhysicalDisk cmdlet in Windows PowerShell, with the MediaType parameter.

Selecting the check box modifies the Specify The Size Of The Virtual Disk page of the wizard, as shown in Figure 2-39. Instead of specifying an overall size for the virtual disk, you specify separate sizes for the Faster Tier and the Standard Tier.

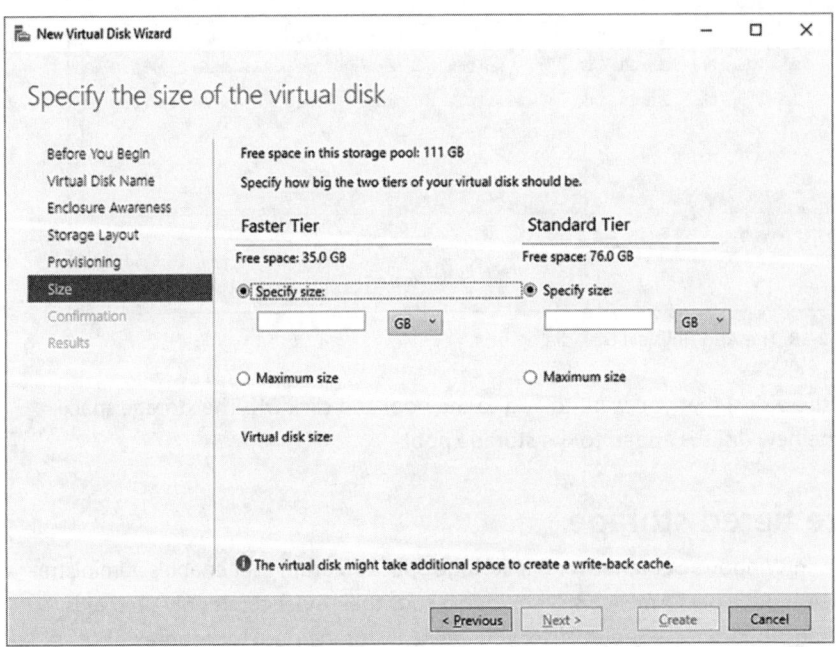

FIGURE 2-39 Tiered storage controls in the New Virtual Disk Wizard

Once the virtual disk is in use, administrators can use Set-FileStorageTier cmdlet to pin specific files to one tier or the other, so that they are always accessed from the specified disk type.

Configure iSCSI target and initiator

A *storage area network (SAN)* is a technology that enterprises use to deploy storage resources and make this storage available to other connected devices. At its most basic level, a SAN is simply a network dedicated solely to high-speed connections between servers and storage devices. Instead of installing disk drives into servers or using directly-connected drive enclosures, a SAN consists of one or more drive arrays equipped with network interface adapters, which connect to servers using standard twisted pair or fiber optic network cables.

The earliest SANs used a serial networking technology called Fibre Channel. Fibre Channel networks provide excellent SAN performance, but the expense and special skills required to install and maintain them have made them a rarity in all but the largest enterprise installations. *Internet Small Computer System Interface (iSCSI,* pronounced *eye-scuzzy*) is an alternative storage area networking technology that enables servers and storage devices to exchange SCSI traffic using a standard IP network instead of a dedicated Fibre Channel network. This makes iSCSI a far more economical and practical solution, placing SAN technology within reach of small and medium-sized installations.

Because iSCSI uses a standard IP network for its lower layer functionality, you can use the same cables, network adapters, switches, and routers for a SAN as you would for a LAN or wide area network (WAN), without any modifications. You simply connect your servers and storage devices to an existing Ethernet network or build a new one using low-cost, widely available components.

Because of its relatively low cost and its simplicity, iSCSI has come to dominate the SAN industry. The addition of widespread support for iSCSI in the Windows Server 2016 and other operating systems has led to the introduction of many iSCSI storage device products at a wide range of price points. Whereas a SAN at one time required a huge investment in money and time, the technology is now available to modest organizations.

Initiators and targets

iSCSI communication is based on two elements: initiators and targets. An *iSCSI initiator*, so-called because it initiates the SCSI communication process, is a hardware or software device running on a computer that accesses the storage devices on the SAN. On an iSCSI network, the initiator takes the place of the host adapter that traditional SCSI implementations used to connect storage devices to a computer. The initiator receives I/O requests from the operating system and sends them, in the form of SCSI commands, to specific storage devices on the SAN.

Hardware-based initiators typically take the form of a host bus adapter (HBA), an expansion card that includes the functionality of a SCSI host adapter and a Gigabit Ethernet network adapter in one device. Hardware-based initiators offload some of the SCSI processing from the computer's main processor.

Initiators can also be software-based, such as the iSCSI Initiator module included in Windows Server 2016. When using a software initiator, the computer connects to the storage devices using a standard Ethernet network adapter.

The other half of the iSCSI equation is the *iSCSI target*, which is integrated into a storage device, such as a drive array or computer. The target receives SCSI commands from the initiator and passes them to a storage device, which is represented by a *logical unit number (LUN)*. A LUN is essentially an address that SCSI devices use to identify a specific storage resource. A single LUN can represent an entire hard disk, part of a disk, or a part of a drive array. Therefore, a single computer or drive array can have many LUNs, represented by multiple targets.

Drive arrays supporting iSCSI have targets implemented in their firmware, automatically making the various volumes in the array available to iSCSI initiators on the network. It is also possible for iSCSI targets to be implemented in software, in the form of a service or daemon that makes all or part of a hard disk in a computer available to initiators.

Windows Server 2016 includes an iSCSI target, in the form of the iSCSI Target Server role service, part of the File and Storage Services role. Using the iSCSI initiator and target capabilities in Windows Server 2016, you can designate a drive on one server as a target, and then access it using the initiator on another computer. On a more practical level, you can also purchase a drive array with an integrated iSCSI target, connect it to your network, and let Windows computers all over the network access it with their initiators.

Creating an iSCSI target

To create an iSCSI target in Windows Server 2016, you must first install the iSCSI Target Server role service, using the Add Roles And Features Wizard in Server Manager, as shown in Figure 2-40, or by running the following command in a Windows PowerShell window with administrative privileges:

```
install-windowsfeature -name fs-iscsitarget-server -includemanagementtools
```

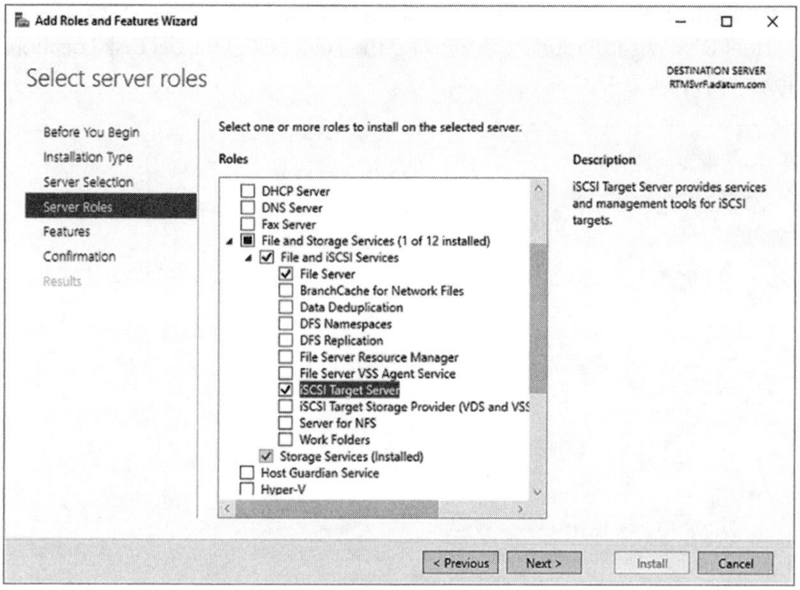

FIGURE 2-40 Installing the iSCSI Target Server role service

Once you have installed the role service, you can proceed to demonstrate the use of iSCSI by creating an iSCSI virtual disk and an iSCSI target, using space on one of the computer's disks, as described in the following procedure.

1. In Server Manager, click the File and Storage Services icon and, in the submenu that appears, click iSCSI. The iSCSI page appears, as shown in Figure 2-41.

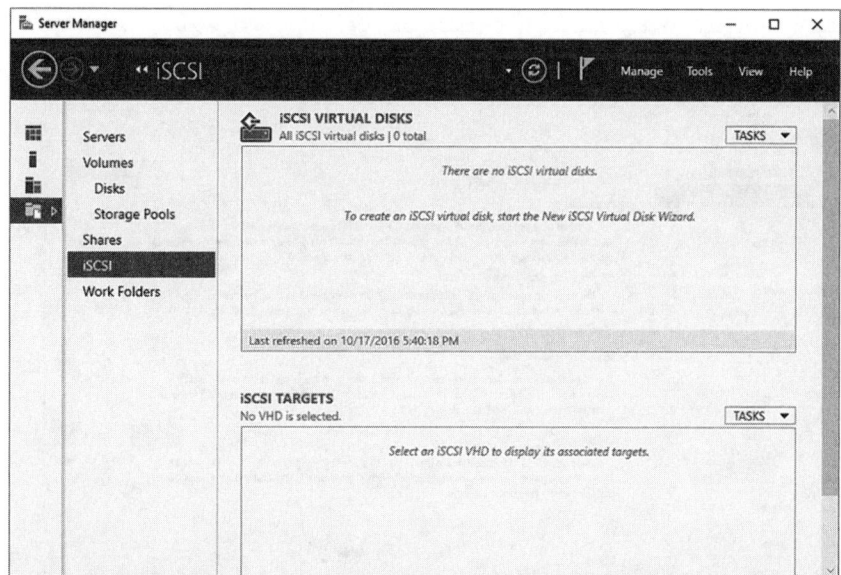

FIGURE 2-41 The iSCSI page in Server Manager

2. From the Tasks menu in the iSCSI Virtual Disks tile, select New iSCSI Virtual Disk. The New iSCSI Virtual Disk Wizard appears, displaying the Select iSCSI Virtual Disk Location page, as shown in Figure 2-42.

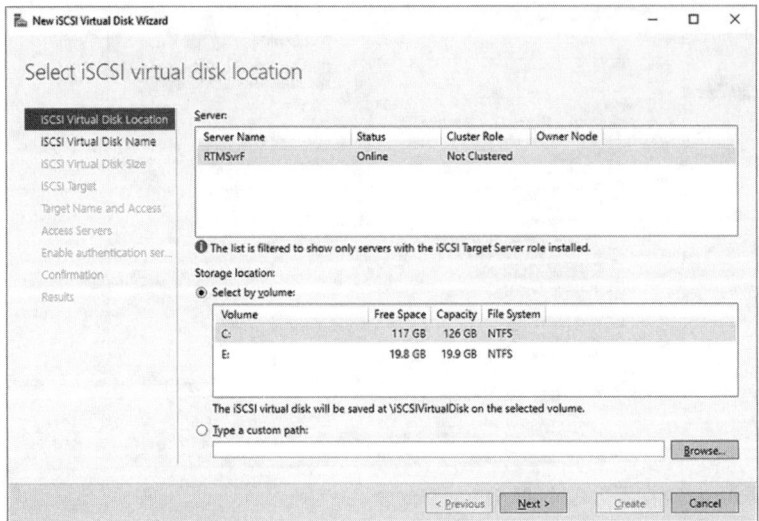

FIGURE 2-42 The Select iSCSI Virtual Disk Location page

3. Select the volume on which you want to create an iSCSI virtual disk and click Next. The Specify iSCSI Virtual Disk Name page appears.

4. Type a name for the iSCSI virtual disk and click Next. The Specify iSCSI Virtual Disk Size page appears, as shown in Figure 2-43.

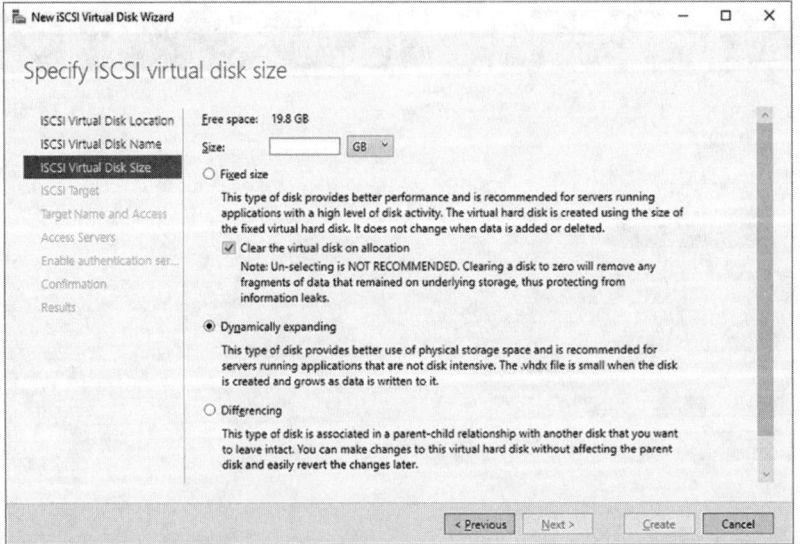

FIGURE 2-43 The Select iSCSI Virtual Disk Size page

5. Specify a size for the iSCSI virtual disk and choose from the Fixed Size, Dynamically Expanding, or Differencing options. The wizard will create a VHDX file, so these options have the same functions as a virtual disk you create in Hyper-V. Click Next. The Assign iSCSI Target page appears.
6. Leave the New iSCSI Target option selected and click Next. The Specify Target Name appears.
7. Type a name for the iSCSI target and click Next. The Specify Access Servers page appears, on which you will identify the iSCSI initiators that will access the new virtual disk.
8. Click Add. The Select A Method To Identify The Initiator dialog box appears, as shown in Figure 2-44.

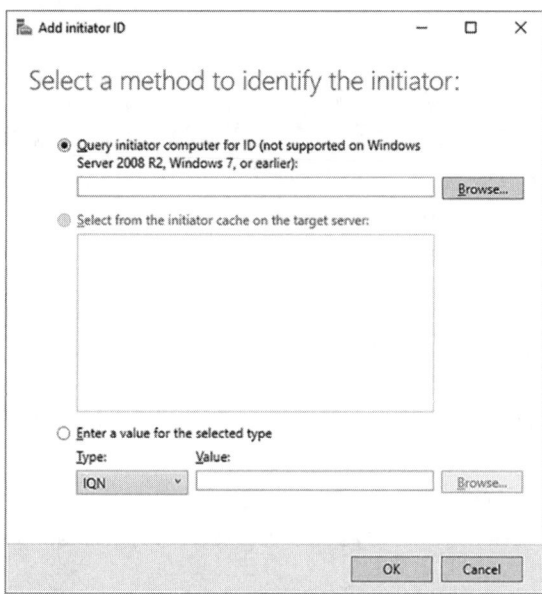

FIGURE 2-44 The Select A Method To Identify the Initiator dialog box

9. Select the Enter A Value For The Selected Type option. Then, select IP Address in the Type drop-down list and type the IP address of the server that will function as the iSCSI initiator and click OK. The initiator computer is added to the wizard.
10. Click Next. The Enable Authentication page appears.
11. Click Next to bypass the optional authentication settings. The Confirm Selections page appears.
12. Click Create. The wizard creates the new iSCSI virtual disk and an iSCSI target.
13. Click Close. The disk and target appear in the tiles on the iSCSI page, as shown in Figure 2-45.

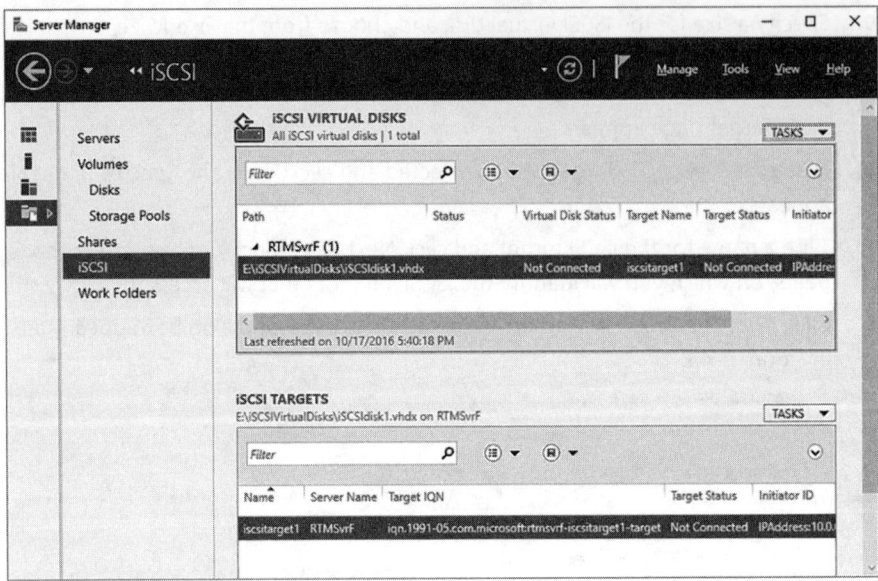

FIGURE 2-45 The iSCSI page in Server Manager

Using iSCSI initiator

When an iSCSI target is available—one you have created on a server or one built into a hardware device—you can connect to it and access its storage using the iSCSI initiator in Windows Server 2016. Unlike the iSCSI Target Server, the iSCSI initiator is installed by default in Windows Server 2016; there is nothing you need to install.

To connect to a target using the iSCSi initiator, use the following procedure.

1. Log on to the computer you have designated as an access server when creating a target in the New iSCSI Virtual Disk Wizard.
2. In Server Manager, click Tools, and iSCSI Initiator. The iSCSI Initiator Properties sheet appears, as shown in Figure 2-46.

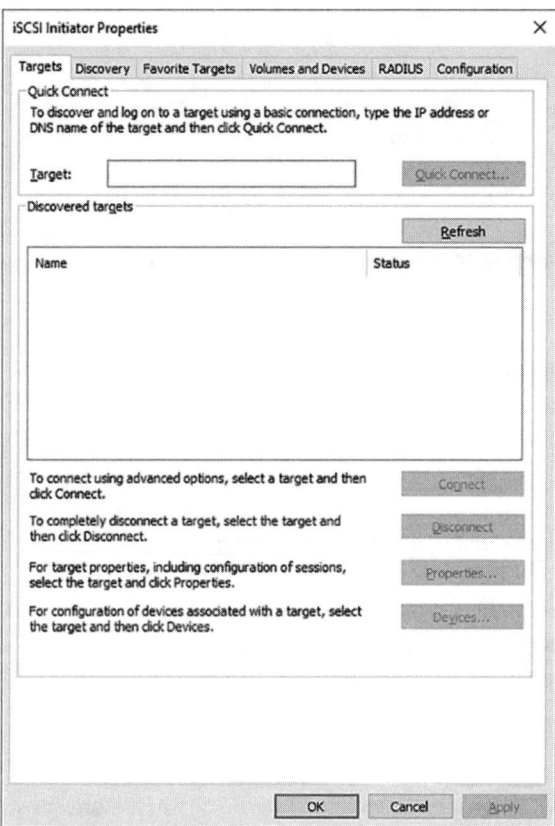

FIGURE 2-46 The iSCSI Initiator Properties sheet

3. On the Targets tab, in the Target text box, type the IP address of the computer where you created the iSCSI target and click Quick Connect. The target appears in the Discovered Targets box.

4. Click OK.

Once the initiator is connected to the target, you can open the Disk Management console and see that the iSCSI virtual disk you created on the target computer is now listed, as shown in Figure 2-47.

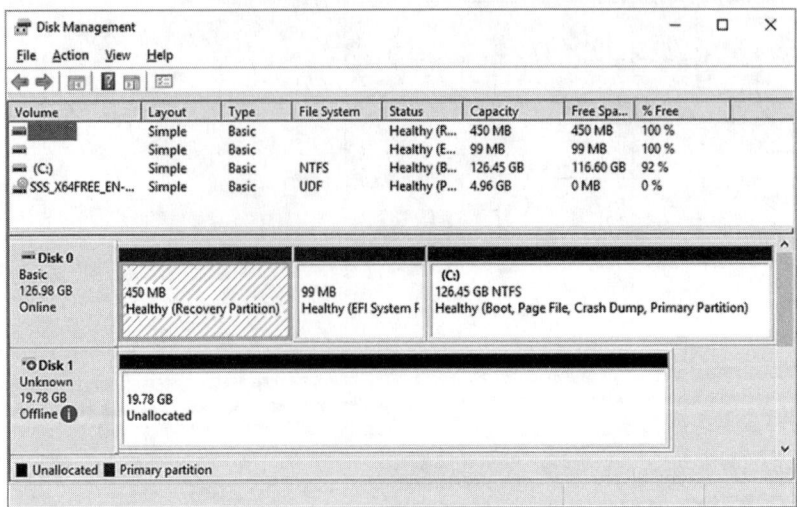

FIGURE 2-47 The Disk Management console, displaying an iSCSi target disk

Because the virtual disk was just created, it appears in the Disk Management console as Offline and Uninitialized. To use the disk, you must bring it online, initialize it, and then create a volume on it, just as if it was a disk in the local system.

Configure iSNS

In a simple demonstration of the iSCSI target and initiator, like the one in the previous section, you can easily determine the IP addresses of the computers involved and use them to establish the iSCSI connection over the network. In an enterprise environment, however, where you might have many iSCSI targets and many initiators accessing them, using IP addresses is not practical.

After the iSCSI targets and initiators are in place, the main problem remaining in iSCSI communications is how the two locate each other. The *Internet Storage Name Service (iSNS)* makes this possible by registering the presence of initiators and targets on a network and responding to queries from iSNS clients. Windows Server 2016 includes an iSNS implementation as a feature, which can provide the identification service for an entire network.

iSNS consists of four components, as follows:

- **iSNS server**   Receives and processes registration requests and queries from clients on the network, using the iSNS database as an information store.
- **iSNS database**   Information store on an iSNS server that contains data supplied by client registrations. The server retrieves the data to respond to client queries.
- **iSNS clients**   Component in iSCSI initiators and targets that registers information about itself with an iSNS server and sends queries to the server for information about other clients.

- **iSNS Protocol (iSNSP)** Protocol used for all registration and query traffic between iSNS servers and clients.

To create an iSNS server on Windows Server 2016, you must install the iSNS feature, using the Add Roles And Features Wizard or the following PowerShell command:

```
install-WindowsFeature -name isns
```

Once the iSNS server is installed, it automatically registers the iSCSI targets available on the network, but you must register your iSCSI initiators with it manually, using the following procedure.

1. In Server Manager, click Tools, iSCSI Initiator. The iSCSI Initiator Properties dialog box appears.
2. Click the Discovery tab, as shown in Figure 2-48.

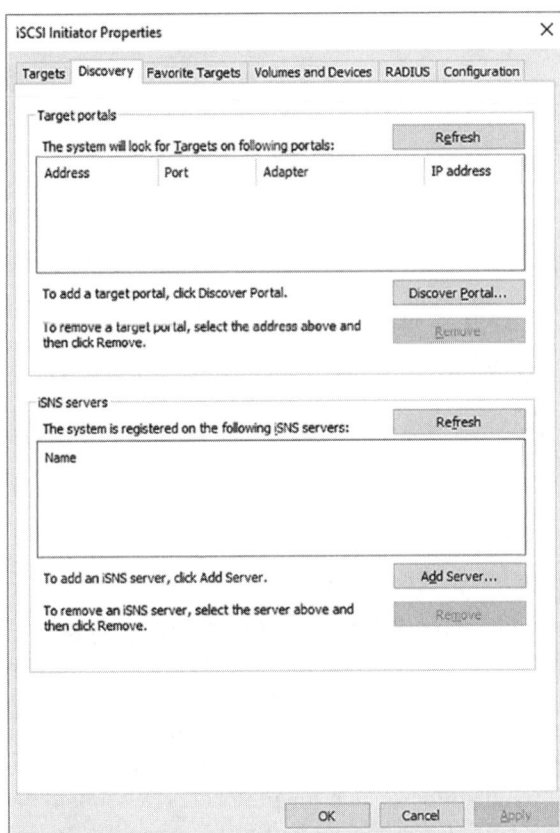

FIGURE 2-48 The Discovery tab in the iSCSI Initiator Properties dialog box

3. In the iSNS Servers box, click Add Server. The Add iSNS Server dialog box appears.

4. Type the IP address or DNS name of the server on which you installed the iSNS Server feature, and click OK.

5. Click OK to close the iSCSI Initiator Properties dialog box.

Once you have added the iSNS server to your iSCSI initiators, they are registered in the iSNS database. When you select Tools, iSNS Server in Server Manager, the iSNS Server Properties sheet appears, as shown in Figure 2-49, listing the iSCSI initiators you have registered.

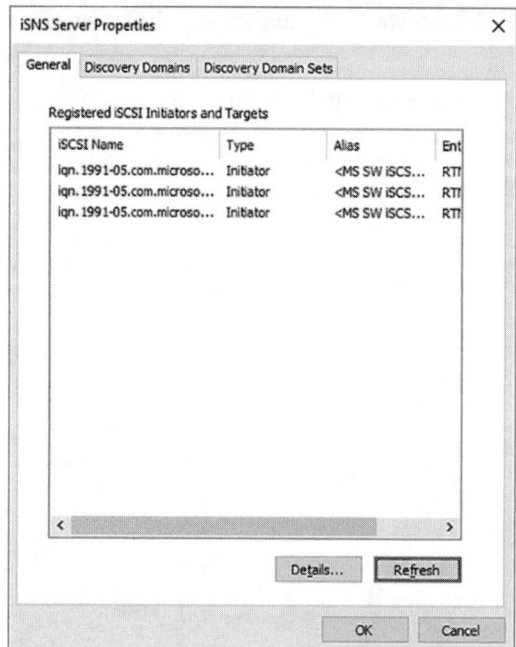

FIGURE 2-49 The iSNS Server Properties sheet

Configure Datacenter Bridging (DCB)

The original concept of the SAN called for a separate network dedicated to storage traffic. Servers already connected to the local area network (LAN) would have an additional network adapter to connect to the SAN, to provide them with access to standalone storage devices. One of the most important innovations of iSCSI is its ability to use a standard Ethernet network for its communications between initiators and targets. Fibre Channel now also has a Fiber Channel over Ethernet (FCoE) standard for running the protocol on a standard network. This raises a question, however. If it is possible to run SAN traffic over a standard Ethernet network, why not just use the network that is already in place and run both SAN and LAN traffic together?

The reasons why this is not a good idea have to do with the way that Ethernet controls access to the network medium. Ethernet is a "lossy" protocol, meaning that packet collisions are an expected occurrence. The more traffic there is on the network, the greater the number of collisions. The TCP/IP traffic running on a LAN has error detection and correction mechanisms in place to deal with the lost packets that result from the collisions. SAN protocols are more finicky about lost packets and are generally in need of an uninterrupted flow of traffic to function efficiently.

The result is that SAN and LAN traffics do not function well together unless there is a mechanism in place to ensure that each gets the bandwidth it needs at all times. This is where datacenter bridging comes into the picture. *Datacenter bridging (DCB)* is a series of standards, published by the Institute of Electrical and Electronics Engineers (IEEE), that define mechanisms for flow control and bandwidth management on a network with multiple traffic types. Windows Server 2016 includes a DCB implementation that enables administrators to allocate a specific amount of bandwidth to the different types of traffic on the network. The result is what is known as a *converged network*. By allocating a percentage of the network bandwidth to iSCSI traffic, for example, the SAN will continue to function properly, even when the LAN is in heavy use.

Windows Server 2016 includes Datacenter Bridging as a feature that you can install in the usual manner, using the Add Roles And Features Wizard in Server Manager or the Install-WindowsFeature cmdlet in PowerShell. However, implementing DCB on your network requires specialized hardware as well as software.

For a server to use DCB, it must have a converged network adapter (CNA) that supports the DCB standards. A CNA is a combination device that includes standard Ethernet networking capabilities, plus a SAN host bus adapter supporting iSCSI, FCoE, or a combination of SAN types. Your storage devices must also support DCB, as must the switches linking your devices together.

The DCB implementation in Windows Server 2016 includes a PowerShell module called DcbQos, which includes cmdlets that enable you to configure the CNA in the server, as described in the following sections.

Set the DCBX Willing bit

DCBX Willing is a single bit function defined in the DCB standards that controls the source of the CNA configuration settings. DCBX is a mechanism by which DCB devices on the network can propagate their configuration settings to other devices. By default, the DCBX Willing bit in a CNA is set to True, enabling your storage devices or switches to alter its settings. Changing the bit to False enables the CNA to receive only local configuration settings, the ones you create with the DcbQos cmdlets in PowerShell.

To set the DCBX Willing bit to false, you use the Set-NetQoSdcbxSetting cmdlet, as in the following example:

```
set-netqosdcbxsetting -willing 0
```

Once the CNA is under your control, you can configure it to function per your specifications.

Create traffic classes

Traffic classes are how you separate the types of traffic on your converged network. By default, there is a single traffic class that gets 100 percent of the network bandwidth and all eight priority ratings. You can create up to seven additional traffic classes, for a total of eight, although you should confirm that all of the other DCB devices on your network can recognize that many.

To create a new traffic class, you use the New-NetQosTrafficClass cmdlet, as in the following example:

```
new-netqostrafficclass -name "smb class" -priority 2 -bandwidthpercentage 60 -algorithm ets
```

In this example, you are creating a new traffic class for SMB traffic, using 60 percent of the network bandwidth, with a priority of 2. The Algorithm parameter specifies which of two transmission selection algorithms, EBS or Strict, defined in the DCB standard the traffic class should use.

Create QoS policies

A quality of service (QoS) policy specifies the type of traffic to which a class is dedicated. To create a QoS policy, you use the New-NetQosPolicy cmdlet, as in the following example:

```
new-netqospolicy -name "smb policy" -smb -priorityvalue8021action 2
```

In this example, the Smb parameter filters the traffic based on Traffic Control Protocol (TCP) and User Datagram Protocol (UDP) port 445, which is the well-known port reserved for SMB traffic. The cmdlet accepts the following filter parameters:

- **SMB** Filters traffic matching TCP or UDP port 445
- **iSCSI** Filters traffic matching TCP or UDP port 3260
- **NFS** Filters traffic matching TCP or UDP port 2049
- **LiveMigration** Filters traffic matching TCP port 6600
- **NetDirect portnumber** Filters traffic matching the specified port number
- **Default** Matches all traffic not otherwise classified

In addition to these predefined filters, you can also identify a traffic type in other ways, using the parameters like the following:

- **AppPathNameMatchCondition** Filters traffic generated by an executable file
- **IPDstPortMatchCondition** Filters traffic based on a specific destination port number
- **IpDstPrefixMatchCondition** Filters traffic based on a specific destination IPv4 or IPv6 address

Enabling Priority-based Flow Control (PFC)

Priority-based Flow Control (PFC), as defined by one of the DCB standards, is a method of regulating network traffic, to provide lossless data transmissions. Typically, you would enable PFC for storage traffic that cannot tolerate packet loss.

To enable PFC for a specific traffic priority, you use the Enable-NetQosFlowControl cmdlet, as in the following example:

```
enable-netqosflowcontrol -priority 3
```

Configure Multipath I/O (MPIO)

Multipath I/O is a Windows Server 2016 feature that enables a server connected to iSCSI, Fibre Channel, or Serial Attached SCSI (SAS) SAN devices to revert to an alternate path through the network when a connection fails.

To implement Multipath I/O, you must have the following components:

- **Multipath I/O feature**   Windows Server 2016 includes a Multipath I/O feature, which you install using the Add Roles And Features Wizard in Server Manager or the Install-WindowsFeature cmdlet in PowerShell.

- **Device Specific Module (DSM)**   Every network adapter or host bus adapter in the server that connects to the SAN must have a DSM. The Multipath I/O implementation in Windows Server 2016 includes a DSM that is compatible with many devices, but some might require a hardware-specific DSM supplied by the manufacturer.

- **Redundant network components**   The server, the network, and the storage device must have redundant components providing separate paths through the network. This means that the server must have at least two network adapters or host bus adapters connected to different network segments and different switches, so that a failure of any component still leaves an available path to the destination. MPIO can support up to 32 redundant paths.

Once you have installed the Multipath I/O feature, you can access the MPIO Properties sheet by selecting Tools | MPIO in Server Manager. By default, the MPIO Devices tab appears, as shown in Figure 2-50.

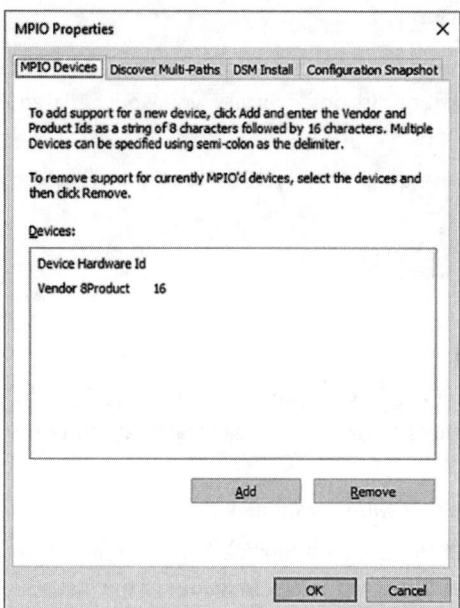

FIGURE 2-50 The MPIO Devices tab on the MPIO Properties sheet

Only the Microsoft DSM appears in the Devices box initially. To add DSMs supplied by the manufacturer of your hardware, select the DSM Install tab, as shown in Figure 2-51, browse to the location of the INF file supplied with the DSM, and click Install. This method only applies to DSMs that are not supplied with their own installation software.

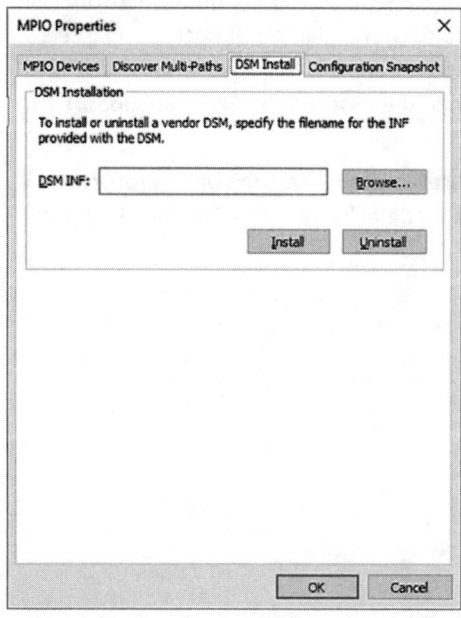

FIGURE 2-51 The DSM Install tab on the MPIO Properties sheet

The Discover Multi-Paths tab, shown in Figure 2-52, displays devices for which MPIO has detected multiple paths through the network. By default, iSCSI devices do not appear on this tab, but you can enable them by selecting the Add Support For iSCSI Devices check box.

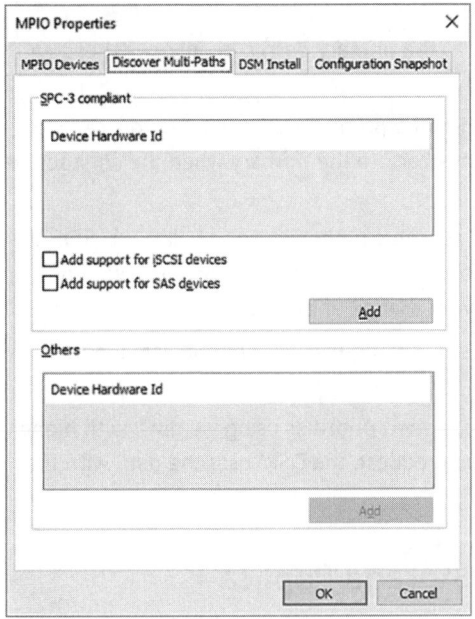

FIGURE 2-52 The Discover Multi-Paths tab on the MPIO Properties sheet

> **NOTE IDENTIFYING DEVICES**
>
> Devices in the MPIO Properties sheet are identified by their hardware IDs, which consist of an eight-character vendor ID (VID) plus a 16-character product ID (PID). The combination is sometimes called a VID/PID.

Detecting devices

Windows Server 2016 relies on Plug and Play (PnP) to detect and identify the storage devices to which the server is connected. Without Multipath I/O, a server with two network interfaces connected to a single storage device would be seen by PnP as two storage devices.

With MPIO installed, each time PnP detects a new storage device, the MPIO driver scans the available DSMs to find the one that corresponds to the device. Once the DSM claims the device, the MPIO driver verifies that the device is active and ready for data. When PnP detects the same device again through a different network interface, the MPIO driver and the DSM identify it as such and create a multipath group that is addressed using a single identifier.

DSM policies

In addition to failover, Multipath I/O can also support load balancing, in which storage requests use different paths to the SAN device to minimize network traffic congestion. The Microsoft DSM supports the following policies:

- **Failover**   The server designates one path as the primary path and only switches to a secondary path when the primary fails.
- **Failback**   The server designates one path as the primary path, switches to a secondary path when the primary fails, and switches back to the primary when the connection is restored.
- **Round Robin**   The DSM uses each of the available paths in turn to balance traffic among them. Variations include a round robin using a set of primary paths, with one or more paths reserved as a standby in the event that all of the primaries fail.
- **Dynamic Least Queue Depth**   For each storage request, the DSM selects the path with the fewest outstanding requests.
- **Weighted Path**   The available paths are assigned priorities using weights, with higher numbers indicating a lower priority. For each request, the DSM uses the path with the lowest weight.

Determine usage scenarios for Storage Replica

Storage Replica (SR) is a Windows Server 2016 feature that enables administrators to replicate volumes, synchronously or asynchronously, for disaster preparedness and disaster recovery purposes. The storage devices to be replicated can be located in the same computer, the same datacenter, or in distant cities.

Storage Replica supports two types of replication: synchronous and asynchronous.

- **Synchronous replication**   Data is written to two destinations at the same time before the acknowledgment of the I/O request to the originating application. In SR, this occurs when the replicated volumes share a fast connection, and data can be mirrored between volumes immediately. This type of replication ensures that there will be no data loss if a failure occurs and the system must fail over to a volume replica.
- **Asynchronous replication**   Data is written to a single destination and acknowledged immediately. Then, it is replicated to a second destination, with acknowledgment sent to the replication partner, but not to the original application that generated the write request. In SR, this occurs when the volumes are connected using a relatively slow technology, usually over longer distances, such as a WAN link. The data write is acknowledged quickly, and the data is mirrored between the volumes, but there is no guarantee that the data will be identical at any given time, in the event of a failure.

Storage Replica is designed to function in three primary scenarios, as follows:

- **Server-to-server**   Provides synchronous or asynchronous replication between local or shared storage volumes on two standalone servers, as shown in Figure 2-53. The servers can be using Storage Spaces with local disks, SAN storage, or shared SAS. Failover of one server to the replica is manual.

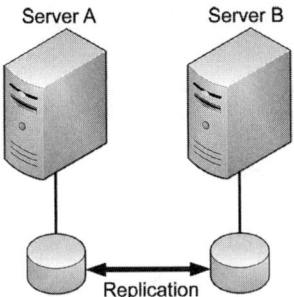

FIGURE 2-53 Storage Replica server-to-server configuration

- **Cluster-to-cluster** Provides synchronous or asynchronous replication between two clusters, as shown in Figure 2-54. The clusters can be using Storage Spaces with SAN storage or shared SAS, or Storage Spaces Direct. Failover of one cluster to the replica is manual.

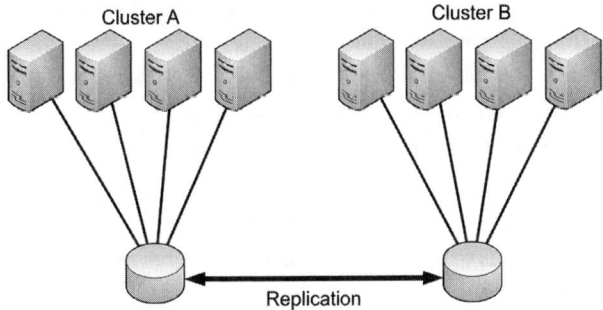

FIGURE 2-54 Storage Replica cluster-to-cluster configuration

- **Stretch cluster** Provides synchronous or asynchronous replication between the storage devices in an asymmetric cluster. In a stretch cluster, the cluster nodes are divided between two sites, each with its own storage, as shown in Figure 2-55. The cluster sites can be using Storage Spaces with SAN storage or shared SAS, or Storage Spaces Direct. The stretch cluster configuration is the only one supported by Storage Replica that includes an automated failover capability.

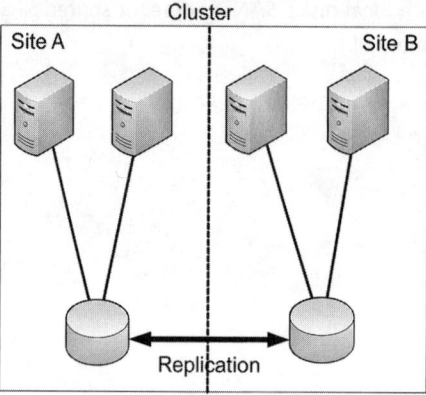

FIGURE 2-55 Storage Replica stretch cluster configuration

While there are many applications for data replication, SR is designed to provide failover capabilities if an equipment failure or other disaster occurs. By replicating your data to another room, another building, or another city, you can easily shift your workload to another location after, or even before, a catastrophic event occurs. In the event of an imminent disaster, such as an approaching hurricane, an organization with its data replicated to a server or node or cluster in another city is prepared to revert to the replica at a few minutes' notice.

SR replication is one-way, from a designated source volume to a destination volume. When you create the replication partnership between them, SR dismounts the destination volume and its drive letter or mount point. The destination volume is therefore not accessible to users while it is involved in a replication partnership. If a failure (or a test) should occur, and you need to access the replication, you remove the partnership and the destination volume becomes available again.

Thus, in a server-to-server or cluster-to-cluster scenario, the failover is manual, but in a stretch cluster, because there are nodes from the same cluster already at the alternate location, along with the replicated data, the failover is automatic.

The replication performed by Storage Replica is designed to improve on Windows tools that administrators might have used in the past, such as Distributed File System (DFS) Replication, which is file-based and exclusively asynchronous. SR uses SMB version 3 for its communication, which provides features such as multichannel link aggregation, data encryption, and digital signatures. The replication is also block-based, not file-based, as in DFS Replication. Because of this, there are no issues of data missing in the replica due to open files that could not be accessed by the replication process.

Even when running asynchronously, RA replication operates continuously; it is not based on checkpoints, which can result is more lost data, depending on the time since the last checkpoint when a failure occurs. The potential for data loss during asynchronous operation is typically based only on the latency of the connection between the replication volumes.

Implement Storage Replica for server-to-server, cluster-to-cluster, and stretch cluster scenarios

Implementing Storage Replica on your network requires careful planning and a lot of prerequisites. Creating the replication partnership is simply a matter of running one PowerShell cmdlet (New-SRPartnership), but this happens at the end of the procedure.

Storage Replica is a Windows feature that is available only in the Datacenter edition of Windows Server 2016. You install the feature through the Add Roles and Features Wizard in Server Manager or by running the following PowerShell command:

```
install-windowsfeature -name storage-replica, fs-fileserver -includemanagementtools -restart
```

> **NOTE INSTALLING FILE SERVER WITH SR**
> The File Server role service (FS-FileServer) is not required for the operation of Storage Replica itself. It is included because it is required to run the Test-SRTopology cmdlet.

The next step is to prepare the storage infrastructure for replication. The individual tasks for this part of the procedure vary depending on whether you are using the server-to-server, cluster-to-cluster, or stretch cluster scenario. After you configure the server or cluster storage infrastructure, all three scenarios proceed with testing the replication topology and creating the SR partnership between servers.

Preparing the storage infrastructure

To use SR, the servers that will function as the replication partners, whether standalone or in a cluster, must be running Windows Server 2016 Datacenter edition. Two gigabytes of memory in each server is the bare minimum; at least four gigabytes is recommended. In addition, the infrastructure should be configured as follows:

- Each server, cluster, or cluster site must have its own storage infrastructure. A server-to-server implementation is the only one that can use internal disks, but all the scenarios can use virtually any kind of external disk technology, including iSCSI, a Fibre Channel SAN, or SAS. In each case, however, a mixture of SSD and HDD drives is recommended.
- To provision the storage, you use Storage Spaces to create at least two virtual disks, one for logs and one for data, with the SSD drives being used for the log volume. All the physical disks used for the logs in both replication partners must use the same sector size, as must all the physical disks used for data. All the disks must use the GPT partition style. None of the replicated storage can be located on the system disk containing the operating system. The data volumes on the two replication partners must be the same size; the log volumes must also be the same size, at least 9 GB. The data volumes can use tiered storage, and mirrored or parity disks.

- The network connecting the replication partners should have sufficient speed and bandwidth to support your workload, with a ~5ms round-trip latency, to support synchronous replication. There is no recommended latency for asynchronous operation.

- All servers must be joined to an Active Directory Domain Services (AD DS) domain, although the domain controllers do not necessarily have to be running Windows Server 2016.

- Firewall rules for the replication partners must allow the following traffic in both directions: Internet Control Message Protocol, SMB (ports 445, and 5445 for SMB Direct), and Web Services Management (WS-MAN, port 5985).

Testing the SR topology

Among the PowerShell cmdlets included with the SR feature is one called Test-SRTopology, which runs a variety of prerequisite and performance tests on the two servers that become replication partners and their network connection, and creates an HTML report containing the results.

The cmdlet takes parameters specifying the names of the servers that become the source and destination replication partners, the volumes to be replicated, the length of the test, and the location for the resulting report, as shown in the following example:

```
test-srtopology -sourcecomputername servera -sourcevolumename f: -sourcelogvolumename e:
-destinationcomputername serverb -destinationvolumename f: -destinationlogvolumename e:
-durationinminutes 30 -resultpath c:temp
```

The cmdlet initially checks whether the servers and the storage subsystems meet the requirements for SR, as shown in Figure 2-56.

Requirements Tests

The following tests were attempted. Hover over each test below to get more details.

Test
Volume Availability Test: Volume **F:** exists on **RTMSvrH**
Volume Availability Test: Volume **E:** exists on **RTMSvrH**
Volume Availability Test: Volume **F:** exists on **RTMSvrI**
Volume Availability Test: Volume **E:** exists on **RTMSvrI**
Partition Style Test: Partition **F:** on **RTMSvrH** is a GPT-style partition
Partition Style Test: Partition **E:** on **RTMSvrH** is a GPT-style partition
Partition Style Test: Partition **F:** on **RTMSvrI** is a GPT-style partition
Partition Style Test: Partition **E:** on **RTMSvrI** is a GPT-style partition
Volume Size Test: Volume **F:** on **RTMSvrH** and **F:** on **RTMSvrI** are identical in size
File System Test: File system on volume **E:** on **RTMSvrH** is **NTFS**
File System Test: File system on volume **E:** on **RTMSvrI** is **NTFS**
Disk Sector Size Test: Sector size of the volume **F:** on **RTMSvrH** and **F:** on **RTMSvrI** is identical
Log Disk Sector Size Test: Sector size of the volume **E:** on **RTMSvrH** and **E:** on **RTMSvrI** is identical
Log Volume Free Disk Space Test: The log volume **E:** in **RTMSvrH** has enough free space to hold the recommended log volume size of **8GB**
Log Volume Free Disk Space Test: The log volume **E:** in **RTMSvrI** has enough free space to hold the recommended log volume size of **8GB**
Remote Server Management Test: Target server **RTMSvrI** can be managed remotely using WMI
SMB Connectivity Test: Firewalls are configured to allow SMB protocol traffic to and from **RTMSvrI**

FIGURE 2-56 Storage Replica requirements test results

Then, the cmdlet runs performance tests for a time interval that you specify in the command line. The ideal way to run this test is while the source server is running under its usual workload. The test proceeds to measure the synchronization performance between the source and the destination, to determine if the throughput is sufficient for synchronous replication, and presents the results in a chart, as shown in Figure 2-57.

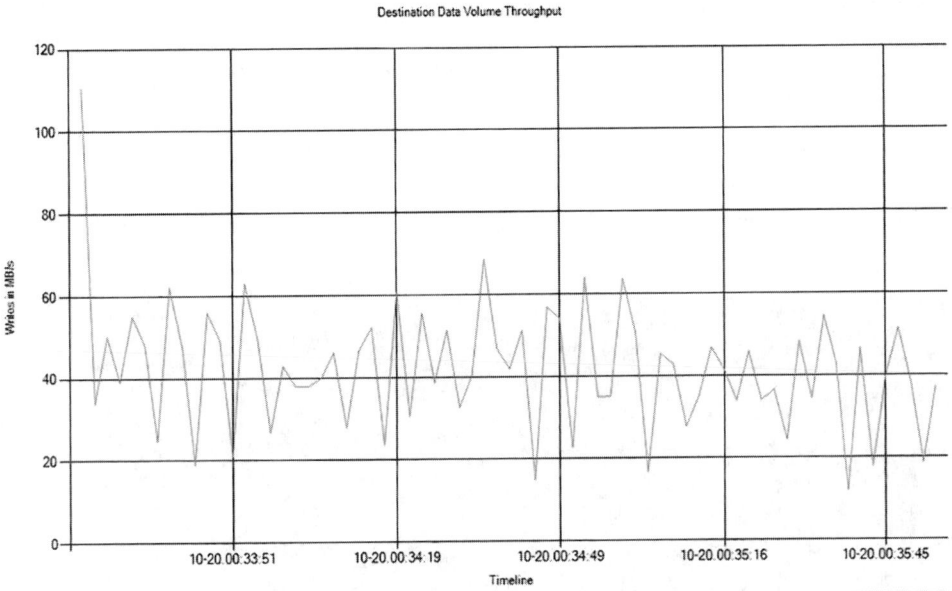

FIGURE 2-57 Storage Replica throughput test results

Configuring clustering

After configuring the replication partners, you can proceed to implement the clustering solution, for the cluster-to-cluster or stretch cluster scenarios. For the cluster-to-cluster scenario, you create two separate failover clusters, in the normal manner. Then, you configure each cluster to have full access to the other, using the Grant-SRAccess cmdlet, as in the following examples:

```
grant-sraccess -computername servera -cluster clustera

grant-sraccess -computername serverb -cluster clusterb
```

For a stretch cluster scenario, you create the cluster and make the replication source disk a cluster shared volume (CSV), using the Add-ClusterSharedVolume cmdlet. You can also do that and create the replication partnership using the graphical Failover Cluster Manager console.

Creating the SR partnership

Assuming that your servers and storage infrastructure have passed the Test-SRTopology checks, and your cluster(s) are in place, you can proceed to establish the actual replication partnership between the source and the destination servers. You do this by running the New-SRPartnership cmdlet, with many of the same parameters as Test-SRTopology, as in the following example:

```
new-srpartnership -sourcecomputername servera -sourcergname group1 -sourcevolumename
f: -sourcelogvolumename e: -destinationcomputername serverb -destinationrgname group2
-destinationvolumename f: -destinationlogvolumename e:
```

Once you create the partnership, the initial synchronization begins, which can take some time, depending on the size of the volumes. To monitor the replication progress, you can use the Get-WinEvent cmdlet to check the Windows event logs for the following codes: 5015, 5002, 5004, 1237, 5001, and 2200, as shown in Figure 2-58.

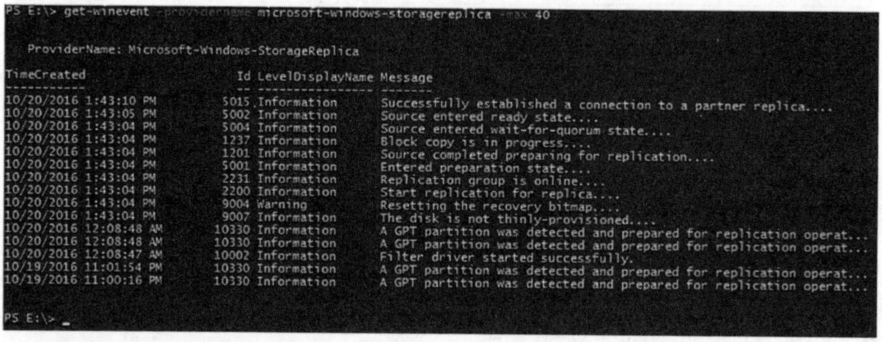

FIGURE 2-58 Storage Replica event log entries

You can also display the status of the partnership using the Get-SRGroup cmdlet, as shown in Figure 2-59.

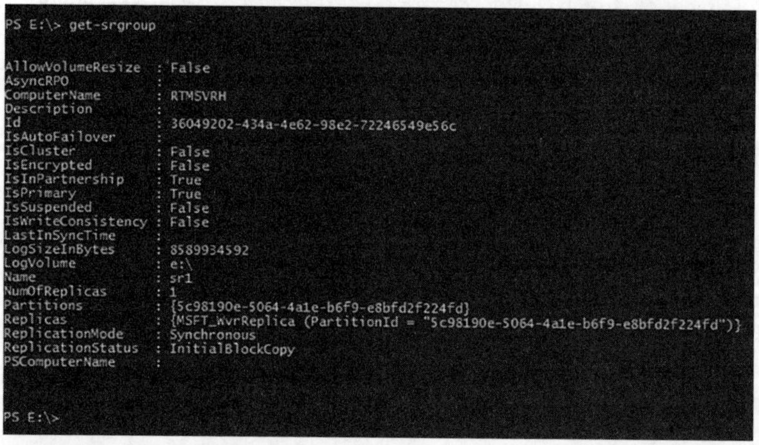

FIGURE 2-59 Storage Replica event log entries

Once the synchronization partnership is in place, you can trigger a failover by using the Set-SRPartnership cmdlet to reverse the source and destination roles, as in the following example. This makes the destination volumes available for use again.

```
set-srpartnership -newsourcecomputername serverb -sourcergname group2
-destinationcomputername servera -destinationrgname group1
```

Skill 2.3: Implement data deduplication

Data deduplication is a role service in Windows Server 2016 that conserves storage space on an NTFS volume by locating redundant data and storing one only copy of that data instead of multiple copies. This is the basic operating principle for many data compression products, but Data Duplication improves on many other technologies by operating at the volume level, and not the file level.

> **This section covers how to:**
> - Implement and configure deduplication
> - Determine appropriate usage scenarios for deduplication
> - Monitor deduplication
> - Implement a backup and restore solution with deduplication

Implement and configure deduplication

To use Data Deduplication on your volumes, you must first install the Data Deduplication role service, which is part of the File and Storage Services Role. You can do this using the Add Roles And Features Wizard, or by using the Install-WindowsFeature cmdlet in PowerShell, as follows:

```
install-windowsfeature -name fs-data-deduplication
```

Once Data Deduplication is installed, you manage it in Server Manager or by using PowerShell cmdlets.

Configuring deduplication using server manager

To use data deduplication, you must enable it on specific volumes. To do this in Server Manager, use the following procedure.

1. In Server Manager, click File And Storage Services, Volumes. The Volumes page appears.
2. Right-click one of the volumes in the Volumes tile and, in the context menu, select Configure Data Deduplication. The Deduplication Settings dialog box for the selected volume appears, as shown in Figure 2-60.

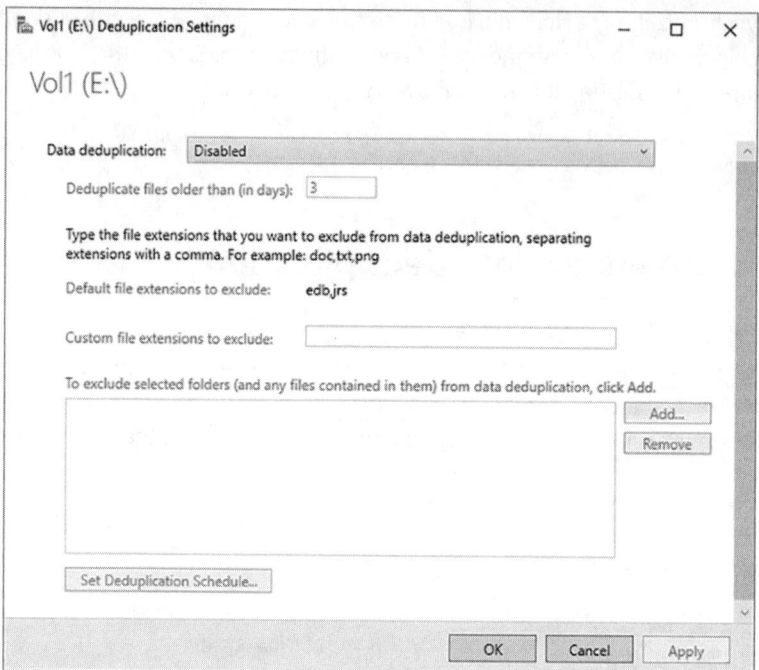

FIGURE 2-60 The Deduplication Settings dialog box

3. In the Data Deduplication drop-down list, select one of the following options:
   - **Disabled**   Prevents any duplication from occurring
   - **General Purpose File Server**   Intended for use with typical file server functions, such as shared folders, Work Folders, and Folder Redirection. Deduplication occurs in the background, and in-use files are ignored.
   - **Virtual Desktop Infrastructure (VDI) Server**   Intended for use with Hyper-V. Deduplication occurs in the background, and in-use and partial files are optimized.
   - **Virtualized Backup Server**   Intended for use with backup applications, such as Microsoft DPM. Deduplication is a priority process, and in-use files are optimized.
4. In the Deduplicate Files Older Than box, specify in days how old files must be before they are deduplicated.
5. The Default File Extensions To Exclude list specifies file types that will not be deduplicated, based on the option you chose in the Data Deduplication drop-down list. To exclude additional file types, specify their file name extensions in the Custom File Extensions To Exclude text box.
6. Click Add to open a Select Folder dialog box, in which you specify any folders that you want to be excluded from the deduplication process.
7. Click Set Duplication Schedule. The Deduplication Schedule dialog box for the selected volume appears, as shown in Figure 2-61.

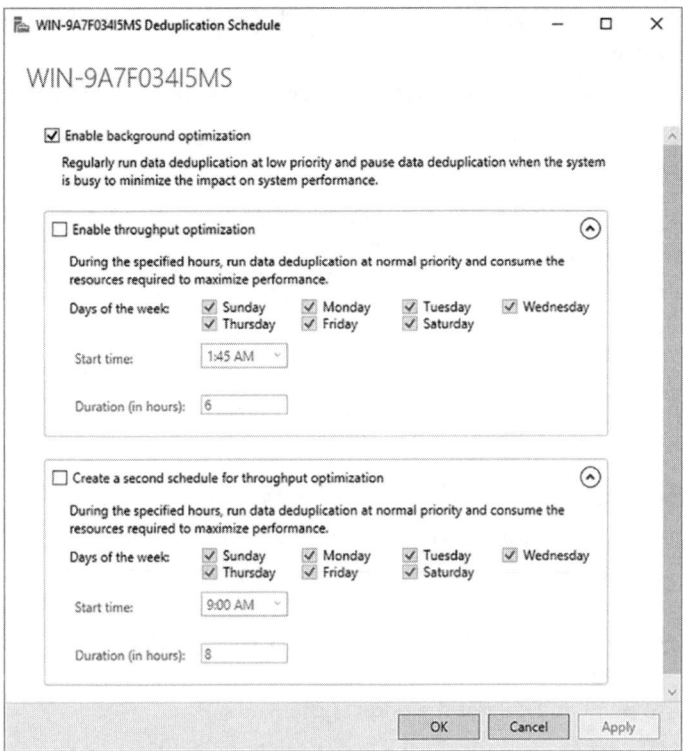

FIGURE 2-61 The Deduplication Schedule dialog box

8. By default, deduplication occurs in the background, as a low-priority process, when the system is not busy. To create a schedule for running the deduplication with normal priority and maximum performance, select the Enable Throughput Optimization check box.
9. Select the days of the week, the time of day, and the duration of the deduplication process.
10. Optionally, create another scheduled deduplication process by selecting the Create A Second Schedule For Throughput Optimization check box and configuring the days, time, and duration. Then click OK.
11. Click OK to close the Deduplication Settings dialog box.

Configuring deduplication using PowerShell

To enable deduplication for a volume using PowerShell, you run the Enable-DedupVolume cmdlet, as in the following example:

```
enable-dedupvolume -volume "e:" -usagetype default
```

The functions of the parameters are as follows:

- **UsageType** Specifies the type of workload for which the selected volume is used. The possible values are as follows:
    - **Default** Corresponds to the General Purpose File Server option in Server Manager
    - **Hyper-V** Corresponds to the Virtual Desktop Infrastructure (VDI) Server option in Server Manager
    - **Backup** Corresponds to the Virtualized Backup Server option in Server Manage
- **Volume** Specifies the volume on which to enable deduplication, using the format "X:" You can separate multiple volumes with commas, or specify a GUID instead of a drive letter, as in the following example:

```
enable-dedupvolume -volume "\\?\volume{26a21bda-a627-11d7-9931-806e6f6e6963}" -usagetype backup
```

Determine appropriate usage scenarios for deduplication

Data deduplication optimizes a volume by selecting the files that are candidates for optimization, breaking them up into variable-sized chunks, and scanning them for their uniqueness. A chunk that is unique is copied to a separate area of the disk, called the *chunk store*, and replaced in its original locations by a special tag called a *reparse point*, directing it to the chunk's new location. If a chunk is identical to one that already exists in the store, the system replaces it with a reparse point and deletes the original chunk.

This principle of deduplication has existed for a long time, but many other products use it on individual files. Data deduplication in Windows Server 2016 works on the entire volume, not on one file at a time. Therefore, instead of having a copy of the same unique chunk in every file, there is only one copy for the entire volume. In the case of the Single Instance Store (SIS) technology in earlier versions of Windows Server, which data deduplication replaces, a volume maintains a single copy of an entire file, instead of multiple duplicates. Chunks, being typically smaller than files, have a much greater chance of being duplicated on a volume, thus generating a greater compression rate.

When an application or a user requests read access to an optimized file, the system uses the reparse points to redirect the request to the appropriate locations in the chunk store. The requestor is completely unaware that the file has been deduplicated.

If the application or user modifies the file, the system writes it back to the volume in its standard, unoptimized form. The file remains unoptimized until the next deduplication job occurs. This accumulation of unoptimized files due to the volume's workload is called *churn*. The post-processing nature of the system prevents any delay or interference with the volume writes.

Data deduplication also performs other jobs besides optimizations. *Garbage collection* is the term for a job that searches the chunk store for chunks that no longer have reparse points associated with them, typically due to modified or deleted files. *Integrity scrubbing* is a job that searches for damage or corruption in the chunk store, replacing the missing data with mirror or parity data. Finally, *unoptimization* is a job that restores all of the optimized files on a volume to their original states, disabling Data Deduplication for that volume in the process.

Optimization rates

The amount of storage space freed up by the application of data deduplication to a volume is dependent on multiple factors, including the formats of the files and the nature of the workload that generated the data. In traditional, file-based compression products, a software binary file might compress at 80 percent, and a bitmap image at 80 percent. If you were to apply the data deduplication process to a single file, the results are likely to be similar.

However, when you apply the deduplication process to an entire volume, you are comparing chunks to a much larger pool. While you might find 10 identical copies of a specific chunk in a single file, comparing that same chunk to an entire volume might yield thousands or millions of copies. Therefore, the space savings resulting from the disk deduplication process tend to be far higher than those from file-based compression.

Take, as an example, a volume that contains many Hyper-V VHD image files, all of which contain Windows 10 guest operating system installations used by a software development team. Since the contents of the VHD files will all be very similar, there will be a great many identical chunks. Microsoft estimates the storage space savings for a volume containing image files like these to be 80 to 95 percent. Thus, a nearly full volume containing 1 TB of data can be reduced to 100 GB or less, leaving 900 GB of newly created free space.

This is a best case example. A volume on a file server containing a typical mixture of user files might optimize at 50 to 60 percent.

Evaluating workloads

Before implementing data deduplication on your volumes, you should consider whether the workloads that generate your data are good candidates for optimization. The factors that can affect this decision include the nature of the work load that generates the data and the nature of the data itself.

The optimization process imposes a burden on a server's processor and memory resources that can have a significant effect on server performance. Because data deduplication uses a post-processing model, there is no effect on performance as the data write occurs. However, you should consider whether your workflow allows for a period when the optimization can occur without compromising production. A workflow that is idle at night is a good candidate for deduplication, in this respect, but one that operates around the clock might not be.

The next consideration is the data itself. The usage scenarios that are predefined in data deduplication are ones in which the data involved is particularly susceptible to redundancy. They are therefore good candidates for optimization. For example, on general purpose file servers, users often tend to store multiple copies of the same files. In the same way, software developers typically store multiple builds that differ only slightly. However, if a volume contains a large amount of encrypted files, the encryption will hide the redundancy, preventing data deduplication from being effective.

Data deduplication includes a Data Deduplication Savings Evaluation Tool (Ddpeval.exe) that you can use to test a volume to see how much storage savings can result from optimization. Ddpeval is a command line tool that you run, by specifying a drive letter to evaluate. The results specify how much saving you can expect in the selected data set, as shown in Figure 2-62.

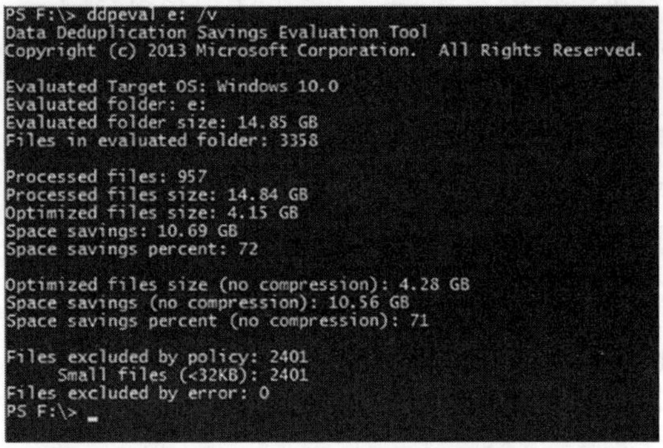

```
PS F:\> ddpeval e: /v
Data Deduplication Savings Evaluation Tool
Copyright (c) 2013 Microsoft Corporation.  All Rights Reserved.

Evaluated Target OS: Windows 10.0
Evaluated folder: e:
Evaluated folder size: 14.85 GB
Files in evaluated folder: 3358

Processed files: 957
Processed files size: 14.84 GB
Optimized files size: 4.15 GB
Space savings: 10.69 GB
Space savings percent: 72

Optimized files size (no compression): 4.28 GB
Space savings (no compression): 10.56 GB
Space savings percent (no compression): 71

Files excluded by policy: 2401
      Small files (<32KB): 2401
Files excluded by error: 0
PS F:\>
```

FIGURE 2-62 Output of the Ddpeval program

Other types of data might not be good candidates for optimization because of the way in which they store and access data. Data deduplication tries to organize the chunk store along file boundaries. A file read request will, in many cases, require access to successive chunks in the store, which enhances performance. Database files, however, tend to have read patterns that are more random, and the way that data deduplication stores a chunked database might require a read process to access chunks scattered all over the disk, decreasing efficiency. Before implementing data deduplication on a production server, you should perform a test deployment, to determine whether the realized savings can offset any performance degradation that might occur.

Monitor deduplication

Once you have installed data deduplication and enabled it on volumes, the Volumes tile in Server Manager is modified to include Deduplication Rate and Deduplication Savings columns, as shown in Figure 2-63. The Deduplication Rate specifies the percentage of the files' original disk space that has been cleared, and the Deduplication Saving specifies the amount of disk space cleared, in gigabytes.

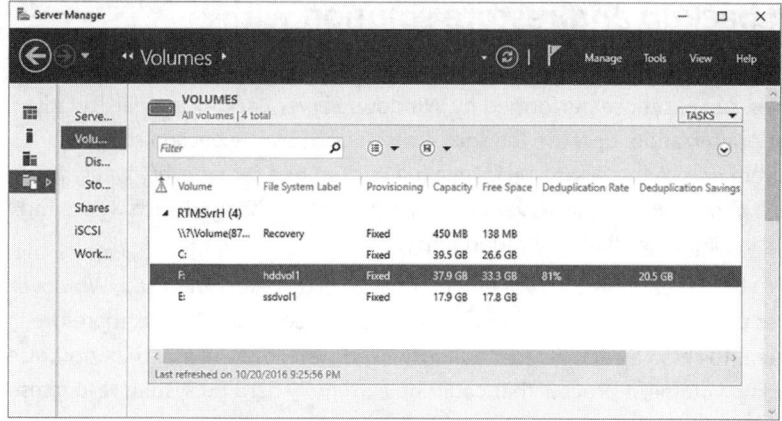

FIGURE 2-63 The Volumes tile in Server Manager

You can also monitor the deduplication process using PowerShell with the Get-Dedup-Status cmdlet. When you run the cmdlet by itself, it displays only a few statistics. To see the entire display, as shown in Figure 2-64, pipe the output to the Format-List cmdlet, as follows:

```
get-dedupostatus | format-list
```

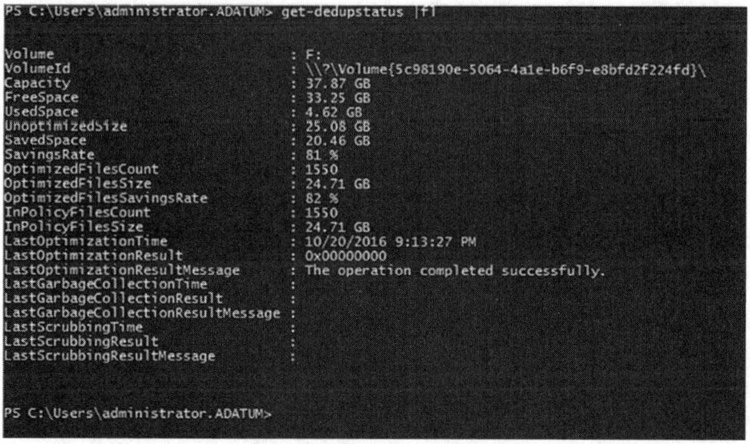

FIGURE 2-64 Output of the Get-DedupStatus cmdlet

A LastOptimizationResult value of zero indicates that the operation was successful. If, after the initial deduplication, jobs start to show as being unsuccessful, it is typically because the deduplication process did not have enough time to keep up with the changes generated by the workload (called the *churn*). You might have to increase the duration of the deduplication jobs, or the priority allotted to them, to resolve the problem.

To monitor the history of a server's deduplication jobs, you can review the Windows event logs. Data deduplication events are located in the Applications and Services Logs\Windows\Deduplication\Operational container.

Implement a backup and restore solution with deduplication

Backups to disk drives, such as those performed by Windows Server Backup, are particularly good candidates for optimization, because the snapshots created by the backup software tend to differ little from each other. If you perform a full backup of a server every week, for example, only a small percentage of the server data is likely to have changed each week, and data deduplication can eliminate all of that redundancy.

In addition, when you are backing up a volume that has already been optimized, Windows Server Backup copies the data to the backup target in its optimized state. There is therefore no need for the system to restore each file to its unoptimized state, copy it, and then optimize the copy on the backup volume, a process that could be extremely hard on system resources.

The Virtualized Backup Server usage option is designed specifically to work with backup software solutions like Microsoft System Center Data Protection Manager (DPM), in which the backup software runs on a Hyper-V virtual machine and stores its backups in VHD or VHDX files on a volume with data deduplication enabled.

Because a backup job can generate a relatively large amount of new data, the optimization settings for the backup scenario differ from those of the other presets, in that they enable the optimization process to run with a high priority on the server. Administrators must monitor the optimization jobs on a regular basis, to ensure that they are keeping up with this higher rate of churn than is typically found on a general-purpose file server.

Chapter summary

- The GUID Partition Table (GPT) is an alternative to the Master Boot Record partition style. GPT supports larger disks than MBR, allows for the creation of more partitions, and provides better recovery from disk errors that corrupt the partition table.
- Windows supports a virtual hard disk (VHD) format that you can use on Hyper-V guests or other purposes. You can create image files using VHD or the newer VHDX format with the Disk Management snap-in or the New-VHD cmdlet in Windows PowerShell.
- VHD and VHDX image files can be mounted on a physical or virtual computer, so that they function just like physical disks.
- Windows Server 2016 includes support for the NTFS file system, as well as the newer ReFS file system, which supports larger volumes, but lacks some of the NTFS capabilities.
- Windows can share folders using SMB, the original standard for Windows drive sharing, and NFS, which the standard used on many UNIX and Linux distributions.

- Windows PowerShell includes a collection of cmdlets that you can use to manage folder shares and their permissions.
- NTFS has a system of permissions that you can use to authorize specific degrees of user access to files and folders.
- Storage Spaces enables administrators to create storage pools out of physical disks. They can then create virtual disks from the pooled storage, irrespective of the boundaries between physical disks.
- Virtual disks in storage pools can be configured to use mirroring, in which data is stored in duplicate, and parity, in which data bits are stored with parity information for data recovery purposes.
- Tiered storage is a feature of virtual disks that uses faster SSD drives in a storage pool to store the most frequently used files.
- iSCSI is a storage area networking protocol that enables Windows servers (called initiators) to connect to storage devices (called targets) using standard Ethernet hardware.
- iSNS is essentially a registry for iSCSI components that enables initiators to locate the targets available on the network.
- Datacenter Bridging (DCB) is a mechanism for separating LAN and SAN traffic on a converged network. DCB works by creating classes of network traffic that are assigned a specific percentage of the available bandwidth.
- Multipath I/O is a fault tolerance mechanism that enables a server to access a networked storage device through redundant paths, in the event of a component failure.
- Storage Replica is a feature in the Datacenter edition that enables administrators to create replication partnerships between servers, between clusters, or within a stretch cluster.
- Data Deduplication is a Windows Server 2016 feature that conserves storage space by splitting files into chunks and storing only one copy each redundant chunk. By operating on entire volumes instead of individual files, the savings rate for many data types can range from 50% to over 90%.
- Data Deduplication has three predefined usage scenarios that contain settings to maximize storage savings and server performance.
- Once enabled, you can use PowerShell cmdlets and Windows Event logs to monitor the ongoing progress of Data Deduplication jobs.
- Data Deduplication is particularly suitable for backup targets because of the redundant nature of the data stored there.

Thought experiment

In this thought experiment, demonstrate your skills and knowledge of the topics covered in this chapter. You can find answer to this thought experiment in the next section.

You are working the help desk for Contoso Corp., a government contractor, and a user named Ralph calls to request access to the files for Alamo, a new classified project. The Alamo project files are stored in a shared folder on a Windows Server 2016 workgroup file server, which is locked in a secured underground data storage facility. After verifying that Ralph has the appropriate security clearance for the project, you create a new group on the file server called ALAMO_USERS and add Ralph's user account to that group. Then, you add the ALAMO_USER group to the access control list for the Alamo folder on the file server, and assign the group the following NTFS permissions:

- Allow Modify
- Allow Read & Execute
- Allow List Folder Contents
- Allow Read
- Allow Write

Sometime later, Ralph calls you to tell you that he is able to access the Alamo folder and read the files stored there, but he has been unable to save changes back to the server. What is the most likely cause of the problem?

Thought experiment answer

This section contains the solution to the thought experiment.

Ralph probably does not have sufficient share permissions for read/write access to the Alamo files. By default, when you share a folder on a workgroup server using File Explorer, the Everyone special identity receives only the Read share permission. After you grant the ALAMO_USER group the Allow Full Control share permission, Ralph should be able to save his changes to the Alamo files.

CHAPTER 3

Implement Hyper-V

Hyper-V is the hypervisor and hardware virtualization platform incorporated into Windows Server 2016 as a role. Using Hyper-V, you can create virtual machines (VMs) that consist of virtualized equivalents of computer hardware, storage resources, and network components, such as network interface adapters and switches. VMs function like physical computers, but administrators can easily save them, move them, and reconfigure them to accommodate their needs.

Skills in this chapter:
- Install and configure Hyper-V
- Configure virtual machine (VM) settings
- Configure Hyper-V storage
- Configure Hyper-V networking

Skill 3.1: Install and configure Hyper-V

Hyper-V is a Windows Server 2016 role that makes it possible to create virtual machines on which you can install an operating system and use as though it is a separate computer. A server running Windows Server 2016 that has the Hyper-V role installed is known as a host. The virtual machines that you create in Hyper-V are known as guests.

> **This section covers how to:**
> - Determine hardware and compatibility requirements for installing Hyper-V
> - Install Hyper-V
> - Install management tools
> - Upgrade from existing versions of Hyper-V
> - Delegate virtual machine management
> - Perform remote management of Hyper-V hosts
> - Configure virtual machines using Windows PowerShell Direct
> - Implement nested virtualization

Determine hardware and compatibility requirements for installing Hyper-V

Windows Server 2016 includes the *Hyper-V* role, which enables you to create virtual machines, each of which runs in its own isolated environment. *Virtual machines (VMs)* are self-contained units that you can easily move from one Hyper-V host server to another, greatly simplifying the process of deploying network applications and services.

Server virtualization in Windows Server 2016 is based on a module called a *hypervisor*. Sometimes called a *virtual machine monitor (VMM)*, the hypervisor is responsible for abstracting the computer's physical hardware and creating a virtualized hardware environment for each virtual machine. Each VM has its own (virtual) hardware configuration and can run a separate copy of an operating system, called a *guest*. Therefore, with sufficient physical hardware and the correct licensing, a single computer running Windows Server 2016 with the Hyper-V role installed can support dozens, or even hundreds, of VMs, which you can manage as though they are standalone computers.

Virtualization architectures

In early virtualization products, including Microsoft Virtual Server, the virtualization software adds the hypervisor component. The hypervisor essentially runs as an application on the host operating system, as shown in Figure 3-1, and enables you to create as many virtual machines as the computer has hardware to support.

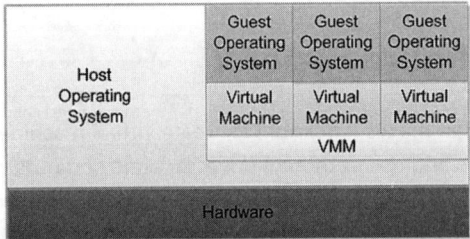

FIGURE 3-1 Type II virtualization

This arrangement, in which the hypervisor runs on top of a host operating system, is called a *Type II virtualization*. The host operating system shares access to the computer's processor with the hypervisor, with each taking the clock cycles it needs and passing control of the processor back to the other.

Type II virtualization can provide adequate virtual machine performance, particularly in classroom and laboratory environments, but it does not provide performance equivalent to separate physical computers. Therefore, it is not recommended for high-traffic servers in production environments.

The Hyper-V virtualization built into Windows Server 2016 uses a different type of architecture. Hyper-V uses *Type I virtualization*, in which the hypervisor is an abstraction layer that interacts directly with the computer's physical hardware—that is, without an intervening host operating system.

The hypervisor creates individual environments called *partitions*, each of which has its own operating system installed and accesses the computer's hardware via the hypervisor. Unlike Type II virtualization, no host operating system shares processor time with the hypervisor. Instead, the hypervisor designates the first partition it creates as the parent partition and all subsequent partitions as child partitions, as shown in Figure 3-2.

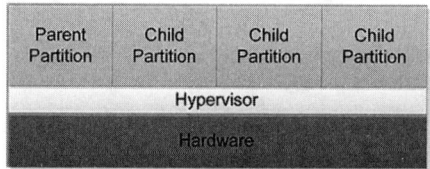

FIGURE 3-2 Type 1 virtualization

The parent partition accesses the system hardware through the hypervisor, just as the child partitions do. The only difference is that the parent runs the virtualization stack, which creates and manages the child partitions. The parent partition is also responsible for the subsystems that directly affect the performance of the computer's physical hardware, such as Plug and Play, power management, and error handling. These subsystems run in the operating systems on the child partitions as well, but they address only virtual hardware, whereas the parent, or root, partition handles the real thing.

Hyper-V hardware limitations

The Windows Server 2016 version of Hyper-V contains improvements in the scalability of the system over previous versions. A Windows Server 2016 Hyper-V host system can have up to 512 logical processors, supporting up to 2,048 virtual CPUs and up to 24 terabytes (TB) of physical memory.

One server can host as many as 1,024 active virtual machines, and each Generation 2 virtual machine can have up to 240 virtual CPUs and up to 12 TB of memory. Generation 1 VMs can have up to 64 virtual CPUs and up to 1 TB of memory.

Hyper-V can also support clusters with up to 64 nodes and 8,000 virtual machines.

> **NOTE HYPER-V SERVER**
>
> Microsoft also provides a dedicated Hyper-V Server product, which is a subset of Windows Server 2016. Hyper-V Server 2016 includes the Hyper-V role, which it installs by default during the operating system installation. Except for some limited File and Storage Services and Remote Desktop capabilities, the operating system includes no other roles.
>
> The Hyper-V Server product is also limited to the Server Core interface, although it also includes Sconfig. a simple, script-based configuration interface, as shown in Figure 3-3. You can also manage Hyper-V Server remotely, using Server Manager and Hyper-V Manager, just as you would with any other Server Core installation.

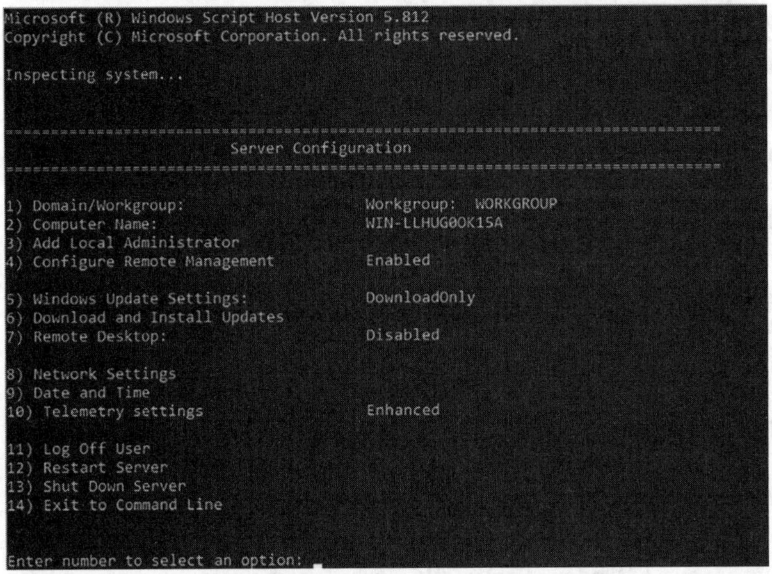

FIGURE 3-3 The Server Core interface in Hyper-V Server

Hyper-V Server is a free product, available for download from the Microsoft website. However, Hyper-V Server does not include any licenses for virtual instances. You must obtain and license all the operating systems you install on the virtual machines you create.

Microsoft recommends that you do not install other roles with Hyper-V. Any other roles that you need the physical computer to perform are better off implemented within one of the virtual machines you create with Hyper-V. You also might want to consider installing Hyper-V on a computer using the Server Core installation option to minimize the overhead expended on the partition. As with other roles, installing Hyper-V on Server Core excludes the management tools, which you must install separately as a feature.

The Hyper-V role has general hardware requirements that exceed those of the Windows Server 2016 operating system itself. Before you can install the Hyper-V role on a server running Windows Server 2016, you must have the following hardware:

- A 64-bit processor that includes hardware-assisted virtualization and second-level address translation (SLAT). This type of virtualization is available in processors that include a virtualization option, such as Intel Virtualization Technology (Intel VT) or AMD Virtualization (AMD-V) technology.
- Hardware-enforced Data Execution Prevention (DEP), which Intel describes as eXecute Disable (XD) and AMD describes as No eXecute (NX). CPUs use this technology to segregate areas of memory for either storage of processor instructions or for storage of data. Specifically, you must enable Intel XD bit (execute disable bit) or AMD NX bit (no execute bit).
- VM Monitor Mode extensions, found on Intel processors as VT-c.
- A system BIOS or UEFI that supports the virtualization hardware and on which the virtualization feature has been enabled.
- A minimum of 4 gigabytes (GB) of memory. In addition to running the Hyper-V host operating system, the computer must have sufficient physical memory for all of the guest operating systems running on the virtual machines.

> **NOTE HYPER-V MANAGEMENT TOOLS**
>
> Virtualization hardware and BIOS/UEFI support is necessary to install the Hyper-V role itself, but it is not necessary to install the Hyper-V management tools. You can manage a Hyper-V server from any remote Windows computer by installing the Hyper-V Management Tools feature.

To determine if a computer has the hardware necessary to install the Hyper-V role, you can open a Windows PowerShell session and run the Systeminfo.exe program, to produce a display like the one shown in Figure 3-4. At the bottom of the listing, the Hyper-V Requirements item lists the computer's hypervisor capabilities.

```
PS C:\Users\Administrator> systeminfo.exe

Host Name:                 CZ10
OS Name:                   Microsoft Windows Server 2016 Datacenter Evaluation
OS Version:                10.0.14393 N/A Build 14393
OS Manufacturer:           Microsoft Corporation
OS Configuration:          Standalone Server
OS Build Type:             Multiprocessor Free
Registered Owner:          N/A
Registered Organization:   N/A
Product ID:                00377-10000-00000-AA360
Original Install Date:     10/17/2016, 10:24:18 PM
System Boot Time:          10/22/2016, 3:55:40 PM
System Manufacturer:       LENOVO
System Model:              Lenovo ThinkServer TS130
System Type:               x64-based PC
Processor(s):              1 Processor(s) Installed.
                           [01]: Intel64 Family 6 Model 58 Stepping 9 GenuineIntel ~1600 Mhz
BIOS Version:              LENOVO FAKT22BUS, 5/29/2013
Windows Directory:         C:\WINDOWS
System Directory:          C:\WINDOWS\system32
Boot Device:               \Device\HarddiskVolume2
System Locale:             en-us;English (United States)
Input Locale:              en-us;English (United States)
Time Zone:                 (UTC-05:00) Eastern Time (US & Canada)
Total Physical Memory:     3,902 MB
Available Physical Memory: 2,923 MB
Virtual Memory: Max Size:  4,606 MB
Virtual Memory: Available: 3,660 MB
Virtual Memory: In Use:    946 MB
Page File Location(s):     C:\pagefile.sys
Domain:                    WORKGROUP
Logon Server:              \\CZ10
Hotfix(s):                 3 Hotfix(s) Installed.
                           [01]: KB3192137
                           [02]: KB3199209
                           [03]: KB3194798
Network Card(s):           1 NIC(s) Installed.
                           [01]: Intel(R) 82579LM Gigabit Network Connection
                                 Connection Name: Ethernet
                                 DHCP Enabled:    Yes
                                 DHCP Server:     192.168.2.2
                                 IP address(es)
                                 [01]: 192.168.2.36
                                 [02]: fe80::d459:e49d:1350:3c5b
Hyper-V Requirements:      VM Monitor Mode Extensions: Yes
                           Virtualization Enabled In Firmware: Yes
                           Second Level Address Translation: Yes
                           Data Execution Prevention Available: Yes

PS C:\Users\Administrator>
```

FIGURE 3-4 Output of the Systeminfo.exe program

Install Hyper-V

As soon as you have the appropriate hardware and the required licenses, you can add the Hyper-V role to Windows Server 2016 using the Add Roles And Features Wizard in Server Manager or the Install-WindowsFeature cmdlet in Windows PowerShell.

Installing Hyper-V using Server Manager

To install the Hyper-V role with Server Manager, use the following procedure.

1. Log on to the server running Windows Server 2016 using an account with administrative privileges.
2. In the Server Manager console, select Manage, Add Roles And Features. The Add Roles And Features Wizard appears, displaying the Before You Begin page.

3. Click Next. The Select Installation Type page appears.
4. Leave the Role-Based Or Feature-Based Installation option selected and click Next. The Select Destination Server page appears.
5. Select the server on which you want to install Hyper-V and click Next. The Select Server Roles page appears.
6. Select the Hyper-V role check box. The Add Features That Are Required For Hyper-V dialog box appears.
7. Click Add Features to accept the dependencies, and then click Next. The Select Features Page appears.
8. Click Next. The Hyper-V page appears.
9. Click Next. The Create Virtual Switches page appears.
10. Select the check box for a network adapter and click Next. The Virtual Machine Migration page appears.
11. Click Next. The Default Stores page appears.
12. Optionally, specify alternatives to the default locations for virtual hard disk and virtual machine configuration files, and click Next. The Confirm Installation Selection page appears.
13. Click Install. The Installation Progress page appears as the wizard installs the role.
14. Click Close to close the wizard.
15. Restart the server.

Installing the role modifies the Windows Server 2016 startup procedure, so that the newly installed hypervisor can address the system hardware directly and then load the operating system as the primary partition on top of that.

Installing Hyper-V using Windows PowerShell

You can also install the Hyper-V role with the Install-WindowsFeature cmdlet, using the following command:

```
install-windowsfeature -name hyper-v -includemanagementtools -restart
```

As always, the Install-WindowsFeature cmdlet does not install the management tools associated with a role by default. You must include the IncludeManagementTools parameter to install Hyper-V Manager and the Hyper-V PowerShell module along with the role.

EXAM TIP

When working with Windows Server 2016 installed as a guest operating system on a Hyper-V host server running an earlier version of Windows Server, such as in a lab or training environment, you cannot install the Hyper-V role using the Add Roles And Features Wizard or the Install WindowsFeature cmdlet. In both cases, the installation terminates with an error message. This is because the virtual machine does not have hardware virtualization capability, and both tools perform prerequisite checks before allowing the installation of the role. However, the Deployment Image Servicing and Management tool (DISM.exe) does not perform these checks, and can install the Hyper-V role on a running system, even if it is a virtual machine. To install Hyper-V using DISM.exe, run the following command from an elevated command prompt:

```
dism /online /enable-feature /featurename:microsoft-hyper-v
```

A Hyper-V installation on a guest operating system is suitable only for training and practice, such as preparing for the 70-740 exam. You can create and configure VMs, but you can't start them, because the requisite hardware is not present. If the Hyper-V host server is running Windows Server 2016 and has the correct hardware, however, Hyper-V nesting is possible.

Install management tools

Adding the Hyper-V role installs the hypervisor software, and, in the case of a Server Manager installation, the management tools as well. The primary tool for creating and managing virtual machines and their components on Hyper-V servers is the Hyper-V Manager console. Hyper-V Manager provides you with a list of all the virtual machines on Windows Server 2016 systems and enables you to configure both the server environments and those of the individual VMs. Windows PowerShell also includes a Hyper-V module containing cmdlets that enable you to exercise complete control over VMs using that interface.

Both the Hyper-V Manager and the PowerShell cmdlets can manage remote Hyper-V servers. To do this, you can install the management tools by themselves, without installing the Hyper-V role. There are no prerequisites for installing or using the tools, so no special hardware is required.

To install the Hyper-V management tools with Server Manager, use the following procedure.

1. Log on to the server running Windows Server 2016 using an account with administrative privileges.
2. In Server Manager, launch the Add Roles And Features Wizard.
3. Leave the default settings selected on the Select Installation Type page and the Select Destination Server page.
4. Click Next to bypass the Select Server Roles page.

5. On the Select Features Page, browse to Remote Server Administration Tools\Role Administration Tools and select the Hyper-V Administration Tools check box. You can also choose to install only the Hyper-V GUI Management Tools or the Hyper-V Module for Windows PowerShell instead, by selecting the appropriate check box. Then click Next.
6. Click Install. The Installation Progress page appears as the wizard installs the features.
7. Click Close to close the wizard.

To install the management tools with Windows PowerShell, you use the Install-Windows-Feature cmdlet, as follows:

```
install-windowsfeature -name rsat-hyper-v-tools
```

To install just the Hyper-V Manager or just the Hyper-V PowerShell module, you use one of the following commands:

```
install-windowsfeature -name hyper-v-tools
```

```
install-windowsfeature -name hyper-v-powershell
```

Upgrade from existing versions of Hyper-V

When you upgrade a server to Windows Server 2016, Hyper-V is an important factor in the planning and execution process. Windows Server 2016 Hyper-V has many new features, and it is worthwhile to take advantage of them, but you must care for your existing virtual machines before you can upgrade the host operating system.

The first step in upgrading a host server to Windows Server 2016 is to get the virtual machines off the host, for their own protection. You can do this in three ways:

- **Export** Saves the VM files, including the virtual disks, to a folder that you specify. Later, you can import the VMs back into the host, after the upgrade is complete. Exporting and importing VMs can be a lengthy process, because you must work with each VM individually. The VMs are also offline while they are stored as exported files. You can import them into another server temporarily and run them there, but this doubles the length of the process.
- **Hyper-V Replica** Creates a copy of a running VM as an offline replica on another host server, including virtual disks. Because the source VM remains online as the replication occurs, downtime is minimal, and production can continue. After the upgrade is complete, you can replicate the copy back to the original host.
- **Share Nothing Live Migration** Moves a running VM with no shared storage to another host server in the same or a trusted domain, with virtually no downtime.

The solution you choose should depend primarily on whether your VMs are production servers that need to be running during the upgrade process. Once the guest VMs are safely located in another location, you can proceed to upgrade the host server, or migrate its roles to a clean Windows Server 2016 installation on another computer (which is the recommended method).

Delegate virtual machine management

To install the Hyper-V role, you must be logged on using an account with local Administrator or Domain Admin privileges, but once the role is installed, it might not be practical to grant this type of access to every person who works with virtual machines on the Hyper-V host.

To address this issue, installing the Hyper-V role in Windows Server 2016 creates a local Hyper-V Administrators group that you can use to grant users and groups permission to create, manage, and connect to virtual machines. Members of this group have no other access to the host operating system, so you can grant this privilege to non-administrators without endangering the rest of the operating system.

> ***NOTE*** **AUTHORIZING HYPER-V ADMINISTRATORS**
>
> In previous versions of Windows Server, there was a tool called Authorization Manager (Azman.msc) that enabled administrators to grant specific privileges to users. For example, you could authorize a user to start and stop virtual machines, but not alter any of their settings. This tool was deprecated in the Windows Server 2012 R2 release, although it still exists in Windows Server 2016. The current approved method for assigning granular Hyper-V administration tasks is to use System Center Virtual Machine Manager (VMM), a separate product that must be purchased.

Perform remote management of Hyper-V hosts

Once the Hyper-V role is installed, you can manage it locally using the Hyper-V Manager console or the cmdlets provided in the Hyper-V PowerShell module. This is frequently not practical, such as when the Hyper-V host server is in a distant data center or server closet. As with many other Windows services, you can manage Hyper-V remotely in a variety of ways.

Remote management using Hyper-V Manager

Like most snap-ins for Microsoft Management Console (MMC), Hyper-V Manager can connect to a remote server and perform the same functions there that it does on the local system. You can install Hyper-V Manager on any computer running Windows Server 2016, whether it has the Hyper-V role installed or not. Using Hyper-V Manager, you can connect to any computer running the Hyper-V role, whether it has Hyper-V Management Tools installed or not.

To run Hyper-V Manager on Windows 10, you must download and install the Remote Server Administration Tools package for Windows 10. The Windows Server 2016 and Windows 10 versions of Hyper-V Manager can connect to Hyper-V running on any Windows version since Windows Server 2012 and Windows 8. The opposite is not necessarily true, however. Earlier versions of Hyper-V Manager are limited in their ability to manage a Windows Server 2016 host server.

To connect the Hyper-V Manager console to a remote server in the same Active Directory Domain Services (AD DS) domain, use the following procedure.

1. Open Hyper-V Manager.
2. In the left pane, right-click Hyper-V Manager and, from the context menu, select Connect To Server. The Select Computer dialog box appears, as shown in Figure 3-5.

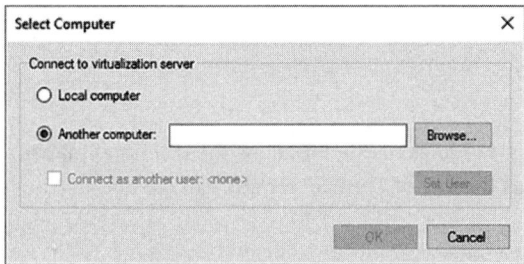

FIGURE 3-5 The Select Computer dialog box

3. With the Another Computer option selected, type the name or IP address of the computer you want to manage. You can also click Browse to open a standard Select Computer search box, as shown in Figure 3-6, in which you can search for a computer name.

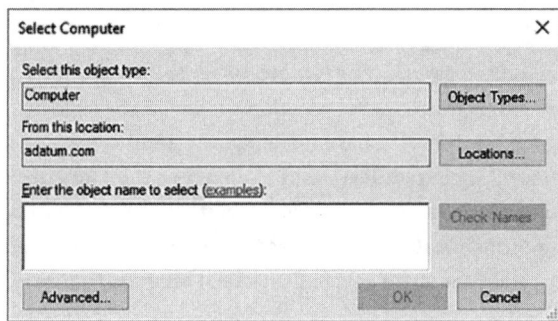

FIGURE 3-6 The Select Computer search box

4. Click OK. The computer you selected appears in the left pane.
5. In the left pane, select the computer you want to manage. The virtual machines on that computer appear in the center pane.

You can now work with the virtual machines and other Hyper-V components of the remote computer, just as if they were on the local system.

Connecting to a remote Hyper-V server when both computers are joined to the same AD DS domain is easy. The computers use Kerberos for authentication, which is brokered by a domain controller. When the computers are not in the same domain, or not in any domain, the authentication process is more complicated, because the computers cannot use Kerberos. Therefore, you must configure them to use the Credential Security Support Provider (CredSSP) authentication protocol instead.

To configure the systems for remote management, run the following commands in an administrative PowerShell session.

On the remote (managed) server:

```
enable-psremoting

enable-wsmancredssp
```

The first command creates the firewall rules needed to allow the incoming management traffic. The second command enables the use of CredSSP for authentication.

On the local (managing) computer:

```
set-item wsman:\localhost\client\trustedhosts -value "hypervserver.domain.com"

enable-wsmancredssp -role client -delegatecomputer "hypervserver.domain.com"
```

The first command adds the fully-qualified domain name of the Hyper-V server to be managed to the local system's WSMan trusted hosts list. The second enables CredSSP on the client.

> *CAUTION* **USING TRUSTED HOSTS**
>
> It should be noted that, while adding the name of the remote server to your trusted hosts list is acceptable on a lab or training network, it is the functional equivalent of leaving your front door wide open and the porch light on. Anyone who knows the address can just walk right in. In a production environment, joining both systems to an Active Directory domain is by far the simplest and best solution. For a situation in which that is not possible, a better alternative is to obtain SSL Server Authentication certificates for both computers from a third-party certification authority and have them authenticate each other using those.

Remote management using Windows PowerShell

The other way to manage Hyper-V on a remote server is to use Windows PowerShell. The Hyper-V PowerShell module includes dozens of cmdlets that provide enormous management flexibility.

There are two main ways to manage Hyper-V with PowerShell:

- **PowerShell remoting** Also called *explicit remoting*, the user on the local (managing) system opens a remote session to the remote (managed) system. In this model, the Hyper-V module must be installed on the remote system, but it does not have to be installed on the local system.

- **Implicit remoting** The user on the local (managing) system runs a cmdlet with a ComputerName parameter, which directs its function to the remote (managed) system. In this model, the local system must have the Hyper-V module installed.

PowerShell remoting

When you establish a remote session to another computer using PowerShell, your command prompt changes to reflect the name of the computer you are managing. Because you are running the cmdlets available on the other computer, the remote server must have the Hyper-V module installed.

PowerShell remoting has some distinct advantages over the Hyper-V Manager console. First, you have access to all of the cmdlets on the remote system, not just those in the Hyper-V module. Second, there are usually no compatibility issues between PowerShell implementations. You can use a Windows Server 2008 PowerShell session to connect to a Windows Server 2016 Hyper-V server with no problem. This is not possible with Hyper-V Manager.

The security issues involved in a remote PowerShell session are like those of a remote Hyper-V Manager session. In this case, you should run the Enable-PSRemoting cmdlet on both computers and again, use Active Directory, SSL certificates, or the trusted hosts list on the managing system, in that order.

To connect to the remote Hyper-V server from an administrative PowerShell session, you must first create a session, using the New-PSSession cmdlet, as in the following example:

```
new-pssession -computername server1
```

The output from this command provides information about the new session, including an ID number. To enter the session, you use the Enter-PSSession cmdlet, specifying the session numbers, as in the following command:

```
enter-pssession #
```

If you are not currently logged on with an account that has administrative privileges on the remote server, you can enter a session using another account with the following command:

```
enter-pssession # -credential (get-credential)
```

This command will cause your system to prompt you for a user name and password with appropriate privileges on the remote server.

When you successfully enter the session, the command prompt changes. You can now run PowerShell commands on the remote server. To leave the session, you use the Exit-PSSession cmdlet, or just type Exit.

For example, Figure 3-7 contains a series of PowerShell commands, as follows.

1. The first command creates a new session with the ID number 5.
2. Still controlling the local system, the Get-VM cmdlet displays a single virtual machine called ServerH-01.

3. Entering remote session 5, the command prompt changes to show the remote server name rtmsvri.
4. This time, the Get-VM cmdlet displays the virtual machine on the remote server, called ServerI-01.
5. The exit command returns the prompt to its original form, and control returns to the local system.

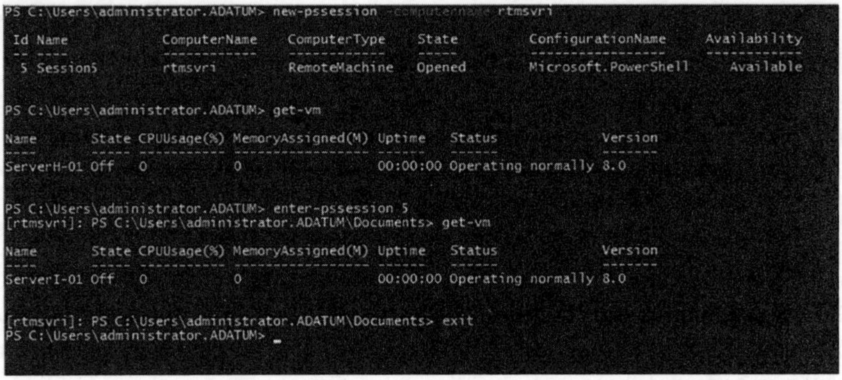

FIGURE 3-7 PowerShell commands demonstrating remote Hyper-V management

Implicit remoting

Implicit remoting does not require you to establish a session with the remote server, instead, the PowerShell cmdlets themselves can address a remote system. The general rule is that if a cmdlet supports a ComputerName parameter, it is capable of implicit remoting. For example, you can use the Get-VM cmdlet to address the local server, with no parameters, or a remote server, with the ComputerName parameter, as shown in Figure 3-8.

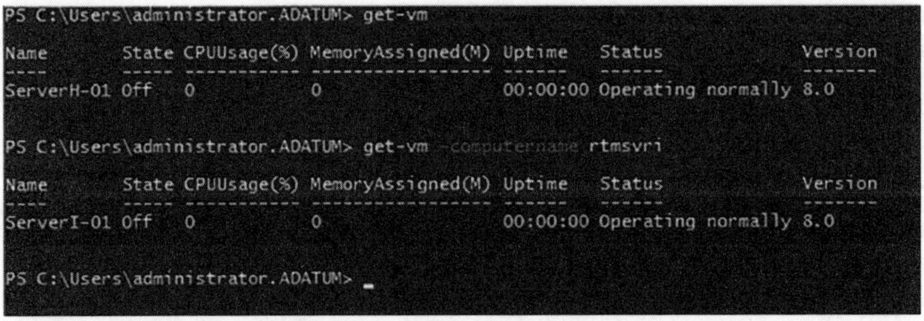

FIGURE 3-8 PowerShell commands demonstrating implicit remoting

Implicit remoting is limited in several ways, including the following:
- Because you are running the cmdlets on your own system, you must have the Hyper-V module installed on your computer.

- There are version limitations to this method, just as there are in Hyper-V Manager. Legally, you are only allowed to install PowerShell modules for the version of Windows you are running on your local computer. If you are trying to manage a server running Windows Server 2016 with a system running a previous version of Windows, your cmdlets might not function properly.
- Not every cmdlet supports the use of the a ComputerName cmdlet, so your capabilities are limited.

One of the powerful benefits of implicit remoting, however, is that some cmdlets support the inclusion of a string array in the ComputerName parameter. This enables you to run a cmdlet against multiple computers at once, as shown in Figure 3-9. This is a tremendous advantage for administrators working with multiple Hyper-V servers, one which Hyper-V Manager and remote PowerShell sessions do not provide.

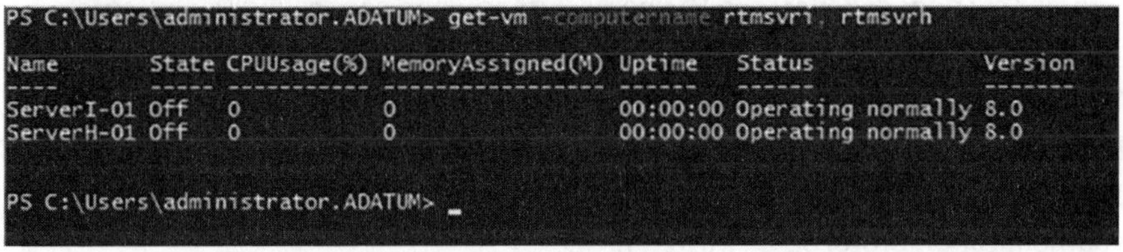

```
PS C:\Users\administrator.ADATUM> get-vm -computername rtmsvri, rtmsvrh

Name         State  CPUUsage(%)  MemoryAssigned(M)  Uptime    Status              Version
----         -----  -----------  -----------------  ------    ------              -------
ServerI-01   Off    0            0                  00:00:00  Operating normally  8.0
ServerH-01   Off    0            0                  00:00:00  Operating normally  8.0

PS C:\Users\administrator.ADATUM>
```

FIGURE 3-9 PowerShell commands demonstrating implicit remoting against multiple computers

> **NOTE GETTING HELP**
>
> The way to tell whether a specific cmdlet supports the inclusion of a string array in the ComputerName parameter is to run Get-Help with the cmdlet name. If the ComputerName parameter has square brackets following its string, as shown in Figure 3-10, you can specify multiple computer names in the command line.

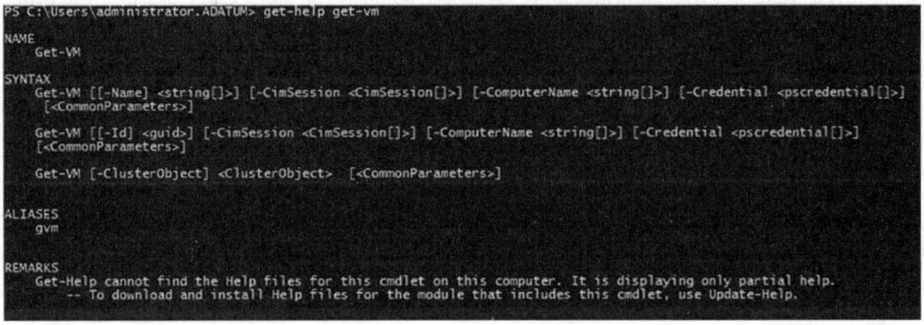

```
PS C:\Users\administrator.ADATUM> get-help get-vm
NAME
    Get-VM

SYNTAX
    Get-VM [[-Name] <string[]>] [-CimSession <CimSession[]>] [-ComputerName <string[]>] [-Credential <pscredential[]>]
    [<CommonParameters>]

    Get-VM [[-Id] <guid>] [-CimSession <CimSession[]>] [-ComputerName <string[]>] [-Credential <pscredential[]>]
    [<CommonParameters>]

    Get-VM [-ClusterObject] <ClusterObject>  [<CommonParameters>]

ALIASES
    gvm

REMARKS
    Get-Help cannot find the Help files for this cmdlet on this computer. It is displaying only partial help.
        -- To download and install Help files for the module that includes this cmdlet, use Update-Help.
```

FIGURE 3-10 PowerShell help

Configure virtual machines using Windows PowerShell Direct

PowerShell Direct is a means of connecting to a Hyper-V guest operating system from the host operating system, using a PowerShell session. For administrators that prefer to use PowerShell, this provides rapid access to a guest VM without having to open a VMConnect window, log on to the guest operating system, and open a PowerShell window.

To connect to a guest operating system, you open a PowerShell session with administrative privileges on the Hyper-V host and use the Enter-PSSession cmdlet, as in the following example:

```
enter-pssession -vmname server1
```

You are then prompted for credentials to access the VM. Once you are authenticated, the command prompt changes to reflect the VM name, just as when connecting to a remote server. You can work in the VM session for as long as you need to; then type Exit to terminate the session.

Using the VmName parameter causes the Enter-PSSession cmdlet to behave differently when establishing the session to the VM. Unlike a session with a remote server, there are no issues with authentication protocols or trusted hosts.

There are also other ways to use this capability. For example, to execute a single PowerShell command on the VM, you can use the Invoke-Command cmdlet, as in the following example:

```
invoke-command -vmname server1 -scriptblock {get-netadapter}
```

This command accesses the VM called server1 and runs the Get-NetAdapter cmdlet there. The resulting output displays on the host, and the session immediately closes.

You can also open a persistent session to the VM using New-PSSession, much as you would do to connect to a remote Hyper-V server, except that here you use the VmName parameter instead of ComputerName. When you do this, you must authenticate during the creation of the session. You then are able to enter and leave the session whenever you need to, using Enter-PSSession and Exit-PSSession, without having to authenticate again. For more advanced PowerShell users, note that creating a persistent session causes all variables you assign within the session to remain available until the session is terminated.

Finally, and perhaps most usefully, you can use the Copy-Item cmdlet to copy files to and from a guest operating system. With a persistent session in place, you can use commands like the following to do this:

```
copy-item -tosession (get-pssession) -path c:\temp\file.txt -destination c:\users

copy-item -fromsession (get-pssession) -path c:\users\file.txt -destination c:\temp
```

Implement nested virtualization

Nested virtualization is the ability to configure a Hyper-V guest VM to function as a Hyper-V host. In previous versions of Windows Server, attempts to install Hyper-V on a guest operating system using Server Manager or PowerShell fail, because the required virtualization hardware support does not exist in the virtual machine. In Windows Server 2016, however, you can configure the VM so that you can install Hyper-V in a guest operating system, create virtual machines within a virtual machine, and even run them.

This capability does not provide much benefit in a production environment, but for testing and training purposes (such as preparing for a certification exam), it can be a boon. This capability also makes it possible to create Hyper-V containers on a virtual machine, which can be an aid to software development efforts and other situations requiring more isolation than standard Windows Server containers can supply.

To create a nested Hyper-V host server, you must have a physical host and a virtual machine on that host that are both running Windows Server 2016. In addition, the physical host must have an Intel processor with VT-x and Extended Page Tables (EPT) virtualization support.

Before you install Hyper-V on the virtual machine, you must provide its virtual processor with access to the virtualization technology on the physical computer. To do this, you must shut down the virtual machine and run a command like the following on the physical host, in an elevated PowerShell session:

```
set-vmprocessor -vmname server1 -exposevirtualizationextensions $true
```

In addition, you must make the following configuration changes on the VM that function as a Hyper-V host. Each is given first as the location in the VM Settings dialog box in Hyper-V Manager, and then as a PowerShell command:

- On the Memory page, disable Dynamic Memory.

  ```
  set-vmmemory -vmname server1 -dynamicmemoryenabled $false
  ```

- On the Processor page, set Number Of Virtual Processors to 2.

  ```
  set-vmprocessor -vmname server1 -count 2
  ```

- On the Network Adapter/Advanced Features page, turn on MAC Address Spoofing.

  ```
  set-vmnetworkadapter -vmname server1 -name "network adapter" -macaddressspoofing on
  ```

Once you have made these changes, you can start the VM, install the Hyper-V role, and create nested virtual machines. While the VMs run on the nested host, there are some Hyper-V features that do not work, such as live memory resizing, checkpoints, Live Migration, and Save/Restore.

Skill 3.2: Configure virtual machine (VM) settings

After installing Hyper-V and configuring Hyper-V Manager, you are ready to create virtual machines and configure the settings that each individual VM uses to operate. Then, you install the guest operating systems on the VMs, just as if they were physical computers. Using Hyper-V Manager or Windows PowerShell, you can create new virtual machines and configure their settings.

> **This section covers how to:**
> - Add or remove memory in running a VM
> - Configure dynamic memory
> - Configure Non-Uniform Memory Access (NUMA) support
> - Configure smart paging
> - Configure Resource Metering
> - Manage Integration Services
> - Create and configure Generation 1 and 2 VMs and determine appropriate usage scenarios
> - Implement enhanced session mode
> - Create Linux and FreeBSD VMs
> - Install and configure Linux Integration Services (LIS)
> - Install and configure FreeBSD Integration Services (BIS)
> - Implement Secure Boot for Windows and Linux environments
> - Move and convert VMs from previous versions of Hyper-V to Windows Server 2016 Hyper-V
> - Export and import VMs
> - Implement Discrete Device Assignment (DDA)

Creating a virtual machine

By default, Hyper-V stores the files that make up virtual machines in the folders you specified on the Default Stores page during the role installation. Each virtual machine uses the following files:

- A virtual machine configuration (.vmc) file in XML format that contains the virtual machine configuration information, including all settings for the virtual machine.
- One or more virtual hard disk (.vhd or .vhdx) files to store the guest operating system, applications, and data for the virtual machine.
- A virtual machine may also use a saved-state (.vsv) file, if the machine has been placed into a saved state.

Creating a VM in Hyper-V Manager

To create a new virtual machine using Hyper-V Manager, use the following procedure.

1. Log on to the Windows Server 2016 host server, using an account with administrative privileges.
2. From the Tools menu of the Server Manager window, select Hyper-V Manager. The Hyper-V Manager console appears, as shown in Figure 3-11.

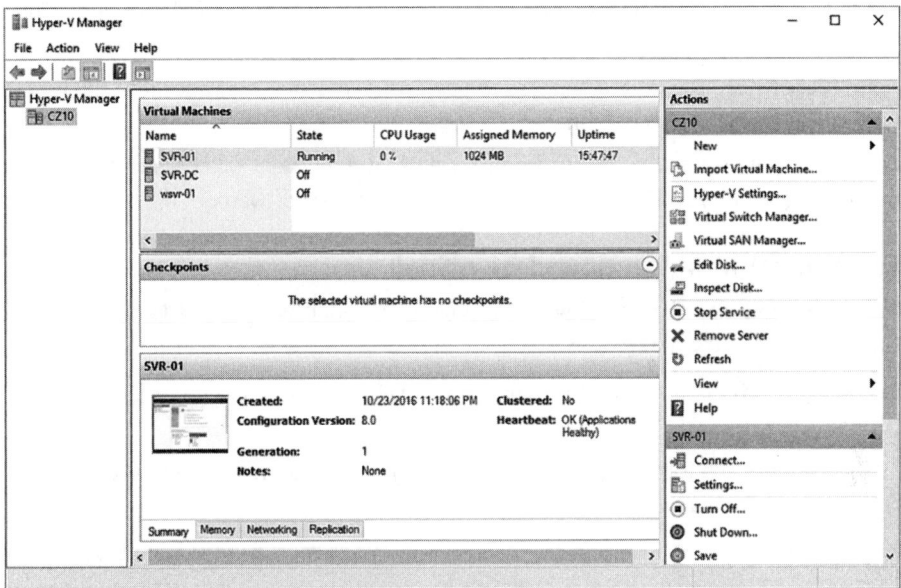

FIGURE 3-11 The Hyper-V Manager console

3. In the left pane of the Hyper-V Manager console, select a Hyper-V server.
4. In the Actions pane, choose New | Virtual Machine. The New Virtual Machine Wizard appears, displaying the Before You Begin page.
5. Click Next. The Specify Name And Location page appears.
6. In the Name text box, type a name for the virtual machine. Hyper-V also uses this name to create the VM files and folders. Then click Next. The Specify Generation page appears.
7. Specify whether you want to create a Generation 1 or Generation 2 virtual machine, and click Next. The Assign Memory page appears.
8. In the Startup Memory text box, type the amount of memory you want the virtual machine to use, and click Next. The Configure Networking page appears.
9. From the Connection drop-down list, select a virtual switch, and click Next. The Connect Virtual Hard Disk page appears.

10. Leave the Create A Virtual Hard Disk option selected, and type values for the following fields:
    - **Name**   Specifies the filename for the virtual hard disk, using the .vhdx format.
    - **Location**   Specifies a location for the virtual hard disk other than the default.
    - **Size**   Specifies the maximum size of the virtual hard disk.
11. Click Next. The Installation Options page appears.
12. Leave the Install An Operating System Later option selected and click Next. The Completing The New Virtual Machine Wizard page appears.
13. Click Finish. The wizard creates the new virtual machine and adds it to the list of virtual machines in Hyper-V Manager.

The virtual machine that this procedure creates is equivalent to a bare metal computer. It has all the (virtual) hardware it needs to run but lacks any software.

Creating a VM in Windows PowerShell

To create a new virtual machine with Windows PowerShell, you use the New-VM cmdlet with the following basic syntax:

```
new-vm -name virtualmachinename -memorystartupbytes memory -generation #
-newvhdsizebytes disksize
```

For example, the following command creates a new Generation 2 VM called Server1 with 1 GB of memory and a new 40 GB virtual hard disk drive:

```
new-vm -name "server1" -generation 2 -memorystartupbytes 1gb -newvhdsizebytes 40gb
```

The New-VM cmdlet has many more parameters, which you can explore through the Get-Help cmdlet.

Configuring VM settings

Each Hyper-V virtual machine consists of settings that specify the virtual hardware resources in the machine and the configuration of those resources. You can manage and modify these settings in Hyper-V Manager by using the Settings dialog box for the particular virtual machine.

Selecting a VM from the Virtual Machines list in Hyper-V Manager displays a series of icons in a separate section of the Actions pane. Clicking the Settings icon opens the Settings dialog box, as shown in Figure 3-12, which is the primary configuration interface for that VM. Here, you can modify any settings that you configured when you created the virtual machine.

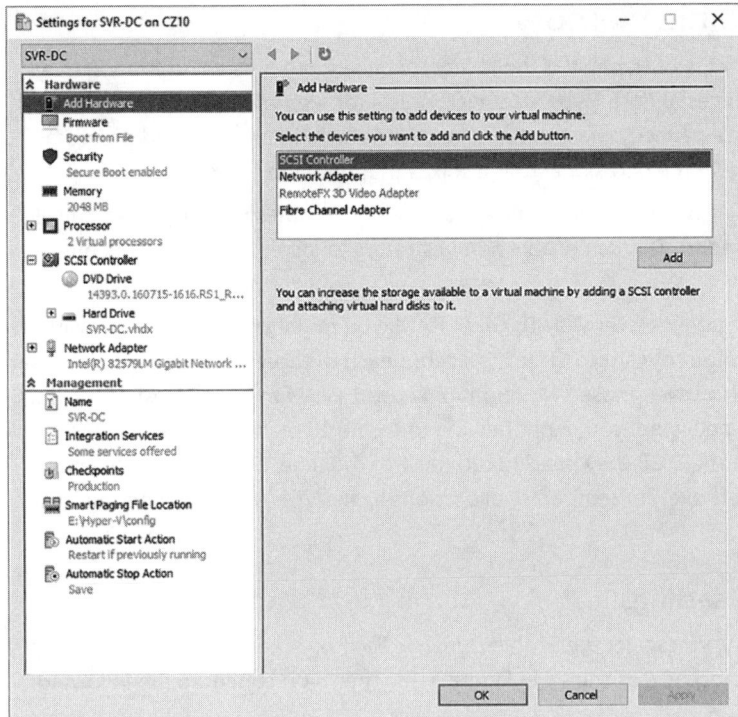

FIGURE 3-12 The Settings dialog box for a virtual machine in Hyper-V Manager

You can also configure the settings of a VM using the PowerShell cmdlets in the Hyper-V module. To list all of the cmdlets in the module, use the following command:

```
get-command -module hyper-v
```

Add or remove memory in running a VM

The Memory page of the Settings dialog box enables you to specify how much of the host server's memory should be allocated to the selected VM. On a Hyper-V server running on Windows Server 2012 R2 or earlier, the Memory page of a VM that is running has all of its settings grayed out. You cannot modify these settings when the VM is running, any more than you can insert memory sticks in a physical computer while it is running.

In Windows Server 2016 Hyper-V, however, this is changed. On the Memory page of a running Generation 1 or Generation 2 VM, as shown in Figure 3-13, the RAM setting is active, and you can increase or decrease the memory allotment for the virtual machine, as it is running. These "hot" changes take effect as soon as you click the OK or the Apply button.

To change the memory allotment with PowerShell, you use the Set-VMMemory cmdlet, as in the following example:

```
set-vmmemory -vmname server1 -startupbytes 1024mb
```

Configure dynamic memory

One of the primary benefits of Hyper-V is the ability to make more efficient utilization of a server's hardware resources. Before Hyper-V, it was typical for a server to operate at 10 to 20 percent of its resource capacity most of the time. The remaining memory and processor power was there to handle the occasional usage spikes that required them.

Dynamic memory is a Hyper-V feature that automatically allocates memory to and deallocates it from VMs as needed. This can enable administrators to increase their server consolidation rates.

For example, on a Hyper-V server with 16 GB of RAM, you might create seven VMs with 2 GB or memory each without dynamic memory, because each of those VMs requires all of that 2GB some of the time. However, those VMs might only use 1 GB of memory most of the time. With dynamic memory activated, you might be able to create 10 or 12 VMs on that same server. All of them have the 1 GB they need to run most of the time, and there are several gigabytes of memory left over for temporary allocations to the VMs during the periods when they need the full 2 GB.

Dynamic memory settings

To use dynamic memory, you select the Enable Dynamic Memory check box on the Memory page of the Settings dialog box, as shown in Figure 3-13. Then, you configure the following memory settings:

- **RAM**   Specifies the amount of memory that Hyper-V allots to the VM when it starts.
- **Minimum RAM**   Specifies the least amount of RAM that can be left to the VM when dynamic memory is reducing the memory allocation. The default setting is 512 MB.
- **Maximum RAM**   Specifies the largest amount of RAM that dynamic memory can ever allocate to the VM. The default setting is 1 TB, the maximum allowable memory in any VM.
- **Memory buffer**   Specifies the percentage of the currently allocated memory that dynamic memory should retain as a buffer for future expansion. Hyper-V resists allocating this buffer memory to another VM, but it does so if necessary.

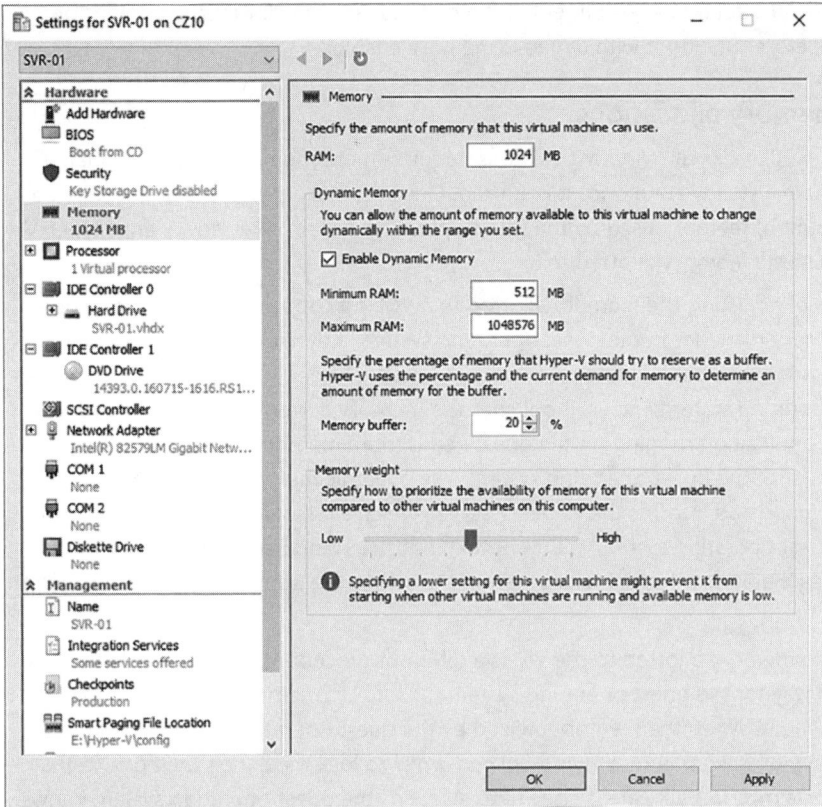

FIGURE 3-13 The Memory page in the Settings dialog box for a virtual machine in Hyper-V Manager

> **NOTE DYNAMIC MEMORY LIMITATIONS**
>
> While you can modify the RAM setting while a VM is running when dynamic memory is not enabled, the following limitations apply:
>
> - You cannot enable or disable dynamic memory while the VM is running.
> - You cannot modify the RAM setting when dynamic memory is enabled.
> - You can lower, but not raise, the Minimum RAM setting while the VM is running.
> - You can raise, but not lower, the Maximum RAM setting while the VM is running.

Not every application running on a VM is a suitable candidate for dynamic memory. For example, Microsoft Exchange is designed to utilize all the memory available to it on a continuous basis. Exchange caches data in RAM when it is not being used for other purposes, so a dynamic reduction in the available memory can cause a reduction in performance. When running VMs in a production environment, it is a good idea to check with the application manufacturer before running it with dynamic memory enabled.

Dynamic memory allocations

Windows Server 2016, like all Windows versions, requires more memory to start up than it needs to maintain a steady state once it is started. Once the startup process is complete on a VM, the amount of memory used by the guest operating system goes down, and Hyper-V reclaims some of the memory allotted to it.

The process of adjusting the memory allotted to a VM is a cooperative arrangement between the memory manager in the guest operating system, a dynamic memory driver in the Hyper-V Integration Services running on the guest, and the Hyper-V host server itself. As far as the guest operating system knows, it only has the memory currently allotted to it to work with. When an application running on the guest needs more memory, it requests it from the memory manager of the guest operating system. The dynamic memory driver on the guest detects this demand and informs the Hyper-V server, which allocates additional memory to the VM. The guest operating system, following the industry standard Hot Add memory function, determines that it now has sufficient memory to satisfy the application's request, and it does so.

Reducing the memory allotted to the VM is a different procedure, because while there is a standardized way for the guest operating system to Hot Add memory, there is no standard for removing it. When the memory utilized by the guest operating system goes down, dynamic memory uses what is known as a *balloon driver* to lock the excess memory, so that Hyper-V can reclaim it and allocate it elsewhere. As far as the guest operating system knows, that memory is still there, and mapping tools show it as still being locked by the driver, but in reality, Hyper-V has taken it back.

Therefore, you might see different memory utilization figures in the guest operating system, when compared to those shown by Hyper-V. In a case like this, the rule to follow is that Hyper-V is correct, and the guest operating system is being deceived by the balloon driver. The guest operating system never sees that driver locked memory released until the VM is restarted.

To view the current memory allocation statistics for a virtual machine, select the Memory tab in the Hyper-V Manager console, as shown in Figure 3-14.

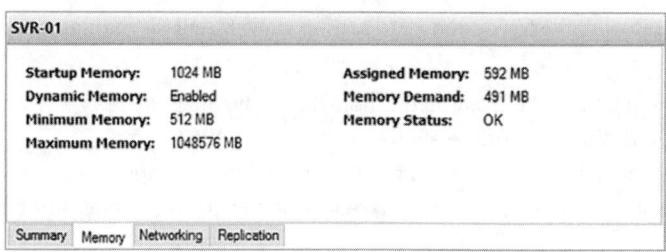

FIGURE 3-14 The Memory tab for a virtual machine

Configure Non-Uniform Memory Access (NUMA) support

Non-Uniform Memory Access (NUMA) is a system architecture used to increase memory efficiency in computers with multiple processors. NUMA is an architecture that divides a system's logical processors and its memory into *NUMA nodes*, with each node containing one or more logical processors and the region of memory nearest to them on a separate bus. These node buses are then interconnected by another bus, enabling the processors to access all of the system memory.

The fundamental rule behind NUMA is "close memory is faster." For any logical processor, the memory within its NUMA node is considered to be *local memory*. Memory in other nodes is called *remote memory* or foreign memory. Processors perform better when accessing local memory than when accessing remote memory because there is less access latency.

For any processor, the difference between accessing local and remote memory is known as its *NUMA ratio*. A system that uses symmetric multiprocessing (SMP), in which all of the processors and all of the memory are connected using a single bus, has a NUMA ratio of 1:1.

To take advantage of the NUMA architecture, certain applications are optimized to utilize processors and memory within the same node wherever possible. Microsoft SQL Server is an example of such an application.

Node spanning

Just as Hyper-V virtualizes the other hardware in a physical computer for use in VMs, it also virtualizes the NUMA architecture. By default, Hyper-V attempts to start a VM using the resources within a single NUMA node. If the physical computer's NUMA architecture does not allow for enough memory within a single node, Hyper-V uses memory from other nodes. This is called *NUMA spanning*.

NUMA spanning enables VMs to utilize any memory available on the host server, regardless of the node in which it is located. However, there are also some potential performance disadvantages.

VM and application performance might vary between restarts because the alignment of the NUMA nodes changes. For example, a VM might have all of its memory allocated from a single NUMA node. Then, after restarting the VM, if memory must be allocated from multiple nodes, the latency in some of the memory accesses increases, diminishing performance.

To avoid this situation, you can configure a Hyper-V server not to allow NUMA spanning. This ensures that the performance of your VMs and your applications is consistent, even after restarts. However, this too has potential disadvantages. If NUMA spanning is disabled and a VM cannot access all of the resources it needs in a single node, it fails to start. In addition, dynamic memory is only able to access the memory in a single node.

To configure NUMA spanning for a Hyper-V server, use the following procedure.

1. In Hyper-V Manager, in the Actions pane, click Hyper-V Settings. The Hyper-V Settings dialog box appears.
2. In the Server list, select NUMA Spanning to display the NUMA Spanning page, as shown in Figure 3-15.

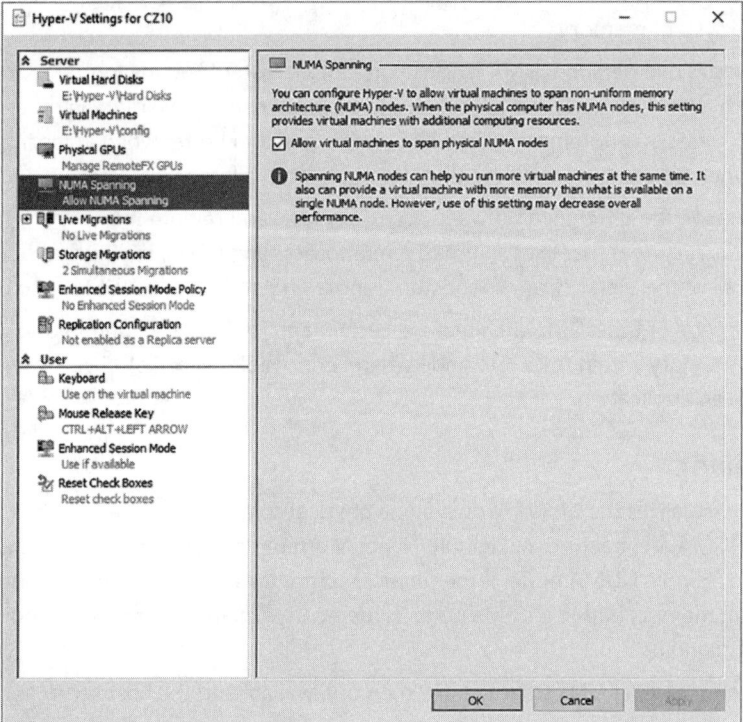

FIGURE 3-15 The NUMA Spanning page in the Hyper-V Settings dialog box

3. Clear the Allow Virtual Machines To Span Physical NUMA Nodes check box.
4. Click OK.

> **NOTE   HYPER-V SETTINGS**
>
> Note that the settings in the Hyper-V Settings dialog box affect all of the virtual machines on the server, and that disabling NUMA spanning prevents all of your VMs from access remote memory.

NUMA topology

When you create a virtual machine, Hyper-V creates a virtual NUMA architecture that corresponds to the host server's physical NUMA architecture. However, it is possible to modify the NUMA node settings for a specific virtual machine.

Why would you want to do this? When you are working with a host server that has multiple NUMA nodes and you are running a NUMA-aware application in a VM, the amount of memory you allocate to that VM can be critical. Microsoft has estimated that a virtual machine's performance can be reduced by as much as eight percent when its memory allocation exceeds the NUMA node boundary.

For example, if each NUMA node on a host server has 16 GB of memory, the VMs should have no more than 16 GB allocated to them. In a case like this, increasing the memory of a VM beyond 16 GB can result in a performance decrease. Therefore, if you have an application that requires more than 16 GB of memory, you can conceivably modify the size of the VM virtual NUMA nodes, to prevent the spanning of (virtual) node boundaries. Of course, the VM might still be spanning the host server's physical node boundaries, and so there will likely be some performance degradation, but not as much as that incurred by spanning in the virtual NUMA architecture.

To configure the NUMA configuration for a virtual machine, use the following procedure.

1. In Hyper-V Manager, open the Settings dialog box for the VM you want to configure.
2. In the Hardware list, expand the Processor entry and select the NUMA subentry. The NUMA Configuration page appears, as shown in Figure 3-16.

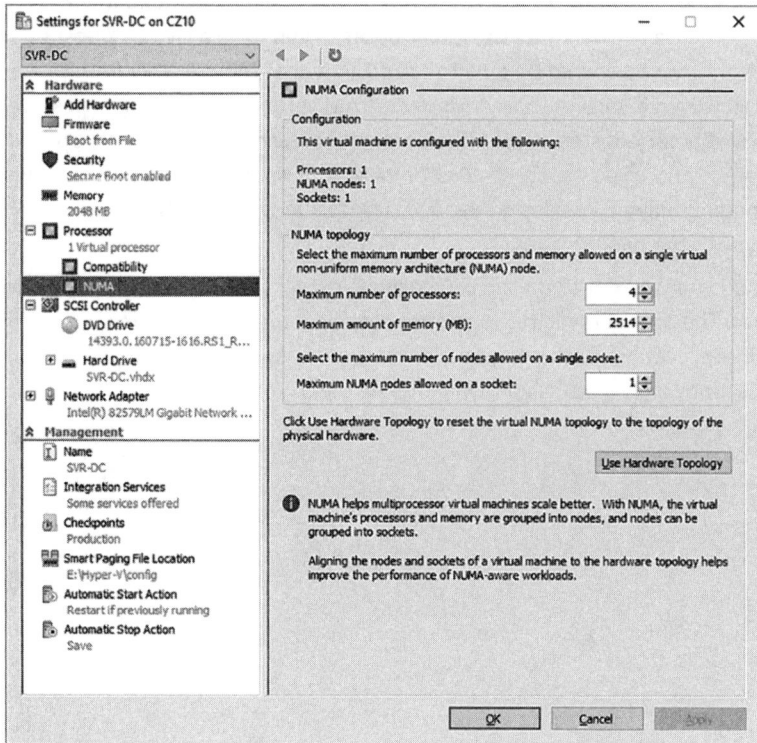

FIGURE 3-16 The NUMA Configuration page in the Settings dialog box

3. In the NUMA Topology box, set values for the following settings:
   - Maximum number of processors
   - Maximum amount of memory (MB)
   - Maximum NUMA nodes allowed on a socket
4. Click OK.

Configure smart paging

Smart paging is a Hyper-V feature that enables the host server to compensate when its memory is overcommitted. If the host lacks the memory needed to start a VM, it uses disk space for memory paging, but only during the boot sequence.

When virtual machines use dynamic memory, they typically have different RAM and Minimum RAM values. This enables the VM to release some of its memory after the startup sequence is completed. Thus, it is possible to have several VMs running simultaneously that together use all the available RAM in the host server. This will work while the VMs are running, but when the VMs restart, there isn't enough memory to supply the amount specified in the RAM setting.

One common scenario in which this might occur is when you have multiple VMs configured to start automatically when the host server boots. If you have a Hyper-V host server with 16 GB of memory, you should be able to run 10 VMs that require 1 GB each to maintain a steady state. However, if each of those VMs has a RAM setting of 2 GB, the host server does not have enough memory to start them all at once. In this case, the host makes up for the memory shortage by using disk space instead of RAM. Disk space might be much slower than RAM, but the paging only occurs during the VM startup. Once the VM is started and releases some of its memory, the paging stops.

Smart paging is transparent to the virtual machine, except possibly for the additional time required to boot. The only administrative control provided over smart paging is the ability to specify an alternate location for the paging file. You do this on the Smart Paging File Location page in a VM Settings dialog box, as shown in Figure 3-17.

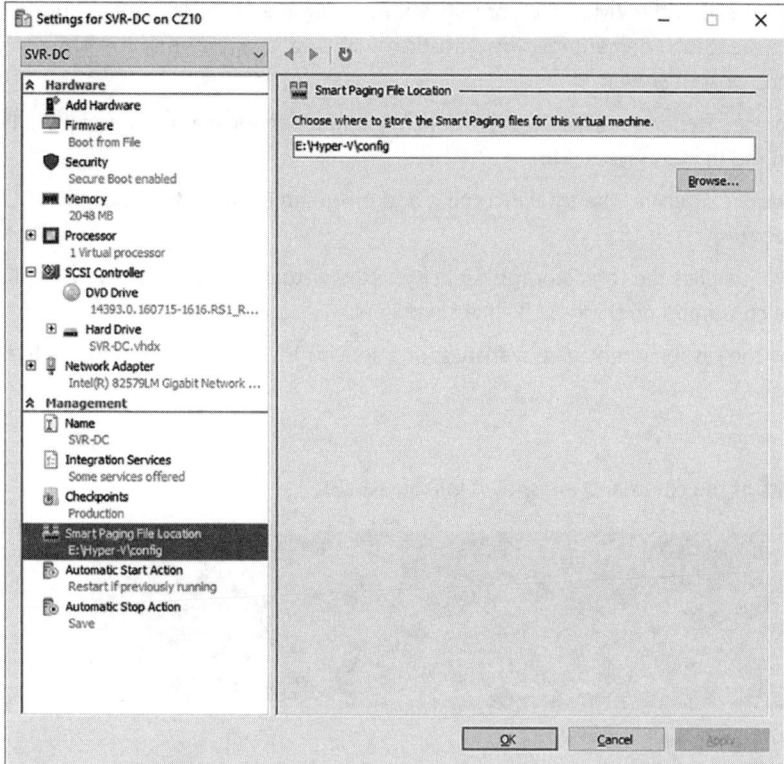

FIGURE 3-17 The Smart Paging File Location page in the Settings dialog box

By default, Hyper-V creates the paging file in the Virtual Machines folder. The only compelling reason to change it is the cost of the disk space on the drive where the designated folder is located. If, for example, the Virtual Machines folder is located on an SSD, you might want to move the smart paging file to a location on a less expensive medium.

Configure resource metering

Resource metering is a Hyper-V feature that makes it possible to track the resources a virtual machine uses as it operates. The feature is designed for fee-based private clouds that host VMs for clients. By metering their resource utilization, vendors can charge clients based on their actual activity, or confirm their compliance with the terms of a contract.

Resource metering is implemented in Windows PowerShell. When you enable metering, the system begins to compile statistics and continues until you reset the metering, at which time the counters are returned to zero.

To enable resource metering, use a command like the following:

```
enable-vmresourcemetering -vmname server1
```

Once metering is enabled, the system tracks usage of the following resources:

- **CPU** Specifies the VM processor utilization in megahertz (MHz). By measuring in MHz instead of a percentage, the statistic remains valid, even when the VM is moved to another host server.
- **Memory** Hyper-V tracks the minimum, maximum, and average allocated memory, measured in megabytes (MB).
- **Network** Specifies the total incoming and outgoing network traffic of the VM, in megabytes.
- **Disk** Specifies the total storage capacity of the virtual hard disks of the VM, plus the space consumed on the host by any snapshots.

To display the resource metering statistics for a specific VM, use a command like the following:

```
measure-vm -vmname server1
```

The results of the command are shown in Figure 3-18.

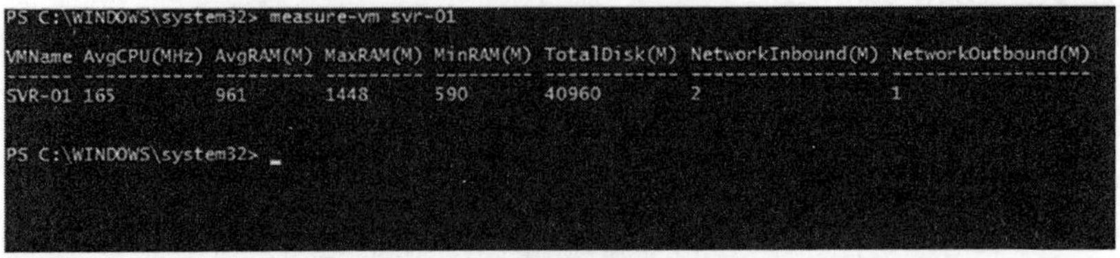

FIGURE 3-18 Output of the Measure-VM cmdlet

To display additional resource metering statistics, you can run the Measure-VM cmdlet and pipe its output to the Format-List cmdlet, as follows. The resulting display is shown in Figure 3-19.

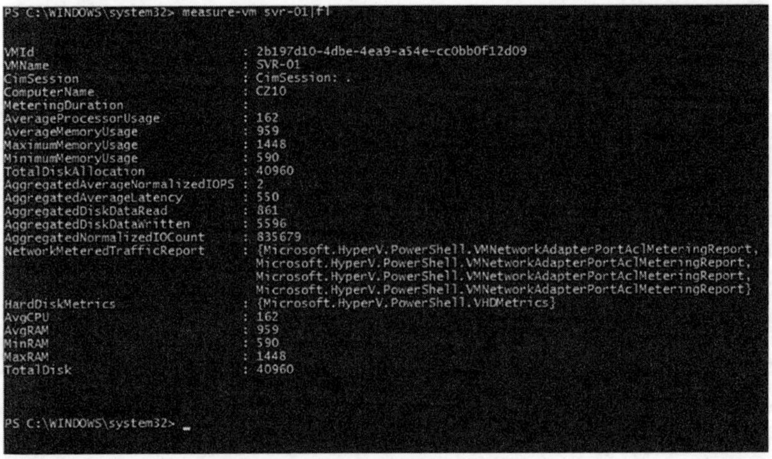

FIGURE 3-19 Formatted output of the Measure-VM cmdlet

To set the resource metering statistics back to zero, use the Reset-VMResourceMetering cmdlet, as in the following example:

```
reset-vmresourcemetering -vmname server1
```

To turn resource metering off for a VM, use the Disable-VMResourceMetering cmdlet, as follows:

```
disable-vmresourcemetering -vmname server1
```

Manage Integration Services

Integration Services is a software package that runs on a guest operating system, enabling it to communicate with the Hyper-V host server. Designed for a specific guest operating system, some of the software components in the Integration Services package run automatically, such as the balloon driver mentioned earlier in this chapter. There are others that administrators can enable or disable as needed.

To select the components that are available on a virtual machine, you open the Integration Services page in the VM Settings dialog box, and select or clear the check boxes, as shown in Figure 3-20.

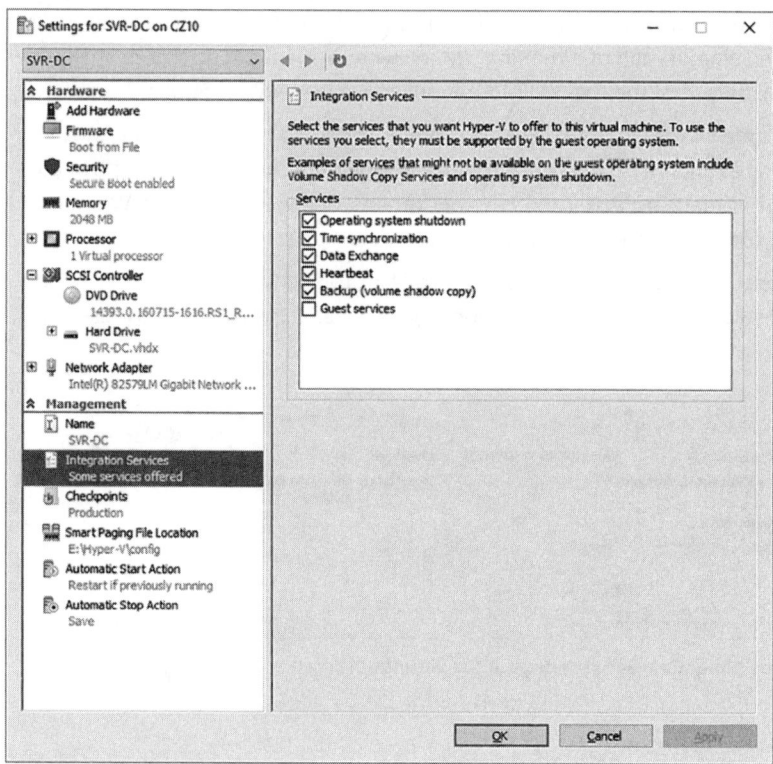

FIGURE 3-20 The Integration Services page in the Settings dialog box

A VM running Windows Server 2016 has six Integration Services components, all of which are enabled by default, except for Guest Services. The functions of the components are as follows:

- **Operating system shutdown**   Enables administrators to perform an orderly shutdown of a VM without having to log on to it. It is possible to shut down a VM using Hyper-V Manager or the Stop-VM cmdlet in PowerShell.

- **Time synchronization**   Synchronizes the clock on the VM the clock on the Hyper-V host server. The only reason to disable this service is when you are using a VM to run an Active Directory Domain Services domain controller, and you have configured the system to sync with the time signal from an external source.

- **Data exchange**   Also known as *key-value pair (KVP)*, this is a service that enables the guest operating system on a VM to share information with the Hyper-V host server operating system using the VMBus. Therefore, no network connection is required. The information is stored in the registry on a Windows guest and in a file on a Linux/UNIX guest. Application developers can use Windows Management Instrumentation (WMI) scripts to store instructions or other information in KVPs that must be seen by the host.

- **Heartbeat**   Causes the VM to generate a signal at regular intervals, indicating that it is running normally. The host server can detect when the heartbeat signal has stopped, indicating that the VM is unresponsive. The current state of the heartbeat signal is displayed on the Summary tab of a running VM in Hyper-V Manager, as shown in Figure 3-21, or in the output of the Get-VMIntegrationService PowerShell cmdlet.

- **Backup (volume shadow copy)**   Enables administrators to back up a VM using backup software running on the host server. This type of backup includes the VM configuration, the virtual hard disks, and any checkpoints. The volumes on the VM must use the NTFS file system and have volume shadow copy enabled.

- **Guest services**   Enables administrators to copy files to and from a running VM using the VMBus instead of a network connection. To copy files this way, you must use the Copy-VMFile PowerShell cmdlet.

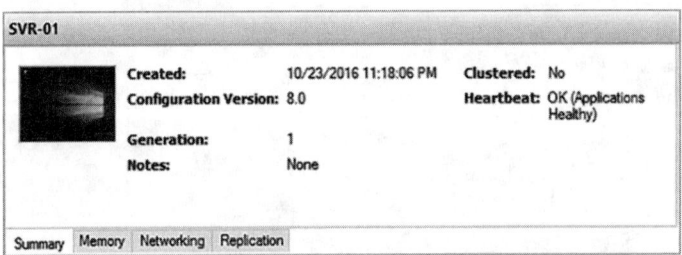

FIGURE 3-21   The Integration Services page in the Settings dialog box

Create and configure Generation 1 and 2 VMs and determine appropriate usage scenarios

When you create a new virtual machine in the Hyper-V manager, the New Virtual Machine Wizard includes a page, shown in Figure 3-22, on which you specify whether you want to create a Generation 1 or Generation 2 VM.

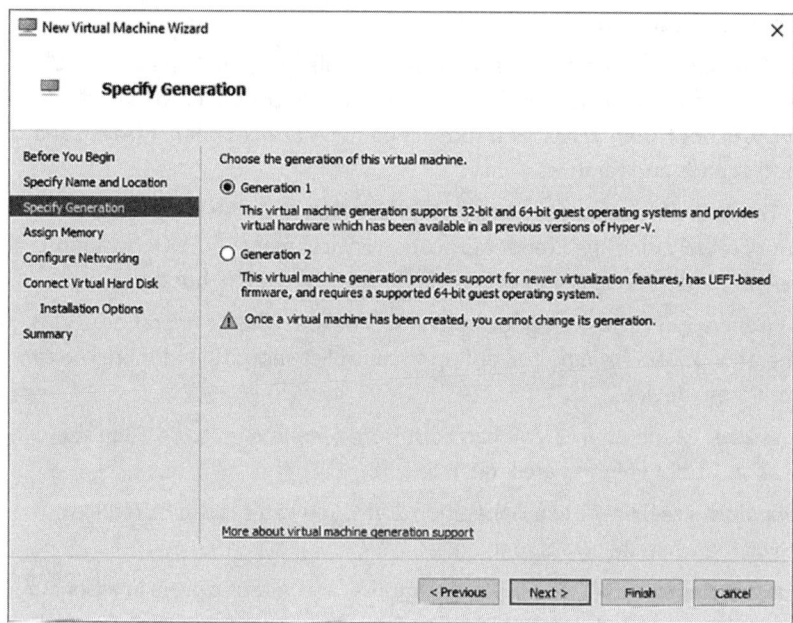

FIGURE 3-22 The Specify Generation page in the New Virtual Machine Wizard

The New-VM PowerShell cmdlet also includes a Generation parameter, which you use in a command like the following:

```
new-vm -name server1 -generation 2 -memorystartupbytes 1gb -newvhdpath
"c:\disks\server1.vhdx"
```

If you omit the Generation parameter from the command line, the cmdlet creates a Generation 1 VM by default.

Generation 2 advantages

Generation 1 VMs are designed to emulate the hardware found in a typical computer, and to do this, they use drivers for specific devices, such as an AMI BIOS, an S3 graphics adapter, and an Intel chipset and network adapter. Generation 1 VMs that you create with Windows Server 2016 Hyper-V are completely compatible with all previous Hyper-V versions.

Generation 2 VMs use synthetic drivers and software-based devices instead, and provide advantages that include the following:

- **UEFI boot** Instead of using the traditional BIOS, Generation 2 VMs support Secure Boot, using the Universal Extensible Firmware Interface (UEFI), which requires a system to boot from digitally signed drivers and enables them to boot from drives larger than 2 TB, with GUID partition tables. UEFI is fully emulated in VMs, regardless of the firmware in the physical host server.

- **SCSI disks** Generation 2 VMs omit the IDE disk controller used by Generation 1 VMs to boot the system and use a high-performance virtual SCSI controller for all disks, enabling the VMs to boot from VHDX files, support up to 64 devices per controller, and perform hot disk adds and removes.

- **PXE boot** The native virtual network adapter in Generation 2 VMs supports booting from a network server using the Preboot Execution Environment (PXE). Generation 1 VMs require you to use the legacy network adapter to support PXE booting.

- **SCSI boot** Generation 2 VMs can boot from a SCSI device, which Generation 1 VMs cannot. Generation 2 VMs have no IDE or floppy controller support, and therefore cannot boot from these devices.

- **Boot volume size** Generation 2 VMs can boot from a volume up to 64 TB in size, while Generation 1 boot volumes are limited to 2 TB.

- **VHDX boot volume resizing** In a Generation 2 VM, you can expand or reduce a VHDX boot volume while the VM is running.

- **Software-based peripherals** The keyboard, mouse, and videos drivers in a Generation 2 VM are software-based, not emulated, so they are less resource-intensive and provide a more secure environment.

- **Hot network adapters** In Generation 2 VMs, you can add and remove virtual network adapters while the VM is running.

- **Enhanced Session Mode** Generation 2 VMs support Enhanced Session Mode, which provides Hyper-V Manager and VMConnect connections to the VM with additional capabilities, such as audio, clipboard support, printer access, and USB devices.

- **Shielded virtual machines** Generation 2 VMs can be shielded, so that the disk and the system state are encrypted and accessible only by authorized administrators.

- **Storage Spaces Direct** Generation 2 VMs running Windows Server 2016 Datacenter Edition support Storage Spaces Direct, which can provide a high-performance, fault-tolerant storage solution using local drives.

Generation 2 limitations

The result in a Generation 2 virtual machine is that the VM deploys much faster than its Generation 1 counterparts, is more secure, and performs better as well. The limitations, however, are that Generation 2 VMs cannot run some guest operating systems, including the following:

- Windows Server 2008 R2
- Windows Server 2008
- Windows 7
- Some older Linux distributions
- All FreeBSD distributions
- All 32-bit operating systems

> **NOTE CONVERTING VM GENERATIONS**
>
> Once you have created a VM using a specific generation, there is no way to change it in Windows Server 2016. However, there is a downloadable script called Convert-VMGeneration available from the Microsoft Developer Network that creates a new Generation 2 VM from an existing Generation 1 VM, omitting some devices such as floppy disk drives, DVD drives using physical media, legacy network adapters, and COM ports. The script is available at *https://code.msdn.microsoft.com/ConvertVMGeneration*.

Choosing a VM generation

Generally speaking, you should use Generation 2 VMs, except in situations where they are not supported or they do not support the features you need, such as the following:

- You want to perform a BIOS boot on the VM.
- You have an existing VHD that does not support UEFI that you want to use in a new VM.
- You want to install a guest operating system version that does not support Generation 2.
- You plan to move the VM to a Windows Server 2008 R2 or other Hyper-V server that does not support Generation 2 VMs.
- You plan to move the VM to Windows Azure.

Implement enhanced session mode

Virtual Machine Connection (VMConnect) is the tool that Hyper-V Manager uses to connect to a running VM and access its desktop. When you select a VM in Hyper-V Manager and click Connect in the Actions pane, you are running VMConnect. However, you can also use the tool without Hyper-V Manager by running VMConnect.exe from the command line.

Enhanced session mode is a Hyper-V feature that enables a virtual machine accessed through VMConnect to utilize resources on the computer where VMConnect is running. For example, with enhanced session mode enabled, a VM can send print jobs to the host system's printer, log on using its smart card reader, share clipboard data, play or record audio, adjust the screen resolution, or access the host's drives.

In Windows Server 2016, enhanced session mode is disabled by default. To use it, you must enable it in the Hyper-V Settings dialog box on the host server, in two places.

- In the Server section, on the Enhanced Session Mode Policy page, select the Allow Enhanced Session Mode check box, as shown in Figure 3-23.
- In the User section, on the Enhanced Session Mode page, select the Use Enhanced Session Mode check box.

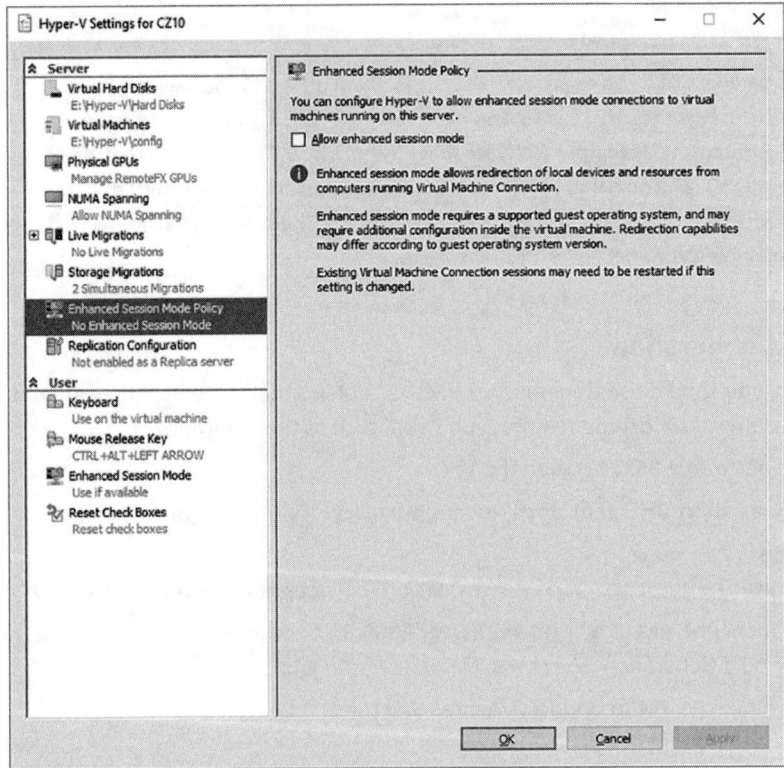

FIGURE 3-23 The Enhanced Session Mode Policy page in the Hyper-V Settings dialog box

To use enhanced session mode, the host system must be running Windows Server 2016, Windows Server 2012 R2, Windows Server 2012, Windows 10, Windows 8.1, or Windows 8. The VM must be Generation 2 and be running Windows Server 2016, Windows Server 2012 R2, Windows 10, or Windows 8.1 as the guest operating system. Remote Desktop must also be enabled in the System Properties sheet.

When you connect to a VM with enhanced session mode enabled, an extra Connect dialog box appears, on which you can select the screen resolution for the VM, as shown in Figure 3-24.

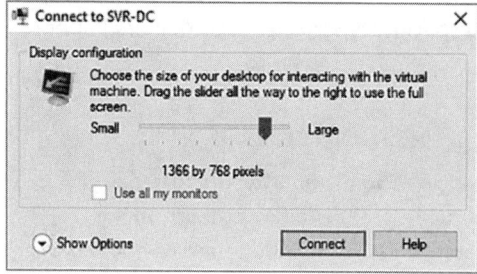

FIGURE 3-24 The Connect dialog box

When you click Show Options, and then select the Local Resources tab, as shown in Figure 3-25, you can select the audio options and local devices you want the VM to be able to use. Clicking Connect then opens the VM desktop in the VMConnect window.

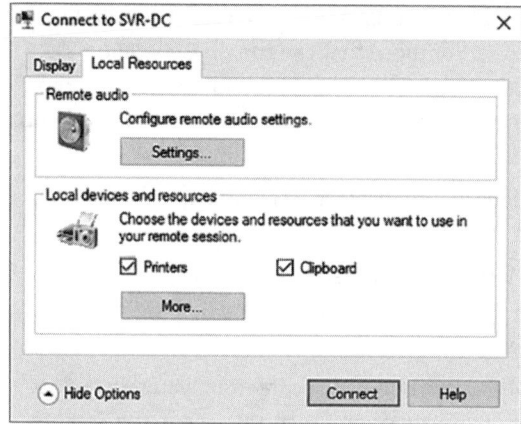

FIGURE 3-25 The Local Resources tab of the Connect dialog box

Create Linux and FreeBSD VMs

Windows Server 2016 Hyper-V is not limited to Windows for guest operating systems. You can install many Linux distributions or FreeBSD in a virtual machine. Installation procedures vary by distribution, as does performance. In some cases, you might have to modify some of the default virtual machine settings to support a particular distribution, but in many cases, the installation process proceeds without problems.

The first step to creating a VM running Linux or FreeBSD is to check whether the distribution and version you want to use is supported. Microsoft has announced support for several Linux distributions, including CentOS, Red Hat, Debian, Oracle, SUSE, and Ubuntu, as well as FreeBSD. These are available in several versions, and you must make sure that the version you want to use is supported, and that it supports the specific Hyper-V features that are important to you.

> **NEED MORE REVIEW? SUPPORTED LINUX AND FREEBSD VERSIONS**
>
> For information on the versions of each Linux and FreeBSD distribution supported as Hyper-V guests, and the features available in each one, see the following page on the Microsoft TechNet site at https://technet.microsoft.com/en-us/windows-server-docs/compute/hyper-v/supported-linux-and-freebsd-virtual-machines-for-hyper-v-on-windows.

Configuring VMs

The next step is to determine what virtual machine settings to use for a VM that uses Linux or FreeBSD as the guest operating system. Here again, the settings you need are generally specific to the individual operating system you plan to run. Some of the recent Linux releases can run on Generation 2 VMs, but others cannot. For those that can run on Generation 2 VMs, you must confirm that they can use Secure Boot. For these operating systems, it is most likely necessary for administrators to do their own testing to determine the optimum settings to provide the best performance.

For example, the Ubuntu distribution of Linux is supported as a Hyper-V guest. However, to create a VM for Ubuntu, you must consider the following:

- For Generation 1 VMs, use the Hyper-V network adapter, not the legacy network adapter. If it is necessary to boot from the network with PXE, use a Generation 2 VM, which supports PXE in the default network adapter.
- Ubuntu can run on a Generation 2 VM. However, to use Secure Boot, you must select the Microsoft UEFI Certificate Authority template on the Security page in the Settings dialog box.
- Many Linux file systems consume unnaturally large amounts of disk space because of the default 32 MB block size that Hyper-V uses when creating a VHDX file. To conserve storage, Microsoft recommends creating a VHDX with a 1 MB block size. To do this, you must use the New-VHD PowerShell cmdlet with the BlockSizeBytes parameter, as in the following example:

  ```
  new-vhd -path c:\disks\server1.vhdx -sizebytes 40gb -dynamic -blocksizebytes 1mb
  ```

- The GRUB boot loader in Ubuntu tends to time out when restarting the VM immediately after the installation. To address this issue after the installation, you can edit the /etc/default/grub file and change the GRUB TIMEOUT value to 100000, as shown in Figure 3-26.

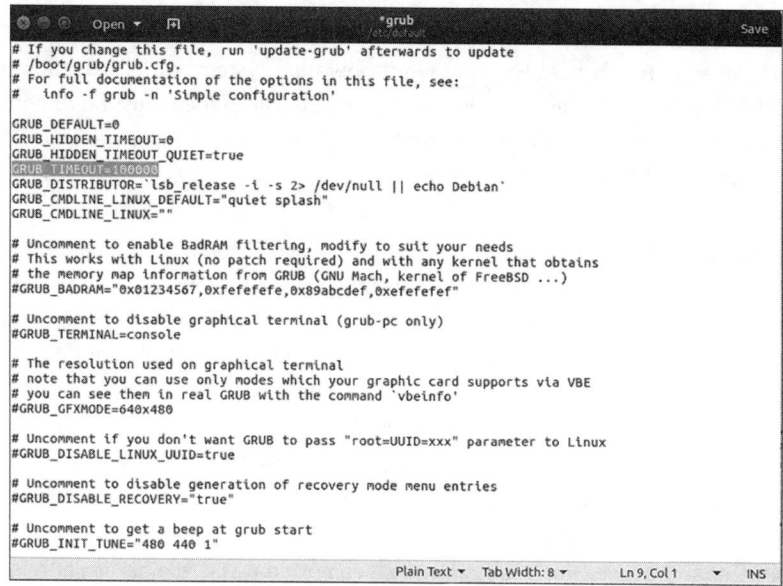

FIGURE 3-26 Editing the grub file

Installing the guest operating system

FreeBSD and most of the supported Linux distributions are available for download in several forms. Most have bootable installation disk images available as ISO files, which you can load into a virtual DVD drive in a VM, to launch the installation program, as shown in Figure 3-27. Many of the current Linux and FreeBSD operating systems have installation programs that rival that of Windows in their simplicity and efficiency, especially in the case of a virtual machine, in which the hardware components are entirely predictable.

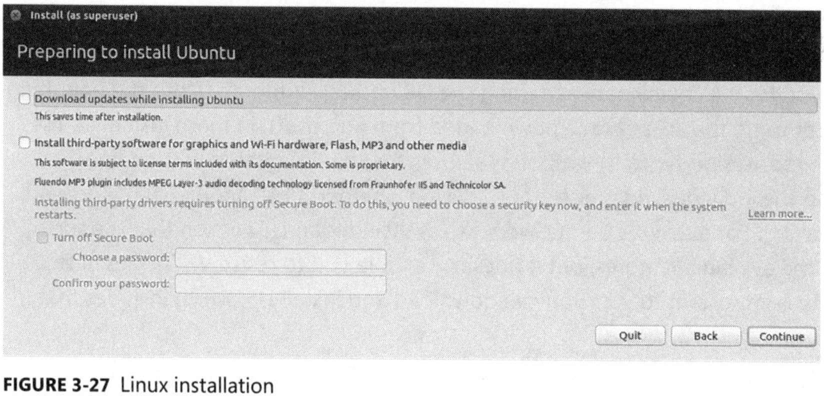

FIGURE 3-27 Linux installation

Install and configure Linux Integration Services (LIS)

As mentioned earlier in this chapter, Hyper-V guest operating systems run a collection of drivers and other components called Integration Services. Because they must be designed to run in the guest operating system environment, there are different implementations for the Linux and FreeBSD operating systems, called Linux Integration Services (LIS) and FreeBSD Integration Services (FIS).

The various Linux distributions that Hyper-V supports have differences in their implementations, but they are all built on the same series of Linux kernel versions. Most of the recent versions in all of the supported distributions have LIS or FIS included as part of the operating system, which Microsoft refers to as "built in" implementations. These implementations are developed as a cooperative effort with the developer community of each distribution, tested by both Microsoft and the operating system contributors. After satisfactory testing, the distribution vendors incorporate LIS into their operating system releases.

However, not all implementations of Integration Services support all of the available Hyper-V features in all versions of the guest operating system. This is due to the nature of the Linux development and distribution methods, which can often result in a particular release not having the latest LIS implementation. For these instances, there are LIS and FIS packages available as free downloads from the Microsoft Download Center.

Depending on the Linux distribution and the version you intend to install, there are three possible solutions for the Integration Services issue, as follows:

- **Do nothing** In older Linux versions that do not include LIS, installing the operating system as a guest creates emulated drivers for the virtualized hardware in the VM. No additional software is needed, but the emulated drivers do not support all of the Hyper-V management features and do not perform as well as the Hyper-V-specific drivers in the LIS package.

- **Download and install LIS** In older Linux versions that do not include LIS, downloading and installing the LIS package provides better performance and additional management features. In some versions of some Linux distributions, such as CentOS and Oracle, you have a choice between using the LIS package integrated into the operating system, or using the LIS package downloaded from Microsoft. In these instances, the downloaded version typically supports features that the integrated version does not. It is up to the individual administrator to decide whether those additional features are worth having. For example, CentOS version 6.4 includes an LIS version that supports most of the available features, but it does not enable you to resize VHDX files. If this capability is important to you, you can download and install LIS, which includes that feature.

- **Use built-in LIS** In some versions of some distributions, such as the most recent Ubuntu releases, LIS is fully implemented in the operating system, and installing the downloadable LIS module is explicitly not recommended. In the latest versions of most distributions, there are few situations in which it is necessary to use the downloaded

LIS package, as the vast majority of Hyper-V features are already integrated into the operating system.

The downloadable versions of the LIS package are assigned version numbers, which the integrated versions are not. If you decide to use the downloaded LIS, you should always obtain the latest version, after ensuring that Microsoft supports it for the version of the guest operating system you are running. Microsoft provides the LIS package in two forms, as a gzipped tar file that you can download to the guest operating system and install, or as a disk image in the ISO format, which you can load into a virtual DVD drive.

Install and configure FreeBSD Integration Services (BIS)

Since version 10, FreeBSD has included full support for FreeBSD Integration Services (BIS) in its operating system releases. There is no need to install additional software unless you are running FreeBSD version 9 or earlier. For versions 8.x and 9.x, there are ports available at: *https://svnweb.freebsd.org/ports/head/emulators/hyperv-is*, which can provide BIS functionality.

Implement Secure Boot for Windows and Linux environments

Secure Boot is a mechanism built into the Unified Extensible Firmware Interface (UEFI) that is designed to ensure that every component loaded during a computer's boot sequence has been digitally signed, and is therefore trusted by the computer's manufacturer. In Hyper-V, Generation 2 VMs support Secure Boot as part of their UEFI implementation.

In a traditional system boot, the computer performs a power-on self-test (POST), after which it initializes the BIOS, detects the system hardware, and loads the firmware into memory. After that, the system runs the bootloader. Because the firmware and the bootloader are not verified, it is possible for them to contain some form of malware, such as a rootkit or bootkit. These are not detectable by ordinary anti-virus software, and can therefore infect the system while remaining invisible to the operating system.

Secure Boot replaces the traditional BIOS firmware with UEFI firmware, which is responsible for verifying that the firmware, the bootloader, and other components originate from trusted sources. UEFI uses trusted certificates for the operating system and a platform key supplied by the computer vendor to ensure that no unauthorized software is being loaded during the boot process.

Windows and Secure Boot

When you create a Generation 2 virtual machine in Hyper-V, the computer manufacturer is Microsoft, and the UEFI firmware includes certificates for the Windows bootloaders. This means that Windows boots on the VM, because there is a chain of trusted certificates going back to the root. If you attempt to boot the VM into a non-Windows operating system, the system silently proceeds to the next item in the boot order. If you find that a VM is constantly trying to boot from the network or from a DVD, no matter what boot order you specify, the problem is likely to be that the Secure Boot failed, and the system is bypassing the hard disk boot.

Secure Boot in enabled by default on Generation 2 VMs. To disable it, you open the Security page in the VM Settings dialog box, and clear the Enable Secure Boot check box, as shown in Figure 3-28.

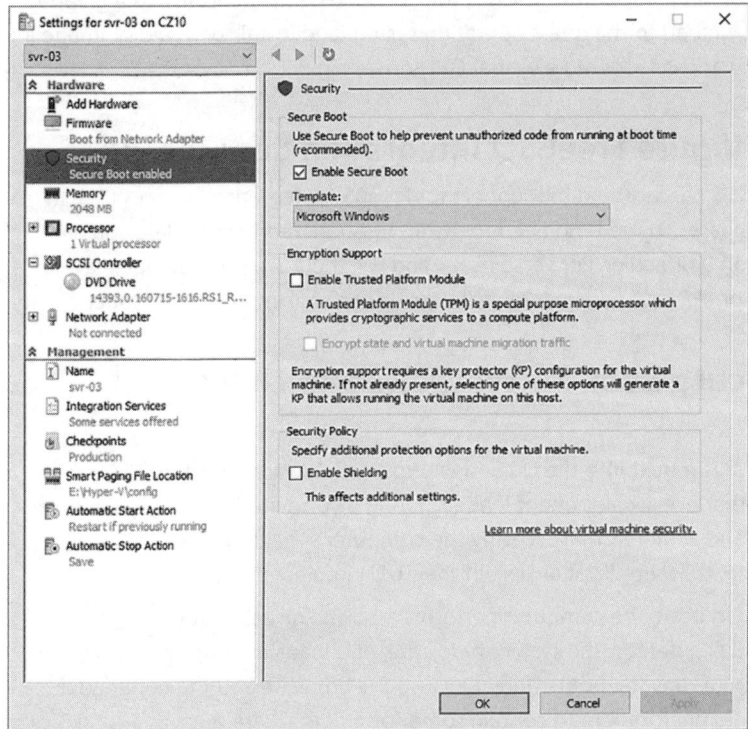

FIGURE 3-28 The Security page of a VM Settings dialog box

You can also disable Secure Boot using the Set-VMFirmware cmdlet in Windows PowerShell, as in the following example:

```
set-vmfirmware -vmname server1 -enablesecureboot off
```

Linux and Secure Boot

When you install a Linux distribution in a Generation 2 VM, the problem described earlier happens when Secure Boot is enabled. UEFI has no certificates for non-Windows operating systems by default, so it cannot run the Linux bootloader and the system keeps trying to boot from the network, as shown in Figure 3-29.

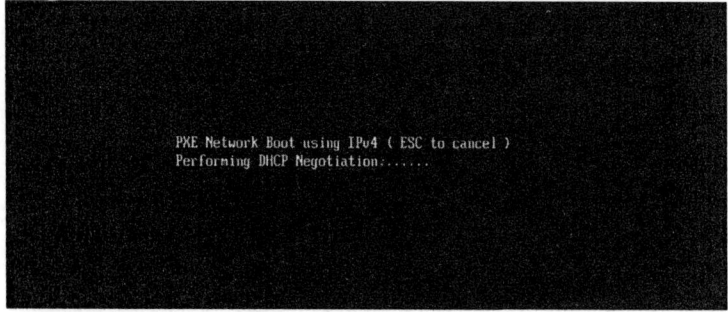

FIGURE 3-29 Secure Boot failure

One of the ways in which certain Linux distributions are supported by Microsoft is the inclusion of certificates for their bootloaders in Windows Server 2016 Hyper-V. To access those certificates and enable the VM to boot into Linux, you must change the Secure Boot template on the Security page in the Settings dialog box. By default, the Microsoft Windows template is selected. The certificates for the Linux operating systems are in the Microsoft UEFI Certificate Authority template, as shown in Figure 3-30.

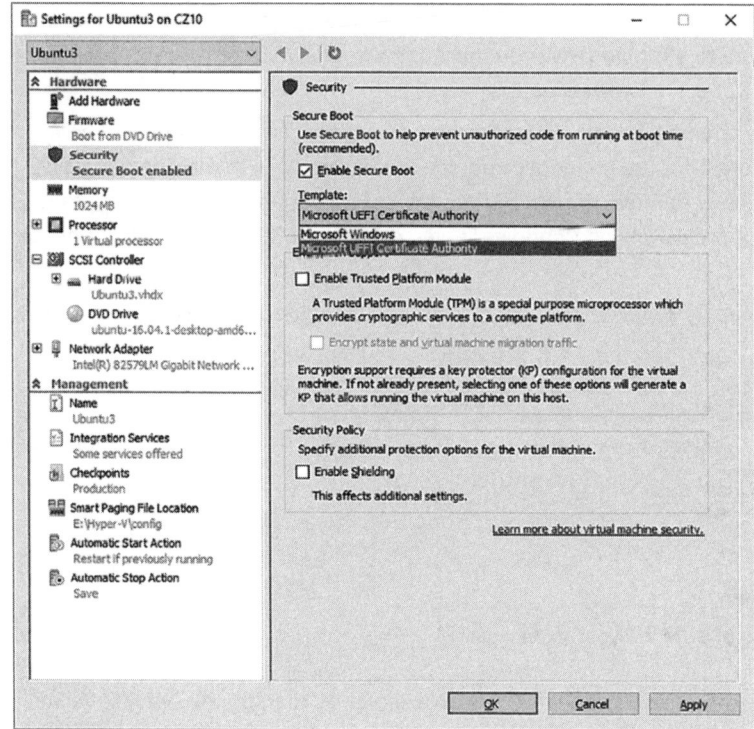

FIGURE 3-30 Secure Boot templates on the Security page of a VM Settings dialog box

To change the template setting using the Set-VMFirmware cmdlet, use a command like the following:

```
set-vmfirmware -vmname server1 -securebootTemplate microsoftueficertificate authority
```

Move and convert VMs from previous versions of Hyper-V to Windows Server 2016 Hyper-V

Each version of Hyper-V creates virtual machines of a specific version. The version indicates the features that are available on that VM. The VMs created in Windows Server 2016 are version 8.0. If you have upgraded a Hyper-V server to Windows Server 2016 from a previous version, you should also consider upgrading your virtual machines as well.

In previous versions of Windows, upgrading the operating system caused the VMs to be upgraded as well. In Windows Server 2016 (and Windows 10), this is not the case, because these versions of Hyper-V enable you to move VMs to servers running different versions of Windows.

For example, if you have virtual machines you created in Windows Server 2012 R2 Hyper-V, you can import them into a Windows Server 2016 Hyper-V, and they run perfectly well. However, if you want to take advantage of the latest Hyper-V features, such as adding a network adapter or memory to a running VM, you must upgrade the VM from version 5.0 (the Windows Server 2012 R2 version) to version 8.0.

Unfortunately, once you upgrade the VM, you can no longer run it on a Windows Server 2012 R2 server. Therefore, VMs are no longer upgrade automatically with the operating system. If you might ever have to move the VM back to the old server, you should not upgrade it. If you intend to run it exclusively on Windows Server 2016 Hyper-V, go ahead and upgrade it.

Each VM Summary tab in Hyper-V Manager displays its Configuration Version, as shown in Figure 3-31.

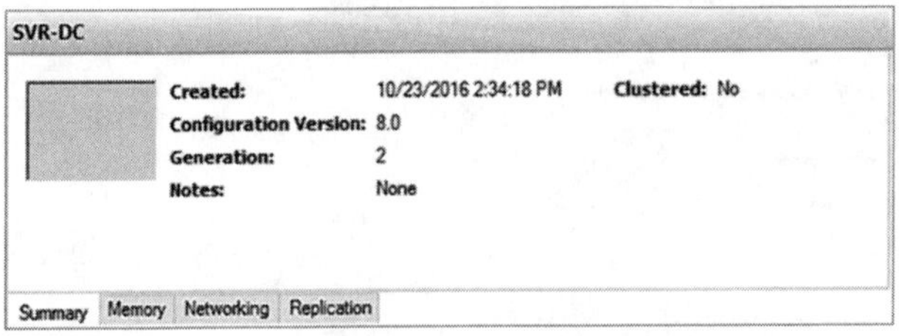

FIGURE 3-31 Summary tab of a VM in Hyper-V Manager

You can also display the versions of all the VMs on a server by running the Get-VM PowerShell cmdlet with the asterisk (*) wildcard character, as shown in Figure 3-32.

```
PS C:\WINDOWS\system32> get-vm

Name       State CPUUsage(%) MemoryAssigned(M) Uptime   Status              Version
----       ----- ----------- ----------------- ------   ------              -------
SVR-01     Off   0           0                 00:00:00 Operating normally  8.0
freebsd1   Off   0           0                 00:00:00 Operating normally  8.0
temptest1  Off   0           0                 00:00:00 Operating normally  5.0
CentOS1    Off   0           0                 00:00:00 Operating normally  8.0
svr-02     Off   0           0                 00:00:00 Operating normally  8.0
Ubuntu3    Off   0           0                 00:00:00 Operating normally  8.0
wsvr-01    Off   0           0                 00:00:00 Operating normally  8.0
svr-03     Off   0           0                 00:00:00 Operating normally  8.0
Ununtu2    Off   0           0                 00:00:00 Operating normally  8.0
SVR-DC     Off   0           0                 00:00:00 Operating normally  8.0

PS C:\WINDOWS\system32>
```

FIGURE 3-32 Output of the Get-VM cmdlet

To move a VM to another server, you can export it in the old one and import it into the new one. To list the VM versions supported on a server, run the Get-VMHostSupportedVersion cmdlet, as shown in Figure 3-33.

```
PS C:\WINDOWS\system32> get-vmhostsupportedversion

Name                                                         Version IsDefault
----                                                         ------- ---------
Microsoft Windows 8.1/Server 2012 R2                         5.0     False
Microsoft Windows 10 1507/Server 2016 Technical Preview 3    6.2     False
Microsoft Windows 10 1511/Server 2016 Technical Preview 4    7.0     False
Microsoft Windows Server 2016 Technical Preview 5            7.1     False
Microsoft Windows 10 Anniversary Update/Server 2016          8.0     True
Prerelease                                                   254.0   False
Experimental                                                 255.0   False

PS C:\WINDOWS\system32>
```

FIGURE 3-33 Output of the Get-VMHostSupportedVersion cmdlet

Then, to upgrade the VM to the version used by the new server, select Upgrade Configuration in the Actions pane, and confirm your action. The version in the Summary tab changes and the new server's features are now available in the VM.

You can also upgrade the VM by using the Update-VMVersion PowerShell cmdlet, as in the following example:

```
update-vmversion -vm server1
```

You can also specify multiple VM names on this command line, to upgrade multiple VMs using a single command.

Export and import VMs

The export and import functions in Hyper-V are a means of moving a virtual machine to a different server or creating a copy of a VM on the same server. When you export a VM, you specify the name of a folder where the system creates a copy of all the files of the VM, including its configuration files, virtual hard disks, and even checkpoints. You can then import the VM into the same or another server.

To export a VM, you select Export in the Actions pane, to display the Export Virtual Machine dialog box, as shown in Figure 3-34. Once you specify a location and click Export, the system begins to copy the files to a subfolder named for the VM. You can export a VM while it is running or stopped.

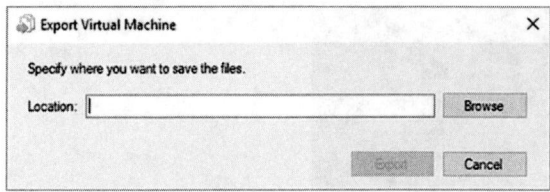

FIGURE 3-34 The Export Virtual Machine dialog box

To export a VM with Windows PowerShell, you use the Export-VM cmdlet, as in the following example:

```
export-vm -name server1 -path c:\export
```

The only indication in Hyper-V Manager that the export is ongoing is that the Actions pane has a Cancel Exporting item in it. Once the export is completed, this item is replaced by the Export item again. At this point, you can copy the export folder to another server, or import it to the same server to make a copy of the VM.

Importing VMs using Hyper-V Manager

To import an exported VM into a Hyper-V server using Hyper-V Manager, use the following procedure:

1. In Hyper-V Manager, in the Actions pane, select Import Virtual Machine. The Import Virtual Machine Wizard appears.
2. On the Locate Folder page, type or browse to the folder containing the exported files.
3. On the Select Virtual Machine page, select the VM to import.
4. On the Choose Import Type page, shown in Figure 3-35, select one of the following options:
    - **Register The Virtual Machine In Place**   Leaves the exported files where they are and registers the VM in the Hyper-V server, using the same ID as the VM from which they were exported. If the VM was exported from the same server, you cannot run both at the same time.
    - **Restore The Virtual Machine**   Copies the exported files, either to the default locations on the server or to different locations that you specify, and registers the VM in the Hyper-V server, using the same ID as the VM from which they were exported. If the VM was exported from the same server, you cannot run both at the same time. Once the import is complete, you can delete the exported files or import them again.
    - **Copy The Virtual Machine**   Copies the exported files, either to the default locations on the server or to different locations that you specify, and registers the VM in the Hyper-V server with a new ID. This enables you to create a copy of an existing VM on the same server and run it together with the original.

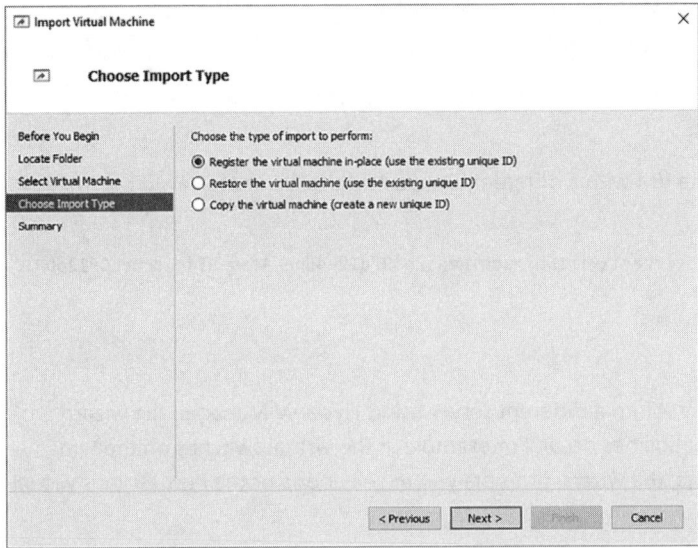

FIGURE 3-35 The Choose Import Type page of the Import Virtual Machine Wizard

5. If you choose either the Restore or Copy option, a Choose Folders For Virtual Machine Files page appears, on which you can specify different locations for the configuration, checkpoint, and Smart Paging files.

6. If you choose either the Restore or Copy option, a Choose Folders To Store Virtual Hard Disks page appears, on which you can specify an alternate location for the VHD files of the virtual machine. If you are importing a VM from the same server, you must specify a different folder, because VHD files with the same names already exist.

7. Click Finish to begin the import process.

Importing VMs using Windows PowerShell

To import a VM with Windows PowerShell, you use the Import-VM cmdlet. To import a VM using the Register option, in which the exported files are not copied, you use a command like the following. Note that, for this cmdlet, you must type the entire path to the VM configuration file:

```
import-vm -path c:\export\server1\virtualmachines\2b197d10-4dbe-4ea9-a54e-cc0bb0f12d09.vcmx
```

To import a VM using the Restore option, you add the Copy parameter, which causes the cmdlet to copy the exported files to the new server's default folders, as follows.

```
import-vm -path c:\export\server1\virtualmachines\2b197d10-4dbe-4ea9-a54e-cc0bb0f12d09.vcmx -copy
```

To specify different locations for the copied files, you can add the following parameters to the command line:

- VirtualMachinePath
- VhdDestinationPath
- SnapshotFilePath
- SmartPagingFilePath

To create a new copy of a VM with a different ID, you add the GenerateNewId parameter, as in the following:

```
import-vm -path c:\export\server1\virtualmachines\2b197d10-4dbe-4ea9-a54e-cc0bb0f12d09.vcmx -copy -generatenewid
```

Handling conflicts

When you are importing a VM into a different server using Hyper-V Manager, the wizard prompts you if any incompatibilities occur. For example, if the virtual switches on the two servers have different names, the wizard prompts you to select one of the new server's virtual switches.

If an incompatibility occurs during a VM import using the Import-VM cmdlet, an error occurs and the command is not completed. You must then use the Compare-VM cmdlet with the same parameters to generate a report that specifies the incompatibility. Depending on the nature of the problem, you then use other cmdlets to rectify the situation. For the virtual switch incompatibility described here, you would use the Disconnect-VMNetwork Adapter cmdlet to remove the switch assignment before reattempting the import.

Implement Discrete Device Assignment (DDA)

Hyper-V has long had the ability to create pass-through disks, in which you assign a physical disk in the Hyper-V host to a guest virtual machine. The VM accesses the disk directly, without using a VHD. *Discrete Device Assignment (DDA)* is a similar concept, except that it enables you to pass any PCI Express device through to a VM.

You can, for example, pass a graphics processing unit (GPU) through to a VM with DDA, providing the VM with graphics performance that was previously impossible. You can also pass a wireless network adapter through to a VM, providing the virtual machine with WiFi capability.

DDA is implemented strictly through PowerShell, presumably to keep all but advanced administrators from playing with it. Any sort of pass-through arrangement between the host server and a guest operating sytem is an inherent security risk. An attack to the guest can use that pass-through conduit to get to the host, possibly bringing down the entire server with an error on the PCI Express bus.

From a high-level perspective, the steps involved in passing through a device using DDA are as follows:

1. Identify the device to be passed.
2. Disable the device on the host.

3. Dismount the device on the host.
4. Attach the device to the virtual machine.

If you think this makes the process look easy, think again. Here are the cmdlets you use to implement each of these steps:

1. The Get-PnpDevice -PresentOnly command generates a long list of the devices that Plug and Play has installed on the computer and displays information about them. By selecting one device and formatting the output of the cmdlet, you can determine the Instance ID of the device, a long string that you need for the next step. The instance ID can also be found in Device Manager on the Details tab, under the name Device Instance Path.

2. The Disable-PnpDevice -InstanceID command disables the device by removing the installed drivers on the host.

3. The Dismount-VmHostAssignableDevice -LocationPath command removes the device from the control of the host. To obtain a value for the LocationPath parameter, you use the Get-PnpDeviceProperty cmdlet, for which you must supply KeyName and InstanceID values. The location path is also available in Device Manager.

4. The Add-VMAssignableDevice -VM -LocationPath cmdlet attaches the device to a specific virtual machine.

Before this last command completes successfully, you must configure the following settings in the virtual machine Settings dialog box:

- The Automatic Stop Action setting must be set to Turn Off The Virtual Machine.
- The VM can use dynamic memory, but the RAM and Minimum RAM settings must be equal.

Finally, and perhaps most important, there are many low-level requirements that the host server BIOS/UEFI and the proposed device must meet. Some of these requirements are visible in software and some are not. The Dismount-VmHostAssignableDevice cmdlet supports a Force parameter that enables it to ignore the Access Control Services (ACS) checks that prevent PCI Express traffic from going to the wrong places. This parameter should only be used with extreme caution.

Skill 3.3: Configure Hyper-V storage

This section covers the various features and mechanisms that Windows Server 2016 uses to enhance the storage subsystem for its virtual machines.

This section covers how to:
- Create VHDs and VHDX files using Hyper-V Manager
- Create shared VHDX files
- Configure differencing disks
- Modify virtual hard disks
- Configure pass-through disks
- Resize a virtual hard disk
- Manage checkpoints
- Implement production checkpoints
- Implement a virtual Fibre Channel adapter
- Configure storage Quality of Service (QoS)

Create VHDs and VHDX files using Hyper-V Manager

When you create a new Generation 1 virtual machine in Hyper-V Manager, the New Virtual Machine Wizard creates a virtual storage subsystem that consists of two IDE (Integrated Drive Electronics) controllers and one SCSI (Small Computer Systems Interface) controller, as shown in Figure 3-36.

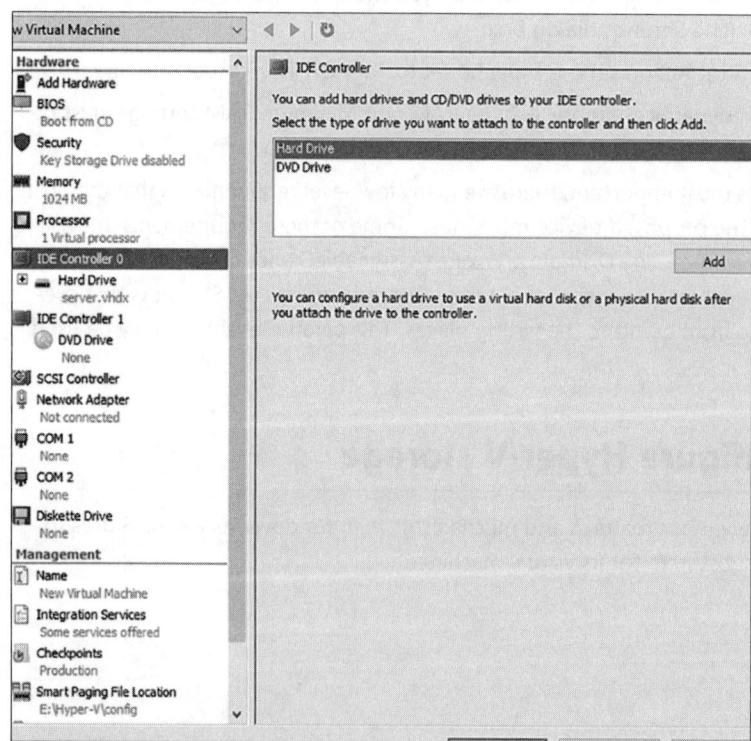

FIGURE 3-36 The default VM drive controller configuration

The IDE controllers host the virtual machine system drive and its DVD drive. As with their physical equivalents, each IDE controller can host two devices, so you can create two additional virtual drives and add them to the system. The SCSI controller is unpopulated; you can create additional disks and add them to that controller to provide the VM with more storage.

In a Generation 2 VM, there is no IDE controller, so the system and DVD drives are both connected to the default SCSI controller. In a VM of either generation, you can also create additional SCSI controllers and add drives to them. By creating multiple drives and controllers, Hyper-V makes it possible to construct virtual storage subsystems that emulate almost any physical storage solution you might devise.

Understanding virtual disk formats

Windows Server 2016 Hyper-V supports the original VHD disk image file and the new VHDX format. The original VHD format is limited to a maximum size of 2 terabytes (TB) and is compatible with all versions of Hyper-V. Windows Server 2012 R2 introduced an updated version of the format, which uses a VHDX filename extension. VHDX image files can be as large as 64 TB, and they also support 4 KB logical sector sizes, to provide compatibility with 4 KB native physical drives. VHDX files can also use larger block sizes (up to 256 MB), which enable you to fine tune the performance level of a virtual storage subsystem to accommodate specific applications and data file types.

However, VHDX files are not backwards compatible and can be read only by the Hyper-V servers in Windows Server 2012 R2 or later and Windows 8.1 or later. If migrating your virtual machines from Windows Server 2016 to an older Hyper-V version is a possibility, you should continue to use the VHD file format.

Creating a Virtual Disk with a VM

Windows Server 2016 Hyper-V provides several ways to create virtual disk files. You can create them as part of a new virtual machine, or create them later and add them to a VM. The graphical interface in Hyper-V Manager provides access to most of the VHD parameters, but the Windows PowerShell cmdlets included in Windows Server 2016 provide the most granular control over the disk image format.

When you create a new VM in Hyper-V Manager, the New Virtual Machine Wizard includes a Connect Virtual Hard Disk page, as shown in Figure 3-37, with which you can add a single disk to your new VM. The options for this disk are limited and consist of the following:

- **Create A Virtual Hard Disk**   Enables you to specify the name, location, and size for a new virtual hard disk, but this option can only create a dynamically expanding disk using the VHDX format.
- **Use An Existing Virtual Hard Disk**   Enables you to specify the location of an existing VHD or VHDX disk, which the VM uses as its system disk.
- **Attach A Virtual Hard Disk Later**   Prevents the wizard from adding any virtual hard disks to the VM configuration. You must manually add a disk later, before you can start the virtual machine.

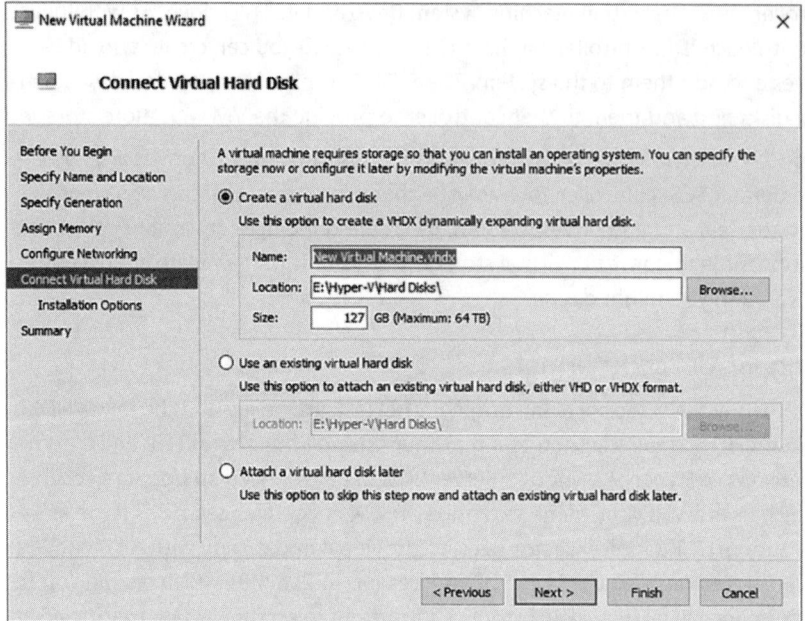

FIGURE 3-37 The Connect Virtual Hard Disk page of the New Virtual Machine Wizard

The object of this wizard page is to create the disk on which you install the guest operating system of the virtual machine, or select an existing disk on which an operating system is already installed. The disk the wizard creates is always a dynamically expanding one, connected to IDE Controller 0 on a Generation 1 VM or the SCSI Controller on a Generation 2 VM. To create a disk using any settings other than the defaults, you must select Attach A Virtual Hard Disk Later, create a new VHD or VHDX using the New Virtual Hard Disk Wizard, and then add the disk to the virtual machine.

> **NOTE DOWNLOADING VHDS**
>
> It is a common practice for Microsoft to release evaluation copies of its products as preinstalled VHD files, as an alternative to the traditional installable disk images. After downloading one of these files, you can create a VM on a Hyper-V server and select the Use An Existing Virtual Hard Disk option to mount the VHD as its system drive.

Creating a new virtual disk in Hyper-V Manager

You can create a virtual hard disk file at any time, without adding it to a virtual machine, by using the New Virtual Hard Disk Wizard in Hyper-V Manager.

To create a new virtual disk, use the following procedure.

1. Log on to the server running Windows Server 2016 using an account with administrative privileges.

2. Launch Hyper-V Manager and, in the left pane, select a Hyper-V server.
3. From the Action menu, select New | Hard Disk. The New Virtual Hard Disk Wizard appears.
4. On the Choose Disk Format page, shown in Figure 3-38, select one of the following disk format options:
   - **VHD** Creates an image no larger than 2 TB, using the highly compatible VHD format
   - **VHDX** Creates an image up to 64 TB in size, using the new VHDX format
   - **VHD Set** Creates an image for disk sharing among guest operating systems that supports features like online disk resizing and host-based backups

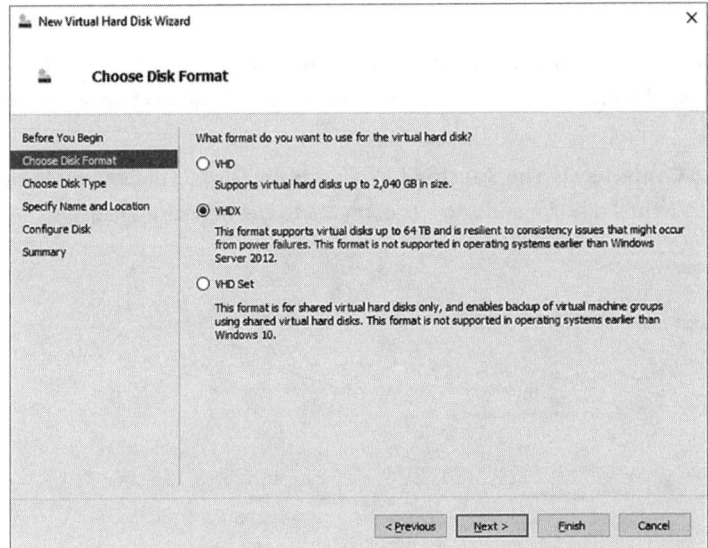

FIGURE 3-38 The Choose Disk Format page of the New Virtual Hard Disk Wizard

5. On the Choose Disk Type page, select one of the following disk type options:
   - **Fixed Size** The image file is a specified size, in which all the disk space required to create the image is allocated during its creation. Fixed disk images can be considered wasteful in terms of storage, because they can contain large amounts of empty space, but they are also efficient from a performance standpoint, because there is no overhead due to dynamic expansion and less fragmentation of the file.
   - **Dynamically Expanding** The image file has a specified maximum size, which starts out small and expands as needed to accommodate the data the system writes to it. Dynamically expanding disks are initially conservative of disk space, but their

continual growth can cause them to be highly fragmented, negatively affecting performance.

- **Differencing** The image file, called a child, is associated with a specific parent image. The system writes all changes made to the data on the parent image file to the child image, to facilitate a rollback later.

6. On the Specify Name And Location page, specify a filename for the disk image in the Name text box and, if desired, specify a location for the file other than the server default.

7. On the Configure Disk page, shown in Figure 3-39, select and configure one of the following options:

    - **Create A New Blank Virtual Hard Disk** Specifies the size (or the maximum size) of the disk image file to create.
    - **Copy The Contents Of The Specified Physical Disk** Enables you to select one of the physical hard disks in the computer and copy its contents to the new disk image.
    - **Copy The Contents Of The Specified Virtual Hard Disk** Enables you to select an existing virtual disk file and copy its contents to the new disk image.

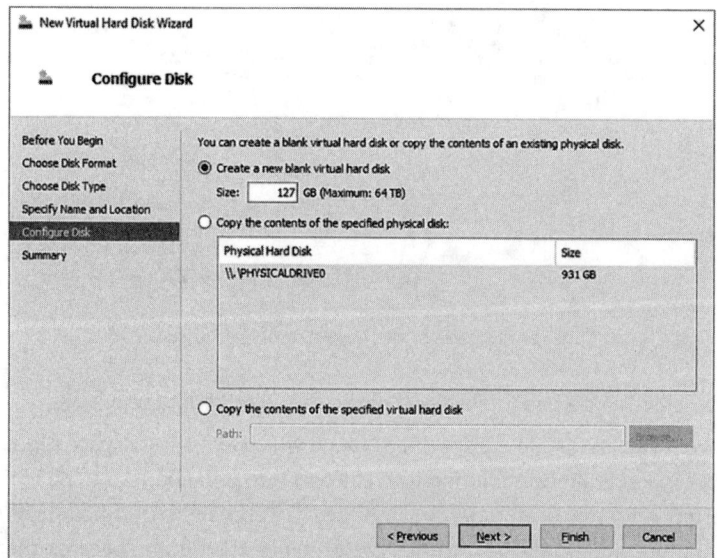

FIGURE 3-39 The Configure Disk page of the New Virtual Hard Disk Wizard

8. On the Completing The New Virtual Hard Disk Wizard page, click Finish.

The wizard creates the new image disk and saves it to the specified location.

Creating a new virtual disk in Windows PowerShell

You can create new virtual hard disk files using Windows PowerShell, with more control than is available through the graphical interface. To create a new disk image, you use the New-VHD cmdlet with the following basic syntax:

```
new-vhd -path c:\filename.vhd|c:\filename.vhdx -fixed|-dynamic|-differencing -sizebytes size [-blocksizebytes blocksize] [-logicalsectorsizebytes 512|4096]
```

When you use the cmdlet to create a virtual disk, the extension you specify for the filename determines the format (VHD or VHDX), and you can specify the block size and the logical sector size for the image, which you cannot do in the GUI. For example, the following command creates a 500 GB fixed VHDX image file with a logical sector size of 4 KB:

```
new-vhd -path c:\diskfile.vhdx -fixed -sizebytes 500gb -logicalsectorsizebytes 4096
```

Adding virtual disks to virtual machines

Creating virtual disk image files as a separate process enables you to exercise more control over their capabilities. After creating the VHD or VHDX files, you can add them to a virtual machine.

To add a hard disk drive to a physical computer, you must connect it to a controller, and the same is true with a virtual machine in Hyper-V. When you open the Settings dialog box for a Generation 1 virtual machine in its default configuration, you see three controllers, labeled IDE Controller 0, IDE Controller 1, and SCSI Controller. Each of the IDE controllers can support two devices, and the default virtual machine configuration uses one channel on IDE Controller 0 for the system hard disk and one channel on IDE Controller 1 for the system's DVD drive.

If you did not create a virtual disk as part of the new Virtual Machine Wizard (that is, if you chose the Attach A Virtual Hard Disk Later option), you must add a hard disk image to IDE Controller 0 to use as a system drive. A Generation 1 virtual machine cannot boot from the SCSI controller.

To add an existing virtual system drive to a virtual machine, use the following procedure.

1. In Hyper-V Manager, select a virtual machine and open its Settings dialog box.
2. Select IDE Controller 0 and, on the IDE Controller page, select Hard Drive, and click Add.
3. On the Hard Drive page, shown in Figure 3-40, in the Controller and Location drop-down lists, select the IDE controller and the channel you want to use for the hard disk.

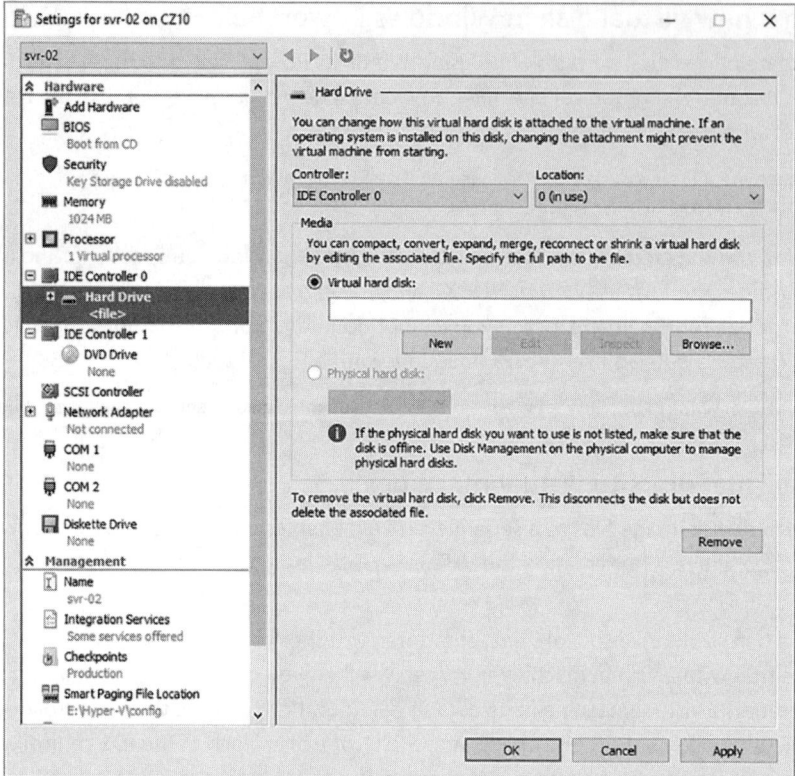

FIGURE 3-40 The Hard Drive page in a Generation 1 VM Settings dialog box

4. With the Virtual Hard Disk option selected, click Browse, and select the disk image file you want to add.

5. Click OK to close the Settings dialog box.

Although you cannot use a SCSI drive as the system disk in a Generation 1 virtual machine, you can add virtual data disks to the SCSI controller, and you must do so on a Generation 2 VM. The procedure is all but identical to that of a Generation 1 VM.

Unlike the IDE Controllers, which support only two devices each, a SCSI connector in Hyper-V can support up to 64 drives. You can also add multiple SCSI controllers to a virtual machine, providing almost unlimited scalability for your virtual storage subsystem.

Create shared VHDX files

Windows Server 2016 Hyper-V can create shared virtual disk files, for use in Hyper-V guest failover clusters. A failover cluster is a group of computers, physical or virtual, that all run the same application. If one of the computers should fail, the others are there to take up the slack. For a failover cluster to function, the computers must access the same data, which means the store hardware—again, physical or virtual—must be shared.

For example, you can create a failover cluster with multiple computers running Microsoft SQL Server. Each computer, called a node, runs its own copy of the application, but all of the nodes must be able to access the same copy of the database. By storing the database on a shared virtual disk, you can configure each of the computers in the cluster to access it, as shown in Figure 3-41.

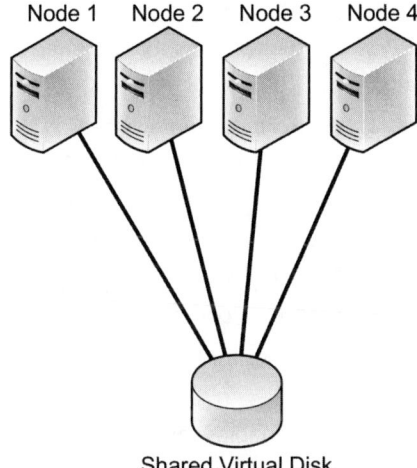

FIGURE 3-41 Failover cluster with a shared virtual disk

Before the release of Windows Server 2012 R2, the only way to create shared storage for clustered virtual machines was to use physical storage hardware. Windows Server 2012 R2 introduced a virtual solution by making it possible to create shared VHDX files. That capability still exists in Windows Server 2016, so that your existing storage configurations remain functional after an upgrade. There is now also a second option, called a *VHD set*.

Shared VHDX files have some shortcomings. You cannot resize them or migrate them, nor can you back up or replicate them from the host server. You can do all these things with VHD sets. Their only drawback is that only Windows Server 2016 can access them.

To create a shared VHDX file or VHD set with Hyper-V Manager, use the following procedure.

1. In Hyper-V Manager, open the Settings dialog box for the VM in which you want to create the shared disk.
2. Select the SCSI Controller and, on the SCSI Controller page, select Shared Drive, and click Add.
3. On the Shared Drive page, click New to launch the New Virtual Hard Disk Wizard.
4. On the Choose Disk Format page, select one of the following options:
   - **VHDX**   Creates a single VHDX file that is accessible by multiple virtual machines running Windows Server 2016 or Windows Server 2012 R2.

- **VHD Set** Creates a 260 MB VHDS file and an AVHDX backing storage file, which will contain the actual stored data. The VHDS file contains metadata used to coordinate the disk activities of the cluster nodes. The AVHDX file is just a standard VHDX file, which has been placed under the control of the hypervisor. VHD sets are only accessible by Windows Server 2016.

5. On the Choose Disk Type page, select one of the following options. Both VHDX files and VHD Sets can use either option:
   - **Fixed size** The image file is a specified size, in which all the disk space required to create the image is allocated during its creation.
   - **Dynamically expanding** The image file has a specified maximum size, which starts out small and expands as needed to accommodate the data the system writes to it.

6. On the Specify Name And Location page, specify a filename for the disk image in the Name text box and a location for the file on a cluster shared volume (CSV).

7. On the Configure Disk page, select and configure one of the following options:
   - **Create A New Blank Virtual Hard Disk** Specifies the size (or the maximum size) of the disk image file to create.
   - **Copy The Contents Of The Specified Physical Disk** Enables you to select one of the physical hard disks in the computer and copy its contents to the new disk image.
   - **Copy The Contents Of The Specified Virtual Hard Disk** Enables you to select an existing virtual disk file and copy its contents to the new disk image.

8. On the Completing the New Virtual Hard Disk Wizard page, click Finish. The wizard creates the new image disk and saves it to the specified location.

9. Click OK to close the Settings dialog box.

To create a VHD set in Windows PowerShell, you use the New-VHD cmdlet, just as you would to create any virtual disk file, except that you use VHDS for the extension of the file you are creating, as in the following example:

```
new-vhd –path c:\diskfile.vhds –dynamic –sizebytes 1tb
```

Configure differencing disks

A differencing disk enables you to preserve an existing virtual disk image file in its original state, while mounting it in an operating system and even modifying its contents. For example, when building a laboratory system, you can create a baseline by installing a clean copy of an operating system on a new virtual disk and configuring the environment to your needs. Then, you can create a new child differencing disk, using your baseline image as the parent. All subsequent changes you make to the system are written to the differencing disk, while the parent remains untouched. You can experiment freely on the system, knowing that you can revert to your baseline configuration by creating a new differencing disk.

You can create multiple differencing disks that point to the same parent image, enabling you to populate a lab network with as many virtual machines as you need, without having to repeatedly install the operating system and while saving on disk space. This can be particularly useful for software development efforts that require testing of subsequent product builds.

You can also create multiple generations of differencing disks, by creating a child of a child. In this case, all of the disks descending from the parent are essential to the disk's functionality.

When you create a differencing disk by using the New Virtual Hard Disk Wizard, selecting the Differencing option on the Choose Disk Type page causes the wizard's Configure Disk page to change, as shown in Figure 3-42. In the Location text box, you must specify the name of the file to use as the parent image.

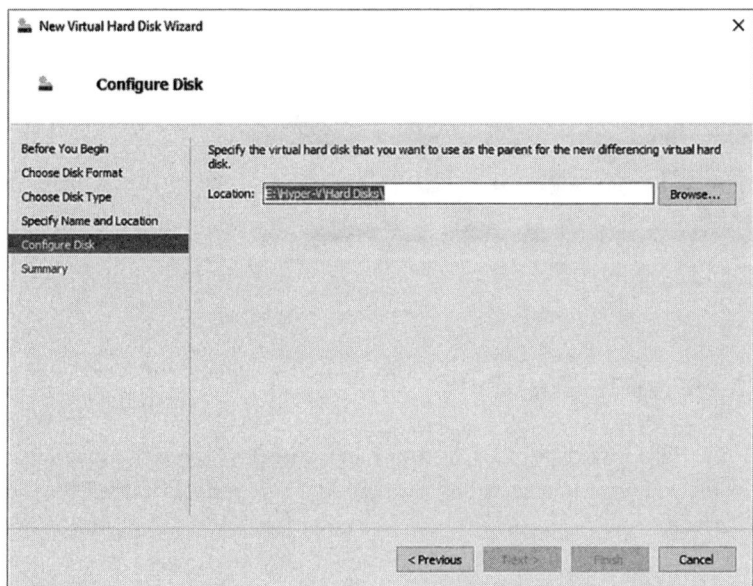

FIGURE 3-42 The Configure Disk page for the Differencing option in the New Virtual Hard Disk Wizard

To create a differencing disk using Windows PowerShell, you must run the New-VHD cmdlet with the Differencing parameter and the ParentPath parameter, specifying the location of the parent disk, as in the following example:

```
new-vhd -path c:\disks\diffdisk.vhdx -sizebytes 1tb -differencing -parentpath c:\disks\parentdisk.vhdx
```

Modify virtual hard disks

Windows Server 2016 provides several ways for you to manage and manipulate virtual hard disk images without adding them to a virtual machine. For example, you can use the Disk Management snap-in or Windows PowerShell to mount a virtual disk in a computer's file system and access its contents, just as if it was a physical disk.

Mounting a VHD

To mount a virtual hard disk file using the Disk Management snap-in, use the following procedure.

1. From the Tools menu in the Server Manager console, select Computer Management.
2. In the left pane of the Computer Management console, select Disk Management.
3. In the Disk Management snap-in, as shown in Figure 3-43, from the Action menu, select Attach VHD.

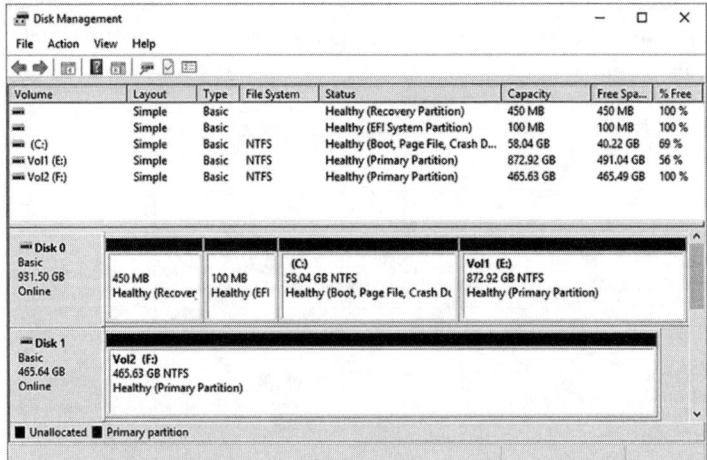

FIGURE 3-43 The Disk Management snap-in

4. In the Attach Virtual Hard Disk dialog box, as shown in Figure 3-44, type or browse to the image disk file you want to attach, and click OK. The disk appears in the Disk Management interface.

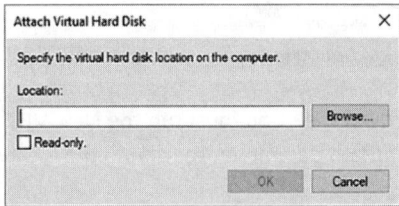

FIGURE 3-44 The Attach Virtual Hard Disk dialog box

5. Close the Computer Management console.

At this point, the contents of the virtual disk are mounted using a drive letter, and you can work with the contents using any standard tools, just as you would the files on a physical hard disk drive. To dismount the disk, saving any changes you have made back to the virtual disk file, you select Detach VHD from the Action menu, and specify the location of the original image file.

You can also mount and dismount a VHD or VHDX file by using the Mount-VHD and Dismount-VHD PowerShell cmdlets, as in the following examples:

```
mount-vhd -path c:\disks\server1.vhdx
```

```
dismount-vhd -path c:\disks\server1.vhdx
```

Installing roles and features offline

To install Windows roles and features on a running virtual machine, you can use the Install-WindowsFeature PowerShell cmdlet. However, you can also use this cmdlet to install roles and features to the VHD or VHDX image of a system disk while it is offline.

To install a Windows role or feature to an offline virtual disk, you add the Vhd parameter to the Install-WindowsFeature command, as in the following example:

```
install-windowsfeature -vhd c:\disks\server1.vhdx -name web-server
-includemanagementtools
```

Configure pass-through disks

The default Hyper-V behavior when creating a VM is to create a virtual hard disk. You also learned how to create VHD or VHDX files, to provide VMs with additional storage. However, it is also possible for VMs to access physical disks in the host server directly.

A *pass-through disk* is a type of virtual disk that points not to a file stored on a physical disk, but to a physical disk drive itself, installed on the host server. When you add a hard drive to any of the controllers in a virtual machine, you can select a physical hard disk, as opposed to a virtual one.

To add a physical hard disk to a virtual machine, however, the VM must have exclusive access to it. That is, you must first take the disk offline in the host operating system, by using the Disk Management snap-in, as shown in Figure 3-45, or the Set-Disk PowerShell cmdlet.

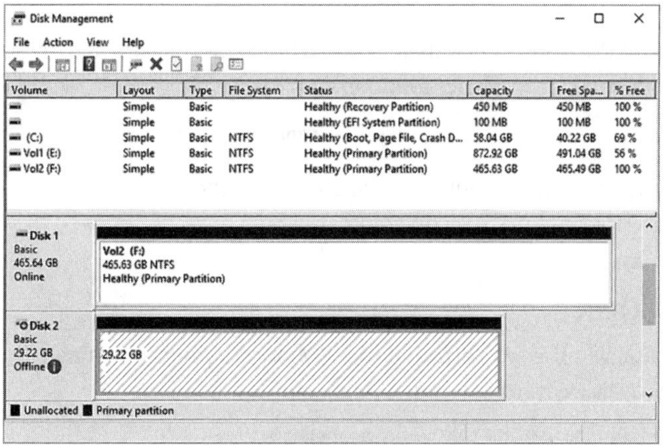

FIGURE 3-45 An offline disk in the Disk Management snap-in

To use the Set-Disk cmdlet to take a disk offline, you must first discover the number of the disk you want to modify by running the Get-Disk cmdlet. You then run Set-Disk using a command like the following:

```
set-disk -number 2 -isoffline $true
```

Once the disk is offline, the Physical Hard Disk option is enabled on the Hard Drive page of the Settings dialog box, as shown in Figure 3-46, and the disk is available for selection in the drop-down list.

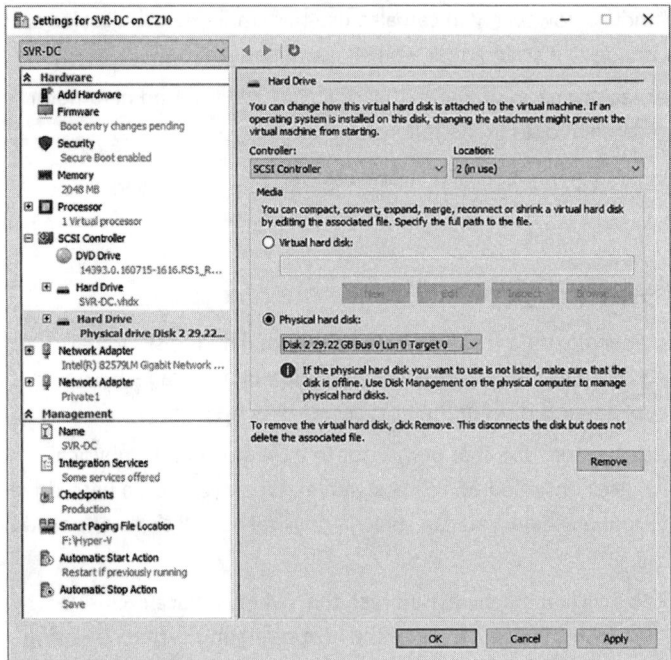

FIGURE 3-46 The Physical Hard Disk option in the Hard Drive page of a Settings dialog box

To create a pass-through disk in Windows PowerShell, you use the Add-VMHardDiskDrive cmdlet with the DiskNumber parameter, as in the following example:

```
add-vmharddiskdrive -vmname server1 -controllertype scsi -disknumber 2
```

When you create a pass-through disk, it is import to understand that the VM will be accessing the actual physical disk; it does not make a copy of it.

Resize a virtual hard disk

After you create a virtual hard disk, whether you attach it to a VM or not, you can manage its size by using the Edit Virtual Hard Disk Wizard in Hyper-V Manager.

To edit an existing VHD or VHDX file, use the following procedure.

1. In Hyper-V Manager, in the Actions pane, select Edit Disk to launch the Edit Virtual Hard Disk Wizard.
2. On the Locate Disk page, type or browse to the name of the VHD or VHDX file you want to open.
3. On the Choose Action page, shown in Figure 3-47, select one of the following functions. The functions that appear depend on the type of disk you have selected.
   - **Compact** Reduces the size of a dynamically expanding or differencing disk by deleting empty space, while leaving the disk's capacity unchanged.
   - **Convert** Creates a copy of the disk image file, enabling you to change the format (VHD or VHDX) or the type (fixed size or dynamically expanding) in the process.
   - **Expand** Increases the capacity of the disk by adding empty storage space to the image file.
   - **Shrink** Reduces the capacity of the disk by deleting empty storage space from the file. The Shrink option only appears when there is unpartitioned space available at the end of the virtual disk.
   - **Merge** Combines the data on a differencing disk with that on its parent disk, to form a single composite image file. The Merge option only appears when you select a differencing disk.

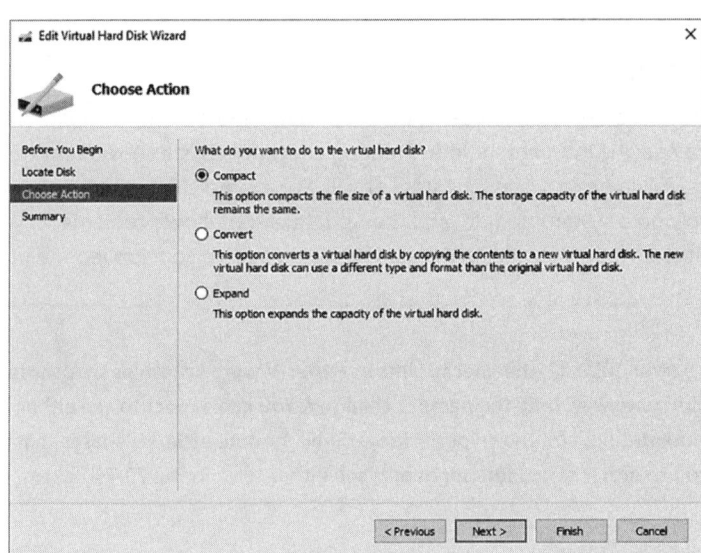

FIGURE 3-47 The Choose Action page in the Edit Virtual Hard Disk Wizard

4. Complete any new pages presented by the wizard based on your selection and click Finish.

You can also execute the functions of the Edit Virtual Hard Disk Wizard using Windows PowerShell cmdlets. To compact a virtual hard disk file (mounted as a read-only disk), you use the Optimize-VHD cmdlet, as in the following example:

```
optimize-vhd -path c:\disks\server1.vhdx -mode full
```

To convert a virtual hard disk file, you use the Convert-VHD cmdlet, as in the following examples that converts a fixed VHD file to a dynamic VHDX:

```
convert-vhd -path c:\disks\server1.vhd -destinationpath c:\disks\server1.vhdx -vhdtype dynamic
```

To expand or shrink a virtual disk, you use the Resize-VHD cmdlet with the SizeBytes parameter, as in the following example. The same command can expand or shrink a disk, depending on its original size. To shrink a disk to is smallest possible size, you can add the ToMinimumSize parameter.

```
resize-vhd -path c:\disks\server1.vhdx -sizebytes 500gb
```

To merge a differencing disk into its parent disk, you use the Merge-VHD cmdlet, as in the following command. If there are multiple generations of child disks involved, merging the youngest child disk into the parent merges all of the intervening child disks as well.

```
merge-vhd -path c:\disks\child.vhdx -destinationpath c:\disks\parent.vhdx
```

Manage checkpoints

In Hyper-V, a *checkpoint* is a captured image of the state, data, and hardware configuration of a virtual machine at a specific moment in time. Creating checkpoints is a convenient way for you to revert a virtual machine to a previous state at will. For example, if you create a checkpoint just before applying a system update, and the update is somehow problematic, you can apply the checkpoint and return the VM to the state it was in before you applied the update.

EXAM TIP

Prior to Windows Server 2012 R2, the checkpoints in Hyper-V were known as snapshots. They function in the same way; only the name is changed. You can expect to see either term used in documentation, and the Hyper-V PowerShell module includes aliases that make it possible to use either term. You might also see either term in the 70-740 exam.

Creating a checkpoint

Creating a checkpoint is as simple as selecting a running virtual machine in Hyper-V Manager and selecting Checkpoint from the Actions pane or running the Checkpoint-VM PowerShell cmdlet with the name of the VM. The system creates a checkpoint file, with an AVHD or AVHDX extension, in the same folder as the virtual hard disk file, and adds the checkpoint to Hyper-V Manager display, as shown in Figure 3-48.

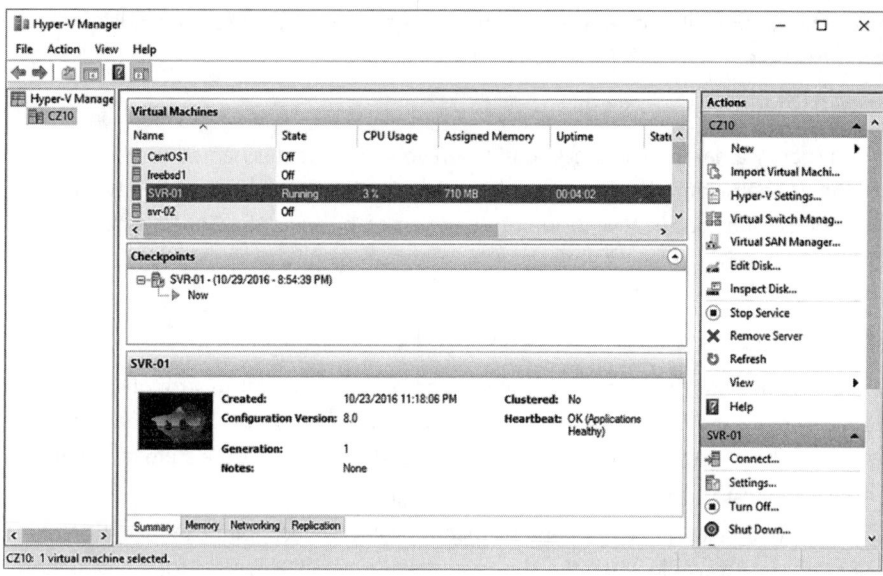

FIGURE 3-48 A checkpoint in Hyper-V Manager

Checkpointing is a useful tool for development and testing environments in Hyper-V, but they are not recommended for use in production environments, nor are they to be considered a replacement for backup software. Apart from consuming disk space, the presence of checkpoints can reduce the overall performance of a virtual machine's storage subsystem.

Applying a checkpoint

To apply a previously created checkpoint, returning the virtual machine to its previous state, you right-click the checkpoint in Hyper-V Manager and select Apply from the Actions menu to open the Apply Checkpoint dialog box, as shown in Figure 3-49.

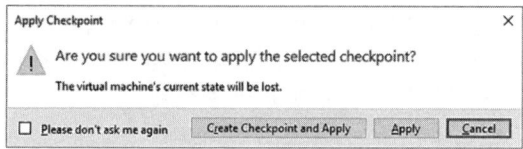

FIGURE 3-49 The Apply Checkpoint dialog box

In this dialog box, you can choose from the following options:

- **Apply**   Applies the selected checkpoint, overwriting the current state of the VM.
- **Create Checkpoint And Apply**   Creates a new checkpoint of the VM, to preserve its current state, and then applies the selected checkpoint.

To apply a checkpoint with PowerShell, you use the Restore-VMCheckpoint cmdlet, as in the following example.

```
restore-vmcheckpoint -name checkpoint1 -vmname server1
```

Unless you specify a name for a checkpoint when you create it, it is named using a combination of the VM name and the timestamp from the creation time. You can display a list of all the checkpoints for a specific VM, including their names, by using the Get-VMCheckpoint cmdlet.

Implement production checkpoints

There is another issue with checkpointing that has compelled Microsoft to strongly recommend that it not be used on production VMs. Before Windows Server 2016, creating a checkpoint saved the memory state of all running applications, not just the state of the virtual machine itself.

This is a boon for a testing environment, so that applying a checkpoint can take the VM back to the exact state it was in when the checkpoint was created. However, for a production VM to which clients are connected, such as a database or mail server, or one that replicates data to other systems, such as domain controller, restoring a previous memory state can interrupt ongoing processes.

For this reason, Windows Server 2016 Hyper-V includes *production checkpoints*, which use the Volume Shadow Copy Service in Windows, or File System Freeze in Linux, to create a snapshot of the data from a VM, without saving its memory state. The use of production checkpoints is now the default on all Windows Server 2016 VMs. The previous type of checkpoint, still available in Windows Server 2016, is now known as a *standard checkpoint*

To administrators, production checkpoints behave exactly like standard checkpoints. You can create them and apply them using the same tools and techniques.

To modify the default checkpointing settings for a VM, you can open its Settings dialog box in Hyper-V Manager to the Checkpoints page, as shown in Figure 3-50, and select the Standard Checkpoints option. You can also use the controls on this page to specify the location for the checkpoint files from the VM, and disable checkpointing entirely.

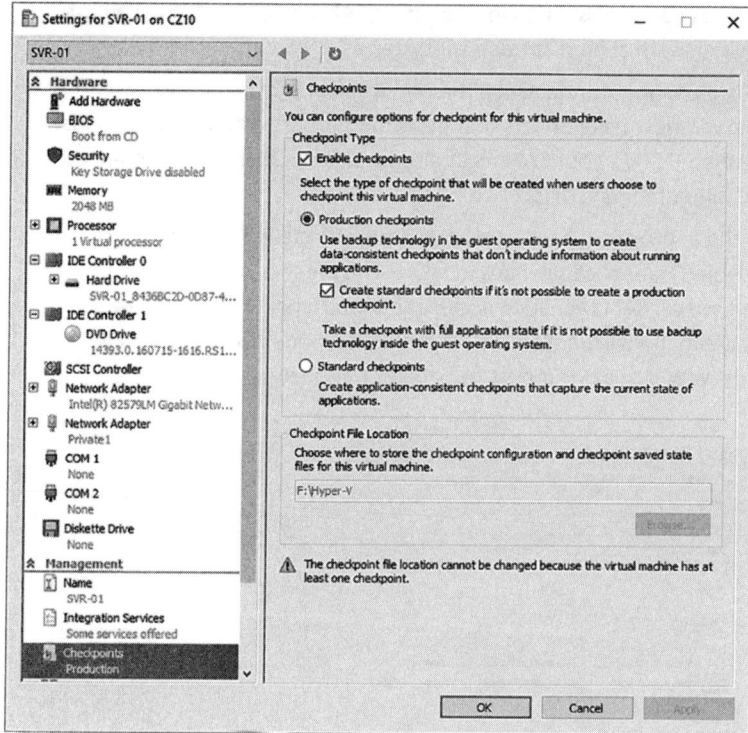

FIGURE 3-50 The Checkpoints page in a VM Settings dialog box

To modify the checkpointing defaults in PowerShell, you use the Set-VM cmdlet, as in the following example:

```
set-vm -name server1 -checkpointtype standard
```

In addition to Standard, the CheckpointType parameter supports the Production value, to return the setting to its default; and the Disabled value, to disable all checkpointing for the VM. You can also use the SnapshotFileLocation parameter to specify where the system should create its checkpoint files.

Implement a virtual fibre channel adapter

In the past, the specialized networking technologies used to build Fibre Channel storage area networks (SANs) made it difficult to use them with virtualized servers. However, since the Windows Server 2012 implementation, Hyper-V has supported the creation of virtual Fibre Channel adapters.

A Hyper-V Fibre Channel adapter is essentially a pass-through device that enables a virtual machine to access a physical Fibre Channel adapter installed in the computer, and through that, the external storage resources connected to the SAN. With this capability, applications running on virtual machines can access data files stored on SAN devices, and you can use VMs to create server clusters with shared storage subsystems.

To support virtual Fibre Channel connectivity, the physical Fibre Channel host bus adapter(s) in the host server must have drivers that explicitly support virtual Fibre Channel and N_Port ID Virtualization (NPIV). Your SAN must also be able to address its connected resources using logical unit numbers (LUNs).

Assuming you have the appropriate hardware and software installed on the host commuter, you implement the Fibre Channel capabilities in Hyper-V by first creating a virtual SAN. You do this by using the Virtual SAN Manager, accessible from Hyper-V Manager, as shown in Figure 3-51. When you create the virtual SAN, the World Wide Node Names (WWNNs) and World Wide Port Names (WWPNs) of your host bus adapter appear.

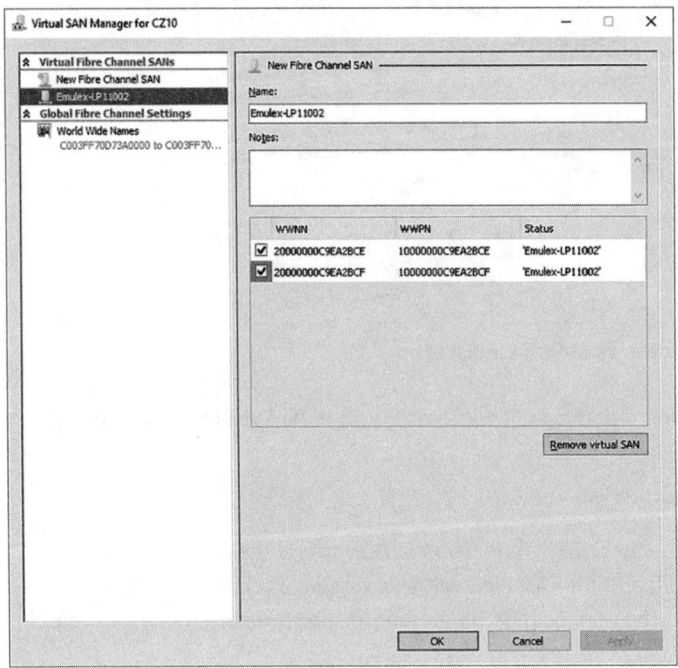

FIGURE 3-51 WWNNs and WWPNs in a virtual SAN

The next step is to add a Fibre Channel Adapter to your virtual machine from the Add Hardware page in the Settings dialog box. Then, the virtual SAN you created previously is available in the Fibre Channel Adapter page, as shown in Figure 3-52. Hyper-V virtualizes the SAN and makes the WWNNs and WWPNs available to the virtual machine.

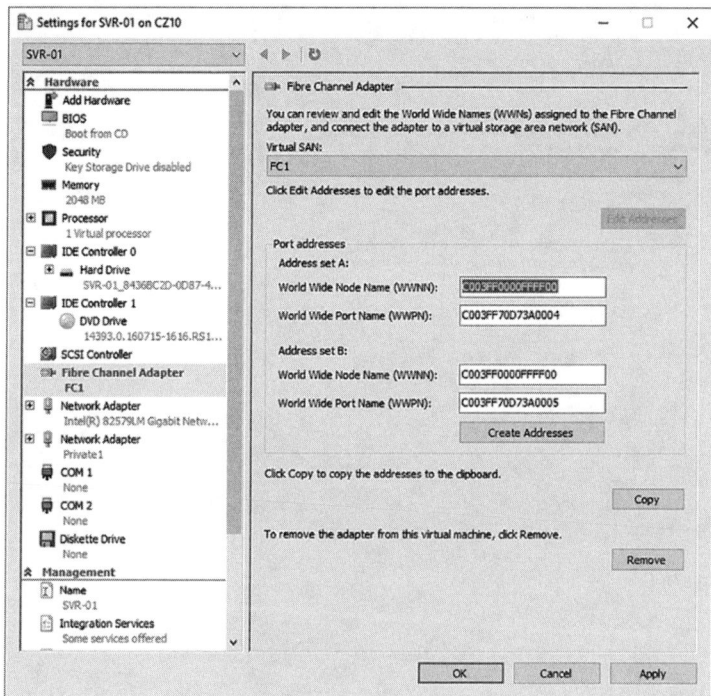

FIGURE 3-52 A Fibre Channel adapter in a VM

Configure Storage Quality of Service (QoS)

When you create virtual machines on a single Hyper-V host, it is common for there to be multiple virtual disks stored on a single physical disk. With VMs running simultaneously and accessing their virtual disks from the same physical disk, it is possible for one virtual disk to monopolize the physical disk's input/output (I/O) capacity, causing the other virtual disks to slow down. To help prevent this, Windows Server 2016 enables you to control the Quality of Service (QoS) for a given virtual hard disk.

QoS management in Hyper-V takes the form of controls that enables you to specify the minimum and maximum input/output operations per second (IOPS) for a disk. To configure storage QoS, you open the Settings dialog box for a VM, expand a hard drive component, select Quality Of Service, and, on the Quality Of Service page, select the Enable Quality Of Service Management check box, as shown in Figure 3-53.

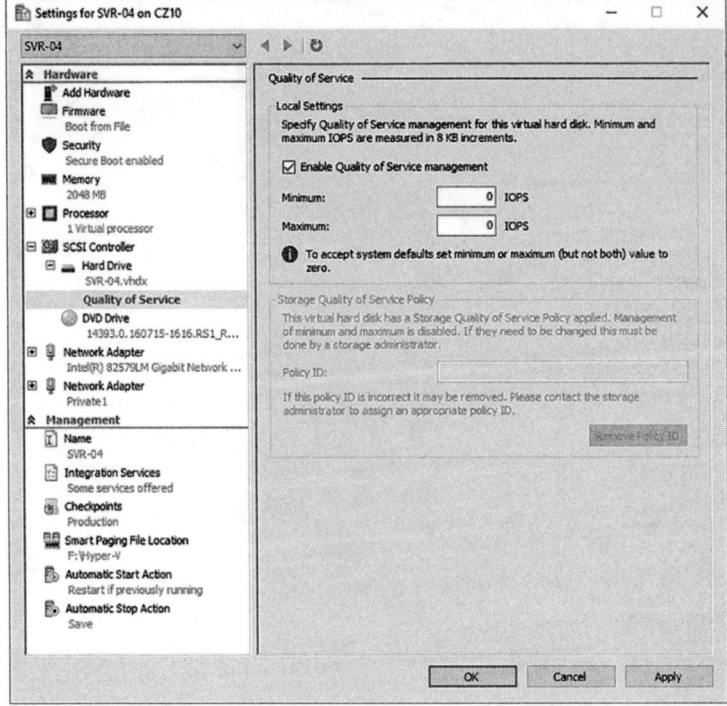

FIGURE 3-53 Quality of Service controls in the Settings dialog box in Hyper-V Manager

After selecting the Enable Quality Of Service Management check box, you can specify minimum and maximum IOPS values for the disk, to throttle its throughout in 8 KB increments. To configure these settings with Windows PowerShell, you use the Set-VMHardDiskDrive cmdlet, as in the following example. The ControllerType and ControllerNumber parameters specify which drive to configure, and the MinimumIOPS and MaximumIOPS parameters specify the QoS settings.

```
set-vmharddiskdrive -vmname server1 -controllertype scsi -controllernumber 0
-minimumiops 10 -maximumiops 500
```

Determining the optimum QoS settings for a specific drive likely takes some monitoring and adjustment. After enabling resource metering on the VM, you can use the Measure-VM cmdlet to display its current disk usage, as shown in the following examples. The output of the Measure-VM cmdlet is shown in Figure 3-54. After checking the IOPS under workload of the VM, you can zero in on appropriate QoS settings.

```
enable-vmresourcemetering -vmname server1

measure-vm -vmname server1 | fl
```

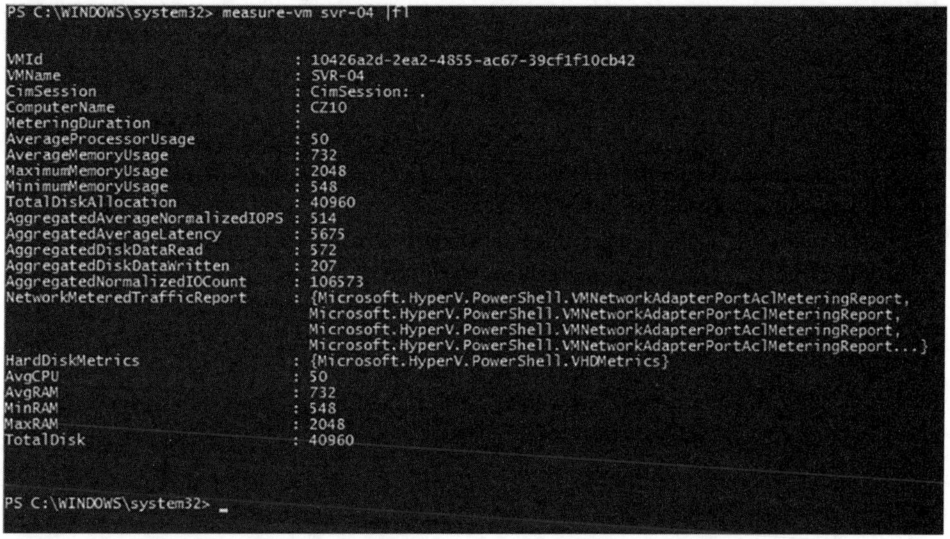

```
PS C:\WINDOWS\system32> measure-vm svr-04 |fl

VMId                            : 10426a2d-2ea2-4855-ac67-39cf1f10cb42
VMName                          : SVR-04
CimSession                      : CimSession: .
ComputerName                    : CZ10
MeteringDuration                :
AverageProcessorUsage           : 50
AverageMemoryUsage              : 732
MaximumMemoryUsage              : 2048
MinimumMemoryUsage              : 548
TotalDiskAllocation             : 40960
AggregatedAverageNormalizedIOPS : 514
AggregatedAverageLatency        : 5675
AggregatedDiskDataRead          : 572
AggregatedDiskDataWritten       : 207
AggregatedNormalizedIOCount     : 106573
NetworkMeteredTrafficReport     : {Microsoft.HyperV.PowerShell.VMNetworkAdapterPortAclMeteringReport,
                                  Microsoft.HyperV.PowerShell.VMNetworkAdapterPortAclMeteringReport,
                                  Microsoft.HyperV.PowerShell.VMNetworkAdapterPortAclMeteringReport,
                                  Microsoft.HyperV.PowerShell.VMNetworkAdapterPortAclMeteringReport...}
HardDiskMetrics                 : {Microsoft.HyperV.PowerShell.VHDMetrics}
AvgCPU                          : 50
AvgRAM                          : 732
MinRAM                          : 548
MaxRAM                          : 2048
TotalDisk                       : 40960

PS C:\WINDOWS\system32>
```

FIGURE 3-54 Output of the Measure-VM cmdlet

Skill 3.4: Configure Hyper-V networking

Hyper-V includes networking capabilities that enable administrators to create a virtualized equivalent of nearly any physical network configuration.

> **This section covers how to:**
> - Add and remove virtual network interface cards (VNICs)
> - Configure Hyper-V virtual switches
> - Optimize network performance
> - Configure MAC addresses
> - Configure network isolation
> - Configure synthetic and legacy virtual network adapters
> - Configure NIC teaming in VMs
> - Configure virtual machine queue (VMQ)
> - Enable Remote Direct Memory Access (RDMA) on network adapters bound to a Hyper-V virtual switch using Switch Embedded Teaming (SET)
> - Configure Bandwidth Management

Add and remove virtual network interface cards (vNICs)

As in a physical computer, a virtual machine can have multiple network interface adapters in it, providing connections to different networks or for carrying different types of traffic. When you create a new virtual machine, the default configuration includes one virtual network adapter. The New Virtual Machine Wizard includes a Configure Networking page, as shown in Figure 3-55, on which you can select one of the virtual switches on the host server.

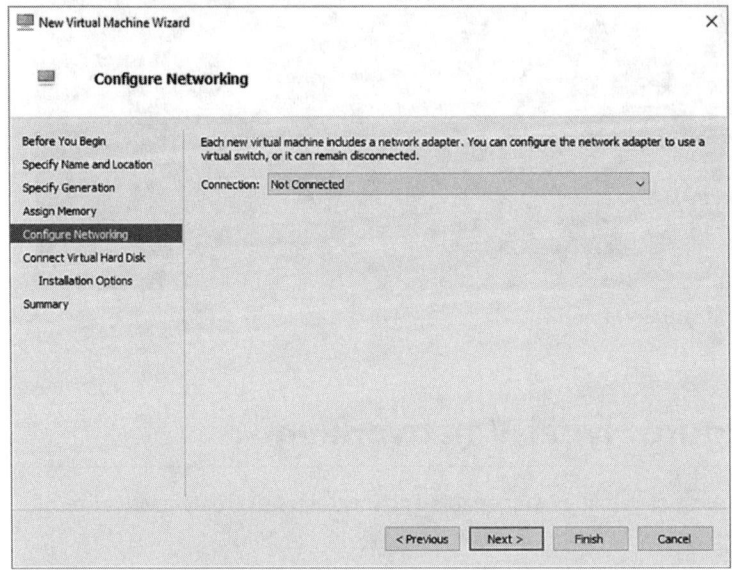

FIGURE 3-55 The Configure Networking page in the New Virtual Machine Wizard

If you create only the default external virtual switch when installing Hyper-V, connecting a virtual machine to the switch joins the system to the physical network. To create additional network adapters in your virtual machines, use the following procedure.

1. Launch Hyper-V Manager, select a virtual machine, and open its Settings dialog box.
2. In the Add Hardware list, select Network Adapter, and click Add.

> **NOTE ADDING NETWORK ADAPTERS**
> On a Generation 2 VM, you can add and configure a network adapter while the system is running. For Generation 1 VMs the system must be shut down.

3. On the new Network Adapter page, shown in Figure 3-56, in the Virtual Switch drop-down list, select the switch to which you want to connect the network adapter.

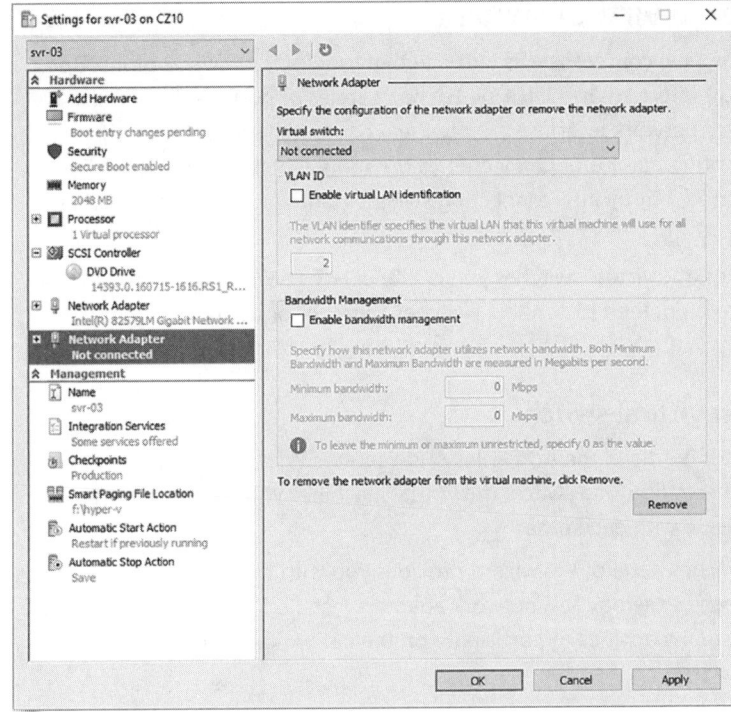

FIGURE 3-56 The Network Adapter page in the Settings dialog box

4. If your host computer is connected to a physical switching infrastructure that uses VLANs to create separate subnets, you can select the Enable Virtual LAN Identification check box and enter a VLAN identifier to associate the network adapter with a specific VLAN on your physical network.

5. Click OK to create the new network adapter and close the Settings dialog box.

You can create up to eight network adapters in a Windows Server 2016 Hyper-V virtual machine. To create a network adapter with PowerShell, you use the Add-VMNetworkAdapter cmdlet, as in the following example:

```
add-vmnetworkadapter -vmname server1 -switchname private1
```

To remove a network adapter in Hyper-V Manager, you select the adapter in the Settings dialog box and click the Remove button. The adapter appears crossed out, until you click the OK or Apply button. To remove a network adapter with PowerShell, you use the Remove-VMNetworkAdapter cmdlet, as in the following example:

```
remove-vmnetworkadapter -vmname server1 -vmnetworkadapter nic1
```

Configure Hyper-V virtual switches

A *virtual switch*, like its physical counterpart, is a device that functions at layer 2 of the Open Systems Interconnect (OSI) reference model. A switch has a series of ports, each of which is connected to a computer's network interface adapter. Any computer connected to the switch can transmit data to any other computer connected to the same switch. The number of ports in a physical switch is limited, but by interconnecting switches, administrators can build networks of nearly any size.

Unlike physical switches, the virtual switches you create in Hyper-V can have an unlimited number of ports, so there is no need to connect switches together or use uplinks and crossover circuits.

Creating the default virtual switch

When you install the Hyper-V role in the Add Roles And Features Wizard, you can create the server's first virtual switches. Without a switch, the virtual machines you create on Hyper-V are not able to communicate with each other.

The Create Virtual Switches page of the wizard provides you with the opportunity to create a virtual switch for each of the physical network adapters installed in the host computer. These switches enable virtual machines to participate on the networks to which the physical adapters are connected.

When you create a virtual switch in this manner, the networking configuration in the host operating system changes. The new virtual switch appears in the Network Connections window. If you examine its properties, notice that the switch is bound to the operating system's TCP/IP client, as shown in Figure 3-57.

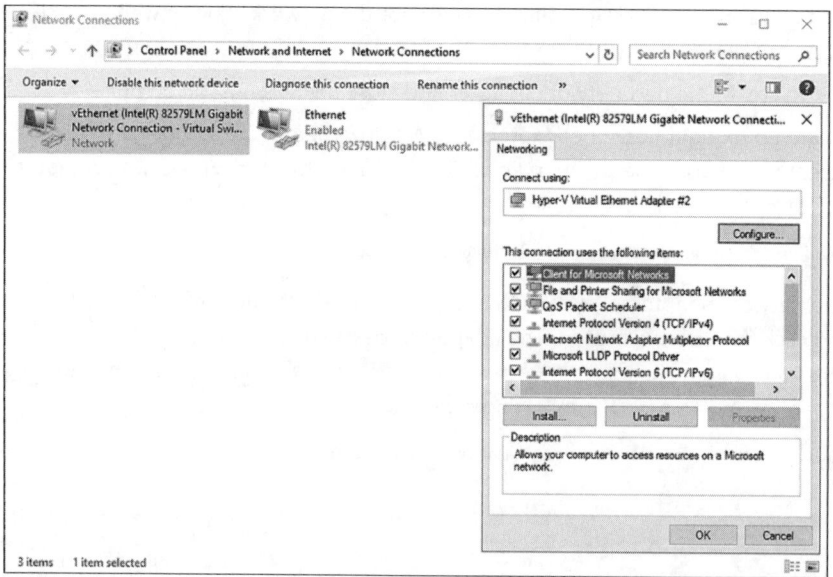

FIGURE 3-57 A virtual switch and its properties, displayed in the host operating system

Meanwhile, Hyper-V also changes the properties of original network connection representing the physical network interface adapter in the computer. The physical network adapter is now bound only to the virtual switch, as shown in Figure 3-58.

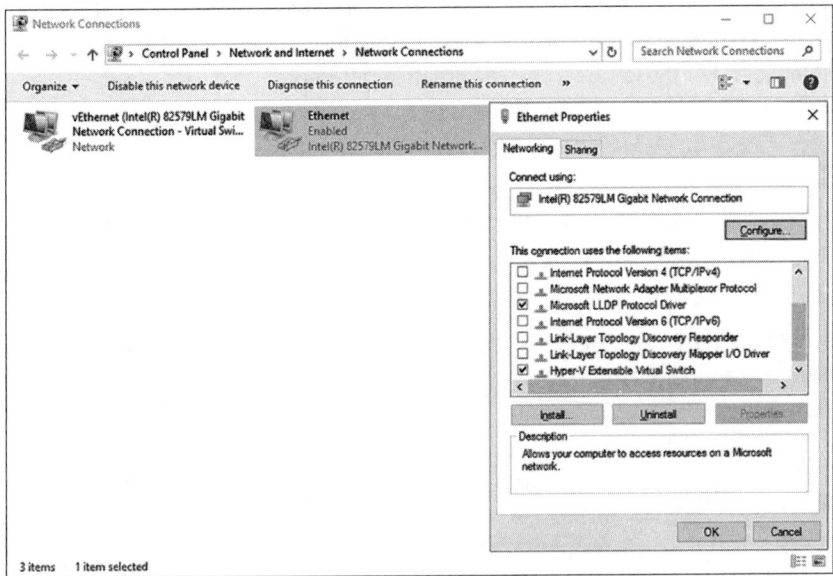

FIGURE 3-58 A network interface adapter in the host operating system, bound to a virtual switch

The result is that the computer's physical network configuration, in which its network adapter is connected to an external physical switch, is overlaid by the virtual network configuration created by Hyper-V. In this virtual configuration, the virtual switch is connected to the physical switch and the network adapter in the host operating system is connected to the virtual switch. The internal virtual network and the external physical network are joined into a single local area network (LAN), just as if you connected two physical switches together.

After Hyper-V creates the virtual switch and makes the configuration changes, any new virtual machines that you connect to the virtual switch become part of this conjoined network, as do any physical computers connected to the physical network through an external switch.

This type of virtual switch is, in Hyper-V terminology, an *external network switch*, because it provides connections external to the Hyper-V environment. This is typically the preferred arrangement for a production network in which Hyper-V virtual machines provide and consume services for the entire network.

For example, a virtual machine connected to this switch automatically obtains an IP address from a DHCP server on the physical network, if one exists. You can also configure a VM as a DHCP server and let it provide addresses to all the system on the network, virtual or physical.

This arrangement also enables your virtual machines to access the Internet by using the router and DNS servers on the external network. The virtual machines can then download operating system updates from servers on the Internet, just as external machines often do.

This type of virtual switch is not appropriate in all situations. If you create a laboratory network for product testing or a classroom network, you might not want it to be connected to the external network. For these cases, you can create a different type of virtual switch, by using the Virtual Switch Manager in Hyper-V Manager.

Creating a new virtual switch

Hyper-V in Windows Server 2016 supports three types of switches that you can create in the Virtual Switch Manager.

To create any of the virtual switch types, use the following procedure.

1. In Hyper-V Manager, in the Actions pane, select Virtual Switch Manager to open the Virtual Switch Manager dialog box, as shown in Figure 3-59.

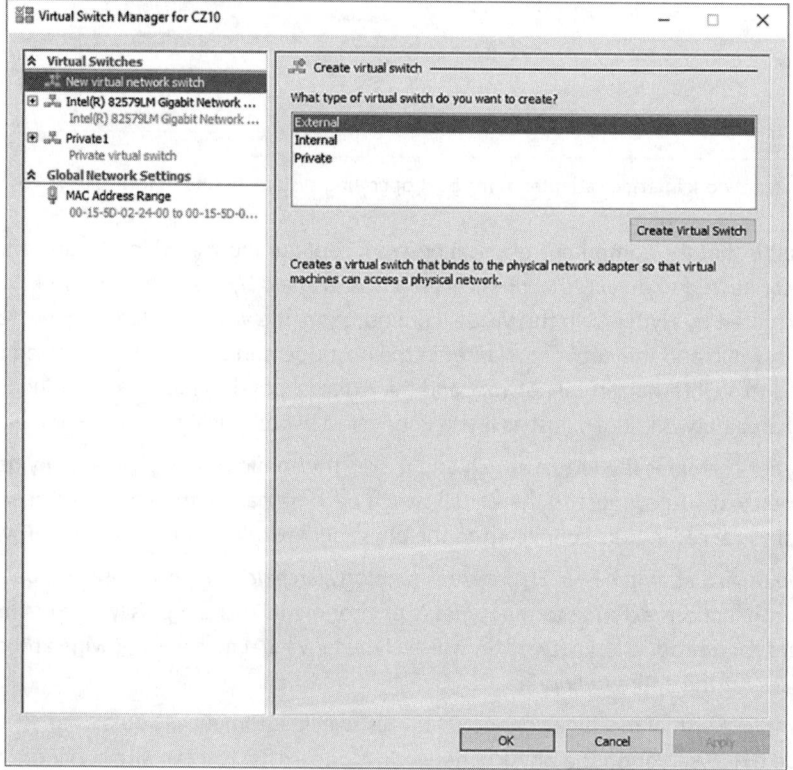

FIGURE 3-59 The Virtual Switch Manager dialog box in Hyper-V Manager

2. In the Create Virtual Switch box, select one of the following switch types, and click Create Virtual Switch.

- **External** The virtual switch is bound to networking protocol stack in the host operating system and connected to a physical network interface adapter in the Hyper-V server. Virtual machines running on the server can access the network to which the physical adapter is connected.
- **Internal** An internal network switch is bound to a separate instance of the networking protocol stack in the host operating system, independent from the physical network interface adapter and its connected network. Virtual machines running on the server can access the virtual network implemented by the virtual switch, and the host operating system can access the physical network through the physical network interface adapter, but the virtual machines cannot access the physical network through the physical adapter.
- **Private** A private network switch exists only in the Hyper-V server and is accessible only to the virtual machines running on the server. The host operating system can still access the physical network through the physical network interface adapter, but it cannot access the virtual network created by the virtual switch.

3. On the Virtual Switch Properties page, as shown in Figure 3-60, type a name for the new switch.

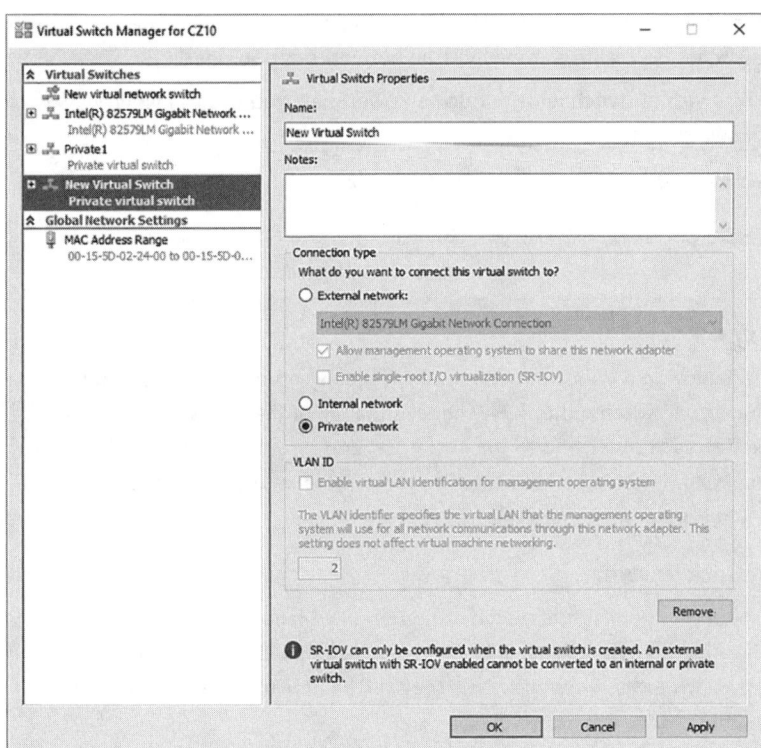

FIGURE 3-60 The Virtual Switch Properties page, with the External Network option selected

4. For an External Network switch, select the physical network adapter to which the virtual switch will be bound, and configure the following options, if desired:

- **Allow Management Operating System To Share This Network Adapter** Selected by default when you create an external virtual switch, clearing this check box excludes the host operating system from the physical network, while allowing access to the virtual machines.
- **Enable Single Root I/O Virtualization (SR-IOV)** Enables you to create an external virtual switch that is associated with a physical network adapter capable of supporting SR-IOV. This option is only available when creating a new virtual switch; you cannot modify an existing switch to use this option.
- **Enable Virtual LAN Identification For Management Operating System** If your host computer is connected to a physical switching infrastructure that uses virtual LANs (VLANs) to create separate subnets, you can select the check box and enter a VLAN identifier to associate the virtual switch with a specific VLAN on your physical network.

5. Click OK. The new virtual switch is created.

You can proceed to create additional virtual switches as needed. You can create only one switch for each physical network adapter in the computer, but you can create multiple internal or private switches, to create as many virtual networks as you need.

To create a new virtual switch with Windows PowerShell, you use the New-VMSwitch cmdlet, as in the following examples:

```
new-vmswitch -name lan1 -netadaptername "ethernet 2"

new-vmswitch -name private1 -switchtype private
```

Quick check

Harold is deploying a Windows Server 2016 Hyper-V server, and he is confused about the virtual switch options. He requires that all of the virtual machines be networked to each other, and to the host operating system as well. Only the host operating system should be connected to the external network and the Internet. How should Harold implement this in Hyper-V?

Quick check answer

Harold should create a virtual switch using Hyper-V Manager in Server Manager. When choosing the type of the virtual switch, he should choose Internal. By connecting the VMs to the Internal switch, they will be able to communicate with each other and the host operating system.

Optimize network performance

Some physical network interface adapters have features that are designed to improve performance by offloading certain functions from the system processor to components built into the adapter itself. Hyper-V includes support for some of these features, if the hardware in the physical network adapter supports them properly.

When you expand a network adapter in the Settings dialog box of a VM, you gain access to the Hardware Acceleration page, as shown in Figure 3-61. On this page, you can configure the following hardware acceleration settings:

- **Enable Virtual Machine Queue**   Virtual machine queue (VMQ) is a technique that stores incoming packets intended for virtual machines in separate queues on the physical network adapter and delivers them directly to the VMs, bypassing the processing normally performed by the virtual switch on the host server.
- **Enable IPsec Task Offloading**   This setting uses the processing capabilities of the network adapter to perform some of the cryptographic functions required by IPsec. You can also specify the maximum number of security associations you want the adapter to be able to calculate.
- **Single-Root I/O Virtualization**   This setting enables the virtual adapter to use the SR-IOV capabilities of the physical adapter. SR-IOV enables virtual machines to share the hardware resources of a PCI Express device, such as a network adapter.

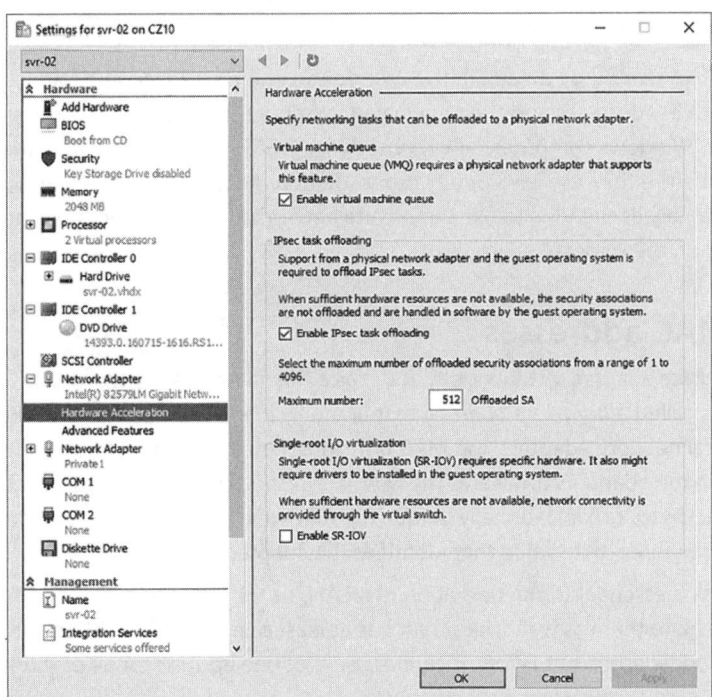

FIGURE 3-61 A network adapter's Hardware Acceleration page in the Settings dialog box

Create multiple switches

If your Hyper-V server has multiple physical network adapters, you should create a virtual switch for each one and split the VMs with network-intensive workloads among them, to achieve best performance.

Create a private network

When you have multiple VMs on a Hyper-V server that frequently communicate with each other, create a private virtual network in Virtual Switch Manager and configure the VMs to use it wherever possible. Network communication is more efficient on a private network than it is on the external network, in which other computers are sharing the same medium.

To create a private network, use the following procedure.

1. Create a private virtual network in Virtual Switch Manager.
2. Add a network adapter to each of your VMs, and assign it to the private switch.
3. Configure the adapter for each VM with a static IP address.
4. Modify the HOSTS file on each VM by adding the names and IP addresses of the other VMs on the Hyper-V server, as in the following example:

```
192.168.10.11    vm-01.contoso.com
192.168.10.12    vm-02.contoso.com
192.168.10.13    vm-03.contoso.com
192.168.10.14    vm-04.contoso.com
192.168.10.15    vm-05.contoso.com
```

HOSTS is a text file, located by default in the \Windows\system32\drivers\etc folder, that contains nothing but IP addresses and their equivalent computer names. When communicating on the network, Windows computers always check the HOSTS file as their first name resolution mechanism, before they use DNS or any other solution. Adding the private network addresses to this file causes the VMs to use the private network first, when communicating with the other VMs on the Hyper-V server.

Configure MAC addresses

Every network interface adapter, virtual or physical, has a Media Access Control (MAC) address (sometimes called a *hardware address*) that uniquely identifies the device on the network. On physical network adapters, the MAC is assigned by the manufacturer and permanently entered in the adapter's firmware. The MAC address is a six-byte hexadecimal value consisting of a three-bytes organizationally unique identifier (OUI) that specifies the manufacturer, and a unique three-byte value that identifies the adapter itself.

The MAC address is essential to the operation of a LAN, so the virtual network adapters on a Hyper-V server require them as well. The server has at least one real MAC address, provided in its physical network adapter, but Hyper-V cannot use that one address for all of the virtual adapters connecting virtual machines to the network.

To provide MAC addresses for the virtual adapters, Hyper-V creates a pool of addresses and assigns them from this pool to virtual network adapters as you create them. To view or modify the MAC address pool for the Hyper-V server, you open the Virtual Switch Manager and select MAC Address Range under Global Network Settings, as shown in Figure 3-62.

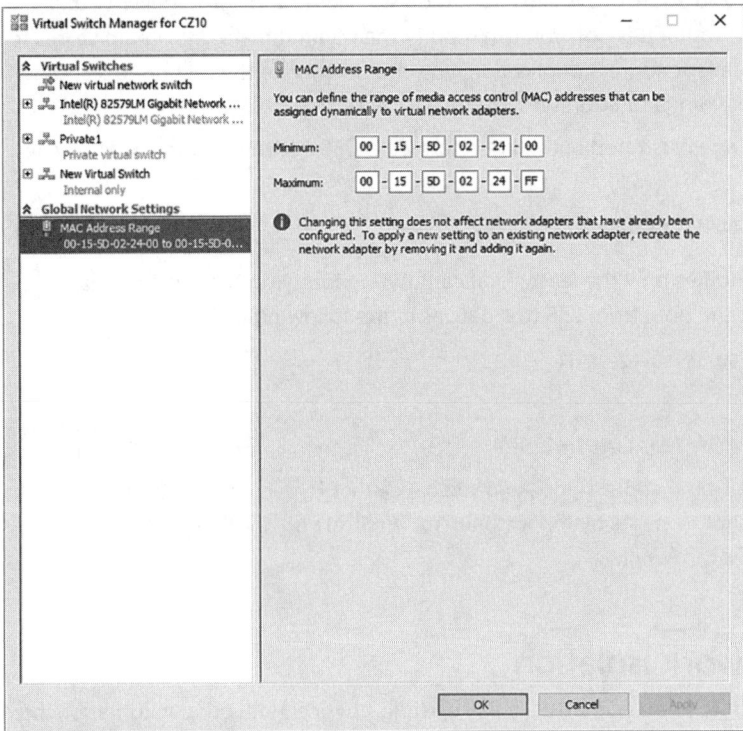

FIGURE 3-62 The MAC Address Range page in Virtual Switch Manager

> **NOTE ASSIGNING MAC ADDRESSES**
>
> Virtual network adapters in Hyper-V receive dynamically assigned MAC addresses by default, but you can choose to configure individual adapters in your virtual machines with static MAC addresses. You do this on the adapter's Advanced Features page in the Settings dialog box.

The Hyper-V MAC address range uses values constructed as follows:

- **Bytes 1 to 3**   Consists of the value 00-15-5D, which is an OUI registered by Microsoft
- **Bytes 4 and 5**   Consists of the last two bytes of the IP address assigned to the server's physical network adapter, converted to hexadecimal notation
- **Byte 6**   Consists of a range of values from 00 to FF, which provides 256 possible addresses

Skill 3.4: Configure Hyper-V networking   **CHAPTER 3**   **245**

The Hyper-V server assigns the MAC addresses to the network adapters in virtual machines as you create the adapters. The adapters retain their MAC addresses permanently, or until the adapter is removed from the virtual machine. The server reclaims any unused addresses and reuses them.

The default pool of 256 addresses is expected to be sufficient for most Hyper-V virtual machine configurations, but if it is not, you can modify the Minimum and Maximum values to enlarge the pool. To prevent address duplication, you should change the second to last byte only, by making it into a range of addresses like the last byte.

For example, the range illustrated in the figure provides 256 addresses with the following values:

`00-15-1D-02-24-00` to `00-15-1D-02-24-FF`

This value range modifies only the least significant byte. Modifying the second to last bytes as well increases the pool from 256 to 4,096, as in the following range:

`00-15-1D-02-20-00` to `00-15-1D-02-2F-FF`

> *CAUTION* **DUPLICATING MAC ADDRESSES**
> When you modify the MAC address pool, and you have other Hyper-V servers on your network, be careful not to create the opportunity for duplicate MAC addresses to occur, or networking problems can result.

Configure network isolation

Hyper-V makes it possible to extend virtually any existing physical network configuration into its virtual space, or create a completely separated and isolated network within the Hyper-V environment.

The basic default configuration of a Hyper-V virtual machine connects its network adapter to an external virtual switch, thus attaching the guest operating system on the virtual machine to the outside network. The VM can then take advantage of services running on the outside network and send traffic through routers to other networks, including the Internet.

This type of arrangement can enable you to consolidate many physical servers into virtual machines on a single Hyper-V server, by providing them all with access to the entire network. There is no distinction here between the physical network and the virtual one in the Hyper-V space.

Extending a production network into virtual space

A Hyper-V server can have multiple physical network adapters installed in it, which might be connected to different networks to separate traffic, or to the same network to increase available bandwidth. You might also have adapters dedicated to SAN connections, for shared storage and server clustering.

Microsoft recommends using at least two physical network adapters in a Hyper-V server, with one adapter servicing the host operating system and the other connected to the VMs. When you have more than two physical adapters in the server, you can create separate external virtual network switches for the physical adapters, and connect each one to a separate VM.

Creating an isolated network

For testing, development, and evaluation purposes, or for classroom situations, you might want to create an isolated network environment. By creating internal or private virtual switches, you can create a network that exists only within the Hyper-V space, with or without the host operating system included.

An isolated network such as this suffers from the weaknesses of its strengths. If you want to install the guest operating systems using Windows Deployment Services or configure the virtual machines using DHCP, you must install and configure these services on the private network. The guest operating systems also do not have access to the Internet, which prevents them from downloading operating system updates. Again, you must deploy appropriate substitutes on the private network.

To provide your systems with software updates, you can install two network adapters on each of your virtual machines and connect one to a private switch and one to an external switch. This procedure enables the virtual machines to access the Internet and the private network.

Another method for creating an isolated network is to use virtual LANs (VLANs). This is particularly helpful if you have virtual machines on different Hyper-V servers that you want to add to the isolated network. By connecting the network adapters to an external switch and configuring them with the same VLAN identifier, you can create a network within a network that isolates the VLAN from other computers. You can, for example, deploy a DHCP server on your VLAN without it interfering with other DHCP servers in your production environment.

Configure synthetic and legacy virtual network adapters

When you select the Network Adapter option in the Add Hardware page of the Settings dialog box, you create what is known in Hyper-V terminology as a *synthetic network adapter*. Generation 1 virtual machines support two types of network and storage adapters: synthetic and legacy (sometimes called emulated).

A synthetic adapter is a virtual device that does not correspond to a real-world product. Synthetic devices in a virtual machine communicate with the host operating system using a high-speed conduit called the VMBus.

Hyper-V virtual switches exist in the host server operating system and are part of a component called the network Virtualization Service Provider (VSP). The synthetic network adapter in the VM is a Virtualization Service Client (VSC). The VSP and the VSC are both connected to the VMBus, which provides communication between the two, as shown in Figure 3-63. The VSP, in the host operating system, provides the VSC, in the guest operating system, with access to the physical hardware in the host computer, that is, the physical network interface adaptor.

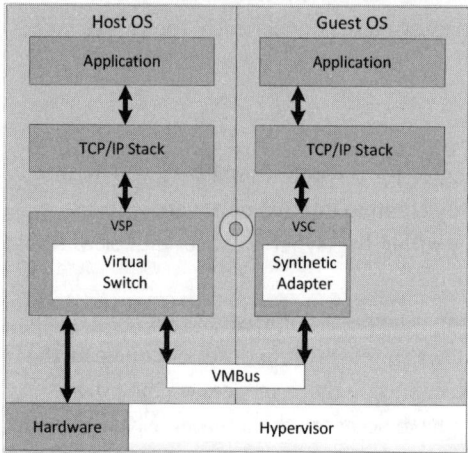

FIGURE 3-63 Synthetic network adapters communicate using the VMBus

Because they have access to the hardware through the VMBus, synthetic adapters provide a much higher level of performance than the alternative—a legacy adapter. Synthetic adapters are implemented as part of the Integration Services package that runs on supported guest operating systems. The one main drawback of synthetic network adapters is that they are not operational until Integration Services is loaded with the operating system on the virtual machine.

A *legacy network adapter* (sometimes called an emulated adapter) is a standard network adapter driver that communicates with the host operating system by making calls directly to the hypervisor, as shown in Figure 3-64. This communication method is substantially slower than the VMBus used by the synthetic network adapters, and is therefore less desirable.

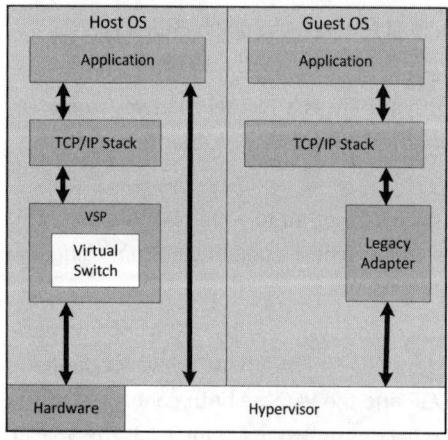

FIGURE 3-64 Legacy network adapter communicating with the host through the hypervisor

The primary advantage of the legacy adapter is that you can use it to boot a Generation 1 VM from the network, using the Preboot Execution Environment (PXE). PXE is a mechanism that software deployment tools, such as Windows Deployment Services (WDS) and System Center Configuration Manager (SCCM), use to install operating systems to new computers over the network. The synthetic network adapter in Generation 1 VMs does not support PXE.

To install a legacy adapter, you use the same procedure described earlier, except that you select Legacy Network Adapter in the Add Hardware list. Unlike synthetic adapters, legacy adapters load their drivers before the operating system, so you can boot the virtual machine using PXE and deploy an operating system over the network. Performance suffers with the legacy adapter, however, so you might consider using a synthetic adapter instead, after the operating system is installed.

This is one of the only scenarios in which an legacy adapter is preferable to a synthetic adapter. The other is when you install an operating system on your virtual machines that does not have an Integration Services package available for it.

In Generation 2 VMs, the distinction between synthetic and legacy adapters disappears. There is no more legacy adapter, and the synthetic adapter is capable of performing a PXE boot.

Configure NIC teaming in VMs

NIC teaming is a Windows feature that enables administrators to join multiple network adapters into a single entity, for performance enhancement or fault tolerance purposes. Hyper-V virtual machines can also take advantage of NIC teaming, but they are limited to teams of only two, as opposed to the host operating system, which can have teams of up to 32 NICs.

To use NIC teaming in Hyper-V, you must complete three basic tasks, as follows:

1. Create the NIC team in the Windows Server 2016 host operating system.
2. In Hyper-V Manager, create an external virtual switch using the NIC team.
3. Configure the network adapter in a virtual machine to connect to the virtual switch representing the NIC team.

Creating the NIC team

NIC teams must consist of physical network interface adapters, so before you can use a NIC team in a virtual machine, you must create it in the host operating system. After installing two physical network adapters in the computer, you can create a NIC team with Server Manager, as shown in Figure 3-65, using the following settings:

- **Teaming Mode**   Switch Independent
- **Load Balancing Mode**   Hyper-V Port
- **Standby Adapter**   None (All Adapters Active)

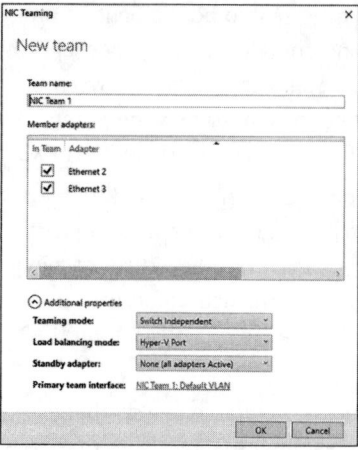

FIGURE 3-65 The NIC Teaming dialog box

Creating the team installs the Microsoft Network Adapter Multiplexor Driver, which appears as one of the components of the network connection representing the team.

Creating the team virtual switch

Once you have created the NIC team, you can open Virtual Switch Manager and create a new virtual switch by selecting the External option and choosing Microsoft Network Adapter Multiplexor Driver from the drop-down list, as shown in Figure 3-66.

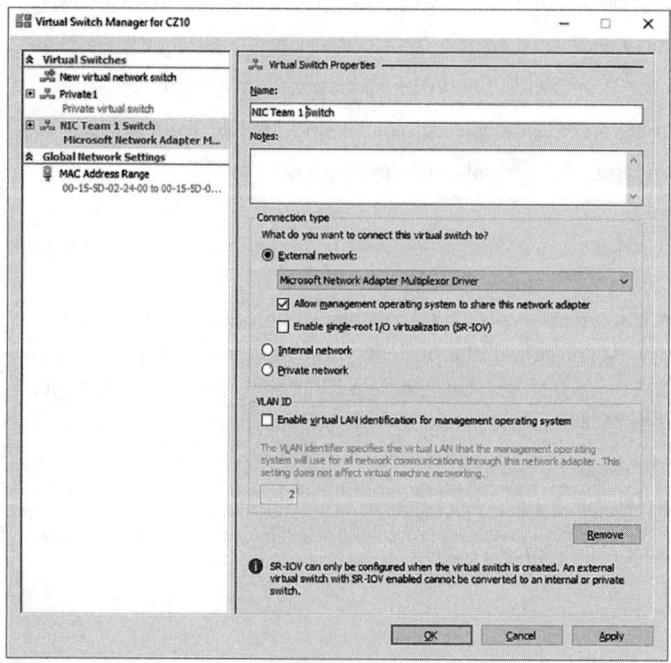

FIGURE 3-66 The Virtual Switch Properties settings for a NIC team switch

Configuring a NIC team virtual network adapter

To configure a virtual machine to use a NIC team, you must use the Settings dialog box to add a virtual network adapter or modify the properties of an existing one, configuring it to use the NIC team switch you created in the previous section, as shown in Figure 3-67.

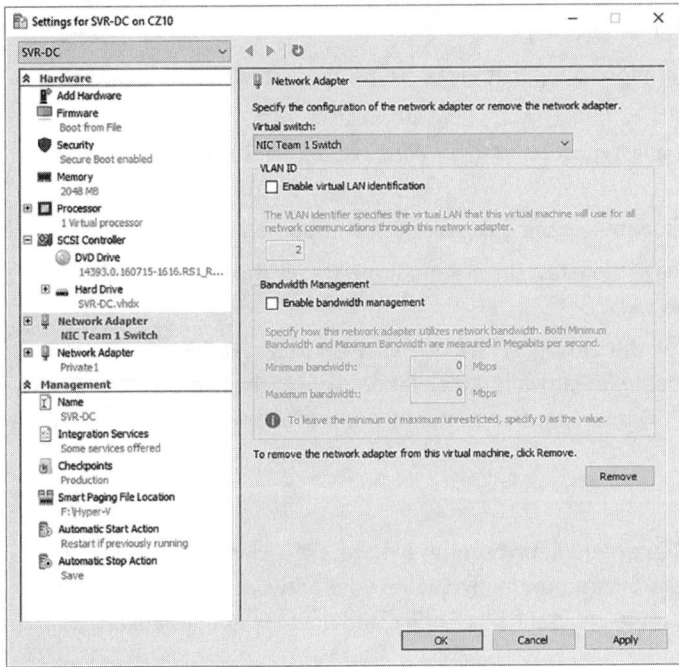

FIGURE 3-67 The Network Adapter settings for a NIC team adapter

Finally, you must open the Advanced Features page for the network adapter and select the Enable This Network Adapter To Be Part Of A Team In The Guest Operating System check box. At this point, the NIC team is operational for the virtual machine. You can unplug one of the network cables, and the system maintains its connection to the network.

Configure virtual machine queue (VMQ)

Virtual machine queue (VMQ) is a network performance enhancement feature that Windows Server 2016 enables automatically when it detects physical network adapters that run at 10 gigabits per second (Gbps) or faster. The VMQ process for incoming network traffic is as follows:

1. A network adapter that supports VMQ performs its own internal packet filtering based on the destination address. The packets for each destination are added to a separate queue.
2. The adapter sends the queued data for each destination to the host operating system.
3. The host operating system forwards each queue to a different logical processor, so that it can handle the traffic for multiple destinations simultaneously.

4. The host operating system sends the packets for each queue to the virtual switch.

5. The virtual switch routes the packets in each queue out through the appropriate port to the destination VM.

Because the filtering takes place in the physical network adapter, there is less processing needed in the virtual switch. Any traffic that does not match the filters is sent to a default queue, which the switch must then process.

For the Hyper-V implementation to support VMQ, it must meet the following requirements:

- Both the host and the guest must be running Windows Server 2016 or Windows Server 2012 R2.
- The physical network adapters in the host server must support VMQ.
- The host server must have the latest drivers and firmware for the physical network adapters installed.
- The network adapters in the VMs must have the Enable Virtual Machine Queue check box selected on the adapter's Hardware Acceleration page in the Settings dialog box. You can also enable VMQ on a specific adapter by running a PowerShell command like the following:

```
enable-netadaptervmq -name nic1
```

Modifying the default VMQ configuration requires a thorough understanding of your hardware's capabilities. You must learn how many queues your network adapters support, how many logical processors there are in the host server, and how the queues are assigned to the processors.

To discover whether your physical network adapters support VMQ, run the Get-NetAdapterVmq cmdlet in a PowerShell window with Administrator privileges. A blank response indicates that your adapters do not support VMQ. If they do, the cmdlet displays the identifying information for the physical adapters it detects in the computer, as well as the following information:

- **Enabled** Indicates whether the adapter is currently using VMQ
- **BaseVmqProcessor** Identifies the first logical processor that VMQ uses to assign queues from the network adapter
- **MaxProcessors** Specifies the maximum number of logical processors that VMQ uses to assign queues from the network adapter
- **NumberOfReceiveQueues** Specifies the number of queues supported by the network adapter

Next, you can use the Get-NetAdapterVmqQueue cmdlet to see which queues are assigned to which logical processors. The information displayed by this cmdlet is as follows:

- **QueueID** Specifies the number of the queue being assigned.

- **MacAddress** Specifies the MAC address to which the queue is assigned. A blank value for this property indicates the default queue used to process all unfiltered traffic.
- **VlanID** Specifies the VLAN to which the queue is assigned, if VLANs are in use.
- **Processor** Specifies the number of the processor to which the queue is assigned.
- **VmFriendlyName** Specifies the name of the virtual machine that is the destination for the queue's traffic. The presence of the host server name in this property indicates the default queue.

To modify the default VMQ settings, you use the Set-NetAdapterVmq PowerShell cmdlet. The parameters that are most commonly modified by administrators are as follows:

- **BaseProcessorNumber** Specifies the number of the lowest logical processor that the system should use when assigning queues. The recommended practice is to leave the first one or two processors for use by the host operating system.
- **MaxProcessorNumber** Specifies the number of the highest logical processor that the system should use when assigning queues.
- **MaxProcessors** Specifies how many of the logical processors in the host server should be used to service queues

For example, the following command sets the network adapter called NIC1 to reserve logical processors 0 and 1 for the host server, and begin assigned queues at processor 2.

```
Set-netadaptervmq -name nic1 -baseprocessornumber 2
```

Enable Remote Direct Memory Access (RDMA) on network adapters bound to a Hyper-V virtual switch using Switch Embedded Teaming (SET)

NIC teaming is a function of Windows Server 2016, which you can use with or without Hyper-V. *Switch Embedded Teaming (SET)* is a Hyper-V-only variation on the concept of NIC teaming that is implemented wholly within a Hyper-V virtual switch.

Remote Direct Memory Access (RDMA) is a high-speed network transmission method that can send large amounts of data with low latency and without processor intervention. RDMA-capable network adapters transfer data directly to and from application memory, without having to buffer it. Networking technologies such as SMB Direct rely on RDMA to achieve their high-performance levels.

Windows Server 2016 can, for the first time, combine these two technologies to provide Hyper-V with a high-performance networking solution using multiple physical network adapters.

To create a Hyper-V virtual switch that uses SET with RDMA adapters, the requirements are as follows:

- The host server can have up to eight physical network adapters.

- All physical network adapters that have passed the Windows Hardware Qualification and Logo (WHQL) test are supported.
- All the physical network adapters must be identical, with the same model, the same firmware, and the same drivers.
- Physical network adapters capable of running at various speeds must all be configured to run at the same speed.
- The physical adapters do not have to be connected to the same physical switch.
- The use of Data Center Bridging (DCB) is strongly recommended, to separate the RDMA from standard networking traffic.

To create a virtual switch with SET enabled, you must run the New-VMSwitch PowerShell cmdlet with the EnableEmbeddedTeaming parameter. There is no graphical equivalent in Virtual Switch Manager. An example of the command is as follows:

```
new-vmswitch -name setswitch -netadaptername "nic1","nic2" -enableembeddedteaming $true
```

After creating the switch, you can add new virtual network adapters to your VMs, using commands like the following:

```
add-vmnetworkadapter -vmname server1 -switchname setswitch -name set1
```

Once you have done this, you can enable RDMA on the adapters in the SET team. The Get-NetAdapterRdma cmdlet displays the current RDMA status of the adapters, plus the names assigned to them. To enable RDMA, you run the Enable-NetAdapterRdma cmdlet with the name listed in the Get-NetAdapterRdma output, as shown in Figure 3-68.

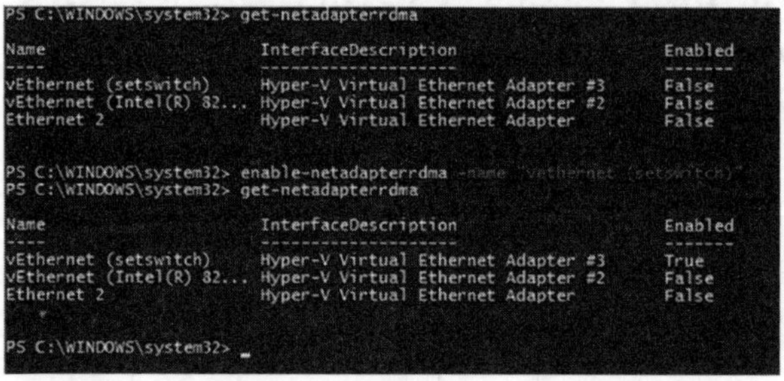

FIGURE 3-68 Enabling RDMA for SET team adapters

Configure bandwidth management

To prevent any one virtual network adapter from monopolizing the bandwidth available in a virtual switch, you can configure the minimum and maximum amount of bandwidth it is permitted to use. When you open the Settings dialog box for a virtual machine and select a network adapter, there is an Enable Bandwidth Management check box the activates the settings shown in Figure 3-69.

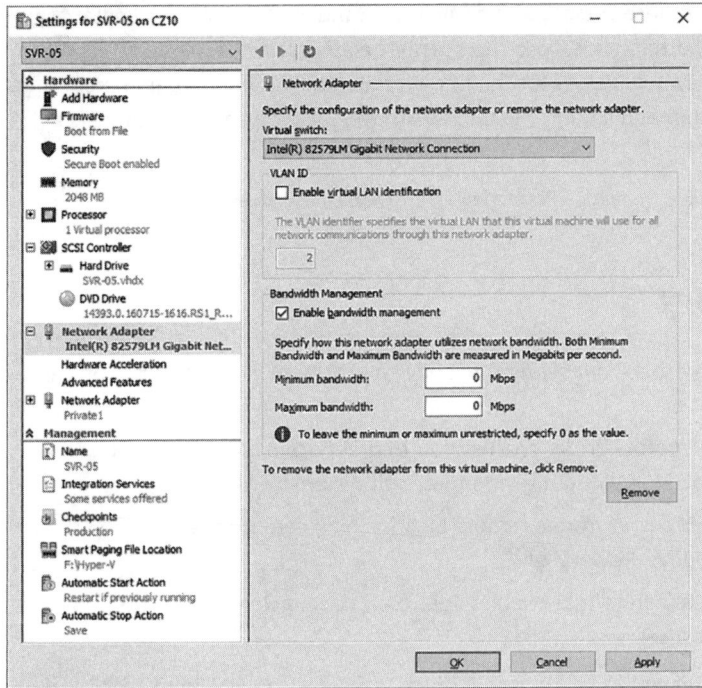

FIGURE 3-69 The Bandwidth Management settings for a virtual network adapter

The Minimum Bandwidth and Maximum Bandwidth settings in Hyper-V Manager are absolute, meaning that they measure the bandwidth in megabits per second (Mbps). Therefore, the settings you use depend on the speed of the physical network adapter in the host server, the number of VMs contending for the available bandwidth of the virtual switch, and the importance of the workloads on the VMs.

The Minimum Bandwidth setting ensures that a specific adapter does not get overwhelmed by the other VMs contending for the same bandwidth. Even if another VM malfunctions and floods the network, this setting should ensure that the adapter is not denied access. The Maximum Bandwidth setting can prevent a malfunctioning or noisy adapter from taking all the bandwidth, shutting the other VMs out.

Make sure that the Maximum Bandwidth settings for all VMs connected to the virtual switch do not exceed the actual bandwidth provided by the physical network adapter. If, for example, the host server has a 1 Gbps physical adapter, and the Maximum Bandwidth settings for the VMs using it add up to more than 1 Gbps, there is contention for the network, and the host server itself might end up being denied access.

You can also configure these settings using the Set-VMNetworkAdapter cmdlet in Windows PowerShell, which also has an additional capability. The parameters corresponding the settings in Hyper-V Manager are MaximumBandwidth and MinimumBandwidthAbsolute.

The latter is so named because there is also a MinimumBandwidthWeight parameter that specifies how much bandwidth to allocate to the adapter relative to the other adapters connected to the same virtual switch. Values for the MinimumBandwidthWeight parameter range from 1 to 100. A typical command setting the bandwidth weight for an adapter appears as follows:

```
set-vmnetworkadapter -vmname server1 -name nic1 -minimumbandwidthweight 75
```

Chapter summary

- To install the Hyper-V role, your server must have a processor with virtualization capabilities.
- The Hyper-V Administrators group enables you to grant users and groups the ability to work with virtual machines without giving them full system privileges.
- To manage a Hyper-V server from a remote location, you can use the Hyper-V Manager console or Windows PowerShell.
- PowerShell Direct is a feature that enables you to establish a PowerShell session with a guest OS from its host server.
- Nested virtualization enables you to install Hyper-V on a virtual machine, essentially creating a host out of a guest.
- In Windows Server 2016, you can modify the amount of memory allotted to a virtual machine while it is running.
- Dynamic Memory is a Hyper-V function that automatically assigns memory to and reclaims it from a virtual machine as it is needed.
- NUMA is a system architecture that pairs processors with local memory for optimum performance. Hyper-V includes a virtualized NUMA architecture that mirrors the one in the physical computer by default, but which you can modify to suit the needs of your VMs.
- Smart Paging is a feature used with Dynamic Memory that enables Hyper-V to restart VMs when the system is short of physical memory by paging to disk during the boot process.
- Integration Services is a suite of programs that runs on the guest operating system and facilitates communication with the host operating system. Hyper-V enables administrators to control which Integration Services components are running for each VM.
- Enhanced Session Mode enables administrators to remotely access virtual machines while taking advantage of local hardware, such as printers and USB devices.
- Hyper-V supports VMs running FreeBSD and various Linux distributions as guest operating systems.

- Secure Boot is part of the UEFI interface that prevents unsigned and unverified software from loading during the system boot process. Hyper-V supports Secure Boot on Generation 2 VMs.
- Discrete Device Assignment is a pass-through technology that enables a VM to access PCI Express devices on the host server, such as GPUs.
- Windows Server 2016 Hyper-V supports two types of shared virtual disks, shared VHDX files and VHD sets. You can use either one to build a Hyper-V cluster in which multiple VMs are accessing the same data.
- By mounting a VHD or VHDX file into the file system, you can work with it offline. You can also use PowerShell cmdlets to install Windows roles and features to an umounted VHD.
- A pass-through disk is a virtual disk that is linked, not to a VHD file, but to a physical disk in the host server.
- Windows Server 2016 supports two types of checkpoints: standard and production. Standard checkpoints contain a copy of a VM's memory state and machine state. A production saves only the machine state, and can be restored without affecting the VM's current memory state.
- Hyper-V supports virtual Fibre Channel adapters, which are pass-through devices to the physical host bus adapters installed on the host server. This enables a VM to access storage devices on a Fibre Channel SAN.
- The virtual disks in Hyper-V support Quality of Service settings that you can use to specify minimum and maximum I/O settings. This can prevent one virtual disk from monopolizing the physical disk on which it is stored.
- Hyper-V uses synthetic network adapters to provide the best performance, but Generation 1 VMs have to use a legacy network adapter to support network booting.
- NIC teaming is a technique for aggregating the bandwidth of multiple network adapters, to provide improved performance and fault tolerance.
- Virtual Machine Queue is a performance-enhancing mechanism in which network adapters filter incoming traffic and send the packets for specific destinations to specific logical processors.
- Windows Server 2016 Hyper-V includes Switch Embedded Teaming, which implements NIC teams in a virtual switch. You can use this capability to combine the RDMA functionality of up to eight physical network adapters.

Thought experiment

In this thought experiment, demonstrate your skills and knowledge of the topics covered in this chapter. You can find answer to this thought experiment in the next section.

Alice has a computer running Windows Server 2016 with 8 GB of memory installed, which she has configured as a Hyper-V server. After creating eight VMs with the New Virtual Machine Wizard, each with a RAM value of 1,024 MB, Alice is having trouble getting all eight VMs to boot. What settings can she modify to resolve the problem without changing the RAM values?

Thought experiment answer

This section contains the solution to the thought experiment.

Alice can enable dynamic memory on each of the eight VMs and set the minimum RAM value on each to 512 MB. This enables each VM to start with 1,024 MB of memory and then reduce its footprint, enabling the next machine to start.

CHAPTER 4

Implement Windows containers

Containers are a means of rapidly deploying virtualized, isolated operating system environments, for application deployment and execution. Windows Server 2016 includes support for containers, in cooperation with an open source container engine called Docker.

Skills in this chapter:
- Deploy Windows containers
- Manage Windows containers

Skill 4.1: Deploy Windows containers

Virtualization has been an important watchword since the early days of Windows. Virtual memory has been around for decades; Windows can use disk space to make the system seem like it has more memory than it has. Hyper-V virtualizes hardware, creating computers within a computer that seem to have their own processors, memory, and disks, when in fact they are sharing the resources of the host server. *Containers* is a new feature in Windows Server 2016 that virtualizes operating systems.

> **This section covers how to:**
> - Determine installation requirements and appropriate scenarios for Windows containers
> - Install and configure Windows Server container host in physical or virtualized environments
> - Install and configure Windows Server container host to Windows Server Core or Nano Server in a physical or virtualized environment
> - Install Docker on Windows Server and Nano Server
> - Configure Docker daemon start-up options
> - Configure Windows PowerShell for use with containers
> - Install a base operating system
> - Tag an image
> - Uninstall an operating system image
> - Create Windows Server containers
> - Create Hyper-V containers

Determine installation requirements and appropriate scenarios for Windows containers

Just as virtual machines provide what appear to be separate computers, containers provide what appear to be separate instances of the operating system, each with its own memory and file system, and running a clean, new copy of the operating system. Unlike virtual machines, however, which run separate copies of the operating system, containers share the operating system of the host system. There is no need to install a separate instance of the operating system for each container, nor does the container perform a boot sequence, load libraries, or devote memory to the operating system files. Containers start in seconds, and you can create more containers on a host system than you can virtual machines.

To users working with containers, what they appear to see at first is a clean operating system installation, ready for applications. The environment is completely separated from the host, and from other containers, using namespace isolation and resource governance.

Namespace isolation means that each container only has access to the resources that are available to it. Files, ports, and running processes all appear to be dedicated to the container, even when they are being shared with the host and with other containers. The working environment appears like that of a virtual machine, but unlike a virtual machine, which maintains separate copies of all the operating system files, a container is sharing these files with the host, not copying them. It is only when a user or application in a container modifies a file that a copy is made in the container's file system.

Resource governance means that a container has access only to a specified amount of processor cycles, system memory, network bandwidth, and other resources, and no more. An application running in a container has a clean sandbox environment, with no access to resources allocated to other containers or to the host.

Container images

The ability to create new containers in seconds, and the isolated nature of each container, make them an ideal platform for application development and software testing. However, there is more to them than that.

Containers are based on images. To create a new container, you download an image from a repository and run it. If you run an image of Windows Server 2016 Server Core, you get a container with a clean instance of the operating system running in it. Alternatively, you can download Windows Server images with roles or applications, such as Internet Information Services (IIS) or Microsoft SQL Server, already installed and ready to run.

The base operating system image never changes. If you install an application in the container and then create a new image, the resulting image contains only the files and settings needed to run the application. Naturally, the new image you created is relatively small, because it does not contain the entire operating system. To share the application with other people, you only have to send them the new, smaller image, as long as they already have the base operating system image.

This process can continue through as many iterations as you need, with layer upon layer of images building on that original base. This can result in an extremely efficient software development environment. Instead of transferring huge VHD files, or constantly creating and installing new virtual machines, you can transfer small container images that run without hardware compatibility issues.

Install and configure Windows Server Container Host in physical or virtualized environments

Windows Server 2016 supports two types of containers: Windows Server Containers and Hyper-V containers. The difference between the two is in the degree of container isolation they provide. Windows Server Containers operate in user mode and share everything with the host computer, including the operating system kernel and the system memory.

Because of this, it is conceivable that an application, whether accidentally or deliberately, might be able to escape from the confines of its container and affect other processes running on the host or in other containers. This option is therefore presumed to be preferable when the applications running in different containers are basically trustworthy.

Hyper-V containers provide an additional level of isolation by using the hypervisor to create a separate copy of the operating system kernel for each container. Although they are not visible or exposed to manual management, Hyper-V creates virtual machines with Windows containers inside them, using the base container images, as shown in Figure 4-1. The container implementation is essentially the same; the difference is in the environments where the two types of containers exist.

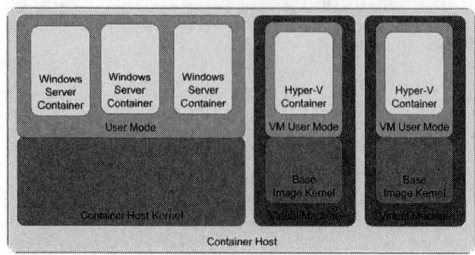

FIGURE 4-1 Windows container architecture

Because they exist inside a VM, Hyper-V containers have their own memory assigned to them, as well as isolated storage and network I/O. This provides a container environment that is suitable for what Microsoft calls "hostile multi-tenant" applications, such as a situation in which a business provides containers to clients for running their own code, which might not be trustworthy. Thus, with the addition of Hyper-V containers, Windows Server 2016 provides three levels of isolation, ranging from the separate operating system installation of Hyper-V virtual machines, to the separate kernel and memory of Hyper-V containers, to the shared kernel and other resources of Windows Server Containers.

Installing a container host

Windows Server 2016 includes a feature called Containers, which you must install to provide container support, but to create and manage containers you must download and install Docker, the application that supports the feature.

To install the Containers feature, you can use the Add Roles And Features Wizard in Hyper-V Manager, selecting Containers on the Select Features page, as shown in Figure 4-2.

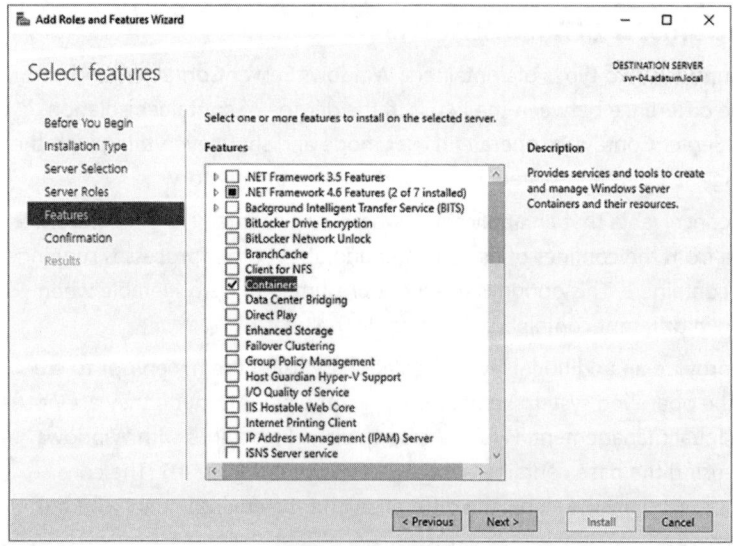

FIGURE 4-2 Installing the Containers feature in Hyper-V Manager

> **NOTE WINDOWS SERVER INSTALLATION**
>
> To create Windows Server containers, the host operating system must be installed on the computer's C drive, which is the installation default. This is to facilitate the sharing the operating system kernel. This is not a requirement for creating Hyper-V containers, as the hypervisor is responsible for providing a copy of the kernel to each container.

To create Hyper-V containers, you must install both the Containers feature and the Hyper-V role. Even though you will not be creating virtual machines for the containers, the Hyper-V role installs the hypervisor that will be needed to create the separate copy of the Windows kernel for each Hyper-V container.

The Hyper-V role has general hardware requirements that exceed those of the Windows Server 2016 operating system itself. Before you can install the Hyper-V role on a server running Windows Server 2016, you must have the following hardware:

- A 64-bit processor that includes hardware-assisted virtualization and second-level address translation (SLAT). This type of virtualization is available in processors that include a virtualization option, such as Intel Virtualization Technology (Intel VT) or AMD Virtualization (AMD-V) technology.
- Hardware-enforced Data Execution Prevention (DEP), which Intel describes as eXecuted Disable (XD) and AMD describes as No eXecute (NX). CPUs use this technology to segregate areas of memory for either storage of processor instructions or for storage of data. Specifically, you must enable Intel XD bit (execute disable bit) or AMD NX bit (no execute bit).
- VM Monitor Mode extensions, found on Intel processors as VT-c.
- A system BIOS or UEFI that supports the virtualization hardware and on which the virtualization feature has been enabled.

When you install the Hyper-V role using Hyper-V Manager, the Add Roles And Features Wizard prompts to install the Hyper-V Management tools as well. If you are creating Hyper-V containers but not Hyper-V virtual machines, there is no need to install the management tools.

Virtualizing containers

Windows Server 2016 supports the use of containers within Hyper-V virtual machines. You can install the Containers feature and the Docker files in any virtual machine. However, to create Hyper-V containers on a virtual machine, the system must meet the requirements for nested virtualization.

To create a nested Hyper-V host server, the physical host and the virtual machine on which you create the Hyper-V containers must both be running Windows Server 2016. The VM can run the full Desktop Experience, Server Core, or Nano Server installation option. In addition, the physical host must have an Intel processor with VT-x and Extended Page Tables (EPT) virtualization support.

Before you install Hyper-V on the virtual machine, you must provide its virtual processor with access to the virtualization technology on the physical computer. To do this, you must shut down the virtual machine and run a command like the following on the physical host, in a PowerShell session with administrator privileges:

```
set-vmprocessor -vmname server1 -exposevirtualizationextensions $true
```

In addition, you must make the following configuration changes on the VM that functions as a Hyper-V host. Each is given first as the location in the VM Settings dialog box in Hyper-V Manager, and then as a PowerShell command:

- On the Memory page, provide the VM with at least 4 gigabytes (GB) of RAM and disable Dynamic Memory.

    ```
    set-vmmemory -vmname server1 -startupbytes 4gb -dynamicmemoryenabled $false
    ```

- On the Processor page, set Number of Virtual Processors to 2.

    ```
    set-vmprocessor -vmname server1 -count 2
    ```

- On the Network Adapter/Advanced Features page, turn on MAC Address Spoofing.

    ```
    set-vmnetworkadapter -vmname server1 -name "network adapter" -macaddressspoofing on
    ```

Once you have made these changes, you can start the VM, install the Hyper-V role, and proceed to use Docker to create Hyper-V containers.

Install and configure Windows Server container host to Windows Server Core or Nano Server in a physical or virtualized environment

A computer installed using the Server Core option can function as a container host. The requirements are the same as for a server installed with the full Desktop Experience, except that you must either use the command line to install the required features or manage the system remotely.

After switching to a PowerShell session, you can install the Containers feature and the Hyper-V role using the following command:

```
install-windowsfeature -name containers, hyper-v
```

Configuring Nano Server as a container host

Nano Server, included with Windows Server 2016, supports both Windows Server containers and Hyper-V containers. The Nano Server implementation includes packages supporting both the Containers feature and the Hyper-V role, which you can add when you create a Nano Server image with the New-NanoServerImage cmdlet in Windows PowerShell, as in the following example:

```
new-nanoserverimage -deploymenttype guest -edition datacenter -mediapath d:\ -targetpath
c:\nano\nano1.vhdx -computername nano1 -domainname contoso -containers
```

This command creates a Nano Server image with the following characteristics:

- **deploymenttype guest**   Creates an image for use on a Hyper-V virtual machine
- **edition datacenter**   Creates an image using the Datacenter edition of Windows Server
- **mediapath d:**   Accesses the Nano Server source files from the D drive
- **targetpath c:\\nano\\nano1.vhdx**   Creates an VHDX image file in the C:\nano folder with the name Nano1.vhdx
- **computername nano1**   Assigns the Nano Server the computer name Nano1
- **domainname contoso**   Joins the computer to the Contoso domain
- **containers**   Installs the Containers feature as part of the image
- **compute**   Installs the Hyper-V role as part of the image

If you plan on creating Hyper-V containers on the guest Nano Server, you must provide it with access to the virtualization capabilities of the Hyper-V server, using the following procedure.

1. Create a new virtual machine, using the Nano Server image file you created, but do not start it.
2. On the Hyper-V host server, grant the virtual machine with access to the virtualization capabilities of the Hyper-V server's physical processor, using a command like the following:

   ```
   set-vmprocessor -vmname nano1 -exposevirtualizationextensions $true
   ```

3. Start the Nano Server virtual machine.

Once the Nano Server virtual machine is running, you must establish a remote PowerShell session from another computer, so you can manage it. To do this, run a command like the following on the computer you use to manage Nano Server:

```
enter-pssession -computername nano1 -credential
```

> **NOTE   REMOTE NANO SERVER MANAGEMENT**
>
> This section assumes that the Nano Server is located on a network with a DHCP server that assigns its TCP/IP settings and that it has successfully joined an Active Directory Domain Services domain. If those are not the case, you must configure the TCP/IP settings for the Nano Server manually, from its console, and then add the Nano Server to the Trusted Hosts list on the computer you use to manage it.

Install Docker on Windows Server and Nano Server

Docker is an open source tool that has been providing container capabilities to the Linux community for years. Now that it has been ported, you can implement those same capabilities in Windows. Docker consists of two files:

- **Dockerd.exe** The Docker engine, also referred to as a service or daemon, which runs in the background on the Windows computer
- **Docker.exe** The Docker client, a command shell that you use to create and manage containers

In addition to these two files, which you must download and install to create containers, Docker also includes the following resources:

- **Dockerfiles** Script files containing instructions for the creation of container images
- **Docker Hub** A cloud-based registry that enables Docker users to link to image and code repositories, as well as build and store their own images
- **Docker Cloud** A cloud-based service you can use to deploy your containerized applications

Installing Docker on Windows Server

Because Docker is an open source product, it is not included with Windows Server 2016. On a Windows Server 2016 Desktop Experience or Server Core computer, you must download Docker and install it before you can create containers. To download Docker, you use OneGet, a cloud-based package manager for Windows.

To access OneGet, you must install the DockerMsftProvider module, using the following command. If you are prompted to install a NuGet provider, answer Yes.

```
install-module -name dockermsftprovider -repository psgallery -force
```

The Install-Module cmdlet downloads the requested module and installs it to the C:\Program Files\Windows PowerShell\Modules folder, where it is accessible from any PowerShell prompt. Next, to download and install Docker, run the following Install-Package command. If the command prompts you to confirm that you want to install an untrusted package, answer Yes.

```
install-package -name docker -providername dockermsftprovider
```

This command, after downloading the Docker files, registers Dockerd.exe as a Windows service and adds the Docker.exe client to the path, so that it is executable from and location in the file system.

Once the installation is completed, restart the computer with the following command:

```
restart-computer -force
```

Installing Docker on Nano Server

Once you have entered a remote PowerShell session with a Nano Server computer, you can install Docker using the same commands as for a Desktop Experience or Server Core system. However, Microsoft recommends that, once the Dockerd service is installed on the Nano Server, you run the Docker client from the remote system.

To do this, you must complete the following tasks:

1. Create a firewall rule. For the Nano Server to allow Docker client traffic into the system, you must create a new firewall rule opening port 2375 to TCP traffic. To do this, run the following command in the Nano Server session:

   ```
   netsh advfirewall firewall add rule name="docker daemon" dir=in action=allow protocol=tcp localport=2375
   ```

2. Configure the Dockerd engine to accept network traffic. Docker has its origins in Linux, and like most Linux applications, it uses text files for configuration. To enable the Dockerd engine to accept client traffic over the network, you must create a text file called daemon.json in the C:\ProgramData\Docker\config directory on the Nano Server that contains the following line:

   ```
   { "hosts": ["tcp://0.0.0.0:2375", "npipe://"] }
   ```

   The following two PowerShell commands create the new file and insert the required text:

   ```
   new-item -type file c:\programdata\docker\config\daemon.json
   ```

   ```
   add-content 'c:\programdata\docker\config\daemon.json' '{ "hosts": ["tcp://0.0.0.0:2375", "npipe://"] }'
   ```

3. Restart the Dockerd engine. Once you have created the daemon.json file, you must restart the Dockerd engine, using the following command:

   ```
   restart-service docker
   ```

4. Download the Docker client. To Manage the Dockerd engine remotely, you must download and install the Docker.exe client on the remote system (not within the Nano Server session). To do this, you can open a browser and type in the following URL to download the Docker package:

   ```
   https://download.docker.com/components/engine/windows-server/cs-1.12/docker.zip
   ```

5. To do this in PowerShell, use the following command:

   ```
   invoke-webrequest "https://download.docker.com/components/engine/windows-server/cs-1.12/docker.zip" -outfile "$env:temp\docker.zip" -usebasicparsing
   ```

6. Install Docker.exe. If you downloaded the Docker. zip file through a browser, you install the application by extracting the Docker.exe file from the zip archive and copying it to a folder you must create called C:\ProgramData\Docker. To do this using PowerShell, run the following command:

   ```
   expand-archive -path "$env:temp\docker.zip" -destinationpath $env:programfiles
   ```

7. Set the PATH environment variable. To run the Docker client from any location on the management system, you must add the C:\ProgramData\Docker folder to the system's PATH environment variable. To do this graphically, open the System Properties sheet from the Control Panel and, on the Advanced tab, click Environment Variables to display the dialog box shown in Figure 4-3.

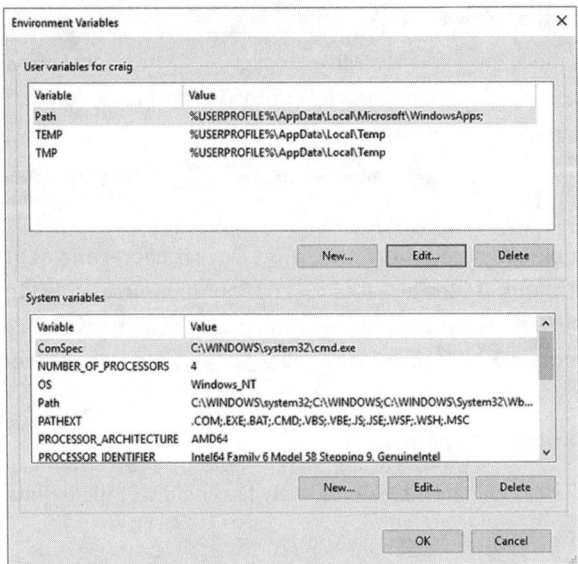

FIGURE 4-3 The Environment Variables dialog box

8. To do this in PowerShell, run the following command:

   [environment]::setenvironmentvariable("path", $env:path + ";c:\program files\docker", [environmentvariabletarget]::machine)

Once you have completed these steps, you can run the Docker.exe client outside of the Nano Server session, but you must include the following parameter in every command, where the ipaddress variable is replaced by the address of the Nano Server you want to manage:

-h tcp://ipaddress:2375

For example, to create a new container with the microsoft/nanoserver image, you would use a command like the following:

docker -h tcp://172.21.96.1:2375 run -it microsoft/nanoserver cmd

To avoid having to add the -h parameter to every command, you can create a new environment variable as follows:

docker_host = "tcp://ipaddress:2375"

To do this in PowerShell, use a command like the following:

$env:docker_host = "tcp://172.21.96.1:2375"

Configure Docker Daemon start-up options

As mentioned in the previous section, the configuration file for the Dockerd engine is a plain text file called daemon.json, which you place in the same folder as the Dockerd.exe file. In addition to the one you used earlier to permit client traffic over the network, there are many other configuration settings you can include in the file. All of the settings you include in a single daemon.json file should be enclosed in a single set of curly braces, as in the following example:

```
{
"graph": "d:\\docker",
 "bridge" : "none",
 "group" : "docker",
{"dns": 192.168.9.2, 192.168.9.6 }
}
```

> **EXAM TIP**
> Be aware that while the Windows port of Docker supports many of the Linux Dockerd configuration settings, it does not support all of them. If you are studying Docker documentation, be sure to look for the Windows version of the documents.

Redirecting images and containers

To configure the Dockerd engine to store image files and containers in an alternate location, you include the following command in the daemon.json file, where d:\\docker is replaced by the location you want to use:

`{ "graph": "d:\\docker" }`

Suppressing NAT

By default, the Dockerd engine creates a network address translation (NAT) environment for containers, enabling them to communicate with each other and with the outside network. To modify this default behavior and prevent the engine from using NAT, you include the following command in the daemon.json file:

`{ "bridge" : "none" }`

Creating an administrative group

By default, only members of the local Administrators group can use the Docker client to control the Dockerd engine when working on the local system. In some cases, you can grant users this ability without giving them Administrators membership. You can configure Dockerd to recognize another group—in this case, the group is called "docker"—by including the following setting in the daemon.json file.

`{ "group" : "docker" }`

Setting DNS server addresses

To specify alternative DNS server addresses for the operating systems in containers, you can add the following setting to the daemon.json file, where address1 and address2 are the IP addresses of DNS servers:

```
{"dns": "address1" , "address2"  }
```

Configure Windows PowerShell for use with containers

The Dockerd engine is supplied with a Docker.exe client shell, but it is not dependent on it. You can also use Windows PowerShell cmdlets to perform the same functions. The Docker PowerShell module, like Docker itself, is in a constant state of cooperative development, and it is therefore not included with Windows Server 2016.

You can download and install the current version of the PowerShell module from a repository called DockerPS-Dev, using the following commands:

```
register-psrepository -name dockerps-dev -sourcelocation https://ci.appveyor.com/nuget/docker-powershell-dev
```

```
install-module docker -repository dockerps-dev -scope currentuser
```

Once the download is completed, you can view a list of the Docker cmdlets by running the following command:

```
get-command -module docker
```

The current resulting output is shown in Figure 4-4.

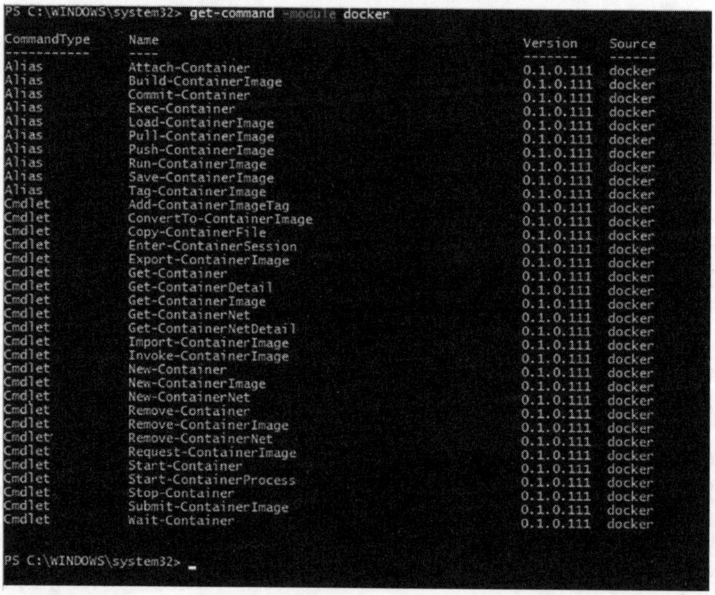

FIGURE 4-4 Cmdlets in the Docker module for Windows PowerShell

Once you have registered the repository and imported the Docker module, you do not have to run those commands again. You can always obtain the latest version of the module by running the following command:

```
update-module docker
```

Install a base operating system

With the Dockerd engine and the Docker client installed and operational, you can take the first step toward creating containers, which is to download a base operating system image from the Docker Hub repository. Microsoft has provided the repository with Windows Server 2016 Server Core and Nano Server images, which you can download and use to create containers and then build your own container images.

To use the Docker client, you execute the Docker.exe file with a command and sometimes additional options and parameters. To download an image, you run Docker with the Pull command and the name of the image. For example, the following command downloads the Server Core image from the repository.

```
docker pull microsoft/windowsservercore
```

The PowerShell equivalent is as follows:

```
request-containerimage -repository microsoft/windowsservercore
```

The output of the command (which can take some time, depending on the speed of your Internet connection) is shown in Figure 4-5.

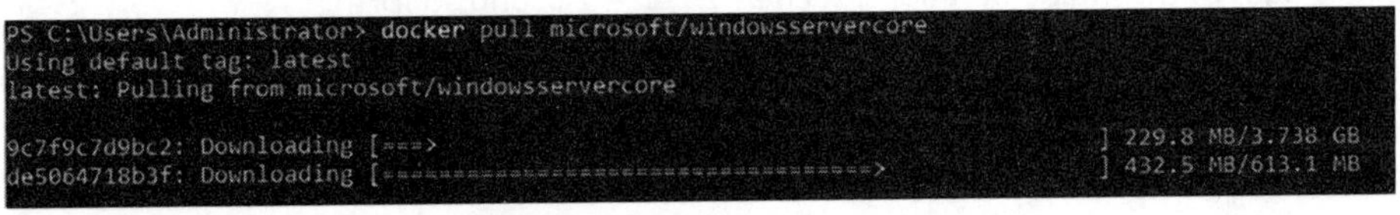

FIGURE 4-5 Output of the Docker Pull command

By default, the Docker Pull command downloads the latest version of the specified image, which is identified by the tag: "latest." When there are multiple versions of the same image available, as in an application development project, for example, you can specify any one of the previous images to download, by specifying its tag. If you run the Docker Pull command with the -a parameter, you get all versions of the image. If the image you are pulling consists of multiple layers, the command automatically downloads all of the layers needed to deploy the image in a container.

If you know that the repository has a Nano Server image, but you are not sure of its name, you can use the Docker Search command to locate it, and then use Docker Pull to download it, as shown in Figure 4-6

```
PS C:\Users\Administrator> docker search microsoft
NAME                                         DESCRIPTION                                       STARS    OFFICIAL    AUTOM
ATED
microsoft/aspnet                             ASP.NET is an open source server-side Web ...    498                  [OK]
microsoft/dotnet                             Official images for .NET Core for Linux an...    327                  [OK]
mono                                         Mono is an open source implementation of M...    195      [OK]
microsoft/windowsservercore                  Windows Server 2016 Server Core base OS im...     69
microsoft/nanoserver                         Windows Server 2016 Nano Server base OS im...     66
microsoft/azure-cli                          Docker image for Microsoft Azure Command L...     66                  [OK]
microsoft/iis                                Internet Information Services (IIS) instal...     50
microsoft/mssql-server-2014-express-windows  Microsoft SQL Server 2014 Express installe...     41
microsoft/aspnetcore                         Official images for running compiled ASP.N...     28                  [OK]
microsoft/mssql-server-2016-express-windows  Microsoft SQL Server 2016 Express installe...     28
microsoft/powershell                         Official PowerShell Core releases from htt...      8                  [OK]
microsoft/oms                                Monitor your containers using the Operatio...      7                  [OK]
microsoft/aspnetcore-build                   Official images for building ASP.NET Core ...      6                  [OK]
microsoft/dotnet35                           The .NET Framework 3.5 image has moved to ...      4
microsoft/vsts-agent                         Official images for the Visual Studio Team...      4
microsoft/applicationinsights                Application Insights for Docker helps you ...      4                  [OK]
microsoft/sample-nginx                       Nginx installed in Windows Server Core and...      4
microsoft/dotnet-nightly                     Preview bits of the .NET Core CLI                  2                  [OK]
microsoft/powershell-nightly                 Nightly builds of PowerShell Core for CI           2                  [OK]
microsoft/sample-dotnet                      .NET Core running in a Nano Server container       1
microsoft/cntk                               CNTK                                               0                  [OK]
dreher/microsoft                             Microsoft Test Repo                                0
microsoft/aspnetcore-build-nightly           Images to build preview versions of ASP.NE...      0                  [OK]
microsoft/dotnet-samples                     .NET Core Docker Samples                           0                  [OK]
berlius/microsoft-malmo                      Microsoft-malmo - artificial intelligence ...      0
PS C:\Users\Administrator> docker pull microsoft/nanoserver
Using default tag: latest
latest: Pulling from microsoft/nanoserver

5496abde368a: Pull complete
94b4ce7ac4c7: Pull complete
Digest: sha256:86cfed90ee6f711086d9cd637b7d8f250270c46cfe4e08f7527aea7968b9c8ff
Status: Downloaded newer image for microsoft/nanoserver:latest
PS C:\Users\Administrator>
```

FIGURE 4-6 Output of the Docker Search command

Tag an image

Tagging, in a container repository, is a version control mechanism. When you create multiple versions of the same image, such as the successive builds of an application, Docker enables you to assign tags to them that identify the versions. Tags are typically numbers indicating the relative ages of the image iterations, such as 1.1, 1.2, 2.0, and so forth.

There are two ways to assign a tag to an image. One is to run Docker with the Tag command, and the other is to run Docker Build with the -t parameter. In both cases, the format of the image identifier is the same.

To tag an image on your local container host, you use the following syntax:

```
docker tag imagename:tag
```

If you are going to be uploading the image to the Docker Hub, you must prefix the image name with your Docker Hub user name and a slash, as follows:

```
docker tag username/imagename:tag
```

For example, a user called Holly Holt might tag the latest build of her new application as follows:

```
docker tag hholt/killerapp:1.5
```

To do the same thing in Windows PowerShell, you would use the Add-ContainerImageTag cmdlet, as follows:

```
add-containerimagetag -imageidorname c452b8c6ee1a -repository hholt/killerapp -tag 1.5
```

If you omit the tag value from the command, Docker automatically assigns the image a tag value of the word "latest," which can lead to some confusion. When you pull an image from a repository without specifying a tag, the repository gives you the image with the "latest" tag. However, this does not necessarily mean that the image you are getting is the newest.

The "latest" tag is supposed to indicate that the image possessing it is the most recent version. However, whether that is true or not depends on the people managing the tags for that repository. Some people think that the "latest" tag is automatically reassigned to the most recent version of an image, but this is not the case. You can assign the "latest" tag to any version of an image, the oldest or the newest. It is solely up to the managers of the repository to maintain the tag values properly. When someone tells you to get the latest build of an image, is the person referring to the most recent build or the build with the "latest" tag? They are not always the same thing.

Uninstall an operating system image

Running Docker with the Images command displays all of the images on the container host, as shown in Figure 4-7.

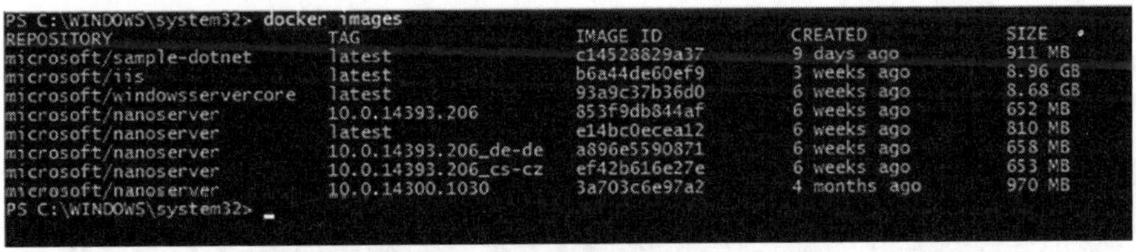

FIGURE 4-7 Output of the Docker Images command

In some instances, you might examine the list of images and find yourself with images that you do not need. In this example, there are two non-English versions of Nano Server that were downloaded accidentally.

To remove images that you do not need and free up the storage space they're consuming, you run Docker with the Rmi command and specify either the repository and tag of the specific image to delete, or the Image ID value, as in the following examples:

```
docker rmi -f microsoft/nanoserver:10.0.14393.206_de-de
```

```
docker rmi -f a896e5590871
```

The PowerShell equivalent is the Remove-ContainerImage cmdlet, as in the following:

```
remove-containerimage microsoft/nanoserver:10.0.14393.206_de-de
```

```
remove-containerimage a896e5590871
```

It is possible for the same image to be listed with multiple tags. You can tell this by the matching Image ID values. If you attempt to remove one of the images using the tag, an error appears, because the image is in use with other tags, Adding the -f parameter forces the command to delete all the tagged references to the same image.

Create Windows Server containers

With the Containers feature in place and Docker installed, you are ready to create a Windows Server container. To do this, you use the Docker Run command and specify the image that you want to run in the container. For example, the following command creates a new container with the Server Core image downloaded from Docker Hub:

```
docker run -it microsoft/windowsservercore powershell
```

In addition to loading the image into the container, the parameters in this command do the following:

- **i**   Creates an interactive session with the container
- **t**   Opens a terminal window into the container
- **powershell**   Executes the PowerShell command in the container session

The result is that after the container loads, a PowerShell session appears, enabling you to work inside the container. If you run the Get-ComputerInfo cmdlet in this session, you can see at the top of the output, shown in Figure 4-8, that Server Core is running in the container, when the full Desktop Experience edition in running on the container host.

FIGURE 4-8 Output of the Get-ComputerInfo cmdlet

You can combine Docker Run switches, so the -I and -t appear as -it. After the name of the image, you can specify any command to run in the container. For example, specifying cmd would open the standard Windows command shell instead of PowerShell.

> **NOTE OBTAINING IMAGES**
>
> Pulling an image from the Docker Hub is not a required step before you can run it. If you execute a Docker Run command, and you don't have the required image on your container host, Docker initiates a pull automatically and then creates the container. For large images, however, pulling them beforehand can save time when creating new containers.

The Docker Run command supports many command line parameters and switches, which you can use to tune the environment of the container you are creating. To display them, you can run the following command:

```
docker run --help
```

> **NOTE** **EXECUTING DOCKER COMMANDS**
>
> Note that this, and other, Docker commands sometimes use double hyphens to process command line parameters.

Figure 4-9 displays roughly half of the available parameters. For example, including the -h parameter enables you to specify a host name for the container, other than the hexadecimal string that the command assigns by default.

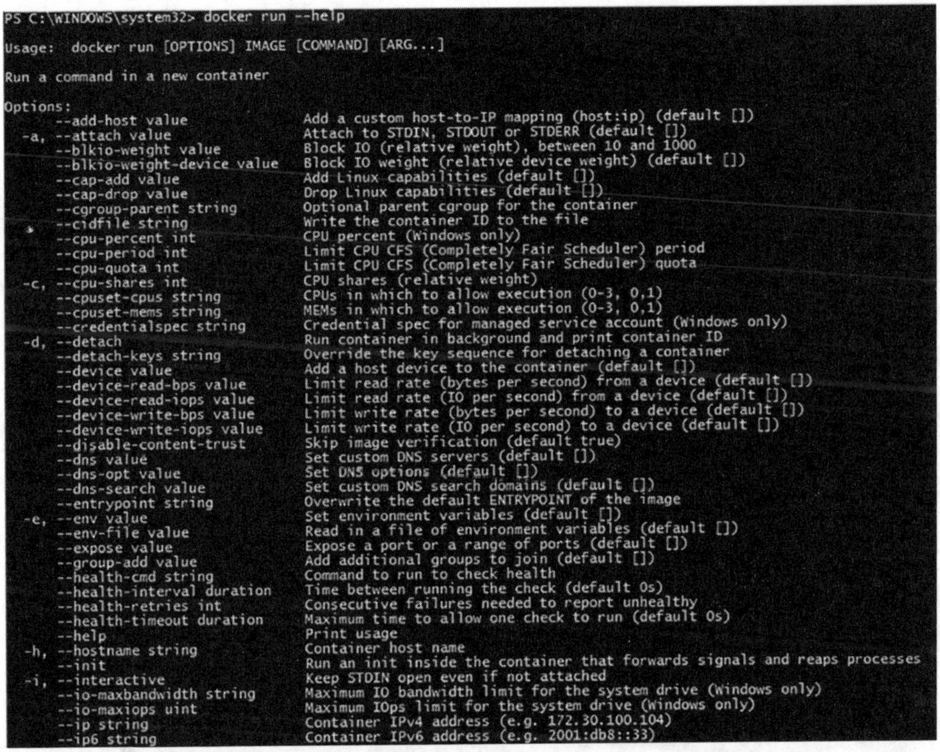

FIGURE 4-9 Output of the Docker Run --help command

The PowerShell equivalent of the Docker Run command uses the New-Container cmdlet, as in the following example:

```
new-container -imageidorname microsoft/windowsservercore -input -terminal -command powershell
```

Create Hyper-V containers

The process of creating a Hyper-V container is almost identical to that of creating a Windows Server container. You use the same Docker Run command, except that you add the --isolation=hyperv parameter, as shown in the following example:

```
docker run -it --isolation=hyperv microsoft/windowsservercore powershell
```

Once you create a Hyper-V container, it is all but indistinguishable from a Windows Server container. One of the few ways to tell the types of containers apart is to examine how they handle processes. For example, you can create two containers and execute a command in each one that starts them pinging themselves continuously, as shown in the following commands:

```
docker run -it microsoft/windowsservercore ping -t localhost
```

```
docker run -it --isolation=hyperv microsoft/windowsservercore ping -t localhost
```

The Windows Server container created by the first command has a PING process running in the container, as shown by the Docker Top command in Figure 4-10. The process ID (PID) number, in this case, is 404. Then, when you run the Get-Process cmdlet, to display the processes (starting with P) running on the container host, you see the same PING process with the 404 ID. This is because the container is sharing the kernel of the container host.

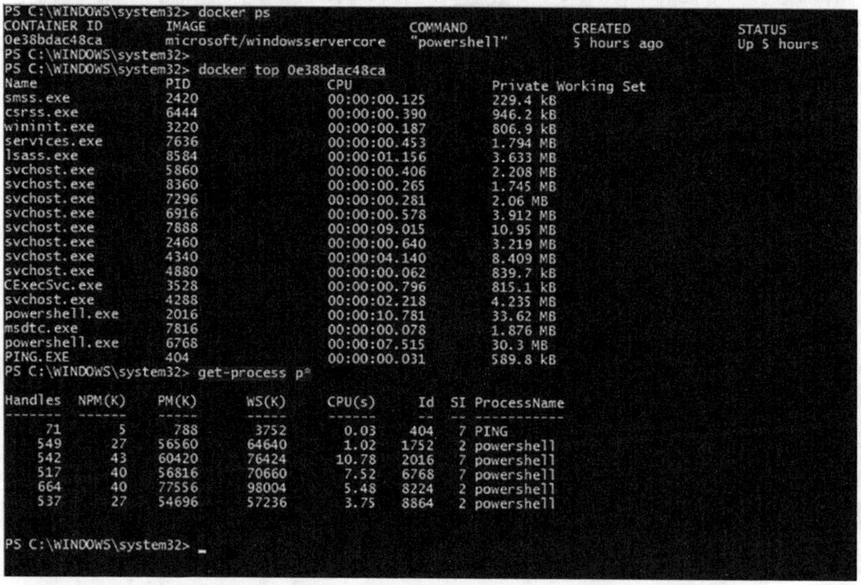

FIGURE 4-10 Output of Docker Top and Get-Process commands for a Windows Server container

On the other hand, when you run the Docker Top command on the Hyper-V container, you again see the PING process, this time with a PID of 1852, as shown in Figure 4-11. However, the Get-Process cmdlet shows no PING process, because this container has its own kernel provided by the hypervisor.

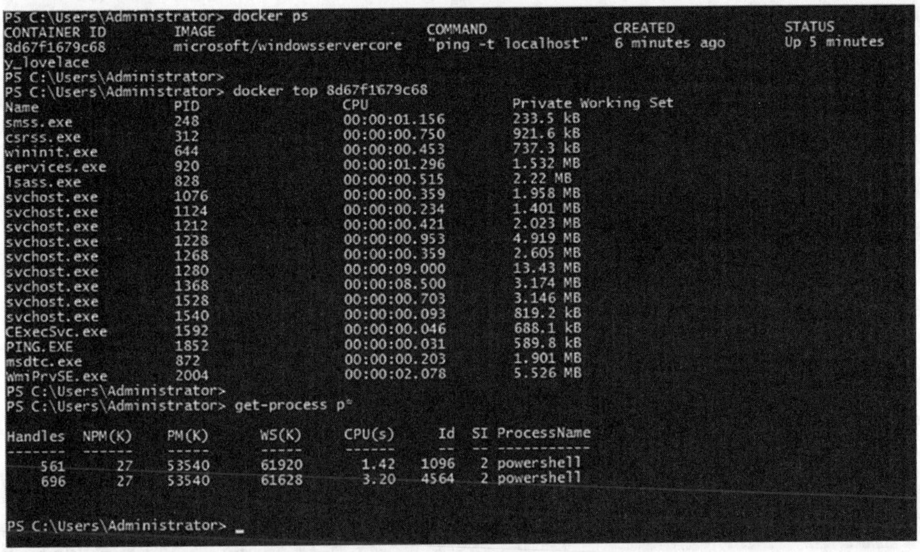

FIGURE 4-11 Output of the Docker Top and Get-Process commands for a Hyper-V container

Skill 4.2: Manage Windows containers

- Manage Windows or Linux containers using the Docker daemon
- Manage Windows or Linux containers using Windows PowerShell
- Manage container networking
- Manage container data volumes
- Manage Resource Control
- Create new container images using Dockerfile
- Manage container images using DockerHub repository for public and private scenarios
- Manage container images using Microsoft Azure

Manage Windows or Linux containers using the Docker daemon

When you use the Docker Run command to create a new container, you can include the -it switches to work with it interactively, or you can omit them and let the container run in the background. Either way, you can continue to use the Docker client to manage container, either Windows or Linux.

Listing containers

To leave a PowerShell or CMD session you started in a container, you can just type the following:

```
exit
```

However, this not only closes the session, it also stops the container. A stopped container still exists on the host; it is just functionally turned off. To exit a session without stopping the container, press Ctrl+P, then Ctrl+Q.

You can display a list of all the running containers on the host by using the Docker PS command. If you add the -a (for all) switch, as in the following example, the command displays all of the containers on the host, whether running or not, as shown in Figure 4-12.

```
docker ps -a
```

FIGURE 4-12 Output of the Docker ps a command

Starting and stopping containers

To start a stopped container, you use the Docker Start command, as in the following example:

```
docker start dbf9674d13b9
```

You can also forcibly stop a container by using the Docker Stop command, as follows:

```
docker stop dbf9674d13b9
```

The six-byte hexadecimal string in these commands is the Container ID that Docker assigns to the container when creating it. You use this value in Docker commands to identify the container that you want to manage. This value also becomes the container's computer name, as you can see if you run Get-ComputerInfo from within a container session.

If you run Docker PS with the --no-trunc (for no truncation) parameter, as shown in Figure 4-13, you can see that the Container ID is a 32-byte hexadecimal string, although it is far more convenient to use just the first six bytes on the command line.

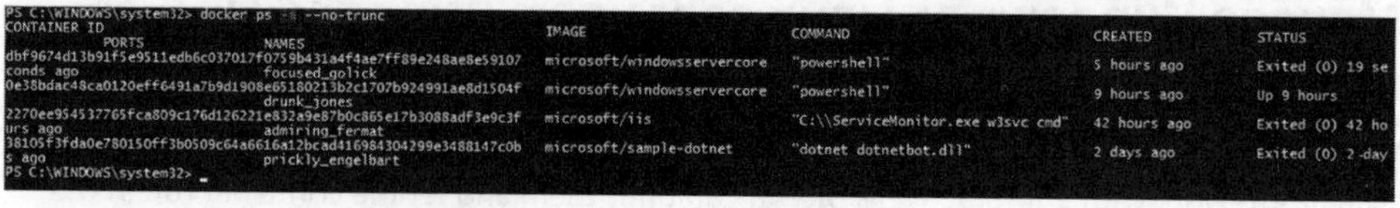

FIGURE 4-13 Output of the Docker ps -a --no-trunc command

Attaching to containers

To connect to a session on a running container, use the Docker Attach command, as in the following example:

```
docker attach dbf9674d13b9
```

Running the command in multiple windows opens additional sessions, enabling you to work in multiple windows at once.

Creating images

If you have modified a container in any way, you can save the modifications to a new image by running the Docker Commit command, as in the following example:

```
docker commit dbf9674d13b9 hholt/killerapp:1.5
```

This command creates a new image called hholt/killerapp with a tag value of 1.5. The Docker Commit command does not create a duplicate of the base image with the changes you have made; it only saves the changes. If, for example, you use the Microsoft/windowsservercore base image to create the container, and then you install your application, running Docker Commit will only save the application. If you provide the new image to a colleague, she must have (or obtain) the base image, in order to run the container.

Removing containers

To remove a container completely, use the Docker RM command, as shown in the following example:

```
docker rm dbf9674d13b9
```

Containers must be in a stopped state before you can remove them this way. However, adding the -f (for force) switch will cause the Docker RM command to remove any container, even one that is running.

Manage Windows or Linux containers using Windows PowerShell

As mentioned earlier, the Dockerd engine does not require the use of the Docker.exe client program. Because Docker is an open source project, it is possible to create an alternative client implementation that you can use with Dockerd, and Microsoft, in cooperation with the Docker community, is doing just that in creating a PowerShell module that you can use to create and manage Docker containers.

Because the Docker module for PowerShell is under development, it does not necessarily support all of the functions possible with the Docker.exe client. However, the primary functions are there, as shown in the following sections.

Listing containers

You can display a list of all the containers on the host by running the Get-Container cmdlet in Windows PowerShell, as shown in Figure 4-14. Unlike the Docker PS command, the Get-Container cmdlet displays all of the containers on the host, whether they are running or stopped.

```
PS C:\WINDOWS\system32> get-container
ID                 Image            Command              Created              Status                Names
--                 -----            -------              -------              ------                -----
080096dce22901167... microsoft/wi... powershell          11/5/2016 9:14:09 AM Up 5 minutes          infallible_mccarthy
d8d297343e8a1c27c... microsoft/wi... powershell          11/5/2016 6:26:51 AM Exited (1067) 54 ...  small_brown
dbf9674d13b91f5e9... microsoft/wi... powershell          11/4/2016 10:39:56 PM Up 4 hours           focused_golick
0e38bdac48ca0120e... microsoft/wi... powershell          11/4/2016 6:09:47 PM Up 16 hours           drunk_jones
2270ee954537765fc... microsoft/iis  C:\ServiceMonitor... 11/3/2016 9:43:16 AM Exited (0) 2 days...  admiring_fermat
38105f3fda0e78015... microsoft/sa.. dotnet dotnetbot.dll 11/2/2016 5:41:28 AM Exited (0) 3 days...  prickly_engelbart

PS C:\WINDOWS\system32>
```

FIGURE 4-14 Output of the Get-Container cmdlet

Starting and stopping containers

When you create a container using the New-Container cmdlet, the container is not started by default. You must explicitly start it. To start a stopped container, you use the Start-Container cmdlet, as in the following example:

`start-container dbf9674d13b9`

You can also stop a container by simply changing the verb to the Stop-Container cmdlet, as follows:

`stop-container dbf9674d13b9`

Attaching to containers

To connect to a session on a running container, use the Enter-ContainerSession cmdlet, as in the following example:

`Enter-containersession dbf9674d13b9`

This cmdlet is also aliased as Attach-Container, enabling to reuse another command with just a verb change.

Creating images

If you have modified a container in any way, you can save the modifications to a new image by running the ConvertTo-ContainerImage cmdlet, as in the following example:

`convertto-containerimage -containeridorname dbf9674d13b9 -repository hholt/killerapp -tag 1.5`

This cmdlet is also aliased as Commit-Container.

Removing containers

To remove a container, use the Remove-Container cmdlet, as shown in the following example:

```
remove-container dbf9674d13b9
```

As with the Docker RM command, containers must be in a stopped state before you can remove them. However, adding the Force switch will cause the cmdlet command to remove any container, even one that is running.

Manage container networking

Containers can access the outside network. This is easy to prove, by pinging a server on the local network or the Internet. However, if you run the Ipconfig /all command in a container session, as shown in Figure 4-15, you might be surprised at what you see.

```
PS C:\> ipconfig /all
ipconfig /all

Windows IP Configuration

   Host Name . . . . . . . . . . . . : f3e054399471
   Primary Dns Suffix  . . . . . . . :
   Node Type . . . . . . . . . . . . : Hybrid
   IP Routing Enabled. . . . . . . . : No
   WINS Proxy Enabled. . . . . . . . : No
   DNS Suffix Search List. . . . . . : zacker

Ethernet adapter vEthernet (Container NIC 76b9f047):

   Connection-specific DNS Suffix  . : zacker
   Description . . . . . . . . . . . : Hyper-V Virtual Ethernet Adapter #7
   Physical Address. . . . . . . . . : 00-15-5D-11-BF-40
   DHCP Enabled. . . . . . . . . . . : No
   Autoconfiguration Enabled . . . . : Yes
   Link-local IPv6 Address . . . . . : fe80::ad08:3832:6ffe:ff4a%44(Preferred)
   IPv4 Address. . . . . . . . . . . : 172.25.117.12(Preferred)
   Subnet Mask . . . . . . . . . . . : 255.255.240.0
   Default Gateway . . . . . . . . . : 172.25.112.1
   DNS Servers . . . . . . . . . . . : 172.25.112.1
                                       192.168.2.2
                                       204.186.110.114
   NetBIOS over Tcpip. . . . . . . . : Disabled
PS C:\>
```

FIGURE 4-15 Output of Ipconfig /all command on a container

In this example, the IP address of the network adapter in the container is 172.25.117.12/20, which is nothing like the address of the network on which the container host is located. However, if you run the Ipconfig /all command on the container host, as shown in Figure 4-16, the situation becomes clearer.

```
PS C:\WINDOWS\system32> ipconfig /all

Windows IP Configuration

   Host Name . . . . . . . . . . . . : CZ10
   Primary Dns Suffix  . . . . . . . :
   Node Type . . . . . . . . . . . . : Hybrid
   IP Routing Enabled. . . . . . . . : No
   WINS Proxy Enabled. . . . . . . . : No
   DNS Suffix Search List. . . . . . : zacker

Ethernet adapter vEthernet (HNS Internal NIC):

   Connection-specific DNS Suffix  . :
   Description . . . . . . . . . . . : Hyper-V Virtual Ethernet Adapter #4
   Physical Address. . . . . . . . . : 00-15-5D-11-BB-AC
   DHCP Enabled. . . . . . . . . . . : Yes
   Autoconfiguration Enabled . . . . : Yes
   Link-local IPv6 Address . . . . . : fe80::49c7:9ebd:f079:2994%29(Preferred)
   IPv4 Address. . . . . . . . . . . : 172.25.112.1(Preferred)
   Subnet Mask . . . . . . . . . . . : 255.255.240.0
   Default Gateway . . . . . . . . . :
   DHCPv6 IAID . . . . . . . . . . . : 486544733
   DHCPv6 Client DUID. . . . . . . . : 00-01-00-01-1F-96-45-81-44-37-E6-C0-9D-DF
   DNS Servers . . . . . . . . . . . : fec0:0:0:ffff::1%1
                                       fec0:0:0:ffff::2%1
                                       fec0:0:0:ffff::3%1
   NetBIOS over Tcpip. . . . . . . . : Enabled

Ethernet adapter vEthernet (Intel(R) 82579LM Gigabit Network Connection):

   Connection-specific DNS Suffix  . : zacker
   Description . . . . . . . . . . . : Hyper-V Virtual Ethernet Adapter #2
   Physical Address. . . . . . . . . : 44-37-E6-C0-9D-DF
   DHCP Enabled. . . . . . . . . . . : Yes
   Autoconfiguration Enabled . . . . : Yes
   Link-local IPv6 Address . . . . . : fe80::e170:47de:5b5a:d24b%4(Preferred)
   IPv4 Address. . . . . . . . . . . : 192.168.2.41(Preferred)
   Subnet Mask . . . . . . . . . . . : 255.255.255.0
   Lease Obtained. . . . . . . . . . : Wednesday, November 2, 2016 12:32:22 AM
   Lease Expires . . . . . . . . . . : Monday, November 14, 2016 12:32:22 AM
   Default Gateway . . . . . . . . . : 192.168.2.99
   DHCP Server . . . . . . . . . . . : 192.168.2.2
   DHCPv6 IAID . . . . . . . . . . . : 205797350
   DHCPv6 Client DUID. . . . . . . . : 00-01-00-01-1F-96-45-81-44-37-E6-C0-9D-DF
   DNS Servers . . . . . . . . . . . : 192.168.2.2
                                       204.186.110.114
   NetBIOS over Tcpip. . . . . . . . : Enabled
```

FIGURE 4-16 Output of Ipconfig /all command on a container host

There are two Ethernet adapters showing on the container host system. One has an IP address on the 192.168.2.0/24 network, which is the address used for the physical network to which the container host is connected. The other adapter has the address 172.25.112.1/20, which is on the same network as the container's address. In fact, looking back at the container's configuration, the container host's address is listed as the Default Gateway and DNS Server address for the container. The container host is, in essence, functioning as a router between the 172.25.112.0/20 network on which the container is located and 192.168.2.0/24, which is the physical network to which the host is connected. The host is also functioning as the DNS server for the container.

If you look at another container on the same host, it has an IP address on the same network as the first container. The two containers can ping each other's addresses, as well as those of systems outside the 172.25.112.0/20 network.

This is possible because the Containers feature and Docker use network address translation (NAT) by default, to create a networking environment for the containers on the host. NAT is a routing solution in which the network packets generated by and destined for a system have their IP addresses modified, to make them appear as though the system is located on another network.

When you ping a computer on the host network from a container session, the container host modifies the ping packets, substituting its own 192.169.2.43 address for the container's

172.25.117.12 address in each one. When the responses arrive from the system being pinged, the process occurs in reverse.

The Dockerd engine creates a NAT network by default when runs for the first time, and assigns each container an address on that NAT network. The use of the 172.25.112.0/20 network address is also a default coded into Docker. However, you can modify these defaults, by specifying a different NAT address or by not using NAT at all.

The network adapters in the containers are, of course, virtual. You can see in the configuration shown earlier that the adapter for that container is identified as vEthernet (Container NIC 76b9f047). On the container host, there is also a virtual adapter, called vEthernet (HNS Internal NIC). HNS is the Host Network Service, which is the NAT implementation used by Docker. If you run the Get-VMSwitch cmdlet on the container host or look in the Virtual Switch Manager in Hyper-V Manager, as shown in Figure 4-17, you can see that Docker has also created virtual switch called nat. This is the switch to which the adapters in the containers are all connected. Therefore, you can see that containers function much like virtual machines, as far as networking is concerned.

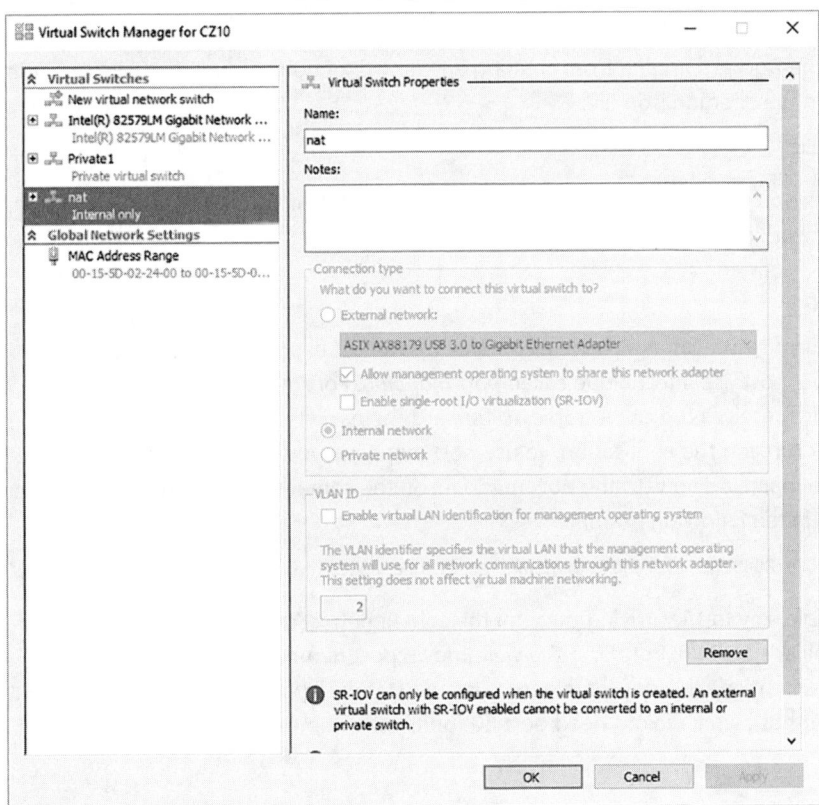

FIGURE 4-17 Nat switch in the Virtual Switch Manager

Modifying NAT defaults

If you want to use a different network address for Docker's NAT configuration, because you already have a network using that same address, for example, it is possible to do so. To specify an alternate address, you must use the daemon.json configuration file, as discussed earlier in the remote Docker client configuration.

Daemon.json is a plain text file that you create in the directory where the Dockerd.exe program is located. To specify an alternate NAT network address, you include the following text in the file:

```
{ "fixed-cidr":"192.168.10.0/24" }
```

You can use any network address for the NAT implementation, but to prevent address conflicts on the Internet, you should use a network in one of the following reserved private network addresses:

- 10.0.0.0/8
- 172.16.0.0/12
- 192.168.0.0/16

To prevent the Dockerd engine from creating any network implementation at all, place the following text in the daemon.json file:

```
{ "bridge":"none" }
```

If you do this, you must manually create a container network, if you want your containers to have any network connectivity.

Port mapping

If you plan to run a server application in a container that must expose ports for incoming client traffic, you must use a technique called *port mapping*. Port mapping enables the container host, which receives the client traffic, to forward the packets to the appropriate port in the container running the application. To use port mapping, you add the -p switch to the Docker Run command, along with the port numbers on the container host and the container, respectively, as in the following example:

```
docker run -it -p 8080:80 microsoft\windowsservercore powershell
```

In this example, any traffic arriving through the container host's port 8080 will be forwarded to the container's port 80. Port 80 is the well-known port number for web server traffic, and this arrangement enables the container to use this standard port without monopolizing it on the container host, which might need port 80 for its own web server.

Creating a transparent network

Instead of using NAT, you can choose to create a transparent network, one in which the containers are connected to the same network as the container host. If the container host is a physical computer, the containers are connected to the physical network. If the container host is a virtual machine, the containers are connected to whatever virtual switch the VM uses.

Docker does not create a transparent network by default, so you must create it, using the Docker Network Create command, as in the following example:

```
docker network create -d transparent trans
```

In this example, the command creates a new network using the transparent driver, signified by the -d switch, and assigns it the name trans. Running the following command displays a list of all the container networks, which now includes the trans network you just created, as shown in Figure 4-18.

```
docker network ls
```

```
PS C:\Users\Administrator> docker network ls
NETWORK ID          NAME                DRIVER              SCOPE
4935e862cb65        nat                 nat                 local
37d5846ae474        none                null                local
9b62d68c1d58        trans               transparent         local
PS C:\Users\Administrator>
```

FIGURE 4-18 Output of the Docker Network LS command

Once you have created the transparent network, you can create containers that use it by adding the network parameter to your Docker Run command, as in the following example:

```
docker run -it --network=trans microsoft/windowsservercore powershell
```

When you run the Ipconfig /all command in this container, you can see that it has an IP address on the 10.0.0.0/24 network, which is the same as the network used by the virtual machine functioning as the container host.

When you create a transparent network and the containers that use it, they all obtain IP addresses from a DHCP on the container host network, if one is available. If there is no DHCP server available, however, you must specify the network address settings when creating the network and manually configure the IP address of each container by specifying it on the Docker Run command line.

To create a transparent network with static IP addresses, you use a command like the following:

```
docker network create -d transparent --subnet=10.0.0.0/24 --gateway=10.0.0.1 trans
```

Then, to create a container with a static IP address on the network you created, you use a Docker Run command like the following:

```
docker run -it --network=trans --ip=10.0.0.16 --dns=10.0.0.10 microsoft/
windowsservercore powershell
```

Manage container data volumes

In some instances, you might want to preserve data files across containers. Docker enables you to do this by creating data volumes on a container that correspond to a folder on the container host. Once created, the data you place in the data volume on the container is also found in the corresponding folder on the container host. The opposite is also true; you can copy files into the folder on the host and access them in the container.

Data volumes persist independent of the container. If you delete the container, the data volume remains on the container host. You can then mount the container host folder in another container, enabling you to retain your data through multiple iterations of an application running in your containers.

To create a data volume, you add the -v switch to a Docker Run command, as in the following example:

```
docker run -it -v c:\appdata microsoft/windowsservercore powershell
```

This command creates a folder called c:\appdata in the new container and links it to a subfolder in C:\ProgramData\docker\volumes on the container host. To learn the exact location, you can run the following command and look in the Mounts section, as shown in Figure 4-19.

```
docker inspect dbf9674d13b9
```

```
"Mounts": [
    {
        "Type": "volume",
        "Name": "85dabc769744f3166aea3dd12a460c3a64f6c31fe5e64414eb56adfd1e87b04c",
        "Source": "C:\ProgramData\\docker\\volumes\\85dabc769744f3166aea3dd12a460c3a64f6c31fe5e64414eb56adfd1e87b04c\\_data",
        "Destination": "c:\\appdata",
        "Driver": "local",
        "Mode": "",
        "RW": true,
        "Propagation": ""
    }
],
```

FIGURE 4-19 Partial output of the Docker Inspect command

The Mounts section (which is small part of a long, comprehensive listing of the container's specifications) contains Source and Destination properties. Destination specifies the folder name in the container, and Source is the folder on the container host. To reuse a data volume, you can specify both the source and destination folders in the Docker Run command, as in the following example:

```
docker run -it -v c:\sourcedata:c:\appdata microsoft/windowsservercore powershell
```

If you create a data volume, specifying a folder on the container that already contains files, the existing contents are overlaid by the data volume, but are not deleted. Those files are accessible again when the data volume is dismounted.

By default, Docker creates data volumes in read/write mode. To create a read-only data volume, you can add :ro to the container folder name, as in the following example:

```
docker run -it -v c:\appdata:ro microsoft/windowsservercore powershell
```

> **NOTE** **ADDING A DATA VOLUME**
>
> To add a data volume to an existing container, your only option is to use Docker Commit to save any changes you've made to the existing container to a new image, and then use Docker Run to create a new container from the new image, including the -v switch to add the data volume.

Manage resource control

As noted earlier, the Docker Run command supports many parameters and switches, some of which have already been demonstrated in this chapter. For example, you have seen how the -it switches create an interactive container that runs a specific shell or other command. To create a container that runs in the background—in what is called detached mode—you use the -d switch, as in the following example:

```
docker run -d -p 80:80 microsoft/iis
```

To interact with a detached container, you can use network connections or file system shared. You can also connect to the container using the Docker Attach command.

Working with container names

By default, when you create a container using the Docker Run command, the Dockerd engine assigns three identifiers to the container, as shown in Figure 4-20:

- **Long UUID** A 32-byte hexadecimal string, represented by 64 digits, as in the following example: 0e38bdac48ca0120eff6491a7b9d1908e65180213b-2c1707b924991ae8d1504f
- **Short UUID** The first six bytes of the long UUID, represented as 12 digits, as in the following example: 0e38bdac48ca.
- **Name** A randomly chosen name consisting of two words separated by an underscore character, as in the following example: drunk_jones

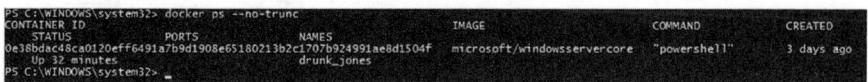

FIGURE 4-20 Output of the Docker ps --no-trunc command

You can use any of the three identifiers when referencing the container on the command line. You can also assign your own name to the container when you create it by adding the name parameter to the Docker Run command line, as in the following example:

```
docker run -it microsoft/windowsservercore powershell --name core1
```

Skill 4.2: Manage Windows containers CHAPTER 4 **287**

Constraining memory

The Docker Run command supports parameters that enable you to specify how much memory a container is permitted to use. By default, container processes can use as much host memory and swap memory as they need. If you are running multiple containers on the same host or a memory intensive application on the host itself, you might to impose limits on the memory certain containers can use.

The memory parameters you can use in a Docker Run command are as follows:

- **-m (or --memory)**   Specifies the amount of memory the container can use. Values consist of an integer and the unit identifier b, k, m, or g (for bytes, kilobytes, megabytes, or gigabytes, respectively).

- **-memory-swap**   Specifies the total amount of memory plus virtual memory that the container can use. Values consist of an integer and the unit identifier b, k, m, or g.

- **-memory-reservation**   Specifies a soft memory limit that the host retains for the container, even when there is contention for system memory. For example, you might use the -m switch to set a hard limit of 1 GB, and a memory reservation value of 750 MB. When other containers or processes require additional memory, the host might reclaim up to 250 MB of the container's memory, but will leave at least 750 MB intact. Values consist of an integer smaller than that of the m or --memory-swap value and the unit identifier b, k, m, or g.

- **-kernel-memory**   Specifies the amount of the memory limit set using the -m switch that can be used for kernel memory. Values consist of an integer and the unit identifier b, k, m, or g.

- **-oom-kill-disable**   Prevents the kernel from killing container processes when an out of memory error occurs. Never use this option without the -m switch, to create a memory limit for the container. Otherwise, the kernel could start to kill processes on the host when an OOM error occurs.

Constraining CPU cycles

You can also specify parameters that limit the CPU cycles allocated to a container. By default, all the containers on a host share the available CPU cycles equally. Using these parameters, you can assign priorities to the containers, which take effect when cpu contention occurs.

The Docker Run parameters that you can use to control container access to CPUs are as follows:

- **-c (or --cpu-shares)**   Specifies a value from 0 to 1024 that specifies the weight of the container in contention for the CPU cycles. The actual amount of processor cycles that a container receives depends on the number of containers running on the host and their respective weights.

- **-cpuset-cpus**   Specifies which CPUs in a multiprocessor host system that the container can use. Values consist of integers representing the CPUs in the host computer, separated by commas.

- **-cpuset-mems** Specifies which nodes on a NUMA host that the container can use. Values consist of integers representing the CPUs in the host computer, separated by commas.

Create new container images using Dockerfile

If you have made changes to a container since you first created it with the Docker Run command, you can save those changes by creating a new container image using Docker Commit. However, the recommended method for creating container images is to build them from scratch using a script called a dockerfile.

A *dockerfile* is a plain text file, with the name dockerfile, which contains the commands needed to build your new image. Once you have created the dockerfile, you use the Docker Build command to execute it and create the new file. The dockerfile is just a mechanism that automates the process of executing the steps you used to modify your container manually. When you run the Docker Build command with the dockerfile, the Dockerd engine runs each command in the script by creating a container, making the modifications you specify, and executing a Docker Commit command to save the changes as a new image.

A dockerfile consists of instructions, such as FROM or RUN, and a statement for each instruction. The accepted format is to capitalize the instruction. You can insert remarks into the script by preceding them with the pound (#) character.

An example of a simple dockerfile is as follows:

```
#install DHCP server
FROM microsoft/windowsservercore
RUN powershell -command install-windowsfeature dhcp -includemanagementtools
RUN powershell -configurationname microsoft.powershell -command add-dhcpserverv4scope -state active -activatepolicies $true  -name scopetest -startrange 10.0.0.100 -endrange 10.0.0.200 -subnetmask 255.255.255.0
RUN md boot
COPY ./bootfile.wim c:/boot/
CMD powershell
```

In this example:

- The FROM instruction specifies the base image from which the new image is created. In this case, the new image starts with the microsoft/windowsservercore image.
- The first RUN command opens a PowerShell session and uses the Install-WindowsFeature cmdlet to install the DHCP role.
- The second RUN command uses the Add-DhcpServerv4Scope cmdlet to create a new scope on the DHCP server.
- The third RUN command creates a new directory called boot.
- The COPY command copies a file called bootfile.wim from the current folder on the container host to the c:\boot folder on the container.
- The CMD command opens a PowerShell session when the image is run.

Once you have created the dockerfile script, you use the Docker Build command to create the new image, as in the following example:

```
docker build -t dhcp .
```

This command reads the dockerfile from the current directory and creates an image called dhcp. As the Dockerd engine builds the image, it displays the results of each command and the IDs of the interim containers it creates, as shown in Figure 4-21. Once you have created the image, you can then create a container from it using the Docker Run command in the usual manner.

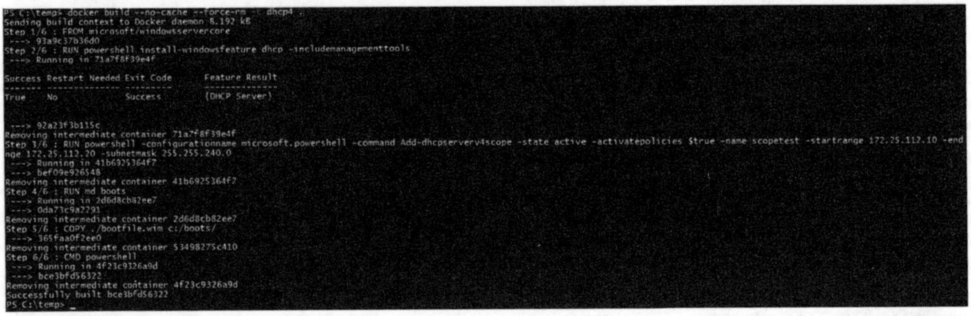

FIGURE 4-21 Output of the Docker Build command

This is a simple example of a dockerfile, but they can be much longer and more complex.

> ✓ **Quick check**
>
> Which of the following Docker commands can you use to create new container image files?
>
> 1. Docker Run
> 2. Docker Commit
> 3. Docker Build
> 4. Docker Images
>
> **Quick check answer**
>
> Answers 2 and 3 are correct. Docker Commit is the command used to create a new image from an existing container. Docker Build is the command used to create a new container image using the instructions in a dockerfile.

Manage container images using DockerHub Repository for public and private scenarios

DockerHub is a public repository that you can use to store and distribute your container images. When you download container images using the Docker Pull command, they come from DockerHub by default, unless you specify another repository in the command. However, you can upload images as well, using the Docker Push command.

Uploading images to DockerHub enables you to share them with your colleagues, and even with yourself, so you don't have to transfer files manually to deploy a container image on another host.

Before you can upload images to the Docker Hub, you must register at the site at *http://hub.docker.com*. Once you have done this, your user name becomes the name of your repository on the service. For example, the microsoft/windowsservercore image you pulled earlier is an image called windowsservercore in the Microsoft repository. If your user name on DockerHub is hholt, your images will all begin with that repository name, followed by the image name, as in the following example:

```
hholt/nano1
```

Once you have an account, you must login to the DockerHub service from the command line before you can push images. You do this with the following command:

```
docker login
```

Docker prompts you for your user name and password, and then provides upload access to your repository.

Searching for images

You can search for images on the DockerHub by using the web site, as shown in Figure 4-22. This interface provides the latest information about the image, as well as comments from other users in the Docker community.

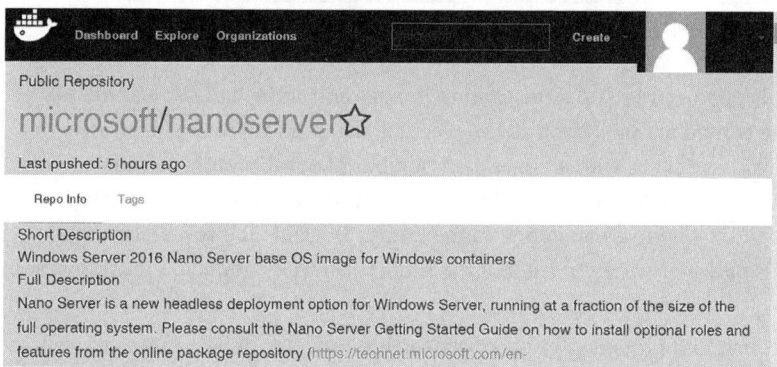

FIGURE 4-22 Screen capture of a DockerHub web search

You can also search the DockerHub from the command line, using the Docker Search command, as in the following example:

```
docker search microsoft --no-trunc
```

Adding the no-trunc parameter prevents the command from truncating the image descriptions, as shown in Figure 4-23.

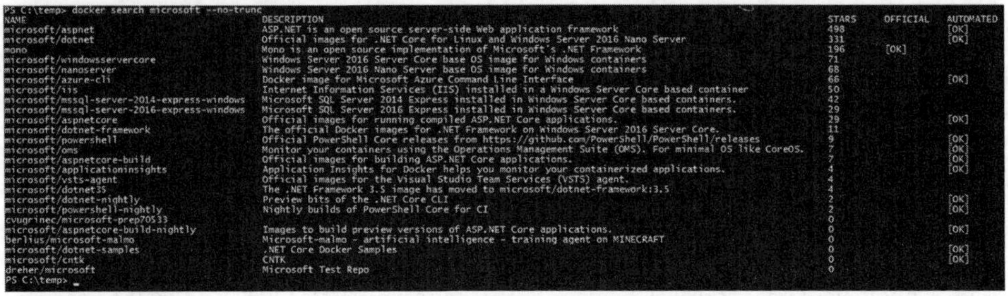

FIGURE 4-23 Output of the Docker Search command

Pushing images

To upload your own images to the repository, you use the Docker Push command, as in the following example:

```
docker push hholt/nano1
```

By default, the Docker Push command uploads the specified image to your public repository on the DockerHub, as shown in Figure 4-24. Anyone can access images pushed in this way.

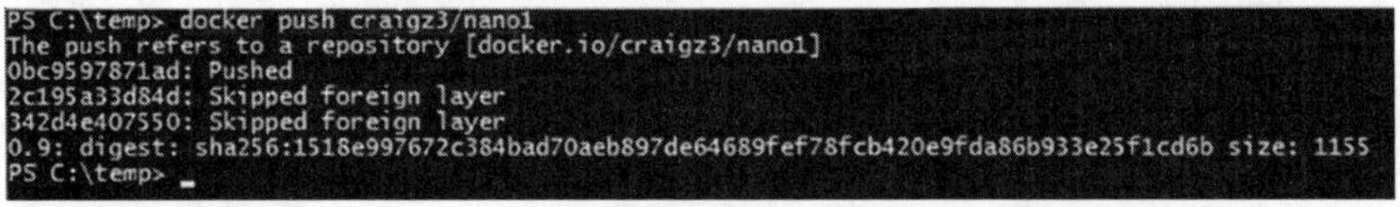

FIGURE 4-24 Output of the Docker Push command

Because Docker is open source software, sharing images and code with the community is a large part of the company's philosophy. However, it is also possible to create private repositories, which you can share with an unlimited number of collaborators you select. This enables you to use DockerHub for secure application development projects or any situation in which you do not want to deploy an image to the public. DockerHub provides a single private repository as part of its free service, but for additional repositories, you must purchase a subscription.

In addition to storing and providing images, DockerHub provides other services as well, such as automated builds. By uploading a dockerfile and any other necessary files to a repository, you can configure DockerHub to automatically execute builds for you, to your exact specifications. The code files are available to your collaborators, and new builds can occur whenever the code changes.

Manage container images using Microsoft Azure

In addition to creating containers locally, you can also use them on Microsoft Azure. By creating a Windows Server 2016 virtual machine on Azure, you can create and manage containers just as you would on a local server. Azure also provides the Azure Container Service (ACS), which enables you to create, configure, and manage a cluster of virtual machines, configured to run container-based applications using various open source technologies.

Microsoft Azure is a subscription-based cloud service that enables you to deploy virtual machines and applications and integrate them into your existing enterprise. By paying a monthly fee, you can create a Windows Server 2016 virtual machine, as shown in Figure 4-25. Once you have created the virtual machine, you can install the Containers feature and the Docker engine. Containers and images that you create on an Azure virtual machine are completely compatible with the Docker implementations on your local computers.

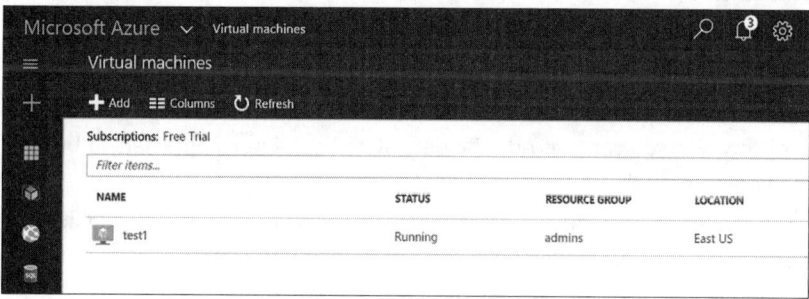

FIGURE 4-25 Microsoft Azure Resource Center

Chapter summary

- Containers are based on images. You create a container by running an image, and you create an image by saving the contents of a container.
- Windows Server 2016 includes the Containers feature, which provides the support environment for the Docker platform.
- Both the Server Core and Nano Server installation options support the creation of Windows Server and Hyper-V containers. In Nano Server, you can run the Docker.exe client on a remote system.
- Docker is an open source container solution that consists of two files: Dockerd.exe, which is the engine that runs as a service on Windows, and Docker.exe, which is the command line client that controls the Dockerd engine.

- Using a text file called daemon.json, you can configure start-up options for the Dockerd engine.
- The Docker client is one way to control the Docker engine, but it is not the only way. You can also use the Docker module for Windows PowerShell to perform the same tasks.
- To download images from the Docker Hub, you use the Docker Pull command.
- Tags are version indicators that developers can use to track the builds or versions of a container image. To assign tag values, you use the Docker Tag command.
- To uninstall a container image, you use the Docker RMI command.
- To create a Windows Server container, you use the Docker Run command, specifying the name of a container image.
- The procedure for creating a Hyper-V container using Docker differs from a Windows Server container only in the inclusion of the --isolation parameter.
- The Docker.exe client enables you to control containers by starting, stopping, saving, and removing them.
- The Docker module for Windows PowerShell provides an alternative to the Docker.exe client that can perform most, if not all, of the same functions.
- By default, Docker uses network address translation to provide containers with network access. However, you can override the default and configure containers to be part of your larger network.
- Docker enables you to create data volumes that exist on the container host and add them to a container. Data volumes remain in place, even if you remove the container itself.
- Using parameters on the Docker Run command line, you can limit the amount of memory and CPU resources a container is permitted to use.
- A dockerfile is a script that contains instructions for building a new container image. You use the Docker Build command to execute the script and create the image.
- Docker Hub is a free repository, based in the cloud, on which you can upload your
- Microsoft Azure enables you to create virtual machines that you can use as container hosts.

Thought experiment

In this thought experiment, demonstrate your skills and knowledge of the topics covered in this chapter. You can find answer to this thought experiment in the next section.

Ralph wants to create a virtual machine called Core1 that functions as a container host for both Windows Server and Hyper-V containers. To create the container host, he plans to perform the following tasks:

- Create a virtual machine.
- Configure the virtual machine with 4 GB of memory, two virtual processors, and MAC address spoofing enabled.
- Install Windows Server 2016 on the virtual machine.
- Install the Containers feature.
- Install the Hyper-V role.
- Install the dockermsftprovider module.
- Install the Docker package.
- Pull the Server Core image from DockerHub.
- Create containers using the Docker Run command.

What step has Ralph forgotten, that prevents him from creating the containers he needs? What task must he perform to complete his plan, and when should he complete it?

Thought experiment answer

This section contains the solution to the thought experiment.

Ralph has forgotten to expose the virtualization extensions of the physical computer's processor to the VM, so that it can run the Hyper-V role. To do this, he must run the following command in a PowerShell session after creating the virtual machine and before he starts it:

```
set-vmprocessor -vmname server1 -exposevirtualizationextensions $true
```

CHAPTER 5

Implement high availability

Keeping applications running at all times is a major priority for many system administrators, and Windows Server 2016 includes features that enable you to create redundant server solutions that can anticipate nearly any type of disaster. Failover clusters enable you to create servers that share data, which ensures that an application runs in spite of multiple failures. Network Load Balancing clusters enable you to provide an application with both fault tolerance and scalability.

Skills in this chapter:

- Implement high availability and disaster recovery options in Hyper-V
- Implement failover clustering
- Implement Storage Spaces Direct
- Manage failover clustering
- Manage VM movement in clustered nodes
- Implement Network Load Balancing (NLB)

Skill 5.1: Implement high availability and disaster recovery options in Hyper-V

Hyper-V enables administrators to consolidate multiple physical servers into a single Hyper-V server. One of the advantages of virtualizing servers in this way is that you can easily move virtual machines (VMs) from one Hyper-V host to another. Whether it is for fault tolerance reasons or load balancing, Hyper-V provides several technologies for replicating and migrating VMs.

> **This section covers how to:**
> - Implement Hyper-V Replica
> - Implement Live Migration
> - Implement Shared Nothing Live Migration
> - Configure CredSSP or Kerberos authentication protocol for Live Migration
> - Implement Storage Migration

Implement Hyper-V Replica

Hyper-V Replica is a feature of the Hyper-V role that enables you to create a replica of the virtual machines on a Hyper-V server to another server, locally or at a remote site. The replication is asynchronous, and the failover process to the replica is not automatic. However, Hyper-V Replica is easy to set up and does not require advanced networking features, such as shared storage or a failover cluster. It is a simple way to create a replica of a Hyper-V server that you can start up whenever the primary server is unavailable.

Hyper-V replica is based on checkpoints, so after the initial replication is completed, only the changes made to the primary server are checkpointed and replicated. This minimizes the amount of data transmitted over the network and enables the replica server to load the virtual machine be accessing its checkpoints.

Hyper-V Replica has a lot of options. It does not require a failover cluster, but it works on one. It does not require certificates for encrypted transmissions, but it can use them. This enables administrators to create as simple or as complex a configuration as they need.

Planning the replication environment

In its simplest form, a Hyper-V Replica implementation uses two servers in the following configuration:

- Hyper-V installed on both servers
- Servers are located behind the same firewall
- Servers are not part of a cluster
- Servers are joined to the same Active Directory Domain Services (AD DS) domain or to domains with mutual trust relationships
- Servers use Kerberos-authenticated, unencrypted communication

Any exceptions to these policies require additional setup procedures, such as the following:

- If the servers are located at different sites, you must configure the intervening firewalls to allow the replication traffic to pass.
- If the replication traffic is to be encrypted, you must obtain a security certificate from an appropriate certification authority (or use a self-signed certificate).
- If the servers are part of a failover cluster, you must configure the Hyper-V Replica Broker role and make note of the client access point name.
- If you want to use a third server to create an additional replica, you must configure Hyper-V Replica to use Extended Replication.

Configuring the Hyper-V Servers

To configure replication in one direction, you must configure Hyper-V Replica on the destination server, also called the replica server. However, to use Hyper-V Replica as a failover solution, the recommended practice is to configure both servers as replica servers. This way, after a failover incident in which you activate a replica server, you can replicate any changes made in the interim back to the original server once it is back online.

To configure a Hyper-V server as a replica server with Hyper-V Manager, use the following procedure:

1. Open Hyper-V Manager, select the server, and, in the Actions pane, click Hyper-V Settings to display the Hyper-V Settings dialog box.

2. On the Replication Configuration page, select the Enable This Computer As A Replica Server checkbox, as shown in Figure 5-1.

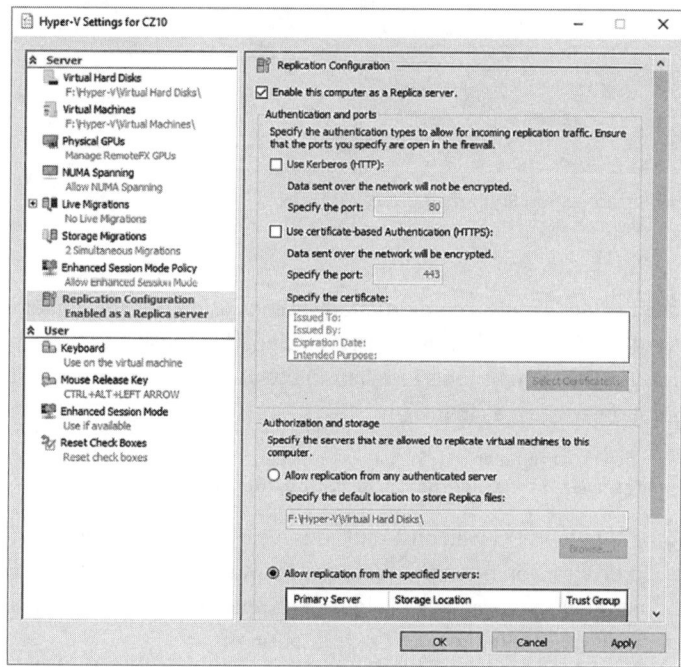

FIGURE 5-1 The Replication Configuration page of the Hyper-V Settings dialog box

3. In the Authentication and Ports box, select one of the following options:

   - **Use Kerberos (HTTP)** Replica traffic will not be encrypted, and the servers must be joined to the same domain (or trusted domains).

   - **Use Certificate-Based Authentication (HTTPS)** Click Select Certificate to specify the certificate to use for replica traffic encryption.

4. In the Authorization and Storage box, select one of the following options:

- **Allow Replication From Any Authenticated Server** Enables replication from any server, and saves replicas to the location you specify.
- **Allowed Replication From The Specified Servers** Click Add to open the Add Authorization Entry dialog box, shown in Figure 5-2, in which you specify a server name, a location for the replicas from that server, and a trust group to which it belongs.

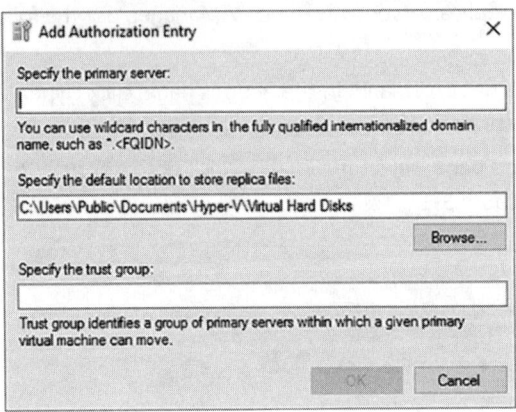

FIGURE 5-2 The Add Authorization Entry dialog box

5. Click OK.

You can also configure a server's replica configuration settings using the Set-VmReplicationServer cmdlet for Windows PowerShell. This cmdlet is included in the Hyper-V module, so you must have the Hyper-V management tools installed to use it. The command for a simple Hyper-V Replica configuration appears as follows:

```
set-vmreplicationserver -replicationenabled $true -allowedauthenticationtype kerberos
-replicationallowedfromanyserver $true -defaultstoragelocation d:\replicas
```

You must also configure Windows Firewall on a replica server to allow incoming traffic from the primary server. To do this, you open the Windows Firewall with Advanced Security console and, on the Inbound Rules page, shown in Figure 5-3, enable one of the following rules, based on your selections on the Replication Configuration page:

- If you selected the Use Kerberos (HTTP) option, enable the Hyper-V Replica HTTP Listener (TCP-In) rule.
- If you selected the Use certificate-based authentication (HTTPS) option, enable the Hyper-V Replica HTTPS Listener (TCP-In) rule.

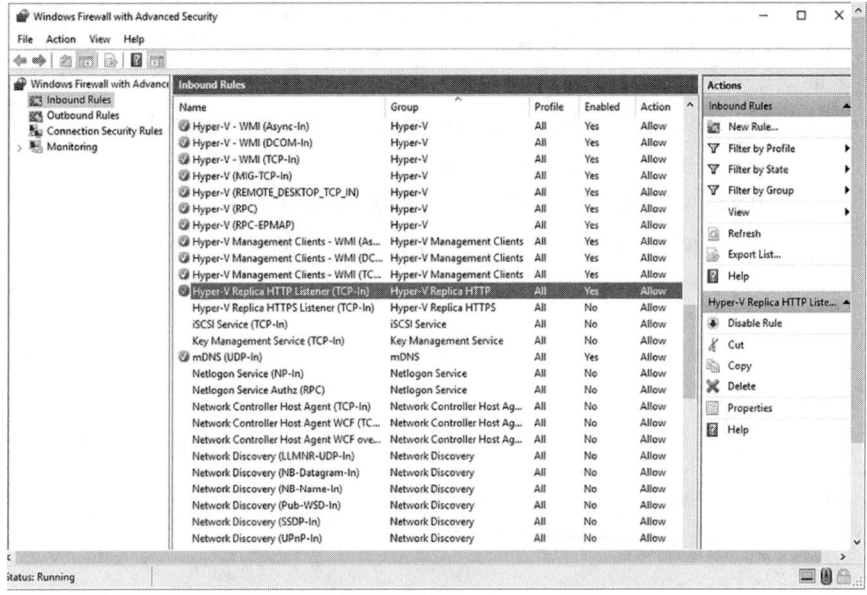

FIGURE 5-3 The Windows Firewall with Advanced Security console

To configure the firewall rule using PowerShell, you use the Enable-NetFirewallRule cmdlet, as in the following examples:

enable-netfirewallrule -displayname "hyper-v replica http listener (tcp-in)"

enable-netfirewallrule -displayname "hyper-v replica https listener (tcp-in)"

As mentioned earlier, this configuration process is only required on the replica server, but you might want to consider configuring the primary server in the same way, in anticipation of a recovery from a failover situation.

Configuring the virtual machines

Once the replica server is configured, you can proceed to configure the virtual machines on the primary server that you intend to replicate. To do this, use the following procedure.

1. In Hyper-V Manager, right-click a virtual machine and in the context menu, select Enable Replication to launch the Enable Replication Wizard.
2. On the Specify Replica Server page, type the name of the replica server you have configured, or click Browse to open a Select Computer dialog box.
3. On the Specify Connection Parameters page, in the Authentication Type box, specify whether to use Kerberos or certificate-based authentication, using the same setting you chose on the replica server. You can also specify whether to compress the replication data.
4. On the Choose Replication VHDs page, clear the checkboxes for any VHDs on the virtual machine that you do not want to replicate.

5. On the Configure Replication Frequency page, specify how often the primary server should send changes to the replica server—every 30 seconds, 5 minutes, or 15 minutes.

6. On the Configure Additional Recovery Points page, select one of the following options:
   - **Maintain Only The Latest Recovery Point** This option creates a replica containing only the state of the primary VM at the time of the last replication event.
   - **Create Additional Hourly Recovery Points** This option enables you to replicate up to 24 hours of recovery points and up to 12 hours of Volume Shadow Copy Service snapshots.

7. On the Choose Initial Replication Method page, shown in Figure 5-4, specify whether you want to perform the initial replication by sending over the network, by hand carrying it on external media, or by creating a virtual machine on the replica server yourself. These options enable you to avoid replicating an entire VM over relatively slow or expensive wide area network (WAN) links.

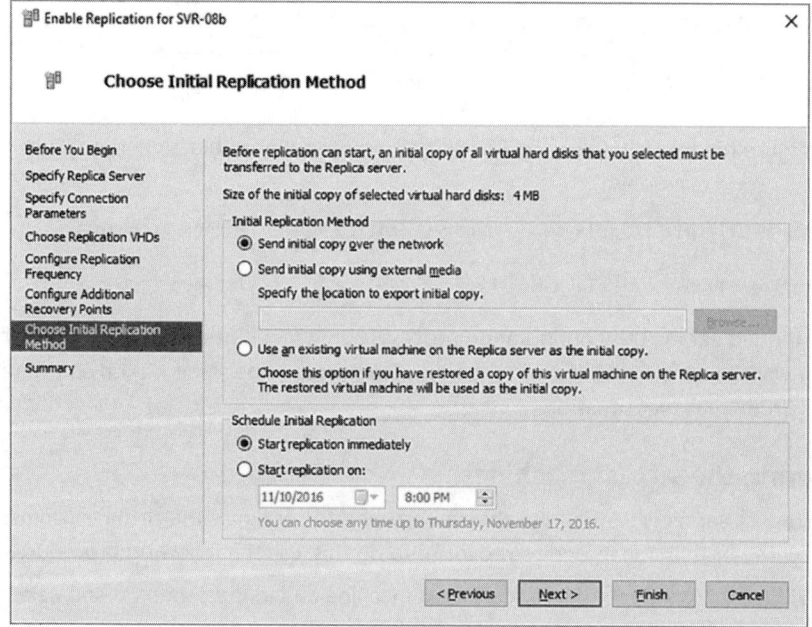

FIGURE 5-4 The Choose Initial Replication Method page of the Enable Replication Wizard

8. In the Schedule Initial Replication box, specify when the replication process should begin—immediately or at a time you specify.

9. Click Finish.

Once the replication process begins, a Replication context menu appears when you right-click the VM, enabling you to initiate a planned failover, pause or remove the replication process, and display a Replication Heath dialog box, as shown in Figure 5-5.

FIGURE 5-5 The Replication Health dialog box

Implement live migration

One of the main advantages of server virtualization, if not the main advantage, is the ability to consolidate multiple physical servers into one Hyper-V server running multiple virtual machines. Because the VMs all run on the same virtualized hardware platform, it is easy to move them around to different Hyper-V hosts, for load balancing or fault tolerance purposes. *Live Migration* is a Hyper-V feature that makes it possible to move a virtual machine from one Hyper-V host to another while it is running, with almost no interruption of service.

Live Migration is not an alternative to Hyper-V Replica; it does not move the virtual machine's data files. Live Migration is designed for environments in which virtual machines already have access to shared data storage; what is migrated is the system state and the live memory contents. If, for example, you have a Hyper-V failover cluster that runs a web server, with the cluster nodes all accessing the same storage array containing the web site files, Live Migration can move a VM from Hyper-V host to another without interrupting the client transactions in progress.

Originally conceived for use on failover clusters with physical shared storage subsystems, Live Migration in Windows Server 2016 can now work with non-clustered systems, systems in different domains, or no domains at all, and systems using nearly any type of shared storage, physical or virtual.

A typical Live Migration of a virtual machine takes place as follows:

1. The source server establishes a connection with the destination server, which creates an unpopulated virtual machine and confirms that it has the resources to recreate the source VM, such as sufficient memory and access to the shared storage containing the VM files.
2. The destination allocates memory and other resources to the new VM, essentially recreating the virtual hardware configuration of the source VM.
3. The source server begins transmitting the VM's memory pages to the destination VM. The source VM is still functioning at this point, servicing clients in the usual manner. As the memory transfer proceeds, however, Hyper-V on the source server starts marking any pages in its memory that have changed since the transfer began.
4. After the initial memory transfer is completed, the process begins again, with the source server transferring any memory pages that have changed since the initial transfer began. This process repeats through several iterations, until the servers reach a critical point at which point their memory states are identical.
5. At this point, processing and I/O are suspended on the source VM and control of the storage resources is transferred to the destination VM.
6. The destination VM now has an up to date "working set" of memory contents, CPU state, and storage resources, and can take over the VM's functionality.
7. With the destination VM up and running, Hyper-V notifies the network switch of the change, causing it to register the MAC addresses of the destination VM and associate them with its IP address, so that network traffic is diverted to the new virtual machine.

Despite all this activity, a live migration is typically completed in less time than the VM's TCP time-to-live interval. The changeover is therefore invisible, both to the clients and to the software running on the virtual machine. There are many factors that can affect the speed of a live migration, including the amount of memory to be transferred, the available bandwidth on the network, and the workload on the source and destination servers. However, any perceptible delay that occurs is usually caused by the time needed for the network to propagate the change in destination.

Live migration in a cluster

When you use the Failover Clustering feature in Windows Server 2016 to create a Hyper-V cluster, you use the Failover Cluster Manager console to initiate the New Virtual Machine Wizard. The wizard itself is the same as the one you can access through the Hyper-V Manager, but after the VM is created, Failover Cluster Manager launches the High Availability Wizard, which configures the VM to support Live Migration. In the PowerShell equivalent, you use the standard cmdlets to create the VM, and then run the Add-ClusterVirtualMachineRole cmdlet to make the virtual machine highly available.

Live migration without a cluster

It is possible, in Windows Server 2016, to perform live migrations between Hyper-V servers that are not clustered, although they must be members of the same domain (or trusted domains). Before you can do this, however, you must configure the Live Migration settings, in both the source and the destination server.

To do this using the Hyper-V Manager, open the Hyper-V Settings dialog box, select the Live Migration page, and select the Enable Incoming And Outgoing Live Migrations checkbox, as shown in Figure 5-6.

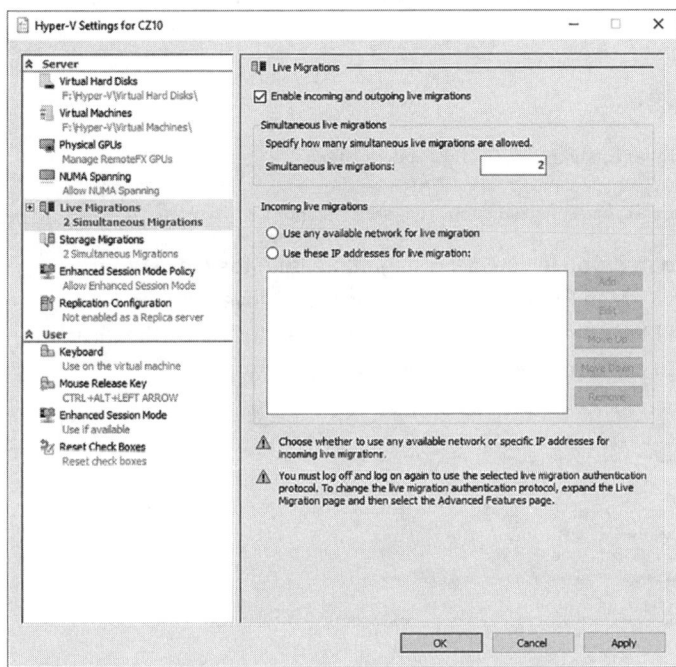

FIGURE 5-6 The Live Migrations page in the Hyper-V Settings dialog box

Then, configure the following settings on that page and the Live Migrations/Advanced Features page:

- **Simultaneous Live Migrations** Enables you to specify how many live migrations the server can perform at the same time, based on the bandwidth and traffic levels of your network and the workload on the server. The default setting is 2.
- **Incoming Live Migrations** If the server is connected to more than one network, this setting enables you to specify which network the server should use for live migration traffic and the order in which multiple networks should be used. Whenever possible, the best practice is to separate live migration traffic from standard local area network traffic (LAN).

- **Authentication Protocol** Enables you to specify whether to use CredSSP or Kerberos for authentication between the servers. Kerberos requires additional configuration of constrained delegation in Active Directory.
- **Performance Options** Enables you to specify whether to use the TCP/IP or Server Message Block (SMB) protocols for the live migration data transfers. If you have a network dedicated to storage traffic, or a network that uses datacenter bridging to separate LAN and storage traffic, SMB is probably a better choice. On a standard LAN connection, use TCP/IP.

To configure these settings using PowerShell, you use commands like the following:

```
enable-vmmigration

set-vmmigrationnetwork 192.168.4.0

Set-VMHost -VirtualMachineMigrationAuthenticationType Kerberos

set-vmhost -virtualmachinemigrationperformanceoption smbtransport
```

Once the servers are configured, you initiate a live migration using the Move Wizard, which you access by selecting a VM in Hyper-V Manager, choosing Move from the Actions pane. On the wizard's Choose Move Type page, shown in Figure 5-7, the Move The Virtual Machine option enables you to perform a live migration.

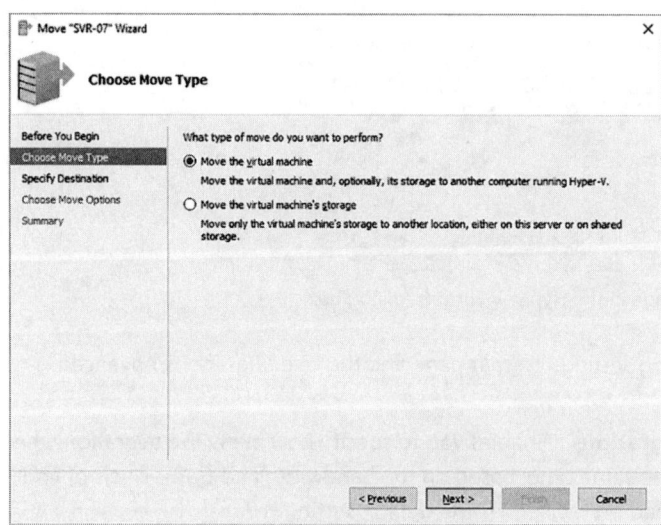

FIGURE 5-7 The Choose Move Type page in the Move Wizard

When you select Move The Virtual Machine, the Choose Move Options page, shown in Figure 5-8, provides the following options:

- **Move The Virtual Machine's Data To A Single location** Causes the wizard to move the virtual machine and its storage to the default location on the destination server

- **Move The Virtual Machine's Data By Selecting Where To Move The Items** Causes the wizard to move the virtual machine and its storage to a location you specify on the destination server.
- **Move Only The Virtual Machine** Causes the wizard to move the virtual machine to the destination server without its storage. This option provided the non-clustered equivalent of a live migration.

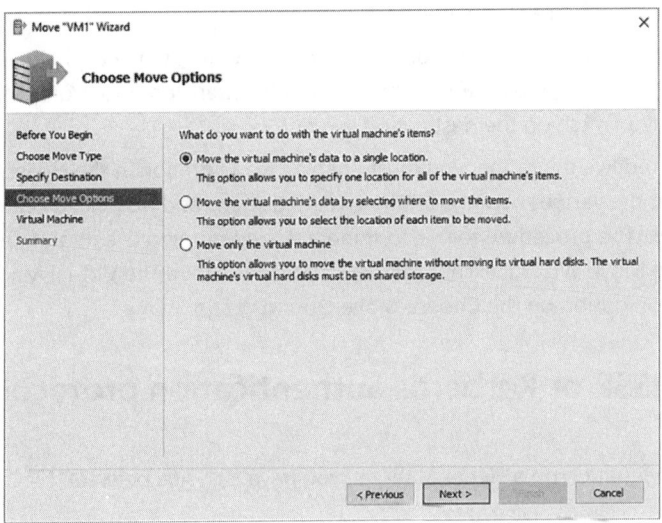

FIGURE 5-8 The Choose Move Options page in the Move Wizard

To perform a live migration with PowerShell, you use the Move-VM cmdlet, as in the following example:

```
Move-vm -vm server1 -destinationhost hyper2
```

Implement shared nothing live migration

Live Migration was originally a tool with highly restrictive requirements. Your servers had to be part of a cluster and the virtual machines had to have access to shared storage. Windows Server 2016 makes it possible to migrate virtual machines between Hyper-V hosts with neither of those requirements, using a feature known as Shared Nothing Live Migration.

Shared Nothing Live Migration is essentially a combination of a live migration and a storage migration. On the surface, the procedure is essentially the same as the one described for a live migration, except that the source server copies the VM's storage to the destination, in addition to its memory and system state. Obviously, the migration process takes much longer than that of a standard live migration, depending on the amount of storage involved and the network bandwidth available, but as with a live migration, the source VM continues to remain active until the data transfer is complete.

A shared nothing live migration has the following prerequisites:

- The source and destination VMs must be members of the same AD DS domain (or trusted domains).
- The source and domain servers must be using the same processor family (Intel or AMD).
- The source and destination servers must be connected by an Ethernet network running at a minimum of 1 gigabit per second (Gbps).
- The source and destination servers should have identical virtual switches that use the same name. If they do not, the migration process will be interrupted to prompt the operator to select a switch on the destination server.

As with a non-clustered live migration, you must enable Live Migration in the Hyper-V Settings dialog box, and the various settings on the Live Migrations and Advanced Features pages apply here as well. The procedure for performing a shared nothing live migration is the same also, using the Move Wizard, except that you select the Move The Virtual Machine's Data To A Single Location option on the Choose Move Options page.

Configure CredSSP or Kerberos authentication protocol for Live Migration

When you enable Live Migration on a Hyper-V server, you have a choice between two authentication protocols:

- **Credential Security Support Provider (CredSSP)**   CredSSP is an authentication protocol that enables a client to delegate a user's credentials for authentication on a remote server. In Hyper-V, CredSSP is the default authentication protocol for Live Migration. The protocol requires no special configuration, but it does require a user to sign in to the source server before performing a live migration.
- **Kerberos**   The default authentication protocol for Active Directory, Kerberos does not require you to sign on, as CredSSP does, but you do have to configure it to use constrained delegation before you can perform live migrations.

Constrained delegation is an element of the Kerberos protocol that enables a server to act on behalf of a user, but only for specific services. To configure constrained delegation, you must be logged on as a domain administrator and use the following procedure.

1. Open the Active Directory Users And Computers console.
2. Browse to the Computers container and locate the computer object for the Live Migration source server.
3. Open the Properties sheet for the source server's computer object and select the Delegation tab, as shown in Figure 5-9.

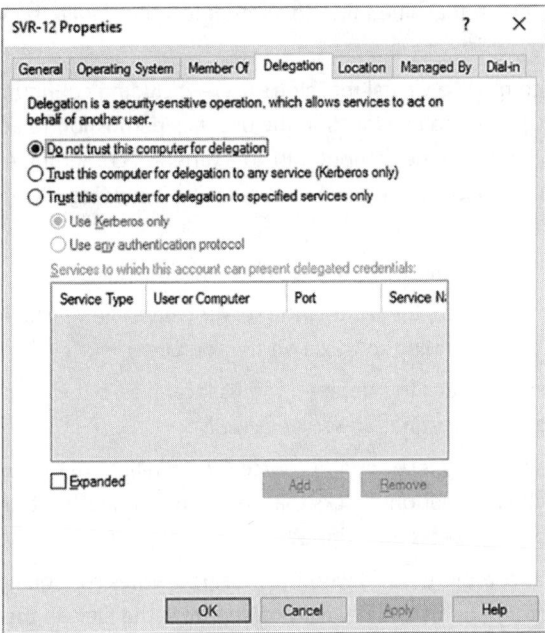

FIGURE 5-9 The Delegation tab of a computer object's Properties sheet

4. Select the Trust This Computer For Delegation To The Specified Services Only option, and leave the Use Kerberos Only option selected.
5. Click Add and, in the Add Services dialog box, click Users or Computers.
6. In the Select Users or Computers dialog box, type the name of the destination server and click OK.
7. In the Available Services box, select one or both of the following services, as needed, and click OK.
   - **cifs**   Enables the computer user to move virtual machine storage, with or without the virtual machine itself.
   - **Microsoft Virtual System Migration Service**   Enables the computer to move virtual machines.
8. Click OK to close the Properties sheet.
9. Repeat the procedure for the Live Migration destination computer, specifying the name of the source computer in the Select Users Or Computers dialog box.

Implement storage migration

Live Migration is designed to move a virtual machine from one Hyper-V host server to another, without touching the files, which are presumed to be accessible on shared storage. Storage Migration (sometimes referred to, somewhat inaccurately, as Storage Live Migration) is the exact opposite; it moves the virtual machine's files to another location, while the VM itself remains in place.

You can use Storage Migration to move a virtual machine's files—including configuration files, checkpoints, and Smart Paging files—to any location the user has permission to access, including another disk or directory on the same computer or to a different computer. As with Live Migration, storage migrations can occur while the virtual machine is running, or while it's stopped.

Compared to a Live Migration, Storage Migration uses a relatively simple process:

1. When you initiate a storage migration, the destination server creates new virtual hard disk files of sizes and types corresponding to those on the source server.
2. The VM on the source server continues to operate using its local files, but Hyper-V begins mirroring disk writes to the destination server as well.
3. While continuing to mirror writes, Hyper-V on the source server initiates a single-pass copy of the source disks to the destination. Blocks that have already been written to the destination by the mirroring process are skipped.
4. When the single-pass copy is completed, and with the mirrored writes continuing, Hyper-V updates the VM configuration and begins working from the files on the destination server.
5. Once the VM is running successfully from the migrated files, Hyper-V deletes the source files.

If the source VM is turned off, there is no need for any special procedure. Hyper-V simply copies the files from the source to the destination, reconfigures the VM to use the destination files, and then deletes the source files.

There are hardly any special requirements for performing a storage migration, except that you cannot migrate VMs that use pass-through disks for their storage. The files must be stored on virtual hard disk (either VHD or VHDX) files.

To perform a storage migration, use the same Move Wizard as for non-clustered live migrations and shared nothing live migrations. On the wizard's Choose Move Type page, you select the Move The Virtual Machine's Storage option. The Choose Options For Moving Storage page appears, as shown in Figure 5-10, with the following options:

- **Move All Of The Virtual Machine's Data To A Single Location** Enables you to specify one destination for all of the source VM's files.
- **Move All Of The Virtual Machine's Data To Different Locations** Adds multiple screen to the wizard, on which you can select the file types to migrate and specify a destination for each type.
- **Move Only The Virtual Machine's Virtual Hard Disks** Enables you to select which VHD/VHDX files to migrate and specify a destination for each one.

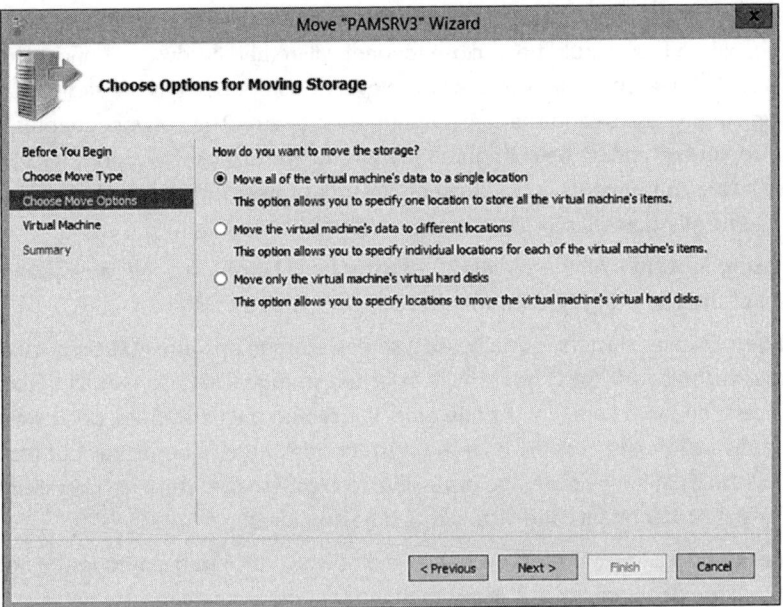

FIGURE 5-10 The Choose Options For Moving Storage page in the Move Wizard

Skill 5.2: Implement failover clustering

A *failover cluster* is a group of two or more computers—physical or virtual, and running the same application—that functions as a single entity to provide a highly available, scalable, and fault tolerant service to clients on the network. Clustered applications typically provide essential user services, such as database and email server applications, or infrastructure services, such as Hyper-V and file servers. With multiple computers—called *nodes*— running the same application, the services are always available, even when a node fails. When demand for the service increases, administrators can easily add more nodes to the cluster, increasing its overall capacity.

In Windows Server 2016, the Failover Clustering feature provides the tools needed to create a cluster of as many as 64 computers, supporting up to 8,000 virtual machines, with a maximum of 1,024 VMs per node. The feature includes a graphical management tool, the Failover Cluster Manager console, plus a Windows PowerShell module with a comprehensive collection of cmdlets.

Although it's possible to create a simple two-node cluster in a lab environment, even on a single Hyper-V server, failover clusters typically have sophisticated hardware and software requirements, especially when they provide vital services to many clients in a production environment. Hardware and software requirements include the following:

- **Servers** The computers that function as cluster nodes are intended to be interchangeable, so they should be as close to identical in their hardware configurations as possible. The ideal situation is one in which every cluster node has the same number and type of processors and the same amount of memory. The network adapters in all of the computers should be configured identically. For Microsoft support, all hardware and software components in the cluster nodes must meet the qualifications for the Certified for Windows Server 2016 logo.

- **Operating System** All the servers in a cluster must be running the same version and edition of the operating system, with the same updates applied to it.

- **Storage** Failover clusters typically use a shared storage implementation, such as a storage area network (SAN) or network attached storage (NAS), so that all the nodes can access the same data files. At one time, this required an elaborate, dedicated storage hardware infrastructure, even if the cluster nodes were to be virtual, but technologies such as iSCSI have now made it possible to create shared storage subsystems using off-the-shelf components and virtual disk infrastructures.

- **Networking** Failover clusters exchange their own control traffic among the nodes, and in a large deployment, it is recommended that there be a separate network dedicated to cluster traffic. In addition, the shared storage infrastructure should typically have its own dedicated network as well. Thus, a failover cluster implementation can have three or more network interfaces per node, supporting these various kinds of traffic, as well as the additional switches, cabling, and other components necessary to support the additional networks. For mission critical applications, it can also be necessary to compound the network implementations with redundant adapters, switches, and cabling, to avoid single points of failure. For smaller deployments, such as in a lab environment, it is also possible to use Quality of Service technologies, such as Datacenter Bridging, to reserve bandwidth on a single network for these various types of traffic.

- **Applications** In addition to the hardware requirements for the cluster itself, you must also consider the requirements for the application that will be running on the cluster nodes. For example, the nodes in a Hyper-V cluster must meet the virtualization hardware requirements specified for the Hyper-V role.

Because the hardware configuration is such an integral part of building a cluster, the Failover Cluster Manager includes a Validate Cluster Wizard that performs a series of tests on the servers you select, to determine if they are eligible for membership in a cluster. You can also use the Test-Cluster PowerShell cmdlet to initiate these tests. The validation process generates a detailed report, like the one shown in Figure 5-11.

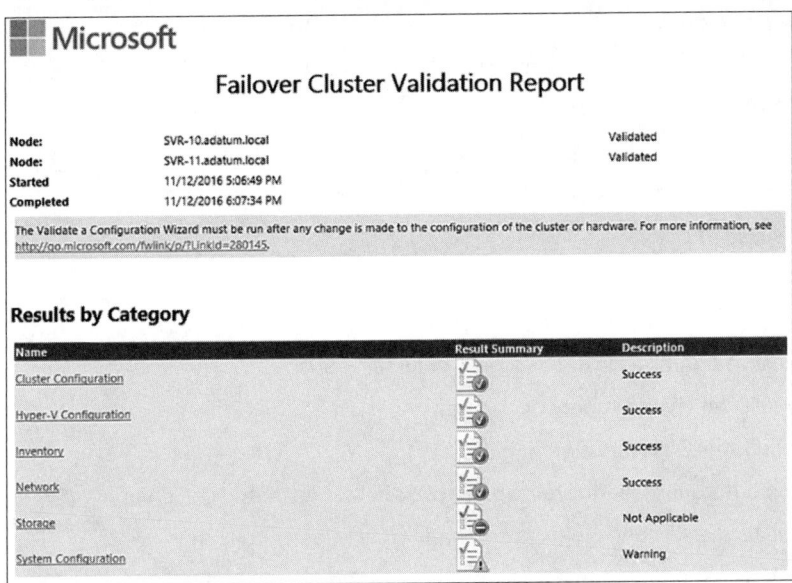

FIGURE 5-11 A Failover Cluster Validation Report

Once the hardware configuration of the cluster has been validated successfully, you can proceed to create the cluster, using the Create Cluster Wizard or the New-Cluster cmdlet. To do this, you specify the name of the servers that you want to add as nodes in the cluster. You also specify a name for the cluster, which is how it will be addressed on the network, as shown in the following example:

```
new-cluster -name cluster1 -node server1,server2
```

The cluster is a separate entity, with its own name and IP address. If there is a DHCP server available on the network, the cluster will obtain an IP address from there. If not, then you must assign the cluster a static address, as in the following example:

```
new-cluster -name cluster1 -node server1,server2 -staticaddress 10.0.0.3
```

The cluster also has its own computer object in Active Directory, called a cluster name object (CNO). Once the application is running on the cluster nodes, the clients will address their requests to the cluster itself, not to an individual server.

This section covers how to:
- Implement Workgroup, Single, and Multi Domain clusters
- Configure quorum
- Configure cluster networking
- Restore single node or cluster configuration
- Configure cluster storage
- Implement Cluster-Aware Updating
- Implement Cluster Operating System Rolling Upgrade
- Configure and optimize clustered shared volumes (CSVs)
- Configure clusters without network names
- Implement Scale-Out File Server (SoFS)
- Determine different scenarios for the use of SoFS vs. Clustered File Server
- Determine usage scenarios for implementing guest clustering
- Implement a Clustered Storage Spaces solution using Shared SAS storage enclosures
- Implement Storage Replica
- Implement Cloud Witness
- Implement VM resiliency
- Implement shared VHDX as a storage solution for guest clusters

Implement workgroup, single, and multi domain clusters

Prior to Windows Server 2016, all of the servers in a failover cluster had to be joined to the same AD DS domain. This is now called a *single domain cluster*. As mentioned earlier, the Create Cluster Wizard and the New-Cluster cmdlet create an AD DS object representing the cluster by default.

Starting in Windows Server 2016, however, it is possible to create a cluster using servers joined to different domains, which is called a *multi-domain cluster*, or servers not joined to any domain at all, which is called a *workgroup cluster*.

Failover Clustering uses Active Directory for a variety of services, not least of which is locating the cluster itself. Without Active Directory support, it is necessary for the cluster to use DNS to register an administrative access point, also known as the cluster network name.

There are also Active Directory issues with some applications that prevent them from running on an multi-domain or workgroup cluster. Microsoft SQL Server functions well without Active Directory because it has its own authentication mechanism. However, a file server cluster without Active Directory authentication would require you to create user accounts on every node in the cluster.

Before you can create a multi-domain or workgroup cluster, you must complete the following tasks.

Create a local account

In a single domain cluster, one domain user account can provide access to all the nodes. Without Active Directory, access to the nodes for cluster communications is an issue. Therefore, you must create a local user account on every node, with the same user name and the same password. Then, you must add the user to the local Administrators group.

You can use the built-in Administrator account for this purpose, which is already a member of the Administrators group, if you assign it the same password on every node. However, if you do not use the Administrator account, you must set a registry key called LocalAccountTokenFilterPolicy on every node, using the following command in a PowerShell session with administrative privileges:

```
new-itemproperty -path hklm:\software\microsoft\windows\currentversion\policies\system
-name localaccounttokenfilterpolicy -value 1
```

Add DNS suffixes

Without Active Directory, a cluster must use DNS to locate the cluster nodes and the cluster itself. You must therefore specify a primary DNS suffix when assigning a name to each node, as shown in Figure 5-12.

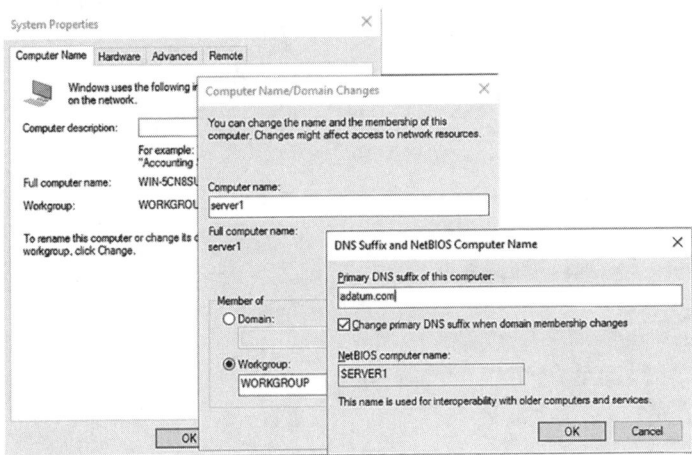

FIGURE 5-12 Assigning a primary DNS suffix

There is no direct way to configure the primary DNS suffix using PowerShell, but you can do so using Group Policy, by browsing to the Computer Configuration\Policies\Administrative Templates\Network\DNS Client folder and enabling the Primary DNS Suffix policy, as shown in Figure 5-13.

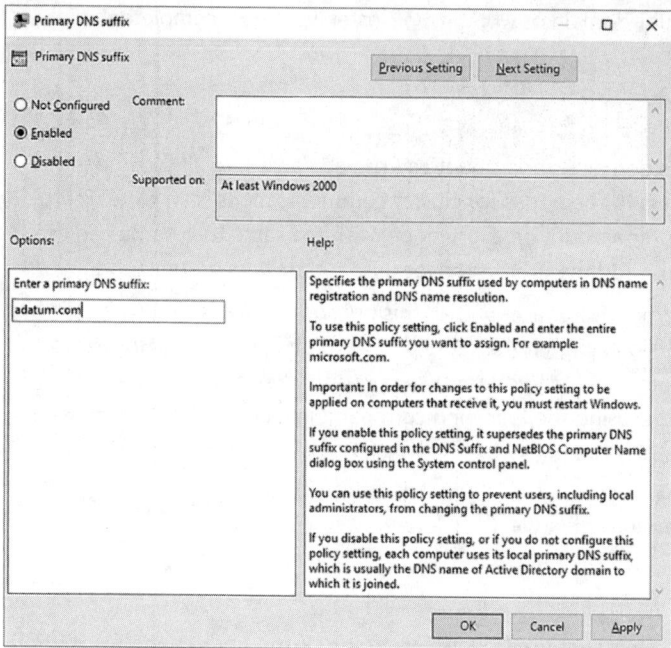

FIGURE 5-13 The Primary DNS Suffix policy dialog box

For a multi-domain cluster, you must also configure the Advanced TCP/IP Settings in every node with the DNS suffixes for all the domains represented in the cluster, as shown in Figure 5-14.

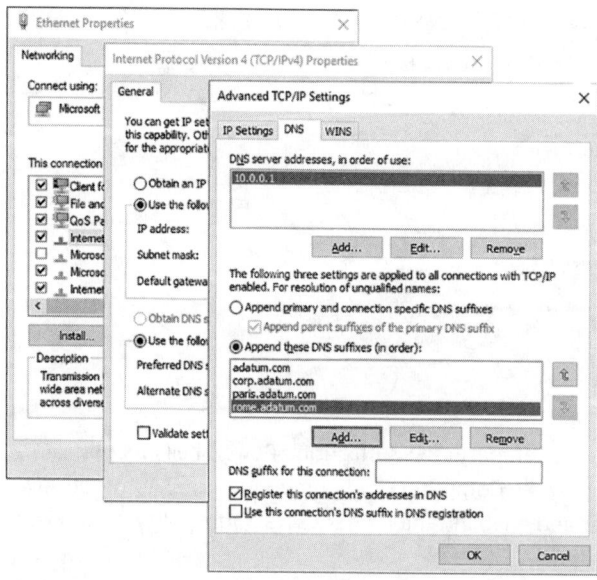

FIGURE 5-14 Specifying additional DNS suffixes

You can also do this using the Set-DnsClientGlobalSettings PowerShell cmdlet, as shown in the following example:

```
set-dnsclientglobalsettings -suffixsearchlist @("adatum.com", "corp.adatum.com", "paris.adatum.com", "rome.adatum.com")
```

Creating a workgroup or multi-domain cluster

With these settings in place, you can proceed to create the cluster. When using PowerShell, you use the New-Cluster cmdlet, just as you would for a single domain cluster, but you must include the AdministrativeAccessPoint parameter with the DNS value, as shown in following example:

```
new-cluster -name cluster1 -node server1,server2,server3 -administrativeaccesspoint dns
```

The AdministrativeAccessPoint parameter causes the cmdlet to use a DNS name for the cluster and prevents it from creating a computer object in Active Directory. You can also use Failover Cluster Manager to create the cluster, if the computer you use is not joined to an AD DS domain.

Configure quorum

The function of *quorum* in failover clustering is to prevent a cluster from being split in two, with both halves continuing to run. This is called a *split-brain* situation. If, for example, a network failure causes a six-node cluster to be split into two three-node clusters, both could continue to function if it wasn't for quorum. If the cluster were running a database application, that would mean that there are two separate copies of the database being accessed and updated by different sets of clients at the same time. This could be disastrous for the integrity of the information in the database.

Quorum provides each node in the cluster with a vote, and in many cases, there is a witness disk adding another vote, to break potential ties. All of the nodes monitor the continual votes from the other nodes and the witness. If a node detects that the vote tally drops below 50 percent +1, it removes itself from the cluster. In the case of the six-node cluster split in half mentioned earlier, all the nodes would see the vote tally drop from 6 to 3. Because 3 is less than 50 percent +1, all the nodes would remove themselves, shutting down both halves of the cluster.

If there was a witness disk somewhere on this cluster, then the half that can contact the witness disk would have a vote tally of 4, which is 50 percent +1 of the original cluster. Therefore, the half with the witness disk would continue to function, while the nodes in the other half, with a tally of 3 votes, would remove themselves.

Quorum witnesses

When you create a failover cluster, the Create Cluster Wizard or the New-Cluster cmdlet creates a quorum configuration that, in most cases, is appropriate for the cluster, based on the number of nodes and the available storage resources. By default, each node gets one vote, and, if there is an even number of nodes, the wizard or cmdlet attempts to create a witness, to function as a tie-breaker. Like the nodes, the witness gets one vote.

A *witness* is a resource that, by its existence, casts a vote for the continued operation of the cluster. Failover clustering in Windows Server 2016 supports three types of witnesses, as follows:

- **Disk Witness**   A dedicated disk in the cluster's shared storage that contains a copy of the cluster database. This is the typical option for a cluster located at a single site.
- **File Share Witness**   An SMB file share on a Windows server with a Witness.log file containing information about the cluster. This is the typical option for clusters divided among multiple sites with replicated storage.
- **Cloud Witness**   A blob stored in the cloud using standard Microsoft Azure services. This is a new option in Windows Server 2016, designed for stretched clusters split among multiple data centers at remote sites, which want to maintain a witness that is independent of all the data centers.

Dynamic quorum management

The default quorum configuration in Windows Server 2016 also includes *dynamic quorum management*, which is a feature that is designed to keep a cluster running in situations where it would be stopped in earlier versions of the Failover Clustering feature.

When a node leaves the cluster, dynamic quorum management automatically removes its vote, so that the functionality of the cluster is based on the quorum of the remaining votes. For example, in a five-node cluster without dynamic quorum management, if three nodes fail, the quorum vote drops to two out of five, and the remaining two nodes remove themselves, shutting down the cluster. In the same cluster with dynamic quorum management, the vote of each failing node is automatically removed from the tally, resulting in a quorum vote of two out of two, so the cluster continues to function. This feature, therefore, can enable a cluster to function, even when all but one of the nodes has failed.

Modifying the Quorum Configuration

Usually, the quorum configuration created by the Create Cluster Wizard or the New-Cluster cmdlet is suitable for the cluster and requires no adjustment. However, you can modify the quorum configuration, by running the Configure Cluster Quorum Wizard in Failover Cluster Manager, or by using the Set-ClusterQuorum cmdlet in Windows PowerShell. Using these tools, you can add or change a witness and specify which nodes should have votes in the quorum.

To run the Configure Cluster Quorum Wizard, you select the cluster in Failover Cluster Manager and, in the Actions pane, select More Actions | Configure Cluster Quorum Settings. On the Select Quorum Configuration Option page, shown in Figure 5-15, you have the following options:

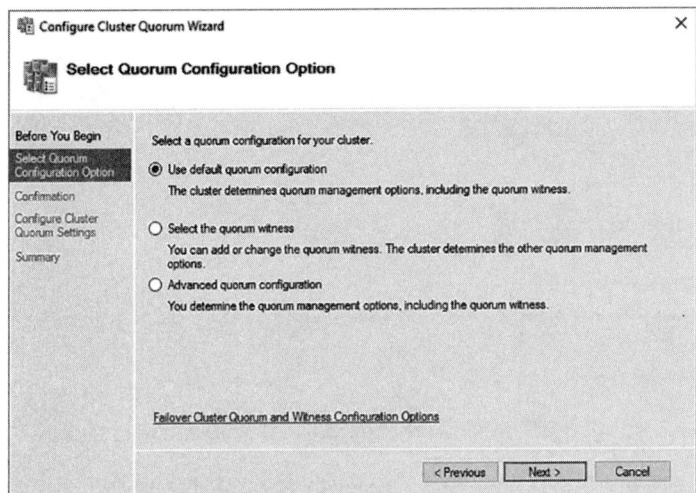

FIGURE 5-15 The Select Quorum Configuration Option page in the Configure Cluster Quorum Wizard

- **Use Default Quorum Configuration** Enables the wizard to configure an appropriate quorum configuration for the cluster without manual input.
- **Select The Quorum Witness** Enables you to add a witness, if none exists, remove an existing witness, and specify the type and location of the witness the quorum should use, as shown in Figure 5-16.

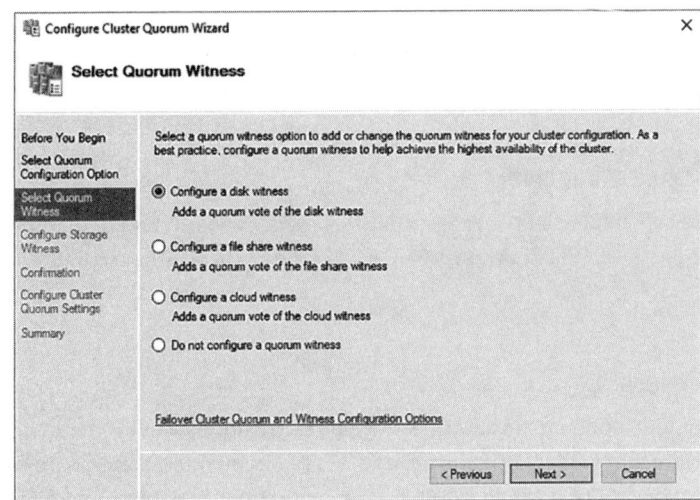

FIGURE 5-16 The Select Quorum Witness page in the Configure Cluster Quorum Wizard

- **Advanced Quorum Configuration** Enables you to specify which nodes should have votes in the quorum, as shown in Figure 5-17. It also configures the same witness settings as the Select the Quorum Witness option.

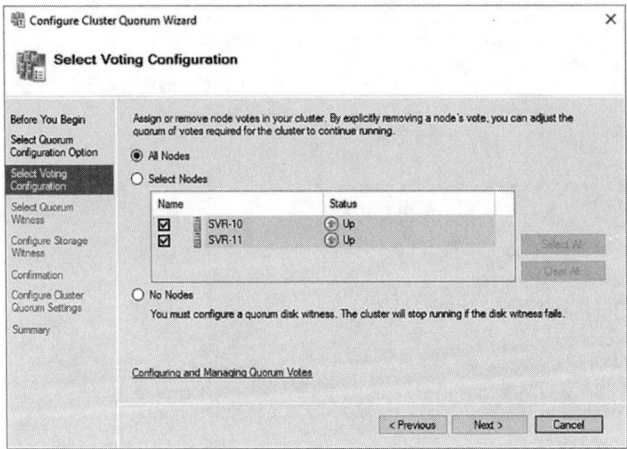

FIGURE 5-17 The Select Voting Configuration page in the Configure Cluster Quorum Wizard

To configure the quorum configuration with Windows PowerShell, you use commands like the following.

To configure the quorum to use a node majority, with no witness:

`set-clusterquorum -cluster cluster1 -nodemajority`

To configure the quorum with votes from each node and a disk witness:

`set-clusterquorum -cluster cluster1 -nodeanddiskmajority "cluster disk 1"`

To configure a cluster node to not have a quorum vote:

`(get-clusternode clusternode1).nodeweight=0`

> **NOTE RUNNING CLUSTERING CMDLETS**
>
> Many of the PowerShell cmdlets in the FailoverClusters module do not function properly from a remote location. Whenever possible, you should try to run the cmdlets on a cluster node.

Configuring a witness

In most cases, Failover Clustering creates a witness when the cluster has an even number of nodes. There can only be one witness in a cluster, and it is recommended that you do not create a witness in a situation where it would result in an even number of votes in the quorum.

When all the nodes in a cluster have access to the same shared storage, then a disk witness is the recommended configuration. The Configure Storage Witness page in the Configure Cluster Quorum Wizard, shown in Figure 5-18, enables you to select the disk that should function as the witness. The witness disk only must contain a small amount of data, so you should create a minimum-sized 512 MB NTFS disk for this purpose.

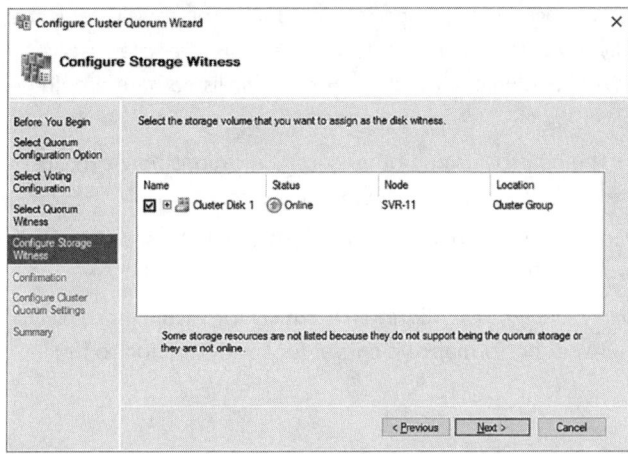

FIGURE 5-18 The Configure Storage Witness page in the Configure Cluster Quorum Wizard

The options to create a file share witness or a cloud witness are similar, enabling you to specify the location for the witness and, in the case of a cloud witness, the name and key for your Azure storage account.

Modifying quorum voting

In most cases, every node in the cluster should have a vote. It is possible to configure a cluster with no voting nodes and just a witness vote, and this might seem at first to be a viable option. If there is a node available that has access to storage, the cluster can run. However, in this configuration, the witness becomes a single point of failure. If the witness becomes inaccessible, the cluster goes down, even if all the nodes and the rest of the storage is functional.

There are situations in which you might want to revoke the votes of specific nodes in the cluster, however. For example, you might have cluster nodes at a remote site that are there strictly as a backup, for manual failover in the event of a disaster. You can revoke their votes so that they are not part of the quorum calculations.

> **NOTE NON-VOTING NODES**
>
> Whether a node has a quorum vote has no bearing on its functionality in the cluster. Nodes that do not participate in the quorum are still fully active in the cluster.

Configure cluster networking

The network connections are critical to maintaining the high availability of a failover cluster. Separating traffic into different networks and providing redundant connections at all point in the network path help to ensure the continued functionality of the cluster.

Depending on the role performed by the cluster, you might want to create separate networks for each of the following types of traffic:

- **Client Communications**   Client access to the application running on the cluster is the highest priority. This is usually the default shared network used for other client/server communications, but whenever possible, the other types of traffic listed here should be kept off this network.
- **Cluster Communications**   The heartbeats and other communications between cluster nodes are essential to the continued functionality of the cluster.
- **iSCSI**   iSCSI and other storage area network communications should be separated from all other types of network traffic.
- **Live Migration**   On a Hyper-V cluster, Live Migration is critical for virtual machines to continue functioning, and network performance is critical for Live Migration to function efficiently.

Selecting network hardware

For the network hardware, the object should be to provide as much redundancy as possible and to avoid single points of failure. Some of the hardware provisioning recommendations are as follows:

- Use separate network adapters, rather than adapters with multiple interfaces, to avoid the adapter card as a single point of failure.
- Use different makes of network adapter when possible, to avoid driver issues from affecting multiple adapters.
- Use separate physical switches, rather than configuring VLANs on a single large switch, to prevent the switch from being a single point of failure.
- Create redundant network connections whenever possible, especially for the client communication network.
- For networks without redundant connections, such as those for cluster communication and Live Migration, use NIC Teaming to provide failover capability in the event of a network adapter malfunction.

Modifying network defaults

When you create a cluster, the system evaluates each of the connected networks and assigns traffic roles to them, based on the following criteria:

- Any network carrying iSCSI traffic is disabled for any cluster communication.
- Networks without a default gateway address are configured for cluster communications only.
- Networks with a default gateway address are configured for both client and cluster communication.

The current states of the detected networks are displayed on the Networks page of Failover Cluster Manager, as shown in Figure 5-19, or by running the Get-ClusterNetwork cmdlet in PowerShell.

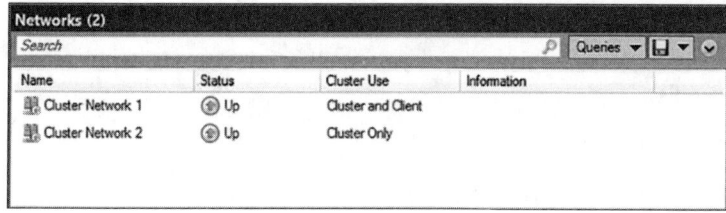

FIGURE 5-19 The Networks page of Failover Cluster Manager

It is possible to modify the default network settings created with the cluster, using Failover Cluster Manager or the Get-ClusterNetwork PowerShell cmdlet. To configure the network in Failover Cluster Manager, use the following procedure.

1. Open Failover Cluster Manager and browse to the Networks page.
2. Select a network and, in the Actions pane, click Properties.
3. On the Properties sheet shown in Figure 5-20, choose from the following options:
   - **Allow Cluster Communication On This Network** Enables the network to be used for cluster communication only.
   - **Allow Clients To Connect Through This Network** Enables the network to be used for client communication, as well as cluster communication.
   - **Do Not Allow Cluster Communication On This Network** Prevents the network from being used for any cluster communication.

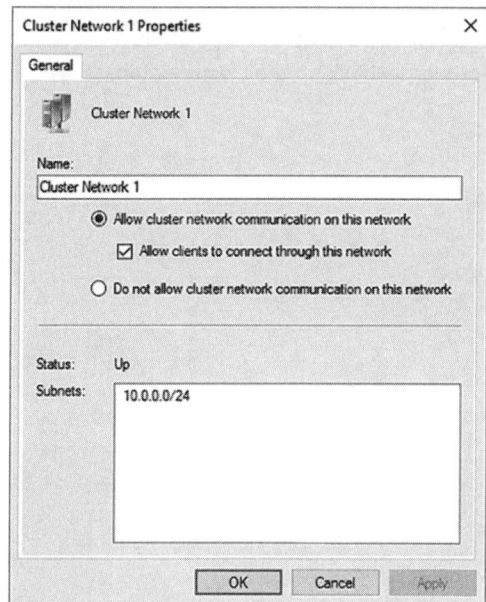

FIGURE 5-20 The Properties sheet for a network

4. Click OK.

To configure these settings in Windows PowerShell, you use the Get-ClusterNetwork cmdlet, as in the following example:

```
(get-clusternetwork "network1").role =1
```

The values for the Role property are as follows:

- 0 Disabled for cluster communication
- 1 Enabled for cluster communication only
- 3 Enabled for client and cluster communication

> **NOTE FAILOVER CLUSTER CMDLETS**
>
> In many instances, the cmdlets in the FailoverClusters PowerShell module are less intuitive than those in other modules. Even experienced PowerShell users might find it more convenient to use Failover Cluster Manager many cluster configuration tasks.

Restore single node or cluster configuration

Failover clusters might provide fault tolerance, but they do not absolve you from the need to back up your servers. Whatever shared storage solution you use for a failover cluster, you should have a backup strategy in place, even if it includes mirrors or parity-based data redundancy. However, the other issue regarding backups is the cluster configuration itself.

Windows Server Backup is limited in its ability to perform backups of Cluster Shared Volumes (CSVs) as part of the server backup, but it can back up the cluster database, as shown in Figure 5-21.

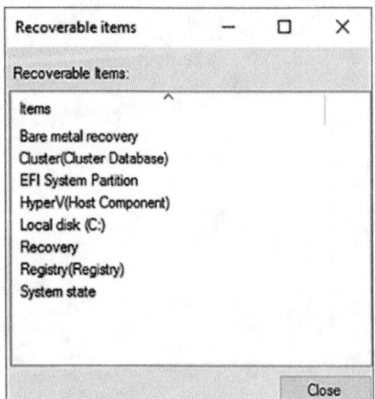

FIGURE 5-21 The Recoverable Items list for a Windows Server Backup job

The cluster database is stored on each node of a cluster, as well as on a disk witness, if one exists. The Cluster Service running on each node is responsible for seeing to it that the most recent version of the cluster database is replicated to each node. When you are performing a restore from backup on a cluster node, you must consider whether you want to perform an authoritative restore of the cluster database.

One of the more likely disaster situations for a failover cluster environment is the loss of a single node. If one node fails, and the rest of the cluster is running, you can probably just perform a full restore of that node from a backup. The version of the cluster database in the backup will be outdated, and the Cluster Service will overwrite it with the latest version as soon as the node comes up as part of the cluster. This is called a non-authoritative backup.

The other situation is when you want to perform an authoritative restore of the cluster database, that is, you want the cluster to use the version of the database from the backup, not the one that it is currently using. To do this with Windows Server Backup, you must perform the restore from the command prompt using the Wbadmin.exe program. You cannot use the GUI for this.

When you run the following Wbadmin command, it displays the backups that are available for restoration. The result is shown in Figure 5-22.

```
wbadmin get versions
```

```
PS C:\Users\administrator.ADATUM> wbadmin get versions
wbadmin 1.0 - Backup command-line tool
(C) Copyright 2013 Microsoft Corporation. All rights reserved.

Backup time: 11/13/2016 9:09 PM
Backup target: Fixed Disk labeled D:
Version identifier: 11/14/2016-05:09
Can recover: Volume(s), File(s), Application(s), Bare Metal Recovery, System State
Snapshot ID: {cfaee8b8-130c-4b2e-9a27-a2758e808a9e}
```

FIGURE 5-22 Results of the Wbadmin get versions command

Using the Version Identifier specified in the listing, you can now display the recoverable contents in the backup— including the cluster database— with a command like the following. The result is shown in Figure 5-23.

```
wbadmin get items -version: 11/14/2016:05:09
```

```
PS C:\Users\administrator.ADATUM> wbadmin get items -version:11/14/2016-05:09
wbadmin 1.0 - Backup command-line tool
(C) Copyright 2013 Microsoft Corporation. All rights reserved.

EFI System Partition
Volume ID = {3d9d7859-d63a-496c-aa59-fea6966f031e}
Volume '', mounted at C:
Volume size = 126.44 GB
Can recover = Full volume

Volume ID = {a84dd41a-1590-40f2-8f75-ece3e0a48112}
Volume 'Recovery', mounted at <not mounted> ('Recovery', mounted at <not mounted> at the time
the backup was created)
Volume size = 450.00 MB
Can recover = Full volume

Application = Cluster
Component = Cluster Database (\Cluster Database)

Application = Registry
Component = Registry (\Registry)

Application = HyperV
VM name: Host Component
VM caption: Host Component
VM identifier: Host Component
Total Size: <Not available>
```

FIGURE 5-23 Results of the Wbadmin get items command

To perform the authoritative restore, you use a command like the following.

```
wbadmin start recovery -itemtype:app -items:cluster -version:01/01/2008-00:00
```

The results, shown in Figure 5-24, indicate that the database has been restored successfully, and provide instructions for restarting the cluster.

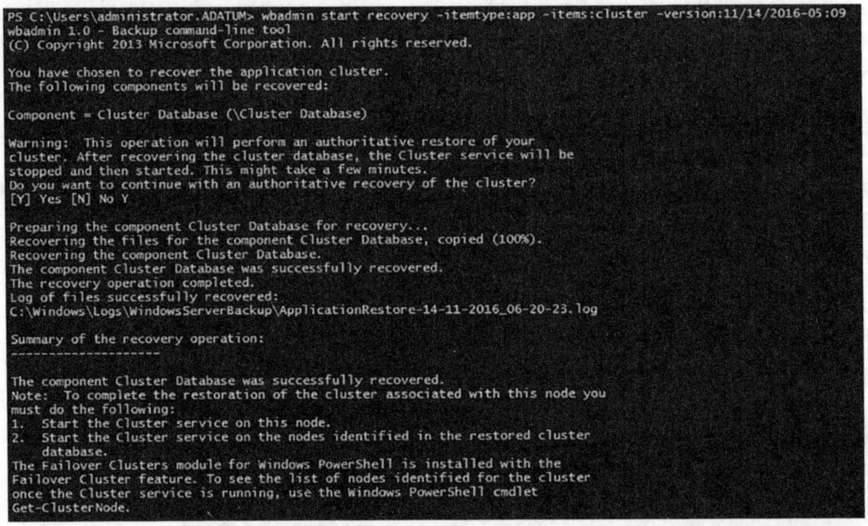

```
PS C:\Users\administrator.ADATUM> wbadmin start recovery -itemtype:app -items:cluster -version:11/14/2016-05:09
wbadmin 1.0 - Backup command-line tool
(C) Copyright 2013 Microsoft Corporation. All rights reserved.

You have chosen to recover the application cluster.
The following components will be recovered:

Component = Cluster Database (\Cluster Database)

Warning:  This operation will perform an authoritative restore of your
cluster. After recovering the cluster database, the Cluster service will be
stopped and then started. This might take a few minutes.
Do you want to continue with an authoritative recovery of the cluster?
[Y] Yes [N] No Y

Preparing the component Cluster Database for recovery...
Recovering the files for the component Cluster Database, copied (100%).
Recovering the component Cluster Database.
The component Cluster Database was successfully recovered.
The recovery operation completed.
Log of files successfully recovered:
C:\Windows\Logs\WindowsServerBackup\ApplicationRestore-14-11-2016_06-20-23.log

Summary of the recovery operation:
--------------------

The component Cluster Database was successfully recovered.
Note:  To complete the restoration of the cluster associated with this node you
must do the following:
1.  Start the Cluster service on this node.
2.  Start the Cluster service on the nodes identified in the restored cluster
    database.
The Failover Clusters module for Windows PowerShell is installed with the
Failover Cluster feature. To see the list of nodes identified for the cluster
once the Cluster service is running, use the Windows PowerShell cmdlet
Get-ClusterNode.
```

FIGURE 5-24 Results of the Wbadmin start recovery command

You can start the Cluster Service on the other nodes remotely, by highlighting them in Failover Cluster Manager and selecting More Actions | Start Cluster Service in the Actions pane.

Configure cluster storage

For a failover cluster to host a highly available application, all the cluster nodes must have access to the application data. Therefore, the cluster must have some form of shared storage. Shared storage is a requirement of the Failover Clustering feature in Windows Server 2016. Before you can add storage to the cluster, you must make sure that all the servers that will become the cluster nodes have access to the storage that will hold the application data.

Windows Server 2016 supports several shared storage technologies, including the following:

- **Fibre Channel** One of the first storage area network (SAN) protocols, Fibre Channel, is a dedicated fiber optic network that, at the time of its introduction, ran at high speeds, but which required specialized equipment and expertise, both of which were extremely expensive. There is now a Fibre Channel variant that runs over standard Ethernet (Fibre Channel over Ethernet, or FCoE), which is more affordable, but is still the esoteric high end of SAN technologies.

- **Serial Attached SCSI (SAS)** Small Computer System Interface (SCSI) is a bus-based storage attachment protocol that, in its parallel form, was at one time the industry standard for high performance local storage. The SAS variant uses serial communications to increase the maximum length of the bus, while using smaller cables and connectors than the original, parallel devices.

- **Internet SCSI (iSCSI)** Another variant of the SCSI protocol that transmits the same SCSI command language over a standard IP network. As with SAS, iSCSI designates storage devices as targets and the servers and other devices that access the storage as initiators. A server running Windows Server 2016 can function as both an iSCSI target and initiator, making it possible to implement an iSCSI SAN wholly in software.

Each of these technologies is less expensive than the ones preceding it, with iSCSI SANs now realizable for little more than the cost of an unsophisticated disk array. While some high-end storage appliances include varying levels of intelligence, fault tolerance, and high availability, there are also storage arrays known as JBODs (Just a Bunch of Disks), which are low cost devices that are little more than standard hard disk drives in a cabinet with a common power supply.

EXAM TIP

Using Hyper-V and iSCSI, it is possible to implement a failover cluster on a single physical server, for evaluation, testing, and educational purposes. The performance level of the cluster is likely to be extremely limited, but an arrangement such as this will enable you to explore the Failover Clustering feature of Windows Server 2016.

Once you create the cluster, any disks that qualify should appear in Failover Cluster Manager when you select Add Disks on the Storage\Disks page, as shown in Figure 5-25. Once you add a disk, it is designated as Available Storage.

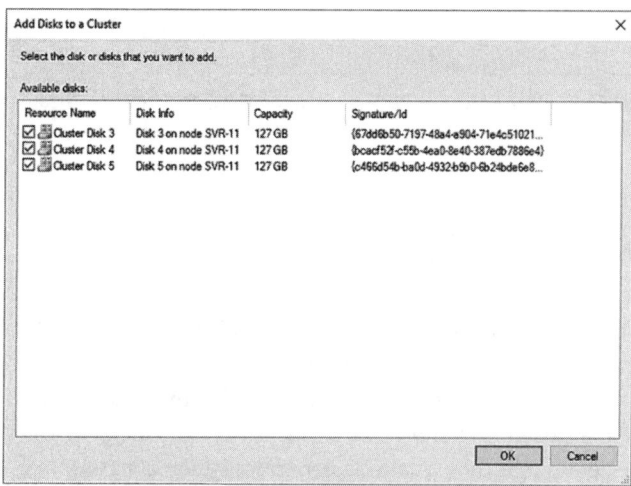

FIGURE 5-25 The Add Disks to a Cluster dialog box in Failover Cluster Manager

Alternatively, you can use the storage on the disks to create a clustered storage pool. The process is like that of creating a pool using Storage Spaces on a single Windows server, except that the storage is shared by all the nodes in the cluster.

A clustered storage pool requires a minimum of three disks of at least 4 GB capacity each, which must be connected to all the cluster nodes using SAS or iSCSI. To create a clustered storage pool, use the following procedure.

1. In Failover Cluster Manager, browse to the Storage\Pools page and click New Storage Pool in the Actions pane to launch the New Storage Pool Wizard.

2. On the Specify a Storage Pool Name and Subsystem page, type a name for the pool and select the primordial pool containing the disks you want to use.

3. On the Select Physical Disks for the Storage Pool page, select the disks you want to add to the pool and specify whether each one should be Automatic, Hot Spare, or Manual, as shown in Figure 5-26.

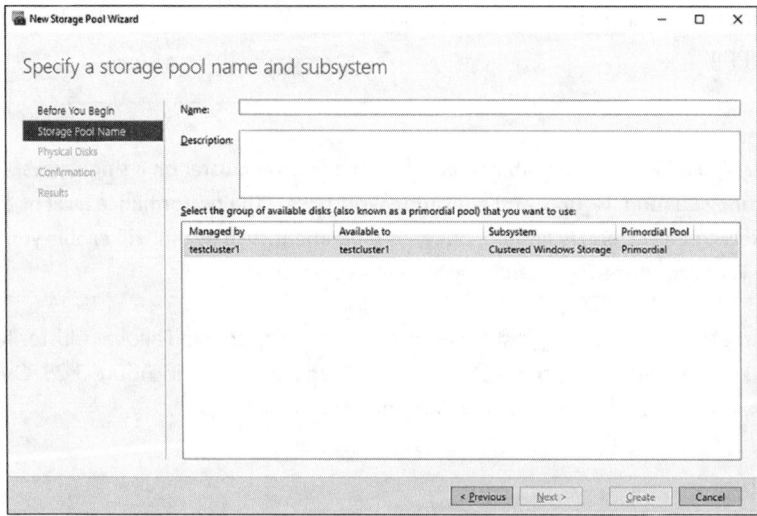

FIGURE 5-26 The Select Physical Disks for the Storage Pool page in the New Storage Pool Wizard

4. Click Create.

Implement cluster-aware updating

One of the important prerequisites for Failover Clustering in Windows Server 2016 is for all the potential cluster nodes to be running the same version of the operating system, with all of the same updates applied to them. The Validate Cluster Wizard issues warnings when it determines that the servers it is checking are not identically updated. What then do you do to keep your nodes updated once the cluster is operational? *Cluster-Aware Updating (CAU)* is a tool supplied with Failover Clustering that can update cluster nodes systematically with a minimum of down time.

CAU applies updates to a cluster in a round-robin fashion, called an Updating Run, using the following procedure:

1. Selects one node to update.
2. Moves any existing roles off the selected node to other nodes in the cluster, using Live Migration or other techniques that minimize client service interruptions.
3. Places the selected node into node maintenance mode.
4. Installs the required updates on the selected node and restarts it, if necessary.
5. Takes the selected node out of maintenance mode.
6. Moves on to the next node in the cluster and repeats the procedure.

This way, each node in turn is taken out of service temporarily and updated, until the entire cluster has had the same updates applied.

CAU requires a computer to function as the Update Coordinator, directing the updating activities for the cluster. The question of which computer performs this function is the primary distinction between the CAU's two operating modes:

- **Self-Updating Mode**   In this mode, one of the cluster nodes has the CAU clustered role installed, enabling it to function as the Update Coordinator. The Update Coordinator node performs Updating Runs according to a schedule configured by an administrator, triggering updates on each of the other nodes in turn. When all of the other nodes have been updated, the CAU role on the Update Coordinator fails over to another node, enabling it to assume the Update Coordinator role. The original coordinator can then be updated itself. In this mode, the entire update process is performed automatically.

- **Remote Updating Mode**   In this mode, a computer outside the cluster is configured to function as the Update Coordinator. From this computer, an administrator can manually trigger an Updating Run on the cluster. The Update Coordinator computer is not updated itself, and the process cannot be automated.

To use CAU in self-updating mode, each node in the cluster must have the Failover Clustering tools installed. The tools are installed by default when you add the Failover Clustering feature using Server Manager. However, if you install the feature using PowerShell, you must add the IncludeManagementTools parameter to the Install-WindowsFeature command.

For remote updating mode, the Update Coordinator must have the Failover Clustering tools installed, but the Failover Clustering feature is not required. The tools themselves are located under Remote Server Administration Tools in the Add Roles and Features Wizard. They are known as RSAT-Clustering in Windows PowerShell.

The CAU tools include a Cluster-Aware Updating console, as shown in Figure 5-27, and a ClusterAwareUpdating module for Windows PowerShell, which contains cmdlets for managing the service.

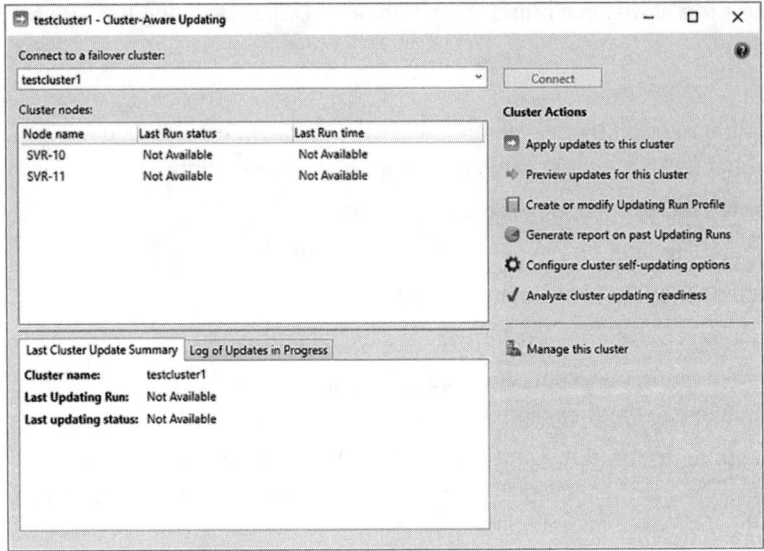

FIGURE 5-27 The Cluster-Aware Updating console

There are other prerequisites for using CAU, most of which are already satisfied in a properly installed Windows Server 2016 failover cluster. Clicking Analyze Cluster Updating Readiness in the console's Cluster Actions list or running the Test-CauSetup cmdlet in PowerShell on a cluster node performs a series of tests that assesses the readiness for the entire cluster, as shown in Figure 5-28.

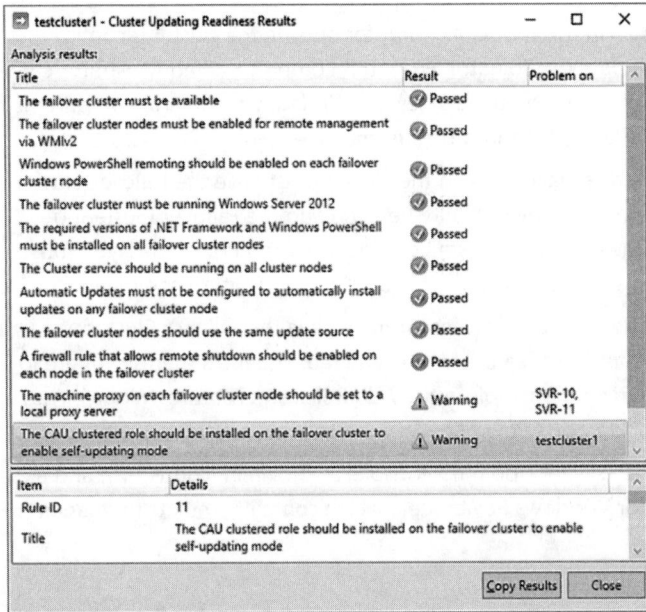

FIGURE 5-28 Cluster Updating Readiness Results

330   CHAPTER 5   Implement high availability

To use self-updating mode, once the cluster meets all the prerequisites, you install the CAU clustered role by clicking Configure Cluster Self-Updating Options in the console. This launches the Configure Self-Updating Options Wizard, which adds the clustered role and creates a schedule for the self-updates, as shown in Figure 5-29. You can also configure advanced updating options, such as the maximum number of retries allowed per node and the order in which nodes should be updated. You can also do these things with the Add-CauClusterRole cmdlet in PowerShell, as in the following example:

```
add-cauclusterrole -clustername "cluster1" -daysofweek sunday -weeksinterval 3
-maxretriespernode -nodeorder node2, node1, node3
```

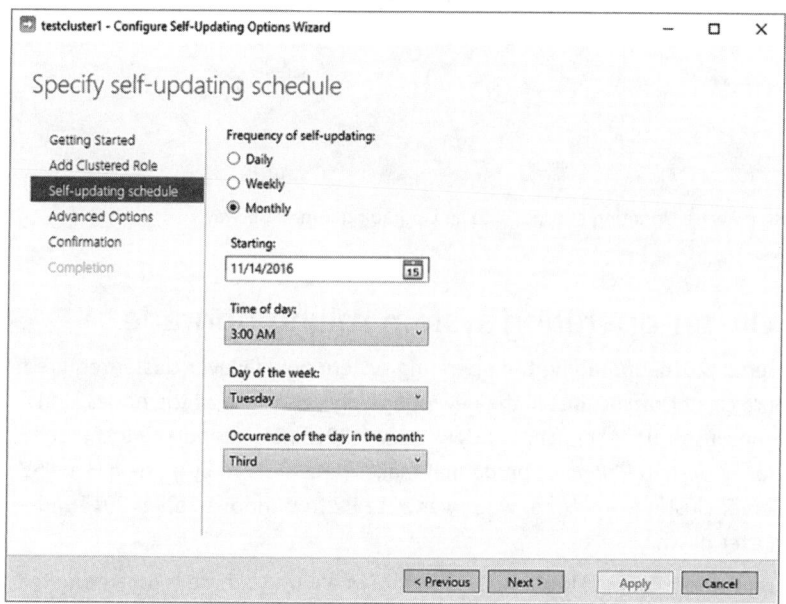

FIGURE 5-29 The Specify Self-Updating page of the Configure Self-Updating Options Wizard

Once the schedule is set, you can wait for it to run, or perform an Updating Run immediately, as shown in Figure 5-30, by clicking Apply Updates to this cluster or running the Invoke-CauRun cmdlet.

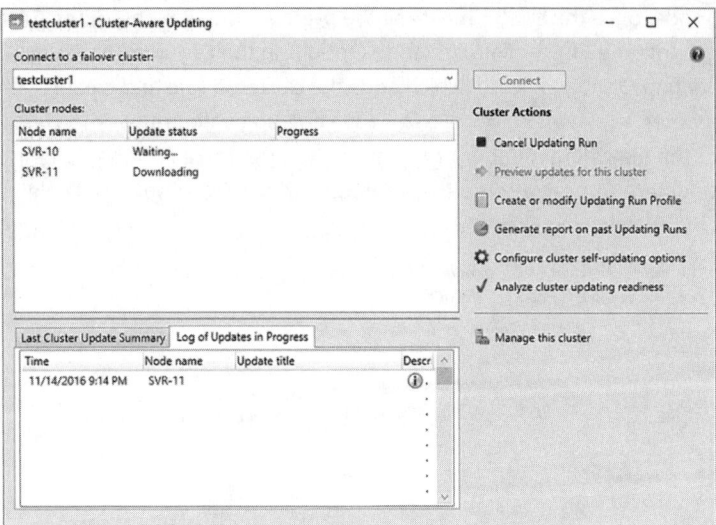

FIGURE 5-30 The Cluster-Aware Updating console with an Upgrading Run underway

Implement cluster operating system rolling upgrade

Prior to Windows Server 2016, upgrading the operating system on a failover cluster required you to take the entire cluster offline, install the new operating system on all the nodes, and essentially rebuild the cluster from scratch. Windows Server 2016 now supports a technique called *Cluster Operating System Rolling Upgrade* that makes it possible to upgrade a Hyper-V or Scale-Out File Server cluster from Windows Server 2012 R2 to Windows Server 2016 without bringing the cluster down.

Cluster Operating System Rolling Upgrade is not a tool or a wizard; there is no automated process for upgrading the cluster. It is rather a technique in which you bring each cluster node down in turn, perform a clean upgrade of the operating system, and add it back into the cluster. The feature that makes this possible is a new operational mode for Failover Clustering called *mixed-OS mode*. Unlike clusters in previous Windows versions, it is possible for a cluster to function, temporarily, with nodes running different operating system versions, specifically Windows Server 2012 R2 and Windows Server 2016.

The process for upgrading each Windows Server 2012 R2 node in the cluster is as follows:

1. Pause the node.
2. Drain the node of its workload by migrating it to other nodes.
3. Evict the node from the cluster.
4. Reformat the system drive and perform a clean installation of Windows Server 2016.
5. Configure network and storage connections.
6. Install the Failover Clustering feature.

7. Add the newly-installed node back into the cluster.
8. Reimplement the cluster workload.

When a newly-installed Windows Server 2016 node is added back into the cluster, it runs in a compatibility mode that enables it to cooperate with the remaining Windows Server 2012 R2 nodes. The cluster continues to operate at the Windows Server 2012 R2 functional level until all of the modes have been upgraded. Any new Failover Clustering features in Windows Server 2016 are not available. All during this period, which can take days or weeks, if necessary, the entire process is reversible. You can reinstall Windows Server 2012 R2 on your nodes and return the cluster to its original state, if necessary.

> **NOTE COMPLETING THE UPGRADES**
>
> Microsoft recommends that all the nodes in a cluster be upgraded within a month. Mixed-OS mode is not intended to be a permanent solution for a failover cluster.

When the upgrades on all the nodes have been completed, you finalize the process by running the Update-ClusterFunctionalLevel cmdlet. This is the "point of no return," when the functional level is permanently raised to Windows Server 2016. At this point, the new features become available, and there is no going back to the previous version.

Configure and optimize clustered shared volumes (CSVs)

When you consider the shared storage prerequisite for Failover Clustering, you are talking about sharing at the hardware level. Every node in the cluster can see the shared disks, but using them is another issue. You can add disks to a cluster in Failover Cluster Manager, or by using the Add-ClusterDisk cmdlet, and they appear as Available Storage, such as Cluster Disk 4 and Cluster Disk 5, shown in Figure 5-31.

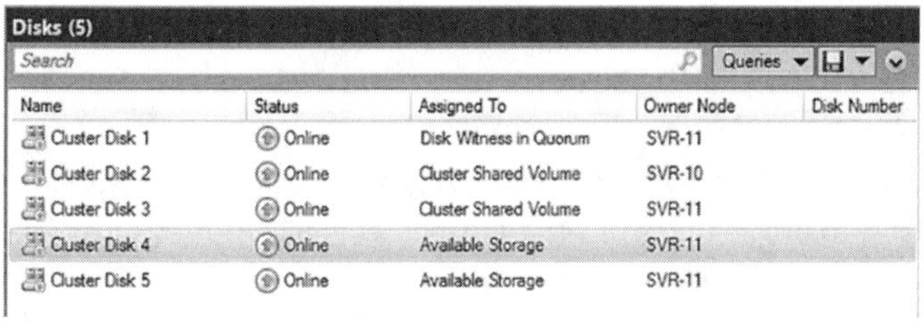

Name	Status	Assigned To	Owner Node	Disk Number
Cluster Disk 1	Online	Disk Witness in Quorum	SVR-11	
Cluster Disk 2	Online	Cluster Shared Volume	SVR-10	
Cluster Disk 3	Online	Cluster Shared Volume	SVR-11	
Cluster Disk 4	Online	Available Storage	SVR-11	
Cluster Disk 5	Online	Available Storage	SVR-11	

FIGURE 5-31 Available Storage in Failover Cluster Manager

These two disks have a node (SVR-11) listed as their designated owner. If you go to that node and open the Disk Management snap-in, those disks appear with drive letters and volume names, healthy and ready to use, as shown in Figure 5-32.

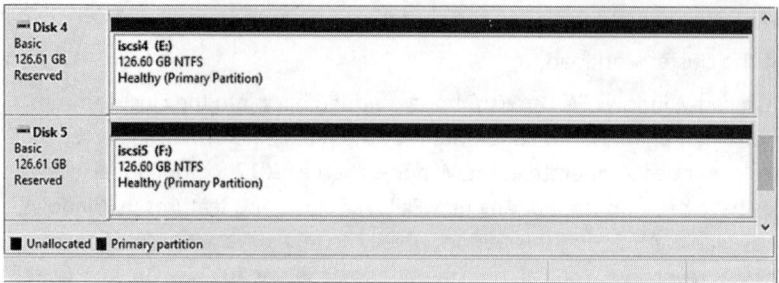

FIGURE 5-32 The Disk Management snap-in with two iSCSI disks mounted

If you go to another node and open the same snap-in, those same two disks have no drive letters, and a status of Reserved, as shown in Figure 5-3. If you try to bring them online, you can't. If this is supposed to be shared storage, why aren't these disks accessible on both nodes?

FIGURE 5-33 The Disk Management snap-in with two iSCSI disks reserved

The issue is not iSCSI, or whatever shared storage protocol you use on your SAN; it's the file system. NTFS is not designed to be accessed and used by more than one operating system instance at one time. Those two drives are mounted on the owner node, and they are usable there. To use them on a different node, you must dismount them from the current node and remounted on the new one. This is possible; but it takes time.

In the original version of Hyper-V in Windows Server 2008, this dismounting and remounting delay was the biggest obstacle to efficient use of virtual machines in a cluster. What's more, since only one node could access a disk at a time, if you want to migrate a VM to another server, you have to migrate all the other VMs using that same disk as well.

The solution to this issue is cluster shared volumes (CSVs). Cluster shared volumes create what is essentially a pseudo-file system (called CSVFS) that is layered on top of the NTFS file system. The problem with multiple nodes accessing an NTFS drive simultaneously is access to the metadata that controls the structure of the disk and the files stored on it. When two systems try to modify that metadata at the same time, corruption occurs and data is lost. CSVFS is essentially a filter that enables multiple nodes to perform data I/O operations on the disk, but restricts metadata access to the designated owner (also known as the coordinator).

You can see this by looking at CSVs in the Disk Management snap-in, as you did earlier with Available Storage disks. On its owner node, shown in Figure 5-34, the iscsi3 disk appears as using the CSVFS file system, and the context menu shows the usual controls for formatting, shrinking, and deleting the volume.

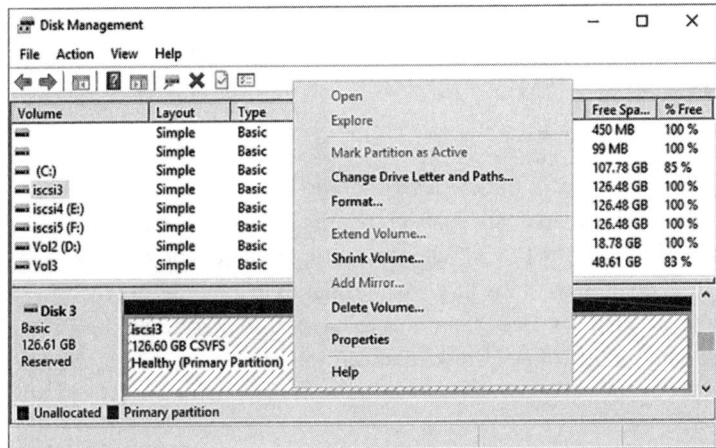

FIGURE 5-34 The Disk Management snap-in, with owner access to a CSVFS disk

On another node, not the owner, shown in Figure 5-35, the same iscsi3 disk looks equally accessible, with the same CSVFS file system, but the context menu is entirely grayed out. This is because those commands for formatting, shrinking, and deleting the volume are the province of the metadata, and only the owner has access to that.

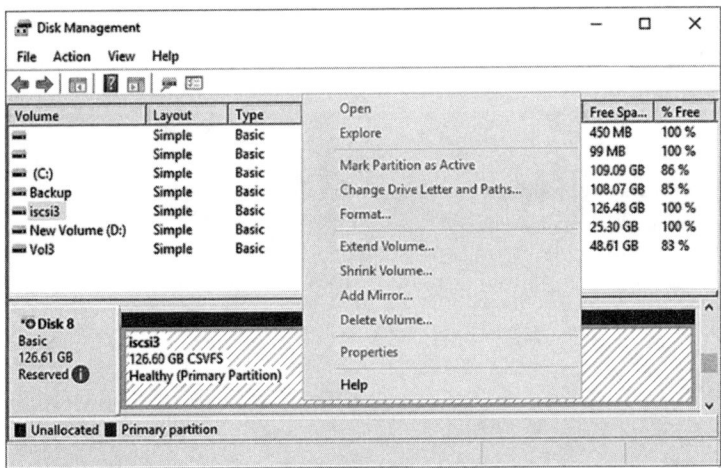

FIGURE 5-35 The Disk Management snap-in, with non-owner access to a CSVFS disk

Skill 5.2: Implement failover clustering   **CHAPTER 5**   **335**

Adding disks to CSVs

Failover Clustering in Windows Server 2016 includes support for CSVs by default. When you add a disk to a cluster, it appears in Failover Cluster Manager as Available Storage. You can then select an Available Storage disk and, in the Actions pane, click Add to Cluster Shared Volumes.

To add available storage to a CSV with PowerShell, use the Add-ClusterSharedVolume cmdlet, as in the following example:

```
add-clustersharedvolume -name "cluster disk 5"
```

Once you do this, the CSV is mounted in the C:\ClusterStorage folder on all the cluster nodes. You can also see in the Disk Management snap-in that the disk is now available on all the cluster's nodes. You can also select the CSV in Failover Cluster Manager and click Move | , Best Possible Node. Watch as ownership of the CSV changes hands in a matter of seconds. This is what makes it possible for Hyper-V Live Migrations to happen so quickly. Before CSVs, it was the dismounting and remounting of NTFS disks that was the bottleneck in the process.

Optimizing CSVs

CSVs include a cache that is designed to improve performance of read-intensive I/O operations. The cache uses an amount of system memory that you specify as a write-through cache, which can benefit clusters running the Hyper-V and Scale-Out File Server roles.

In Windows Server 2016 Failover Clustering, the cache exists by default, but the default cache size is 0, effectively disabling it. The maximum size for the cache is 80% of system memory. To enable the CSV cache, you must specify an amount of memory for it, in megabytes, using the following PowerShell command:

```
(get-cluster).blockcachesize = 512
```

 Quick check

> Which of the following storage components prevents a shared disk from being accessed by two cluster nodes simultaneously?
>
> 1. iSCSI
> 2. NTFS
> 3. CSVFS
> 4. SAS
>
> **Quick check answer**
>
> NTFS is not designed for access by two operating system instances at the same time. If two systems both modify the NTFS metadata, the file system tables can be corrupted and data lost.

Configure clusters without network names

Failover clusters rely on Active Directory Domain Services for authentication and naming services. By default, creating a cluster causes AD DS to create a computer object, called a cluster name object (CNO), to represent the cluster itself. This is the cluster's *administrative access point*. Some clustered applications also create AD DS objects representing client access points, called virtual computer objects (VCOs).

However, it is possible to create a cluster that does not use these AD DS objects, even though the cluster nodes are joined to a domain. This is called an *Active Directory-detached cluster*. Because there are no objects created in Active Directory, it is not necessary for the person creating the cluster to have the permissions needed to create objects or have the computer objects prestaged in AD DS.

In an Active Directory-detached cluster, the name of the cluster and any names used for client access points are registered in the DNS instead of Active Directory. However, the nodes still must be joined to an AD DS domain, and the cluster still uses Kerberos to authenticate cluster communications between the nodes. Authentication for the cluster name uses NTLM.

Because of these changes, some applications will not function properly when you deploy them on an Active Directory-detached cluster. Hyper-V, for example, relies on Kerberos authentication for Live Migration, so it is not a suitable candidate for this type of cluster. You also cannot use BitLocker drive encryption or Cluster-Aware Updating in self-updating mode. Microsoft SQL Server has its own internal authentication mechanism, however, which enables it to function properly on an Active Directory-detached cluster.

To create an Active Directory-detached cluster, you must use the New-Cluster PowerShell cmdlet and include the AdministrativeAccessPoint parameter, specifying a value of DNS instead of the default ActiveDirectoryAndDns value, as in the following example:

```
new-cluster cluster1 -node node1,node2 -staticaddress 10.0.0.1 -nostorage -
administrativeaccesspoint dns
```

This parameter setting causes the cmdlet to create the cluster's network name, and the network names on all clustered roles you install later, in DNS instead of Active Directory.

> **NOTE CLUSTERS WITH NO NAME**
>
> It is also possible to create a cluster with no administrative access point at all, by specifying a value of None for the AdministrativeAccessPoint parameter in the New-Cluster command. If you do this, however, you cannot use Failover Cluster Manager to administer the cluster, and the functionality of some cluster roles might be impaired.

Implement Scale-Out File Server (SoFS)

Scale-out File Server is a clustered role that is designed to provide highly available storage for applications, such as Hyper-V and SQL Server. Unlike a file server intended for general use, an SoFS creates shares that are accessible on all the cluster nodes at the same time. This is known as an active/active (or dual active) system, as opposed to an active/passive system, in which one node provides accessible shares and the others remain dormant until a failover occurs.

An SoFS ensures the continuous availability of data to applications that require that continuity. When a node goes down, due to a hardware failure, a maintenance cycle, or any other reason, the data remains available through the shares on the other nodes. Even if a node loses access to the SAN, CSV can redirect the I/O traffic over the network to another node.

> *NOTE* **CLUSTER NETWORK METRICS**
>
> A cluster assigns metric values to the available networks, based on their speeds and other characteristics, as shown by the Get-ClusterNetwork command in Figure 5-36. CSV uses the network with the lowest metric value for its redirection traffic. In some situations, it might be necessary to adjust the metrics, to ensure that the CSV redirection traffic for a SoFS uses a specific network. To modify the network metrics manually, you use a command like the following:
>
> (get-clusternetwork -name "cluster network 3").metric = 30000

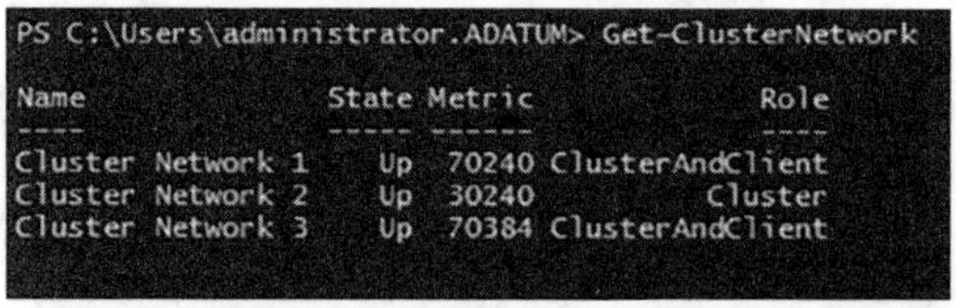

```
PS C:\Users\administrator.ADATUM> Get-ClusterNetwork

Name               State Metric   Role
----               ----- ------   ----
Cluster Network 1  Up    70240    ClusterAndClient
Cluster Network 2  Up    30240             Cluster
Cluster Network 3  Up    70384    ClusterAndClient
```

FIGURE 5-36 Results of the Get-ClusterNetwork command

SoFS also increases the efficiency of the cluster by using the combined bandwidth of all the nodes for file system I/O. To increase the available bandwidth, administrators can add more nodes to the cluster. Finally, SoFS automatically rebalances connections, to ensure that each client is directed to the node with the best access to the requested data.

The prerequisites for creating a Scale-out File Server are essentially the same as those for Failover Clustering. The hardware configuration of the cluster nodes should be as nearly identical as possible, and all the nodes should have access to shared storage using iSCSI, SAS, Fibre Channel, or a similar technology. As SoFS is a clustered role, you must install the Failover Clustering feature on all your nodes and create the cluster before you can install SoFS. You also must allocate your available storage as Cluster Shared Volumes, as these are required for a Scale-out File Server.

Once the cluster is in place and operational, you install SoFS using the following procedure.

1. Open Failover Cluster Manager and select the Roles page.
2. Click Configure Role to launch the High Availability Wizard.
3. On the File Server Type page, select the Scale-Out File Server for Application Data option, as shown in Figure 5-37.

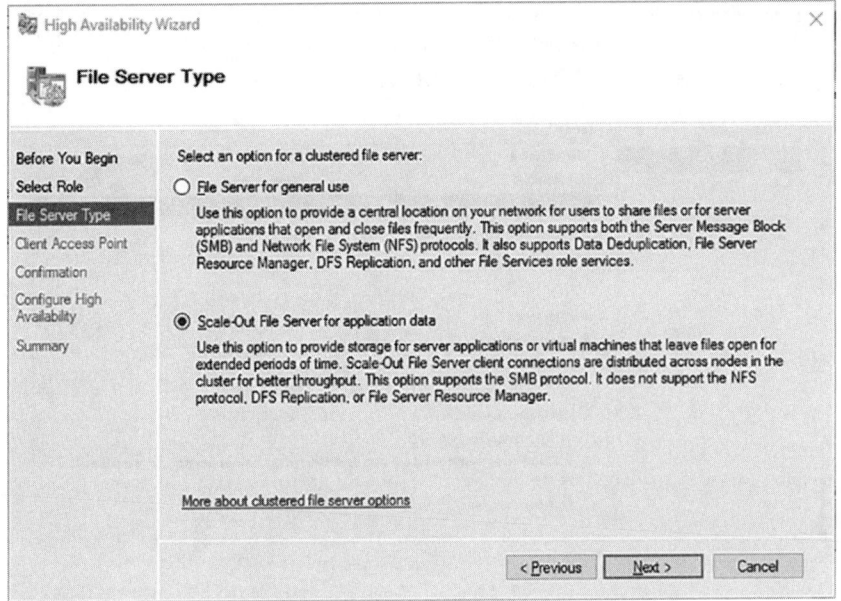

FIGURE 5-37 The File Server Type page in the High Availability Wizard

4. On the Client Access Point page, specify a name that clients will use to access the role. The wizard will create an AD DS computer object using this name.
5. Click Finish. The Scale-out File Server appears on the Roles page.

> **NOTE USING POWERSHELL**
>
> To install the Scale-out File Server role with Windows PowerShell, you run the Add-ClusterScaleOutFileServer cmdlet without parameters.

With the Scale-out File Server role installed, you can proceed to create a file share, using the following procedure.

1. In Failover Cluster Manager, on the Roles page, select the Scale-out File Server role you just created and, in the Actions pane, select Add File Share to launch the New Share Wizard.
2. On the Select the Profile for this Share page, select SMB Share - Applications
3. Note that despite this wizard's similarity to the New Share Wizard in Server Manager, you must use Failover Cluster Manager or the New-SmbShare cmdlet to create SoFS file shares.
4. On the Select the Server and Path for this Share page, select the Scale-out File Server role you created, as shown in Figure 5-38.

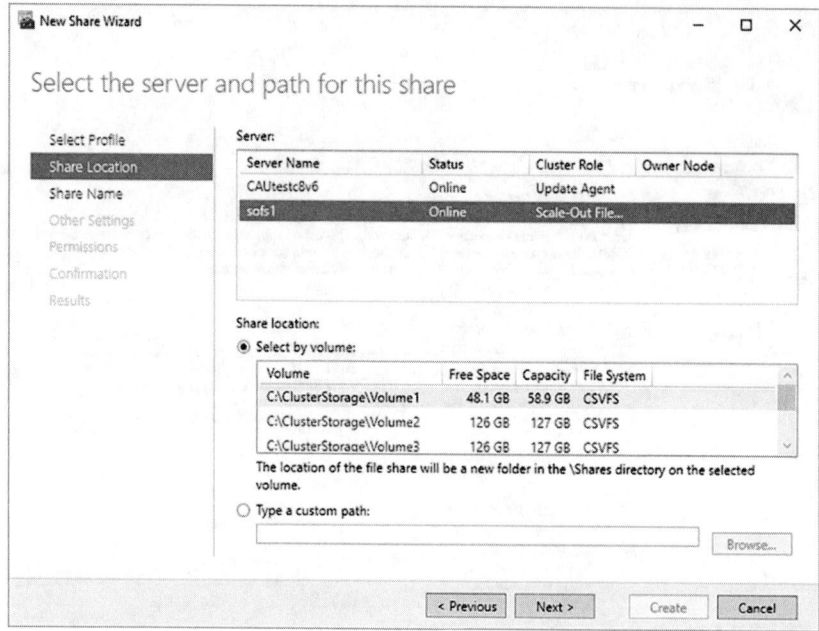

FIGURE 5-38 The Select the Server and Path for this Share page of the new Share Wizard

5. In the Share Location box, select a Cluster Shared Volume.
6. On the Specify Share Name page, type a name and, optionally, a description for the share.
7. On the Configure Share Settings page, make sure that the Enable Continuous Availability checkbox is selected, and that the Enable Access-based Enumeration checkbox is cleared.
8. On the Specify Permissions to Control Access page, click Customize Permissions and make sure that the AD DS computer objects for the cluster and the nodes using the SoFS share all have the Full Control permission.
9. Click Create.

To create an SoFS share with PowerShell, you use the New-SmbShare cmdlet to create the share, as in the following example. The Set-SmbPathAcl cmdlet configures the file system permissions of the folder to match those of the share.

```
new-smbshare -name share1 -path c:\clusterstorsge\volume1 -fullaccess adatum\cluster1,
adatum\node1, adatum\node2
-continuouslyavailable set-smbpathacl -sharename share1
```

Determine different scenarios for the use of SoFS vs. clustered file server

The File Server Type page in the High Availability Wizard provides a choice between the standard File Server cluster role, intended for general use, and the Scale-out File Server role, which is intended for use by clustered applications. In some cases, it might not be clear which one is the better choice for a particular workload.

SoFS shares are located on Cluster Shared Volumes, and the underlying nature of CSVs largely determines what roles and applications are best suited to a Scale-out File Server. SoFS makes its shares available on all the cluster's nodes, meaning that any node can process disk read and write requests. However, the underlying CSVFS file system still requires the disk coordinator (that is, the node that owns the disk) to perform all metadata-related activities. This means that all requests to open, close, create, and rename files on an SoFS share, no matter which node receives them, must be redirected to the coordinator node.

This makes it easier to understand why the SoFS role is specifically recommended for use on Hyper-V and SQL Server clusters. Both of those applications routinely open large files—VHDs and databases—and leave them open for long periods of time. Metadata requests are infrequent in this type of application, so the burden on the disk's coordinator node is minimized.

For many other applications, however, including the general file server activities performed by typical users and administrators, the burden on the disk coordinator node can become a bottleneck. This is because there are many more requests that require access to the file system metadata, including common file server administrator activities, such as modifying NTFS permissions and other file system attributes.

Continuous availability of SoFS shares can also affect the overall performance of a file server. To ensure the integrity of the data, write requests are sent straight to the disk, rather than being cached on the node. This way, if a node fails, there is less chance of data being lost due to cache failure.

As a result, you must consider the nature of your cluster's workload before deciding which option to select on the File Server Type page. The greater the proportion of file management requests the application generates, the less likely that it is a suitable candidate for a Scale-out File Server.

Determine usage scenarios for implementing guest clustering

A guest failover cluster is a cluster that consists solely of virtual machines running on a single Hyper-V host server. You can create two or more identical VMs, install the Failover Clustering feature on all of them, and create a cluster out of them, just as if they were physical computers. In fact, you are less likely to have cluster validation issues with a guest cluster, because the (virtual) hardware configuration of each node is identical. For the shared storage that a guest cluster needs, you can use any of the standard storage area networking technologies, including Fibre Channel, SAS, or iSCSI, as pass-through disks.

Building a guest cluster is a great way to learn about Failover Clustering and a useful tool for evaluating clustered applications, without having to invest in a lot of hardware. For education and testing purposes, you can create a guest cluster with a virtualized SAN by using the iSCSI target capability in Windows Server 2016 to mount a virtual hard disk, which your VMs can access using the iSCSI initiator. Performance levels probably won't be suitable for production applications, but the cluster will function.

In addition, with the nested virtualization capabilities built into Windows Server 2016, you can even create a guest cluster by installing Hyper-V on a single virtual machine and clustering nested VMs.

Guest clusters have practical functions as well, including the following:

- **Node Monitoring**   Clusters can monitor resources, such as the storage subsystem, the network connectivity, and the clustered application itself, and automatically take action when a problem occurs, by migrating or failing over the role to another node.
- **Application Migration**   By deploying an application as a role on a guest cluster, you can maintain availability by migrating the application to different nodes in the cluster. For example, rather than deploying an application on a single network server, you can configure the server as a Hyper-V host and create a cluster that runs the application. That way, if a VM fails or requires maintenance, the application can fail over to another node.
- **Host Availability**   You can create a guest cluster from virtual machines located on different Hyper-V hosts. If a host should experience a failure, the nodes running on other hosts will detect the absence of its VMs and bring any clustered applications that were running there online.
- **VM Migration**   If you have multiple Hyper-V hosts available, you can migrate virtual machines between hosts as needed, to perform maintenance tasks that require you to take a host offline temporarily.
- **Nested Clustering**   It is possible to create a "guest cluster within a cluster," by joining two or more physical servers into a Hyper-V cluster, and then guest clustering virtual machines running on the Hyper-V host nodes. This will enable the system to automatically react to the failure of a Hyper-V host, by migrating its virtual machines to the other hosts; or the failure of a VM, by migrating its clustered applications.

Implement a clustered Storage Spaces solution using shared SAS storage enclosures

Storage Spaces is the Windows Server 2016 tool that enables you to add the data storage provided by multiple physical disks to a storage pool. You can then use the storage in the pool to create virtual disks of any size, irrespective of the boundaries between the physical disks. By combining Storage Spaces with Failover Clustering, you can create a solution that highly available and resistant to both hard drive and server failures. This solution is commonly known as Clustered Storage Spaces.

A Clustered Storage Spaces solution begins with one or more Serial-Attached SCSI (SAS) disk arrays, simple just-a-bunch-of-disks (JBOD) enclosures that do not provide additional functions, such as Redundant Array of Independent Disks (RAID). In a Storage Spaces deployment, data fault tolerance is provided in the software; you don't want to duplicate those functions in the hardware. If the disk arrays include those functions, you must disable them to be able to use the disks with Storage Spaces.

Storage Spaces provides data resiliency in the form of data mirroring, in which two or three copies of all files are written to different disks; or parity, a bit-level technique that provides the ability to recover from a disk failure by reconstructing the lost data using parity bits.

The second element of the solution is the failover cluster, typically a group of two to four servers that are connected to the disk enclosures using redundant hardware. To create a truly reliable solution for enterprise productivity, there should be hardware redundancy at all levels, including multiple host bus adapters in each server, redundant power supplies in the disk enclosures, and even redundant disk enclosures.

With the hardware in place, the rest of the solution consists of a storage pool that provides redundant data storage, the failover cluster that provides redundant servers, Cluster Shared Volumes, which provide a unified namespace across the cluster, and highly available file shares, which is how users access the data. The entire solution is shown in Figure 5-39.

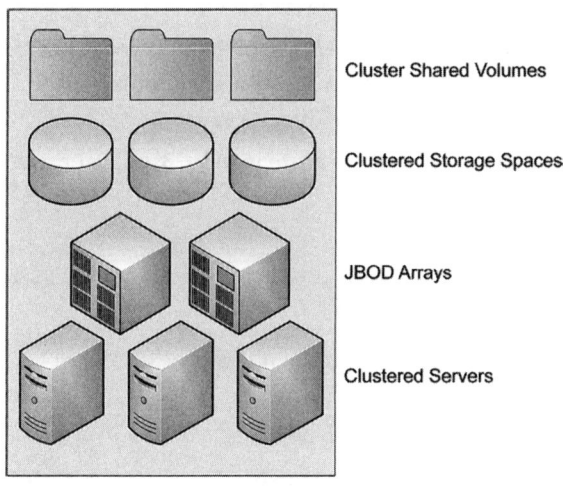

FIGURE 5-39 Diagram of a Cluster Shared Volume installation

Once the hardware components are in place and you have installed Windows Server 2016 on all the servers, you must confirm that the storage is accessible from all of the servers. Then, you can proceed to build a Clustered Storage Spaces solution in two ways:

- **Storage Pool First** If you have an existing storage pool, or if you are building a cluster from scratch, you can create the storage pool using Server Manager or the New-StoragePool cmdlet before you create the cluster. Once you have created the cluster, the storage pool will be available to it.
- **Failover Cluster First** If you have an existing cluster, you can create the storage pool in Failover Cluster Manager.

To create Clustered Storage Spaces in an existing cluster with Failover Cluster Manager, use the following procedure.

1. In Failover Cluster Manager, select Storage | Pools, to display the Pools page.
2. Click Add Storage Pool to launch the New Storage Pool Wizard.
3. On the Specify a Storage Pool Name and Subsystem page, specify a name for the pool and select the primordial pool containing the disks you want to add.
4. On the Select Physical Disks for the Storage Pool page, select the checkboxes for the disks you want to add to the pool. To create a clustered storage pool, you must select a minimum of three disks; for three-way mirroring, you must select a minimum of five disks.
5. Click Create.
6. On the View Results page, select the Create a Virtual Disk When This Wizard Closes checkbox and click Close. The New Virtual Disk Wizard appears.
7. On the Select the Storage Pool page, select the pool you just created.
8. On the Specify the Virtual Disk Name page, type a name for the disk.
9. On the Select the Storage Layout page, select Simple, Mirror, or Parity. If you select Mirror, and there are five disks in the pool, a Configure The Resiliency Settings page appears, prompting you to choose Two-Way Mirror or Three-Way Mirror.
10. On the Specify The Size Of The Virtual Disk page, type a size in MB, GB, or TB, or select the Maximum Size checkbox.
11. Click Create.
12. On the View Results page, select the Create A Volume When This Wizard Closes checkbox and click Close. The New Volume Wizard appears.
13. On the Select The Server And Disk page, select your cluster and the virtual disk you just created.
14. On the Specify The Size Of The Volume page, type a volume size.
15. On the Assign To A Drive Letter Or Folder page, select a drive letter or a folder where you want to mount the volume.
16. On the Select File System Settings page, select the NTFS or ReFS file system, specify an Allocation Unit Size, and type a volume label.
17. Click Create. Then click Close.

The resilient storage is now available to the cluster. You can create CSVs from it to create highly available shares using a single unified name space.

Implement Storage Replica

Storage Replica is a Windows Server 2016 feature that enables you to replicate volumes, synchronously or asynchronously, for disaster preparedness and recovery purposes. You can perform replications between storage devices located in the same computer, in the same datacenter, or in distant cities.

Using Storage Replica, you can create a stretch cluster, which is a cluster that is split between two or more sites, without shared storage connecting the sites. For example, you might have a four-node cluster with one data set, but two of the nodes are in the New York branch office and two are in the San Francisco headquarters. The idea is that the nodes in the New York site function as a failover backup, should the San Francisco office suffer a disaster.

Each site has shared storage for its two nodes, but they do not have access to the storage at the opposite sites. This is called asymmetric storage. However, for the two sites to function as a true failover cluster, they must have the same data. Storage Replica can replicate the data between the two sites, either synchronously or asynchronously.

> **NEED MORE REVIEW?** **USING STORAGE REPLICA**
>
> For more information on implementing Storage Replica in a cluster environment, see Chapter 2.

Implement cloud witness

A cloud witness is a new type of quorum witness for a failover cluster. Instead of storing the witness on a disk or a file share, it is stored in the cloud, in a Windows Azure Storage Account. The function of a cloud witness is to keep a cluster running, even when half of its nodes are down or in a split-brain state.

When a cluster is split evenly between two sites, previous versions of Failover Clustering force you to store the witness at one site or the other, effectively declaring one the primary site and one the secondary. The only other option is to create a third site at another location, with a server just to store the witness, which is an expensive proposition.

The reason for this is to enable either half of the cluster to continue running if the other half suffers a power failure or other disaster. If the witness is stored at one of the sites, as shown in Figure 5-40, then that site has most the quorum votes.

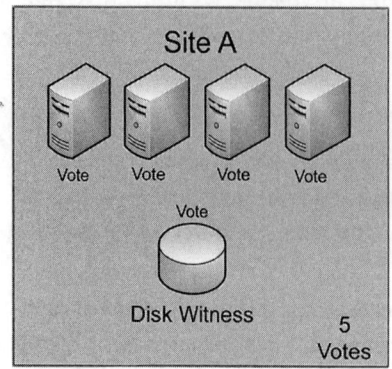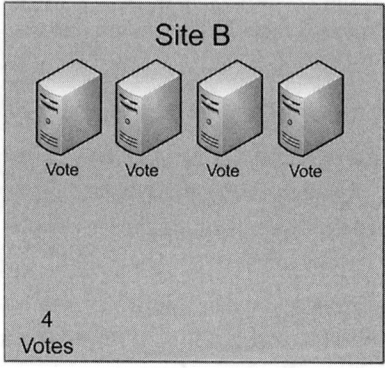

FIGURE 5-40 Diagram of a split cluster with a disk witness

If the minority site went down, the cluster at the majority site continues to run, because it has quorum. However, if the majority site goes down, the minority site has to stop as well, because it did not have quorum. Now, in Windows Server 2016 Failover Clustering, if the witness is stored in the cloud, as shown in Figure 5-41.If the surviving cluster can connect to the Internet, to obtain the witness vote, either one of the cluster halves can continue to run if the other fails. Microsoft is recommending the use of a cloud witness for any failover cluster in which all the nodes have access to the Internet.

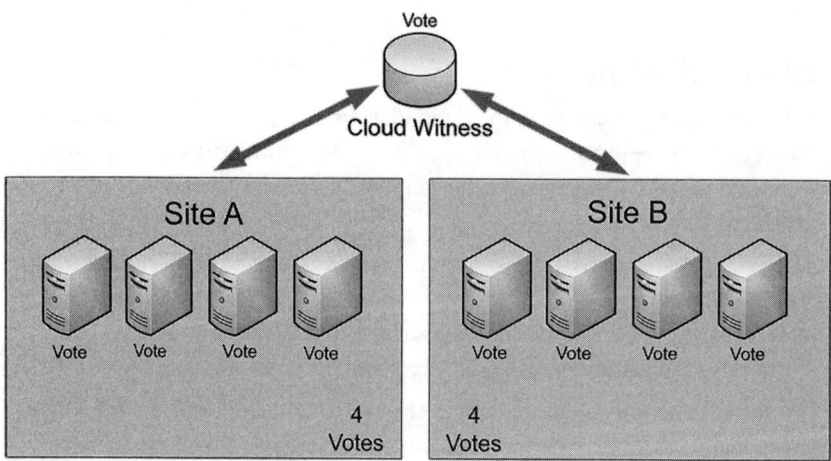

FIGURE 5-41 Diagram of a split cluster with a cloud witness

A cloud witness is stored in the cloud using a Microsoft Azure Storage Account, which is an inexpensive way to store small amounts of data in the cloud, without having to maintain a virtual server solely for that purpose. The witness is stored as a binary large object (called a blob).

To create a cloud witness, you must first create a Storage Account in Microsoft Azure, and then configure the cloud witness for the cluster to use that account. To create the storage account, use the following procedure.

1. In the Azure portal, select New | Storage | Storage Account, as shown in Figure 5-42.

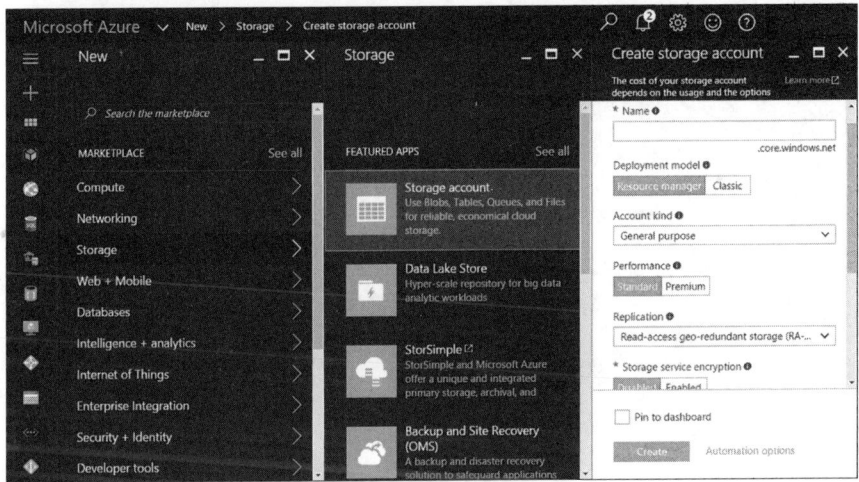

FIGURE 5-42 Creating a Storage Account in the Azure portal

2. In the Name field, type a name for the account.
3. In the Account Kind drop-down list, select Blob Storage.
4. In the Replication drop-down list, select Locally Redundant Storage (LRS).
5. Click Create.
6. When the Storage Account is created, select it on the Azure dashboard and click the keys icon.
7. Note the following information that appears on the page, which you will need to configure the witness:
   - Storage account name
   - Key
   - Blob service endpoint

With this information in hand, you can proceed to configure your cluster with a cloud witness, using the following procedure.

1. In Failover Cluster Manager, on the main page for your cluster, select More Actions | Configure Cluster Quorum Settings, to launch the Configure Cluster Quorum Wizard.
2. On the Select Quorum Configuration Option pane, select the Select the Quorum Witness option.
3. On the Select Quorum Witness page, select Configure a Cloud Witness.

Skill 5.2: Implement failover clustering **CHAPTER 5** **347**

4. On the Configure Cloud Witness page, shown in Figure 5-43, type in the information you gathered from the Azure portal.

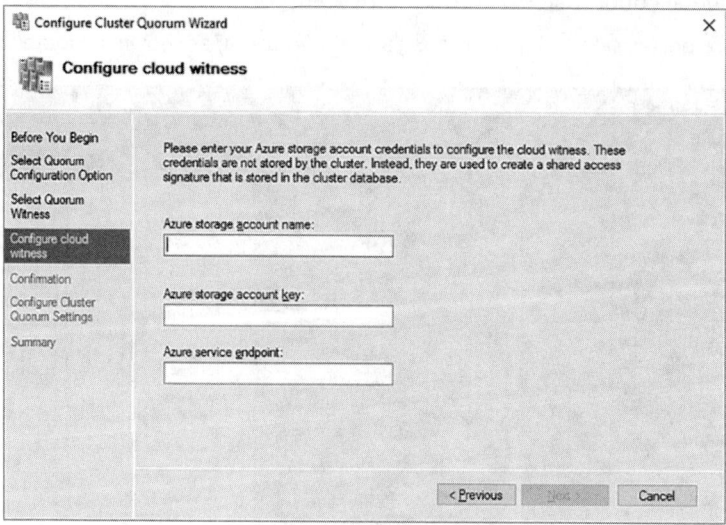

FIGURE 5-43 The Configure Cloud Witness page of the Configure Cluster Quorum Wizard

5. Click Finish.

To configure a cloud witness with PowerShell, you use a command like the following:

```
set-clusterquorum -cloudwitness -accountname clusterstorage1 -accesskey oyhmhpi1x9q5htonrcxhcnpz0xzw2zgf49lgdwmexn5lr7xcdrenuxtlxujdpfwcqcknzea8xx12ye25g8jdxw==
```

Implement VM resiliency

The entire idea behind clustering is to provide services that can continue functioning despite catastrophic events. However, in today's climate, localized transient failures occur more frequently than major catastrophes. For this reason, the Windows Server 2016 Failover Clustering release includes enhancements that increase the resiliency of individual virtual machines in several ways.

Cluster nodes communicate constantly— at least, they are supposed to communicate constantly. However, it is a common occurrence for a single VM to lose contact with the cluster temporarily. There are many possible causes for this: for example, the Cluster Service on a VM might shut down, due to a memory or software problem; network communication might be disrupted, due to a driver or IP addressing issue; or the network cable might be damaged or simply unplugged.

To help administrators address issues like these, Windows Server 2016 has introduced new VM states, which appear in Failover Cluster Manager as the Status of a role or node. These states include the following:

- **Unmonitored** Indicates that the VM owning a role is not being monitored by the Cluster Service.
- **Isolated** Indicates that the node is not currently in active member of the cluster, but is still in possession of a role. During a transient failure, a VM is first placed in the Isolated state, and then passes to the Unmonitored state when it is removed from the active cluster.
- **Quarantine** Indicates a node that has been drained of its roles and removed from the cluster for a specified length of time after having left and reentered the cluster three times in the previous hour.

You can also configure the way the cluster uses these states, using the following settings in Windows PowerShell:

- **ResiliencyLevel** A value of 1 enables the use of the Isolated state only if the node supplies a known reason for disconnecting from the cluster. Otherwise, the node fails immediately. A value of 2 (which is the default) enables the free use of the Isolated state and allows the node time to recover.

    ```
    (get-cluster).resiliencylevel = 2
    ```

- **ResiliencyDefaultPeriod** Specifies how long the nodes in the entire cluster are permitted to remain in the Isolated state (in seconds). The default value is 240.

    ```
    (get-cluster).resiliencydefaultperiod = 240
    ```

- **ResiliencyPeriod** Specifies how long the nodes in a particular group are permitted to remain in the Isolated state (in seconds). A value of -1 causes the group to revert to the ResiliencyDefaultPeriod setting. The default value is 240.

    ```
    (get-clustergroup "group1").resiliencyperiod = 240
    ```

- **QuarantineThreshold** Specifies the number of failures that a node can experience in a one hour period before being placed in a Quarantine state. The default value is 3.

    ```
    (get-cluster).quarantinethreshold = 3
    ```

- **QuarantineDuration** Specifies the length of time (in seconds) that a node remains in quarantine. The default value is 7200.

    ```
    (get-cluster).quarantineduration = 7200
    ```

Implement shared VHDX as a storage solution for guest clusters

Creating a guest cluster on an existing failover cluster can complicate the issue of shared storage. However, it is possible to use the shared storage provided by a physical cluster to create a shared VHDX file for the guest cluster.

In this scenario, you have two or more physical Hyper-V servers, functioning as nodes in a failover cluster. These physical servers are connected to shared storage hardware, using iSCSI, SAS, or Fibre Channel, as shown in Figure 5-44. The shared storage is configured as cluster shared volumes or SMB 3.0 shares.

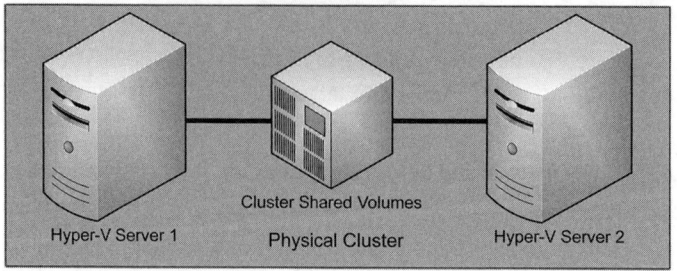

FIGURE 5-44 Diagram of a physical cluster with shared storage

To create the guest cluster, each of the Hyper-V servers hosts a virtual machine. To create the shared storage needed by the guest cluster, you can create a shared VHDX file on the physical cluster's CSVs, as shown in Figure 5-45.

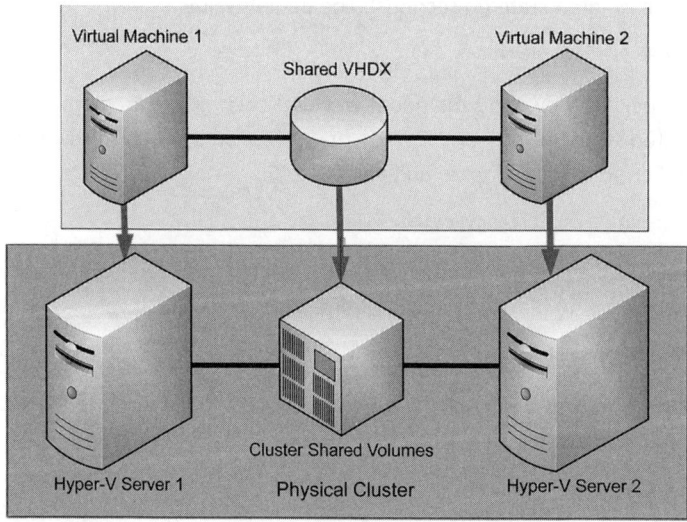

FIGURE 5-45 Diagram of a guest cluster with a shared VHDX file

Windows Server 2016 supports two types of shared virtual hard disk files, as follows:

- **VHDX** Introduced in Windows Server 2012 R2, VHDX files created on a shared storage infrastructure can be shared between virtual machines in a guest cluster. Shared

VHDX files are still supported in Windows Server 2016, to provide backward compatibility for existing clusters, but Microsoft recommends creating VHD Sets for new files.

- **VHD Set**   Introduced in Windows Server 2016, a VHD Set consists of a 260 KB VHDS file, which contains metadata, and an AVHDX file, which contains the actual data. VHD Sets provide online resizing capabilities and support for host-based backups that VHDX files lack.

> *NOTE* **CONVERTING VHD FORMATS**
>
> You can convert a VHDX file to the new VHD Set format by using the Convert-VHD cmdlet in Windows PowerShell. The cmdlet works by creating a new file of the appropriate format and copying the data into it from the original file. The format of the destination is specified by the filename extension, which for a VHD Set is VHDS. A typical command appears as follows:
>
> ```
> convert-vhd -path disk.vhdx -destinationpath disk.vhds
> ```

To create a new shared VHDX or VHD Set file for a guest cluster, you open the Settings dialog box in Failover Cluster Manager, select the SCSI Controller, select Shared Drive, and click Add. You can then launch and run the New Virtual Hard Disk Wizard, just as you would on a non-clustered Hyper-V server. The only difference is a Choose Disk Format page, shown in Figure 5-46, on which you specify whether to create a VHDX or VHD Set file.

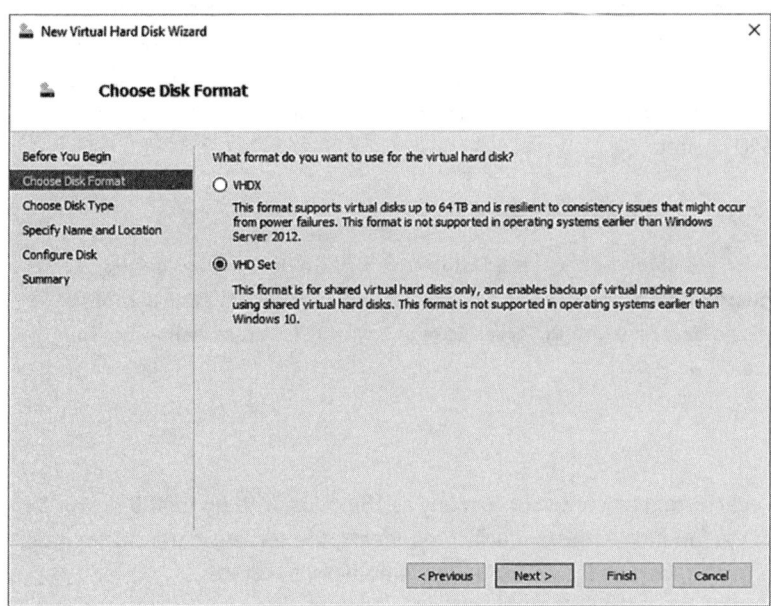

FIGURE 5-46 The Choose Disk Format page of the Add Virtual Hard Disk Wizard

Skill 5.3: Implement Storage Spaces Direct

Storage Spaces Direct (S2D) is the next stage in the evolution of the software-defined storage technology that first appeared in servers as Storage Spaces in Windows Server 2012. Storage Spaces makes it possible to create pools containing the space from multiple physical disk drives, and then create virtual disks out of the pooled storage, irrespective of the physical disk boundaries. Storage Spaces Direct provides the same type of services in a clustered environment, making it possible to create shared storage pools using the standard local SAS, SATA or NVMe drives inside the cluster nodes. For the first time, it is not necessary to purchase expensive external storage arrays to deploy a failover cluster.

> **This section covers how to:**
> - Determine scenario requirements for implementing Storage Spaces Direct
> - Enable Storage Spaces direct using Windows PowerShell
> - Implement a disaggregated Storage Spaces Direct scenario in a cluster
> - Implement a hyper-converged Storage Spaces Direct scenario in a cluster

Determine scenario requirements for implementing Storage Spaces Direct

Storage Spaces Direct provides many of the same benefits as Storage Spaces, such as data redundancy and tiered storage, and it does so in software, using standard, off-the-shelf disk drives and common networking components. However, this is not to say that S2D has no special requirements. The following sections explain some of the factors you must consider before deploying a S2D cluster.

> **NOTE STORAGE SPACES DIRECT AVAILABILITY**
>
> Storage Spaces Direct is included only in the Datacenter edition of Windows Server 2016, not the Standard edition. You can use S2D on a Datacenter server using any of the installation options, however, including Server Core and Nano Server, as well as the full Desktop Experience.

Servers

A Storage Spaces Direct cluster can consist of as many as 16 nodes, with up to 400 drives. Despite the ability of S2D to function with standard components, the servers in the cluster must be able to support large numbers of drives and multiple network interfaces.

Disk drives

The recommended drive configuration for a node in an S2D cluster is a minimum of six drives, with at least two solid state drives (SSDs) and at least four hard disk drives (HDDs). Whatever the form factor of the drive enclosure, internal or external, there must not be any RAID or other intelligence that cannot be disabled. S2D provides fault tolerance and high performance; competing hardware will only have a negative effect on overall functionality of the cluster.

For S2D to detect them and use them, the disks must be initialized (typically using GPT), but they must not be partitioned. Disks with partitions or volumes on them will not be considered as eligible for use by Storage Spaces Direct.

Networking

The key to Storage Spaces Direct is the *software storage bus*, a logical network conduit that connects the local data drives in all of the cluster nodes. This bus theoretically falls between the servers and the disk drives inside them, as shown in Figure 5-47.

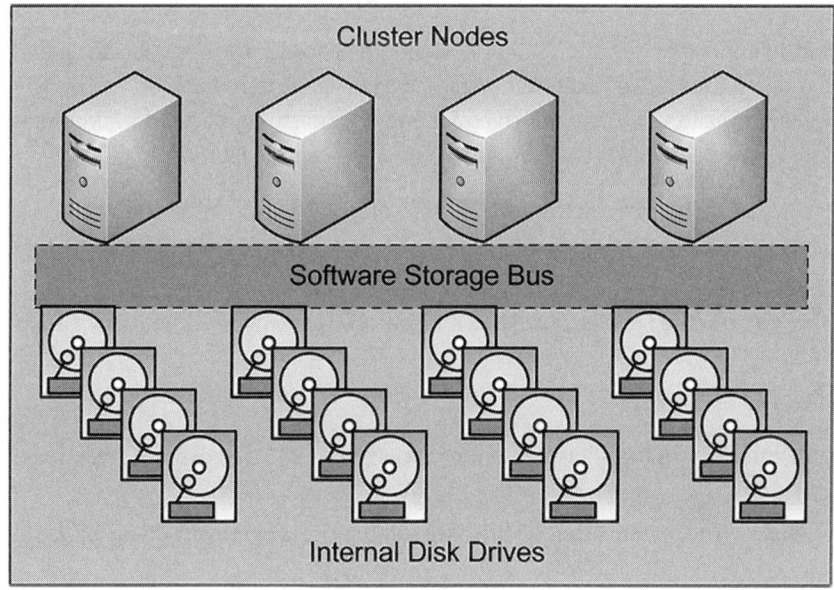

FIGURE 5-47 The software storage bus

Because S2D creates a pool out of the internal storage in different computers, all storage traffic is carried over standard Ethernet networks using SMB3 and RDMA. There is no traditional storage network fabric, such as SAS or Fibre Channel, eliminating distance limitations and the need for different types of cabling. However, traffic management is therefore a critical part of any production S2D cluster deployment.

The physical realization of the logical software storage bus must transfer data as though the disks in the various cluster node is a single entity. In addition, the networks must carry the redundant data generated by the mirroring and parity arrangements on virtual disks created from the pool. Thus, efficient S2D performance requires intra-node Ethernet communications that provide both high bandwidth and low latency.

At the physical layer, Microsoft recommends the use of at least two 10 Gbps Ethernet adapters per node, preferably adapters that use RDMA, so that they can offload some of the processor burden from the servers.

S2D uses Server Message Block version 3 (SMB3) for communications between cluster nodes, employing the protocol's advanced features, such as SMB Direct and SMB Multichannel, whenever possible.

Enable Storage Spaces Direct using Windows PowerShell

Most of the deployment process for a cluster using Storage Spaces Direct is nearly the same as that for any other cluster. You install Windows Server 2016 on the cluster nodes, update them identically, add the Failover Clustering feature and the Hyper-V node, and create the cluster.

Here you find an important deviation from the standard procedure. While you can create the cluster using the graphical Create Cluster Wizard in Failover Cluster Manager, you must prevent the system from automatically searching for and adding storage. Therefore, you must create the cluster in Windows PowerShell, using a command like the following:

```
new-cluster -name cluster1 -node server1,server2,server3,server4 -nostorage
```

The NoStorage parameter is important here, and the lack of storage will generate an error during the creation of the cluster. The storage will be added when you enable Storage Spaces Direct. To do this, you run the Enable-ClusterStorageSpacesDirect cmdlet without any parameters, as follows:

```
enable-clusterstoragespacesdirect
```

This one cmdlet performs several tasks that are crucial to the S2D deployment, including the following:

- **Locates Disks** The system scans all the nodes in the cluster for local, unpartitioned disks.
- **Creates Caches** The system classifies the disks in each node by their respective bus and media types and establishes bindings between them to create partnerships in each server that use the faster disks for read and write caching.
- **Creates a Pool** The system adds all of the available disks in all of the nodes into a single cluster-wide storage pool.

Once the storage pool is created, you can proceed to create virtual disks on it (just as you do in Storage Spaces in Server Manager on a standalone server). In Failover Cluster Manager, you select the storage pool, as shown in Figure 5-48, and launch the New Virtual Disk Wizard (Storage Spaces Direct). In the wizard, you specify a size, and it creates a disk using the default two-way mirror resiliency setting.

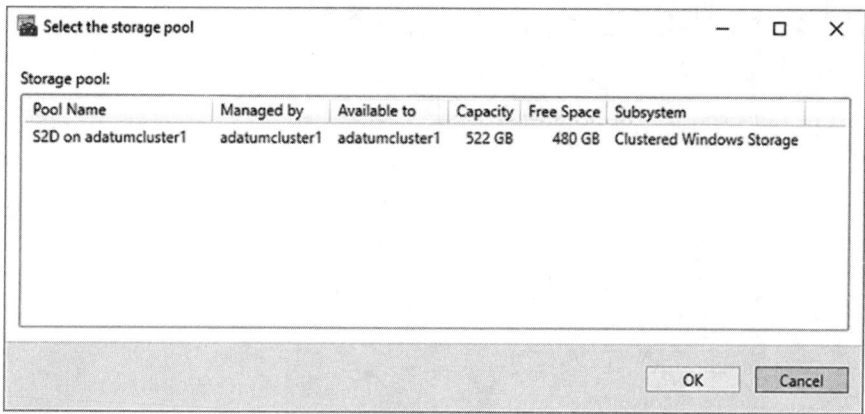

FIGURE 5-48 The Select the Storage Pool dialog box

However, S2D virtual disks can support simple, mirror, and parity resiliency types, as well as customized storage tiers. For more flexibility in creating virtual disks, you can use the New-Volume cmdlet in Windows PowerShell. This cmdlet can perform, in one step, tasks that at one time required several separate operations, including creating, partitioning, and formatting the virtual disk, converting it to the CSVFS file system, and adding it to the cluster.

For example, to create a virtual disk that uses parity resiliency and two tiers, with the default friendly names of Performance for SSDs and Capacity for HDDS, you can use a command like the following:

```
new-volume -storagepool "s2d*" -friendlyname vdisk1 -filesystem csvfs_refs
-resiliencysettingname parity -storagetiersfriendlynames performance, capacity
-storagetiersizes 10gb, 100gb
```

Once you have created the virtual disks, you can add them to cluster shared volumes, to make them accessible in every node.

Implement a disaggregated Storage Spaces Direct scenario in a cluster

The designated application for Storage Spaces Direct, as defined in Microsoft's two deployment scenarios, is to support a Hyper-V cluster. In the first scenario, called a disaggregated or converged deployment, there are two distinct clusters. The first is a Scale-out File Server cluster that uses Storage Spaces Direct to provide the storage for the second, a Hyper-V cluster hosting virtual machines, as shown in Figure 5-49.

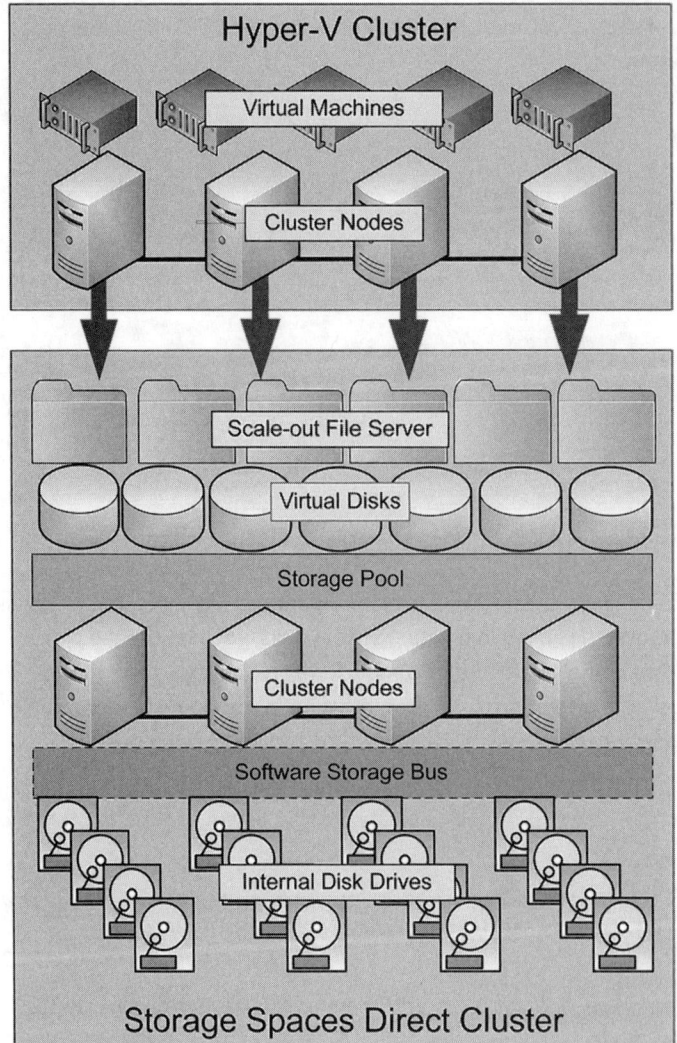

FIGURE 5-49 A disaggregated Storage Spaces Direct deployment

In this scenario, the function of the S2D cluster is to provide the storage that the Hyper-V cluster needs for its virtual machines. As such, S2D is essentially a replacement for a SAN. Because it requires two separate clusters, this model requires more servers and is, therefore, more expensive to implement. However, the advantage to this type of deployment is that the S2D cluster and the Hyper-V cluster can scale independently.

Storage Spaces Direct creates a highly scalable environment in which you can add drives to the nodes or add nodes to the cluster. Either way, S2D will assimilate any new storage detected into the pool. In a disaggregated deployment, you can add storage to the S2D cluster without affecting the Hyper-V cluster. In the same way, you can add nodes to the Hyper-V cluster without affecting the storage infrastructure.

To implement the disaggregated scenario, you proceed as described earlier to create a cluster, enable S2D, create virtual disks, and add them to CSVs. Then you add the Scale-out File Server role, to complete the configuration of the storage cluster. The second cluster is a standard Hyper-V cluster that uses the shares provided by the SoFS cluster to store its virtual machines.

Implement a hyper-converged Storage Spaces Direct scenario in a cluster

The second Storage Spaces Direct scenarios is called hyper-converged because it combines Storage Services Direct with Hyper-V in a single cluster, as shown in Figure 5-50. There is less hardware involved in this solution, and it certainly generates less network traffic; it is also far less expensive and requires less maintenance. There is no need to configure file server permissions or monitor two clusters.

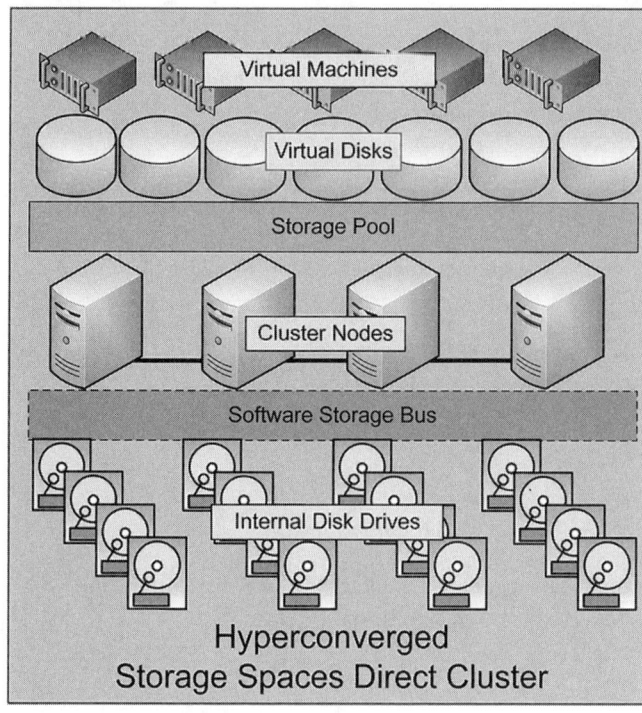

FIGURE 5-50 A hyper-converged Storage Spaces Direct deployment

EXAM TIP

With Windows Server 2016, it is possible to create a hyper-converged S2D cluster on a single Hyper-V server, for testing and educational purposes. After installing Failover Clustering and Hyper-V, you can create two or more virtual machines with several VHDX files on each, cluster them, and enable Storage Spaces Direct. Then, after exposing the host server's virtualization extensions, you can install Hyper-V on the VMs, created nested VMs, and cluster those. It won't be fast, and the storm of disk requests handled by the host server's physical disks will be chaotic if you could see them, but it does work.

The drawback of this scenario is that you can't scale the SoFS and Hyper-V services independently. If you want to add a server to provide more storage to the pool, you must add a node to the Hyper-V cluster as well.

The deployment of a hyper-converged Storage Spaces Direct cluster is not much different from that of a standard Hyper-V cluster, except that you must enable S2D after you create the cluster. One of the positive aspects of S2D is that it leverages skills administrators probably already know. If you've worked with Windows failover clusters before, there should not be a great deal that is new to you in a S2D deployment. In fact, when compared to setting up a SAN, Storage Spaces Direct is much easier.

NEED MORE REVIEW?

For a detailed procedure outlining a hyper-converged Storage Spaces Direct cluster deployment, see *https://technet.microsoft.com/en-us/windows-server-docs/storage/storage-spaces/hyper-converged-solution-using-storage-spaces-direct*.

 Quick check

Which of the following shared storage solutions enables clusters to utilize the local disks inside of a computer?

1. Fibre Channel
2. Cluster Shared Volumes
3. Serial Attached SCSI
4. Storage Spaces Direct

Quick check answer

Storage Spaces Direct (#4) can create a pool consisting of the local disk storage in all of the cluster nodes combined and shared with the entire cluster.

Skill 5.4: Manage failover clustering

Once you have installed and configured a failover cluster, there are ongoing maintenance and management tasks to perform, using tools such as Failover Cluster Manager and Windows PowerShell cmdlets in the FailoverClusters module.

> **This section covers how to:**
> - Configure role-specific settings, including continuously available shares
> - Configure VM monitoring
> - Configure failover and preference setting
> - Implement stretch and site-aware failover clusters
> - Enable and configure node fairness

Configure role-specific settings, including continuously available shares

Every cluster role you install in Failover Cluster Manager or by using a PowerShell cmdlet has its own settings that are specific to the role's function. On the Roles page in Failover Cluster Manager, when you select one of your roles, a section for it appears in the Actions pane, as shown in Figure 5-51. Some of the actions in the pane are role-specific, and some are generic actions that appear in every role pane.

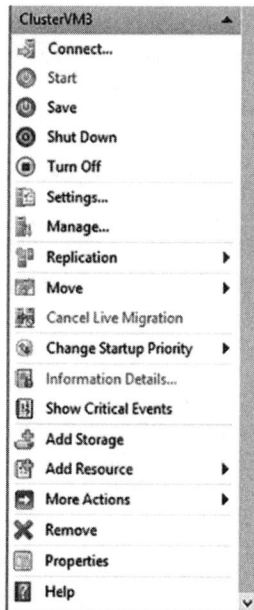

FIGURE 5-51 The Actions list for the Virtual Machine cluster roll

Skill 5.4: Manage failover clustering   CHAPTER 5   **359**

Virtual Machine Role Settings

In this example, for the Virtual Machine role, there are actions like those in Hyper-V Manager, which enable you to start, stop, and connect to the VM, as well as open its Settings dialog box. The Move menu enables you to perform live migrations, quick migrations, and migrate virtual machine storage, using the interface shown in Figure 5-52.

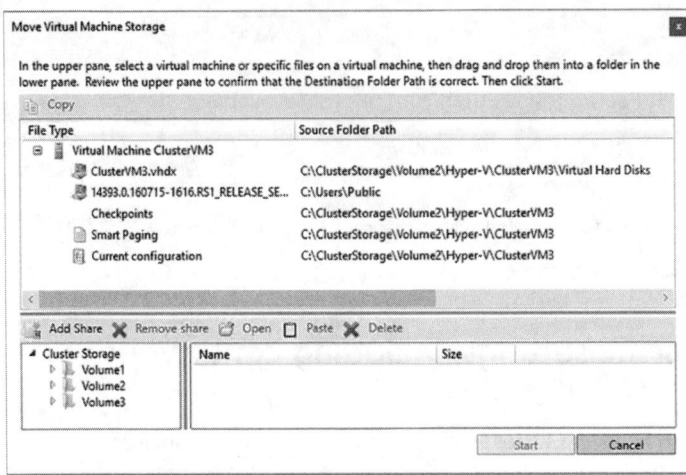

FIGURE 5-52 The Move Virtual Machine Storage dialog box

Continuously available share settings

When you install the File Server cluster role, you have a choice of creating a general use file server or a Scale-out File Server designed to provide storage to applications, such as Hyper-V and SQL Server. Both roles enable you to create shares that are continuously available through the use the SMB 3.0 protocol.

Version 3.0 of the SMB protocol includes enhancements that are particularly useful in a clustered environment, including the following:

- **SMB Transparent Failover** Enables a client session to be transferred from one cluster node to another without interruption. This is implemented by default on all Failover Cluster file server shares. Both the client and the server must support SMB 3.0 (Windows Server 2012 or Windows 8).

- **SMB Scale-out** Enables shares to be accessible by clients from all nodes in the cluster simultaneously. This effectively increases the share's available bandwidth to the combined bandwidth of the nodes. Scale-out shares are only accessible to clients running SMB versions 2 and 3.

- **SMB Multichannel** Enables file servers to combine the bandwidth from multiple network interface adapters, to achieve enhanced throughout and fault tolerance. SMB can automatically detect the existence of multiple adapters and configure itself to make use of them.

- **SMB Direct** Uses Remote Direct Memory Access (RDMA) to perform direct memory-to-memory data transfers between remote systems, minimizing system processor utilization. Both the client and the server must be using SMB 3.0.
- **SMB Encryption** Provides end-to-end AES encryption between servers and clients using SMB 3.0.

When you create or modify a file server share in Failover Cluster Manager, the New Share Wizard presents a Configure Share Settings page, as shown in Figure 5-53. The Enable Continuous Availability checkbox, selected by default, activates the SMB Transparent Failover feature, and the Encrypt Data Access checkbox enables SMB Encryption.

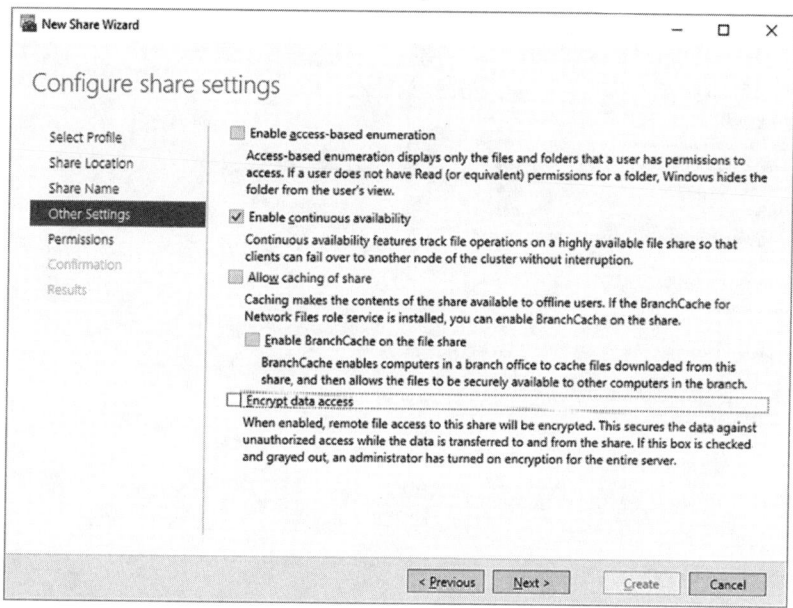

FIGURE 5-53 The Configure Share Settings page of the New Share Wizard

Configure VM monitoring

One of the advantages of running Hyper-V in a cluster is that the cluster is capable of monitoring specific services on the virtual machines, reporting when a problem occurs, and taking action that you can configure. This way, you can select the service associated with a critical application on the VM and configure the VM to restart it or failover to another node when a problem occurs.

To use VM Monitoring in Failover Clustering, the virtual machine must meet the following prerequisites:

- The VM must be in the same domain as the Hyper-V host.
- Windows Firewall on the VM must have the inbound rules in the Virtual Machine Monitoring group enabled.

- The Hyper-V cluster administrator must be a member of the local Administrators group on the VM.

To configure monitoring for a specific virtual machine, use the following procedure.

1. Open Failover Cluster Manager and click Roles to display the Roles page.
2. Select the Virtual Machine role you want to monitor and, on the Actions pane, select **More Actions, Configure Monitoring**.
3. On the Select Services dialog box appears, as shown in Figure 5-54, select the checkbox for the service you want to monitor and click OK.

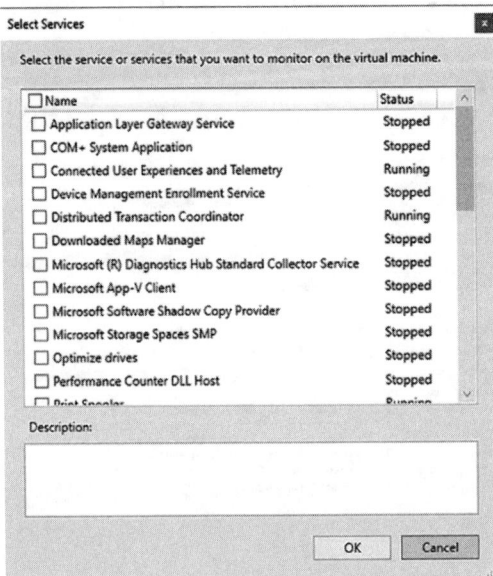

FIGURE 5-54 The Select Services dialog box

You can also configure monitoring using the Add-ClusterVMMonitoredItem cmdlet in a Windows PowerShell window, as in the following example:

```
add-clustervmmonitoreditem -virtualmachine clustervm3 -service spooler
```

When a service you've selected experiences problems, they are handled first by the Service Control Manager on the VM, which uses the properties of the individual service to control its actions, as shown in Figure 5-55. You can modify these properties to specify what actions the Service Control Manager should take, and how often.

FIGURE 5-55 A service's Properties sheet

If the Service Control Manager's efforts fail, and the service is still malfunctioning, the cluster takes over and performs its own recovery actions, as follows:

- The cluster creates an entry in the host's System log with the Event ID 1250.
- The cluster changes the status of the Virtual Machine to Application in VM Critical.
- The cluster restarts the Virtual Machine on the same node. If the service continues to fail, the cluster fails the role over to another node.

You can modify these default restart activities by opening the Virtual Machine Cluster WMI Properties sheet, as shown in Figure 5-56. This is located on the cluster's main page, in the Cluster Core Resources box.

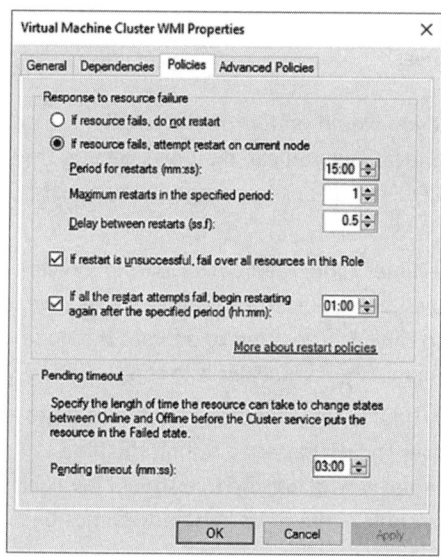

FIGURE 5-56 The Virtual Machine Cluster WMI Properties sheet

Configure failover and preference settings

A *failover* is when a role running on a cluster node can no longer continue to run, and the cluster moves it to another node. There are any number of reasons why a failover might occur: there could be a power failure, the software could malfunction, or an administrator might have to shut the node down for maintenance. A *failback* is when the cluster moves the role back to its original node, after the problem that caused the failover is fixed.

Administrators can control the behavior of the cluster with regard to node selections and failover behavior for a specific role by modifying its properties. In Failover Cluster Manager, on the Roles page, selecting a role and clicking Properties in the Actions pane displays the role's Properties sheet, as shown in Figure 5-57.

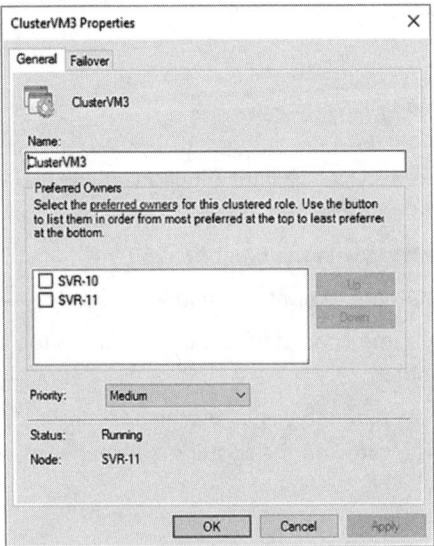

FIGURE 5-57 The General tab on a cluster role's Properties sheet

On the General tab, you can specify the node that you would prefer run the role. It shouldn't matter, since the nodes are functionally identical, but you can do it by selecting the checkbox for one of the nodes and using the Up and Down buttons to change the order of preference.

In the Priority drop-down list, you can specify the values High, Medium, or Low to indicate when the role should start, in relation to the other roles in the cluster. The values are relative only to those of the other roles, and there is also a No Auto Start setting to prevent the node from starting with the cluster. You must then start it manually, if you want it to run.

On the Failover tab, shown in Figure 5-58, you can specify the maximum number of times the cluster should attempt to restart a role or fail it over to another node during the time interval specified by the Period setting. You can also specify whether the role should fail back to the preferred node, and whether it should do so as soon as the preferred node comes back online, or wait an interval that you specify.

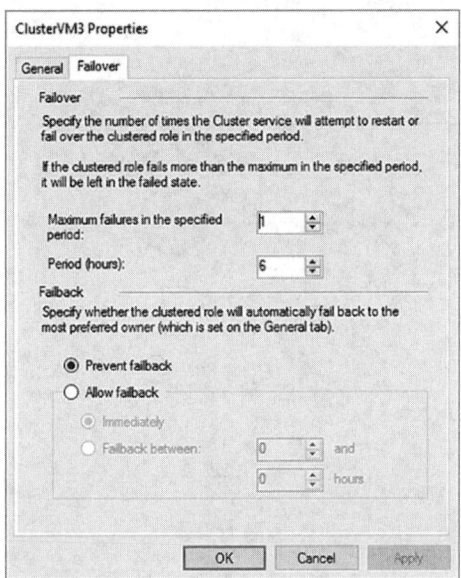

FIGURE 5-58 The Failover tab on a cluster role's Properties sheet

Implement stretch and site-aware failover clusters

Fault tolerance is about planning for any eventuality, and failover clusters are a means of anticipating hardware and software failures. However, sometimes failures occur on a larger scale, in which it's not hard drives and servers that are affected, but rather building and cities. For this reason, organizations that want to keep their applications running in any eventuality can create stretch (or stretched) clusters.

A *stretch cluster* is a cluster that has it nodes divided among different sites, often in different cities. This way, if a catastrophe occurs, such as a hurricane or earthquake, the cluster can failover its roles to nodes that are located far away from the problem. However, stretch clustering presents administrators with some difficult problems, such as how to ensure that cluster nodes in different cities are working with the same data and how to control failover behavior in a situation in which the nodes are not interchangeable.

Because it is usually not practical to create a shared storage solution that can connect all the nodes in a stretch cluster to the same disk drives, many stretch clusters use asymmetric storage, in which each site has its own shared storage solution. Administrators can then use the Storage Replica feature in Windows Server 2016 to synchronize the data between sites, as shown in Figure 5-59.

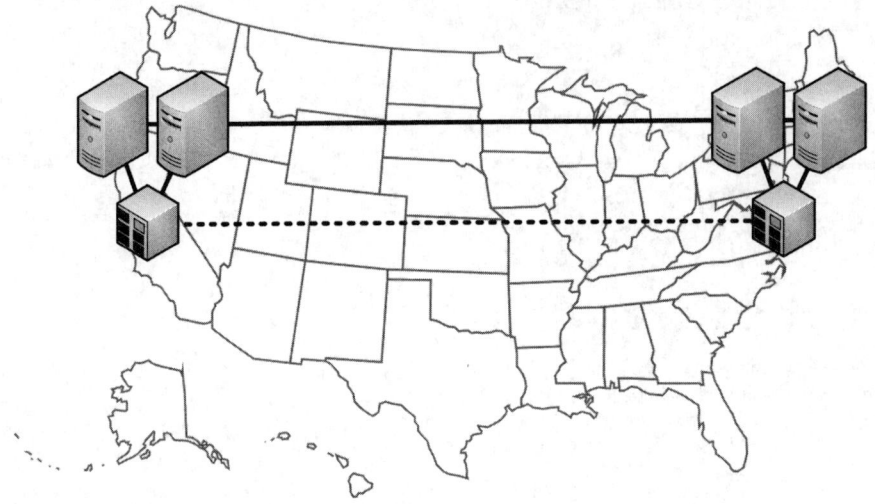

FIGURE 5-59 A stretched cluster with replicated storage

Even with the shared data problem resolved, however, there are other issues involved in stretch clustering. For example, in a failover situation, how is the cluster supposed to distinguish between the nodes located in New York and the nodes in San Francisco? Windows Server 2016 Failover Clustering addresses this issue by providing the ability to create site-aware failover clusters.

A *site-aware failover cluster* is a cluster that contains fault domains based on the values of a site property configured for each node. The cluster uses these fault domains to determine its behavior during failovers and other role transfers. To create a site-aware cluster, you first use the New-ClusterFaultDomain PowerShell cmdlet to define the sites. Then you use the Set-ClusterFaultDomain cmdlet to assign the cluster nodes to the sites you've created.

For example, to create sites for offices in New York and San Francisco, you could use commands like the following:

```
new-clusterfaultdomain -name ny -type site -description "primary" -location "new york ny"

new-clusterfaultdomain -name sf -type site -description "secondary" -location "san francisco ca"
```

Then, for a four-node cluster with two nodes at each site, you would assign the nodes to the sites using commands like the following:

```
set-clusterfaultdomain -name node1 -parent ny

set-clusterfaultdomain -name node2 -parent ny

set-clusterfaultdomain -name node3 -parent sf

set-clusterfaultdomain -name node4 -parent sf
```

Once these properties are configured, the cluster uses the site information to control activities involving resource transfers between nodes. When a node fails, for example, the cluster will attempt to fail it over to another node in the same site first. Only when all the nodes in that site are found to be unavailable will it fail over to a node at another site. This is known as *failover affinity*.

In the same way, when an administrator drains a node of its roles prior to bringing it down for maintenance, the cluster will move the roles to a node in the same site. Cluster Shared Volumes will also distribute connections among nodes in the same site, whenever possible.

It is also possible to configure the heartbeat settings that a cluster uses to determine that nodes are functional. In a stretch cluster, there are bound to be longer latency delays in communication between sites than between subnets, so you can modify the following settings to prevent nodes from being incorrectly designated as having failed:

- **CrossSiteDelay** Specifies the amount of time (in milliseconds) between heartbeats sent to nodes in different sites. The default setting is 1000.
- **CrossSiteThreshold** Specifies the number of missed heartbeats that must occur before a node at a different site is considered to have failed. The default setting is 20.

To configure these settings, you use PowerShell commands like the following:

```
(get-cluster).crosssitedelay = 2000
```

```
(get-cluster).crosssitethreshold = 30
```

You can also configure one of the sites you have created to be the preferred site for the cluster, using a command like the following:

```
(get-cluster).preferredsite = ny
```

When you do this, roles start at the preferred site during a cold start of the cluster, and the preferred site receives precedence during quorum negotiations, keeping the preferred site alive at the expense of the other sites, if necessary.

Enable and configure node fairness

Maintenance, failovers, and other activities can cause virtual machines on a Hyper-V cluster to be migrated in such a way that some nodes are overcommitted, while others are hardly being utilized. Windows Server 2016 includes a feature called *node fairness*, which attempts to balance the distribution among the nodes.

Node fairness works by evaluating the memory and CPU loads on each node over time, attempting to identify those that are overcommitted. When cluster detects an overloaded node, it balances the load by live migrating VMs to other nodes that are idle, while still observing fault domains and preferred owners.

Node fairness is enabled by default, but you can configure whether it runs and when load balancing occurs. You can also configure the aggressiveness of the load balancing that occurs. You do this in the cluster's Properties sheet, on the Balancer tab, as shown in Figure 5-60.

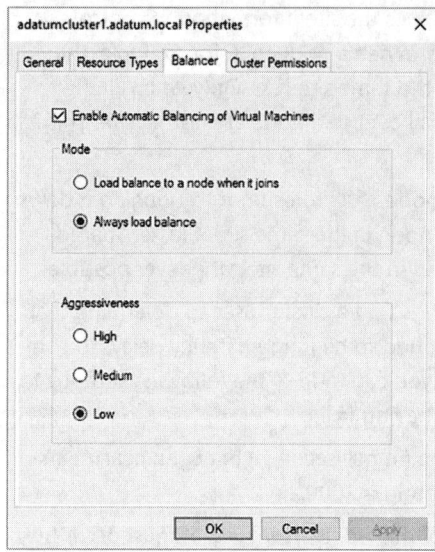

FIGURE 5-60 The Balancer tab of a cluster's Properties sheet

You can also configure these settings using Windows PowerShell, using the following commands:

- **(Get-Cluster).AutoBalancerMode**   Specifies whether node fairness should run and how often it should balance the load, using the following values:
    - 0   Node fairness is disabled
    - 1   Load balancing occurs when a node joins the cluster
    - 2   Load balancing occurs when a node joins the cluster and every 30 minutes thereafter. This is the default.
- **(Get-Cluster).AutoBalancerLevel**   Specifies the aggressiveness with which node fairness should evaluate the load on each node, using the following values:
    - 1   Low. Migrates VMs when the host is more than 80 percent loaded. This is the default.
    - 2   Medium. Migrates VMs when the host is more than 70 percent loaded.
    - 3   High. Migrates VMs when the host is more than 60 percent loaded.

Skill 5.5: Manage VM movement in clustered nodes

Once you have a cluster installed, configured, and operational, you will be likely to encounter situations in which it is necessary to change the distribution of virtual machines among the cluster nodes. Windows Server 2016 provides several methods for moving VMs and controlling their behavior when they are moved.

This section covers how to:
- Perform a live migration
- Perform a quick migration
- Perform a storage migration
- Import, export, and copy VMs
- Configure VM network health protection
- Configure drain on shutdown

Perform a live migration

When you create a Virtual Machine role on a cluster, you create the VM itself and then configure it for high availability. This latter action, which you perform with the High Availability Wizard or the Add-ClusterVirtualMachineRole cmdlet in PowerShell, enables Live Migration for the role. There is no need to manually configure the Hyper-V server to enable Live Migration or select an authentication protocol.

Once the virtual machine is created in the cluster, performing a live migration is simply a matter of right-clicking the VM on the Roles page and, on the context menu, selecting Move | Live Migration. You can let the cluster choose the best node or select any of the nodes in the cluster as the target, as shown in Figure 5-61.

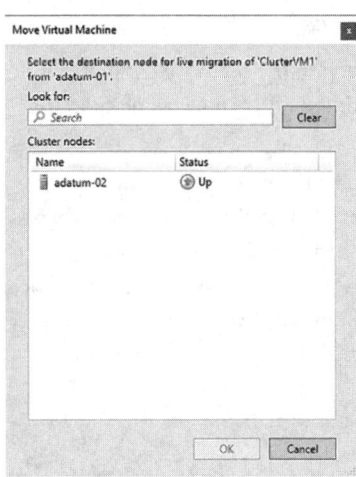

FIGURE 5-61 The Move Virtual Machine dialog box

To initiate a live migration in PowerShell, you use the Move-ClusterVirtualMachineRole cmdlet, as in the following example:

```
move-clustervirtualmachinerole -name clustervm1 -node server2
```

Perform a quick migration

Quick Migration is the predecessor to Live Migration, and was the original tool for moving a virtual machine from one cluster node to another. Largely replaced by Live Migration on Windows Server 2012, Quick Migration is still included in Windows Server 2016, because there are situations in which it is still useful.

Compared to Live Migration, in which the handover of a VM from one node to the other is, in most cases, nearly instantaneous, Quick Migration involves what is usually a brief pause. As with a live migration, the data files do not move during a quick migration. However, you can perform a quick migration on VMs that are either running or stopped. For a live migration, the VMs must be running. In practice, administrators typically use Quick Migration only when they can't perform a Live Migration.

A typical quick migration of a running virtual machine role proceeds as follows:

1. The cluster pauses the virtual machine role, suspending the I/O and CPU functions of the VM.
2. The cluster saves the source VM's memory contents and system state to shared storage and places the VM into the Saved state.
3. The cluster copies the symbolic link specifying the location of the source VM's files to the destination node and transfers ownership of the source VM's files to the destination VM.
4. The cluster removes the symbolic link from the source VM.
5. The cluster resumes the role from the Saved state, copying the memory contents and the system state from shared storage to the destination VM, now running on the destination node.

The fundamental difference between Quick Migration and Live Migration is that a quick migration copies the VM's memory first to disk and then from disk to the destination, while a live migration copies the memory directly from the source to the destination. The length of the pause in a quick migration depends on the size of the VM's memory and the performance of the storage subsystem. The only data copied directly from the source to the destination VM is the tiny symbolic link.

> **NOTE QUICK MIGRATION IN STOPPED VMS**
>
> When the virtual machine is stopped, a quick migration requires only the transfer of the symbolic link from the source to the destination. In this case, the process is nearly instantaneous.

The effect of the pause on the clustered role depends on the applications running on the VM. Some applications can recover easily from a pause of a few seconds, while others might not. However, the situation was important enough to the Windows Server 2012 developers that the creation of a nearly instantaneous migration tool, Live Migration, was a top priority for them.

The process of performing a quick migration is nearly identical to that of a live migration. You right-click the VM on the Roles page and, on the context menu, selecting Move | Quick Migration, and choose the desired destination node. As the migration proceeds, you can see the role enter the Saved state and then the Starting state as the role is resumed.

Perform a storage migration

Live Migration and Quick Migration are designed to move the memory contents and the system state from one virtual machine to another. They do not move the virtual hard disk files that the VM uses to store its operating system, application files, and data. In a failover cluster, these files are expected to be located on shared storage, so the destination VM already has access to them.

Storage Migration has the opposite effect: it moves a VM's virtual hard disk files, but not its memory and system state. There are relatively few limitations on Storage Migration. The virtual machine does not have to be part of a cluster, so you see it implemented in Hyper-V as well as Failover Clustering.

On a standalone Hyper-V server, you can move the files to any destination you have permission to access, including a different location on the same computer. This is helpful, because it updates the VM with the new locations of the files as it migrates them.

In Hyper-V, you use the Move Wizard to perform storage migrations, but there is a different tool in Failover Cluster Manager. When you select a virtual machine cluster role and click Move | Virtual Machine Storage, the Move Virtual Machine Storage dialog box appears, as shown in Figure 5-62.

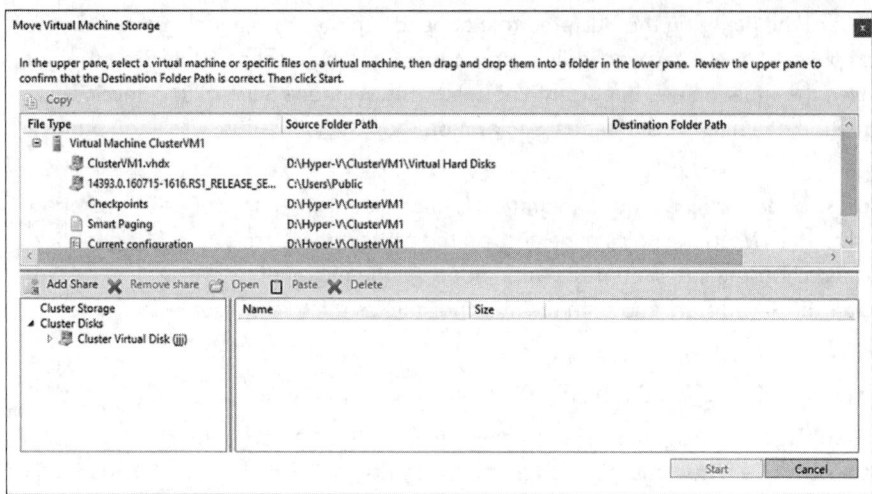

FIGURE 5-62 The Move Virtual Machine Storage dialog box

> **EXAM TIP**
>
> When preparing for the 70-740 exam, keep in mind that Storage Migration and Live Migration are separate processes. In Hyper-V Manager, the Move Wizard integrates Live Migration and Storage Migration capabilities into one interface, which can be confusing. Using this wizard, you can move a virtual machine to a different Hyper-V host; you can move a VM's storage, while leaving the VM in place; or you can move both the VM and its storage to a different host, effectively combining Live Migration and Storage Migration. Remember, however, that these are two separate tools and two separate procedures, although the wizard makes it seem as though it is one process.

In this dialog box, you can select any of the virtual machine's stored resources, including individual VHD and VHDX files, checkpoints, and Smart Paging files, and drag and drop them to a location anywhere in cluster storage. A new Destination Folder Path value appears, specifying to where the tool will move the file. When you have selected destinations for all of the files you want to move, you can click the Start button to close the dialog box and begin the storage migration process.

Import, export, and copy VMs

In Hyper-V, the ability to export and import VMs has several useful purposes. It is a simple, although tedious, way to move a VM from one host to another, complete with all its virtual hard disk, checkpoint, and Smart Paging files, without the prerequisites needed for Live Migration or Quick Migration. It is also a way to copy—or clone— a virtual machine, with all its updates, configuration settings, and applications intact.

Hyper-V Manager provides access to an Export Virtual Machine dialog box and an Import Virtual Machine Wizard, as described in Chapter 3, but there is no such interface accessible in Failover Cluster Manager. You can, however, use the Export-VM and Import-VM cmdlets in Windows PowerShell to effectively clone a clustered virtual machine.

To export a virtual machine, running or stopped, you use a command like the following:

```
export-vm -name clustervm1 -path d:\vm
```

You can run the command from any node in the cluster, but if you specify a local, unshared disk for the Path parameter, the VM will be exported to the specified path on the node where it is running. Specifying shared storage for the Path value is therefore preferable.

To import the virtual machine into the Hyper-V host, copy the files to the host's default folders and generate a new security identifier (SID) for the VM. To prevent conflicts, use a command like the following:

```
import-vm -path "d:\vm\virtual machines\5ae40946-3a98-428e-8c83-081a3c68d18c.xml" -copy -generatenewid
```

Once the process is complete, you will have a new virtual machine on that host. If the Hyper-V host is configured to store VM files on shared storage by default, you can then use Failover Cluster Manager to add that VM as a Virtual Machine role, configuring it for high availability.

Configure VM network health protection

Network health protection is a feature that detects whether a VM on a cluster node has a functional connection to a designated network. If it does not, the cluster automatically live migrates the VM role to another node that does have a connection to that network.

Without this feature, clustered virtual machines can lose contact with the network they are supposed to be servicing, and will continue to run as though nothing is wrong. If the problem is a simple one, such as an unplugged cable, other nodes in the cluster might still have access to that network, and migrating the VM to one of those nodes can keep it operational until the network fault is repaired.

Network health protection is enabled by default, but there are situations in which an administrator might not want a live migration to occur automatically. For example, if the cluster nodes are equipped with connections to redundant networks, you might not want live migrations to occur in response to one network's failure, when the node has access to others already.

To control whether network health protection is applied, open the Settings dialog box for the VM, either in Failover Cluster Manager or Hyper-V Manager, expand the network adapter providing the connection to the network in question, and display the Advanced Features page, as shown in Figure 5-63. When you clear the Protected Network checkbox, you prevent live migrations from occurring due to faults detected on that particular network.

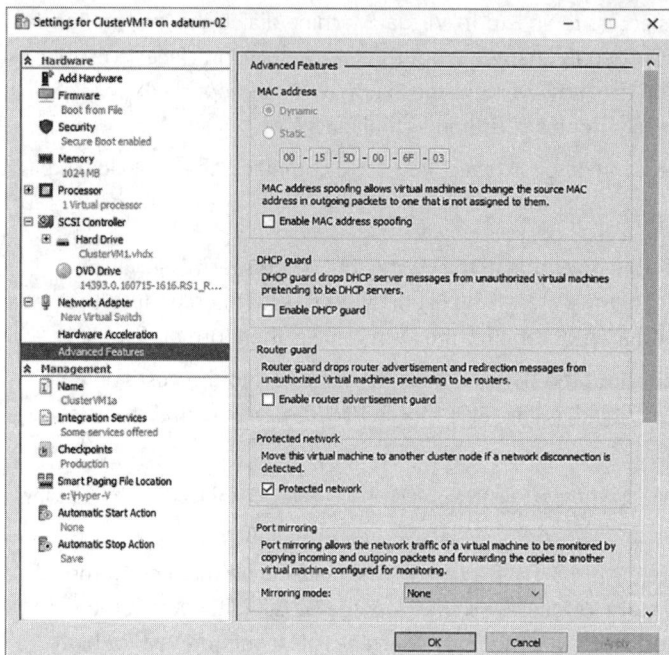

FIGURE 5-63 The Advanced Settings page for a network adapter in a VM's Setting's dialog box

Configure drain on shutdown

When you want to shut down a cluster node containing VMs, for maintenance or any other reason, the proper procedure is to drain the roles off the node (that is, live migrate them to other nodes) before you shut down the machine. In Failover Cluster Manager, you do this by selecting a node and clicking Pause | Drain Roles in the Actions pane. If you click the Roles tab at the bottom of the page, you should see each one live migrated to another node in the cluster.

In PowerShell, you can drain a node using the Suspend-ClusterNode cmdlet, as in the following example:

```
suspend-clusternode
```

At one time, if you failed to drain the node and just shut it down with the roles running, the roles would be placed into a Saved state, causing a service outage until the VMs could be moved to another node and resumed. Now, Windows Server 2016 Failover Clustering includes a feature called drain on shutdown, which automatically live migrates all the roles on a node before shutting down the system. It is worth noting, however, that Microsoft still recommends pausing a node and draining it before initiating a shutdown.

Drain on shutdown is enabled by default, as you can tell by running the (Get-Cluster). DrainOnShutdown command, as shown in Figure 5-64. A value of 1 indicates that the feature is enabled, and 0 is disabled.

```
PS C:\Users\administrator.ADATUM> (get-cluster).DrainOnShutdown
1
PS C:\Users\administrator.ADATUM>
```

FIGURE 5-64 Output of the (Get-Cluster).DrainOnShutdown command

To disable drain on shutdown, you would therefore use the following command:

(get-cluster).drainonshutdown = 0

Skill 5.6: Implement Network Load Balancing (NLB)

The basic philosophy of a failover cluster is one of fault tolerance, in which one computer performs a service while others remain idle, waiting to serve as replacements in the event of a failure. *Network load balancing*, by contrast, is based on the idea that many computers are all providing the same service simultaneously. This arrangement provides fault tolerance also, but the primary objective is to distribute the traffic load among many computers, enabling the cluster to service more clients at once than a single computer ever could.

> **This section covers how to:**
> - Configure NLB prerequisites
> - Install NLB nodes
> - Configure affinity
> - Configure port rules
> - Configure cluster operation mode
> - Upgrade an NLB cluster

Configure NLB prerequisites

A Network Load Balancing (NLB) cluster can consist of 2 to 32 servers—called hosts— each of which runs a separate copy of the desired application. NLB then uses TCP/IP addressing to send incoming client requests to the different hosts, balancing the load among them. NLB is best suited for stateless applications, such as web servers, with variable client loads. As traffic increases, it is possible to add hosts to the cluster, increasing its capacity. You can easily remove hosts as well, when the client load is diminished.

> **EXAM TIP**
>
> Failover Clustering clusters consist of *nodes*, while Network Load Balancing clusters consist of *hosts*. Remember this distinction for the 70-740 exam.

Skill 5.6: Implement Network Load Balancing (NLB)   **CHAPTER 5**   **375**

The NLB hosts in a cluster exchange messages called *heartbeats* once a second. These messages enable them to track the continued functionality of the other hosts. When the heartbeats from a single host stop for a given length of time, the other hosts remove it from the cluster. Whenever a host is added or removed, the NLB cluster performs a process known as *convergence*, during which it evaluates the current cluster membership and determines how client requests should be distributed among the hosts.

As with Failover Clustering, an NLB cluster has its own virtual identity on the network, with a name and IP address that clients use to connect to the application. For example, when you connect to any large web site on the Internet, you are connecting to a cluster address with some mechanism like NLB that forwards your request to one of the computers in a server farm. You have no idea which server you are accessing, and it doesn't matter, because they all provide the same service.

Because the application runs on all the hosts in the cluster, many of the complicated negotiations required for failover clustering are not needed. There is no quorum, and there are no questions of which the server is performing a specific role. They are all active. Thus, NLB is much simpler to set up and administer than Failover Clustering, and has fewer prerequisites.

Hardware prerequisites

NLB clusters can support up to 32 hosts. In general, there is no shared storage or other specialized hardware required for NLB. Unlike a failover cluster, the computers you use to create NLB hosts must not be identical. However, they should be similar in their capabilities, so that some hosts do not perform substantially worse than others.

All the hosts in an NLB cluster must be connected to the same subnet, and network latency must be minimized to allow the convergence process to proceed normally. The hosts don't need to be in the same server closet or data center, but dispersing the computers over long distances could result in hosts being dropped from the cluster.

> **NOTE** **SITE-BASED FAULT TOLERANCE FOR NLB**
>
> To provide site-based fault tolerance, in the event of a large-scale disaster, the best practice is to create separate NLB clusters at different locations, and use another mechanism to distribute client requests between the two sites. For example, *DNS round robin* is a technique that enables the DNS servers resolving the cluster name to supply different IP addresses to successive requests. This would effective split the incoming traffic between the sites, and NLB would split it again among the hosts at each site.

The NLB hosts can have as many network interface adapters as needed for other purposes, but the network adapters used for NLB must all use either multicast or unicast transmissions. The cluster parameters—and specifically the Cluster Operation Mode—influence the hardware configuration of your network. Because this is selected when setting up the NLB cluster, you will have to consider this point at that time.

Software prerequisites

Network Load Balancing has some software configuration requirements that you must consider before creating an NLB cluster, including the following:

- **Operating System** Windows Server has supported Network Load Balancing through several versions, and the implementations since Windows Server 2008 are largely the same. However, the best practice is to have all the hosts in an NLB cluster run the same version and the same edition of Windows Server.

- **IP Addresses** All the hosts in an NLB cluster must have static IP addresses. NLB does not support the use of Dynamic Host Configuration Protocol (DHCP), and will disable the DHCP client on the computers you configure as hosts. Therefore, you must be aware of the IP addressing used on the subnet and have appropriate IP addresses that you can assign to the hosts and the cluster. If the subnet uses DHCP for its other computers, you must have addresses that fall outside of the DHCP scope.

- **Local User Accounts** All the hosts in an NLB cluster should have an identical user account, with membership in the local Administrators group, which the Network Load Balancing Manager will use to access them. Without identical accounts, you must supply authentication credentials for each host you access. While membership in an Active Directory Domain Services domain is not required for an NLB cluster, it makes management easier, because the AD DS Domain Admins group is a member of the local Administrators group on every joined computer.

Install NLB nodes

Network Load Balancing, like Failover Clustering, is a feature included in Windows Server 2016. You must install the feature on all servers that will function as NLB hosts, by using the Add Roles and Features Wizard in Server Manager. Or, you can install this feature using the Install-WindowsFeature cmdlet in Windows PowerShell, using the following command:

```
install-windowsfeature -name nlb -includemanagementtools
```

You can also install the NLB management tools without the NLB feature, to administer a cluster from a remote workstation, using the following command:

```
install-windowsfeature -name rsat-nlb
```

Once the feature is installed on all the servers, you can proceed to create an NLB cluster, using the following procedure.

1. Launch the Network Load Balancing Manager console, shown in Figure 5-65, from the Tools menu in Server Manager.

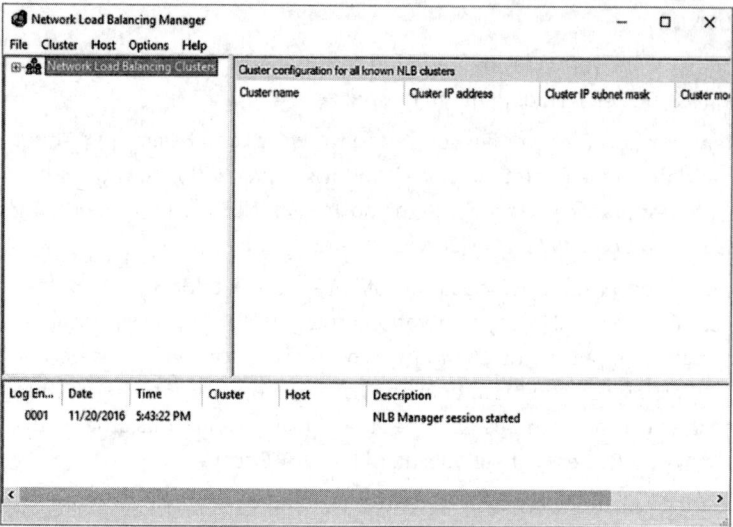

FIGURE 5-65 The Network Load Balancing Manager console

2. On the Cluster menu, click New.
3. On the New Cluster: Connect page, shown in Figure 5-66, in the Host text box, type the name of the first host you want to add to the cluster (even if it is the name of the local computer) and click Connect. The interface(s) and IP address(es) of the computer appear.

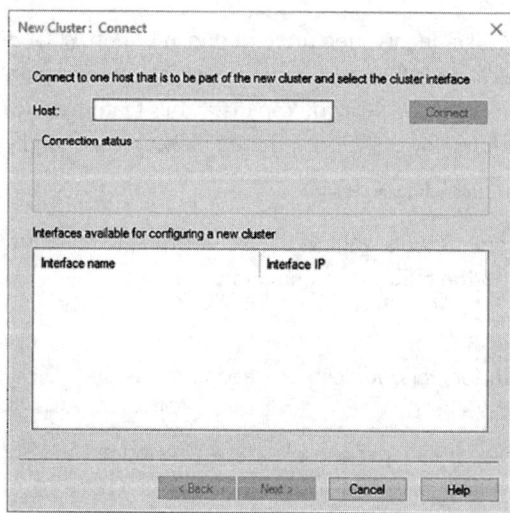

FIGURE 5-66 The New Cluster: Connect page

4. Select the interface the host will use for the cluster.

5. On the New Cluster: Host Parameters page, specify a Priority (Unique Host Identifier) value using the drop-down list. This value must be unique on each host you install. Any traffic that does not conform to the port rules configured for the cluster will be forwarded to the host with the lowest priority value.

6. On the New Cluster: Cluster IP Addresses page, click Add.

7. In the Add IP Address dialog box, shown in Figure 5-67, specify the IPv4 Address and Subnet Mask values that the cluster will use, and click OK. This creates the virtual identity for the cluster, which will be added to the network adapter configuration of every host in the cluster.

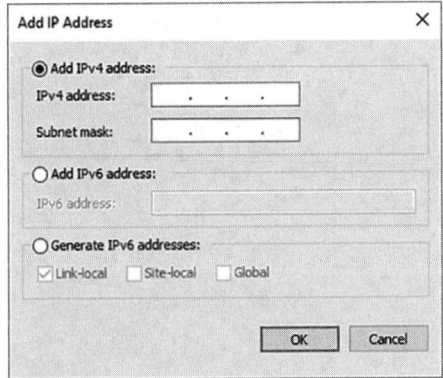

FIGURE 5-67 The Add IP Address dialog box

8. On the New Cluster: Cluster Parameters page, shown in Figure 5-68, specify the Full Internet Name value for the cluster. This is the name that clients will use to connect to the application running on the cluster. For a web server cluster, for example, this will be the server name in the web site's URL.

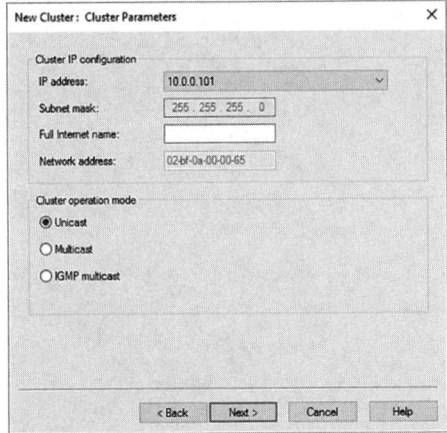

FIGURE 5-68 The New Cluster: Cluster Parameters page

9. In the Cluster Operation Mode box, select one of the following values:
   - **Unicast**   Specifies that the cluster should use a unicast media access control (MAC) address for cluster communications.
   - **Multicast**   Specifies that the cluster should use a multicast MAC address for cluster communications.
   - **IGMP Multicast**   Specifies that the cluster should use a multicast MAC address for cluster communications, with Internet Group Messaging Protocol (IGMP), to prevent port flooding.
10. On the New Cluster: Port Rules page, shown in Figure 5-69, click Edit to modify the default port rule.

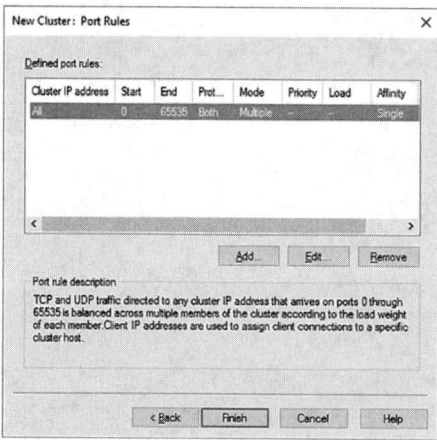

FIGURE 5-69 The New Cluster: Port Rules page

11. In the Add/Edit Port Rule dialog box, shown in Figure 5-70, modify the Port Range settings to specify the port(s) for the application the cluster will be running.

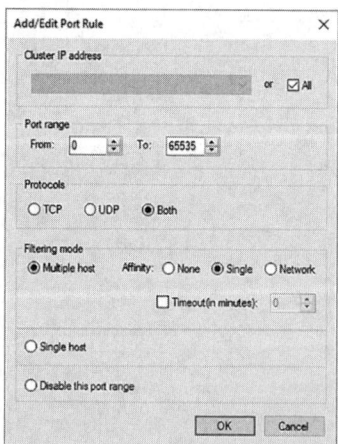

FIGURE 5-70 The Add/Edit Port Rule dialog box

12. In the Filtering Mode box, select one of the following options, and click OK to revise the settings in the port rule.

- **Multiple Host** Enables incoming traffic conforming to the port rule to be handled by multiple cluster hosts. Select an Affinity setting to specify how repeat traffic from clients is distributed among hosts.
- **Single Host** Enables incoming traffic conforming to the port rule to be handled by a single cluster host.
- **Disable This Port Range** Causes the cluster to block all traffic confirming to the port rule.

13. Click Finish.

You have now created an NLB cluster and configured its first host. To add additional hosts to the cluster, select it in the console and click Cluster | Add Host. For each host you add, you must configure only the Connect, Host Parameters, and Port Rules pages. As you add each host, the cluster converges, until all the hosts have been recognized and incorporated into the cluster, as shown in Figure 5-71.

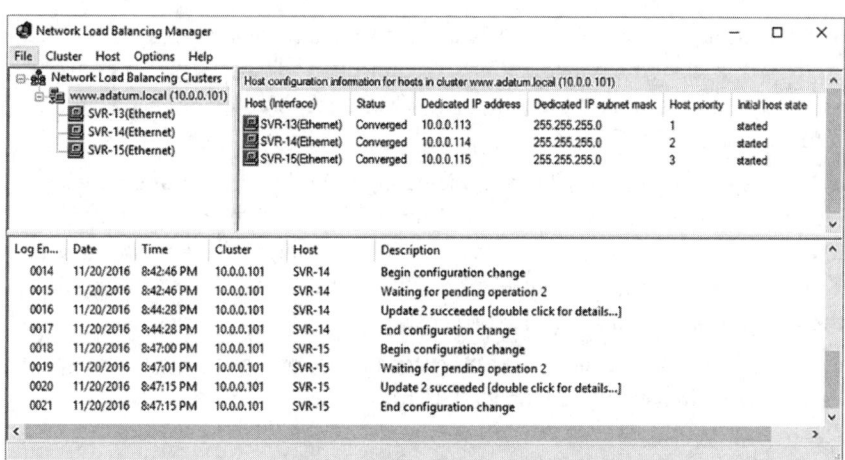

FIGURE 5-71 The Network Load Balancing Manager console, with a three-node cluster

Configure affinity

When you configure the Filtering Mode setting in a port rule, you specify how the cluster handles the traffic conforming to that port rule. If you select Single, you are essentially using NLB as a failover cluster for that rule, with fault tolerance, but no scalability. Only the host with the lowest Priority value will handle traffic for that rule. If that host should fail, then the next lowest priority host would take over.

Selecting Disable prevents the cluster from accepting any traffic conforming to the rule. You use this setting to creating a rule that blocks traffic using a specific IP address or port.

When you select the Multiple Host option, then the traffic conforming to that rule is distributed among all the hosts of the cluster. This provides both fault tolerance and scalability. The potential problem with this arrangement is that a client could conceivably disconnect and reconnect to the cluster, and be sent to a different host.

For some applications, this is not a problem. If, for example, you are running a web server that provides only static pages, then it doesn't matter if a client is shifted from one host to another. However, for an e-commerce web site, interrupting a session and moving the client to another host would interrupt the transaction. The Affinity settings for the Multiple Hosts option address this problem.

The Affinity setting you choose specifies how the cluster should react to repeated requests from the same client. The available settings are as follows:

- **None** With no client affinity, incoming requests from the same IP address can be handled by any host. You should avoid this setting for transaction based applications that require consistent connections to one host. You should also avoid this setting when the rule uses UDP or Both for the Protocols setting, so that IP fragments are not sent to different hosts.

- **Single** This setting ensures that all traffic coming from a single IP address is sent to the same host. If a client disconnects, then a reconnection will use the same source IP address, and NLB will recognize this and forward the traffic accordingly, allowing the session to continue.

- **Network** This setting enables all traffic originating from the same Class C network to be sent to the same host. In some cases, clients might use different proxy servers on the same network when connecting to the cluster. As long as those proxy servers are located on the same subnet, NLB will recognize that the traffic probably originates from the same client and send it to a single host.

Select the timeout checkbox to specify the maximum amount of time that can pass between connections before the affinity rule no longer applies.

Configure port rules

Port rules define what types of TCP/IP traffic the NLB cluster should handle and how it should handle each type. When you first create a cluster, the default port rule admits traffic using all IP address and all ports. You can modify this rule as needed, and create others to specify different settings for different types of traffic.

In addition to the Filter Mode and Affinity settings already described, the settings available in a port rule are as follows:

- **Cluster IP Address** A cluster can have multiple IP addresses, representing different services, such as different web sites hosted by Internet Information Services (IIS). By selecting a specific address, you can create a different rule for each service. Selecting the All checkbox creates a global rule for all the cluster's IP addresses.

- **Port Range** A cluster can also provide services that use different ports. For example, the well-known port for a web server is 80, but the well-known port for a secured web server is 443. If you are using NLB to balance traffic for a web server that runs multiple sites, you can create a rule for each site by specifying its IP address and/or its port number. A site that provides static web pages can use the Multiple Host filtering mode with no client affinity, but for a secure e-commerce site supported on only one host, you might use the Single filtering mode.

- **Protocols** Specifies whether the rule should apply to TCP, or UDP traffic, or both. TCP is typically used for longer transactions that require multiple packets, while UDP is often used for quick request/response transactions. Depending on the application you are running on the cluster, you might want to configure different affinity settings for each protocol.

When you access the port rules through the Properties sheet for one of the hosts, as shown in Figure 5-72, you cannot modify the rule settings listed earlier, but there are two host-specific settings that you can configure, as follows:

- **Load Weight** Accessible only in multiple host mode, specifies how much of the traffic conforming to the rule should be handled by the selected host. The default setting is to balance the traffic equally, but you can specify a relative value from 0 to 100.

- **Handling Priority** Accessible only in single host mode, specifies a priority for the host's handling of the traffic conforming to the rule. The host with the lowest value will handle all the traffic for the rule.

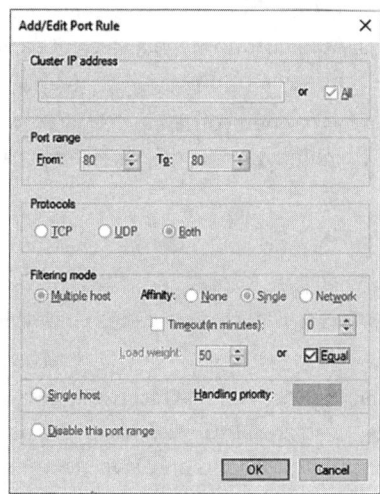

FIGURE 5-72 The Port Rules settings in a host's Properties sheet

Configure cluster operation mode

The Cluster Operation Mode setting specified what kind of TCP/IP traffic the cluster hosts should use. A unicast is a TCP/IP transmission that is addressed to a single destination. A multicast is a transmission sent to multiple destinations, using a special multicast IP address.

The MAC address is a unique six-byte value encoded into network interface adapters at the factory. When you select the unicast mode for a cluster, NLB replaces the hardware MAC address on the interface you select for each host with the cluster's virtual MAC address. This causes traffic addressed to the cluster to go to all its hosts. This practice also confuses your network switches, which are unable to determine which port the cluster MAC address belongs to, and therefore must forward the traffic out through all its ports, flooding the network in the process.

Unicast mode also prevents cluster hosts from communicating with each other using their designated cluster adapters. Because all the hosts use the same MAC address, outgoing traffic loops back and never reaches the network. You should therefore install a second network adapter in each host if you plan to use unicast mode and require normal communication between the hosts.

When you select the multicast option, NLB adds a second MAC address to the network interface on each host, which is a multicast MAC address that does not replace the original one. Because each host retains its unique MAC address, there is no need for a second network adapter. The multicast option also causes switch flooding, by default, but there are solutions for it. The IGMP multicast option uses the Internet Group Management Protocol to program the switches, so that traffic destined for the cluster's MAC address is only forwarded out through the switch ports connected to NLB hosts. Administrators can also create a virtual local area network (VLAN) in the switch that achieves the same results.

Multicast mode is the preferable option, except in cases when your network hardware does not support multicast transmissions or the use of multicasts seriously diminishes cluster performance.

Upgrade an NLB cluster

There are two ways to upgrade an existing Windows Server NLB cluster to the Windows Server 2016 version:

- **Simultaneous Upgrade** In this option, you bring the entire NLB cluster down, upgrade all the hosts, and then bring the cluster up again. Obviously, this entails a significant amount of downtime for the clustered application. This is only a viable option if you are comfortable with leaving your application unavailable for a time, or if you have a backup cluster available to take its place.

- **Rolling Upgrade** In this option, you remove the hosts from the cluster, one at a time, upgrade each one, and then add it back into the cluster. NLB is designed to accommodate the addition and removal of hosts, so the cluster will converge each time you remove or add one of the servers.

Chapter summary

- Hyper-V Replica is a feature that can duplicate virtual machine storage, either synchronously or asynchronously.
- Live Migration is the process by which the memory and system state of a virtual machine are transferred from one cluster node to another almost instantaneously.
- Storage Migration is a process by which a VM's virtual hard disk files are moved from one location to another, either on the same or a different Hyper-V host.
- Windows Server 2016 supports failover clusters containing nodes in a single domain, in multiple domains, and in workgroups.
- Quorum is the voting procedure that clusters use to determine whether it should continue to run or shut down during a failure.
- Failover Clusters require shared storage, so that the applications running on the cluster nodes can continue to function, despite a node failure.
- Cluster-aware Updating is a feature that ensures that all the nodes in a failover cluster receive the same updates in a timely manner.
- Cluster Operating System Rolling Upgrade is a new operational mode that enables cluster nodes with different operating systems to coexist temporarily.
- Cluster Shared Volumes are shared storage that is available on all a cluster's nodes simultaneously.
- Guest clustering is when you create a failover cluster using virtual machines on Hyper-V servers.
- A cloud witness is a voting quorum member that resides in Microsoft Azure, providing the decisive vote for multisite clusters.
- Storage Spaces Direct enables you to create cluster shared storage using the local disks in the nodes.
- Storage Spaces Direct can provide shared storage for a separate cluster or for roles running in the same cluster.
- VM monitoring enables you to specify a service running on a virtual machine, so that the cluster can take action if the service fails.
- A stretch cluster is one that is split between two or more sites. Site awareness is the ability to configure cluster nodes with their sites, to control their failover behavior.
- To perform Live Migrations and Storage Migrations, you can use Failover Cluster Manager or Windows PowerShell cmdlets.
- Quick Migration, the predecessor to Live Migration, copies memory contents to shared storage and then to the destination node.
- Network health protection automatically fails over a role to a different node when a network is inaccessible.

- Network Load Balancing is a Windows Server 2016 feature that enables you to create clusters in which all the servers are running the same application simultaneously.
- NLB clusters have their own identities, with names and IP addresses that clients use to access them.
- To create an NLB cluster, you use the Network Load Balancing Manager to add each host and configure the settings for the hosts and the cluster.
- Port rules enable you to identify the types of traffic that NLB cluster hosts can handle, by specifying IP addresses, protocols, and ports.

Thought experiment

In this thought experiment, demonstrate your skills and knowledge of the topics covered in this chapter. You can find answer to this thought experiment in the next section.

Alice is setting up a Network Load Balancing cluster consisting of five hosts running IIS to host an e-commerce web site. Each of the host servers has a single network adapter, and they are all connected to the same subnet. When creating the NLB cluster, Alice works at the first host server, adding the local machine, configuring the cluster to use Unicast transmissions, and modifying the default port rule to use the Multiple Host filtering mode with the Single affinity setting.

After adding the first host to the NLB cluster, Alice discovers that she cannot communicate with the four computers that are to be the other hosts in the cluster. She tries adding them to the cluster, and she is unable to connect. She tries pinging them, and the destination is unreachable. She even tries shutting down Windows Firewall, to no avail.

What is preventing the communication and what are two possible solutions Alice can use to remedy the situation?

Thought experiment answer

This section contains the solution to the thought experiment.

The unicast transmission setting has caused the MAC address on the host's network adapter to be replaced by the virtual MAC address of the cluster. Because that MAC address resolves to the cluster, Alice is, in effect, pinging herself when she tries to contact the other servers. To remedy the situation, she can either add a second network adapter to all of the host servers, or reconfigure the cluster to use multicast transmissions, which does not suppress the server's own MAC address.

CHAPTER 6

Maintain and monitor server environments

Once servers are installed and configured, there are still tasks for administrators to perform. Servers require maintenance, to ensure that they are updated and protected, and their performance must be monitored, to ensure their continued efficiency.

Skills in this chapter:
- Maintain server installations
- Monitor server installations

Skill 6.1: Maintain server installations

No matter what fault tolerance mechanisms you are using on your network, servers require regular maintenance to function efficiently. Administrators must apply updates to operating systems and applications, monitor antimalware software products, and perform regular backups to ensure data is protected against loss. Windows Server 2016 includes features that can perform these tasks, as described in the following sections.

> **This section covers how to:**
> - Implement Windows Server Update Services (WSUS) solutions
> - Configure WSUS groups
> - Manage patch management in mixed environments
> - Implement an antimalware solution with Windows Defender
> - Integrate Windows Defender with WSUS and Windows Update
> - Perform backup and restore operations using Windows Server Backup
> - Determine backup strategies for different Windows Server roles and workloads, including Hyper-V Host, Hyper-V Guests, Active Directory, File Servers, and Web Servers using Windows Server 2016 native tools and solutions

Implement Windows Server Update Services (WSUS) solutions

Windows Server 2016 is equipped with a Windows Update client that automatically downloads operating system updates from Microsoft's web servers and installs them. By enabling an optional setting, you can enable Windows Update to download updates for other Microsoft products as well.

The simplest software update strategy you can implement on a network is to simply let Windows Update run using its default settings. The client typically downloads and installs updates about once a month. However, in an enterprise environment, this practice can result in some problems, including the following:

- **Bandwidth Utilization** Each computer running the Windows Update client downloads its own copy of every update from the Microsoft servers on the Internet. A large network can therefore consume a huge amount of Internet bandwidth downloading hundreds of copies of the same files.
- **Update Approval** The Windows Update client defaults do not provide users or administrators with an opportunity to evaluate the updates before it installs them. You can specify a time during which the system will reboot, if it is necessary, but this would require someone to manage each computer individually.
- **Compliance** The default Windows Update configuration provides no means for administrators to confirm that the client has installed all the required updates successfully, except to examine the Update History on each computer individually.

On all but the smallest networks, the Windows Update client with its default settings is not a reliable update solution. To address these problems, you can design an alternative update deployment strategy for your network, using Group Policy settings and Windows Server Update Services (WSUS).

WSUS architectures

Windows Server Update Services (WSUS) is a role included in Windows Server 2016 that enables a local server on your network to function as the back end for the Windows Update client, just as the Microsoft Update servers do on the Internet.

After installing a WSUS server, you can use it to supply updates to all the other servers and workstations on your network. WSUS downloads all new updates from the Microsoft Update servers on the Internet, and your other computers download the updates from the WSUS server. This way, you are only paying for the bandwidth needed to download one copy of every update.

In addition to conserving bandwidth, WSUS enables administrators to screen the available updates, test them in a lab environment, and approve them for deployment to the clients.

Administrators can therefore retain ultimate authority over which updates get installed and when the installations occur.

A single WSUS server can support many Windows Update clients, which means that one server is theoretically enough for all but the largest networks. However, WSUS also supports a few architectural variations, to accommodate topologies of various sizes that include remote users and branch offices with limited communication capabilities.

There are five basic WSUS architecture configurations, as follows:

- **Single WSUS Server**   A single WSUS server downloads updates from the Microsoft Update website and all the other computers on the network download the updates from that WSUS server, as shown in Figure 6-1. A single WSUS server can support as many as 25,000 clients, so this configuration is suitable for most enterprise networks.

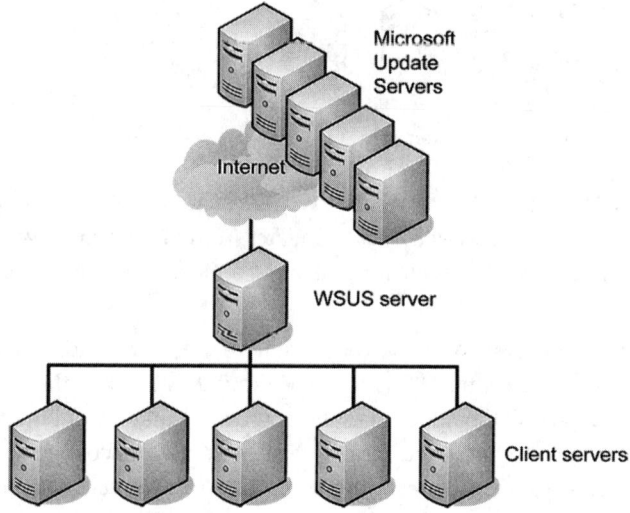

FIGURE 6-1 The WSUS single server architecture

- **Replica WSUS Servers**   One central WSUS server downloads updates from the Microsoft Update site on the Internet. Administrators at that central site evaluate and approve the downloaded updates, and WSUS servers at remote locations— called downstream servers— obtain the approved updates from that first server, as shown in Figure 6-2. Intended for networks with well-connected branch offices, this arrangement enables clients to access their updates from a local source, minimizes the Internet bandwidth used, and enables the administrators of the central server to manage the updates for the entire enterprise.

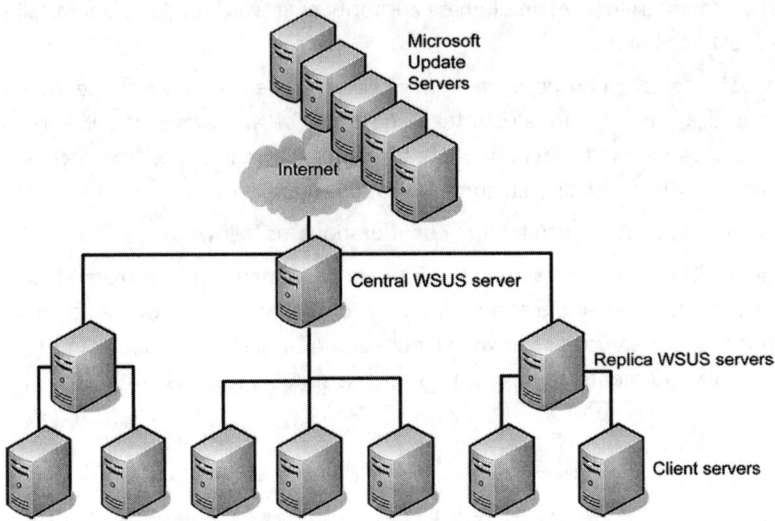

FIGURE 6-2 The WSUS remote server architecture

- **Autonomous WSUS Servers** Like the replica WSUS server architecture, except that the remote WSUS servers download all available updates from the central server, and administrators at each site are responsible for evaluating and approving updates for their own users.

- **Low-bandwidth WSUS Servers** WSUS servers at remote sites download only the list of approved updates from the central WSUS server, without downloading the updates themselves. The remote servers then download the approved updates from the Microsoft Update servers on the Internet, using their relatively fast Internet connection to do so. This arrangement enables remote sites with low-bandwidth or metered Wide Area Network (WAN) connections to the main office to minimize WAN traffic

- **Disconnected WSUS Servers** Administrators at the main office save the updates to an offline medium, such as portable drives or DVD-ROMs, and ship them to the remote sites, where other administrators import them for deployment. This enables the main office administrators to exercise control over the update process while utilizing no WAN or Internet bandwidth.

When you use multiple WSUS servers on your enterprise network, you create an architecture by specifying the upstream server from which each server should obtain its updates. For your central WSUS server, the upstream server is always the Microsoft Update servers on the Internet. You can then configure second level servers to use the central server as their upstream server.

It is also possible to create a three-level architecture by configuring WSUS to use a second-level server as its upstream server. While Microsoft has tested WSUS architectures up to five levels deep, they recommend using no more than three layers.

>  **Quick check**
>
> Which of the following is not one of the basic WSUS server types?
>
> 1. Disconnected WSUS server
> 2. Autonomous WSUS server
> 3. Replica WSUS server
> 4. High-bandwidth WSUS server
>
> **Quick check answer**
>
> High-bandwidth (#4) is not one of the standard WSUS server types.

WSUS Database

WSUS requires a SQL Server database, to store configuration settings for the WSUS server, metadata for each update, and information about client/server interaction. By default, WSUS installs the Windows Internal Database feature for this purpose on Windows Server 2016, but you can also use Microsoft SQL Server 2008 SP2 or later, in the Enterprise, Standard, or Express edition.

When you install the Windows Server Update Services role using the Add Roles and Features Wizard in Server Manager, the Select Role Services page, shown in Figure 6-3, has the WID Connectivity role service selected by default. To use a full version of SQL Server, you must first clear the WID Connectivity checkbox and then select the SQL Server Connectivity role service instead.

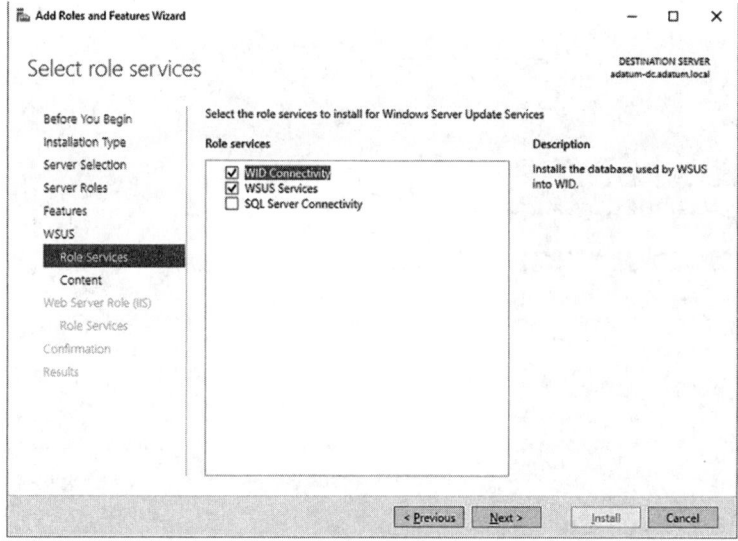

FIGURE 6-3 The Select Role Services page for a WSUS role installation

For a single WSUS server configuration, there is no performance advantage to using SQL Server over Windows Internal Database. SQL Server includes database management tools, which Windows Internal Database does not, but WSUS is designed to function without direct administrative access to its database.

A full version of SQL Server does provide the ability to house the database on a back-end server, separate from WSUS. This enables administrators to provide shared database access to a failover cluster of WSUS servers. A multiple server configuration consisting of two front-end WSUS servers and a single back-end SQL Server database server can conceivably service as many as 100,000 clients.

To use a full version of SQL Server with WSUS, you must configure the servers as follows:

- The computer running SQL Server cannot be a domain controller
- The WSUS server cannot be configured to use Remote Desktop Services
- The servers running WSUS and SQL Server must be members of the same, or a trusted, AD DS domain
- The servers running WSUS and SQL Server must be in the same time zone or be synchronized to use Coordinated Universal Time.
- Every WSUS server must have its own database instance. SQL Server can provide multiple instances, which enables administrators to use the server for other purposes.

WSUS storage

The Content Location Selection page, as shown in Figure 6-4, appears in the Add Roles and Features Wizard. On this page, you can specify whether you want to store downloaded updates on the server's local NTFS drive. The Store Updates In the Following Location checkbox is selected by default, and you can specify the drive and folder where you want the server to store the update files.

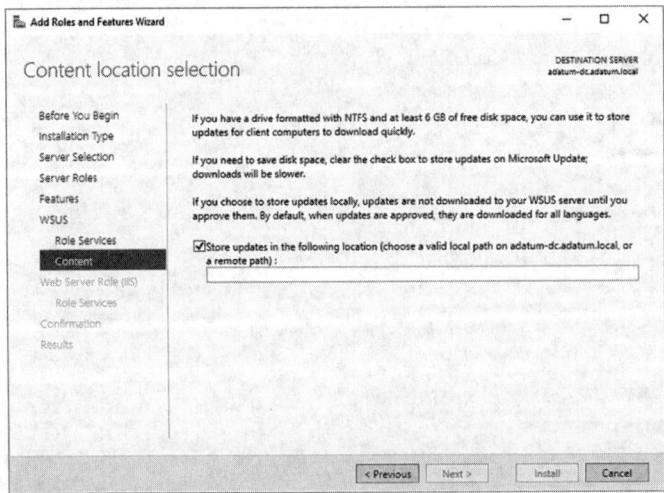

FIGURE 6-4 The Content Location Selection page in the Add Roles and Features Wizard

If you clear the checkbox, the WSUS server will only download metadata regarding the available updates, not the updates themselves. This conserves disk space on the server and essentially configures WSUS to function as a clearing house for the updates available on the Microsoft Update web servers. Administrators can select the updates they want to deploy, and the Windows Update clients on the network download the actual update files from the Microsoft servers on the Internet.

Deploying WSUS

To install WSUS on Windows Server 2016, you must add the Windows Server Update Services role. You can do this in Server Manager, using the Add Roles and Features Wizard in the usual manner. The wizard adds the additional pages where you can select the SQL Server Connectivity role service and specify where to store the downloaded updates. The wizard also installs the Web Server role and provides you with a Select Role Services page for it.

WSUS is just a local version of a Microsoft Update server, so it needs a web server to which clients can connect. By default, the wizard installs the Web Server role with the components WSUS needs, but the Select Role Services page enables you to select any other components you might need for other purposes. If the Web Server (IIS) role is already installed on the server, then the wizard installs any additional role services that WSUS requires.

When the wizard finishes installing the roles, click the Launch Post-Installation Tasks link to open the Complete WSUS Installation dialog box, in which you click Run to complete the installation tasks.

It is also possible to install the WSUS role from the command line, using the Install-WindowsFeature cmdlet for PowerShell and the Wsusutil.exe tool. The command for installing the role with its default settings in PowerShell is as follows:

```
install-windowsfeature -name updateservices -includemanagementtools
```

You can't use the Install-WindowsFeature cmdlet to configure extra parameters for a role, so after this command, you must run the Wsusutil.exe tool to specify the location for the downloaded updates, as in the following example:

```
wsusutil.exe postinstall content_dir=d:\wsus
```

When you install the UpdateServices feature with PowerShell, the cmdlet includes the WID Connectivity role service. If you want to use a separate SQL server, then you would run the following command:

```
install-windowsfeature -name updateservices-services,updateservices-db -includemanagementtools
```

When you specify the UpdateServices-Services feature, no database connectivity is installed, so you must include the SQL database features, UpdateServices-Db, as well. Then, to specify the database server and instance WSUS should use, you run Wsusutil.exe, as in the following example

```
wsusutil.exe postinstall sql_instance_name="db1\sqlinstance1"- content_dir=d:\wsus
```

Configuring WSUS

Once you have installed the role, you must launch the Update Services console. The first time you do this, the Windows Server Update Services Configuration Wizard appears, enabling you to complete the process of setting up WSUS.

> **NOTE REOPENING THE WIZARD**
> The Windows Server Update Services Configuration Wizard only runs the first time you open the Update Services console. If you do not complete the wizard during its first appearance, you can launch it again from the console, where it is well-hidden at the bottom of the Options page.

To configure WSUS, use the following procedure.

1. In Server Manager, click Tools | Windows Server Update Services. The Windows Server Update Services Configuration Wizard appears.
2. On the Choose Upstream Server page, select one of the following options:
   - **Synchronize From Microsoft Update** Configures the server to download all update information and updates from the Microsoft Update servers on the Internet. Use this option for single server WSUS implementations or for the first WSUS server you install at the top of a WSUS hierarchy.
   - **Synchronize From Another Windows Software Update Services Server** Configures the server to download all update information from another WSUS server on your network. Use this option to create the lower levels of a WSUS server hierarchy on your network. When you select this option, as shown in Figure 6-5, you must specify the name and port number for an upstream WSUS server on your network and specify whether the connection between the servers should use SSL encryption. Select the This Is A Replica Of The Upstream Server checkbox to download only the updates approved at the upstream server.

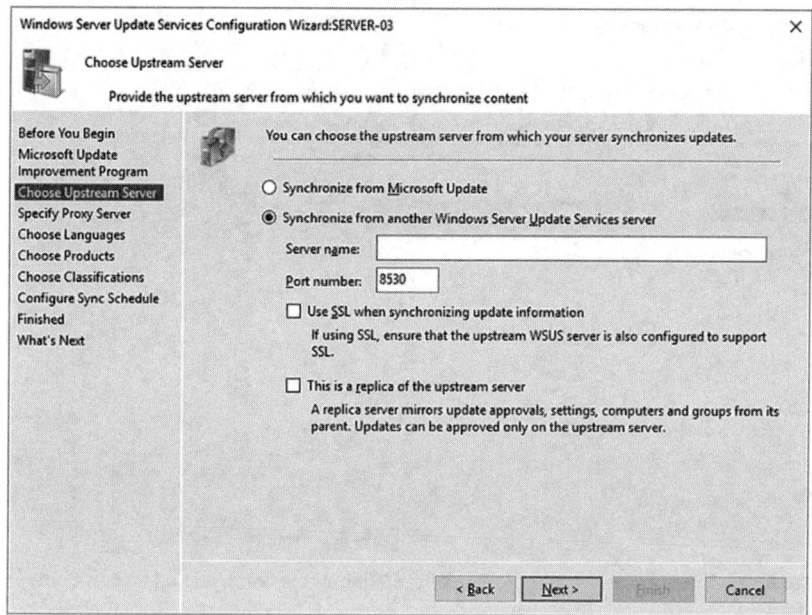

FIGURE 6-5 The Choose Upstream Server page in the Windows Server Update Services Configuration Wizard

3. On the Specify Proxy Server page, select the Use A Proxy Server When Synchronizing checkbox if the server requires a proxy server to access the Internet or the upstream server you specified. Then, specify the proxy server name and port number, as well as the credentials needed to access the proxy server, if necessary.

4. On the Connect to Upstream Server page, click Start Connecting to access the upstream server you selected and download information about the available updates. This process is called synchronization in WSUS.

5. By default, WSUS downloads updates in all available languages, which can consume a lot of unnecessary bandwidth and disk space. On the Choose Languages page, shown in Figure 6-6, you can select the Download Updates Only In These Languages option and specify which languages your WSUS clients use. This configures the WSUS server to download updates only in the selected languages.

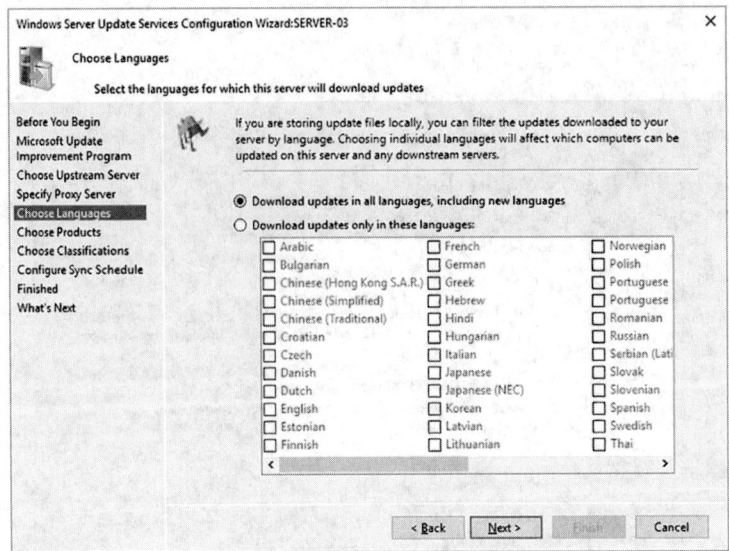

FIGURE 6-6 The Choose Languages page of the Windows Server Update Services Configuration Wizard

6. On the Choose Products page, shown in Figure 6-7, you select the Microsoft products and versions for which you want to download updates. By default, all the Windows products and versions are selected. If you do not use some of the selections on your network, you can clear their checkboxes and save more bandwidth and disk space.

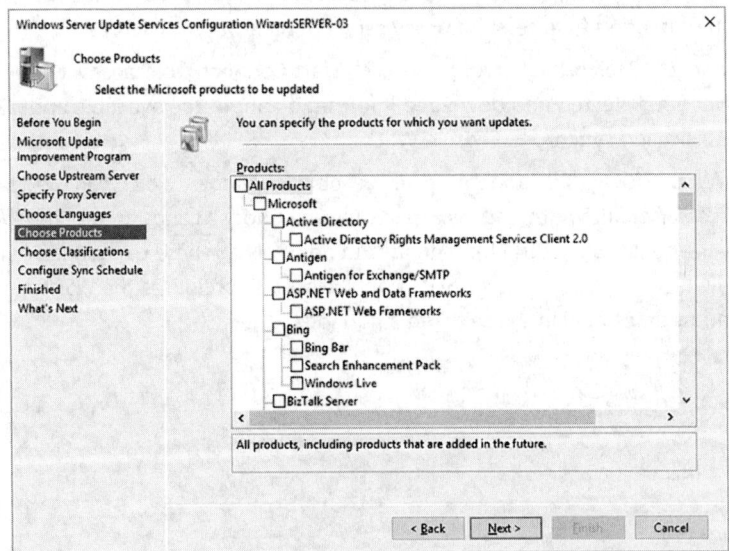

FIGURE 6-7 The Choose Products page of the Windows Server Update Services Configuration Wizard

7. On the Choose Classifications page, shown in Figure 6-8, you specify what types of updates you want the server to download. By default, Critical, Definition, and Security Updates are selected, as well as Upgrades. You can select other classifications, but be mindful that some of these classifications, such as the Service Packs for older Windows versions, can be very large.

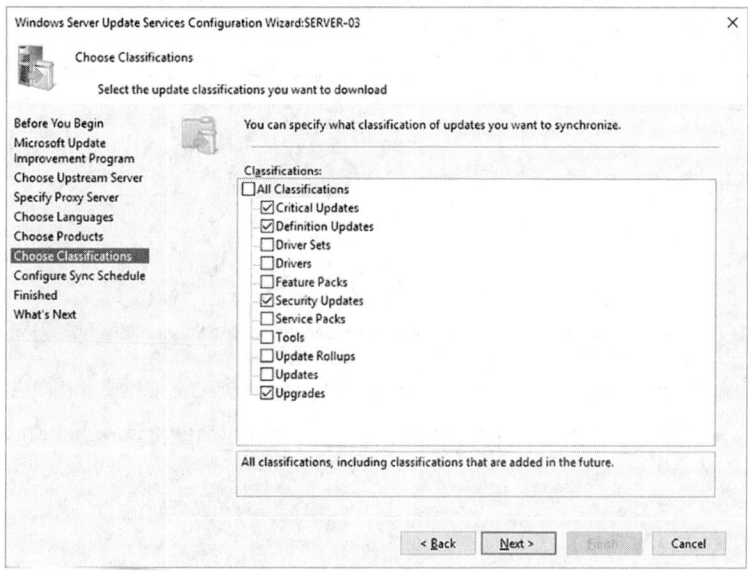

FIGURE 6-8 The Choose Classification page of the Windows Server Update Services Configuration Wizard

EXAM TIP

What's the difference between an update and an upgrade? Semantically, update means to bring something up to its current level, while upgrade means to improve something, or bring it to a higher level. In most cases, these definitions apply to software. An update typically addresses problems in the software or adds support for new technology, while an upgrade adds new features or capabilities. In terms of version numbers, updates typically increment numbers after the decimal point, as in 2.1 and 2.2, while upgrades increment the number before the decimal point, as in 2.0 and 3.0. At one time, these definitions were applicable to Microsoft products. With Windows Server 2016 and Windows 10, however, the terms update and upgrade have become increasingly nebulous. Build number increments have replaced version numbers, and what appear to be updates are major upgrades containing significant new features.

8. On the Set Sync Schedule page, Synchronize Manually is the default option, requiring you to start a synchronization to download new updates. You can also select the Synchronize Automatically option, as shown in Figure 6-9, to set a scheduled start time and the number of times each day that synchronization should occur.

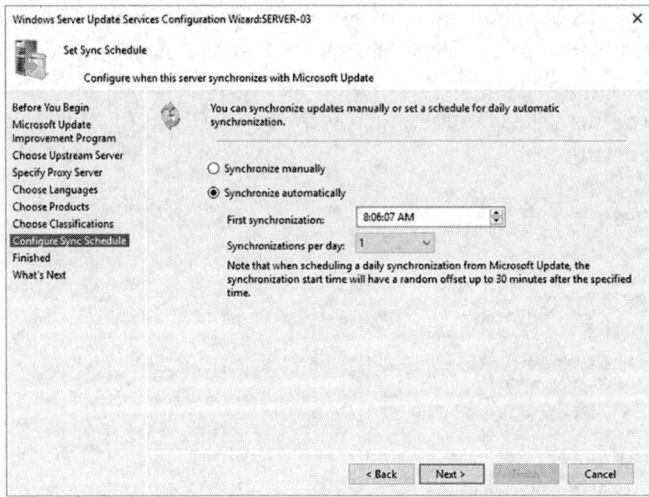

FIGURE 6-9 The Set Sync Schedule page of the Windows Server Update Services Configuration Wizard

9. On the Finished page, select the Begin Initial Synchronization check box and click Finish.

WSUS begins synchronizing with its upstream server and downloading information about the updates that are available.

Configure WSUS groups

To exercise control over which Windows Update clients on the network receive specific updates, WSUS uses a system of groups, which are independent of the security groups in AD DS and the local groups in Windows. When you approve updates for deployment, you select the groups that should receive it, as shown in Figure 6-10.

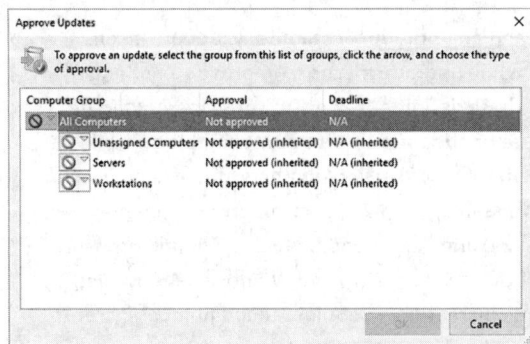

FIGURE 6-10 The Approve Updates dialog box

To create and manage WSUS groups, you use the Update Services console, as shown in Figure 6-11. There are two default groups, called All Computers and Unassigned Computers. Each Windows Update client computer that connects to the WSUS server gets added automatically into these two groups.

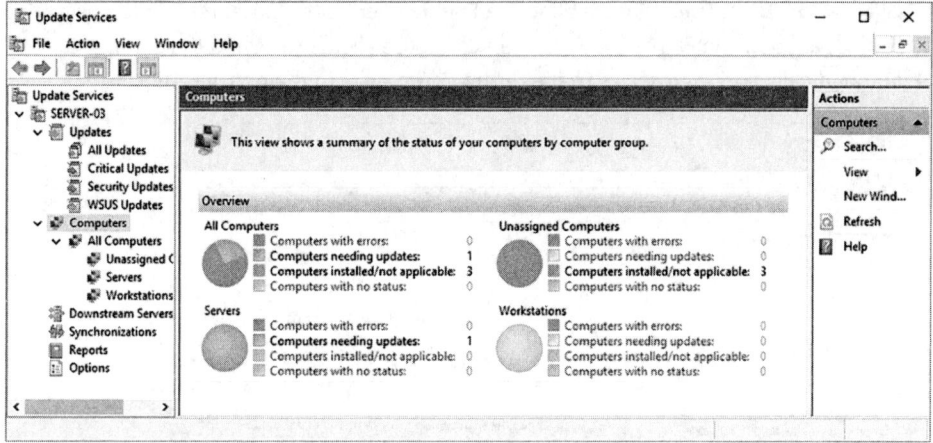

FIGURE 6-11 Computer groups in the Update Services console

To create a new group, right-click the All Computers group and, from the context menu, select Add Computer Group to open the Add Computer Group dialog box, in which you specify a name.

After creating your own groups in the console, you can then move computers from the Unassigned Computers group to the group of your choice in one of two ways:

- **Server-Side Targeting** By manually selecting a computer in the Update Services console, you can change its membership to any existing group by right-clicking it and selecting Change Membership, to open the Set Computer Group Membership dialog box, shown in Figure 6-12.

FIGURE 6-12 The Set Computer Group Membership dialog box

Skill 6.1: Maintain server installations   CHAPTER 6   **399**

- **Client-Side Targeting** By enabling the Enable Client-side Targeting Group Policy setting, as shown in Figure 6-13, you can configure clients receiving the setting to automatically add themselves to the group you specify in the policy setting.

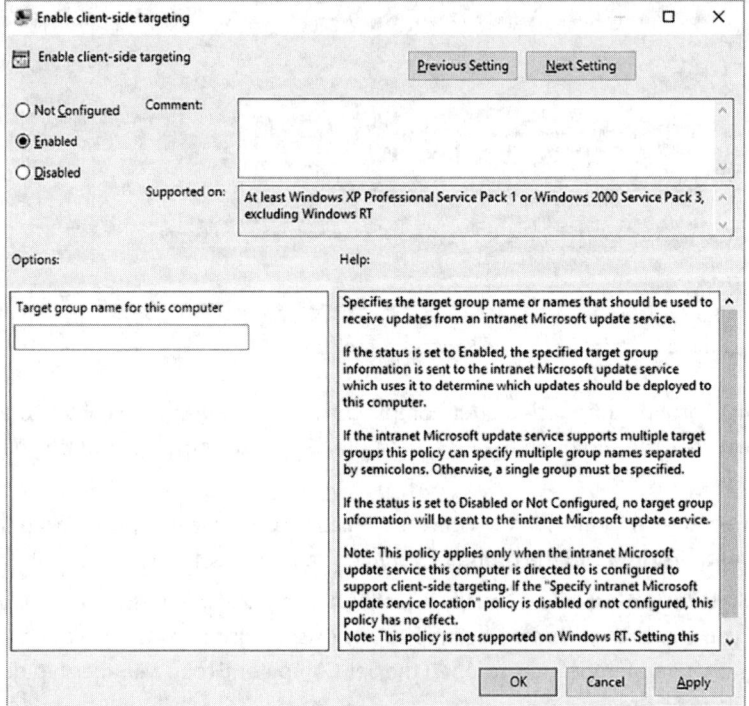

FIGURE 6-13 The Enable Client-side Targeting policy

>  **Quick check**
>
> Which of the following best describes the function of the Enable Client-side Targeting Group Policy setting?
>
> 1. Enables clients to download updates from a WSUS server instead of the Microsoft Update servers on the Internet
> 2. Automatically creates WSUS computer groups
> 3. Enables client computers to automatically add themselves to a WSUS group
> 4. Enables administrators to manually add WSUS client computers to groups
>
> **Quick check answer**
>
> The Enable client-side targeting Group Policy setting enables client computers to automatically add themselves to a WSUS group (#3).

Manage patch management in mixed environments

One of the primary advantages of WSUS is that it provides administrators with an opportunity to evaluate and test updates before deploying them on production networks. The process of evaluating and testing updates is one that must be developed by the network administrator. Microsoft tests its updates carefully before releasing them to the public, but they cannot possibly test every combination of operating systems, device drivers, applications, and other software components that exist in a mixed environment. Conflicts and incompatibilities might occur, and it is up to the administrator to develop policies that screen updates for these types of issues before they deploy them.

Depending on the nature of the updates and the complexity of the workstation configurations, the update evaluation process might consist of any or all of the following:

- An evaluation of the documentation included with the update release
- A waiting period, to determine whether other users experience problems
- A pilot deployment on a small subsection of the network
- An internal testing regimen conducted on a laboratory network

In a mixed environment with computers running many versions and editions of Windows, the regimen for the evaluation of new updates is likely to vary. Server updates, for example, should be evaluated and tested more thoroughly than workstation updates. Older operating system versions typically require many more updates than newer ones, and might require an adjustment of priorities to evaluate them all.

Approving updates

Once the evaluation process for a specific update is completed, an administrator can approve the update for deployment using the Update Services console on the WSUS server. By right-clicking an update and selecting Approve from the context menu, you open the Approve Updates dialog box, as shown earlier, in which you specify which groups you want to receive that update.

Configuring WSUS clients

Before the client computers on the network can download updates from the WSUS server, you must configure their Windows Update clients. The Windows Update page in the Windows Server 2016 and Windows 10 operating systems does not provide any means of configuring the client to use an internal WSUS server instead of the Microsoft Update servers, and even if it did, individual client configuration would not be a practical solution for a large network. Instead, you configure the Windows Update clients on your network using Group Policy settings.

As usual, in an AD DS environment, the recommended practice for deploying Group Policy settings is to create a new Group Policy object (GPO), configure the required Windows Update settings, and link the GPO to an appropriate domain, site, or organizational unit object. If you are using multiple WSUS servers, you can distribute the client load among them by creating a separate GPO for each server and linking them to different objects.

> **NOTE WINDOWS UPDATE AND OS VERSIONS**
>
> The Windows Update Group Policy settings apply to all Windows server and workstation versions, going back to Windows 2000. There is no need to create different GPOs or AD DS objects for different Windows versions, to configure Windows Update.

In a GPO, the Windows Update settings are located in the Computer Configuration\Policies\Administrative Templates\Windows Components\Windows Update folder. The key Group Policy setting for the Windows Update client is Configure Automatic Updates, as shown in Figure 6-14.

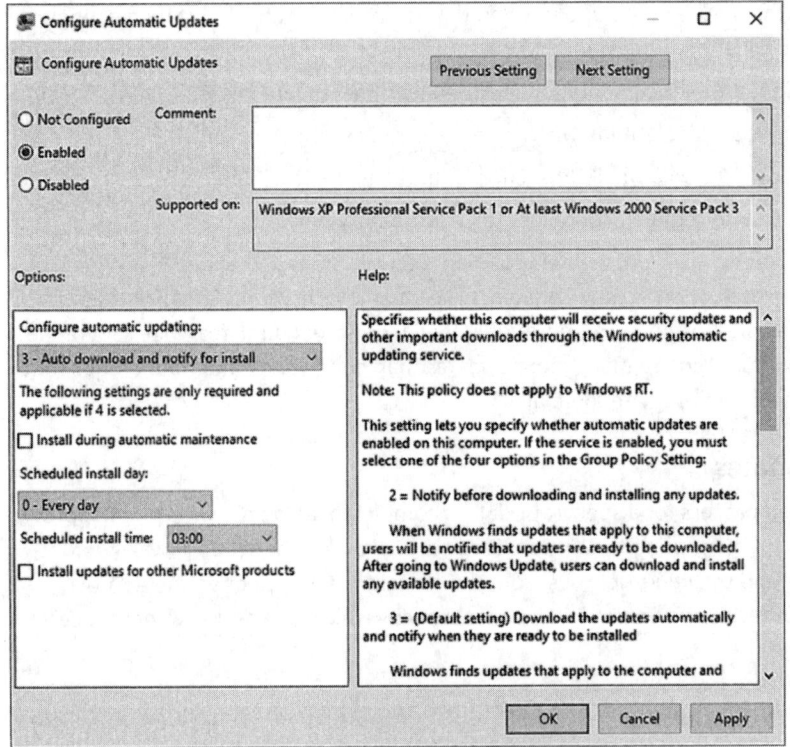

FIGURE 6-14 The Configure Automatic Updates dialog box

This setting, when enabled, activates the client, specifies the degree of user interactivity in the update process, and schedules the time and day when automated update installations should occur. In an enterprise environment, it is typical for administrators to completely automate the update process, leaving no choice to the user whether the computer should download and install updates.

There are two main issues that can complicate an automated update process of this type.

1. The first is that some updates must replace files that are in use while the operating system is running. The client therefore requires the system to restart to replace these files. An involuntary restart can cause problems for the user working at the workstation, so there are Group Policy settings that can modify the default behavior of the client in this respect.

    - **Delay Restart For Scheduled Installations**   When enabled, it specifies the time interval (in minutes) that the client waits after completing an update installation before it restarts the system. When disabled or not configured, the default time interval is 15 minutes.

    - **Re-Prompt For Restart With Scheduled Installations**   When a user postpones a restart requested by the client, this setting, when enabled, specifies the time interval (in minutes) before the client prompts the user again.

    - **No Auto-Restart With Logged On Users For Scheduled Automatic Updates Installations**   When enabled, prevents the client from automatically restarting the computer when a user is logged on. Instead, the client notifies the user to restart the system to complete the update installation.

2. The second issue is the behavior of the Windows Update client when the computer is shut off during the time of a scheduled update. Obviously, when the computer is not running, an update cannot occur. The next time that the computer starts, the client performs all scheduled tasks that it has missed. However, the following Group Policy settings can control the behavior of the client when this occurs:

    - **Enabling Windows Update Power Management To Automatically Wake Up The System To Install Scheduled Updates**   When enabled, causes the computer to wake from a hibernation state when there are updates to be installed. If the computer is running on battery power, the client aborts the update installation and returns the computer to the hibernation state after two minutes.

    - **Reschedule Automatic Updates Scheduled Installations**   When enabled, specifies the time interval (in minutes) that the client should wait after system startup before it performs a missed, scheduled update installation. When not configured, the client waits a default time interval of 1 minute before initiating a missed, scheduled installation. When disabled, the client defers the update until the next scheduled installation.

For WSUS clients, the key Group Policy setting is Specify Intranet Microsoft Update Service Location, as shown in Figure 6-15.

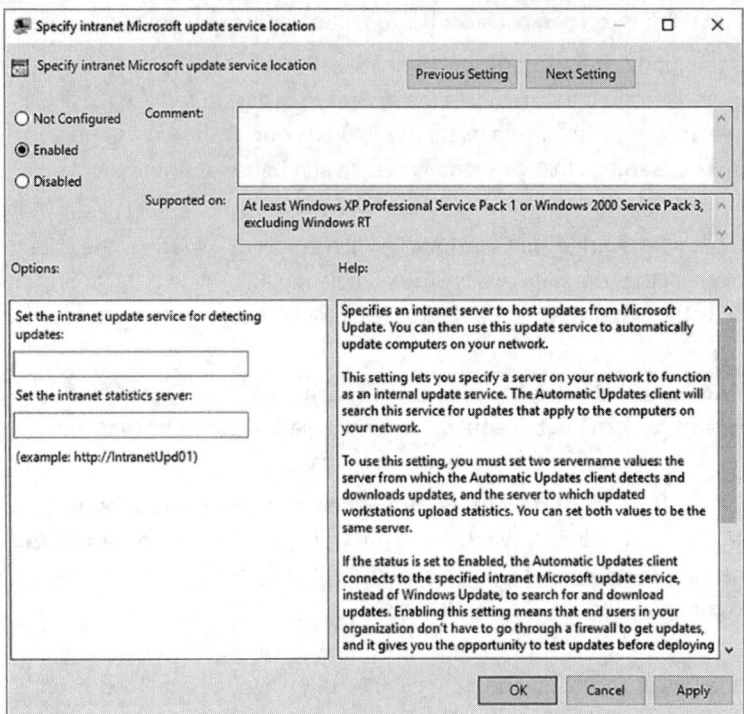

FIGURE 6-15 The Specify Intranet Microsoft Update Service Location dialog box

In the Set The Intranet Update Device For Detecting Updates and Set The Intranet Statistics Server text boxes, type the URL for the WSUS server you want the clients to use. By default, this will take a form like the following:

```
http://server1:8530
```

> **NOTE   WSUS PORT NUMBER**
>
> WSUS uses port number 8530 by default when configuring IIS to host its web site. If you modify the default IIS configuration, you must change the URL accordingly.

This setting causes the Windows Update client to connect to your WSUS server for updates, rather than the Microsoft Update servers. If you have configured your WSUS server not to store updates locally, then the client will contact the WSUS server to determine which files it needs and then download those files from the Internet servers.

In addition, you can configure the following settings, which only take effect when you enable the Specify Intranet Microsoft Update Service Location setting:

- **Automatic Updates Detection Frequency**   When enabled, specifies the interval (in hours) at which the client checks the server for new updates.

- **Allow Signed Updates From An Intranet Microsoft Update Service Location** When enabled, allows clients to download and install updates not signed by Microsoft. However, updates must be signed with a certificate found in the computer's Trusted Publishers store. This enables administrators to deploy their own updates using WSUS.

Implement an antimalware solution with Windows Defender

Windows Defender is the antimalware feature included in Windows Server 2016, Running as a service called Windefend, the feature is installed and activated by default on all Windows Server 2016 installations. Defender continuously monitors the system for spyware, viruses, and other threats, and generates notifications and system events when a threat is detected.

Because Defender is activated by default, there is nothing to be done to install it. However, you might want to deactivate it, such as when you are going to run a third-party antimalware product with which it is incompatible. To uninstall Windows Defender, you can use the Remove Roles and Features Wizard in Server Manager or the Uninstall-WindowsFeature PowerShell cmdlet, as in the following example:

```
uninstall-windowsfeature -name windowsserverantimalware
```

Configuring Defender Graphically

To configure Windows Defender, you open the Settings window and select the Windows Defender page, as shown in Figure 6-16.

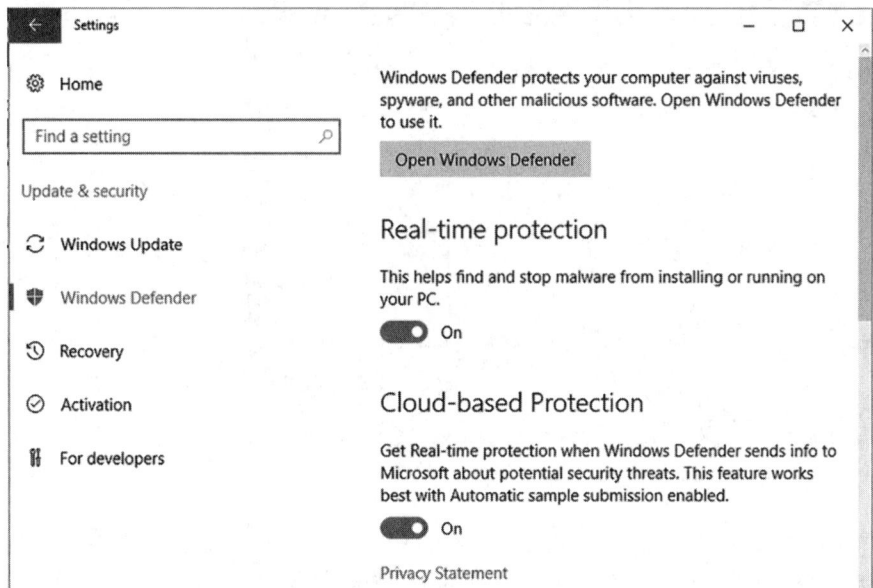

FIGURE 6-16 The Windows Defender page in the Settings window

On this page, you can configure the following Defender properties:

- **Real-Time Protection**   Enables Windows Defender to continuously scan the system for malware. If you turn this option off, Windows will eventually attempt to turn it on again. If you turn it off to install another antimalware solution that is incompatible with Windows Defender, the system will generate errors when it is unable to turn real-time protection on again. The best practice is to uninstall Windows Defender entirely if you plan to use another product.
- **Cloud-Based Protection**   Enables Windows Defender to send information about its findings to Microsoft servers in the cloud for research purposes.
- **Automatic Sample Submission**   Enables Windows Defender to send samples of infected files to Microsoft servers in the cloud without prompting. Disabling this option causes Windows Defender to prompt the user before uploading samples.
- **Exclusions**   Enables users to specify files, folders, file types, and processes that should be excluded from Windows Defender's scans.
- **Enhanced Notifications**   Enables Windows Defender to generate notifications regarding its activities. Disabling its features causes Defender to suppress all but critical notifications.

Windows Defender performs regular scans of the system, but it is also possible to perform manual scans and examine Defender's activities. Clicking Open Windows Defender launches Defender's graphical interface, as shown in Figure 6-17.

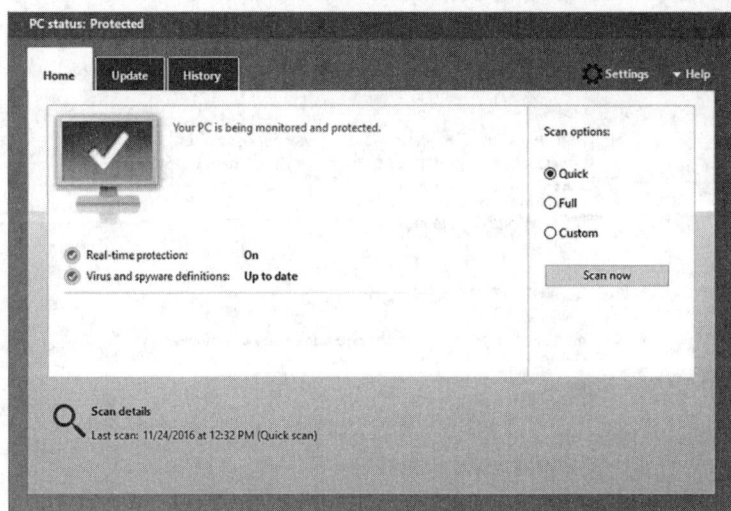

FIGURE 6-17 The Windows Defender graphical interface

This window displays Defender's status and enables you to scan all or part of the system. You can also click the Update tab to check the status of Defender's virus and spyware definitions, or click the History tab to examine the results of Defender's scans.

Configuring defender using PowerShell

The graphical Windows Defender interface provides control over only a few basic settings. For more granular control, Windows Defender includes a Windows PowerShell module, also called Defender, which contains cmdlets that enable you to monitor and control Defender's activities in greater detail. For example, the Get-MpComputerStatus cmdlet displays whether Windows Defender's functions are enabled and the dates of the most recent updates and scans, as shown in Figure 6-18.

```
PS C:\Users\administrator.ADATUM> Get-MpComputerStatus

AMEngineVersion                  : 1.1.13303.0
AMProductVersion                 : 4.10.14393.0
AMServiceEnabled                 : True
AMServiceVersion                 : 4.10.14393.0
AntispywareEnabled               : True
AntispywareSignatureAge          : 1
AntispywareSignatureLastUpdated  : 11/26/2016 7:07:34 AM
AntispywareSignatureVersion      : 1.233.672.0
AntivirusEnabled                 : True
AntivirusSignatureAge            : 1
AntivirusSignatureLastUpdated    : 11/26/2016 7:07:35 AM
AntivirusSignatureVersion        : 1.233.672.0
BehaviorMonitorEnabled           : True
ComputerID                       : C7C703DC-CC17-4CDC-B097-32A5F06EB730
ComputerState                    : 0
FullScanAge                      : 4294967295
FullScanEndTime                  :
FullScanStartTime                :
IoavProtectionEnabled            : True
LastFullScanSource               : 0
LastQuickScanSource              : 2
NISEnabled                       : True
NISEngineVersion                 : 2.1.12706.0
NISSignatureAge                  : 4294967295
NISSignatureLastUpdated          :
NISSignatureVersion              : 116.67.0.0
OnAccessProtectionEnabled        : True
QuickScanAge                     : 2
QuickScanEndTime                 : 11/24/2016 12:37:57 PM
QuickScanStartTime               : 11/24/2016 12:32:18 PM
RealTimeProtectionEnabled        : True
RealTimeScanDirection            : 0
PSComputerName                   :
```

FIGURE 6-18 Output of the **Get-MpComputerStatus cmdlet**

The primary cmdlet for configuring Windows Defender is Set-MpPreference, which supports dozens of parameters that control Defender's features. Some of the parameters that you can use with Set-MpPreference are as follows:

- **CheckForSignaturesBeforeRunningScan**   Specifies whether Defender should check for new definition releases before beginning a scan.
- **DisableArchiveScanning**   Specifies whether Defender should scan the contents of archive files, such as zips and cabs.
- **DisableEmailScanning**   Specifies whether Defender should scan the contents of standard mailbox files.
- **DisableIOAVProtection**   Specifies whether Defender should scan downloaded files and attachments.
- **DisableRealtimeMonitoring**   Specifies whether Defender should use real-time protection. This parameter conforms to the Real-time Protection switch in the Settings window.

- **ExclusionPath**   Specifies a path that Defender should exclude from its scans. There are similar parameters that enable you to exclude extensions and processes.
- **LowThreatDefaultAction {Clean | Quarantine | Remove | Allow | UserDefined | NoAction | Block}**   Specifies what remediation action Defender should take when it detects a low level threat. There are similar parameters for moderate and high level threats.
- **ScanParameters {QuickScan | FullScan}**   Specifies what type of scan Defender should perform during its scheduled scans.

Configuring defender using group policy

Configuring Windows Defender on servers individually, or leaving the configuration to individual server administrators, is not a practical solution for an enterprise that takes security seriously, the preferred alternative in this type of environment is to configure Windows Defender settings at the network level. You can use Group Policy to assign Windows Defender settings for all the computers in Active Directory Domain Services (AD DS) domains, sites, or organizational units.

Windows Defender settings are located in Group Policy objects in the Computer Configuration/Policies/Administrative Templates/Windows Components/Windows Defender folder, as shown in Figure 6-19.

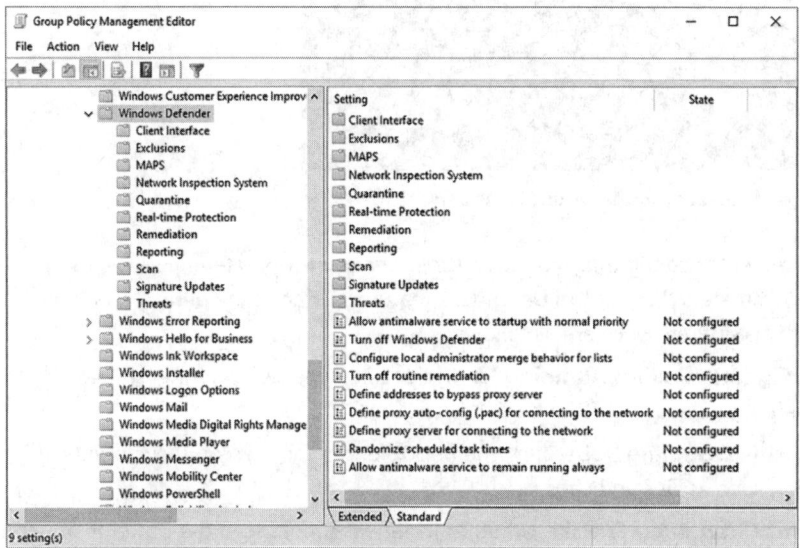

FIGURE 6-19 The Windows Defender folder in a Group Policy object

Group Policy provides even more granular control over Windows Defender than Windows PowerShell. There are nearly one hundred Defender policy settings in a Group Policy object, enabling you to configure every aspect of Defender's performance, as well as the information that is presented to users.

Integrate Windows Defender with WSUS and Windows Update

To maintain the protection it provides, Windows Defender must have updates to its spyware and virus signature definitions on a regular basis. These signatures tell Windows Defender what to look for during its scans.

By default, Windows Server 2016 updates Windows Defender along with the operating system updates, by downloading them directly from the Internet using Windows Update. However, if you use WSUS to deploy updates to your network computer, you might want to ensure that Windows Defender definition updates are approved automatically, so they can be deployed as quickly as possible. You can do this by completing the following tasks in the Update Services console.

1. Launch Update Services, expand the server icon, and select the Options page.
2. Select Products and Classification.
3. On the Products tab, scroll down and select the Windows Defender checkbox, shown in Figure 6-20, and click Apply.

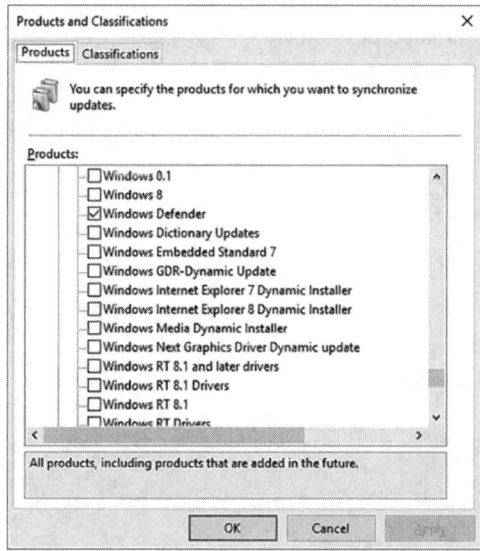

FIGURE 6-20 The Products tab of the Products and Classifications dialog box

4. On the Classification tab, select the Definition Updates checkbox and click OK.
5. Click Automatic Approvals.
6. On the Update Rules tab, click New Rule.
7. In the Add Rule dialog box, shown in Figure 6-21, in the Step 1 box, select the When An Update Is In A Specific Classification checkbox.

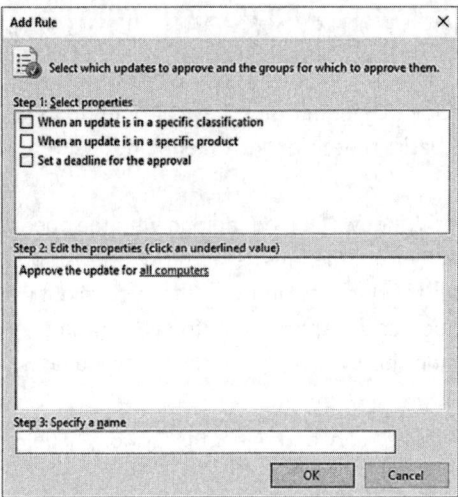

FIGURE 6-21 The Add Rule dialog box

8. In the Step 2 box, click the Any Classification link.
9. In the Choose Update Classifications dialog box, shown in Figure 6-22, clear all the checkboxes except for Definition Updates, and click OK.

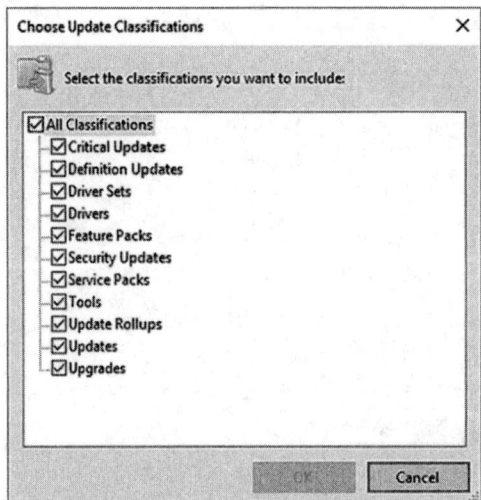

FIGURE 6-22 The Choose Update Classifications dialog box

10. In the Step 2 box, click the All Computers link.
11. In the Choose Computer Groups dialog box, clear all the checkboxes except those of the groups you want to receive the updates, and click OK.
12. In the Step 3 box, type a name for the rule and click OK.
13. Click OK to close the Automatic Approvals dialog box.

Perform backup and restore operations using Windows Server Backup

Windows Server 2016 includes a backup software program that you can use to back up your volumes to an internal or external hard drive, to a writable DVD drive, or to a network share. Windows Server Backup is designed primarily to create backups of entire server volumes on an external hard disk drive. Thus, many of the more advanced backup software features included in third-party products are absent from Windows Server Backup.

Some of the most important factors that administrators must understand about Windows Server Backup are as follows:

- **Limited Drive Support** Windows Server Backup does not support tape or optical drives that are not accessible through the file system. The program is designed primarily for use with external hard disk drives, using a USB or IEEE 1394 connection.
- **Limited Scheduling** Windows Server Backup can only schedule a single job, and is limited to running the job either daily or multiple times per day. You cannot schedule a job for a future date, or specify a interval of more than 24 hours between jobs.
- **Limited Job Types** Windows Server Backup does not enable you to perform full, incremental, and differential backups on a per-job basis. You can configure all of your backups to be either full or incremental, or select full or incremental for each target volume. The program does not support differential jobs.
- **Different Backup Format** Windows Server Backup writes its backup files in VHDX (Virtual Hard Disk) format, which makes them accessible using Hyper-V or the Disk Management snap-in.

Windows Server Backup takes the form of a feature that you must install using the Add Roles and Features Wizard in Server Manager or the Install-WindowsFeature cmdlet in Windows PowerShell. Adding the feature installs the Windows Server Backup console, as shown in Figure 6-23.

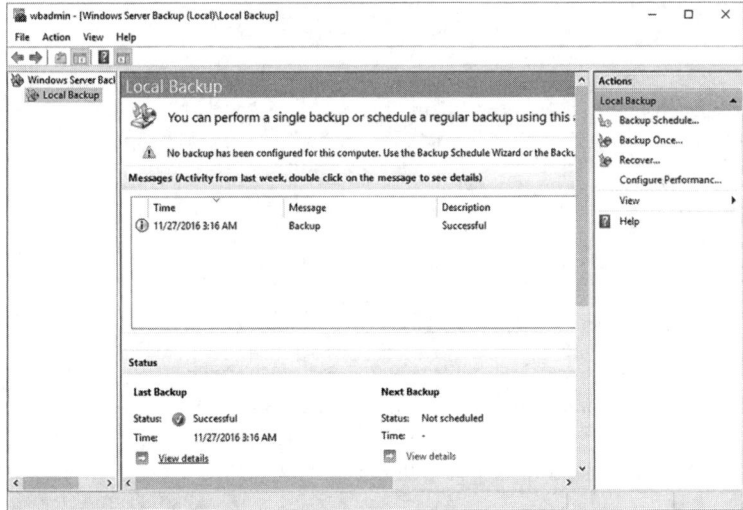

FIGURE 6-23 The Windows Server Backup console

In addition to installing the Windows Server Backup feature, you must have a backup device accessible to the system, either a hard disk or a network share. Once you have installed Windows Server Backup, you can begin creating your backup jobs.

Creating a single backup job

Windows Server Backup can perform single, interactive backup jobs that begin immediately, or automated jobs that you schedule to commence later. Single backup jobs provide more flexibility than scheduled ones, with the obvious disadvantage that someone must be there to create and start the job. You can use a local disk or a network share for your backups. If there is not enough space for the backup job on the selected target, the job fails.

To create a single backup job using a local disk as the job destination, use the following procedure.

1. Open the Windows Server Backup console and, in the Actions pane, click Backup Once to launch the Backup Once Wizard.

2. On the Backup Options page, leave the Different Options option selected. If you already have a scheduled backup job configured on the system, you can select Scheduled Backup Options to run a single instance of that job immediately.

3. On the Select Backup Configuration page appears, shown in Figure 6-24, select the Custom option.

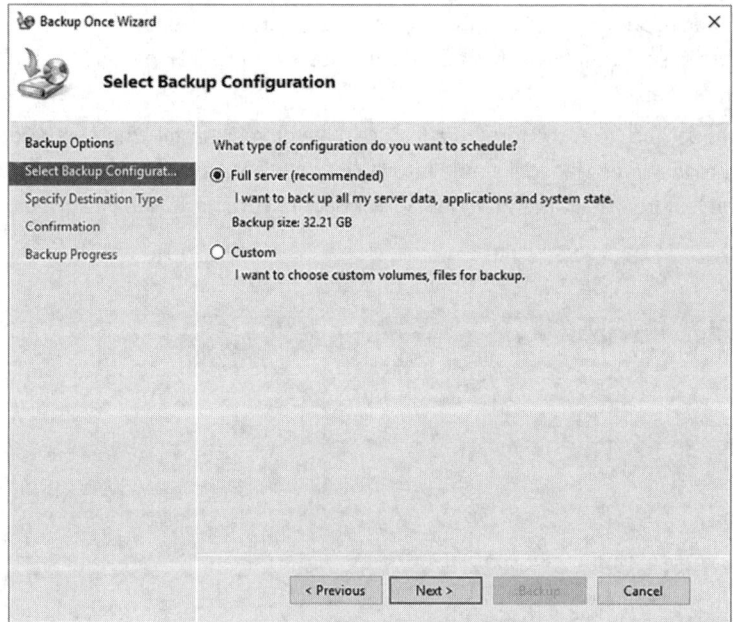

FIGURE 6-24 The Select Backup Configuration page of the Backup Once Wizard

4. On the Select Items for Backup page, click Add Items.

> **NOTE EXCLUDING FILE TYPES**
>
> Click the Advanced Settings button on the Select Items for Backup page to create exclusions that prevent specified file types from being backed up during the job.

5. In the Select Items dialog box, as shown in Figure 6-25, select the system elements you want to back up.

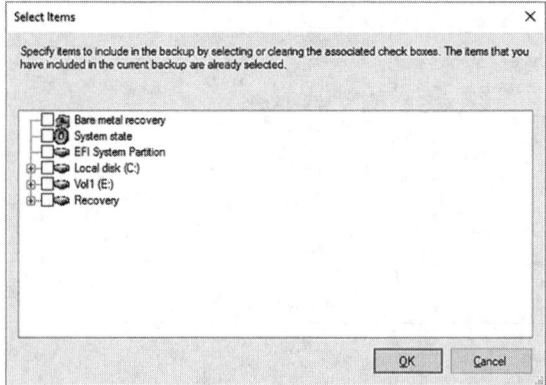

FIGURE 6-25 The Select Items dialog box of the Backup Once Wizard

6. On the Specify Destination Type page, shown in Figure 6-26, leave the Local drives option selected.

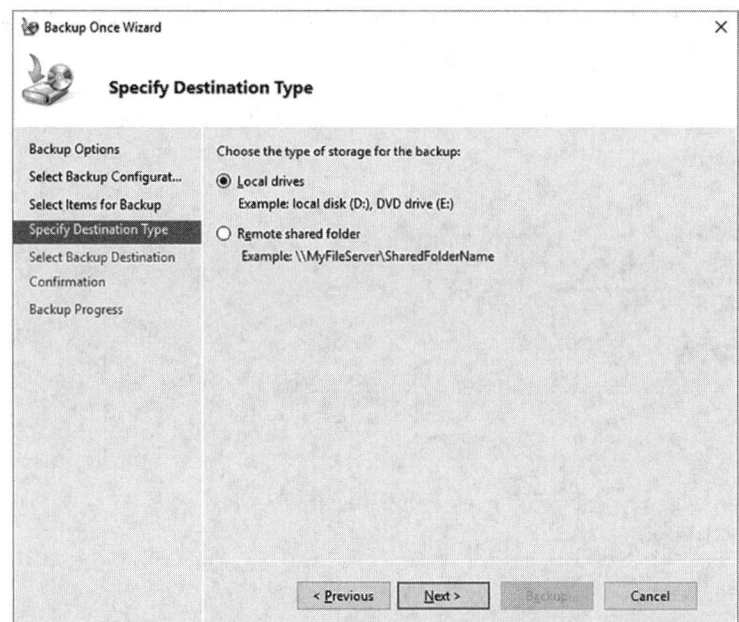

FIGURE 6-26 The Specify Destination Type page of the Backup Once Wizard

7. On the Select Backup Destination page, shown in Figure 6-27, use the Backup Destination drop-down list to select the volume where you want the program to store the backups.

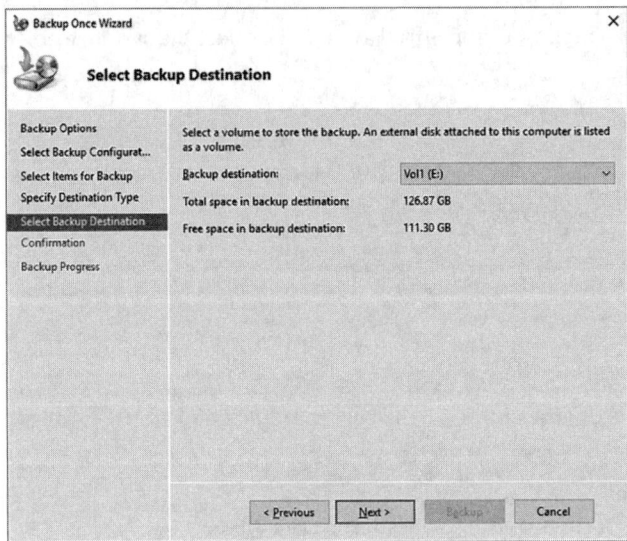

FIGURE 6-27 The Select Backup Destination page of the Backup Once Wizard

8. On the Confirmation page, click Backup to begin the job.
9. On the Backup Progress page, shown in Figure 6-28, you can monitor the job as it proceeds.

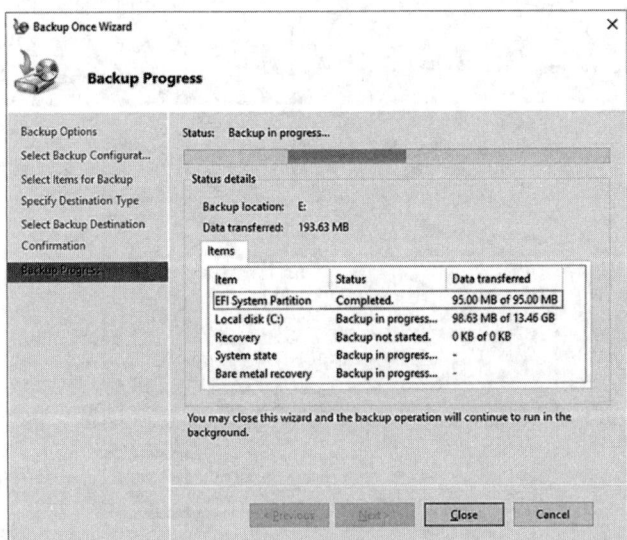

FIGURE 6-28 The Backup Progress page of the Backup Once Wizard

10. Click Close. The backup job continues in the background, even after you close the wizard and the console.

Performing a scheduled backup

Windows Server backup makes it possible to schedule a backup job to execute at the same time(s) each day. When you create a scheduled backup job, the options are somewhat different from a single, interactive job. First, you cannot use optical disks or network shares as backup drives; you must use a hard disk connected to the computer, either internal, or external. Second, you cannot simply perform a backup to a file stored anywhere on the computer and manage it using Windows Explorer, as you would any other file. Windows Server Backup reformats the backup disk you select and uses it for backups exclusively.

To create a scheduled backup job, use the following procedure.

1. Open the Windows Server Backup console and, in the Actions pane, click Backup Schedule to launch the Backup Schedule Wizard.
2. On the Select Backup Configuration page appears, select the Custom option.
3. On the Select Items for Backup page, click Add Items.
4. In the Select Items dialog box, select the system elements you want to back up.
5. On the Specify Backup Time page, shown in Figure 6-29, leave the Once a Day option selected and use the Select Time of Day drop-down list to specify when the backup should occur.

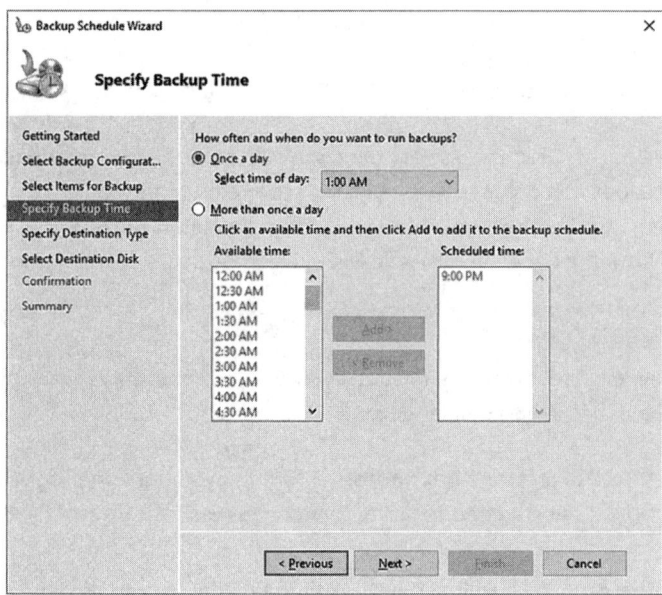

FIGURE 6-29 The Specify Backup Time page of the Backup Schedule Wizard

> **NOTE RUNNING MULTIPLE DAILY BACKUPS**
>
> For a computer running a volatile application, such as a Web server, you might want to select the More Than Once a Day option and select multiple times for the backup to occur each day.

6. On the Specify Destination Type page, shown in Figure 6-30, select the Back Up To A Hard Disk That Is Dedicated For Backups option.

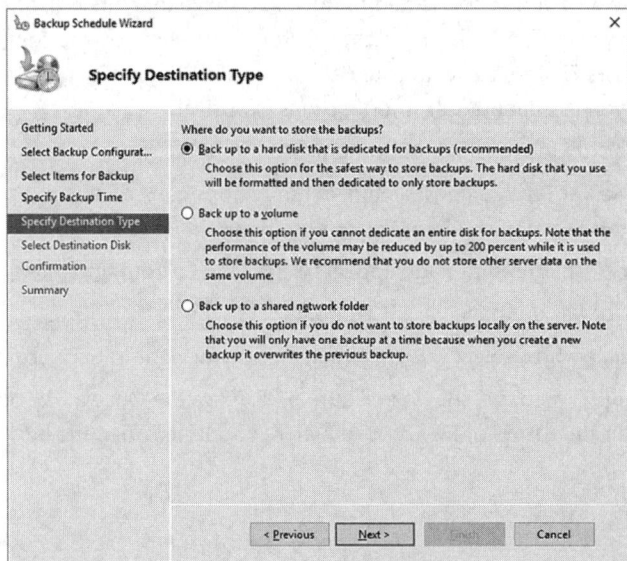

FIGURE 6-30 The Specify Destination Type page of the Backup Schedule Wizard

7. On the Select Destination Disk page, select the disk you want to use for your backups. The Available Disks box lists only the external disks connected to the computer. To use an internal disk, you must click Show All Available Disks and select the disk(s) you want to add to the list from the Show All Available Disks dialog box.

> **NOTE CREATING MIRRORED BACKUPS**
>
> If you select multiple disks on the Select Destination Disk page, Windows Server Backup will create identical copies of the backup files on each disk.

8. A Windows Server Backup message box appears, informing you that the program will reformat the disk(s) you selected and dedicate them exclusively to backups. Click Yes to continue.

9. On the Confirmation page, click Finish. The wizard formats the backup disk and schedules the backup job to begin at the time you specified.

10. Click Close.

Windows Server Backup only enables you to schedule one backup job, so the next time you start the Backup Schedule Wizard, your only options are to modify or stop the current backup job.

Configuring incremental backups

Windows Server Backup supports incremental jobs, but in a manner that is different from some other backup software products. When Windows Server Backup takes control of a backup disk, it creates new, separate files for the backup job(s) it performs each day. The system retains the files for all the old jobs until the disk is filled or 512 jobs are stored on the disk, whichever comes first. Then, the system begins deleting the oldest jobs as needed.

Unlike most backup software programs, Windows Server Backup does not enable you to specify a job type for each individual job you perform. You cannot choose to perform a full backup on Saturday, and an incremental or differential backup on each weekday, for example. Therefore, traditional job planning strategies and tape rotation methods do not apply here.

Windows Server Backup does support incremental backups, but only as a general setting that applies to all your backup jobs. When you select Configure Performance Settings from the actions pane in the Windows Server Backup console, an Optimize Backup Performance dialog box appears, as shown in Figure 6-31.

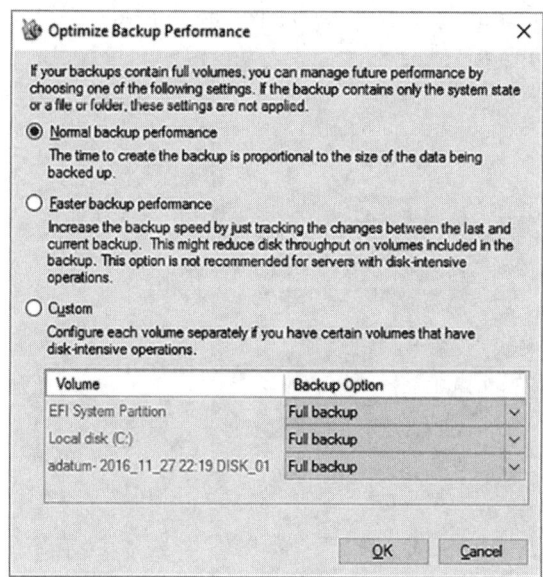

FIGURE 6-31 The Optimize Backup Performance dialog box

The Normal Backup Performance option, which is the default, causes the program to copy every file on the selected volume(s) to the backup medium, every time you perform a backup. This means that the program copies all the operating system and application files on the volume(s), files which never change, to the backup disk over and over, possibly occupying a great deal of space to no useful end.

When you select the Faster Backup Performance option, the program only copies the files that have changed since the previous backup, which is called an incremental backup. The first backup job is always a full backup, of course, but subsequent jobs use much less storage space, enabling the program to maintain a longer backup history. The Custom option enables you to specify whether to perform full or incremental backups for each of the volumes on the computer.

Performing a restore

Windows Server Backup enables you to restore entire volumes or selected files, folders, and applications, using a wizard-based interface in the Windows Server Backup console. Once you have completed at least one backup job, you can use the Windows Server Backup console to restore all or part of the data on your backup disk. Administrators should perform test restores at regular intervals, to ensure that the backups are completing correctly.

To perform a restore of selected files or folders, use the following procedure.

1. Open the Windows Server Backup console and, in the Actions pane, click Recover to launch the Recovery Wizard.
2. On the Getting Started page, leave the This Server option selected.
3. On the Select Backup Date page, shown in Figure 6-32, in the Available Backups box, select the date of the backup you want to restore from, and if you performed more than one backup on that date, the time as well.

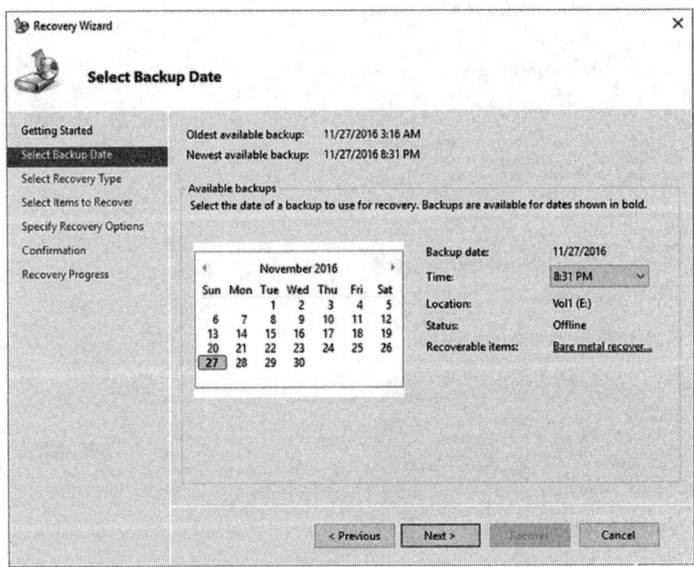

FIGURE 6-32 The Select Backup Date page, in the Recovery Wizard

4. On the Select Recovery Type page, shown in Figure 6-33, leave the Files And Folders option selected.

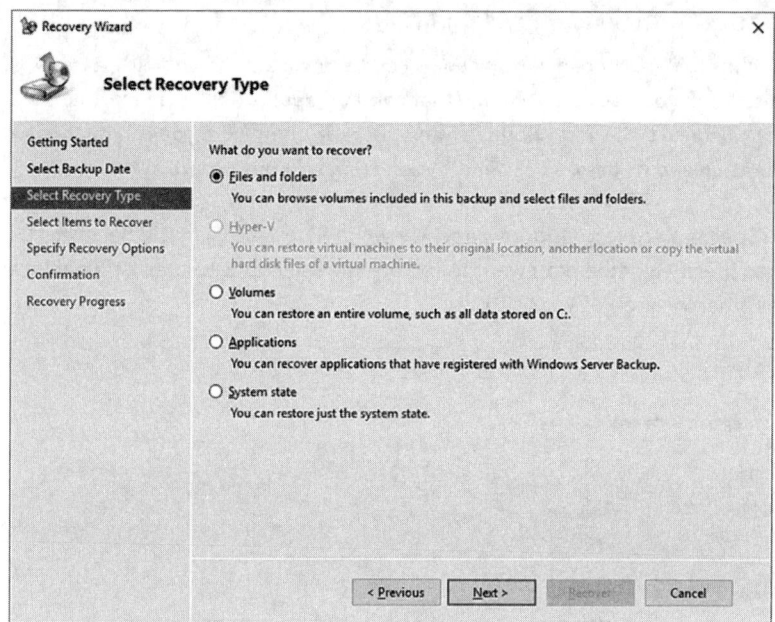

FIGURE 6-33 The Select Recovery Type page, in the Recovery Wizard

5. On the Select Items to Recover page, expand the server folder, as shown in Figure 6-34, and select the files or subfolders you want to restore.

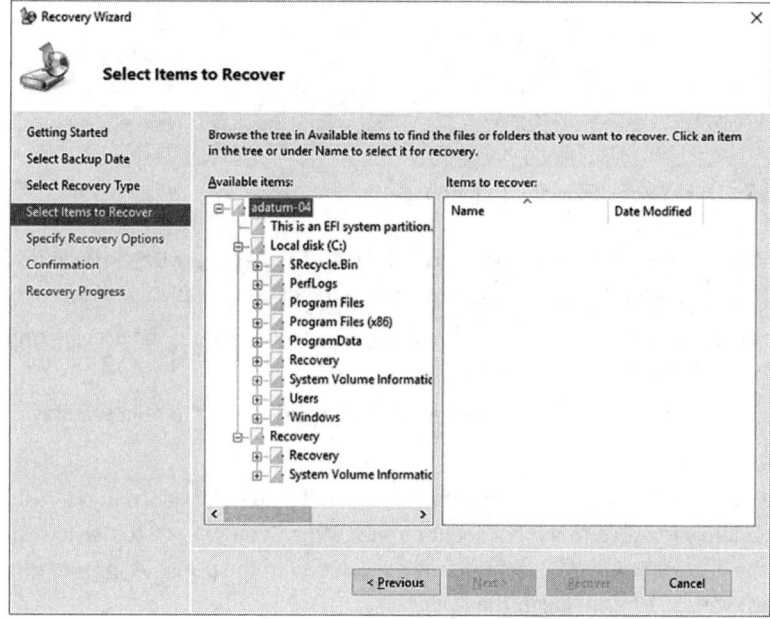

FIGURE 6-34 The Select Items to Recover page, in the Recovery Wizard

> **NOTE** **RESTORING VOLUMES AND APPLICATIONS**
>
> The Select Items to Recover page also enables you to restore entire volumes, as well as applications. When you back up a volume that contains applications that are Volume Shadow Copy Service (VSS) and Windows Server Backup compliant, you can restore an entire application and its data, all at once, by selecting it in the wizard.

6. On the Specify Recovery Options page, shown in Figure 6-35, in the Recovery Destination box, specify whether you want to restore the selections to their original locations or to another location of your choice.

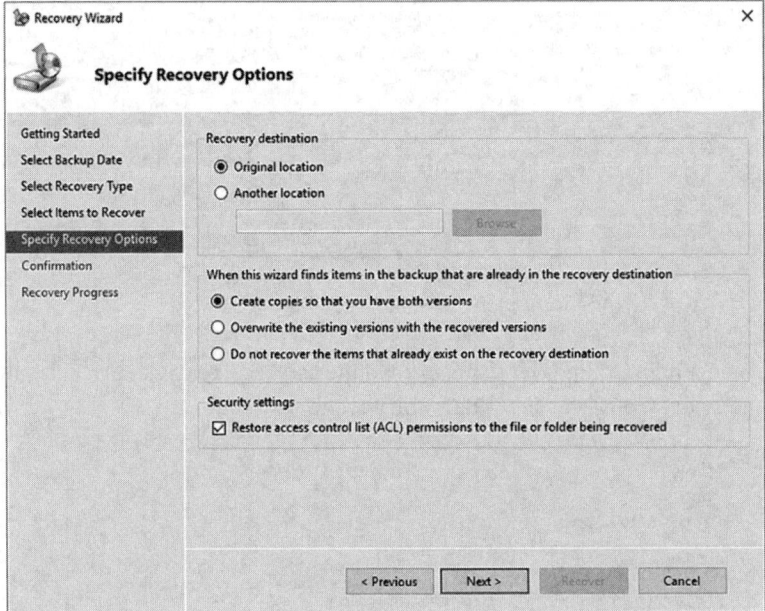

FIGURE 6-35 The Specify Recovery Options page, in the Recovery Wizard

7. In the When The Wizard Finds Files And Folders In The Recovery Destination box, specify whether you want to copy, overwrite, or skip the existing files and folders.

8. In the Security Settings box, specify whether you want to restore the access control lists of the selected files and folders.

9. On the Confirmation page, click Recover. The wizard restores the selected files.

10. Click Close.

Unlike many backup software products, the handling of incremental jobs in the restore process is completely invisible to the console operator. When you select a folder to restore, for example, the Recovery Wizard automatically accesses all of the previous jobs needed to locate the latest version of each file in the folder.

>  **Quick check**
>
> Which of the following device types is Windows Server Backup unable to use for a backup drive?
>
> 1. magnetic tape drives
> 2. internal disk drives
> 3. external hard disk drives
> 4. remote network shares
>
> **Quick check answer**
>
> Windows Server Backup does not support magnetic tape drives (#1), but can back up to internal or external disk drives, as well as remote network shares.

Determine backup strategies for different Windows Server roles and workloads, including Hyper-V Host, Hyper-V Guests, Active Directory, File Servers, and Web Servers using Windows Server 2016 native tools and solutions

Some Windows Server 2016 components present special difficulties for a backup solution, and yet at the same time, those components are often the ones most worth protecting.

Backing Up Active Directory

The Active Directory database is a crucial resource on most Windows networks, one that backup administrators must not ignore. However, backing up and restoring Active Directory is an exceptional process in nearly every way. When you perform a scheduled backup of an Active Directory domain controller, or perform a single backup with the System State checkbox selected, Windows Server Backup includes the Active Directory database as part of the system state, among other things.

Active Directory domains should have at least two domain controllers, and if that is the case, and one of them fails or is lost, it should not be necessary to restore the Active Directory database from a backup. Instead, you can reinstall the Active Directory Domain Services role, promote the computer to a domain controller, and allow the replication process to rebuild the database on the new domain controller.

Performing a full server restoration includes the system state, and consequently the Active Directory database, but there might be occasions when you want to retrieve parts of Active Directory, such as objects you have inadvertently deleted.

> **NOTE BACKING UP THE SYSTEM STATE**
>
> You can only work with the system state as a single entity. You cannot back up or restore individual elements within the system state.

It is possible to restore just the system state from a backup, but you must use the Wbadmin.exe command line tool, as in the following example:

```
wbadmin start systemstaterecovery -version:11/27/2016-11:07
```

The date and time value following the version: parameter is the version identifier for the backup from which you want to restore the system state. To list the version identifiers of the available backups, use the following command, as shown in Figure 6-36:

```
wbadmin get versions
```

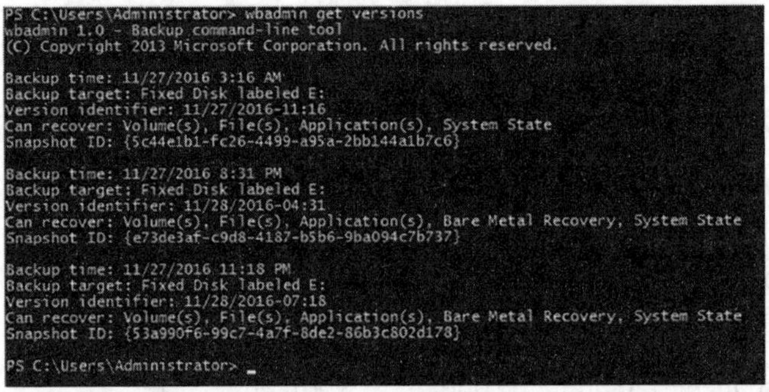

FIGURE 6-36 Output of the wbadmin get versions command

It is important for the administrator to understand that there are two types of system state restores: *authoritative* and *nonauthoritative*.

- **Nonauthoritative** When you open a Command Prompt window in a standard Windows session and restore the system state, you are performing a nonauthoritative restore. This means that the program will restore the Active Directory database to the exact state it was in at the time of the backup. However, the next time an Active Directory replication occurs, the other domain controllers will update the newly restored system with any changes that have occurred since the backup took place. This means that if you are trying to recover AD objects that you accidentally deleted, the replication process will cause the system to delete the newly restored objects.

- **Authoritative** To restore deleted objects, you must perform an authoritative restore, and to do this, you must restart the computer in Directory Services Repair Mode (DSRM) by pressing F8 during the boot process and selecting the appropriate entry from the Advanced Boot Options menu. After logging on using the Administrator account and the DSRM password specified during the Active Directory Domain Services installation, you can perform the system state restore using Wbadmin.exe. Once the restoration of the system state is complete, you can use the Ntdsutil.exe tool to specify the objects that you want restored authoritatively.

Backing up group policy objects

Group policy objects (GPOs) are a special case. You cannot use the authoritative restore procedure to restore GPOs that you have accidentally deleted. To back up and restore GPOs, you must use the Group Policy Management console. When you right-click a GPO in the console and select Back Up from the context menu, a Back Up Group Policy Object dialog box appears, as shown in Figure 6-37, in which you can specify the location for the backup.

FIGURE 6-37 The Back Up Group Policy Object dialog box

To restore a GPO, right-click the Group Policy Objects container and, from the context menu, select Manage Backups. The Manage Backups dialog box appears, as shown in Figure 6-38, in which you can select the GPO you want to recover and click the Restore button.

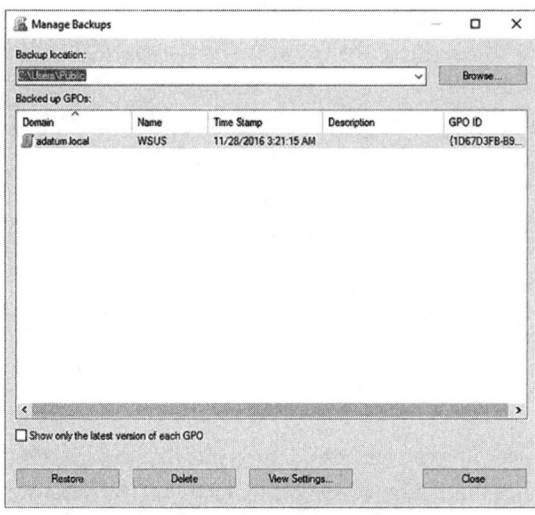

FIGURE 6-38 The Manage Backups dialog box

Backing Up Hyper-V

Hyper-V presents a problem for backup administrators. You can conceivably back up virtual machines as though they are separate systems, by running Windows Server Backup in the guest operating system. You can also back them up as part of the host server, by backing up the virtual machine files and the virtual hard disks.

Backing up from within the guest OS can provide access to resources that are not available through the host, such as pass-through disks, but it saves none of the virtual machine settings. If you must perform a restore of the guest, you must recreate the virtual machine first, with the appropriate settings, and then restore the guest OS. Microsoft recommends that administrators use this method in addition to a host backup, not in place of it.

Backing up virtual machines from the Hyper-V host uses the Hyper-V Volume Shadow Copy Requestor service in the guest operating system to enable the host to back up the VM while it is running. The requestor service in the guest communicates with the Volume Shadow Copy Service (VSS) in the host, enabling it to back up the virtual machine configuration files, the virtual hard disks, and any checkpoints associated with the VM. You can then restore the virtual machine from the host, if needed, without having to first configure it in Hyper-V.

Windows Server Backup includes support for the VSS writer and the guest requestor service, making it a simple matter to backup virtual machines and their host settings. When you create a backup of a Hyper-V host, the Select Items dialog box includes a Hyper-V item, as shown in Figure 6-39, that enables you to select the host components and the individual VMs running on the server.

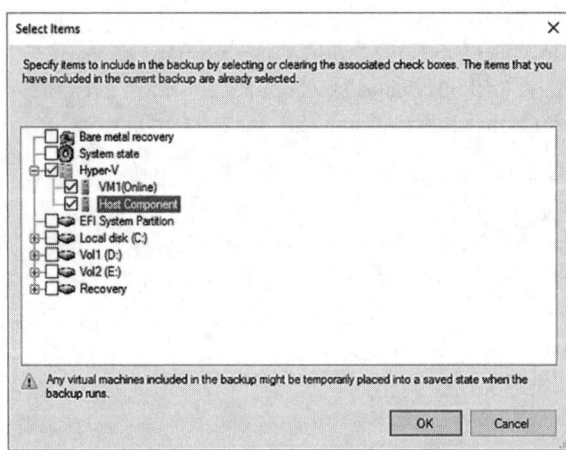

FIGURE 6-39 The Select Items dialog box on a Hyper-V host

Backing up IIS

Web sites running Internet Information Services (IIS) can include components that complicate the process of backing them up. The static files that make up a web site, such as HTML files, are not a problem, because they can be treated as files on a file server and backed up accordingly.

However, many web sites are connected to back-end databases, hosted by Microsoft SQL Server or other applications. The database can be located on the server running IIS or another server. To back these up, you must use a product that supports SQL Server backups. Windows Server Backup can perform VSS backups of SQL Server databases.

The third possible components of an IIS web site are the configuration files, including ApplicationHost.config, Administration.config, and Redirection.config. These are XML files, located in the Windows\System32\inetsrv folder, which contain the configuration settings for the IIS sites and applications.

Because these are XML files, they are not a problem to back up, but administrators must remember to select them for backup. It is also possible to back these configuration files up using an IIS utility called Appcmd.exe. To perform a backup of the IIS configuration files, you run a command like the following in the Windows\System32\inetsrv folder:

```
appcmd add backup configbackup1
```

To restore the configuration files from a previously performed backup, you use a command like the following:

```
appcmd restore backup configbackup1
```

Skill 6.2: Monitor server installations

Server performance can change over time for a variety of reasons. Workloads can change, and so can hardware components. Part of the server administrator's job is to track the ongoing performance of servers, to ensure that they continue to function efficiently. Windows Server 2016 includes tools that you can use for this performance tracking, such as the Performance Monitor console.

> **This section covers how to:**
> - Monitor workloads using Performance Monitor
> - Configure Data Collector Sets
> - Determine appropriate CPU, memory, disk, and networking counters for storage and compute workloads
> - Configure alerts
> - Monitor workloads using Resource Monitor

Monitor workloads using Performance Monitor

Performance Monitor is a tool that displays system performance statistics in real time. Using Performance Monitor, you can display hundreds of different statistics (called performance counters) and create customized graphs containing any information you choose.

When you open the Performance Monitor console from the Windows Administrative Tools group, you see an Overview page containing a system summary. Click the Performance Monitor icon and you see a line graph, updated in real time, showing the current level for the % Processor Time performance counter, as shown in Figure 6-40.

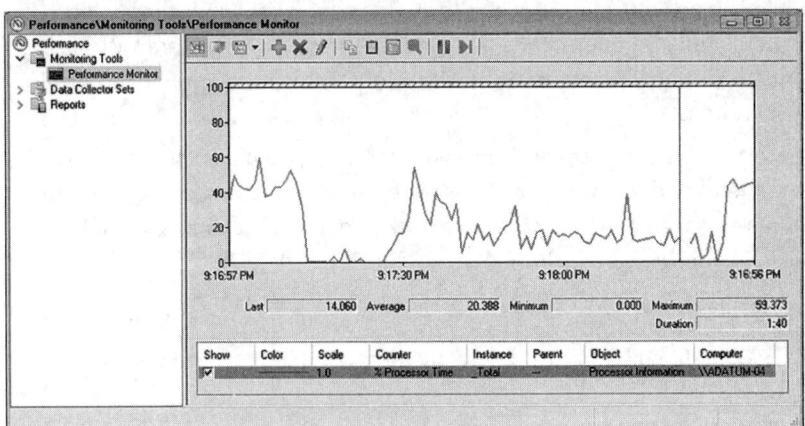

FIGURE 6-40 The default Performance Monitor display

A performance counter is a measure of the current activity in one aspect of a specific hardware or software component. The % Processor Time counter measures the percentage of the system processor's clock cycles that are being utilized by non-idle tasks. This is one of the basic measures of computer activity. A % Processor Time counter that is consistently pegged at 100 percent indicates that the processor is unable to keep up with the tasks it must perform.

There are counters available that measure processor performance in other ways, as well as counters for many other system components. You can add as many counters to the graph as you want, although adding too many can make the display difficult to interpret. By viewing the statistics generated by these counters and learning their significance, you can evaluate the performance of the computer in many ways.

Modifying the graph view

The legend beneath the Performance Monitor graph specifies the line color for each counter added to the display, the scale of values for each counter, and other identifying information. When you select a counter in the legend, its current values appear in numerical form at the bottom of the graph.

> **NOTE HIGHLIGHTING COUNTERS**
>
> When you have multiple counters in the Performance Monitor graph, clicking the Highlight button in the toolbar (or pressing Ctrl+H) changes the selected counter to a broad line that is easier to distinguish from the others.

If your computer is otherwise idle, you will probably notice that the line in the default graph is hovering near the bottom of the scale, making it difficult to see its exact value. You can address this problem by modifying the scale of the graph's Y (that is, vertical) axis. Click the Properties button in the toolbar (or press Ctrl+Q) to display the Performance Monitor Properties sheet and click the Graph tab, as shown in Figure 6-41. In the Vertical Scale box, you can reduce the maximum value for the Y axis, thereby using more of the graph to display the counter data.

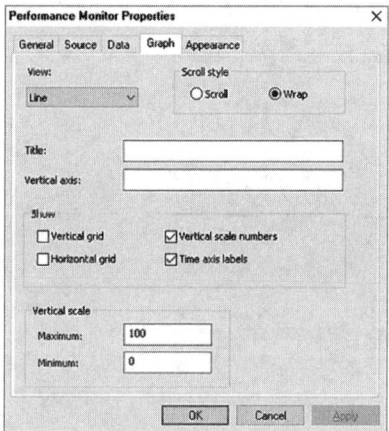

FIGURE 6-41 The Graph tab on the Performance Monitor Properties sheet

Depending on the nature of counters displayed in the graph, you might want to raise or lower the Maximum and Minimum values in the Vertical Scale box to create an ideal range for the Y axis. Different counters use different units of measurement for the data they present; they are not all percentages. Part of the skill in using Performance Monitor effectively is selecting counters with units of measurement and value ranges that work well together on the same graph.

On the General tab of the Performance Monitor Properties sheet, you can also modify the sample rate of the graph. By default, the graph updates the counter values every one second and displays 100 seconds worth of data at a time, but you can increase this value to display data for a longer period of time on a single page of the graph. This can make it easier to detect long-term trends in counter values.

> **NOTE MODIFYING THE GRAPH APPEARANCE**
>
> The Performance Monitor Properties sheet contains a few other controls that you can use to modify the appearance of the graph. For example, on the Graph tab, you can add axis titles and gridlines, and in the Appearance tab, you can control the graph's background and select a different font.

Other graph views

In addition to the line graph, Performance Monitor has two other views of the same data, a histogram bar graph and a report view. You can change the display to one of these views by clicking the Change Graph Type toolbar button. The histogram view is a bar graph with a separate vertical bar for each counter, as shown in Figure 6-42. In this view, it is easier to monitor large numbers of counters, because the lines do not overlap.

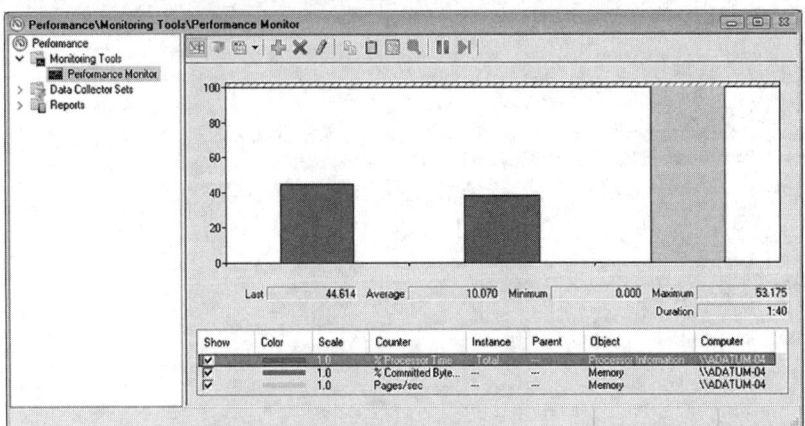

FIGURE 6-42 The Performance Monitor histogram view

The report view, shown in Figure 6-43, displays the numerical value for each of the performance counters.

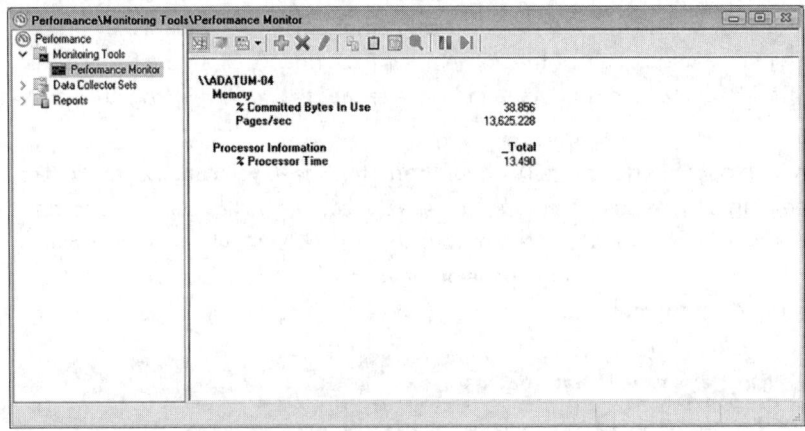

FIGURE 6-43 The Performance Monitor report view

As with the line graph, the histogram and report views both update their counter values at the interval specified on the General tab of the Performance Monitor Properties sheet. The main drawback of these two views, however, is that they do not display a history of the counter values, only the current value. Each new sampling overwrites the previous one in the display, unlike the line graph, which displays the previous values as well.

Adding performance counters

To add counters to the Performance Monitor display, click the Add button in the toolbar or press Ctrl+I, to display the Add Counters dialog box, as shown in Figure 6-44.

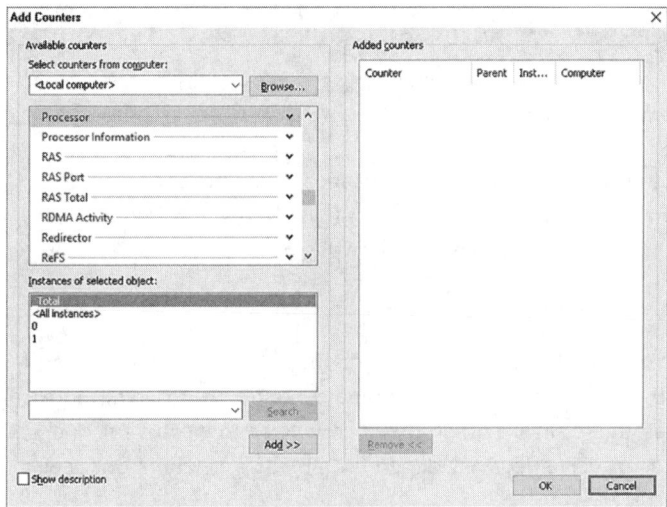

FIGURE 6-44 The Add Counters dialog box

In the Add Counters dialog box, you must specify the following four pieces of information to add a counter to the display:

- **Computer**   Specifies the name of the computer you want to monitor with the selected counter. Unlike most MMC snap-ins, you cannot redirect the entire focus of Performance Monitor to another computer on the network. Instead, you specify a computer name for each counter you add to the display. This enables you to create a display showing counters for various computers on the network, such as a single graph of the processor activity for all your servers.
- **Performance Object**   Specifies the hardware or software component in the computer you want to monitor. Click the down arrow on a performance object to display the performance counters related to that component.
- **Performance Counter**   Identifies a statistic representing a specific aspect of the selected performance object's activities.
- **Instance**   Identifies a specific occurrence of the selected performance counter. For example, on a computer with two network interface adapters, each counter in the Network Interface performance object has two instances, enabling you to track the performance of each adapter individually. Some counters also have instances such as

Total or Average, enabling you to track the performance of all instances combined or the median value of all instances.

Once you have selected a computer name, a performance object, a performance counter in that object, and an instance of that counter, click Add to add the counter to the Added Counters list. The dialog box remains open so that you can add more counters. Click OK when you are finished to update the graph with your selected counters.

> **NOTE UNDERSTANDING PERFORMANCE OBJECTS**
>
> Select the Show Description checkbox to display a detailed explanation of the selected performance object or performance counter.

The performance objects, performance counters, and instances that appear in the Add Counters dialog box depend on the computer's hardware configuration, the software installed on the computer, and the computer's role on the network.

Controlling the display

In many cases, when users first discover Performance Monitor, they see the hundreds of available performance counters and proceed to create a line graph containing a dozen or more different statistics. In most cases, the result is a graph that is crowded and incoherent. The number of counters that you can display effectively depends on the size of your monitor and the resolution of your video display.

Consider the following tips when selecting counters:

- **Limit The Number Of Counters**   Too many counters make the graph more difficult to understand. To display a large number of statistics, you can display multiple console windows (by right-clicking Performance Monitor and selecting New Window From Here) and select different counters in each one, or use the histogram or report view to display a large number of counters in a more compact form.

- **Modify The Counter Display Properties**   Depending on the size and capabilities of your monitor, the default colors and line widths that Performance Monitor uses in its graph might make it difficult to distinguish counters from each other. On the Data tab in the Performance Monitor Properties sheet, you can modify the color, style, and width of each counter's line in the graph, to make it easier to distinguish.

- **Choose Counters With Comparable Values**   Performance Monitor imposes no limitations on the combinations of counters you can select for a single graph, but some statistics are not practical to display together, because of their disparate values. When a graph contains a counter with a typical value that is under twenty and another counter with a value in the hundreds, it is difficult to arrange the display so that both counters are readable. Choose counters with values that are reasonably comparable, so that you can display them legibly. Here again, if you must display counters with different value ranges, you might prefer to use the report view instead of the graph view.

Configure data collector sets

Performance bottlenecks can develop on a server over a long period, and it can often be difficult to detect them by observing performance levels at one point in time. This is why it is a good idea to use tools like Performance Monitor to establish baseline levels for a server. A *baseline* is a set of readings, captured under normal operating conditions, which you can save and compare to readings taken later. By comparing the baseline readings to the server's current readings at regular intervals, you can discern trends that might eventually affect the computer's performance.

To capture counter statistics in Performance Monitor console for later review, you must create a *data collector set*, using the following procedure.

1. Open the Performance Monitor console and expand the Data Collector Sets folder.
2. Right-click the User Defined folder and, on the context menu, click New | Data Collector Set. The Create New Data Collector Set Wizard appears, displaying the How Would You Like To Create This New Data Collector Set page, as shown in Figure 6-45.

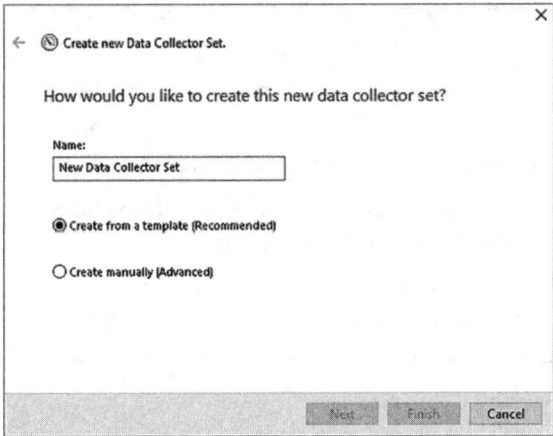

FIGURE 6-45 The How Would You Like To Create This New Data Collector Set page of the Create New Data Collector Set Wizard

3. In the Name text box, type a name for the data collector set. Then, select the Create Manually (Advanced) option.
4. On the What Type Of Data Do You Want To Include? page, shown in Figure 6-46, leave the Create Data Logs option selected and select the Performance Counter check box.

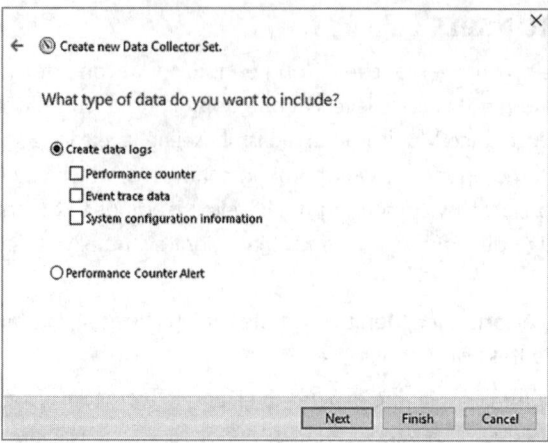

FIGURE 6-46 The What Type Of Data Do You Want To Include? page of the Create New Data Collector Set Wizard

5. On the Which Performance Counters Would You Like To Log page, click Add, to display the Add Counters dialog box.
6. Select the counters you want to log in the usual manner and click OK. The counters appear in the Performance Counters box.
7. Select the interval at which Performance Monitor should collect samples.
8. On the Where Would You Like The Data To Be Saved Page, type the name of or browse to the folder where you want to store the data collector set.
9. On the Create The Data Collector Set page, if the account you are currently using does not have the privileges needed to gather the log information, click Change to display a Performance Monitor dialog box in which you can supply alternative credentials.
10. Select one of the following options:
    - **Open Properties For This Data Collector Set** Saves the data collector set to the specified location and opens its Properties sheet for further modifications.
    - **Start This Data Collector Set Now** Saves the data collector set to the specified location and starts collecting data immediately.
    - **Save and Close** Saves the data collector set to the specified location and closes the wizard.
11. Click Finish. The new data collector set appears in the User Defined folder.
12. Right-click the new data collector set and, in the context menu, select Start. The console begins collecting data until you right-click and select Stop.

Once you have captured data using the collector set, you can display the data by double-clicking the Performance Monitor file in the folder you specified during its creation. This opens a Performance Monitor window containing a graph of the collected data, as shown in Figure 6-47, instead of real time activity.

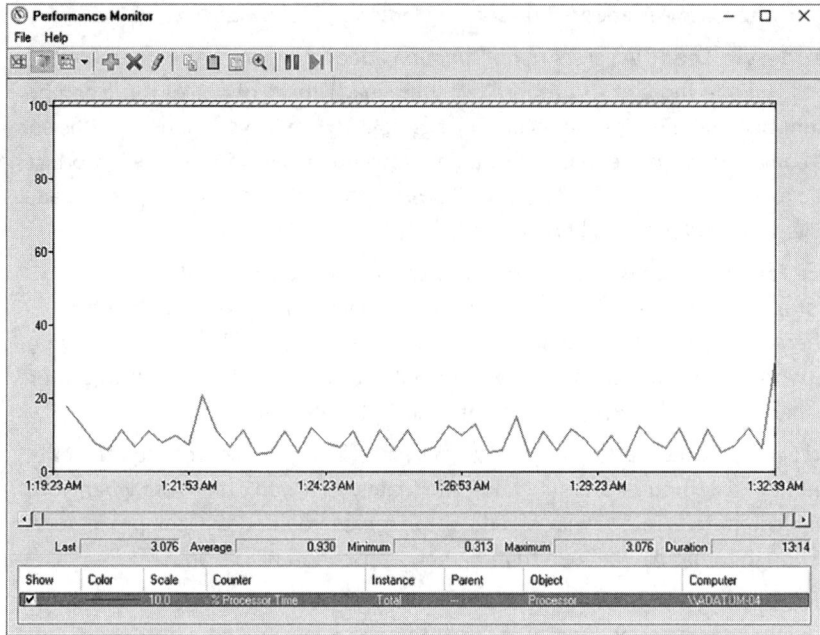

FIGURE 6-47 Performance Monitor information collected using a data collector set

By repeating this process later and comparing the information in the two data collector sets, you can often detect performance trends that indicate the presence of bottlenecks.

Determine appropriate CPU, memory, disk, and networking counters for storage and compute workloads

Once you learn how to operate the Performance Monitor console, the next step is to learn how to use it to monitor and troubleshoot a computer. Server administrators often encounter performance problems that are not attributable to an obvious cause, such as a hardware or service failure. Users might complain that a server's performance is slow at certain times of the day, or that performance has been declining gradually over the course of weeks or months. When this occurs, one of the most common causes is a performance bottleneck somewhere in the server.

A *bottleneck* is a component that is not providing an acceptable level of performance, compared with the other components in the system. For example, users might complain that their file server performance is slow, and you might spend a great deal of time and money upgrading your network, expecting to see a dramatic improvement. However, if the server is an older computer using an outdated processor, the improvement might be minimal because it is the processor, not the network, that is the bottleneck. All the other components might be running well, but the processor cannot keep up with the data capacity of the new, faster network.

Bottlenecks can appear for a variety of reasons, including the following:

- **Increased Server Load**   A server might function adequately in a particular role at first, but as you add more users or more tasks, the inadequacy of one or more components might become more pronounced. For example, a web server might be sufficient to host a company's web site at first, but then the company introduces a new product and traffic to the site triples. Suddenly, you find that the web server's disk performance is insufficient to handle the additional traffic.

- **Hardware Failure**   Hardware failures do not always manifest themselves as catastrophic stoppages. A component might malfunction intermittently for a long time, causing degraded server performance that is maddeningly inconsistent. For example, a faulty network cable connecting a server to a switch can cause occasional traffic interruptions that show up as degraded performance in the server.

- **Changed Server Roles**   Different applications have different resource requirements. You might have a computer that functions adequately as a web server, but when you change the computer's role to that of a database server, you find that the processor is not fast enough to handle the load that the new application places on it.

Locating the bottleneck that is hindering performance can be a complicated task, but the Performance Monitor console provides most of the tools you need. To find a bottleneck, you usually examine the four main subsystems of a computer, which are covered in the following sections.

CPU counters

An inadequate or malfunctioning processor array can cause a server to queue incoming client requests, preventing the server from fulfilling them promptly. For general monitoring of the processor subsystem, consider using the following performance counters:

- **Processor: % Processor Time**   Specifies the percentage of time that the processor is busy. This value should be as low as possible, with anything below 85 percent being acceptable. If this value is consistently too high, you should attempt to determine which processes are using too much processor time, upgrade the processor, or add another processor, if possible.

- **System: Processor Queue Length**   Specifies the number of program threads waiting to be executed by the processor. This value should be as low as possible, with values less than 10 being acceptable. If the value is too high, upgrade the processor or add another processor.

- **Server Work Queues: Queue Length**   Specifies the number of requests waiting to use a specific processor. This value should be as low as possible, with values less than four being acceptable. If the value is too high, upgrade the processor or add another processor.

- **Processor: Interrupts/Sec** Specifies the number of hardware interrupts the processor is servicing each second. The value of this counter can vary greatly and is significant only in relation to an established baseline. A hardware device that is generating too many interrupts can monopolize the processor, preventing it from performing other tasks. If the value increases precipitously, examine the various other hardware components in the system to determine which one is generating too many interrupts.

Memory counters

An inadequate amount of memory in a server can prevent the computer from caching frequently-used data aggressively enough, causing processes to rely on disk reads more than memory reads and slowing down the entire system. Memory is the single most important subsystem to monitor because memory problems can affect all the other subsystems. For example, when a memory condition causes excessive disk paging, the system might appear to have a problem in the storage subsystem, although memory is the culprit.

One of the most common conditions that can cause memory-related problems is a memory leak. A memory leak is the result of a program allocating memory for use but not freeing up that memory when it is finished using it. Over time, the computer's free memory can be totally consumed, degrading performance and ultimately halting the system. Memory leaks can be fast, causing an almost immediate degradation in overall server performance, but they can also be slow and difficult to detect, gradually degrading system performance over a period of days or weeks. In most cases, memory leaks are caused by third-party applications, but operating system leaks are not unprecedented.

To monitor basic memory performance, use the following counters:

- **Memory: Page Faults/Sec** Specifies the number of times per second that the code or data needed for processing is not found in memory. This value should be as low as possible, with values below 5 being acceptable. This counter includes both soft faults (in which the required page is found elsewhere in memory) and hard faults (in which the requested page must be accessed from a disk). Soft faults are generally not a major problem, but hard faults can cause significant delays because disk accesses are much slower than memory accesses. If this value is too high, you should determine whether the system is experiencing an inordinate number of hard faults by examining the Memory: Pages/Sec counter. If the number of hard page faults is excessive, you should either determine what process is causing the excessive paging or install more random access memory (RAM) in the system.

- **Memory: Pages/Sec** Specifies the number of times per second that required information was not in RAM and had to be accessed from disk or had to be written to disk to make room in RAM. This value should be as low as possible, with values from 0 to 20 being acceptable. If the value is too high, you should either determine what process is causing the excessive paging or install more RAM in the system.

- **Memory: Available MBytes**   Specifies the amount of available physical memory in megabytes. This value should be as high as possible and should not fall below 5 percent of the system's total physical memory, as this might be an indication of a memory leak. If the value is too low, consider installing additional RAM in the system.
- **Memory: Committed Bytes**   Specifies the amount of virtual memory that has space reserved on the disk paging files. This value should be as low as possible and should always be less than the amount of physical RAM in the computer. If the value is too high, this could be an indication of a memory leak or the need for additional RAM in the system.
- **Memory: Pool Non-Paged Bytes**   Specifies the size of an area in memory used by the operating system for objects that cannot be written to disk. This value should be a stable number that does not grow without a corresponding growth in server activity. If the value increases over time, this could be an indication of a memory leak.

Disk counters

A storage subsystem that is overburdened with read and write commands can slow down the rate at which the system processes client requests. The server's hard disk drives carry a greater physical burden than the other three subsystems because, in satisfying the I/O requests of many clients, the drive heads must continually move to different locations on the drive platters. The drive head mechanism can move only so fast, however, and once the drive reaches its maximum read/write speed, additional requests can begin to pile up in the queue, waiting to be processed. For this reason, the storage subsystem is a prime location for a bottleneck.

To monitor the storage subsystem in Performance Monitor, you can use the following counters:

- **PhysicalDisk: Disk Bytes/Sec**   Specifies the average number of bytes transferred to or from the disk each second. This value should be equivalent to the levels established in the original baseline readings or higher. A decrease in this value could indicate a malfunctioning disk that could eventually fail. If this is the case, consider upgrading the storage subsystem.
- **PhysicalDisk: Avg. Disk Bytes/Transfer**   Specifies the average number of bytes transferred during read and write operations. This value should be equivalent to the levels established in the original baseline readings or higher. A decrease in this value indicate a malfunctioning disk that could eventually fail. If this is the case, consider upgrading the storage subsystem.
- **PhysicalDisk: Current Disk Queue Length**   Specifies the number of pending disk read or write requests. This value should be as low as possible, with values less than 2 being acceptable per disk spindle. High values for this counter can indicate that the drive is malfunctioning or that it is incapable of keeping up with the activities demanded of it. If this is the case, consider upgrading the storage subsystem.

- **PhysicalDisk: % Disk Time**   Specifies the percentage of time that the disk drive is busy. This value should be as low as possible, with values less than 80 percent being acceptable. High values for this counter can indicate that the drive is malfunctioning, that it is incapable of keeping up with the activities demanded of it, or that a memory problem is causing excess disk paging. Check for memory leaks or related problems and, if none are found, consider upgrading the storage subsystem.
- **LogicalDisk: % Free Space**   Specifies the percentage of free space on the disk. This value should be as high as possible, with values greater than 20 percent being acceptable. If the value is too low, consider adding more disk space.

Most storage subsystem problems, when not caused by malfunctioning hardware, are resolvable by upgrading the storage system. These upgrades can include any of the following measures:

- Install faster hard disk drives, such as solid state drives (SSDs).
- Install additional hard disk drives and split your data among them, reducing the I/O burden on each drive.
- Replace standalone drives with a RAID (Redundant Array of Independent Disks) array.
- Add more disk drives to an existing RAID array.

Network counters

Monitoring network performance is more complicated than monitoring the other three subsystems because many factors outside the computer can affect network performance. You can use the following counters to try to determine if a network problem exists, but if you suspect one, you should begin looking for causes external to the computer:

- **Network Interface: Bytes Total/Sec**   Specifies the number of bytes sent and received per second by the selected network interface adapter. This value should be equivalent to the levels established in the original baseline readings or higher. A decrease in this value could indicate malfunctioning network hardware or other network problems.
- **Network Interface: Output Queue Length**   Specifies the number of packets waiting to be transmitted by the network interface adapter. This value should be as low as possible, and preferably zero, although values of two or less are acceptable. If the value is too high, the network interface adapter could be malfunctioning or another network problem might exist.
- **Server: Bytes Total/Sec**   Specifies the total number of bytes sent and received by the server over all its network interfaces. This value should be no more than 50 percent of the total bandwidth capacity of the network interfaces in the server. If the value is too high, consider migrating some applications to other servers or upgrading to a faster network.

The bandwidth of the network connections limits the amount of traffic reaching the server through its network interfaces. If these counter values indicate that the network itself is the bottleneck, there are two ways to upgrade the network, and neither one is a simple fix:

- **Increase The Speed Of The Network**   This means replacing the network interface adapters in all the computers, as well as the switches, routers, and other devices on the network, and possibly replacing the cabling as well.

- **Install Additional Network Adapters In The Server And Redistribute The Network**   If traffic frequently saturates the network interfaces already in the server, the only way to increase the network throughput without increasing the network's speed is to install more network interfaces. However, connecting more interfaces to the same network will not permit any more traffic to reach the server. Instead, you must create additional subnets on the network and redistribute the computers among them, so that there is less traffic on each subnet.

Configure alerts

Performance Monitor is a useful tool, but few administrators have the time to sit around watching line graphs track server performance counters. This is why you can also use the Create New Data Collector Set wizard to create *performance counter alerts*, which monitor the values of specific counters and perform a task, such as sending an email to an administrator, when the counters reach a specific value.

To create an alert, you use a procedure like that of creating a data collector set, as follows.

1. Open the Performance Monitor console and expand the Data Collector Sets folder.
2. Right-click the User Defined folder and, on the context menu, click New, Data Collector Set.
3. On the How Would You Like To Create This New Data Collector Set? page, type a name for the data collector set and select the Create Manually (Advanced) option.
4. On the What Type Of Data Do You Want To Include? page, select the Performance Counter Alert option.
5. On the Which Performance Counters Would You Like To Log? page, click Add and select the counter you want to monitor.
6. In the Alert When drop-down list and the Limit text box, specify the value at which Performance Monitor should trigger an alert. The values you use for these fields depend on the nature of counter you select. For example, when monitoring the % Processor Time counter, you might want to trigger an alert when the value goes above 95 percent. Counters that do not measure percentages might use values based on other factors, however.
7. On the Create The Data Collector Set? page, if the account you are currently using does not have the privileges needed to gather the log information, click Change to display a Performance Monitor dialog box in which you can supply alternative credentials.

8. Select one of the following options:
   - **Open Properties For This Data Collector Set** Saves the data collector set to the specified location and opens its Properties sheet for further modifications
   - **Start This Data Collector Set Now** Saves the data collector set to the specified location and starts collecting data immediately
   - **Save And Close** Saves the data collector set to the specified location and closes the wizard
9. Click Finish. The new data collector set appears in the User Defined folder.
10. Select the new data collector set under the User Defined folder.
11. Right-click the alert and select Properties.
12. In the Properties sheet for the alert, select the Alert Task tab, as shown in Figure 6-48.

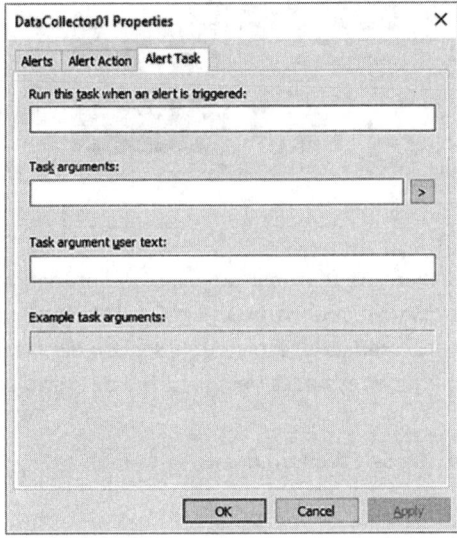

FIGURE 6-48 The Alert Task tab of a Properties sheet for a performance counter alert

13. In the fields provided, specify a Windows Management Instrumentation task or a script to run when the alert is triggered.
14. Click OK.

When you start the alert, it will monitor the selected counter and execute the task when it reaches the specified value. In the same Properties sheet, on the Alert tab, you can also configure the sample interval for the alert, so that it does not interfere with server performance or trigger unwanted alerts too often.

Monitor workloads using Resource Monitor

When you launch the Performance Monitor console, you can right-click the Monitoring Tools folder and, from the context menu, select Resource Monitor, to display the Resource Monitor window, as shown in Figure 6-49.

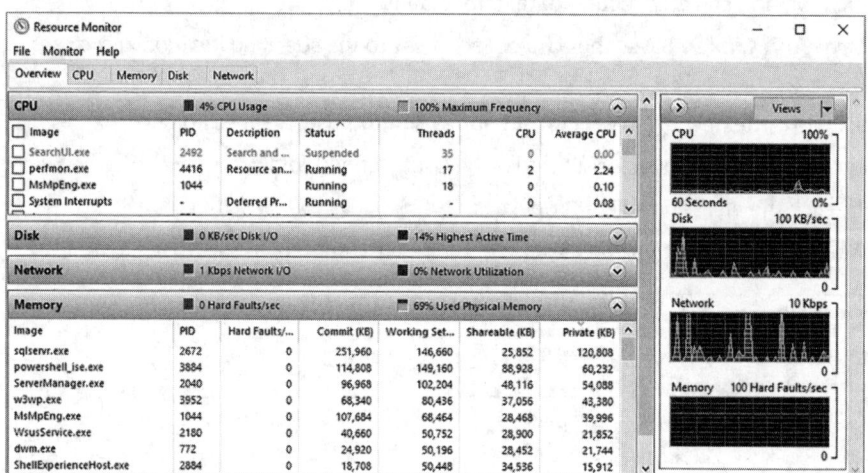

FIGURE 6-49 The Resource Monitor console

On the Resource Monitor's Overview tab, there are four real-time line graphs that display information about the server's four main hardware components: CPU, Disk, Network, and Memory. Each of the four components also has a separate, expandable section displaying more detailed information in text form, such as the resources being utilized by individual applications and processes.

The statistics displayed by the graphs and the text sections are listed in Table 6-1.

TABLE 6-1 Resource Monitor Line Graphs and Text Statistics

Component	Line graph statistics	Text statistics
CPU	■ Overall CPU Utilization (%)	■ **Image** The application using CPU resources ■ **PID** The Process ID of the application ■ **Status** Specifies whether the application is currently running or suspended ■ **Threads** The number of active threads generated by the application ■ **CPU** The number of CPU cycles currently being used by the application ■ **Average CPU** The percentage of the total CPU capacity being used by the application
Disk	■ Total Current Disk I/O Rate (In KB/Sec)	■ **Image** The application using disk resources ■ **PID** The Process ID of the application ■ **File** The file currently being read or written by the application ■ **Read** The speed of the current read operation (in bytes/sec) ■ **Write** The speed of the current write operation (in bytes/sec) ■ **Total** The speed of the current combined read/write operations (in bytes/sec) ■ **I/O Priority** The priority of the I/O task currently being performed by the application ■ **Response Time** The interval between the issuance of a command to the disk and its response (in milliseconds)
Network	■ Current Total Network Traffic (In Kb/Sec)	■ **Image** The application using network resources ■ **PID** The Process ID of the application ■ **Address** The network address or computer name of the system with which the computer is communicating ■ **Send** The speed of the current network send operation (in bytes/sec) ■ **Receive** The speed of the current network receive operation (in bytes/sec) ■ **Total** The combined bandwidth of the current network send and receive processes (in bytes/sec)
Memory	■ Current Hard Faults Per Second ■ Percentage Of Physical Memory Currently In Use (%)	■ **Image** The application using memory resources ■ **PID** The Process ID of the application ■ **Hard Faults/Sec** The number of hard faults currently being generated by the application ■ **Commit** The amount of memory (in KB) committed by the application ■ **Working Set** The amount of physical memory (in KB) currently being used by the application ■ **Shareable** The amount of memory (in KB) being used by the application that it can share with other applications ■ **Private** The amount of memory (in KB) being used by the application that it cannot share with other applications

Examining the resources utilized by specific applications and processes over time can help you to determine ways to improve the performance of a computer. For example, if all the system's physical memory is frequently being utilized, then the system is probably being slowed by large amounts of disk paging. Increasing the amount of physical memory or reducing the application load will probably improve the overall performance level of the computer.

Chapter summary

- Windows Server Update Services (WSUS) is a feature included in Windows Server 2016 that enables a local server on your network to function as the back end for the Windows Update client, just as the Microsoft Update servers do on the Internet.
- When you use multiple WSUS servers on your enterprise network, you create an architecture by specifying the upstream server from which each server should obtain its updates.
- In a replica WSUS server configuration, one central WSUS server downloads updates from the Microsoft Update site on the Internet, and the WSUS servers at other sites obtain the approved updates from that first server.
- Autonomous WSUS servers download all available updates from the central server, and administrators at each site are responsible for evaluating and approving updates for their own users.
- The process by which a WSUS downloads updates from an upstream server is called synchronization.
- To exercise control over which Windows Update clients on the network receive specific updates, WSUS uses a system of groups.
- Windows Defender is an antimalware solution that is automatically installed an enabled on all servers running Windows Server 2016.
- For Windows Defender to remain effective, it must have regular updates to its antispyware and antivirus definitions.
- In Windows Server Backup, single backup jobs provide more flexibility than scheduled ones, with the obvious disadvantage that someone must be there to create and start the job.
- When you create a scheduled backup job, the options are somewhat different from a single, interactive job.
- When you perform a scheduled backup of an Active Directory domain controller, or perform a single backup with the System State checkbox selected, Windows Server Backup includes the Active Directory database as part of the job.
- Windows Server Backup can back up Hyper-V hosts and the guest virtual machines as well.

- Performance Monitor is a tool that displays system performance statistics in real time. Performance Monitor can display hundreds of different statistics (called performance counters); you can create a customized graph containing any statistics you choose.
- A bottleneck is a component that is not providing an acceptable level of performance compared with the other components in the system.
- The Resource Monitor console contains four real-time line graphs that display information about four of the server's main hardware components.

Thought experiment

In this thought experiment, demonstrate your skills and knowledge of the topics covered in this chapter. You can find answer to this thought experiment in the next section.

Norton, an administrator at Adatum, Ltd., has been assigned the task of deploying new servers throughout the enterprise. The servers will be running Windows Server 2016, and Norton is in the process of creating a long-term plan to replace the servers at each of the company's five offices. He wants to install Windows Server Update Services on one of the servers at each office, so that clients can download updates from a local source, but is running into some administrative problems in the process.

The one Canadian office, in Winnipeg, operates under another name and has its own IT staff. However, their Internet connection is considerably more expensive than those of the US offices and is priced based on the bandwidth they use. The Minneapolis and Detroit offices have high-speed connections to the company headquarters in Chicago, but they do not maintain their own IT administrators. The newly-created branch office in St. Louis is tiny, with only two sales associates. They have a high-speed Internet connection, but use a VPN connection to connect to the headquarters network.

How should Norton configure the WSUS architecture for the home office and the four branches?

Thought experiment answer

This section contains the solution to the thought experiment.

The WSUS server at the headquarters in Chicago should be configured as the central server and should obtain its updates from the Microsoft Update servers on the Internet. The server at the Winnipeg office should download updates from the Chicago server, but the administrators there should evaluate and approve updates for themselves. The WSUS servers in the Minneapolis and Detroit offices should be replicas of the Chicago server. The server in the St. Louis office should have the Chicago server as its upstream server, but the Do Not Store Update Files Locally; Computers Install From Microsoft Update option on the Update Files and Languages dialog box should be selected, so that the server downloads the approval list from Chicago and the actual updates from the Microsoft Update servers on the Internet.

Index

A

access control entries (ACEs) 112, 115
access control lists (ACLs) 112
ACEs. *See* Access Control Entries (ACEs); *See* access control entries (ACEs)
ACLL. *See* Attempt Copy Last Logs
ACLs. *See* access control lists (ACLs)
activation models 35–42
   Active-Directory based 39–41
   Automatic Virtual Machine Activation 41–42
   Key Management Service 36–39
   multiple activation keys 35–36
activation threshold 37
activation validity interval 37
Active Directory
   backing up 421–422
Active Directory-based activation 39–41
Active Directory-detached clusters 337
Active Directory Domain Services (AD DS) 337
Add-ClusterSharedVolume cmdlet 153
Add-ClusterVirtualMachineRole cmdlet 304
Add-ClusterVMMonitoredItem cmdlet 362
Add-Computer cmdlet 20
Add-ContainerImageTag cmdlet 272
Add Roles And Features Wizard 11–15
Add-VMNetworkAdapter cmdlet 237
administrative access points 337
Administrators groups 269
advanced permissions 114–115, 120–121
allocation unit size 82–84
antimalware solution 405–410
asynchronous replication 148
Attach-Container cmdlet 280
authentication protocols
   for Live Migration 308–309
authorization 113
Automatic Virtual Machine Activation (AVMA) 41–42
AVMA. *See* Automatic Virtual Machine Activation
AVMAkey variable 42
Azure
   managing container images using 293
Azure Access Panel. *See* Access Panel

B

backups
   Active Directory 421–422
   before upgrading 30
   data deduplication and 162
   failover clusters and 324–326
   group policy objects 423
   Hyper-V 424–425
   IIS 424–425
   incremental 417–418
   mirrored 416
   restores from 418–421
   scheduled 415–417
   single job creation 412–415
   strategies for 421–425
   Windows Server Backup 411–421
balloon driver 188
bandwidth management 254–256
Basic Input/Output System (BIOS) 86
basic permissions 114, 117–120
BIOS settings 7
blob files 45, 46–47
Block-SmbShareAccess cmdlet 109
boot
   Secure Boot 205–208
   traditional 205
bottlenecks 433–434

C

cabinet (CAB) files 48, 74
checkpoints
   applying 229–230
   creating 228–229
   managing 228–230
   production 230–231
   standard 230
child partitions 167
Chkdsk.exe 94
chunks 159
chunk store 158
churn 158, 161
Close-SmbOpenFile cmdlet 108
Close-SmbSession cmdlet 107
cloud-based services 43
cloud deployment 4
cloud witnesses 345–348
Cluster-Aware Updating (CAU) 328–332
Clustered Storage Spaces 342–345
cluster name object (CNO) 313, 337
Cluster Operating System Rolling Upgrade 332–333
cluster shared volume (CSV) 153
cluster shared volumes (CSVs) 333–336, 341
cluster-to-cluster configurations 149, 151–155
CNA. *See* converged network adapter (CNA)
collector technologies 65
Compare-VM cmdlet 212
connectors. *See also* receive connectors;
     See also send connectors
containers. *See* Linux containers;
     See Windows containers
converged network adapter (CNA) 143
converged networks 143
convergence 376
ConvertTo-ContainerImage cmdlet 280
Convert-VHD cmdlet 228
Copy-Item cmdlet 180
CPU counters 434–435
CPU cycles 288–289
Create New Data Collector Set wizard 438–439
Credential Security Support Provider (CredSSP) 308–309
CSV. *See* cluster shared volume (CSV)

D

DAC. *See* Datacenter Activation Coordination
daemon.json 269–270
DAGs. *See* Database Availability Groups
DAS. *See* Direct-Attached Storage
databases. *See* mailbox databases
datacenter bridging (DCB) 142–145
Datacenter edition 4, 5, 41
data collector sets 431–433
data deduplication 155–162
   backup and restore solution with 162
   configuration of 155–158
   monitoring 160–161
   optimization rates 159
   usage scenarios for 158–160
   workload evaluation 159–160
Data Deduplication Savings Evaluation Tool 160
Data Protection Manager (DPM) 162
data replication 148–155
data storage. *See also* storage architectures; *See also* storage requirements
data volumes 286–287
DCB. *See* datacenter bridging (DCB)
DCBX Willing bit 143
DDA. *See* Discrete Device Assignment (DDA)
Ddpeval.exe 160
deduplication. *See* data deduplication
Deployment Image Servicing and Management (DISM.exe) 172
   adding drivers to image files using 72–74
   /disable-feature command 76
   /enable-feature command 76–77
   installing roles and features in offline images with 75–77
   umounting image with 74
   updating images with 70–72
   Windows PowerShell equivalents for 77–79
Desired State Configuration (DSC) 26–28
   creating configuration scripts 26
   deploying configurations 27–28
Desktop Experience 2
devices
   detecting 147
Device Specific Module (DSM) 145
   policies 148
DFS. *See* Distributed File Share

differencing disks 222–223
/disable-feature command 76
Discrete Device Assignment (DDA) 212–213
discretionary access control lists (DACLs) 93
disk counters 436–437
disk fragmentation 83
Disk Management console 84, 139–140
    creating VHD or VHDX files using 88–90
    mounting VHD and VHDX files with 91–92
disk partitions 9–10
disks
    adding to CSVs 336
    differencing 222–223
    GUID partition table 84–88
    initializing new 84–85
    MBR 84–85
    partition style selection 87
    pass-through 212, 225–226
    physical 125, 225–226
    storage layout options 125–131
    virtual. *See* virtual disks
disk sectors
    size configuration 82–84
disk volume
    allocation unit size 82–84
DISM.exe. *See* Deployment Image Servicing
        and Management
Dismount-VHD cmdlet 92
Distributed Component Object Model (DCOM) 25
Distributed File System (DFS) Replication 150
Djoin.exe tool 46
DNS round robin 376
DNS server addresses 270
Docker
    Attach command 279
    Build command 290
    Commit command 279
    Images command 273
    installation
        on Nano Server 267–268
        on Windows Server 266
    managing containers with 277–279
    Network Create command 285
    PowerShell and 270–271
    Pull command 271
    Push command 292
    RM command 279
    Run command 274–276, 285, 287, 288
    Start command 278
    start-up options 269–270
    Stop command 278
Dockerd.exe 266, 269
Docker.exe 266
dockerfile 289–290
DockerHub 271, 291–293
Domain Name System (DNS) 39
domains
    joining, with Nano Server 45–47
drive arrays 134
drivers
    adding to image files 72–74
DSC. *See* Desired State Configuration (DSC)
Dynamic Host Configuration Protocol (DHCP) 51
Dynamic Host Configuration Protocol (DHCP) server 11
dynamic least queue depth 148
dynamic memory
    allocations 188
    configuration 186–188
    limitations 187
    settings 186–188
dynamic quorum management 318

E

Edit-NanoServerImage cmdlet 49, 51, 77
EFS. *See* Encrypting File System
emulated adapters 248–249
Enable-DedupVolume cmdlet 157–158
/enable-feature command 76–77
Encrypting File System (EFS) 94
enhanced session mode 199–201
Enter-ContainerSession cmdlet 280
Enter-PsSession cmdlet 22, 56
ESRA. *See* EdgeSync replication account (ESRA)
Essentials edition 5, 6
Ethernet 142–143
Exit-PsSession cmdlet 22, 57
Exit-PSSession cmdlet 177
explicit remoting 176
Export-SmigServerSetting cmdlet 33
Export-VM cmdlet 210
Extended Page Tables (EPT) 263
Extensible Firmware Interface (EFI)-based
        boot partition 87
external network switches 239, 241

F

failback policy 148
failbacks 364
failover affinity 367
failover clusters 153, 220–221, 304, 311–351
   cloud witnesses 345–348
   Cluster-Aware Updating 328–332
   cluster configuration 324–326
   Clustered Storage Spaces 342–345
   cluster networking 321–324
   Cluster Operating System Rolling Upgrade 332–333
   cluster shared volumes 333–336, 341
   configurating without network names 337
   guest clustering 341–342, 349–351
   managing 359–368
   monitoring VMs in 361–363
   node fairness 367–368
   quorum 317–321
   role-specific settings 359–361
   Scale-out File Server 337–341
   shared VHDX files 349–351
   site-aware 365–367
   storage configuration 326–328
   stretch 365–367
   VM resiliency and 348–349
   workgroup, single, and multi-domain 314–317
failover policy 148
failovers 150
failover settings 364–365
fault tolerance 128–131
features
   implemention on Nano Server 48–50
   installation of 13–15
      in offline images 75–77
   offline installation 225
Fiber Channel over Ethernet (FCoE) 142
Fibre Channel 133, 326
   adapter 231–233
file compression 94
file ownership 122
file permissions 112–122
File Server cluster role 360
File Server Resource Manager (FSRM) 103
File Server role service 96
File Sharing dialog box 95
file systems
   NTFS 93–95
   ReFS 93–95
folder ownership 122
folder permissions 112–122
folder shares. *See* shares
Format-List cmdlet 161
FreeBSD
   virtual machines 201–203
FreeBSD deployments 61
FreeBSD Integration Services (BIS) 61
FreeBSD Integration Services (FIS) 204, 205
FSW. *See* File Share Witness

G

garbage collection 158
Generation 1 VMs 197, 214
Generation 2 VMs 197–199, 205, 215
generic volume licensing keys (GVLKs) 39
Get-Command cmdlet 21
Get-ComputerInfo cmdlet 274
Get-Container cmdlet 280
Get-DedupStatus cmdlet 161
Get-help cmdlet 21
Get-NetAdapter cmdlet 19
Get-NetAdapterVmqQueue cmdlet 252–253
Get-SmbClientConfiguration cmdlet 111–112
Get-SmbOpenFile cmdlet 108
Get-SmbServerConfiguration cmdlet 109–110
Get-SmbSession cmdlet 107
Get-SmbShareAccess cmdlet 108
Get-SmigServerFeature cmdlet 33
Get-SRGroup cmdlet 154
Get-VM cmdlet 177
Get-VMHostSupportedVersion cmdlet 209
Get-VM PowerShell cmdlet 208
Get-WindowsFeature cmdlet 15
globally-unique identifier (GUID) 86
GPT. *See* GUID partition table (GPT) disks
Grant-SmbShareAccess cmdlet 109
Grant-SRAccess cmdlet 153
Group policy objects (GPOs) 401–403, 409
   backing up 423
GRUB boot loader 202
GUID partition table (GPT) disks
   advantages of 86
   booting from 87–88
   compared with MBR 87
   configuration of 84–88

H

hard disk drives (HDDs) 131
hard disks. *See* disks
hardware address 244–246
hardware requirements 3–4
high availability 297–386
   failover clustering 311–351, 359–368
   in Hyper-V 297–310
   Live Migration 303–309, 369–370
   network load balancing 375–384
   Storage Migration 309–311
   Storage Spaces Direct (S2D) 352–358
   VM movement in clustered nodes 369–375
host bus adapter (HBA) 134
hotfixes 74–75
hot spares 130–131
hygiene. *See* message hygiene
hyperthreading 4
Hyper-V 165–258
   backing up 424–425
   checkpoints 228–231
   containers 261–264, 275–277
   converting from previous versions 208–209
   Discrete Device Assignment 212–213
   enhanced session mode 199–201
   export and import functions 209–212
   Fibre Channel adapter 231–233
   guest operating systems 203–208
   guests 165, 166
   hardware limitations 167–169
   high availability in 297–310
   hosts 165, 174–179
   installation 165–173
      hardware and compatibility requirements 166–170
      management tools 172–173
      using PowerShell 171
      using Server Manager 170–171
   Integration Services 195–196, 204
   Nano Server and 43
   nested virtualization 181
   networking 235–256
      bandwidth management 254–256
      MAC address configuration 244–246
      network isolation 246–247
      NIC teaming 249–251
      performance optimization 243–244
      Switch Embedded Teaming 253–254
      synthetic network adapters 247–249
      virtual machine queue 251–253
      virtual network interface cards 236–237
      virtual switches 238–242, 244, 247
   New Virtual Hard Disk Wizard 88
   permissions 174
   PowerShell Direct 180
   remote management 174–179
   resource metering 193–195
   smart paging 192–193
   storage 213–235
      differencing disks 222–223
      quality of service 233–235
      shared VHDX files 220–222
      VHDs 214–220, 223–225
      VHDX files 214–220
   supported guest VMs 61
   upgrading from existing versions of 173
   virtual machine configuration 182–213
hypervisor 166–167
Hyper-V Manager 172–173
   conflict handling 212
   container host installation in 262–263
   creating VHDs and VHDX files using 214–220
   creating virtual hard disks in 216–218
   importing VMs using 210–211
   remote management using 174–176
   virtual machine creation in 183–184
Hyper-V Replica 298–303
Hyper-V Server 168
Hyper-V Server edition 5

I

image files
   adding drivers to 72–74
   adding updates to 74–75
   committing 74
   container 261, 291–293
   for deployment 58–79
   installing roles and features in offline 75–77
   managing, using Windows PowerShell 76–78
   mounting 71–72
   removing 273–274
   umounting 74
   updating 70–75
implicit remoting 177, 178–179
Import-SmigServerSetting cmdlet 33
Import-VM cmdlet 211–212
inheritance
   permission 115–116

initiators
  iSCSI 133–140
in-place upgrades 28–32
installation
  MAP Toolkit 63
  Nano Server 44–48
  Server Core 17–19
  upgrades 28–32
  Windows Server 2016 1–18
    activation models 35
    clean installation 6–9
    features and roles 11–17
    mass deployment 11
    partitions 9–10
    requirements 2–4
  Windows Server Migration Tools 33–34
Install-WindowsFeature cmdlet 15, 171, 377
Install-WindowsFeature PowerShell cmdlet 225
Institute of Electrical and Electronics Engineers (IEEE) 143
Integration Services 195–196, 204
integrity scrubbing 158–159
internal network switches 241
Internet Information Services (IIS)
  backing up 424–425
Internet SCSI (iSCSI) 327
Internet Small Computer System Interface (iSCSI) 133–140
  creating targets 134–138
  initiators and targets 133–134
  using initiators 138–140
Internet Storage Name Service (iSNS) 140–142
Inventory And Assessment Wizard 65–67
Invoke-Command cmdlet 180
IP addresses
  configuration
    Nano Server 51–53
iSNS Protocol (iSNSP) 141

J

just-a-bunch-of-disks (JBOD) arrays 123

K

Kerberos 308–309
Key Management Service (KMS) 36–39
  client configuration 39
  host installation 37–39
  limitations 36–37
KMS. *See* Key Management Service

L

legacy network adapters 248–249
Lightweight Directory Access Protocol (LDAP) 66
Linux
  Secure Boot and 206–208
  virtual machines 201–203
Linux containers
  managing
    using Docker daemon 277–279
    using PowerShell 279–281
Linux deployments 61
Linux Integration Services (LIS) 61, 204–205
Live Migration
  CredSSP or Kerberos authentication protocol for 308–309
  implementing 303–308
  in cluster 304
  of VM 369–370
  Shared Nothing 307–308
  without a cluster 305–307
local area network (LAN) 142
Local Configuration Manager (LCM) 26
local Hyper-V Administrators 174
local memory 189
log files. *See* transaction log files
logical unit number (LUN) 134
Lync Online. *See* Skype for Business

M

MAK Volume Licensing agreements 35–36
Management Object Format (MOF) files 27
MapSetup.exe 63–64
MAP Toolkit. *See* Microsoft Assessment and Planning (MAP) Toolkit
master boot record (MBR) 84–85, 87
maximum hardware configurations 4
MBR. *See* master boot record (MBR)
Measure-VM cmdlet 194, 234–235
Media Access Control (MAC) address
  configuration of 244–246
memory
  adding or removing, in VM 185–186
  containers 288

dynamic 186–188
local 189
Non-Uniform Memory Access 189–192
remote 189
virtual 259
memory counters 435–436
Merge-VHD cmdlet 228
message transport. *See* transport
Microsoft Assessment and Planning (MAP) Toolkit 61–69
  collection of inventory information 64–68
  discovery methods 66
  evaluation of results 68–69
  functions of 62
  installation 63–64
Microsoft Azure. *See* Azure
Microsoft Azure Active Directory. *See* Azure Active Directory (Azure AD)
Microsoft Management Console (MMC) snap-ins
  using remotely 25–26
migrations. *See also* Live Migration
  migration guides 34–35
  P2V 60
  Quick Migration 370–371
  roles 32–33
  servers 32–35
  Storage Migration 309–311, 371–372
  virtual machines 369–372
mirror storage layout 128
MOF files. *See* Management Object Format (MOF) files
Mount-DiskImage cmdlet 92
mounting
  virtual hard disks 91–93, 224–225
mounting images
  images 71–72
Mount-VHD cmdlet 92
MSU files 74
multi-domain clusters 314–317
Multipath I/O (MPIO) 145–148
multiple activation keys (MAKs) 35–36
Multipoint edition 5

N

namespace isolation 260
Nano Server 2, 4, 42–57
  as container host 264–265
  authentication screen 50
  configuration 50–55

  firewall rules 54–55
  IP address 51–53
  Docker installation on 267–268
  features of 42, 43
  image creation 44–45
  installation 44–48
  joining a domain 45–47
  managing, using Windows PowerShell 76–78
  remote management 265
  remote management of 55–57
  roles and features implementation on 48–50
  shortcomings of 44
  usage scenarios and requirements for 43–44
  virtual machine creation 47–48
Nano Server Recovery Console 50–54
NAS. *See* network attached storage (NAS)
NAT. *See* network address translation (NAT)
nested virtualization 181
Netdom.exe tool 21
network adapters 246–247
  enabling RMDA on 253–254
  legacy 248–249
  NIC teaming 249–251
  synthetic 247–249
  virtual 251, 283
network address translation (NAT) 269, 284
network attached storage (NAS) 123
network counters 437–438
Network File System (NFS) shares 96
  creation of 101–103
network hardware 322
network health protection 373–374
networking
  cluster 321–324
  container 281–285
  Hyper-V 235–256
    bandwidth management 254–256
    MAC address configuration 244–246
    network isolation 246–247
    NIC teaming 249–251
    performance optimization 243–244
    Switch Embedded Teaming 253–254
    synthetic network adapters 247–249
    virtual machine queue 251–253
    virtual network interface cards 236–237
    virtual switches 238–242, 244, 247
  S2D 353–354
  transparent networks 285
network load balancing (NLB) 375–384
  affinity configuration 381–382

cluster operation mode configuration 384
cluster upgrades 384
node installation 377–381
port rules 382–383
prerequisites 375–377
New-Cluster cmdlet 337
New-Container cmdlet 275, 280
New-NanoServerImage cmdlet 44–49, 51, 52, 264
New-NetIpAddress cmdlet 19, 20
New-NetQosPolicy cmdlet 144
New-NetQosTrafficClass cmdlet 144
New-PsSession cmdlet 21–22, 55
New-PSSession cmdlet 177, 180
New-SmbShare cmdlet 106–107, 340
New-SRPartnership cmdlet 151
New-VHD cmdlet 90, 219, 223
New Virtual Hard Disk Wizard 88
New-VM cmdlet 47, 184
New-VM PowerShell cmdlet 197
NICs. *See* network interface cards (NICs)
NIC teaming 249–251
NLB. *See* network load balancing (NLB)
node fairness 367–368
nodes 311, 375
Non-Uniform Memory Access (NUMA) 189–192
  nodes 189
  node spanning 189–190
  ratio 189
  topology 190–192
N_Port ID Virtualization (NPIV) 232
NTFS file system 93–95
NTFS permissions 112–114, 117–122

O

Office Telemetry. *See* telemetry
operating system environments (OSEs) 5
Optimize-VHD cmdlet 228
organizationally unique identifier (OUI) 244

P

P2V migration 60
packages
  Nano Server 48–49
parent partitions 167
parity storage layout 129
partitions 9–10, 167

pass-through disks 212, 225–226
patches 74–75
performance counter alerts 438–439
Performance Metrics Wizard 68
Performance Monitor
  bottlenecks and 433–434
  CPU counters 434–435
  data collector sets 431–433
  disk counters 436–437
  memory counters 435–436
  monitoring workloads using 425–430
  network counters 437–438
permissions
  advanced 114–115, 120–121
  allowing 115, 116
  assigning 117–121
  basic 114, 117–120
  configuration 112–122
  denying 115, 116
  Hyper-V 174
  inheritance 115–116
  NTFS 112–114, 117–122
  resource ownership and 122
  share 96, 104–106, 108–109, 112–113
  understanding effective access 116–117
physical disks 225–226
  adding 125
physical servers
  migration to virtual 60
platform-as-a-service. *See* PaaS
Plug and Play (PnP) 147
port mapping 284
power-on self-test (POST) 205
PowerShell. *See* Windows PowerShell
PowerShell Core 57
Preboot Execution Environment (PXE) 198, 249
Preboot Execution Environment (PXE) feature 11
Priority-based Flow Control (PFC) 145
private networks 244
private network switches 241
production checkpoints 230–231
Pull Server 27–28

Q

quality of service (QoS) policies 144, 233–235
Quick Migration 370–371

quorum 317–321
    dynamic quorum management 318
    modifying configuration of 318–320
    voting 321
    witnesses 317–318, 320–321
quotas 94

R

Receive-SmigServerData cmdlet 33
redundancy 128, 145
ReFS (Resilient File System) 93–95
Remote Direct Memory Access (RDMA) 253–254
remote management
    configuration of 55
    Hyper-V 174–179
    Nano Server 265
    of Nano Server 55–57
    using MMC snap-ins 25–26
    using PowerShell 21–22
    using Server Manager 22–24
remote memory 189
Remote Server Administration Tools 174
Remove-Container cmdlet 281
Remove-ContainerImage cmdlet 273
Remove-SmbShare cmdlet 108
reparse point 158
replica servers 299–301
replication
    asynchronous 148
    DFS 150
    Hyper-V Replica 298–303
    Storage Replica 148–155
    synchronous 148
Reset-VMResourceMetering cmdlet 195
Resize-VHD cmdlet 228
resource governance 260–261
resource metering 193–195
Resource Monitor 440–442
resource ownership 122
restores
    data deduplication and 162
    from backups 418–421
Revoke-SmbShareAccess cmdlet 109
roles
    implemention on Nano Server 48–50

installation 11–17
    in offline images 75–77
migration of 32–33
offline installation 225
round robin policy 148

S

SAN. *See* storage area network (SAN)
saved-state (.vsv) files 182
Scale-out File Server (SoFS) 337–341
SCCM. *See* System Center Configuration Manager
SCSI (Small Computer Systems Interface) controllers 214–215
sector sizes 82–84
Secure Boot 205–208
security identifiers (SIDs) 113
security principal 112
self-service deployment. *See* user-driven client deployments
Send-SmigServerData cmdlet 33
Serial Attached SCSI (SAS) 327
Server Core 2, 4, 42
    configuration 19–20
    Hyper-V Server and 168
    installation 17–19
    management of 21–25
        using Windows PowerShell 76–78
    Windows containers and 264
server folders
    sharing 95–109
Server for NFS role service 97
server installations
    maintaining 387–425
        backup strategies 421–425
        patch management 401–405
        Windows Defender 405–410
        Windows Server Backup 411–421
        Windows Server Update Services 388–405
    monitoring 425–442
        performance counter alerts 438–439
        using Performance Monitor 425–430, 431–438
        using Resource Monitor 440–442
Server Manager
    deduplication configuration using 155–157
    Hyper-V installation using 170–171
    installing roles using 11–15
    managing Server Core using 22–24
    share configuration using 95–106

453

Server Message Blocks (SMB) clients
  configuration settings 111–112
Server Message Blocks (SMB) server
  configuration settings 109–111
Server Message Blocks (SMB) shares 96
  configuration of 106–108
  creation of 97–101
servers. *See also* Windows Server 2016
  adding, in Server Manager 22–24
  choosing, to virtualize 59–60
  configuration of multiple 13
  DHCP 11, 51
  fault tolerance 128–131
  mass deployment of 11
  migration of 32–35
  replica 299–301
  SMB 109–111
  upgrades 28–32
server-to-server configurations 148–149, 151–155
Server Virtualization And Consolidation Wizard 68–69
Set-Disk cmdlet 226
Set-DnsClientServerAddress cmdlet 20
Set-FileStorageTier cmdlet 133
Set-Item cmdlet 56
Set-NetAdapterVmq PowerShell cmdlet 253
Set-NetQoSbcdxSetting cmdlet 143
Set-SmbPathAcl cmdlet 340
Set-SmbServerConfiguration cmdlet 109–111
Set-SRPartnership cmdlet 155
Set-VM cmdlet 231
Set-VMFirmware cmdlet 208
Set-VMMemory cmdlet 185
Set-VMNetworkAdapter cmdlet 255
Set-VmReplicationServer cmdlet 300
Shared Nothing Live Migration 307–308
shares
  advanced 103–104
  configuration
    using Windows PowerShell 106–108
  configuration, using Server Manager 95–106
  continuously available 360–361
  NFS 96
    creation of 101–103
  permissions 96, 104–106, 108–109, 112–113
  removing 108
  sessions management 107–108
  SMB 96
    creation of 97–101
shielded virtual machines 198

simple storage layout 128
single domain clusters 314–317
Single Instance Store (SIS) technology 158
single-root I/O virtualization (SR-IOV) 243
site-aware failover clusters 365–367
site-based fault tolerance 376
slack space 82, 83
Small Computer System Interface (SCSI) 327
smart paging 192–193
SMB 3.0 protocol 360
SmbShare 106–112
SMTP. *See* Single Mail Transfer Protocol (SMTP)
snapshots 228. *See also* checkpoints
software patches 401–405
software storage bus 353
solid state drives (SSDs) 131–132
SPF. *See* send policy framework (SPF) records
standard checkpoints 230
Standard edition 5
Start-DscConfiguration cmdlet 27
storage area network (SAN) 123, 133, 142
storage area networks (SANs) 231
storage infrastructure 151–152
Storage Migration 309–311, 371–372
storage pools 123–125, 342–343, 344
  expanding 131
  hot spares 130–131
Storage Replica (SR)
  clustering configuration 153
  event log entries 154
  implementing 151–155, 345
  replication partnerships 154–155
  storage infrastructure for 151–152
  testing topology 152–153
  usage scenarios for 148–150
Storage Server edition 5
storage solutions 81–164
  clusters 326–328
  datacenter bridging 142–144
  data depulication 155–162
  fault tolerance and 128–131
  GUID partition table (GPT) disks 84–88
  Hyper-V 213–235
  implementation of 123–155
  Internet Storage Name Service (iSNS) 140–142
  iSCSI targets and initiators 133–140
  NTFS file system 93–95
  permissions configuration 112–122

virtual hard disks (VHDs)

Quality of Service for 233–235
ReFS file system 93–95
sector size configuration 82–84
shared VHDX files 349–351
shares configuration
    using Server Manager 95–106
    using Windows PowerShell 106–108
storage layout options 125–131
storage pools 123–125
Storage Replica 148–155
tiered storage 131–133
virtual disks 125–128
virtual hard disks
    creating 88–91
    mounting 91–93
Storage Spaces 123
    Clustered 342–345
    expanding storage pools 131
    fault tolerance in 128–131
    tiered storage 131–133
Storage Spaces Direct 198
Storage Spaces Direct (S2D) 352–358
    disaggregated 355–357
    disk drives 353
    enabling, using PowerShell 354–355
    hyper-converged 357–358
    networking 353–354
    scenario requirements for 352–354
    servers 352
stretch clusters 149–150, 151–155, 345, 365–367
Suspend-ClusterNode cmdlet 374
Switch Embedded Teaming (SET) 253–254
symmetric multiprocessing (SMP) 189
synchronous replication 148
synthetic network adapters 247–249
system boot 205
System Center Configuration Manager (SCCM) 66, 249
Systeminfo.exe 169–170

T

targets
    iSCSI 134–138
Test-SRTopology cmdlet 152–153
thin provisioning 126
tiered storage 131–133
traffic classes 144
Traffic Control Protocol (TCP) 144
transparent networks 285

Type II virtualization 166
Type I virtualization 167

U

Unblock-SmbShareAccess cmdlet 109
Unified Extensible Firmware Interface (UEFI) 86, 205, 206
Universal Extensible Firmware Interface (UEFI) 198
unoptimization 159
updates
    patch management 401–405
    Windows Server Update Services 388–405
Update-VMVersion cmdlet 209
upgrades
    Hyper-V 173
    in-place 28–32
    paths 28
    preparing for 29–30
    procedure for 30–32
    virtual machines 208
user accounts. *See also* identities
User Datagram Protocol (UDP) 144
user identities. *See* identities

V

VAMT. *See* Volume Activation Management Tool
VHD Set files 351
VHD sets 221
VHDX files 182
    creating
        shared 220–222
        using Hyper-V Manager 214–220
    creation of 88–91
        using Disk Management 88–90
        with Windows PowerShell 90–91
    mounting 91–93
    shared 349–351
virtual disks
    creating 123, 125–128, 132
virtual hard disks (VHDs) 44, 60, 182
    adding to virtual machines 219–220
    creating
        in PowerShell 219
        using Hyper-V Manager 214–220
        with VMs 215–216
    creation of 88–91
        using Disk Management 88–90
        with Windows PowerShell 90–91

virtualization

formats 215
managing, using Windows PowerShell 76–78
modifying 223, 223–225
mounting 91–93, 224–225
resizing 226–228
virtualization 259. *See also* Hyper-V
   advantages of 303
   architectures 166–167
   defining scope of 59–60
   deployment considerations 69–70
   maximum hardware configurations and 4
   nested 181
   N_Port ID Virtualization (NPIV) 232
   planning for 58–60
   single-root I/O virtualization (SR-IOV) 243
   strategy 3
   Type I 167
   Type II 166
   Windows containers 263–264
   workload assessment 61–69
Virtualization Service Client (VSC) 247–248
Virtualization Service Provider (VSP) 247–248
Virtualized Backup Server 162
virtual LANs (VLANs) 247
virtual machine configuration (.vmc) files 182
Virtual Machine Connection (VMConnect) 199
virtual machine monitor (VMM) 166
virtual machine queue (VMQ) 243, 251–253
Virtual Machine role 360
virtual machines (VMs) 166
  adding or removing memory 185
  adding virtual disks to 219–220
  advantages of 58–59
  Automatic Virtual Machine Activation 41–42
  configuration
    dynamic memory 186–188
    FreeBSD 202–203
    Integration Services 195–196
    Linux 202–203
    resource metering 193–195
    settings 184–185
    smart paging 192–193
    using PowerShell Direct 180
  configuration of 301–303
  containers with 263–264
  converting generations 199
  creating 47–48, 182–184, 201–202
  delegating management of 174
  drain on shutdown configuration 374–375

enhanced session mode 199–201
exporting and importing 209–212
FreeBDS deployment 61
FreeBSD 201–203
Generation 1 197, 214
Generation 2 197–199, 205, 215
import, export, and copy of 372–373
installation
    guest operating system 203
Linux 201–203
Linux deployment 61
Live Migration of 303–309, 369–370
monitoring 361–363
movement of, in clustered nodes 369–375
moving between hosts 297–310
Nano Server for 43, 47–48
network health protection 373–374
Quick Migration 370–371
resiliency 348–349
shielded 198
storage 213–235
Storage Migration 309–311, 371–372
upgrading to Windows Server 2016 Hyper-V 208–209
virtual memory 259
virtual network adapters 283
virtual network interface cards (vNICs) 236–237
virtual switches 238–242, 244, 247, 250
Volume Activation Management Tool (VAMT) 36
Volume Activation Tools Wizard 38, 41
volume shadow copies 94
Volume Shadow Copy Service (VSS) 424

W

Wbadmin command 325–326
WDS. *See* Windows Deployment Services
weighted paths 148
WIM. *See* Windows Imaging Format (WIM)
Windows
  Secure Boot and 205–206
Windows containers 259–296
  architecture 262
  attaching 279, 280
  container names 287
  CPU cycles 288–289
  creating 274–277
  creating images 279, 280, 289–290
  deployment of 259–277

Docker and 266–270
Hyper-V 261–264, 275–277
images 261
image tagging 272–273
installation
    base operating system 271–272
    container host 262–263
    requirements 260–261
listing 278, 280
managing
    data volumes 286–287
    networking 281–285
    resource control 287–289
    using Docker daemon 277–279
    using Microsoft Azure 293
    using PowerShell 279–281
    with DockerHub 291–293
memory constraints 288
Nano Server as container host 264–265
PowerShell and 270–271
removing 279, 281
Server Core and 264
starting and stopping 278, 280
uninstalling operating system image 273–274
use scenarios for 260–261
virtualizing 263–264
Windows Server 261, 264–265, 274–275
Windows Defender 405–410
    configuration of 405–408
    integration with WSUS and Windows Update 409–410
Windows Deployment Services (WDS) 11, 249
Windows Firewall 300–301
    configuration 54–55
Windows PowerShell
    container management using 279–281
    creating virtual disks in 219
    deduplication configuration in 157–158
    Desired State Configuration 26–28
    DISM.exe command equivalents 77–79
    displaying cmdlets 21
    enabling S2D using 354–355
    Hyper-V installation using 171
    importing VMs using 211–212
    installing roles using 15–16
    managing Nano Server using 77–79
    managing Server Core using 21–22, 77–79
    mounting VHD and VHDX files in 92–93
    remote management of Nano Server using 55–57
    remote management using 176–179

SMB share configuration using 106–108
using containers with 270–271
VHD and VHDX file creation in 90–91
VM creation in 184
Windows Defender configuration using 407–408
Windows PowerShell Direct
    VM configuration using 180
Windows Remote Management (WinRM) 21
    configuration 55
Windows Server 2012
    upgrading 28
Windows Server 2012 R2
    upgrading 28
Windows Server 2016
    Docker installation on 266
    editions 2, 4–6
    images for deployment 58–73
    installation 1–18
        activation model for 35–42
        clean 6–9
        features and roles 11–17
        mass deployment 11
        requirements 2–4
    migrations 32–35
    permissions management 112–122
    upgrades to 28–32
    virtualization
        planning for 58–60
    working with partitions in 9–10
Windows Server Backup 324–325, 411–421, 424
Windows Server Migration Tools 32, 33–34
Windows Server Update Services (WSUS) 388–400
    architectures 388–391
    client configuration 401–405
    configuration of 394–398
    database 391–392
    deploying 393
    groups 398–400
    storage 392–393
    Windows Defender integration 409–410
Windows Setup page 7
Windows Update Stand-Alone Installer (MSU) files 74
Winrm.exe tool 56
witnesses
    cloud 345–348
    quorum 317–318, 320–321
workgroup clusters 314–317
workload monitoring 425–430, 440–442

World Wide Node Names (WWNNs)

workloads
  virtualization considerations for 69–70
World Wide Node Names (WWNNs) 232
World Wide Port Names (WWPNs) 232
WSUS. *See* Windows Server Update Services (WSUS)

About the author

CRAIG ZACKER is the author or co-author of dozens of books, manuals, articles, and web sites on computer and networking topics. He has also been an English professor, an editor, a network administrator, a webmaster, a corporate trainer, a technical support engineer, a minicomputer operator, a literature and philosophy student, a library clerk, a photographic darkroom technician, a shipping clerk, and a newspaper boy. He lives in a little house with his beautiful wife and a neurotic cat.